KT-561-699

PAGE 36

ON THE ROAD

YOUR COMPLETE DESTINATION GUIDE
In-depth reviews, detailed listings
and insider tips

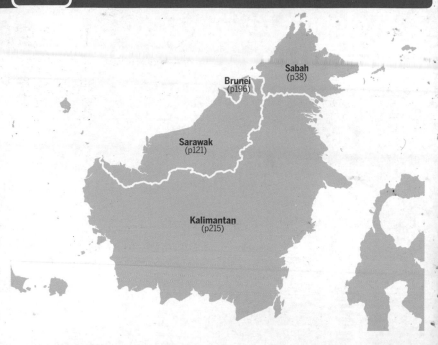

Sabah (p38)

Brunei (p196)

Sarawak (p121)

Kalimantan (p215)

THIS EDITION WRITTEN AND RESEARCHED BY

Daniel Robinson
Adam Karlin, Paul Stiles

welcome to Borneo

Ancient Rainforests

If you love tropical greenhouses and can't wait to be enveloped by the humid fecundity of a real equatorial rainforest, Borneo will fulfil your wildest dreams. The island's jungles conjure up remoteness and peril, bringing to mind impenetrable foliage and river trips into the 'heart of darkness'. But look a little closer – on a nature walk with a park ranger, for instance – and nuances emerge: the pitcher plants, lianas and orchids of the lowland forest give way to conifers, rhododendrons and different kinds of orchids as you ascend the flanks of Mt Kinabalu. The vegetation changes just as radically as you sail upriver from the mangroves along the South China Sea.

Deforestation makes for depressing headlines, but significant parts of the Bornean rainforest – among the most ancient ecosystems on earth – remain intact, protected by conservation projects whose viability depends, in part, on income from tourists.

Jungle Wildlife

For many visitors to Borneo, their most memorable moment is a personal encounter with a living creature: glimpsing a wild orangutan swinging through the jungle canopy, spotting an Irrawaddy dolphin in the shimmering waters of the South China Sea, or locking eyes with the reptilian gaze of a saltwater croc. Jungle animals are shy by nature, but a good guide can

It's a jungle out there! Borneo boasts some of the world's most species-rich equatorial rainforests — prime patches are easily accessible from multiethnic cities with great food.

(left) Hiking towards caves in Gunung Mulu National Park (p180)
(below) Orangutans at play, Sepilok (p77)

help you tell the difference between a vine and vine snake (not as easy as you might think) and between a twig and a stick insect as long and thin as a pencil. They can also help you differentiate between the call of a gibbon and the cry of a hornbill, and identify a dominant male orangutan (hint: size counts but so do the cheeks). If you're keen to have close encounters of the animal kind, Borneo's jungles offer a unique combination of extraordinary biodiversity, unspoilt habitats and practical accessibility.

Cultural Riches

Borneo brings together an astonishing array of cultures, religions, languages and cuisines and, thanks to age-old traditions of hospitality, they're all a cinch for visitors to approach. The cities of Sarawak and Sabah have significant Chinese communities and the picturesque coastal *kampung* (villages) are populated mainly by Malays, but head inland and the dominant culture is indigenous. Borneo's Dayak groups stopped nabbing noggins long ago, but many other ancient customs and ceremonies live on, in harmony with a few mod cons, in longhouse communities. There's no better way to experience a slice of the Dayak way of life than to drop by for a visit – it's easy to arrange this with a local guide.

Borneo

Maliau Basin
Truly untouched
rainforest (p101)

**Gunung Mulu
National Park**
Hiking, caves and bats (p180)

SOUTH
CHINA
SEA

ELEVATION

2000m
1000m
500m
200m
100m
0

0
0
200 miles
400 km

11°E

5°N

Bako National Park
Proboscis monkeys, pitcher
plants and beaches (p142)

Kuching
Stylish, sophisticated
and multicultural (p124)

**Semenggoh
Nature Reserve**
Semi-wild orangutans (p149)

Sarawak
Dayak longhouses and
traditional life (p121)

**Tanjung Puting
National Park**
Amazing jungle cruise (p251)

Pulau
Natuna

Anambas
Archipelago

Serasan
Strait

Teluk Datu

Sematan

Gunung Gading
National Park

Sambas

Bau

Pemangkat

Benkayang

Singkawang

Tembelan
Archipelago

Mempawah

Equator (0°)

Pontianak

Rambai

Sanggau

Tanjung

Ananah
Rais

Semenggoh
Nature
Reserve

Serian

Bako
National
Park

Bitangor

Kabong

Pusa

Sarikei

Sri
Aman

Lubok
Antu

Sintang

Kuching

Mukah

Dalat

Sibu

Kanowit

Batang Rejang

Igan

Kapuas Hulu Range

Danau
Sentarum
National Park

Betung Kerihun
National Park

Kapuas

Lambir Hills
National Park

Niah
National Park

Similajau
National Park

Bintulu

Belaga

SARAWAK
MALAYSIA

Schwaner Range

Telukbatang

Pulau
Maya

Pulau
Karimata

Ketapang

Teluk
Sukadana

Gunung Palung
National Park

Nanga
Tayap

Kudangan

Tumbangjul

Tumbangsamba

Kuala Kuayan

Kuala Kuru

Kasungan

Petakbehandang

Bukit Baka-
Bukit Raya
National Park

Tandjungpandan

Manggar

SUMATRA
INDONESIA

Pulau
Belitung

Karimata
Strait

Kendawangan

Sukamara

Pangkalan
Bun

Sampit

Teluk
Kumai

Tanjung Puting
National Park

Teluk
Sampit

Kuala Pembuang

Palangka
Raya

Sebangau
National
Park

Pembuang

Java
Sea

Top Experiences ›

Mt Kinabalu
By far Borneo's
highest peak (p56)

**Sepilok Orang-Utan
Rehabilitation Centre**
Orangutans up close (p77)

Sungai Kinabatangan
River banks teeming
with animals (p82)

Danum Valley
Primeval jungle, pygmy
elephants, orangutans (p88)

Kelabit Highlands
Cool air, smiles, great
trekking (p186)

Derawan Archipelago
Unspoilt tropical
islands (p239)

Loksado
Mountain retreat (p263)

Balabac Strait
Pulau
Balambangan
Pulau Banggi

Kudat
Cagayan
Sulu
Island
Pulau
Malawali
11°30'E
Kpg
Datong
Pulau
Jambongan
*Sulu
Sea*
12°E
Kota
Belud
Mt Kinabalu
(4095m)
Turtle Islands
National Park
Parang
Jolo
Island

**Tunku Abdul
Rahman
National Park**
Ranau
Beluran
Sandakan
Siasi
5°N
Kota Kinabalu
Papar
Tambunan
Sepilok
*Sungai
Kinabatangan*
Tawitawi
Island

**Crocker Range
National Park**
Mt Trus-Madi
(2642m)
**SABAH
MALAYSIA**
Lahad
Datu
Tungku
PHILIPPINES

BANDAR
SERI
GAWAN
*Teluk
Brunei*
Tenom
Keningau
**Maliau Basin
Conservation
Area**
Danum Valley
Conservation
Area
*Teluk Lahad
Datu*

utong
eria
Lawas
Limbang
Sipitang
Kuala
Tomani
Sapulot
Kalabakan
Semporna

abi
BRUNEI
Kalabakan
**Gunung
Mulu (2337m)**
Sebuku
Sembakung
National Park
Nunukan
Timur
Island
Tawau
*Pulau
Sipadan*
*Celebes
Sea*

Baram
**Gunung
Mulu
National Park**
**Kelabit
Highlands**
Tarakan
*Teluk
Sekatak*
*Teluk
Sebuko*
Pulau
Bunyu

**Kayan Mentarang
National Park**
Tanjung
Batu
Derawan
Archipelago

Iran Range
Berau
Semerut
*Tiung
Estuary*

Kayan
Sangkulirang
Sambaliung Mountains

**KALIMANTAN
INDONESIA**
Muara Wahau
**Kutai
National
Park**
Equator (0°)

Longiram
Bontang
*Lake Lake
Semayang Melintang*
Tenggarong
Palu

*Lake
Jempang*
Samarinda
*Makassar
Strait*

Muara Teweh
**SULAWESI
INDONESIA**

Barito
*Teluk
Adang*
*Teluk
Apar*

Tanahgrogot

Amuntai
Loksado
Kandangan
Rantau
Kotabaru
Pulau
Sebuku

**Pegunungan
Meratus**
Martapura
Pagatan
Pulau
Laut
Palopo

Pelaihari
Batakam

15 TOP EXPERIENCES

Gunung Mulu National Park

1 If the only marvel at Mulu (p180) were the biggest cavern on earth, sprouting a phantasmagorical forest of stalactites and stalagmites, this park would be on any list of Borneo's best. If the only fauna were the twirling, spiralling clouds of bats that emerge from the Deer Cave each day at dusk, it would deserve Unesco World Heritage status. And if the only activity were spotting 20cm-long stick insects on a night walk, the flight from Miri would be worth it. But add in towering Gunung Mulu and the Pinnacles and you have one of Southeast Asia's wonders. The Pinnacles, Gunung Mulu National Park

Maliau Basin

2 You came to Borneo looking for something wild, right? The Maliau Basin (p101) is as wild as it gets. The basin is a rock-rimmed depression filled with primary rainforest – that's untouched, uncut jungle, as old as the hills. We asked a local ranger what he thought of the Maliau, and his Malay response was *'Adan da Hawa'* – Adam and Eve. That's how fresh and perfect this forest feels, and while it may look expensive to enter, with a bit of initiative you too can experience the world as it once was. Flying gecko, Maliau Basin

ANDREW WATSON/GETTY IMAGES ©

Sarawak's Dayak Longhouses

3 There's no better way to get a sense of indigenous tribal culture than to visit a longhouse (p146) – or, better yet, stay over. Essentially a whole village under a single roof, these dwellings can be longer than two football pitches and contain dozens of family units, each of which opens onto a covered common verandah used for economic activities, socialising and celebrations. Although these days all longhouses enjoy some modern amenities, many still have at least a few headhunted skulls on display.

Kuching

4 Borneo's most sophisticated and stylish city (p124) brings together an atmospheric old town, a romantic waterfront, fine cuisine for all budgets, and chic nightspots that would be right at home in London. But the city's biggest draw is what's nearby: some of Sarawak's finest natural sites, easy to visit on day trips. You can spot semi-wild orangutans or search out a giant Rafflesia flower in the morning, look for proboscis monkeys and wild crocs on a sundown cruise in the South China Sea, and then dine on super-fresh seafood or crunchy *midin* fern tips.
Kuching's waterfront at dusk

Loksado

5 If you'd like to escape a bit from the jungle, if not the world, this small hamlet will do the trick. Nestled by a rushing stream in the foothills of the Meratus, scenic Loksado (p263) feels more like a mountain retreat than part of Borneo. There's a vibrant market, diverse trekking opportunities, bamboo rafting, and lots of friendly locals. Accommodation options are sparse but include a great riverside budget hotel with everything you need for an extended stay. Backpackers take note: if you need to re-energise, this is the place. Bamboo rafting

Mt Kinabalu

6 Mt Kinabalu (p56) is so many things we don't know where to start. Highest mountain in Borneo and Malaysia? Check. Climbable even by novices but great fun for veteran trekkers? Check. Abode of the spirits of local indigenous tribes? Check. Home to several unique-in-Borneo ecosystems and some 6000 plant species, many of them endemic? Check. Even on an island bursting with astonishing natural beauty, the sight of Mt Kinabalu's peak early in the morning causes most folks to lose their breath.

Cross-Borneo Trek

7 Welcome to the triathlon of adventure travel! Starting on Borneo's east coast, you'll travel hundreds of kilometres upriver, deep into the heart of one of the world's most fabled jungles, trek through back-of-beyond hills like the explorers of old, and then head down to the west coast on a thrilling white-water canoe ride. Along the way you'll sample everything Kalimantan has to offer: wildlife, Dayak culture and pure adrenalin. If you can't do it all, the first stage of the Cross-Borneo Trek (p219) is great by itself.

NORA CAROL PHOTOGRAPHY/GETTY IMAGES ©

PETER PTSCHELINZEW/GETTY IMAGES ©

8

Semenggoh Nature Reserve

8 Watching Homo sapiens encounter orangutans for the first time is almost as entertaining as watching our shaggy jungle cousins stuff half a dozen bananas into their mouths, grab a coconut and scramble back up into the jungle canopy. Both primate encounters are a twice-daily feature at Semenggoh Nature Reserve (p149) near Kuching, one of the best places in the world to see semi-wild orangutans swing from tree to tree, dangle nonchalantly from vines and take care of their adorable and very curious infants. Orangutan at Semenggoh Wildlife Centre

Danum Valley

9 If Danum Valley's primeval jungle (p88) makes you think of dinosaurs, we'll understand – the area really does look like Jurassic Park. Confirmed sightings of a *T. rex* eating a lawyer? Not that we know of, but visitors often spot pygmy elephants, wild orangutans and clouds of bird life. Some, though, don't actually *see* any animals at all as the jungle is so thick it can cloak fauna mere metres from where you're standing. But that's part of Danum's enchanting and timeless appeal. Fiddle beetle, Danum Valley

Kinabatangan River Safaris

10 Indiana Jones would love the Sungai Kinabatangan (Kinabatangan River). Like a muddy brown python, Sabah's longest river wends its way through the epic jungles south of Sandakan, bracketed by riverine forest teeming with civet cats, orangutans, proboscis monkeys, saltwater crocodiles, monitor lizards, hornbills, kingfishers and hawks. Book yourself into one of several jungle camps in the villages of Sukau and Bilit, or stay with locals in a homestay, and set out on a river cruise (p83) for an excellent shot at spotting some of Borneo's most iconic animals.

Sepilok Orang-Utan Rehabilitation Centre

11 Most people find orangutans to be meltingly cute ambassadors of the great ape family. If you fit into this demographic, you'll love the Sepilok sanctuary (p77), one of the better dedicated research and rehabilitation facilities in Borneo. You're likely not going to see orangutans gambolling as they would in the wild, but it's still magical to watch these ginger giants during feeding times, when they bend their way over ropes and branches and turn their meal of bananas into so many scattered peels.

Derawan Archipelago

12 These diverse islands (p239) offer something wonderful for everyone. The sandy streets and waterfront losmen (budget guesthouses) of Pulau Derawan are a first-rate backpacker destination, while the postcard-pretty twin resort isles of Nabucco and Nunukan offer some truly extraordinary diving, along with high-end bungalow accommodation. And for those intent on finding an authentic tropical paradise, massive Maratua atoll and the virtually untouristed islands beyond offer a shot at bliss that is increasingly hard to find. Homestay visits here have been known to stretch on for weeks.

Tanjung Puting National Park

13 Arguably one of the best places in the world to experience close-up encounters with semi-wild orangutans, Tanjung Puting (p251) offers an unforgettable upriver journey on a chugging *klotok* (a boat that's both your home and your lookout tower): the Milky Way glittering above you as you sleep alfresco on the top deck, the call of gibbons waking you in the morning, and the emotional and fascinating experience of seeing Borneo's critically endangered orangutans so intimately you're often almost rubbing shoulders with them. *Klotok* in Tanjung Puting National Park

Bako National Park

14 Wild jungle animals – think proboscis monkeys, bearded pigs and entire families of long-tailed macaques – are easier to spot on the rocky Bako Peninsula than almost anywhere else in Borneo, although the park (p142) is just a short trip (by road and then motorboat) from the bustle of Kuching. Over a dozen hiking trails take you to sandstone plateaus, waterfalls, secret bays and secluded beaches, passing through endangered lowland ecosystems – mangroves, heath forest, dipterocarp forest – that provide the ideal conditions for pitcher plants and terrestrial orchids.

Kelabit Highlands

15 The air is clean and cool, the rice fields impossibly green, the local cuisine scrumptious, and the trekking – from long-house to longhouse – some of the best in Borneo, but the star attraction in the Kelabit Highlands (p186) is the people, justifiably famous for their ready smiles and easy way with visitors. Getting to Sarawak's remote north-eastern corner is half the fun – you can either bust your butt on logging roads for 12 hours or take an exhilarating flight in a 19-seat Twin Otter turboprop. Portrait of a Kelabit man

need to know

Currency

» Malaysian ringgit (RM), Brunei dollar (B$), Indonesian rupiah (Rp)

Language

» Bahasa Malaysia, Bahasa Indonesia, Chinese dialects, Dayak languages such as Kadazan–Dusun, Iban, Bidayuh and Kelabit

When to Go

Tropical climate, rain year-round

Kota Kinabalu
• GO year-round

Bandar Seri Begawan
GO year-round •

Kuching
• GO year-round

Pontianak
• GO year-round

Balikpapan
GO year-round

Banjarmasin
• GO year-round

Year-round

» No especially good or bad season to visit.

» Lowland areas hot and humid.

» Rain a possibility every day, all year (but without rain, as they say, it wouldn't be a rainforest).

'Wet' Season
(Oct-Feb)

» Indistinct wet season October to February; can affect boat links to islands and diving visibility.

» Rains can render Kalimantan's dirt roads impassable (October to April).

High Season
(Jul-Sep)

» Accommodation and trekking guides may be booked out in some areas in July, August and perhaps September.

Your Daily Budget

Budget less than
US$30

» Dorm bed: US$4–7

» Meals at food stalls, self-catering at fruit and vegie markets

» National park admission: US$3

» Almost all museums are free

Midrange
US $30–80

» Air-con double with bathroom: from US$20

» Meals at all but the priciest restaurants

» Taxis, chartered motorboats or tours to nature sites

Top end over
US$80

» Luxury double room: US$100

» Seafood dinner: US$8–20 per kilo

Money

» ATMs widely available in cities and larger towns. Credit cards usually accepted at top-end establishments.

Visas

» Generally not required for Malaysia and Brunei. Needed for Indonesia *except* if entering Kalimantan at Balikpapan, Pontianak or Tebedu Entikong.

Mobile Phones

» Cheap international direct-dial calls can be made with a local SIM card in a 900/1800MHz phone. Settled areas have good coverage

Transport

» Aeroplanes, express ferries and motorised longboats go where roads don't. Frequent buses link major cities in Sarawak, Brunei and Sabah.

Websites

» **Brunei Tourism** (www.bruneitourism. travel) Oodles of info.

» **Google Earth** (www .google.com/earth) Vivid satellite imagery.

» **Lonely Planet** (www .lonelyplanet.com) Information, bookings, forums and more.

» **Sabah Parks** (www .sabahparks.org) Sabah's national parks.

» **Sabah Tourism** (www.sabahtourism .com) Official site.

» **Sarawak Forestry** (www.sarawakforestry .com) Sarawak's national parks.

» **Sarawak Tourism** (www.sarawaktourism .com) Official site.

» **Mongabay** (www .mongabay.com) Rainforest conservation news.

Exchange Rates

		RM	B$	Rp
Australia	A$1	3.21	1.28	10,036
Canada	C$1	3.07	1.22	9587
Euro zone	€1	4.15	1.65	12,896
Japan	¥100	3.31	1.32	10,346
New Zealand	NZ$1	2.63	1.05	8207
Singapore	S$1	2.51	1.00	7845
UK	UK£1	4.79	1.90	14,964
USA	US$1	3.10	1.24	9700

For current exchange rates see www.xe.com.

Important Numbers

Country codes for Borneo:

Brunei	☎673
Indonesia	☎62
Malaysia	☎60

Emergency police numbers:

Brunei	☎993
Indonesia	☎110
Malaysia	☎999

Arriving in Borneo

» **Malaysia**
Major airports, such as Kuching, Kota Kinabalu and Miri, have ATMs, car rental desks, kiosks selling SIM cards, and orderly taxi queues with fixed prices and vouchers for trips into town.

» **Brunei**
Brunei International Airport has ATMs, car rental and good bus connections with the centre of Bandar Seri Begawan. City tours available for transit passengers. Singapore dollars are universally accepted, with a conversion rate of one to one.

» **Kalimantan**
Taxis and other conveyances meet all incoming flights.

Well Dressed in Borneo

Despite the heat and humidity, adult men in Malaysian Borneo don't wear short pants in cities or towns, particularly not in smart restaurants or hotels. In Kalimantan, however, shorts are very popular among men, especially younger ones.

Likewise, women should remember that much of Borneo is largely Muslim and relatively discreet clothing is recommended. You certainly don't have to cover your hair (except inside mosques), but walking around with a tank top or bikini top is unwise.

Cotton clothing never really dries in the jungle, so bring at least a few fast-drying synthetic items.

if you like...

Orangutans

You scan the canopy and wait, straining to hear the rustle of branches above the drone of cicadas. Suddenly, a fluttering of leaves and – a flash of orange-brown fur! It's a female orangutan, her baby hanging onto her long chest hair as the two of them swing through their native habitat, high in the rainforest canopy. Later, dangling in space, the mother crams bright-yellow bananas into her mouth and casually hands fruit to her hungry infant.

Semenggoh Wildlife Centre One of the easiest places to see semi-wild orangutans (p149)

Sepilok Orang-Utan Rehabilitation Centre Rescued orangutans, living free in the forest, drop by for fruit (p77)

Sungai Kinabatangan Home to lots of truly wild orangutans (p82)

Camp Leakey, Tanjung Puting National Park Great for sighting semi-wild orangutans at feeding times (p251)

Jungle Trekking

There's nothing quite like being a day or two's walk from the nearest road, entirely surrounded by old-growth rainforest as you tramp from one longhouse to the next. It's a challenging slog – the heat, the humidity and the leeches take their toll, and the trail itself sometimes disappears into a bog or, on muddy inclines, becomes as slippery as ice – but to be surrounded with such fecundity and botanical richness...the feeling is indescribable!

Kinabalu National Park Much more than just the famous summit climb (p56)

Gunung Mulu National Park Options include the Headhunters' Trail (p180)

Maliau Basin Conservation Area Remote hikes through old-growth forest (p101)

Bario to Ba Kelalan A classic trek through the Kelabit Highlands (p191)

Pegunungan Meratus (Meratus Mountains) Trails from Loksado criss-cross forested valleys (p263)

Muller Mountains Borneo's remotest mountain range (p219)

Indigenous Culture

Borneo's Dayak groups – (in)famous for having once practised headhunting – have lived in harmony with the rainforest for thousands of years, in remote communities based on mutual reliance and responsibility. Even a short longhouse visit offers insights into their age-old traditions – and the ways they're adapting to modern life. Come during a festival and you may be asked to join in the merriment, liberally lubricated with *tuak* (rice wine).

Kelabit Highlands One of the best places in Borneo to trek from longhouse to longhouse (p186)

Batang Ai Region Old-time Iban longhouses, many accessible only by boat (p158)

Upper Sungai Mahakam Dayak culture in the heart of Borneo (p228)

Upper Sungai Kapuas Linked by boat with Putussibau (p249)

Pegunungan Meratus Animist beliefs are strong and shamans have plenty of work in these remote hills (p263)

Western Sarawak Bidayuh longhouses and the Sarawak Cultural Village (p142)

» Food stall at night market (p162), Sibu

Jungle River Trips

From time immemorial, rivers were the only transport arteries into Borneo's interior, and in some areas – especially in Kalimantan – ferries, longboats and canoes are still the only way to get around. Make a virtue of necessity by treating your floating transport as part of the roaring adventure.

Tanjung Puting National Park The shores of Sungai Sekonyer teem with macaques, orang-utans and crocs up towards Camp Leakey (p251)

Sungai Mahakam The further upriver you go, the wilder the wildlife (p235)

Sungai Bungan Borneo's most thrilling canoe trip (p250)

Sungai Kinabatangan Spot an ark's worth of animals, including pygmy elephants (p83)

Batang Rejang Take a 'flying coffin' river express to Belaga (p163)

Bandar Seri Begawan to Bangar Slap through palm-lined waterways and weave among mangroves (p210)

Multicultural Cities

Nowhere is Borneo's extraordinary ethnic gumbo more colourful – and delicious – than in the cities. The minarets of Malay mosques tower over the streetscape a few blocks from bright-red Chinese temples, and both are just a short walk from colonial-era shophouses and hawker centres with a tongue-boggling array of bubbling soups, barbecuing satay and fresh-squeezed juices. Many cities take special pride in their parks, promenades and festivals.

Kuching Fantastic for strolling and aimless exploration, with 19th-century forts, two China-towns and excellent cuisine for every budget (p124)

Bandar Seri Begawan Blessed with picturesque water villages, two stunning mosques and some outstanding food stalls, BSB is as polite and unassuming as its people (p198)

Sibu The mostly Chinese 'Swan City' boasts a busy ferry port, 22 community parks and a great night market (p159)

Singkawang Kalimantan's most Chinese city sometimes feels like Shanghai circa 1930 (p246)

Exploring Caves

Borneo has an incredible variety of underground wonders. While some of the most breathtaking caves must be visited with a professional guide, others are easily accessible on plankwalks. Daily at dusk, millions of bats head out of Borneo's caves to hunt insects – an awesome sight.

Gunung Mulu National Park Some of the world's most spectacular caves, dripping with fantastic stalactites, are home to millions of bats and swiftlets (p180)

Gomantong Caves The cathedral-like grand chamber is speckled with rays of sunlight (p82)

Niah National Park Niah's enormous caverns, once home to prehistoric humans, are easy to explore on boardwalks (p171)

Wind Cave & Fairy Cave Stairs and paths make it possible to visit unaccompanied (p153, p154)

Kuching Caving This small spelunking outfit mounts adventurous day expeditions to Kuching-area caves (p154)

month by month

Muslim and Chinese festivals follow lunar or lunisolar calendars and so vary relative to the Western calendar. Approximate dates for 2013 to 2016 appear below; celebrations often begin the night before these dates.

February

The weather is hot and humid, with rain always likely. February is one of the wettest months of the year in Kuching (Sarawak) and Banjarmasin (South Kalimantan). The seas off Sarawak and around Kalimantan's Derawan Archipelago can be rough.

Chinese New Year

Borneo's Chinese communities, especially large in Sarawak's Kuching, Sibu and Singkawang, welcome the New Year with bright-red lanterns, sweets, lion and dragon dances, drum performances, night markets and, often, a raucous (and illegal) display of firecrackers and fireworks. Falls on 31 January 2014, 19 February 2015 and 8 February 2016.

April

The weather is hot and humid, with rain always likely, even in Sandakan (Sabah), where months don't get any drier.

Regatta Lepa

Bajau Sea Gypsies deck out their *lepa* (boats) with streamers, bunting, flags, ceremonial umbrellas and gorgeously decorated sails. The mid-April weekend festivities are further animated with violin, cymbal and drum music, duck-catching competitions and tug-of-war contests with boats; see p94 for more.

May

The weather is hot and humid, with rain always likely. May is not the wettest month anywhere on the island, but neither is it the driest, so be prepared to be rained on.

Borneo Jazz Festival

An eclectic assemblage of artists from Europe, North America and Southeast Asia makes the Borneo Jazz Festival (www.jazzborneo .com), held on a weekend in mid-May, Borneo's premier jazz event. Formerly known as the Miri International Jazz Festival.

Harvest Festival

Rice is the basis of Sabah's indigenous way of life. To mark the annual harvest, native peoples gather in their home villages on 30 and 31 May for a colourful thanksgiving festival that's also known as Pesta Ka'amatan.

June

The weather is hot and humid, with rain always likely. June is the wettest month of the year in Balikpapan (West Kalimantan). Tourist numbers rise because of the northern hemisphere summer.

Gawai Dayak

An official holiday in Sarawak (it's also marked by the Iban in Brunei), this Dayak festival (p280) celebrates the end of the rice harvest season. City-dwelling, Dayaks return to their longhouses to socialise, make music, eat and get happy with *tuak* (rice wine). Held statewide from the evening of 31 May to 2 June, in some villages on other dates in June.

July

The weather is hot and humid, with rain likely even in Kuching, where this is the driest month. Northern hemisphere tourists flock to Borneo so consider booking treks, caving, guides and tours in advance.

Ramadan
During the month of Ramadan, Muslims are not allowed to eat, drink or have sexual relations from dawn to sunset. Celebratory break-the-fast meals are held after sundown. Many offices have shorter hours and some restaurants close during daylight. Begins on 9 July 2013, 28 June 2014 and 18 June 2015.

Borneo Cultural Festival
Brings to Sibu (Sarawak) music, dance, cultural performances and food representing central Sarawak's Chinese, Malay-Melanau and Dayak traditions. Held over 10 days in early July.

Rainforest World Music Festival
This three-day musical extravaganza (www.rwmf. net), held in the Sarawak Cultural Village near Kuching on the second weekend in July, brings

together Dayak bands and international artists. Area accommodation fills up long in advance.

Sultan of Brunei's Birthday
Colourful official ceremonies are held on 15 July to mark the birthday of Sultan Hassanal Bolkiah. In Bandar Seri Begawan, events include an elaborate military ceremony presided over by the supremo himself, smartly dressed in a medal-bedecked uniform.

August

The weather is hot and humid, with rain likely everywhere even though August is the driest month in Banjarmasin (South Kalimantan). Northern hemisphere tourists are numerous so consider booking treks, caving, guides and tours in advance.

Hungry Ghost Festival
On the 15th (full moon) day of the seventh Chinese lunar month, when spirits are free to roam the earth, offerings of food, prayer, incense and (fake) paper money are made to appease the spirits of the deceased. Falls on 21 August 2013, 10 August 2014 and 28 August 2015.

Hari Raya Puasa
This festive three-day Muslim holiday marks the end of the fasting month of Ramadan. Many people travel to their hometowns, creating traffic jams and a shortage of air, boat and

bus tickets. Begins 8 August 2013, 28 July 2014 and 17 July 2015.

September

The weather is hot and humid. September isn't the driest month anywhere on the island, so be prepared for rain.

Belaga Rainforest Challenge
Orang Ulu longhouses along the Batang Rejang joyously share their music, dance, traditional costumes and cuisines with each other and with visitors. Competitions include boat races and a 12km jungle run. Held in even-numbered years, it lasts for three days.

Borneo International Kite Festival
Held on the runway of the old airport in Bintulu (Sarawak), this festival (www.borncokite.com) brings colourful, strange and marvellous kites to Borneo's natural-gas capital. Takes place over four or five days in late September or early October.

Erau Festival
Held in late September, the Erau Festival sees thousands of Dayaks from all over Kalimantan converging on Tenggarong, on the mighty Sungai Mahakam (Mahakam River), in a whirl of tribal costumes, ceremony and dance.

Adventure Borneo

Best Wildlife Spotting

Tanjung Puting National Park (p251)
Mancong, Sungai Mahakam (p233)
Bako National Park (p142)
Wildlife River Boat Cruises, Sungai Kinabatangan (p83)
Kuching Wetlands National Park (p148)
Gunung Mulu National Park (p180)

Best Mountain Climbing

Mt Kinabalu, Sabah (p56)
Gunung Mulu, Sarawak (p180)
Mt Besar, Kalimantan (p263)

Best Jungle Day Hikes

Rafflesia Loop Trail, Gunung Gading National Park (p156)
Wehea Forest, Kalimantan (p237)
Danum Valley Conservation Area (p84)
Gunung Mulu National Park (p180)
Bako National Park (p142)

Best Rainforest Canopy Walks

Gunung Mulu National Park (p180)
Ulu Temburong National Park (p212)
Poring Hot Springs (p65)
Danum Valley, Sabah (p88)
Sepilok Rainforest Discovery Centre (p79)

Borneo is one of Southeast Asia's premier outdoor adventure destinations, with a spectacular mix of jungle, rock, water and thrills that will wow both nature lovers and adrenalin junkies. If you like to experience a place by trekking it, climbing it, crawling through it or floating on it, you'll love Borneo.

Jungle Trekking
When to Go

Borneo has some of the best jungle trekking anywhere in the world. While the island's forests are disappearing at an alarming rate, vast swaths of old-growth (primary) tropical rainforest still cover the middle of the island and much of Brunei, and pristine patches remain in parts of Sabah and Sarawak. If you've never walked through genuine tropical jungle, the experience – even if you don't see many mammals, which tend to be nocturnal, very shy or both – is likely to be a revelation: you simply won't believe the teeming fecundity.

Borneo has wet months and less-wet months – the timing depends on where you are – but precipitation varies so widely from year to year that a month that's usually dry can be very rainy and vice versa. In short, no matter when you go you are likely to get wet.

What is seasonal, however, is the number of other travellers you'll be competing with for experienced guides and lodgings. For obvious reasons, northern hemisphere residents often come to Borneo (especially Sabah and Sarawak) during summer holidays in their home countries, so if you'd like

TRAVEL LITERATURE: STORIES OF ADVENTURE

Borneo has fired the world's imagination for centuries. Perhaps the best recent title is *Stranger in the Forest* (1988) by Eric Hansen, in which the author recounts his journey across the island in the company of Penan guides. It is not just the difficulty of the feat but the author's brilliant and sensitive storytelling that make the book a classic. One cannot read it without a sense of sadness, for the world and the people described are now almost completely gone.

The most popular book about Borneo is Redmond O'Hanlon's *Into the Heart of Borneo* (1984), a humorous account of the author's 1983 journey up a river in Sarawak. While O'Hanlon makes a bit much of what was a fairly unremarkable journey, one cannot help but enjoy his colourful narrative.

Espresso with Headhunters: A Journey Through the Jungles of Borneo (2001) by John Wassner tells of a more extensive trip by an Australian traveller (and inveterate caffeine and nicotine addict). Not nearly as famous as O'Hanlon's book, this gives a more realistic account of what life is like in Sarawak. We only wish he had chosen a different title – it's time to let the whole Borneo-headhunter thing die a quiet death.

If you climb Mt Kinabalu, you'll notice the gaping chasm of Low's Gully to your right as you ascend the final summit pyramid. *Kinabalu Escape: The Soldiers' Story* (1997) by Rich Mayfield tells of the British Army's ill-fated 1994 attempt to descend the gully. The expedition, a textbook case in how not to run an expedition, led to an expensive rescue operation and the near deaths of several team members.

to trek – particularly in popular national parks such as Gunung Mulu, Kinabalu and Tanjung Puting – in July, August or September, it's a good idea to book a guide or tour in advance.

Guides

Many national parks have well-marked day trails that can be tramped unaccompanied. But for almost all overnight trails, only a fool would set out without a local guide. Remember, trail maps of any sort are completely unavailable and signage along remote trails nonexistent.

Especially in Sabah, Brunei and Sarawak, national parks are very strict about allowing only licensed guides to show visitors around. We've heard stories of groups being turned back when they arrived with an uncertified leader. Before you fork over any cash, compare notes with other travellers and ask to see the guide's national park certification.

Guides for day walks can sometimes be hired at national park headquarters, but for overnight trekking you'll generally need to contact either a freelance guide or a tour agency before you arrive.

Physical Demands

Hiking in the tropics is much more strenuous than in temperate zones. One kilometre of slogging through Borneo is roughly equivalent to two in Europe or North America. Thanks to the combination of high temperatures and high humidity, you will sweat enough to discover what eyebrows are for, so be sure to drink plenty of water. In *kerangas* (heath forests) and on high mountains, prepare for intense sun by wearing a hat and sunscreen. Make sure your guide is aware of the pace you can handle.

Borneo is hardly the Himalayas, but even in places like the Kelabit Highlands (1500m) you may feel the altitude, at least for a few days.

Pre-Trip Preparation

To the uninitiated, jungle trekking can be something of a shock – like marching all day in a sauna with a floor as slippery as ice. To make the experience as safe and painless as possible, it's necessary to prepare ahead:

» On overnight trips, bring two sets of clothing: one for hiking and one to wear at the end of the day (keep your night kit dry in a plastic bag). Within minutes of starting, your hiking kit will be drenched and will stay that way throughout your trip. Never blur the distinction between your day and night kits, or you'll find that you have two sets of wet clothes.

» If you'll be hiking through dense vegetation, wear long trousers and a long-sleeved shirt. Otherwise, shorts and a T-shirt will suffice. Whatever you wear, make sure it's loose fitting.

LEECHES SUCK (BLOOD)

There's just no getting around it: if you want to experience Borneo's magnificent tropical rainforests, at some point you're going to find yourself getting up close and intimate with a leech (www.invertebrate.us/leech) – or, more likely, with lots of them. If you can't stand the sight of blood, wear dark-coloured socks.

Common Leech Varieties

There are two main varieties of leech in Borneo: the ground-dwelling brown leech and the striped yellow-reddish tiger leech, which often lives higher up on foliage. Leeches, which are attracted by the vibrations and carbon dioxide you produce, are probably the jungle's quietest creatures. Since you can't feel the bite of the brown leech, you'll only realise what's going on when you actually spot him-and-her (leeches are hermaphrodites), or when you notice blood seeping through your clothing. But you can feel the bite of a tiger leech – it's similar to an ant sting – which means that if you're quick, you can take action before making an involuntary blood donation.

While leeches are horrible creatures, they are almost completely harmless. In Borneo they don't generally carry parasites, bacteria or viruses that can infect humans. However, a bite may itch and bleed profusely for a few hours due to the anticoagulant juices (hirudin) the leech injects. The spot may itch for another week, and then it will scab over and resolve into a small dark spot that completely disappears after several weeks. The only danger is that the bite may get infected, which is why it's important to disinfect the bite and keep it dry.

Self-Defence Against Leeches

Like hangover cures, everyone has a favourite method of protecting themselves from leeches. Problem is, most don't work. Putting tobacco in your socks or on your shoes is an old standby. We tried this one and it only seemed to encourage the little bastards.

» Bring fast-drying synthetic clothes. Once cotton gets wet, it won't dry until you bring it back to town.

» Evenings can be cool in the mountains, so if you'll be spending time in higher altitudes, bring a fleece top to keep warm.

» If you're going to be trekking on well-used trails (eg in the Kelabit Highlands) and don't need a lot of ankle support, consider hiking in running shoes with good traction. For serious trekking, though, it's crucial to have serious hiking boots with cleats, properly broken in, for the muddy slopes.

» To keep the leeches at bay, buy spandex pants or a pair of light-coloured leech socks. It's not always possible to find these in Borneo (guesthouses in Miri may carry them), so buy them online before coming.

» Drink plenty of water. If you're going long distances, you'll have to bring either a water filter or a water-purification agent such as iodine (most people opt for the latter to keep weight down).

» Get in shape long before coming to Borneo and start slowly. Try day hikes before longer treks.

» Always go with a guide unless you're on a well-marked, commonly travelled trail. Navigating in the jungle is extremely difficult because most of the time – even when you're on top of a hill – all you can see is trees.

» Bring talcum powder to cope with the chafing caused by wet undergarments. Wearing loose underwear will also help prevent chafing.

» If you wear glasses, you might want to treat them with an antifog solution (ask your optician). Otherwise, you may find yourself in a foggy whiteout within minutes of setting out.

» Your sweat will soak through the back of your backpack. Consider putting something waterproof over the back padding to keep the sweat out; otherwise, consider a waterproof stuff sack.

» Keep your camera gear, including extra batteries, in an airtight plastic container, with a pouch of silica gel or other desiccant.

Guides & Agencies

Tour agencies and guides can help you head for the hills.

Sabah

» Adventure Alternative Borneo (p45)

» Borneo Adventure (p45)

» Borneo Eco Tours (p46)

» Borneo Nature Tours (p46)

» Fieldskills Adventures (p45)

Many Kelabit people swear that spraying your shoes with a powerful insecticide works (that's insecticide, not insect repellent); we didn't try this one for fear of unwelcome side effects, nor did we use Dettol disinfectant, which can be toxic. Yet other people wear pantyhose or spandex cycling pants, slather on the baby oil (said to cause leeches to slide off your skin) or use tropical-strength mosquito repellent – though since this last item is water-soluble, it's likely to wash off if you ford a river or sweat.

There is only one really effective method of keeping leeches at bay: wearing an impenetrable fabric barrier. Knee-length leech socks, made from tightly knit calico, work as does Spandex. The best leech socks are light coloured so you can see the leeches ascending your legs and pick them off. You can find these online; guesthouses in Miri may also sell them.

If you do discover a leech making a pass at you, don't panic. Yanking off a leech can leave part of its jaws in the wound, and burning it or dousing it with vinegar, lemon juice or alcohol can cause it to regurgitate its stomach contents, increasing the likelihood of infection. Instead, slide your fingernail along your skin at the point where the leech is attached to break the suction. The leech will try to grab your finger with its other end so roll it around to prevent it from getting a grip and flick it away. If there are other people around, it's good form to chop the leech in half with your *parang* (Bornean machete). Don't squirt DEET directly on sucking leeches as the chemical may get in your wound.

One more thing to remember: salt is to leeches as kryptonite is to Superman. Some people put a teaspoon of salt inside some thin cloth and tie it to the top of a stick – touch a leech with something salty and it will recoil like the Wicked Witch of the West.

If you find a few leech bites on your feet, console yourself with the thought that you have had the privilege and the honour of making a very real contribution to sustaining Borneo's endangered ecosystem.

Sarawak

Guides can also be found at Gunung Mulu National Park (p180) and in the Kelabit Highlands (p186)

Brunei

Kalimantan

For day trekking, many of the agencies specialising in river trips (p25) also offer hikes. Trekking in remote areas can be dangerous, so for a multiday expedition we recommend two outfits:

Mountain Climbing

Towering above the forests of Borneo are some brilliant mountains. Even nonclimbers know about 4095m Mt Kinabalu, the highest peak between the Himalayas and the island of New Guinea. This craggy monster simply begs to be climbed, and there is something magical about starting the ascent in humid tropical jungle and emerging into a bare, rocky alpine zone so cold that snow has been known to fall. But beyond the transition from hot to cold, it's the weird world of the summit plateau that makes Mt Kinabalu among the world's most interesting peaks. It's got a dash of Yosemite and a pinch of Torres del Paine, but at the end of the day, it's pure Borneo.

Gunung Mulu (2377m) isn't quite as high but it's almost as famous, thanks in part to being a Unesco World Heritage site. If you're a glutton for punishment, you'll probably find the five-day return trek to the summit of this peak to your liking. Those who make the journey experience a variety of pristine natural environments, starting with lowland dipterocarp forest and ending with rhododendron and montane forest.

AL'S JUNGLE KIT LIST *AL DAVIES*

General Kit
☐ backpack
☐ pack liner (waterproof)
☐ waterproof bags
☐ day pack
☐ water bottles
☐ personal medical kit
☐ water purifier
☐ insect repellent (containing DEET)
☐ pocket knife
☐ head torch (flashlight)
☐ spare mini-torch
☐ small binoculars
☐ notepad and pencil

Clothing
☐ jungle boots
☐ breathable waterproof socks or boot liners

☐ sandals
☐ socks
☐ underwear
☐ lycra bras
☐ long trousers (2)
☐ shorts
☐ leech socks
☐ long-sleeve shirts (2)
☐ lightweight waterproof jacket
☐ swimwear
☐ warm top
☐ sunhat
☐ sarong
☐ sweat rag

Sleeping
☐ basha (tarpaulin) sheet
☐ hammock

☐ mosquito net
☐ bungee cords
☐ sleeping mat
☐ sleeping bag
☐ sleeping-bag liner

Cooking & Eating
☐ mess tin
☐ spoon
☐ mug

Miscellaneous
☐ wash kit
☐ sunscreen
☐ towel
☐ toilet paper
☐ sewing kit
☐ waterproof freezer bags

Pre-Trip Preparation

Climbing one of Borneo's iconic mountains is like a jungle trek except more so – more exhausting, more psychologically challenging and especially more vertical. Be prepared for ascents that turn your legs to rubber and for much colder weather. Book well ahead.

Guides & Agencies

Many of the agencies that handle trekking (p22) also offer mountain ascents. Some more experienced guides in the Kelabit Highlands can take you to two rarely climbed peaks, Batu Lawi and Gunung Murud.

Caving

Slice one of Borneo's limestone hills in half and chances are you'll find that the inside looks like Swiss cheese. Borneans have been living, harvesting birds' nests, planning insurgencies and burying their dead in these caves for tens of thousands of years.

These days, the island's subterranean spaces – including some of the largest caverns anywhere on earth – are quiet, except for the flow of underground streams, the drip of stalactites and the whoosh of bat and swiftlet wings.

Sarawak's Gunung Mulu National Park is a place of spelunking superlatives. It has the world's second-largest cave passage (Deer Cave, which is 2km in length and 174m in height), the world's largest cave chamber (Sarawak Chamber, at 700m long, 400m wide and 70m high) and Asia's longest cave (Clearwater Cave, with 225km of passages). Several of the park's finest caves are – like their counterparts in Niah National Park and Sabah's Gomantong Caves – accessible to nonspelunkers on raised walkways.

A pitch-black passageway deep in the bowels of the earth is not the ideal place to discover that you can't deal with narrow, confined spaces. Before heading underground, seriously consider your susceptibility to claustrophobia and fear of heights (some caves require scaling underground cliffs). If you have any concerns about a specific route, discuss these with your guide beforehand.

Be prepared to crawl through muck, including bat guano, and bring clothes you won't mind getting filthy in (some guides and agencies supply these).

When to Go

Rain can flood the interior of some caves at any time of the year.

Gunung Mulu National Park has a shortage of trained spelunking guides, so unless you'll be hiring a private guide or going with a tour agency, make your reservations well in advance. Some dates in July, August and September are likely to be booked out months ahead.

Guides & Agencies

» Gunung Mulu National Park (p180)

» Kuching Caving (p192)

Jungle River Trips

The mountains and jungles of Borneo are drained by some of Southeast Asia's longest rivers. Whether it's tearing up a mainline *batang* (Iban for 'large river') in a speedboat, rafting down a *sungai* (Bahasa Malaysia for 'river') or kayaking on a narrow *ai* (Iban for 'small river') in an *ulu* (upriver) part of the interior, you'll find that these watery highways are perhaps the best way to experience Borneo.

Many parts of Borneo's interior can be reached only by river, so hopping on a boat is a necessity. There's something magical about heading to a human settlement connected by road to absolutely nowhere, especially if you're in the safe hands of an experienced boatman and accompanied by locals.

On larger rivers, transport is often by 'flying coffin' – long, narrow passenger boats with about 70 seats, not including the people sitting on the roof. Thanks to their mighty engines, these craft can power upriver against very strong currents. Ferry safety is a major issue in Kalimantan.

In a smaller upriver craft, such as a *temuai* (shallow-draft Iban longboat), be prepared for you and your (hopefully waterproofed) kit to get dunked – and to get out and push if it hasn't rained for a while. Whatever the size of the vessel, be aware that rivers can suddenly rise by 2m or more after a downpour. If a boat looks unseaworthy or lacks basic safety equipment (especially life vests), don't be shy about speaking up.

Sea-going craft travelling along the coast and out to offshore islands have to deal with rougher waters than their inland counterparts. In Sarawak and parts of Kalimantan, this is especially true from November to March, when the northeast monsoon can bring choppy conditions.

Costs

Travel by boat does not come cheap, mainly because marine engines and outboard motors, which must shove aside prodigious quantities of water, really slurp up the petrol.

For a small motorboat with a capacity of four to six people, count on paying about RM7 per kilometre, or roughly RM100 to RM150 per hour of actual sailing time. While the boat is moored somewhere – at an island or a remote beach, for instance – you'll have to remunerate the driver but, obviously, there are no fuel costs when the motor is off.

Guides & Agencies

Following are some of the agencies that can organise longboat trips, rafting, kayaking and other water-borne adventures (and in many cases day hikes too).

Sabah

» Borneo Authentic (p46)

» Borneo Eco Tours (p46)

» Borneo Nature Tours (p46)

» GogoSabah (p45)

» Only in Borneo (p107)

» Riverbug (p45)

» SI Tours (p74)

» Uncle Tan (p74)

» River Junkie (p106)

Sarawak

» Gunung Mulu National Park (p180)

» Rainforest Kayaking (p132)

» Stu Roach, Bario, Kelabit Highlands (p187)

Kalimantan

Guides can be found in Banjarmasin (p259), Loksado (p263), Tanjung Puting National Park (p251) and the Sungai Mahakam (p228). Other options:

» Borneo Orangutan Adventure Tour (p253)

» Borneo Wisata Permai Tours (p253)

» Kalimantan Tour Destinations (p257)

Diving Pulau Sipadan

Best Times for Diving

April–September This is turtle time, when sea turtles come to the archipelago to lay their eggs in the soft sand. You're unlikely to actually see turtles laying eggs, but you may spot them dancing their slow ballet beneath the waves. That said, turtles are always present in these waters – they're just highly concentrated during this period.

July–August Visibility is often stunning at this time of year, and clear views to 25m are common. You'll likely have to deal with more crowds as well, as this is prime holiday time in the northern hemisphere. Book well in advance if you want to visit during this period.

December–February This is the local wet season. The rain doesn't impact visibility too badly, but monsoon winds may keep boats from accessing Sipadan and the other Semporna islands. On the other hand, by January crowds have thinned out a bit. The rains sometimes continue into March.

The waters off the island of Sipadan were declared 'one of the world's best diving sites' by no less an expert than Jacques Cousteau. Every year, his assessment is confirmed by thousands of divers who come here to explore Sipadan's plunging sea wall, home and transit point for a staggering array of marine life, including green and hawksbill sea turtles, hammerhead sharks, parrotfish, manta rays and schools of fish so massive they resemble silver tornadoes or shimmering walls of armour.

But those same divers make it hard for Sipadan to remain 'an untouched piece of art', as Cousteau put it. Sipadan is many things, including one of Borneo's most popular tourism destinations, but untouched it is not. The Malaysian government has seen the need to preserve the integrity of Sipadan and, as a result, visiting the island is a tightly regulated process (although visitors never deal with the paperwork themselves). In fact, no tourists are even allowed on the island of Sipadan; rather, its surrounding waters attract mobs of divers, many of whom have travelled great distances to embark on the marine trek of a lifetime.

Planning
When to Go

The good news: there isn't a bad time to dive Sipadan, at least as far as visibility and wildlife go. But consider how much you want to balance factors like weather (ie rain or no rain), crowds and abundance of marine life. The general rule of thumb: the better the conditions, the larger the crowds. The corollary: wildlife spotting is almost always good, and thanks to the strict permit process, crowds rarely feel overwhelming.

Getting to Sipadan

Sipadan is an island in the Semporna Archipelago, situated just off Sabah's eastern tip. Eight islands within the archipelago form the Semporna Marine Park, the largest marine park in Malaysia. The closest town is also named Semporna; a nearby naval station has the area's only decompression chamber.

The closest airport is at Tawau, 72km west of Semporna town; a taxi from the airport to Semporna runs around RM100. Otherwise, there are numerous bus connections between Semporna and the rest of Sabah – for more information, see p92. Note that unless you arrive in Semporna town early in the day, you'll likely have to stay there overnight.

Permits & Dive Operators

Access to Sipadan is regulated by a tightly controlled permitting process. You can't get out there on your own; you must book with a tour operator, who will determine the day(s) you are allowed to dive Sipadan (note: you can dive other sites in the Semporna Archipelago without a permit). A list of dive operators can be found on p94.

The dive operators also run places to stay. Most accommodation, and all budget options, are on the small island of Mabul. Other possibilities include ritzier choices on the islands of Mataking, Kapalai and Pom Pom; for a complete list, see p95. Note that diving is the main event here – while the islands mentioned are pretty, they're too small to be enjoyed as island retreats in and of themselves.

Best Diving Sites
Around Sipadan

There are roughly a dozen delineated dive sites orbiting Sipadan island:

The Sea Wall The water here drops into a blue abyss some 2000m deep. Arising from this cleft

ARE YOU EXPERIENCED?

Sipadan rewards experienced divers, but you don't have to be a scuba veteran to enjoy the island, and nearby places like Mabul are easy for beginners. Even if you've never dived, every tour company we list (p94) can get you open-water certified, for reasonable prices compared to most of the world. Snorkellers are accommodated in Semporna as well; all the outfits we recommend offer snorkelling packages for less than diving packages (see p93).

are clouds of marine life – the abundance of which almost defies hyperbole. It's the most famous marine destination in the Semporna Archipelago.

Mid Reef The central, eastern-facing portion of the Sea Wall often contains one of the finest concentrations of marine life in the archipelago.

Barracuda Point Schools of undulating barracuda form seemingly impenetrable walls of scales and fins.

Coral Garden A sloped wall inhabited by macro sea life. White tip reef sharks sometimes roll by, pecking the coral clean – but don't worry, they'll leave you alone.

Hanging Garden Sea fans peek out among the many overhangs that give this area its name.

South Point Excellent spot for larger marine life like manta rays.

Turtle Tombs/Caves You can't fit into these coral caverns, which may be for the best, as they shelter the bones and shells of countless sea turtles who got lost inside and drowned.

Other diving locations around Semporna:

Mabul Rich in all types of marine life, and particularly good for muck diving (ie searching out smaller life forms in the sea mud), although you'll also likely spot rays and sea turtles.

Mataking Vertical wall dives here lead you past grey reef sharks and manta rays, among other outstanding forms of marine life.

Kapalai Relatively easy but offers exceedingly rewarding diving in conditions that are often shallow and sandy.

TIM ROCK/GETTY IMAGES ©

» (above) Diver passing coral fans in waters near Sipadan (p93)
» (left) Sea turtle swimming near reefs off Sipadan (p93)

WATERY WAYPOINT

Travellers know Sipadan as a diving destination. But if you're a marine biologist (or a fish), you'll know Sipadan as the grand highway interchange for the Indo-Pacific basin, one of the world's seminal marine habitats. Any tropical fish worth its fins ends up swimming by here at some point. OK, that's a bit of an exaggeration, but the Semporna Archipelago does sit atop a pretty incredible watery confluence, and Sipadan is the crossroads of that confluence. Part of the reason is the excellent condition of local reefs; sadly, much of the nearby coral, especially in the Philippines and Indonesia, has been seriously degraded by pollution and dynamite fishing.

Elsewhere in Borneo

Layang Layang A remote island renowned for wall dives, pristine coral and real adventure.

Pulau Mantanani Two little flecks of land ringed by a halo of colourful coral.

Derawan Archipelago Has some brilliant pier, cave and wall dives.

Miri Visibility is variable but the area has some interesting wrecks.

Responsible Diving

Here's how you can do your part to keep the Semporna Archipelago healthy for future generations of fish and divers:

» Avoid touching or standing on coral. Even a strong flipper kick can irreparably damage a reef.

» Practise neutral buoyancy. It's useful for all divers and keeps you off the coral.

» Keep your gear tight. Gauges, fins and other accessories can scrape the sea floor or coral.

» Observe animals – without trying to handle them. This goes double for sea turtles; trying to handle them stresses them out and can be especially detrimental to egg-bearing females.

» Don't feed sea creatures. When you feed wildlife, it stops being wild.

» Ask your operators not to anchor on coral (this isn't much of an issue in Semporna, where operators are conscientious, but it's good to be vigilant).

» Throw all rubbish, including cigarette butts, into a bag and take it with you when you leave.

» If you wish, participate in local conservation efforts. Every now and then accommodation owners in Mabul try to clean up rubbish in the local Malay and Bajau villages – visitors are welcome to join in.

» Avoid eating the local marine life, especially shark fin soup at Chinese restaurants.

itineraries

Whether you've got six days or 60, these itineraries provide a starting point for the trip of a lifetime. Want more inspiration? Head online to lonelyplanet.com/thorntree to chat with other travellers.

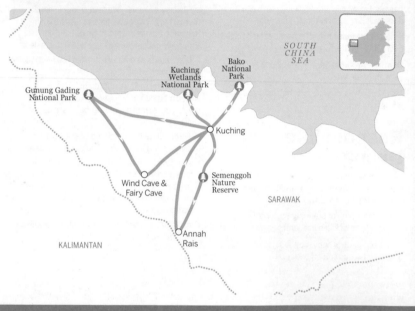

One Week
Kuching Excursions

> Spend your first day in **Kuching** tuning into the vibe of the city's kaleidoscopic mix of cultures and cuisines. Explore the narrow streets of Old Chinatown, ride a tiny passenger ferry to the English Renaissance–style Fort Margherita, and take a sunset stroll along the Waterfront Promenade. If it's Saturday, head to the Satok Weekend Market in the afternoon; if it's Sunday, visit in the morning; and if a giant Rafflesia flower happens to be in bloom in **Gunung Gading National Park**, drop everything and rush over before it fades away. On the way back, explore the **Wind Cave** and the **Fairy Cave**. On other days, combine a daytime excursion with an evening enjoying Kuching's fine eateries and chic but laid-back nightlife. Spend a half-day spotting orangutans at **Semenggoh Nature Reserve**, then drive further inland to the longhouse of **Annah Rais**, where you can stay overnight. Take a boat to **Bako National Park**, keeping an eye out for proboscis monkeys, macaques and pitcher plants as you hike around the peninsula. One day spend the sunset hour cruising around **Kuching Wetlands National Park**, alert for fireflies, crocs and proboscis monkeys.

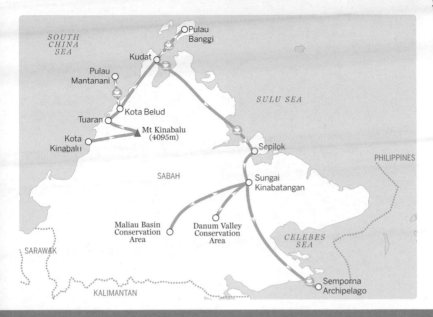

Around Sabah

> Arrive in **Kota Kinabalu** (KK) and give yourself two days to pre-book accommodation in places like Sungai Kinabatangan, the Semporna Archipelago (if you plan on diving) and Mt Kinabalu – accommodation at the latter should ideally be booked before you get to Sabah. Whilst in KK, make sure to eat at the Night Market and take a trip to the Mari Mari Cultural Village, Sabah Museum and Lok Kawi Wildlife Park – you can get a taste of the cultures, landscapes and animal life you're about to encounter firsthand. Party on the KK waterfront your first night in town, but try to keep your head clear the morning you leave Sabah's capital.

If you decide to climb **Mt Kinabalu**, it's easiest to leave from KK. You'll need to allow two to three days for the mountain – there's the climb itself, and the day of rest you'll need afterwards! Whether you climb the highest mountain in Borneo or not, give yourself a few days to explore northwest Sabah. In the vicinity of **Tuaran** you can visit a lovely water village, while in **Kota Belud** you can relax at Mañana guesthouse and see, if you time things right, the famous Sunday *tamu* (market). Heading north are the hidden beaches of **Kudat**, and offshore, the isolated, off-the-tourist-trail islands of **Pulau Mantanani** (easier to get to from Kota Belud) and **Pulau Banggi**. This area is great for homestays.

Now a little over a week into your trip, head east to **Sepilok** and its famous orangutan sanctuary. After watching our arboreal cousins being fed in a wildlife reserve, try to spot them in the wild during a river cruise down the **Sungai Kinabatangan**. There are great lodges and homestays out this way. Relaxing in these two spots could easily fill four days to a week. Now decide – do you want to finish by diving in the **Semporna Archipelago**? Or trekking in the **Danum Valley** or **Maliau Basin**? All of these options are possible, but to be practical and give these destinations the time they deserve, allow five days for each. If you want to both dive and see Danum or Maliau, cut out the days allotted above for exploring northwest Sabah.

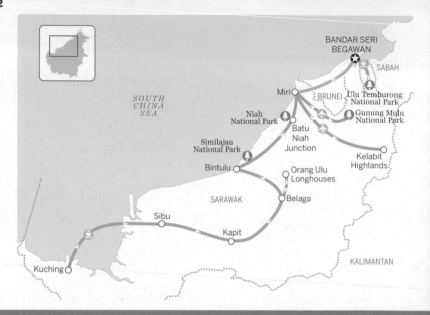

Three Weeks
Kuching to Brunei

Fly into **Kuching** and spend a few days exploring this multicultural mini-metropolis, delving into its scrumptious cuisine scene for breakfast (Sarawak laksa), lunch and dinner. Take day trips to nearby national parks in search of orangutans, proboscis monkeys and exotic flora. Then hop on the daily express ferry to the mostly Chinese river port of **Sibu**, where you can continue to eat well – don't miss the Foochow specialities on offer in the vast Central Market.

Sibu serves as the gateway to the mighty Batang Rejang (Rejang River), the 'Amazon of Borneo'. Board an early-morning 'flying coffin' express boat and head upriver to **Kapit**, a bustling trading centre founded in the days of the White Rajahs. If the river level is high enough, continue on to back-of-beyond **Belaga**, jumping-off point for short treks to a number of fascinating **Orang Ulu longhouses**.

A bone-jarring 4WD ride will get you down to the coastal city of **Bintulu**, Borneo's natural gas capital. Avoid the less-than-fetching city centre and head straight to the beaches, rainforest trails and bungalows of oft-overlooked **Similajau National Park**, which stretches along the coast for 30km.

Hop on a bus heading northeast to **Batu Niah Junction**, situated just a few kilometres from the vast caves, chirping bat colonies and prehistoric archaeological sites of **Niah National Park**. Next stop is the shiny petroleum city of **Miri**, home to a flourishing guesthouse scene that nicely complements the excellent dining options (especially fish). Chilling here amid mod cons is a great way to spend a day or two before flying into Borneo's interior for a few days – travellers speak glowingly of both **Gunung Mulu National Park**, a Unesco World Heritage site, and the gorgeously green and amazingly friendly **Kelabit Highlands**.

After flying back to Miri, take a bus – or the newspaper delivery van – to **Bandar Seri Begawan**, the surprisingly laid-back capital of the tiny, oil-rich sultanate of Brunei. Several museums showcase Bruneian culture, and culinary creations can be enjoyed at BSB's superb – and surprisingly inexpensive – hawker centres. End your Bornean odyssey back in the primeval rainforest by taking a speedboat, a car and finally a longboat to the pristine jungles of **Ulu Temburong National Park**.

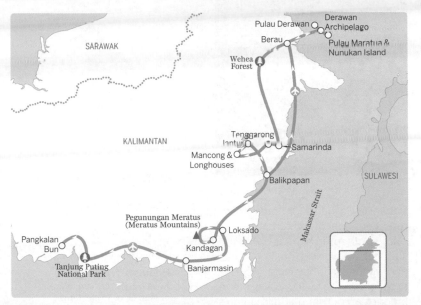

Three Weeks
Around Kalimantan

Fly into **Berau**, preferably via hopping **Balikpapan** (where you can get your visa on arrival), and explore the nearby **Derawan Archipelago**, home to some world-class diving. You can spend the night swapping stories with backpackers on **Pulau Derawan**, or head to the little-touristed outer islands, like **Pulau Maratua** (backpacker heaven) or tiny **Nunukan Island**, a resort perched on a blackened reef. Once back in Berau, head south to unspoiled **Wehea Forest** where you will find virgin rainforest at its very best. Look for rare wildlife and stay overnight in an ecolodge on a rushing stream. From there it's on to exotic **Samarinda**, gateway to the **Sungai Mahakam** and home to an eye-popping mosque. Head upriver to **Tenggarong**, with its resplendent *keraton* (palace) and golden *lembuswana* (mythical winged creature with an elephant's trunk); take a gaily-coloured *ces* (longtail canoe) on an unforgettable journey through the marshes and waterways around **Mancong**; and overnight on a *kapal biasa*, a river ferry that acts like a floating hostel. Side trips to **longhouses** reveal local Dayak culture past and present. Don't miss fascinating **Jantur**, a large town with riverside boardwalks on the edge of an enormous wetland. After returning to Balikpapan, take a bus to the pleasant village of **Kandagan**, gateway to the **Pegunungan Meratus (Meratus Mountains)**, and then a car to **Loksado**, a charming mountain hamlet that will capture your heart, where you can equally enjoy trekking, bamboo rafting or doing nothing. Continue on to **Banjarmasin**, where you can catch the floating market in the early hours, then fly to **Tanjung Puting National Park**, where you can cruise the Sungai Sekonyer in search of wildlife and watch wild orangutans emerge from the forest to feed, in one of Indonesia's most popular destinations. Then it's onto nearby **Pangkalan Bun** airport, where you'll wonder how you ever packed all that into three weeks.

regions at a glance

Sabah, in Borneo's far north, brings together unspoilt rainforests – prime orangutan habitat – with some of the world's most phenomenal scuba diving. More excellent diving awaits south of the Indonesian border on Kalimantan's east coast, and there's plenty of jungle adventure to be had inland, along and between Kalimantan's major rivers. On the north coast, Sarawak is home to the island's most accessible national parks – based in the sophisticated but laid-back city of Kuching, you can take day trips to see orangutans and (if you're lucky) a 75cm-wide Rafflesia flower, hike in the jungle and visit longhouse communities. Tiny Brunei, with a tempo and culinary customs all its own, offers visitors pristine habitats and a modernising take on Malay traditions.

Sabah

Hiking & Trekking ✓✓✓
Diving ✓✓✓
Jungle Wildlife ✓✓

Hiking & Trekking
Novice explorers can take a night trek near the Sungai Kinabatangan or inch across a canopy walkway in Poring Hot Springs, while the fit can test their endurance at the limestone outcrops of Batu Punggul or on the icy peak of Mt Kinabalu.

Diving & Snorkelling
To say Sabah is known for its scuba scene is like saying France is known for its cuisine. The diving in spots like Pulau Mantanani, Layang Layang and, of course, the famous Sipadan is – no exaggeration – some of the finest in the world.

Jungle Wildlife
Hornbills shriek in trees inhabited by pot-bellied proboscis monkeys, and slow-swinging through the canopy comes the ginger mass of an orangutan – to see one of these primates in the wild is to be reduced to grinning awe.

p38

Sarawak

Hiking & Trekking ✓✓✓
Cave Exploration ✓✓✓
Jungle Wildlife ✓✓

Hiking & Trekking
Trekking from Bario to
Ba Kelalan or assaulting
the summit of Gunung
Mulu will exhilarate experienced hikers, but even a
relaxed stroll through one
of Sarawak's Kuching-area
national parks will envelop
you in the wonders of the
equatorial rainforest.

Cave Exploration
The Wind Cave, Fairy Cave
and Niah National Park
boast huge caverns with
stalactites and bats, but for
sheer size and spectacle you
can't beat Gunung Mulu
National Park, renowned
for the Deer Cave and
the 700m-long Sarawak
Chamber.

Jungle Wildlife
Wild proboscis monkeys
munch leaves at Bako
National Park, orangutans
swing through the canopy
at Semenggoh Nature
Reserve, and estuarine
crocodiles lurk in the
muddy waters of Kuching
Wetlands National Park.

p121

Brunei

Culture ✓✓
Food ✓✓
Boat Rides ✓✓

Culture
Bandar Seri Begawan's
two opulent 20th-century
mosques feature eye-
popping architecture and
sumptuous interior decor,
but many visitors find the
traditional lifestyle and
architecture of Kampung
Ayer, a Malay stilt village,
more engaging.

Food
Bruneian cuisine may not
be well known, but we can
guarantee you've never eaten
anything like *ambuyat*
(made from sago starch),
and that the delicious *kuih*
(baked sweets) available in
night markets will perfectly
complement a quick satay or
curry chicken meal.

Boat Rides
The speedboat ride from
Bandar Seri Begawan to
Bangar is the biggest thrill
B$6 can buy, but nothing
beats starting the day
heading upriver to Ulu
Temburong National Park
in a shallow-draft Iban
longboat.

p196

Kalimantan

Hiking & Trekking ✓✓✓
Jungle Wildlife ✓✓✓
Diving ✓✓

Hiking & Trekking
The supremely fit and truly
adventurous can take the
2½-week Cross-Borneo
Trek, but the easiest area for
jungle exploration – with
a wide range of guides
available – is the stunning
Pegunungan Meratus
(Meratus Mountains), using
Loksado as base camp.

Jungle Wildlife
If you're an amateur
naturalist, Kalimantan's
rainforests will exceed
even your wildest dreams.
A good guide can help you
spot orangutans, gibbons,
macaques, flying squirrels,
monitor lizards, crocodiles
and giant butterflies.

Diving & Snorkelling
In the Derawan Archi-
pelago, surrounded by the
Celebes Sea, you can swim
in coral-blue water with
giant green turtles, manta
rays, myriad reef fish,
sharks and whales. Borneo's
best-kept secret!

p215

> **Every listing is recommended by our authors, and their favourite places are listed first**

> **Look out for these icons:**

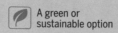 Our author's top recommendation

A green or sustainable option

 No payment required

See the Index for a full list of destinations covered in this book.

On the Road

Sabah

POP 3.39 MILLION / AREA 76,115 SQ KM

Includes »

Best Places to Eat

- » KK's Night Market (p40)
- » Alu-Alu Cafe (p48)
- » Moon Bell (p48)
- » Sim Sim Seafood Restaurant (p76)

Best Places to Stay

- » Mañana (p68)
- » Lupa Masa (p65)
- » Tampat Do Aman (p69)
- » Orou Sapulot (p105)

Why Go?

Sabah's beauty is quite simply gut-wrenching. This is one of the most physically stunning places on Earth, a land of deep green jungle, craggy mountains and shockingly blue ocean that all seems to collide into one moving, magnificent vista.

It's a land for adventure enthusiasts and yet, we must stress, not only adventure enthusiasts. Many treks around Mt Kinabalu, for example, really consist of vigorous hikes, jaunts you want to be fit to attempt, but don't need to be in Olympic shape to finish. Similarly, the diving in East Sabah – some of the best in the world – is easily accessible to beginners. And anyone can sit on a boat and appreciate the majesty of spotting clever lizards, prowling civets, doe-eyed loris and great ginger orangutans in the wild.

In addition, there is a thriving yet laid-back culture here. Sabah's citizens are wonderful: cosmopolitan, friendly, famously relaxed folks who are quick to laugh and slow to rile. Their good-humoured presence is the perfect accompaniment to the awe-inspiring scenery of their home.

When to Go

Kota Kinabalu

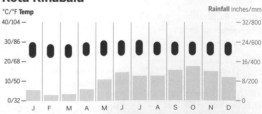

Jan–Apr A dry, pleasant time, exploding with celebrations for Chinese New Year.

Mar–Jul The water calms; this is the best time for diving.

Jun–Sep Hot and often (but definitely not always) rainy.

Sabah Highlights

1 Admiring the sea turtles among the **Semporna Archipelago's** (p93) reefs

2 Hoofing it over pitcher plants and granite moonscapes for the ultimate Bornean sunrise atop **Mt Kinabalu** (p59)

3 Breathing in the air of an actual virgin rainforest in the

Maliau Basin Conservation Area (p101)

4 Watching orangutans in **Sepilok** (p77)

5 Discovering the hidden beaches of northern Borneo near **Kudat** (p69)

6 Floating down a river through primary jungle to the

Batu Punggul rock formation in **Sapulot** (p105)

7 Enjoying the nightlife and eating opportunities of **Kota Kinabalu** (p48)

8 Staying in a homestay and spotting primates from a boat on the **Sungai Kinabatangan** (p86)

KOTA KINABALU

POP 630,000

We realise you almost certainly didn't come to Sabah for the urban scene, but you have to book permits somewhere, you gotta sleep after climbing Mt Kinabalu/diving in Sipadan/exploring the jungle etc, and you need some place to connect to onward travel, and KK, as everyone calls it, is a good place (sometimes the only place) to do all of the above. The centre is walkable. The population is a spicy mix of expats, Chinese, indigenous Kadazan and of course, Malays. The food is good – surprisingly good, given you're in Malaysia's hinterlands. Nightlife is fun, a testament to Sabah's laid-back approach to life; there aren't a lot of bars. The downside is out of control construction; KK desperately seems to want to answer the question, 'How many empty malls can we build in one city?', but past this one demerit, it's hard not to love this town.

◉ Sights & Activities

CITY CENTRE & WATERFRONT

Night Market   MARKET

(Map p42; Jln Tun Fuad Stephens; ◷late afternoon-11pm) KK's main market is a place of delicious contrasts. Huddled beneath the imposing Le Meridien, the market is divided into two main sections: the southwest end is given over mostly to produce, while the northeast end (the area around the main entrance) is a huge hawker centre where you can eat your way right through the entire Malay gastronomy. A fish-and-food market extends to the waterfront; the closer you get to the ocean, the more the scent of salt water, death, blood and spices envelops you – an oddly intoxicating experience. If you've never seen a proper Southeast Asian market, this place will be a revelation.

Signal Hill   LANDMARK

(Map p42) There's a UFO-like observation pavilion on this hill at the eastern edge of the city centre. Come here to escape the traffic and get another take on the squatters' stilt village at Pulau Gaya. The view is best as the sun sets over the islands. From the top, it's also possible to hike down to the Wetland Centre on the other side, but it's a longer way than it looks – don't try this if it's getting dark, as the walk can take up to two hours. Near here are some shells of unfinshed building sites that were rumored to

ANIMAL ALERT

During KK's big Sunday Market, animals lovers may want to stay away from the market area where Jln Gaya intersects Beach Street; pet kittens and puppies are put out for sale in mesh cages and they don't look happy in the midday heat. Locals don't seem to mind, and to be fair, most vendors try to provide water and shade for the animals, but many Western travellers are put off by the sight.

be haunted; the ghosts drove away the construction crews, presumably because they liked the idea of ugly concrete foundations overlooking KK.

Atkinson Clock Tower   LANDMARK

(Map p42) The modest timepiece at the foot of the hill is one of the only structures to survive the Allied bombing of Jesselton in 1945. It's a square, 15.7m-high wooden structure that was completed in 1905 and named after the first district officer of the town, FG Atkinson, who died of malaria aged 28.

Central Market   MARKET

(Map p42; Jln Tun Fuad Stephens; ◷6.30am-6pm) The Central Market is fun to wander about, and a nice spot for people watching as locals transact their daily business. Nearby, the **Handicraft Market** (Filipino Market; Jln Tun Fuad Stephens; ◷10am-6pm) is a good place to shop for inexpensive souvenirs. Offerings include pearls, textiles, seashell crafts, jewellery and bamboo goods, some from the Philippines, some from Malaysia and some from other parts of Asia. Needless to say, bargaining is a must.

KK Heritage Walk   WALKING TOUR

(www.kkheritagewalk.com; admission RM200; ◷walks 9am Tue & Thu) This two-hour tour, which can be booked through any of KK's many tour operators (just ask at your hotel front desk), explores colonial KK and its hidden delights. Stops include Chinese herbal shops, bulk produce stalls, a *kopitiam* (coffee shop), and Jln Gaya (known as Bond St when the British were in charge). There's also a quirky treasure hunt at the end leading tourists to the Jesselton Hotel. Guides speak English, Chinese and Bahasa Malaysia.

Sunday Market
MARKET

(Map p42; Jln Gaya; ⊘7am-3pm Sun) On Sundays, a lively Chinese street fair takes over the entire length of Jln Gaya. It's a pretty manic scene and a perfect spot for souvenir shopping, but animal lovers may want to avoid some sections.

BEYOND THE CITY CENTRE

Some of KK's best attractions are located beyond the city centre, and it's well worth putting in the effort to check them out.

Sabah Museum
MUSEUM

(☑253199; www.museum.sabah.gov.my; Jln Muzium; admission RM20; ⊘9am-5pm Sat-Thu; P) Centred on a modern four-storey structure inspired by the longhouses of the Rungus and Murut tribes, this is the best place to go in KK for an introduction to Sabah's ethnicities and environments. It's slightly south of the city centre, on the hilly corner of Jln Tunku Abdul Rahman and Jln Penampang.

In the main building there are good permanent collections of tribal and historical artefacts including ceramics and exhibits of flora and fauna – some dusty, others well presented (including a centrepiece whale skeleton). The prehistory gallery has a replica limestone cave, in case you don't make it to any of the real ones. In the gardens, the **Heritage Village** offers the chance to wander round examples of traditional tribal dwellings, including Kadazan bamboo houses and a Chinese farmhouse, all nicely set on a lily-pad lake.

The adjoining **Science & Education Centre** has an informative exhibition on the petroleum industry, from drilling to refining and processing. The **Sabah Art Gallery** features regular shows and exhibitions by local artists. If you're heading east after KK, keep

FIND YOUR WAY IN KK

Downtown KK is a dense grid of concrete buildings nestled between the waterfront and a range of low, forested hills to the east. It's compact, walkable and easy to navigate – most of the restaurants, markets, accommodation, tourist offices and tour operators are located here. Transport terminals bookend the city on either side.

hold of your admission ticket – it also allows entry to Agnes Keith House in Sandakan.

Mari Mari Cultural Village
MUSEUM

(☑019-820 4921; www.traversetours.com/culturalvillage.php; Jln Kiansom; adult/child RM160/140; P) Mari Mari is an entertaining combination of semi-corny and semi-educational. It's supposed to offer insight into the living cultures of Sabah via a three-hour show-tour (beginning at 10am, 3pm and 7pm), which winds through the jungle passing various tribal dwellings along the way. At each stop, tourists learn about indigenous folkways and can try their hand at bamboo cooking, rice-wine making (and drinking!), fire starting, tattooing, blowpipe shooting etc. A short dance recital and meal are included in the visit – the centre must be notified of any dietary restrictions in advance. A trip to the cultural village can be combined with a white-water rafting tour; contact Riverbug for more information. The village is a 20-minute to 30-minute drive north of central KK, so most people visit it on a package tour, but if you come on your own the admission is RM80/70 for adults/children.

Rather than portraying living cultures, Mari Mari sort of freezes local ethnic groups into museum pieces. No one is dressing in

THE SOUTHSIDE CONNECTION

A paved road makes a frowning arc from KK to Tawau, passing Mt Kinabalu, Sepilok, Sandakan, Lahad Datu and Semporna (the gateway to Sipadan) along the way. It takes around 10 hours to complete the circuit.

Getting from KK to Tawau via the northern half of the island, via a big frown, is easy. Doing the smile side of the loop (going back to KK through the south from Tawau): not so much. The road here is not entirely paved, but there's at least finely crushed gravel the whole way through. A 2WD or even motorbike can make the drive, but drive carefully. An infrastructure of public buses does not yet exist here; minivans occasionally ran this stretch of road, but only when needed by logging camps. If you can get a lift to Keningau, the rest of the journey to KK is a breeze.

Kota Kinabalu

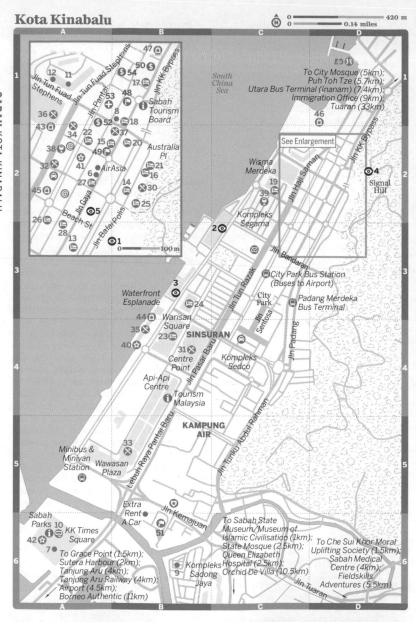

loincloths and feathers in Sabah, except maybe in the very deepest, remote interior. The Rungus and Murut may live in longhouses, but many of those longhouses have satellite television and air-con, and they hunt with guns, not blowpipes.

There is also a small waterfall – **Kiansom Waterfall** (admission RM1; ☉dawn-dusk) – about 400m beyond the cultural village, which is easily accessible by private transport or on foot. The area around the cascade lends itself well to swimming and

Kota Kinabalu

it's a great place to cool off after a visit to Mari Mari.

Lok Kawi Wildlife Park ZOO
(☏765710; www.lokkawiwildlifepark.com; Jln Penampang; adult/child RM20/10; ◎9.30am-5.30pm, last entry at 4:30pm; P) If you'd like to check out the orangutans but won't make it out to Sepilok or the Kinabatangan, a visit to this wildlife park is highly recommended, especially for those with children in tow. There are plen-

ty of other animals as well, from tarsiers to Sumatran rhinos. Don't miss the giant aviary at the top of the hill, with its ominous warning sign 'beware of attacking birds'.

It's best to arrive by 9.50am at the latest – feedings take place throughout the park at 10am. After the various feedings, an interactive show takes place at the stage around 11.15am everyday. After feeding time, most of the animals take their daily siesta – only the humans are silly enough to stay out in the scorching midday sun.

The 17B minibus goes to Lok Kawi (RM2). Visitors with a private vehicle can access the park via the Papar–Penampang road or the Putatan–Papar road. Travel agents offer half-day tours, or you can hire a taxi, which will cost around RM150, including a two-hour wait.

Monsopiad Cultural Village   MUSEUM
(☎774337; www.monsopiad.com; admission adult/ student/child RM75/50/free; ☺9am-5pm; ℗) On the banks of Sungai Moyog, Monsopiad is named after a legendary warrior and head-hunter, whose direct descendants established this private heritage centre in 1996. The highlight is the House of Skulls, which supposedly contains the ancient crania of Monsopiad's unfortunate enemies, as well as artefacts illustrating native rituals from the time when the *bobolian* (priest) was the most important figure in the community.

Many tour companies include Monsopiad on local itineraries. To get here independently, take a bus from central KK to Donggongon (RM1.50), where you can catch a minivan to the cultural village (RM1). You can also take a taxi or charter a minivan direct from KK for around RM40.

🖉 Kota Kinabalu
Wetland Centre   MUSEUM
(☎246955; www.sabahwetlands.org; Jln Bukit Bendera Upper; adult/child RM10/5; ☺8am-6pm Tue-Sun; ℗) This spot encompasses the last 24 hectares of a mangrove swamp that once stretched across what is now KK. A series of wooden walkways leads into a wetland rife with fiddler crabs, mangrove crabs, mud lobsters, mudskippers, skinks, turtles, water monitors and the adorably turd-like mangrove slug, among other swamp fauna (sadly, there are also plastic bottles). For many, the big attraction is a stunning variety of migratory birds, some from as far away as Siberia. The walkway ends at a spot that looks out over a flat marshscape that would feel virgin were it not for the high rise buildings behind it. Staff are cheerful but not always that helpful.

To get here, head north on Jln Fuad Stephens (the main road north out of town; in town it's also called Jln KK Bypass) and follow it as it curves around the coast. You'll then turn right at Jln Istidat and follow that for about 1km; signs for the Wetland Centre will be on your right.

Che Sui Khor Moral
Uplifting Society   CHINESE TEMPLE
(Jln Tuaran; ℗) About four minutes north of KK, this complex is anchored by an 11-storey pagoda that shimmers in orange and green. Tourists can't enter the actual pagoda, but the friendly members of the society don't mind you poking around the rest of their library. The Society espouses believing in the best Islam, Taoism, Buddhism and Christianity have to offer. You can get here via the bus terminal at Wawasan Plaza going north on the Jln Tuaran route (RM3). To get home, just stand outside the temple on the main road and a minibus or regular bus will pick you up. A return taxi should cost around RM20.

Puh Toh Tze
Buddhist Temple   CHINESE TEMPLE
(Jln Tuaran; ℗) Also spelled 'Poh Toh Tse', this temple is 20 minutes north of KK, at Mile (Batu) 5.5. It's quite impressive: a stone staircase-pavilion flanked by 10 Chinese deities leads up to a main temple complex dominated by Kwan Yin, Goddess of Mercy. A Chinese-style reclining Buddha rests inside. You can to enter and wander around. The temple is on a small hill west of the main highway junction north; you can get here by taking the Jln Tuaran bus again or, more easily, hire a taxi; a round-trip shouldn't be more than RM36.

Museum of Islamic Civilisation   MUSEUM
(☎538234; admission incl in Sabah Museum ticket; ☺9am-5pm Sat-Thu; ℗) This museum consists of six galleries devoted to Muslim culture and history in Malaysia and beyond. The five domes represent the holy Five Pillars of Islam. It's in need of a facelift and an update, but can fill up an hour or two of a boring afternoon.

To get to the museum complex, catch a bus (RM1) along Jln Tunku Abdul Rahman and get off just before the mosque. Be warned: it's a short but steep walk uphill to the museum. Bus 13 also goes right round past the Queen Elizabeth Hospital and stops near Jln Muzium (look for the Sacred Heart Church). Taxi fare will run between RM10 and RM15.

City Mosque   MOSQUE
(off Jln Tun Fuad Stephens) Overlooking the South China Sea, this mosque is built in classical style, and is far more attractive than the State Mosque in terms of setting and design. Completed in 2000, it can hold up to 12,000 worshippers. It can be entered by

non-Muslims outside regular prayer times, but dress modestly (long trousers and arms covered is a good rule of thumb, although you may get away with just shoulders covered) and remove your shoes before entering. To get here, take bus 5A from Wawasan Plaza going toward UMS (RM1.50). Just ask the conductor to drop you off outside the City Mosque after the Tanjung Lipat roundabout.

State Mosque   MOSQUE
(Jln Tunku Abdul Rahman) Sabah's state mosque is a perfect example of contemporary Malay Muslim architecture: all modernist facade and geometric angles. The building is south of the city centre past the Kampung Air stilt village, not far from the Sabah Museum; you'll see the striped minaret and chevronned dome on your way to or from the airport. Non-Muslim visitors are allowed inside, but dress appropriately.

Tanjung Aru   BEACH
This pretty sweep of sand begins around the Shangri-La's Tanjung Aru Resort and stretches south to the airport. Tanjung Aru is a locals' beach, full of picnic spots, swoony-eyed couples and much familial goodwill. Food stalls are plentiful, most closing up a bit after dark, which reminds us: sunsets here are pretty perfect. We would advise against swimming here; the water may look nice, and some locals may tell you it's fine, but others claim it's tainted by run-off from KK and nearby water villages.

Orchid De Villa   FARM
(☏380611; www.orchid-de-villa.com.my; Jln Kiansom; ☺8am-5pm; ℗) If you're just as crazy about flora as fauna, head to this farm, about 3 km from central KK, along the road to Penampang. The farm specialises in rare Bornean orchids, hybrid orchids, cacti and herbal plants.

Tours
KK has a huge number of tour companies, enough to suit every taste and budget. Head to Wisma Sabah – this office building is full of agents and operators. We have highlighted three companies that specialise in off-the-beaten-track and/or ecotourism activities.

[TOP CHOICE] GogoSabah   SIGHTS
(Map p42; ☏316385, 317385; www.gogosabah.com; Lot G-4, ground fl, Wisma Sabah, Jln Tun Razak) Gogo is a fantastic tour company that does a great job of booking just about anything, anywhere in Sabah. It's especially excellent for motorbike rentals – staff will help map out some of the choicest areas for exploration in Sabah. It also offers car rentals and a serviced apartment, too. It's a good go-to organisation for package tours, but can also help independent travellers out with logistics, itineraries and information.

[TOP CHOICE] Sticky Rice   TOURS
(☏250588; www.stickyricetravel.com) The Sticky Rice guys are extremely helpful, knowledgable about Borneo, and committed to natural immersion, community engagement and independent travel.

[TOP CHOICE] Adventure Alternative Borneo   NATURE
(Map p42; ☏019-802 0549; www.adventurealternativeborneo.com; 97 Jln Gaya) Adventure Alternative specialises in getting Sabah visitors off the beaten/package tour path, and is an excellent resource for independent travellers, especially those who are interested in sustainable and responsible tourism.

Bike Borneo   BICYCLE RENTAL
(☏484734; www.bikeborneo.com; City Mall, Jln Lintas, Kota Kinabalu; 1-day tours from RM245) Our favourite means of getting around Sabah on two wheels (with no motor) is mountain biking, and the guys at Fieldskills Adventures, who run Bike Borneo, are the experts on the topic. They run their mountain biking activities largely out of Tuaran; packages include a day ride in the vicinity of town that crosses three (count 'em) swinging bridges and a four-day cycling adventure across the foothills of Mt Kinabalu.

Riverbug/Traverse Tours   SIGHTS
(Map p42; ☏260501; www.traversetours.com; Lot 227, Wisma Sabah, Jln Tun Fuad Stephens) An excellent and forward-thinking operator that has a wide variety of tours across Sabah. It makes admirable efforts to engage in sustainable travel practices.

Fieldskills Adventures   ADVENTURE TOUR
(☏484734; fieldskills.com.my; City Mall, Jln Lintas) If you're into outdoor activities and adventure, get in touch with these guys. This outfit leads well-regarded cycling, rock climbing, trekking and diving trips across Sabah.

Borneo Adventure   ADVENTURE TOUR
(Map p42; ☏486800; www.borneoadventure.com; Block E-27-3A, Signature Office, KK Times Square)

Award-winning Sarawak-based company with very professional staff, imaginative sightseeing and activity itineraries and a genuine interest in local people and the environment.

Borneo Authentic   BOAT TOUR
(☑773066; www.borneo-authentic.com; Lot 3, 1st fl, Putatan Point, Jln JKR) A friendly operation offering a variety of package tours including day-trip cruises on the Sungai Klias.

Equator Adventure Tours   CULTURAL TOUR
(☑766351, 013-889 9535; http://equator-adventure.com) Offers plenty of nature and adventure tours, as well as the Hajah Halimah Traditional cooking course (RM135), one of the few cooking courses currently offered in Sabah. Participants check out the local fresh and wet markets and prepare a meal in a Malaysian kitchen with an English-speaking guide. Its head office is in Putatan, 9km east of the city centre.

Borneo Divers   DIVING
(Map p42; ☑222226; www.borneodivers.net; 9th fl, Menara Jubili, 53 Jln Gaya) This is the longest-established Borneo dive outfit; it can arrange courses and dives just about anywhere and has its own dive shop. It's possible to get discounted rates as a walk-in.

Downbelow Marine & Wildlife Adventures   DIVING
(Map p42; ☑012-866 1935; www.divedownbelow.com; Lot 67 & 68, 5th fl, KK Time Square Block) A well-respected dive outfit with a PADI Centre on Pulau Gaya that can arrange all kinds of travel packages across Borneo.

Borneo Eco Tours   SIGHTS
(☑438300; www.borneoecotours.com; Pusat Perindustrian Kolombong Jaya, Mile 5.5 Jln Kolombong) This is a place with a good reputation, arranging tours throughout Malaysian Borneo, including travel to the Kinabatangan area.

Borneo Nature Tours   NATURE
(Map p42; ☑267637; www.borneonaturetours.com; Block D, Lot 10, Kompleks Sadong Jaya, Ikan Juara 4) A professional and knowledgeable operation that manages bookings for Danum Valley's Borneo Rainforest Lodge. Its office building is on the corner near a canal.

Scuba Junkie/River Junkie   DIVING, RAFTING
(Map p42; ☑255816; www.scuba-junkie.com; ground fl, Lot G7, Wisma Sabah, Jln Haji Saman) Runs diving trips in the Semporna Archipelago and white-water rafting trips in southwest Sabah aimed at the Western backpacker (and flashpacker) crowd.

Sutera Harbour   CLIMBING
(Sutera Sanctuary Lodges; Map p42; ☑308914/5; www.suteraharbour.com; ground fl, Lot G15, Wisma Sabah, Jln Haji Saman) Sutera runs a lot of the tourism activities in Sabah, and has a monopoly on accommodation within the Mt Kinabalu ark. Make this your first stop in KK if you're planning to climb Kinabalu and didn't book your bed in advance.

🛏 Sleeping

Check out the **Sabah Backpacker Operators Association** (SBA; www.sabahbackpackers.com) which was set up in an effort to help shoestring travellers in the region. Check out its website for discount deals on accommodation and tours. KK's midrange options seem to be sliding towards either end of the budget spectrum. Although backpacker hangouts and top-end treats are in great proliferation, there are still several spots around town suiting those Goldilockses out there.

🔝 Sarangnova Hotel   HOTEL $$
(Map p42; ☑233750; www.sarangnova.com; 98 Jln Gaya; s/d from RM120/170) It's hard not to miss this fascinating hotel; there's a conceptual, woodsy slat fixture attached to the front. The rooms are just as distinctive as the exterior, seeing as they're themed after Borneo's birds. No, no feathers on the walls or anything, but the attractively minimalist decor is offset by gallery-style portraits of local avian life; this includes some picture compositions that are downright Warhol-ian. For being a little different, and still offering superlative service in all the ways that count (helpful staff, central location), we give the Sarangnova two beaks up.

Hotel Eden 54   BOUTIQUE HOTEL $$
(Map p42; ☑266054; www.eden54.com; 54 Jln Gaya; r RM119-179; ❅ 🜁) This smart choice would likely cost five times what it does were it plopped in the West. Fortunately this Eden's contrasting solid dark and light colours, geometric design sensibility and immaculate furniture have turned up in Kota Kinabalu. A fine choice for flashpackers, couples, even families. One warning: the cheapest rooms are windowless and should be avoided.

Rainforest Lodge   HOTEL $$
(Map p42; ☑258228; www.rainforestlodgekk.com; Jln Pantai; dm/s/d/ste from RM40/115/135/165;

⊛@) Located in the swinging centre of the 'Beach Street' complex, the Rainforest is all of a stairward stumble from some of KK's best nightlife. Rooms are refreshingly chic, a nice mix of modern and Sabah-tribal style, and many have cool balconies that look onto the Beach St parade below. Just be warned: it gets loud at night.

Hotel Sixty3
HOTEL **$$**

(Map p42; ☑212663; www.hotelsixty3.com; Jln Gaya 63; r from RM190; ⊛⊚) This smart hotel offers business-class standard accommodation, with chilly air-con, flat-screen TVs and big soft beds, all in the heart of KK. The rooms, with their clean white lines and geometric accents, are popular with families and travellers needing a little pampering.

Le Meridien Kota Kinabalu
HOTEL **$$$**

(Map p42; ☑322222; www.starwoodhotels.com; Jln Tun Fuad Stephens; r from RM300; P⊛⊚⊛) 'If you can't undercut 'em, outclass 'em' seems to be the motto at KK's most central five-star venture, which just reeks of luxury, from the incredible views from the pool deck to the flat-screen TVs and DVD players. The eye-watering prices come down a little in low season, and may even get as low as RM200 if you catch the right discounts.

Klagan Hotel
HOTEL **$$**

(Map p42; ☑488908; www.theklagan.com/; Block D, Warisan Square, Jln Tun Fuad Stephens; r RM180-260; ⊛⊚) Funky molded recliners and bright yellows and reds in the superior rooms make this midrange option a cut above the competition.

Le Hotel
HOTEL **$$**

(Map p42; ☑319696; www.lehotel.com.my; Block B, 3rd fl, Warisan Sq, Jln Tun Fuad Stephens; r RM120-198; ⊛⊚) Rooms at the Le are a little smallish, but there's a cool blue colour scheme and midrange amenities, plus nice views of the waterfront at the higher end of the price scale.

Summer Lodge
HOSTEL **$**

(Map p42; ☑244499; www.summerlodge.com.my; Lot 120, Jln Gaya; dm/d RM28/70; ⊛⊚) Summer Lodge feels like a bed factory, but it's got that social vibe backpackers adore – 'How long have you been travelling? Where did you come from/where are you going? Isn't it funny when foreigners do that thing they do? Fancy a drink?' The answer to the last question is easily solved – the Beach St bar complex is just below.

Jesselton Hotel
HOTEL **$$$**

(Map p42; ☑223333; www.jesseltonhotel.com; 69 Jln Gaya; r/ste from RM180/450; ⊛⊚) The oldest hotel in KK doesn't need to manufacture character – it fairly drips it, in a dignified if dated way. Mock-colonial wood and marble make you want to don black-tie formal clothes, and the single suite even has its own fishpond. There's also a very good restaurant, coffee shop, business centre and red London cab to shuttle you to the airport.

Kinabalu Daya
HOTEL **$$**

(Map p42; ☑240000; www.kkdayahotel.com; Lot 3-4, Block 9, Jln Pantai; r/ste incl breakfast from RM140/270; ⊛⊚) Oddly angled hallways and strangely placed lifts give Kinabalu Daya a certain '10-year-old's-Lego-project' vibe. Nevertheless, tons of tourists swear by this midrange stalwart – and justifiably so – it's in the centre of the action, the Best Western branding ensures a certain amount of familiar comfort, and many rooms actually exude a stylish, boutique chic.

Akinabalu Youth Hostel
HOSTEL **$**

(Map p42; ☑272188; www.akinabaluyh.com/; Lot 133, Jln Gaya; dm/r incl breakfast from RM22/60; ⊛⊚) Friendly staff, fuchsia accent walls and trickling Zen fountains make this a solid option among KK's hostels, particularly if you find a quiet time to take advantage of the gratis internet and DVDs. Accommodation is mostly in basic four-bed rooms, with windows facing an interior hallway.

Lucy's Homestay
HOSTEL **$**

(Backpacker's Lodge; Map p42; ☑261495; lucyhomestay.go-2.net; Lot 25, Lg Dewan, Australia Pl; dm/s/d incl breakfast RM28/45/50; ⊚) Lucy's is one of the oldest of the old school hostels in Australia Pl. There's loads of charm, with wooden walls smothered in stickers, business cards and crinkled photographs. It may not suit if you're a party person or want cushy extras, and we get the sense Lucy is a bit more motherly to women than male guests.

Hyatt Regency Kota Kinabalu
HOTEL **$$$**

(Map p42; ☑221234; http://kinabalu.regency.hyatt.com; Jln Datuk Salleh Sulong; r from RM350; P⊛⊚⊛) Located in the city centre, this branch of the Hyatt chain is all corporate glitz – a good spot to take a businessman for lunch while enjoying impressive views out of a top-storey suite. Rooms are done up in warm earth tones and packed with amenities, including quite possibly the best selection of cable-TV channels in the city.

Shangri-La's Tanjung Aru Resort & Spa
RESORT **$$$**

(STAR; ⏰327888; www.shangri-la.com/kotakinaba lu/tanjungaruresort; Tanjung Aru; r from RM550; ⓟ❋⏰✈) The Shangri-La is a good choice for those who want to combine the attractions of Kota Kinabalu with the features of a tropical resort. It's a sprawling complex, dotted with swaying palms and metal gongs, located in the Tanjung Aru area about 3km south of the city centre. Dozens of uniformed staff are constantly on hand to respond to your every whim.

Borneo Gaya Lodge
HOSTEL **$**

(Map p42; ⏰242477; www.borneogayalodge.com; 78 Jln Gaya; dm/d from RM25/65; ❋⏰) A typical high-volume hostel. Staff are a peach, and will help organise nearly anything, and you're as centrally located in KK as can be.

Myne Hotel
HOTEL **$$$**

(Map p42; ⏰448787; http://hotel.myne.com.my; Lot 21, Warisan Sq; r/ste from RM270/430; ❋⏰) It might be located within a mall, but the Myne, with its deep red and gold accents and brass fixtures, feels as gaudy as a chandelier. As high-end spots go, this is an executive-class kind of place, lacking the space of a resort but making up for it with a more central location.

Borneo Backpackers
HOSTEL **$**

(Map p42; ⏰234009; www.borneobackpackers. com; 24 Lg Dewan, Australia Pl; dm/s/d incl breakfast from RM20/40/60; ❋⏰) This long-running backpackers is a bit cramped, but it's very popular, especially with younger travellers.

Bunibon
HOSTEL **$**

(Map p42; ⏰210801; www.bunibonlodge.com/; Lot 21, Lorong Dewan; dm/s/d from RM25/50/68; ❋⏰) An attractive, friendly hostel with a social vibe and surprisingly nice private doubles.

Kinabalu Backpackers
HOSTEL **$**

(Map p42; ⏰253385; www.kinabalubackpackers. com; Lot 4, Lorong Dewan; dm/s/d from RM25/55/68; ❋⏰) A bit bare, but cheap, cheerful and clean. It can organise onward travel and tours.

✕ Eating

KK is one of the few cities in Borneo with an eating scene diverse enough to refresh the noodle-jaded palate. Besides the ubiquitous Chinese *kedai kopi* (coffee shops) and Malay halal restaurants, you'll find plenty of interesting options around the city centre – head to the suburbs if you're looking for some truly unique local fare.

CITY CENTRE

TOP CHOICE Moon Bell
CHINESE **$$**

(Map p42; ⏰019-861 1605; 33 Jln Haji Saman; mains RM15-35; ⏰11am-9pm, closed Mon; ❋) Never had Xinjiang cuisine? This is the food of China's northwest frontier: spicy, rich and meaty, and damned delicious anytime of day. Moon Bell, run by a superlatively friendly Chinese granny, blows us away with spicy eggplant fried in a sweet, caramelized laquer of dark sauce, gamey roast lamb, crispy-skinned duck and hearty clay hotpots. It's best to come here with a big group and eat family-style, just as all the locals do.

TOP CHOICE Alu-Alu Cafe
SEAFOOD **$$**

(Map p42; Jesselton Point; mains from RM10-30; ⏰10:30am-2:30pm & 6:30am-10pm; ❋) Technically part of the Gayana Eco Resort, Alu-Alu is a delicious restaurant that sources its ingredients from Borneo Eco-Fish, an organisation dedicated to harvesting and distributing seafood from sustainable sources – no shark fin here. Besides having a bit of a moral mission, Alu-Alu is legitimately delicious. It takes the Chinese seafood concept to new levels – lightly breading fish chunks and serving them drowned in a mouth-watering buttermilk sauce, or simmering amid diced chilies. Even the vegetables, simply steamed with a side of pungent garlic, are a main event as opposed to an afterthought.

Ya Kee Bah Kut Teh
CHINESE **$**

(Map p42; ⏰221192; 74 Jln Gaya; mains from RM5; ⏰4pm-11pm) Kosher and halal readers need not apply because this spot is all about the pork. Pork, pork, pork, in herbal soup form (ie *Bah Kut The*). Fatty pork. Pork ribs. Pork belly. Pork with ginger and chillies. Pork offal. With all apologies to *Babe*, we gotta highly recommend this delicious option.

Grazie
ITALIAN **$$**

(Map p42; ⏰019-821 6936; ground fl, Wawasan Plaza; mains from RM17; ⏰noon-3pm Fri-Sun, noon-6pm Mon-Thu; ❋) KK is chock-full of Italian places, but Grazie, run by Italian expat Salvatore Marcello, tops them all handily. Many ingredients are imported (including a fine shot of grappa we finished our meal with); the pizza is thin crust and divine; the pasta and other mains sent from on high. Grazie, *grazie* indeed.

Chili Vanilla
FUSION $$

(Map p42; 35 Jln Haji Sama; mains RM12-20; ☺10am-10pm, closed Sun; ❋☎) KK is not the first city that springs to mind when we think 'Sure could use some goulash,' but then Chili Vanilla comes along. Run by a Hungarian chef and her local busines partner, this adorable spot dishes out some unexpected delights; besides the goulash there's Moroccan lamb stew, spicy duck tortillas and, just to bring it back to Asia, rich braised oxtail. Wash it all down with the incredible house lime juice, or order off the extensive wine menu.

El Centro
FUSION $

(Map p42; 32 Jln Haji Saman; RM9-16; ☺5pm-midnight, closed Mon; ☎) El Centro serves up lovely Malaysian dishes, but honestly, we come here when we need a Western food fix (also: good music, nice atmosphere and tasteful decor). The burgers taste like real beef and the pasta dishes are comforting enough to make us long for home.

Borneo 1945 Museum Kopitiam
CAFE $

(Map p42; ☏272945; 24 Jln Dewan, Australia Pl; mains from RM3; ☺7:30am-midnight; ❋) Odd name for a restaurant-cum-cafe? Yes, because this is a restaurant-cum-cafe-cum-museum, dedicated to the Allied fighting forces in Borneo during WWII. Perhaps the best iced coffee in KK is served here, alongside breakfast favourites like toast and *kaya* (coconut jam), indigenous fare like pandan chicken and rice, and (why not?) reproductions of Anzac biscuits. The on-site mini-museum is worth a visit by itself.

Kohinoor
INDIAN $$$

(Map p42; ☏235160; Lot 4, Waterfront Esplanade; dinner about RM50; ☺11.30am-2.30pm & 5.30pm-11pm; ❋♪) There are several excellent restaurants along the Waterfront Esplanade, but this Indian place is an easy favourite. Take advantage of its authentic tandoori oven and don't forget to grab a side of pillowy garlic naan.

MAKAN: KOTA KINABALU STYLE

Kota Kinabalu (KK) may be light on sights, and its urban core isn't a stunner, but the city comes up trumps in the food category. KK's veritable melting pot of cultures has fostered a lively dining scene that differentiates itself from the rest of Malaysia with a host of recipes fusing foreign recipes and local ingredients. KK's four essential eats:

Sayur Manis Also known as 'Sabah vegie', this bright-green jungle fern can be found at any Chinese restaurant worth its salt. It's best served fried with garlic, or mixed with fermented shrimp paste. The *sayur manis* plant is a perennial and can grow about 3m high. It is harvested year round so it tends to be very fresh. Adventurous eaters might want to try other local produce like *tarap*, a fleshy fruit encased in a bristly skin, or *sukun*, a sweet-tasting tuber used to make fritters.

Filipino Barbecue Located at the north end of the KK Night Market, the Filipino Barbecue Market is the best place in town for grilled seafood at unbeatable prices. Hunker down at one of the crowded tables and point to your prey. Once the waitress has sent your order off to the grill, she'll hand you a cup (for drinking), a basin (to wash your hands) and a small plate to prepare your dipping sauce (mix up the chilli sauce, soy sauce, salt and fresh lime for your own special concoction). No cutlery here! Just dig in with your bare hands and enjoy steaming piles of fresher-than-fresh seafood. Figure around RM15 for a gut-busting meal.

Hinava Perhaps the most popular indigenous appetiser, colourful *hinava* is raw fish pickled with fresh lime juice, *chilli padi*, sliced shallots and grated ginger. The melange of tangy tastes masks the fishy smell quite well. The best place to try *hinava* is Grace Point, a posh local food court near Tanjung Aru. You'll find it at the 'Local Counter' for around RM2 per plate (the portions are small – the perfect size for a little nibble).

Roti Canai The ubiquitous *roti canai*, a flaky flat bread fried on a skillet, is served from dawn till dusk at any Indian Muslim *kedai kopi* (coffee shop) around town. Although the dish may appear simple, there's actually a lot of skill that goes into preparing the perfect platter. The cook must carefully and continuously flip the dough (à la pizza chef) to create its signature flakiness. *Roti canai* is almost always served with sauce, usually dhal (lentil curry) or another curry made from either chicken or fish.

KOTA KINABALU'S HAWKER CENTRES & FOOD COURTS

As in any Southeast Asian city, the best food in KK is the street food and hawker stalls. If you're worried about sanitation, you really shouldn't be, but assuage your fears by looking for popular stalls, especially those frequented by families.

Night Market (p40) The night market is the best, cheapest and most interesting place in KK for dinner. Vegetarian options available.

Centre Point Basement Food Court (Map p42; Basement fl, Centre Point Shopping Centre, Jln Pasar Baru; mains RM3-10; ⊘11am-10pm) Your ringgit will go a long way at this popular and varied basement food court in the Centre Point Mall. There are Malay, Chinese and Indian options, as well as drink and dessert specialists.

Grace Point (Grace Point; mains RM2-8; ⊘11am-3pm) Take bus 15 out near Tanjung Aru for some local grub at this KK mainstay. The development is actually quite chic compared to the smoke-swathed food courts in the city centre. Go for the Sabahan food stall (located in the far right corner when facing the row of counters) and try *hinava* (raw fish pickled with fresh lime juice, chilli padi, sliced shallots and grated ginger).

Wisma Merdeka Food Court   FOOD COURT **$**
(Map p42; Wisma Merdeka; mains from RM3; ⊘9am-5pm) For cheap, excellent eats, head to the top floor of the Wisma Merdeka mall and get stuck into the local food court. There's a nice diversity of stalls serving mainly Asian street food; the Chinese dumpling stand is delicious and cheap as chips. Note the above hours do not apply to each stall; some close shop earlier in the day and some stick around into the evening, but in general this is a breakfast and lunch food court.

Nagisa   JAPANESE **$$$**
(Map p42; ☑221234; Jln Datuk Salleh Sulong; sushi from RM15; ⊘noon-10pm; ✳🍴) For our money – and you'll spend a bit here – this is the best Japanese in KK. Why? Well, it's the sushi spot of choice for Japanese businessmen on return visits, which oughta tell you something. If they've got roe (caviar) on the menu, get it, and thank us later. Located in the Hyatt Regency.

Kedai Kopi Fatt Kee   CHINESE **$**
(Map p42; 28 Jln Bakau; mains from RM5; ⊘noon-10pm Mon-Sat) The woks are always sizzlin' at this popular Chinese place next to Ang's Hotel. Its *sayur manis* cooked in *belacan* (shrimp paste) is a classic, and the salt-and-pepper prawns are tasty.

TANJUNG ARU

In the early evening, head to Tanjung Aru at the south end of town near the airport for sunset cocktails and light snacks along the ocean. The area has three beaches – First Beach offers up a few restaurants, Second Beach has steamy local stalls, and Third Beach is a great place to bring a picnic as there are no establishments along the sand. A taxi to Tanjung Aru costs RM20, or you can take public transport (RM1.80) – take bus 16, 16A or city bus 2.

Self-Catering

There are a variety of places to stock up on picnic items and hiking snacks, including the centrally located **Milimewa Superstore** (Map p42; Jln Haji Saman) and **Tong Hing Supermarket** (Map p42; Jln Gaya). **7-Eleven** (Map p42; Jln Haji Saman; ⊘24hr) is conveniently open throughout the evening.

🍸 Drinking & Entertainment

Get ready for loads of karaoke bars and big, booming nightclubs, clustered around the Waterfront Esplanade, KK Times Square – where the newest hot spots are congregating, and Beach St, in the centre of town, a semipedestrian street cluttered with bars and eateries.

TOP CHOICE El Centro   BAR
(Map p42; 32 Jln Haji Saman; ⊘5pm-midnight, closed Mon) This fantastic spot, which doubles as a restaurant (p49), was sorely needed in KK. El Centro is the traveller's hangout you've been looking for: cool, Asian-mod decor, soft lighting, good music that isn't the same recycled pop every other Malaysian bar plays, and a general sense of chilled-ed-ness that makes it easy to meet other wanderers and form new friendships. Also: the drinks are strong. Stupid strong. And El Centro hosts impromptu quiz nights, costume parties and live music shows.

Bed NIGHTCLUB

(Map p42; 251901; Waterfront Esplanade) It's big, it's crowded, it's cheesy – chances are you'll end up in Bed on one of your KK nights out. Yes, get those bed puns ready, as well as your dancing shoes and patience for a *lot* of hip Chinese and locals in outfits that are alternatively slinky/shiny/skimpy. Bands play from 9pm, followed by DJs till closing.

White Room NIGHTCLUB

(Map p42; 017-836 7718; KK Times Sq) The hot thing with KK's young folks, the White Room is two levels of sweat, loud music, beautiful bodies and expensive drinks.

Shenanigan's BAR

(Map p42; 221234; Hyatt Regency Hotel) Shenanigan's is a hot mess, so we kinda love it, even though, honestly, it's just a hot mess. Live bands perform most nights from 9pm and the place is packed on weekends. Prices are horrendous (up to RM30 for a small beer) but get better during happy hour.

Shamrock BAR

(Map p42; 249829; 6 Anjung Samudra, Waterfront Esplanade) This bar is as authentically Irish as, well, Borneo, but it is an authentic Irish Bar, Model 1.0: green, Guinness, meat stew, luck o' the lass o' the laddish behaviour. Still a nice place to shoot some stick and watch KK's monied elite get silly.

Hunter's BAR

(Map p42; 016-825 7085; Kinabalu Daya Hotel) A favourite for local guides and expats, Hunter's offers up karaoke, sport on the plasma TV and balmy outdoor seating in the heart of the city.

Upperstar BAR

(Map p42; Jln Datuk Saleh Sulong) Opposite the Hilton, this pleasant semi-outdoor bar offers cheap booze and decent pub grub.

Black World KARAOKE

(Map p42; Jln Pantai; ⊙24hrs) We know. This is the only spot that stays open past 2am in central KK. But here's what to expect: cheap beer served in iced buckets, ear-shredding karaoke and dance music, sleazy male clientele, ladies of negotiable affection and bathrooms from the deepest pits of hell.

Suria Sabah CINEMA

(Map p42; Suria Sabah Mall, Jn Haji Saman) The Suria Sabah mall houses a huge multiplex that shows all the Hollywood hits, usually in the original English with subtitles.

🛍 Shopping

Like any Malaysian metropolis, KK is all about shopping. Malls seem to pop up every year; at the time of research the big new complex was **Suria Sabah**, which is full of Western retail chains and very few people.

Borneo Trading Post CRAFTS

(Map p42; 232655; Lot 16, Waterfront Esplanade, Jln Tun Fuad Stephens) Upmarket tribal art and souvenirs.

Borneo Books BOOKSHOP

(Map p42; 538077/241050; www.borneobooks. com; ground fl, Phase 1, Wisma Merdeka; ⊙10am-7pm) A brilliant selection of Borneo-related books, maps and a small used-book section. Plenty of Lonely Planet guides, too.

ℹ Information

Free maps of central KK and Sabah are available at almost every hostel or hotel.

Emergency

Ambulance (999, 218166)
Fire (994)
Police (241161, 999; Jln Dewan)

Immigration Office

Immigration office (488700; Kompleks Persekutuan Pentadbiran Kerajaan, Jln UMS; ⊙7am-1pm & 2-5:30pm Mon-Fri) In an office complex near the Universiti Malaysia Sabah (UMS), 9km north of town. Open on weekends, but only for Malaysian passport processing.

Internet Access

Every sleeping spot we list has some form of internet connection, be it dial-up or wi-fi.

Borneo Net (Jln Haji Saman; per hr RM3; ⊙9am-midnight) Twenty terminals, fast connections and loud headbanger music wafting through the air.

Net Access (Jln Pantai; per hr RM3; ⊙9-2am) Plenty of connections and less noise than other net places in KK. LAN connections are available for using your own laptop.

Medical Services

Permai Polyclinic (Map p42; 232100; 4 Jln Pantai) Excellent private outpatient clinic.

Sabah Medical Centre (211333; www. sabamedicalcentre.com/; Lorong Bersatu, off Jalan Damai) Good private hospital care, located about 6km southeast of the city centre.

Money

Central KK is chock-a-block with 24-hour ATMs.
HSBC (Map p42; 212622; 56 Jln Gaya; ⊙9am-4.30pm Mon-Thu, 9am-4pm Fri)

Maybank (Map p42; ☑254295; 9 Jln Pantai; ⏱9am-4.30pm Mon-Thu, 9am-4pm Fri) 24hr ATM.

Standard Chartered Bank (Map p42; ☑298111; 20 Jln Haji Saman; ⏱9.15am-3.45pm Mon-Fri)

Post

Main Post Office (☑210855; Jln Tun Razak; ⏱8am-5pm Mon-Fri) Western Union cheques and money orders can be cashed here.

Tourist Information

Sabah Parks (☑523500, 486430; www.sabah parks.org.my; 1st-5th fl, Lot 45 & 46, Block H, Signature Office; ⏱8am-1pm & 2-4.30pm Mon-Thu, 8-11.30am & 2-4.30pm Fri, 8am-12.50pm Sat) Source of information on the state's parks.

Sabah Tourism Board (☑212121; www.sabah tourism.com; 51 Jln Gaya; ⏱8am-5pm Mon-Fri, 8am-4pm Sat, 9am-4pm Sun) Housed in the historic post office building, KK's main tourist office has eager staff and a wide range of brochures. Fair warning, they're going to direct you towards package tours, so don't expect much in the way of independent travel advice.

Tourism Malaysia (☑248698; www.tourism. gov.my; ground fl, Api-Api Centre, Jln Pasar Baru; ⏱8am-4.30pm Mon-Thu, 8am-noon & 1.30-4.30pm Fri) This office is of limited use for travellers, but does offer a few interesting brochures on sights in Peninsular Malaysia.

ⓘ Getting There & Away

Air

KK is well served by **Malaysia Airlines** (☑1-300 883 000, 088-515555; www.malaysiaair lines.com; MAS; 1st fl, Departure Hall, KKIA; ⏱5.30am-7.30pm) and **AirAsia** (☑03-2171 9333; www.airasia.com; ground fl, Wisma Sabah, Jln Gaya) offer the following international flights to/from KK: Brunei, Shenzhen, Jakarta, Manila, Singapore and Tapei. Within Malaysia, flights go to/from Johor Bahru, Kuala Lumpur and Penang in Peninsular Malaysia, and Kuching, Labuan, Miri, Sandakan, and Tawau in Borneo. **Jetstar** (www.jetstar.com) and **Tiger Airways** (www.tigerairways.com) both offer flights to Singapore.

Boat

All passengers must pay an adult/child RM3.60/1.80 terminal fee for ferries departing from KK. Passenger boats connect KK to Pulau Labuan twice daily at 8am and 1:30pm (adult first/economy class RM36/31, child first/economy class RM23/18), with onward service to Brunei and to Tunku Abdul Rahman National

MAIN DESTINATIONS & FARES FROM KOTA KINABALU

The following bus and minivan transport information was provided to us by the Sabah Tourism Board and should be used as an estimate only: transport times can fluctuate due to weather, prices may change, and the transport authority has been known to alter departure points.

DESTINATION	DURATION (HR)	PRICE (RM)	TERMINAL	DEPARTURES
Beaufort	2	12	Padang Merdeka	7am-5pm (frequent)
Keningau	2½	17	Padang Merdeka	7am-5pm (8 daily)
Kota Belud	1	10	Padang Merdeka	7am-5pm (frequent)
Kuala Penyu	2	20	Segama Bridge	8-11am (hourly)
Kudat	3	22	Padang Merdeka	7am-4pm (frequent)
Lahad Datu	8	40	Inanam	7am, 8.30am, 9am, 8pm
Lawas (Sarawak)	4	25	Padang Merdeka	8.30am & 1.30pm
Mt Kinabalu NP	2	15-20	Inanam & Padang Merdeka	7am-8pm (very frequent)
Ranau	2	15	Padang Merdeka	7am-5pm
Sandakan	6	35-40	Inanam	7.30am-2pm (frequent) & 8pm
Semporna	9	50	Inanam	7am, 8.30am, 9am, 8pm
Tawau	9	55	Inanam	7.30am, 2pm, 8pm
Tenom	3½	25	Padang Merdeka	8am, noon, 4pm

DON'T MISS

RIDING THE BORNEO RAILS

Back in the late 19th-century, colonials used to swan around the western Sabah coast on the **North Borneo Railway**, which eventually fell into disuse and disrepair. Recently, the old rail line has been revived, not as a viable means of train travel but as a nostalgic attraction in its own right. The old iron horse has been restored, with natural wood interiors and the original exterior colour scheme of green and cream, set off with the railway's old brass emblem of a crown surmounting a tiger holding a rail wheel.

The train leaves KK at 9:30am and arrives in Papar at 11:45am, taking in mountains and rice paddies, with stops for a look at a Chinese temple and the Papar wet market. On the trip back to KK (12.20–1.40pm) a smashing colonially inspired tiffin lunch of cucumber sandwiches and satay (plus some other goodies) is served.

The railway is operated by Sutera Harbour (p46); adult/child tickets cost RM270/170. The train leaves the station in Tanjung Aru twice a week, on Wednesday and Saturday. For more information or to book tickets, contact Sutera Harbour at 308500 or nbrinfo@suteraharbour.com.my.

Park. Ferries depart from Jesselton Point, located a little way north of the **Suria Sabah shopping mall** (Map p42).

Bus & Minivan

Several different stations around KK serve a variety of out-of-town destinations. There is a bus to Brunei.

In general, land transport heading east departs from Inanam (Utara Terminal; 9km north of the city) while those heading north and south on the west coast leave from Padang Merdeka (Merdeka Field) Bus Station (also called Wawasan or 'old bus station'; at the south end of town). Local buses (RM1.80) from Wawasan can take tourists to Inanam if you don't want to splurge on the RM20 taxi. Have your hotel call ahead to the bus station to book your seat in advance. Same-day bookings are usually fine, although weekends are busier than weekdays. It's always good to ring ahead because sometimes transport will be halted due to flooding caused by heavy rains.

Taxi

Share taxis operate from the Padang Merdeka Bus Station. Several share taxis do a daily run between KK and Ranau, passing the entrance road to the Kinabalu National Park office. The fare to Ranau or Kinabalu National Park is RM25, or you can charter a taxi for RM100 per car (note that a normal city taxi will charge around RM200 for a charter).

ⓘ Getting Around

To/From the Airport

The international airport is in Tanjung Aru, 7km south of central KK. Please note that the two terminals of Kota Kinabalu International Airport (KKIA) are not connected – they feel like two different airports. Most airlines operate out of Terminal 1, but an increasing amount of carriers, including AirAsia, depart from Terminal 2. City bus 2 and bus 16A (RM1.50) service Terminal 2 and can be boarded at City Park station downtown. Minibuses (RM3) leave from City Park station for Terminal 1 (look for city bus 1 to access this terminal in the future). Public transport runs from 6am to 7pm daily. Taxis heading from terminals into town operate on a voucher system (RM38) sold at a taxi desk on the terminal's ground floor. Taxis heading to the airport should not charge over RM40 if you catch one in the city centre.

Car

Major car-rental agencies have counters on the first floor at KKIA and branch offices elsewhere in town. Manual cars start at around RM120 to RM140 per day and most agencies can arrange chauffeured vehicles as well.

Borneo Express (☑016-886 0793, In Sandakan 016-886 0789; http://borneocar. com/; Lot 1-L01 C4, Kota Kinabalu Airport)

Kinabalu Heritage Tours & Car Rental (☑318311; www.travelborneotours.com; Block F, Tanjung Aru Plaza)

Extra Rent A Car (☑251529, 218160; www.e-erac-online.com; 2nd fl, Beverly Hotel, Jln Kemajuan)

Minivans

Minivans operate from several stops, including Padang Merdeka Bus Station and the car park outside Milimewa Superstore. They circulate the town looking for passengers. Since most destinations in the city are within walking distance, it's unlikely that you'll need to catch a minivan, although they're handy for getting to the airport or to KK Times Square. Most destinations within the city cost RM1 to RM2.

Taxi

Expect to pay roughly between RM7 to RM10 for a ride in the city centre. Taxis can be found throughout the city and at all bus stations and shopping centres. There's a stand by Milimewa Supermarket (near the intersection of Jln Haji Saman and Beach St) and another 200m southwest of City Park.

AROUND KOTA KINABALU

Tunku Abdul Rahman National Park

Whenever one enjoys a sunset off KK, the view tends to be improved by the five jungly humps of Manukan, Gaya, Sapi, Mamutik and Sulug islands. These swaths of sand, plus the reefs and cerulean waters in between them, make up **Tunku Abdul Rahman National Park** (adult/child RM10/6), covering a total area of just over 49 sq km (two-thirds of which is water). Only a short boat ride from KK, the islands are individually quite pretty, but in an effort to accommodate the ever-increasing tourist flow (especially large numbers of Chinese), barbecue stalls and restaurants now crowd the beaches. On weekends the islands can get *very* crowded, but on weekdays you can find some serenity. Accommodation tends to be expensive, but most travellers come here for day trips anyway, and there are camping options.

Although it's no Sipadan, diving in the park is a popular activity, and the area is considered a good spot for getting open water certified. **Borneo Dream** (☏088-244064; www.borneodream.com; F-G-1 Plaza Tanjung Arum, Jalan Mat Salleh, Kota Kinabalu) and Downbelow (p46) both run diving programs on Pulau Gaya.

PULAU MANUKAN

Manukan is the most popular destination for KK residents and has plenty of facilities. It is the second-largest island in the group, its 20 hectares largely covered in dense vegetation. There's a good beach with coral reefs off the southern and eastern shores, a walking trail around the perimeter and a network of nature trails – if you want to thoroughly explore all of the above it shouldn't take more than two hours, and you don't need to be particularly fit. There's little clouds of tropical fish swimming around, many of which

can be seen simply by looking down from the jetty. When you depart the boat you'll likely be pointed towards a kiosk that hires equipment masks and snorkels (RM15), beach mats (RM5) and body boards (RM10).

Manukan Island Resort (☏017-833 5022; www.suterasanctuarylodges.com; villa from RM1120; ❄❢), managed by Sutera Sanctuary Lodges, has the only accommodation on the island. It comprises a restaurant, swimming pool and tennis courts, as well as 20 dark-wood villas, all overlooking the South China Sea and decked out in tasteful Bali-chic style; the cool stone showers hemmed in by flowering plants are a nice touch.

PULAU MAMUTIK

Mamutik is the smallest island out here, a mere 300m from end to end. A nice beach runs up and down the east coast of the island, although it can get pretty kelp-y after bad weather. Snorkelling here is pretty good, but you may want to avoid the shallow area; the coral here will do a number on your bare feet. There's no resort, but camping (RM5 per person, pay on arrival) is possible. There's a small store-restaurant-snorkel-rental place, but it's a good idea to bring supplies.

PULAU SAPI

They should really rename Pulau Sapi (Cow Island) to Pulau Biawak (Monitor Lizard Island). This little speck also offers snorkelling and attractive beaches, but Sapi can also get very cramped with day-tripping families. The island is separated from Gaya by a very shallow 200m channel that you can swim across if you feel up to it, but be careful; there are definitely no life guards on duty. Otherwise, the main activities include wading, relaxing on the beach around the jetty or exploring the trails through the forest; it takes about 45 minutes to walk around the island. There are changing rooms, toilets, barbecue pits, and a small snack kiosk, plus an outfitted campsite (RM5 per person), but you'll need to bring most supplies from the mainland.

PULAU GAYA

With an area of about 15 sq km, Pulau Gaya is the Goliath of KK's offshore islands, rising to an elevation of 300m. It's also the closest to KK and covered in virtually undisturbed tropical forest. The bays on the east end are filled with bustling water villages, inhabited by Filipino immigrants (legal and otherwise) who live in cramped houses built on stilts in the shallow water, with mosques, schools and simple shops, also built on stilts. Residents of KK warn against exploring these water villages, saying that incidences of theft and other crimes have occurred.

🛏 Sleeping

Bunga Raya Island Resort   RESORT $$$
(🖉380390; http://bungarayaresort.com, villas from RM1715; ❄🛜🏊) Six stunning villas occupy a fertile patch of beachfront. The Plunge Pool has just that – its own deep body of water that looks over the beach and ocean – while the incredibly romantic Treehouse perches over a jacuzzi, lounge and its own private swimming hole. Operated by the owners of Gayana Eco Resort.

Gaya Island Resort   RESORT $$$
(🖉KL number 3 2783 1000; www.gayaislandresort. com; villas from RM1100; ❄🛜🏊) Six immaculate villas that blend modernity with open air accents, earth tones with cool whites, and a subtle integration of the ocean with green jungle perch over a half-moon bay. Attentive service makes for a property that drips with refined indugence.

Gayana Eco Resort   RESORT $$$
(🖉380390; www.gayana-eco-resort.com; villas from RM1200; ❄🛜🏊) Five stunning villas stuffed with modern amenities and island chic touches make up posh Gayana. The Bakau (mangrove) Villa overlooks a series of tangled flooded forest, while the Palm Villa's deceptive simplicity masks steps that lead into the warm heart of Tunku Rahman's protected waters.

PULAU SULUG
Shaped like a cartoon speech bubble, Sulug has an area of 8.1 hectares and is the least visited of the group, probably because it's the furthest away from KK. It only has one beach, on a spit of land extending from its eastern shore. Unfortunately, the snorkelling is pretty poor. If you want a quiet getaway, Sulug is a decent choice, but you'll have to charter a boat to get here; the normal ferries don't stop here. If you want a secluded beach and don't want to lay out for a charter (at least RM240), you'll do better by heading to Manukan and walking down the beach to escape the crowds.

ℹ Getting There & Away
Boat
Boats to the park leave from 8.30am to 4.15pm when full from KK's Jesselton Point Ferry Terminal (commonly known as 'The Jetty' by locals and taxi drivers); the last boats leave the islands for KK around 5pm. Service is every 30 minutes, but on slower days this can be every hour. Inquire at the counter for the next available boat, sign up for your chosen destination and take a seat until there are enough passengers to depart. Catch a boat in the morning, as it's much harder to make up boat numbers in the afternoon. Boats also run from Sutera Harbour – more convenient for those staying near Tanjung Aru (or for those wanting to reach Pulau Gaya). Return fares to Mamutik, Manukan and Sapi hover around RM30. You can also buy two-/three-island passes for RM40/48.

WATER MONITORING

If you look around the edge of the barbecue pits on Sapi, you may spot a fence cordoning off some of the jungle, and at said fence you'll usually find a hissing band of great, grey-green dragons: water monitor lizards, known locally as *biawak*. They're some of the largest reptiles in the world, with males averaging a length of 1.5m to 2m, sometimes growing as large as 3m, weighing anywhere from 19kg to 50kg. Within the lizard family they are only outstripped by Komodo Dragons.

These mini-Godzillas are found all over Malaysia, but on Pulau Sapi they are the king of the jungle – and the waves. It's amazing watching these lumbering beasts take to the water, where they instantly transform into graceful sea monsters reminiscent of aquatic dinosaurs (which, indeed, are believed to be the ancestors of monitor lizards). Despite their size, water monitors aren't apex predators in the vein of crocodiles or their Komodo Dragon cousins. Instead, they serve the purpose of coyotes in North America, or jackals in Africa: adaptable, clever scavengers that seem to thrive, rather than suffer, when humans are near, making use of our refuse dumps as their larders.

Water monitors are awesome creatures, but don't be an idiot like some tourists and try to pose next to them or hand feed them. Their mouths are filled with deadly bacteria and their claws can rip a gash in your flesh you won't soon forget.

The set fee for charter to one island is RM250, but this can be negotiated. Try to deal directly with a boatperson if you do this – don't talk to the touts who prowl the area. And don't consider paying until you return to the dock.

A RM3 terminal fee is added to all boat journeys, and a RM10 entrance fee to the marine park, paid when you purchase your ticket (if you are chartering a boat this should be included).

NORTHWESTERN SABAH

The northern edge of Sabah manages to compact, into a relatively small space, much of the geographic and cultural minutiae that makes Borneo so special. The ocean? Lapping at miles of sandy beach, sky blue to stormy grey, and concealing superlative dive sites. The people? Kadazan-Dusun, Rungus, rice farmers, mountain hunters, ship builders and deep-sea fishermen. And then, of course, 'the' mountain: Gunung Kinabalu, or Mt Kinabalu, the focal point of the island's altitude, trekkers, folklore and spiritual energy. For generations, the people of Sabah have been drawn to the mountain; don't be surprised when you fall under its spell too.

Mt Kinabalu & Kinabalu National Park

Gunung Kinabalu, as it is known in Malay, is more than the highest thing on the world's third largest island. And it is more than scenery. Mt Kinabalu is ubiquitous in Sabah to the point of being inextricable. It graces the state's flag and is a constant presence at the edge of your eyes, catching the clouds and shading the valleys. It is only when you give the mountain your full attention that you realise how special this peak, the region's biggest tourist attraction, truly is.

The 4095m peak of Mt Kinabalu may not be a Himalayan sky-poker, but Malaysia's first Unesco World Heritage site is by no means an easy jaunt. The main trail up is essentially a very long walk up a very steep hill, past alpine jungle and sunlit moonscapes, with a little scrabbling thrown in for good measure. If you don't feel up to reaching the mountain top, its base has some worthy attractions, including a large network of nature trails.

That said, the main detriment to climbing is not the physical challenge, but the cost. Things are expensive within Mt Kinabalu National Park. Bottled water costs four or five times what it goes for in KK and Sutera Sanctuary Lodges has a monopoly on accommodation. You'll have to decide if you want to accept these fees because they are basically the cost of climbing the mountain.

Amazingly, the mountain is still growing: researchers have found it increases in height by about 5mm a year. On a clear day you can see the Philippines from the summit; usually, though, the mountain is thoroughly wreathed in fog by midmorning.

History

Although it is commonly believed that local tribesmen climbed Kinabalu many years earlier, it was Sir Hugh Low, the British colonial secretary on Pulau Labuan, who recorded the first official ascent of Mt Kinabalu in 1851. Today Kinabalu's tallest peak is named after him, thus Borneo's highest point is ironically known as Low's Peak.

In those days the difficulty of climbing Mt Kinabalu lay not in the ascent, but in getting through the jungle to the mountain's base. Finding willing local porters was another tricky matter – the tribesmen who accompanied Low believed the spirits of the dead inhabited the mountain. Low was therefore obliged to protect the party by supplying a large basket of quartz crystals and teeth, as was the custom back then. During the subsequent years, the spirit-appeasement ceremonies became more and more elaborate, so that by the 1920s they had come to include loud prayers, gunshots, and the sacrifice of seven eggs and seven white chickens. You have to wonder at what point explorers started thinking the locals might be taking the mickey...

These days, the elaborate chicken dances are no more, although climbing the mountain can still feel like a rite of passage.

Check out Mountain Torq's website (www.mountaintorq.com) for more fun facts about Kinabalu's history.

Geology

Many visitors to Borneo assume Mt Kinabalu is a volcano, but the mountain is actually a huge granite dome that rose from the depths below some nine million years ago. In geological terms, Mt Kinabalu is still young. Little erosion has occurred on the exposed granite rock faces around the summit, though the effects of glaciers that used to cover much of the mountain can be detected by striations on the rock. There's no longer a

Mt Kinabalu Summit Trail

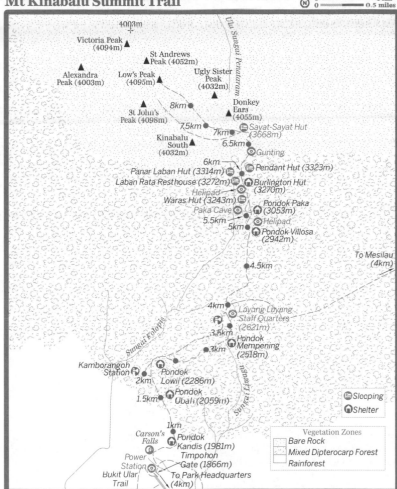

snowline and the glaciers have disappeared, but at times ice forms in the rock pools near the summit.

Orientation & Information

Kinabalu National Park HQ is 88km by road northeast of KK and set in gardens with a magnificent view of the mountain. At 1588m the climate is refreshingly cool compared to the coast; the average temperatures are 20°C in the day and 13°C at night. The hike to the summit is difficult.

On the morning of your arrival, pay your park entry fee, present your lodging reservation slip to the Sutera Sanctuary Lodges office to receive your official room assignment, and check in with the Sabah Parks office to pay your registration and guide fees. Advance accommodation bookings are *essential* if you plan on climbing the mountain.

PERMITS, FEES & GUIDES

A park fee, climbing permit, insurance and a guide fee are *mandatory* if you intend to climb Mt Kinabalu. All permits and guides must be arranged at the **Sabah Parks office** (⊙7am-7pm), which is directly next door to the Sutera Sanctuary Lodges office, immediately on your right after you pass through the main gate of the park. Pay all fees at park HQ before you climb and don't ponder an 'unofficial' climb as permits (laminated cards worn on a string necklace) are scrupulously checked at two points you cannot avoid passing on the way up the mountain.

Virtually every tour operator in KK can hook you up with a trip to the mountain; solo travellers are often charged around RM1400. It's possible, and a little cheaper, to do it on your own – but plan ahead. Packages are obviously easier if pricey, so if you find one that sounds enticing, go for it.

All visitors entering the park are required to pay a park entrance fee: RM15 for adults and RM10 for children under 18 (Malaysians pay RM3 and RM1, respectively). A climbing permit costs RM100/RM40 for adults/children, while Malaysian nationals pay RM30/RM12. Climbing insurance costs a flat rate of RM7 per person. Guide fees for the summit trek cost RM100. Climbers ascending Kinabalu along the Mesilau Trail will pay an extra RM10 (small group) or RM20 (large group) for their guide. Your guide will be assigned to you on the morning you begin your hike. If you ask, the park staff will try to attach individual travellers to a group so that guide fees can be shared. Couples can expect to be given their own guide. Guides are mostly Kadazan from a village nearby and many of them have travelled to the summit several hundred times. Try to ask for a guide who speaks English – he or she (usually he) might point out a few interesting specimens of plant life. The path up the mountain is pretty straightforward, and the guides walk behind the slowest member of the group, so think of them as safety supervisors rather than trailblazers.

All this does not include at least RM415 for room-and-board on the mountain at Laban Rata. With said lodging, plus buses or taxis to the park, you're looking at spending over RM800 for the common two-day, one-night trip to the mountain. That said, you *can* do a one-day hike if you show up at the park entrance when it opens (7am) and are judged physically fit by a ranger. This allows you to cut the cost of lodging, but there are two catches. First, when we say you need to be fit, we mean *fit*. A friend – one of those annoyingly healthy mountaineers who probably sleepwalks up the Alps – couldn't walk upstairs for two days after managing the one-day hike. Second, and more worryingly, there are rumours the park will discontinue allowing one-day hikes in the future.

Optional extra fees include a taxi ride from the park office to the Timpohon Gate (RM16.50 per vehicle, one-way, four-person maximum), a climbing certificate (RM10) and a porter (RM102 per trip to the summit or RM84 to Laban Rata) who can be hired to carry a maximum load of 10kg.

If you need a helicopter lift off the mountain for emergency reasons, the going rate is RM2500.

EQUIPMENT & CLOTHING
No special equipment is required to successfully summit the mountain, however a headlamp is strongly advised for the predawn jaunt to the top – you'll need your hands free to climb the ropes on the summit massif. Expect freezing temperatures near the summit, not to mention strong winds and

CAN I AVOID PLAYING MONOPOLY?
One of the most common questions travellers in Sabah ask is: is there any way to go up Mt Kinabalu that is less expensive? The best way to do so is the one-day climb, but that prospect is tough unless you're fit, and even then it is discouraged by park officials, and may be discontinued in the future.

Many travellers hate that Sutera has a monopoly on accommodation, or that they are encouraged to book their climb months in advance, which discourages just showing up and walking. If you feel this way, it may be best to walk the trails at the base of Mt Kinabalu or attempt the Mesilau Trail up to the first park checkpoint, which offers much of the full climb's scenery.

Sabah Parks won't allow a night climb, and permits are carefully checked at several points on the mountain. We did meet hikers who wanted to try the above, but this would involve a lot of sneaking around and tempting fate, be it a trekking accident or arrest, and we don't recommend this. If you're set against giving Sabah Parks or Sutera your money, trust us, there are plenty of other things to see and do here.

KINABALU PACKING LIST

» Headlamp (with spare batteries)
» Comfortable running shoes
» Wool socks and athletic socks
» Hiking shorts or breathable pants
» Three T-shirts (one made of lightweight synthetic material)
» Fleece jacket
» Lightweight shell jacket or rain jacket
» Fleece or wool hat
» Fleece gloves
» Long johns
» Hand towel
» Water bottle
» Sunscreen
» Insect repellent
» Light, high-energy snacks
» Camera
» Money
» Earplugs for dorms

The above items should easily fit into a small waterproof backpack. Apply a dab of sunscreen and insect repellent before you depart.

the occasional rainstorm. Don't forget a water bottle, which can be refilled at unfiltered (but potable) tanks en route.

THE CLIMB TO THE SUMMIT

This schedule assumes you're doing a two-day/one-night ascent of the mountain. You'll want to check in at park headquarters at around 9am (8.45am at the latest for *via ferrata* participants) to pay your park fees, grab your guide and start the ascent (four to six hours) to Laban Rata (3272m) where you'll spend the night before finishing the climb. On the following day you'll finish scrambling to the top at about 2.30am in order to reach the summit for a breathtaking sunrise over Borneo.

A climb up Kinabalu is only advised for those in adequate physical condition. The trek is tough, and *every step you take* will be uphill. You will negotiate several obstacles along the way, including slippery stones, blinding humidity, frigid winds and slow-paced trekkers. Mountain Torq compares the experience to squeezing five days of hiking into a 38-hour (or less, if you do the one-day climb) trek.

There are two trail options leading up the mountain – the Timpohon Trail and the Mesilau Trail. If this is your first time climbing Kinabalu, we advise taking the Timpohon Trail – it's shorter, easier (but by no means easy!) and more convenient from the park headquarters (an hour's walk or short park shuttle ride; RM16.50 one-way per vehicle, four-person maximum). If you are participating in Mountain Torq's *via ferrata,* you are required to take the Timpohon Trail in order to reach Laban Rata in time for your safety briefing at 4pm. The Mesilau Trail offers second-time climbers (or fit hikers) the opportunity to really enjoy some of the park's natural wonders. This trail is less trodden so the chances of seeing unique flora and fauna are higher.

As you journey up to the summit, you'll happen upon signboards showing your progress – there's a marker every 500m. There are also rest shelters *(pondok)* at regular intervals, with basic toilets and tanks of unfiltered (but potable) drinking water. The walking times that follow are conservative estimates – don't be surprised if you move at a slightly speedier pace, and certainly don't be discouraged if you take longer – everyone's quest for the summit is different.

ADDING INSULT TO INJURY

As your two-day Kinabalu adventure comes to an end and you limp across the Timpohon Gate a shrivelled bundle of aching muscles and bones, don't forget to glance at the climbing records chart. Every year the **Kinabalu International Climbathon** (http://climbathon.sabahtourism.com) attracts the fittest athletes from around the world for a competitive climb-off as dozens of hikers zoom up the mountain a la the Road Runner. The oldest person to reach the summit was a Japanese lady who battled her way to the top at the grand old age of 90. So just remember, when you're smugly slinking by slower hikers, there are pensioners out there who would leave you for dead...

TIMPOHON GATE TO LAYANG LAYANG

'Why am I sweating this much *already?*'

The trip to the summit officially starts at the Timpohon Gate (1866m) and from there it's an 8.72km march to the summit. There is a small bathroom outhouse located 700m before the Timpohon Gate, and a convenience shop at the gate itself for impulse snack and beverage purchases.

After a short, deceptive descent, the trail leads up steep stairs through the dense forest and continues winding up and up for the rest of the trip. There's a charming waterfall, **Carson's Falls**, beside the track shortly after the start, and the forest can be alive with birds and squirrels in the morning. Five *pondok* (shelters) are spaced at intervals of 15 to 35 minutes between Timpohon Gate and Layang Layang and it's about three hours to the Layang Layang (2621m) rest stop. Near **Pondok Lowii** (2286m) the trail follows an open ridge giving great views over the valleys and up to the peaks.

LAYANG LAYANG TO PONDOK PAKA

'Why did I put all that extra crap in my rucksack?'

This part of the climb can be the most difficult for some – especially around the 4.5km marker. You've definitely made some headway but there's still a long trek to go – no light at the end of the jungly tunnel quite yet. It takes about 1¾ hours to reach **Pondok Paka** (3053m), the seventh shelter on the trail, 5.5km from the start.

PONDOK PAKA TO LABAN RATA

'Why did I pay all that money just to climb a freakin' mountain?!'

Also known as the 'can't I pay someone to finish this for me?' phase, this part of the climb is where beleaguered hikers get a second wind as the treeline ends and the summit starts to feel closer. At the end of this leg you'll reach **Laban Rata** (3272m), your 'home sweet home' on the mountain. Take a good look at the slender signpost announcing your arrival – it's the propeller of the helicopter once used to hoist the construction materials to build the elaborate rest station. This leg takes around 45 minutes.

LABAN RATA TO SAYAT-SAYAT HUT

'Why am I waking up at the time I usually go to bed back home?'

It's 2am and your alarm just went off. Is this a dream? Nope. You're about to climb the last part of the mountain in order to reach the summit before sunrise.

Most people set off at around 2.45am, and it's worth heading out at this time even if you're in great shape (don't forget your torch). The one-hour climb to **Sayat-Sayat** hut (3668m) involves a lot of hiker traffic and the crossing of the sheer Panar Laban rock face. There is little vegetation, except where overhangs provide some respite from the wind. It is one of the toughest parts of the climb, especially in the cold and dark of the predawn hours.

SAYAT-SAYAT HUT TO SUMMIT

'Why is it so darn cold out?! I'm standing near the equator!'

After checking in at Sayat-Sayat, the crowd of hikers begins to thin as stronger walkers forge ahead and slower adventurers pause for sips from their water bottle. Despite the stunning surroundings, the last stretch of the summit ascent is, of course, the steepest and hardest part of the climb.

From just beyond Sayat-Sayat, the summit looks deceptively close and, though it's just over 1km, the last burst will take between one to three hours depending on your stamina. You might even see shattered climbers crawling on hands and knees as they reach out for the top of Borneo.

THE SUMMIT

[Speechless...]

This is it – the million-dollar moment (or the RM800+ moment for those who are keeping score...). Don't forget the sunrise can be glimpsed from anywhere on the mountain. The summit warms up quickly as the sun starts its own ascent between 5.45am and 6.20am, and the weary suddenly smile; the climb up a distant memory, the trek down an afterthought.

Consider signing up with Mountain Torq to climb back to Laban Rata along the world's highest *via ferrata*.

THE JOURNEY BACK TO THE BOTTOM

'Why didn't I believe anyone when they said that going down was just as hard as going up?!'

You'll probably leave the summit at around 7.30am and you should aim to leave Laban Rata no later than 12.30pm. The gruelling descent back down to Timpohon Gate from Laban Rata takes between three and four hours (if you're returning to the bottom along the Mesilau Trail it will take more time than descending to the Timpohon Gate). The weather can close in very quickly and the granite is slippery even when dry. During rainstorms the downward trek feels like walking through a river. Slower walkers often find that their legs hurt more the day after – quicker paces lighten the constant pounding as legs negotiate each descending step. If you participated in the *via ferrata*

you will be absolutely knackered during your descent and will stumble into Timpohon Gate just before sunset (around 6pm to 6.30pm).

A 1st-class certificate can be purchased for RM10 by those who complete the climb; 2nd-class certificates are issued for making it to Laban Rata. These can be collected at the park office.

WALKS AROUND THE BASE

It's well worth spending a day exploring the marked trails around park headquarters; if you have time, it may be better to do it before you climb the mountain, as chances are you won't really feel like it afterwards. There are various trails and lookouts.

The base trails interconnect with one another like a tied shoelace, so you can spend the day, or indeed days, walking at a leisurely pace through the beautiful forest. Some interesting plants, plenty of birds and, if you're lucky, the occasional mammal can be seen along the **Liwagu Trail** (6km), which follows the river of the same name. When it rains, watch out for slippery paths and legions of leeches.

At 11am each day a **guided walk** (per person RM3) starts from the Sabah Parks office and lasts for one to two hours. The knowledgeable guide points out flowers, plants, birds and insects along the way. If you set

VIA FERRATA

Mountain Torq has dramatically changed the Kinabalu climbing experience by creating an intricate system of rungs and rails crowning the mountain's summit. Known as *via ferrata* (literally 'iron road' in Italian), this alternative style of mountaineering has been a big hit in Europe for the last century and is just starting to take Asia by storm. In fact, Mountain Torq is Asia's first *via ferrata* system, and, according to the Guinness Book of World Records, it's the highest 'iron road' in the world.

After ascending Kinabalu in the traditional fashion, participants use the network of levers to return to the Laban Rata rest camp along the mountain's dramatic granite walls. Mountain Torq's star attraction, the **Low's Peak Circuit** (RM550; minimum age 17), is a four-to-five-hour scramble down metres upon metres of sheer rock face. This route starts at 3800m, passing a variety of obstacles before linking up to the Walk the Torq path for the last part of the journey. The route's threadlike tightrope walks and swinging planks will have you convinced that the course designers are sadistic, but that's what makes it so darn fun – testing your limits without putting your safety in jeopardy. Those who don't want to see their heart leaping out of their chest should try the **Walk the Torq** (RM400; minimum age 10) route. This two-to-three-hour escapade is an exciting initiation into the world of *via ferrata*, offering dramatic mountain vistas with a few less knee-shaking moments. No matter which course you tackle, you'll undoubtedly think that the dramatic vertical drops are nothing short of exhilarating.

Via ferrata may be an Italian import, but Mountain Torq is pure Bornean fun. For more information about Mountain Torq, check out www.mountaintorq.com.

FLORA & FAUNA OF MT KINABALU

Mt Kinabalu is a botanical paradise, designated a Centre of Plant Diversity as well as a Unesco-listed World Heritage site. The wide range of habitats supports an even wider range of natural history, and over half the species growing above 900m are unique to the area.

Among the more spectacular flowers are orchids, rhododendrons and the *Insectivorous nepenthes* (pitcher plant). Around park HQ, there's dipterocarp forest (rainforest); creepers, ferns and orchids festoon the canopy, while fungi grow on the forest floor. Between 900m and 1800m, there are oaks, laurels and chestnuts, while higher up there's dense rhododendron forest. On the windswept slopes above Laban Rata vegetation is stunted, with *sayat-sayat* a common shrub. The mountain's uppermost slopes are bare of plant life.

Deer and monkeys are no longer common around park HQ, but you can see squirrels, including the handsome Prevost's squirrel and the mountain ground squirrel. Tree shrews can sometimes be seen raiding rubbish bins. Common birds are Bornean treepies, fantails, bulbuls, sunbirds and laughing-thrushes, while birds seen only at higher altitudes are the Kinabalu friendly warbler, the mountain blackeye and the mountain blackbird. Other wildlife includes colourful butterflies and the huge green moon moth.

out from KK early enough, it's possible to arrive at the park in time for the guided walk.

Many of the plants found on the mountain are cultivated in the **Mountain Garden** (Map p63; admission RM5; ☺9am-1pm, 2:30am-4pm) behind the visitors centre. Guided tours of the garden depart at 9am, noon and 3pm and cost RM5.

🛏 Sleeping

LABAN RATA (ON THE MOUNTAIN)
Camping is not allowed on the mountain, and thus access to the summit is limited by access to the huts on the mountain at Laban Rata (3272m). This *must* be booked in advance, the earlier the better. In order to have any hope of clear weather when you reach the summit, you must arrive around dawn, and the only way to do this is by spending a night at Laban Rata. If you attempt a one-day ascent starting around 7am, by the time you get to the summit it will almost certainly be clouded over or raining.

Sutera Sanctuary Lodges (☎088-308470, 088-318888, info 243 629; suterasanctuary lodges.com.my; Jln Haji Saman, Lot G15, ground fl, Wisma Sabah; ☺8:30am-4:30pm Mon-Sat, 8:30am-12:30pm Sun) in Kota Kinabalu operates almost all of the accommodation here, but space is limited. Be mindful that travellers often report frustration with booking huts on the mountain – claiming the booking system is disorganised and inefficient, the huts are often full, or aren't full when

they're told they are. Bookings can be made online (but only if you book at least two nights) in person or over the phone – our experience was that it was best to book at Sutera's offices in KK if you haven't done so in advance.

The most common sleeping option is the heated dormitory (bedding included) in the Laban Rata Resthouse, which sells for RM485 per person. If you need privacy, twin shares are available for RM920. Three meals are included in the price. Non-heated facilities surrounding the Laban Rata building are also available for RM415 per person (meals included).

The other option at Laban Rata is to stay at **Pendant Hut**, which is owned and operated by **Mountain Torq** (pricing is on par with Sutera). All guests sleeping at Pendant Hut take two of three meals at Sutera's cafeteria, and are required to participate in (or at least pay for) the *via ferrata* circuit. Pendant Hut is slightly more basic (there's no heat, although climbers sleep in uberwarm sleeping bags). However, there's a bit of a summer-camp vibe here while Laban Rata feels more like a Himalayan orphanage. Prices for Pendant Hut are comparable to Sutera.

PARK HEADQUARTERS (AT THE BASE)
The following sleeping options are located at the base of the mountain and are operated by Sutera Sanctuary Lodges. They're overpriced compared to sleeping spots just outside the park.

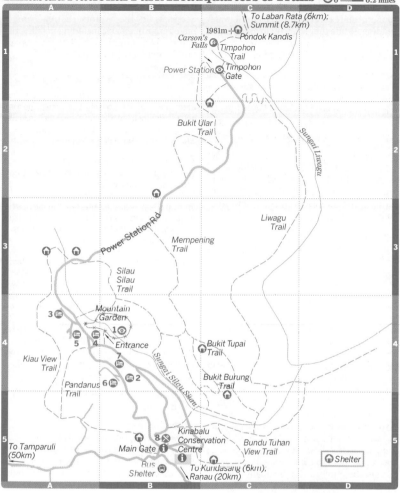

Kinabalu National Park Headquarters & Trails

Grace Hostel　　　　　　　　　HOSTEL **$$**

(Map p63; dm RM192) Clean, comfortable 20-bed dorm with fireplace and drink-making area.

Hill Lodge　　　　　　　　　CABIN **$$$**

(Map p63; cabin RM580) These semidetached cabins are a good option for those who can't face a night in the hostels. They're clean and comfortable, with private bathrooms.

Liwagu Suites
HOTEL $$$

(Map p63; ste RM700) These hotel-like rooms (four in total) can be found in the Liwagu Building. While they sleep up to four people, they're best for couples as they contain only one bedroom and one living room.

Nepenthes Villa
HOTEL, LODGE $$$

(Map p63; lodge RM1078) These two-storey units fall somewhere between hotel rooms and private lodges. They have two bedrooms (one with a twin bed, one with a queen) and verandahs offering limited mountain views.

Peak Lodge
UNIT $$$

(Map p63; lodge RM940) These semidetached units have two bedrooms (one with a bunk bed and one with two twin beds), pleasant sitting rooms, fireplaces and nice views from their verandahs.

Rock Hostel
HOSTEL $$

(Map p63; dm RM192) Somewhat institutional 20-bed hostel.

Eating

LABAN RATA (ON THE MOUNTAIN)
At Laban Rata the cafeteria-style restaurant in the **Laban Rata Resthouse** has a simple menu and also offers buffet meals coordinated with the usual climbing times. Most hikers staying at Laban Rata (either in one of Sutera's huts or at Pendant Hut) have three meals (dinner, breakfast and lunch) included in their accommodation packages. It is possible to negotiate a price reduction if you plan on bringing your own food (boiling water can be purchased for RM1 if you bring dried noodles). Note: you will have to lug said food up to Laban Rata. Buffet meals can also be purchased individually – dinner costs RM45. A counter in the dining area sells soft drinks, chocolate, pain relievers and postcards.

PARK HEADQUARTERS (AT THE BASE)
Restoran Kinabalu Balsam
CAFETERIA $$

(Map p63; dishes RM5-15; ☺6am-10pm, to 11pm weekends) The cheaper and more popular of the two options in the park is this canteen-style spot directly below the park HQ. It offers basic but decent Malaysian, Chinese and Western dishes at reasonable prices. There is also a small but well-stocked shop in Balsam selling tinned and dried foods, chocolate, beer, spirits, cigarettes, T-shirts, bread, eggs and margarine.

Liwagu Restaurant
CAFETERIA $$

(Map p63; dishes RM10-30; ☺6am-10pm, to 11pm weekends) In the visitors centre, there's a huge range of dishes, including noodles, rice and seafood standards. An 'American breakfast' is pretty ordinary here.

🛈 Getting There & Away
It is highly advised that summit-seekers check in at the park headquarters by 9am, which means if you're coming from KK, you should plan to leave by 7am, or consider spending the night somewhere near the base of the mountain.

Bus
Express buses (RM25) leave KK from the Utara Terminal bus station every hour on the hour from 7am to 10am and at 12:30pm, 2pm and 3pm, and leaves at the same times in the reverse directions; minivans (RM15) leave from the same area when full. A shuttle bus (RM40) also runs from the Pacific Sutera (9am), the Magellan Sutera (9.10am) and Wisma Sabah (9.20am) to Kinabalu National Park HQ, arriving at 11.30am (RM40). In the reverse direction, it leaves Kinabalu National Park HQ at 3.30pm. There is also a shuttle bus from Kinabalu National Park HQ to Poring Hot Springs at noon (RM25) and another at 3.30pm (RM25) to Mesilau Nature Resort. Express buses and minivans travelling between KK and Ranau (and Sandakan) pass the park turnoff, 100m uphill from the park entrance. You can go to Sandakan (RM40) if the bus has room.

Taxi
Share taxis leave KK from Inanam and Padang Merdeka Bus Stations (RM150 to RM200).

Jeep
Share jeeps park just outside of the park gates and leave when full for KK (RM150) and Sandakan (RM400); each jeep can hold around five passengers, but they can be chartered by individuals.

Around Mt Kinabalu
Kinabalu National Park is home to Borneo's highest mountain and some of the island's best-preserved forest. Most travellers make a beeline for the mountain and the main park headquarters area, but the following spots are also worth exploring.

👁 Sights & Activities
MESILAU NATURE RESORT
This lovely slice of country is the trailhead for an alternative approach up Mt Kinabalu, often favoured by trekkers as it's more challenging than the main route and less crowd-

ed than park headquarters. The Mesilau route wanders up the mountain and links up with the Timpohon route to continue the ascent to Laban Rata. Arrange your trip with (who else?) Sutera Sanctuary Lodges and your guide will meet you at Mesilau.

KUNDASANG MEMORIAL

The junction for the Mesilau Nature Resort on the KK–Ranau Hwy is the site of the **Kundasang War Memorial** (admission RM10; ⊘8am-5.30pm), which commemorates the Australian and British prisoners who died on the infamous Sandakan Death Marches. Four gardens, manicured in that bucolic yet tame fashion that is so very English, are separated by a series of marbled pavilions. In the Anzac Garden you can see a full list of the dead and at the back of the gardens is a viewpoint that offers a stunning view of Mt Kinabalu.

The memorial is in Kundasang, 6km east of Kinabalu National Park headquarters. You'll know you're in Kundasang when you see the market stalls on either side of the road. Take the turn on the left for Mesilau Nature Resort. The memorial is on the right 150m after the turn-off. Look for the flags and the stone fort-like structure above the road.

RANAU

Ranau is a collection of concrete shop blocks on the road between KK and Sandakan. There's a busy Saturday **night market**, but otherwise this a good town for passing through: rampant construction is scarring the lovely valley it sits in. That said, there is a podiatry experience here you don't want to miss (we don't often use those words). After your epic Kinabalu climb, head to **Tagal Sungai Moroli** (admission RM10) in Kampung Luanti for a truly unique massage experience. The term *tagal* means 'no fishing' in the local Kadazan–Dusun language, as the fish in the river (a species known locally as *ikan pelian*) are not to be captured – they are special massage fish. The townsfolk claim that they've trained the little swimmers to gently nibble at weary feet.

Sabah Tea Garden   TEA PLANTATION
(⏏440882; www.sabahtea.net; factory tour RM12, with set lunch RM34, 2-day, 1-night package from RM190) A pretty tea plantation that looks like a cluster of giant mossy tussocks huddles in the mountains near Ranau. Contact the tea garden to arrange tours of both

the plantation and surrounding rainforests and river valleys. Overnight packages are available; you get to sleep in an on-site property in a tarted-up version of a traditional longhouse. Also offers tours of the facilities coupled with a trip to the fish foot massage (RM110).

PORING HOT SPRINGS

One of the few positive contributions the Japanese made to Borneo during WWII, **Poring Hot Springs** (adult/child RM15/10) has become a popular weekend retreat for locals. The complex is actually part of the Kinabalu National Park, but it's 43km away from the park headquarters, on the other side of Ranau.

The hot springs are located in a well-maintained forest park that does a fine job of giving casual visitors a small slice of the jungle – there's various nature paths and the like that the elderly and children can enjoy. But the springs themselves are not natural puddles. Steaming (seriously, it's hot), sulphurous water is channelled into man-made pools and tubs, some of which feel a little rundown. For some, it's a huge anticlimax, but others enjoy it. Don't forget a towel and your swimming trunks.

For our ringgit, the highlight of the place is actually way above the springs: a **Canopy Walkway** (admission RM15; ⊘9am-4pm) that consists of a series of walkways suspended from trees, up to 40m above the jungle floor, providing unique views of the surrounding forest.

Get there early if you want to see birds or other wildlife. A **tropical garden** (adult/child RM3/1.50; ⊘9am-4pm), **butterfly farm** (adult/ child RM4/2; ⊘9am-4pm Tue-Sun) and **orchid garden** (adult/child RM10/5; ⊘9am-4pm) are also part of the Poring complex. Rafflesia sometimes bloom in the area; look out for signs in the visitors centre and along the road.

🛌 Sleeping

It's worth spending a night around the base of Kinabalu before your ascent, and there are plenty of accommodation options suiting everyone's budget. All of the following have attached restaurants:

The accommodation at Mesilau and Poring is run by Sutera Sanctuary Lodges with a notable exception. At forested Mesilau, the **lodging** (dm from RM428 per person) is in functional dorms and doubles, but if you want to splurge there are some oddly shaped chalets (they look like they were designed by Frank Gehry on a bad day) that start at RM1285 for a three-bed property. Mesilau Nature Resort is 30 minutes beyond the entrance to Kinabalu (when driving towards Ranau from KK). The Sutera lodging in Poring is located within the hot-springs complex and is same-same in terms of the room experience and prices.

There are privately owned sleeping options looping around Kinabalu's base. Most of these are located along the road between the park headquarters and Kundasang (east of the park's entrance).

Two homestays in Kundasang, **Walai Tokou** (☑088-888166, 019-860 2270; koch_homestay@yahoo.com; Ranau; Packages from RM240) and **Mesilou Atamis** (☑017-832 5578, 019-580 2474; http://www.mesilau-homestay.com/; 2-day/1-night packages from RM350; P) are another option.

TOP CHOICE **Lupa Masa** ECO-CAMP $
(☑019-802 0549, SMS advised 016-8068194; www.facebook.com/lupa.masa; dm with stretcher hammock RM50) About a 10-minute drive from Poring you'll find this incredible ecolodge; the name comes from the Malay for 'forget time', which is pretty easy to do here. The green friendly spot contributes money to local communities and very much caters to independent travellers, which is a bit of a rarity in Sabah.

That said, Lupa Masa isn't for everyone. It's rustic here. There are bugs in the camp and leeches just outside. You get three good meals a day (vegetarian on demand), but there's no TV, no air-con and you're using squat toilets.

Accommodation is in raised tents and traditional lodging made from local bamboo, roofed with palm leaves and kitted with stretcher hammocks and mosquito nets. You are in the jungle, folks. On the other hand: *what a jungle*. There are a few 'pools' on the property – incredible natural pools fed by mountain streams and waterfalls where you feel like you're in true, wild Borneo.

The owners offer guided treks and there's a great chance you'll run into local wildlife, especially on night walks. The trekking options include night, day and overnight treks (starting at RM20), as well as jungle survival courses. You can also opt for rooms in a traditional-style longhouse if you want a bit more privacy.

Wind Paradise YURT $$
(☑714563, 012-820 3360; http://windparadise2011.blogspot.com/; Jln Mesilau, Cinta Mata, Kundasang; d from RM170, yurt (4-person) RM300; P) There are elements of Wind Paradise that resemble just another (albeit well-executed) Mt Kinabalu resort: lodge-y rooms with attractive hardwood floors and an odd mix of modern, minimalist furniture and rather garish bedsheets. Then there are the yurts. If you're scratching your head, a yurt is the traditional tent used by Mongolian nomads. While these ones aren't really suitable for those wanting to pillage Eurasia from Korea to Poland, they are attractive, white-and-blue structures that also come with hardwood floors and cosy beds (one queen and two twins). Almost all lodging, rooms and yurts, comes with great views over the alpine jungle that surrounds Mt Kinabalu.

Mountain Guest House GUESTHOUSE $
(☑888632, 016-837 4040; dm/s/d incl breakfast from RM30/60/70) The closest non-Sutera accommodation to Mt Kinabalu park is about 4km from the trailhead that leads up the mountain. This guesthouse consists of bare but clean rooms plopped into huts and chalets that seem to precariously lean out from the side of Mt Kinabalu. Free breakfast and vegetarian dinners (RM8) are available.

D'Villa Rina Ria Lodge LODGE $$
(☑889282; www.dvillalodge.com.my; dm/r RM30/120; @) This charming lodge is run by friendly staff that maintains cute, cosy rooms and a dining area that overlooks a lovely view over the mountain ranges/thick clouds of afternoon fog, depending on the mercy of the weather gods.

❶ Getting There & Around

Bus & Van

KK round-trip buses stop in front of park headquarters and in Ranau (RM15 to RM20, two hours) from 7am to 8pm. Minivans operate from a blue-roofed shelter in Ranau servicing the nearby attractions (park HQ, Poring etc) for RM5. The national park operates a van service between the headquarters and Poring for RM25 – it leaves the park HQ at noon.

Northwest Coast

The northwest coast of Sabah is criminally underexplored. The A1 runs north from KK to Kudat and the tip of Borneo past wide headlands, rice paddies and hidden beaches.

This is a good area for renting a car or motorbike – the roads are pretty level, and public transport links aren't reliable for getting off the main road.

TUARAN

Tuaran, 33km from KK, is a bustling little town with tree-lined boulevard-style streets and the distinctive nine-storey **Ling Sang Pagoda**, whose approaches are dominated by vividly painted guardian deities. There's little point stopping in the town itself unless you happen to pass through on a market day (Tuaran is likely named for the Malay word *tawaran*, or 'sale', reflecting its history as a trading post), but the surrounding area conceals a few cool sights. You'll see signs for **Mengkabong Water Village**, a Bajau stilt village built over an estuary, but development and pollution has diminished this spot's charms.

◉ Sights & Activities

Rumah Terbalik HOUSE
(The Upside Down House; ☑088-260263; www.upsidedownhouse.com.my/; Kg. Telibong, Batu 21, Jln Telibong Tamparuli; adult/child RM18/5; ⊗8am-10pm Mon-Sun; P👶) Sabah has many great sights of the natural beauty sort, but very few that we'd call 'quirky'. And then there's Rumah Terbalik: the Upside Down House. Which is like a modern, tastefully designed and decorated house, but...wait for it...upside down! Crazy. Even the furniture and the car parked in the *garage sticks to the ceiling*. This is an amusing spot to visit, as much for the reaction of local Malaysians (who seem to find this place the funniest thing under the sun) as the actual novelty of the place.

🛏 Sleeping & Eating

Given the town's proximity to KK (with its heaps of accommodation options), you probably won't need to stay in town. However, if for some reason you need a room, try **Orchid Hotel** (☑012-820 8894, 088-793789; http://www.orchidhotel.notmyno.com/; 1 Jln Teo Teck Ong; r from RM80; ❋). It's somewhat overpriced but it'll do the trick for a night. Just a few doors away is **Tai Fatt** (Jln Teo Teck Ong; meals RM4; ⊗7am-10pm), which has the best *kedai kopi* in Tuaran. It excels at *char mien/mee goreng*, the local, mouth-watering take on Chinese fried noodles, overflowing with vegetables, pork, oil, pork, egg, pork, wheat noodles and, yes, pork.

Shangri La Rasa Ria Resort RESORT $$
(☑088-792888; www.shangri-la.com; Pantai Dalit; r from RM450; P❋@🛜🏊) This sister resort of the Shangri La Tanjung Aru Resort in Kota Kinabalu occupies a fine stretch of peach-hued dunes about 45 minutes north of the KK airport. It's a sprawling resort complete with its own 18-hole golf course, several fine restaurants, an amoeba-esque pool and a relaxing spa. The resort's best feature is the small nature sanctuary.

❶ Getting There & Away

All buses north pass through Tuaran, and minivans shuttle regularly to and from KK (RM5 to RM10, 30 minutes). Minivans to Mengkabong are less frequent and cost RM1. Regular minivans go from Tuaran to Kota Belud (around RM15, 30 minutes).

KOTA BELUD

You might think Kota Belud isn't much to look at, and frankly, you'd be right, but the town's Sunday **tamu**, or market, is definitely worth your time. It's a congested, colourful and dusty melee of vendors, hagglers, browsers, gawpers and hawkers, all brought together by a slew of everyday goods in a bustle that consumes the whole town every

DON'T MISS

THE ORANGUTANS OF SHANGRI-LA

Sounds like a movie starring adorable primates in Tibet, right? No, we're just referring to the Sanctuary at Shangri-La's Rasa Ria Resort, sister resort of the Shangri La Tanjung Aru Resort in Kota Kinabalu, located near Tuaran.

The Sanctuary is a makeshift wildlife reserve owned and managed by the resort. There's all kinds of daily activities, from bird-watching trips to night walks (there are civets and loris on the reserve) to viewing the Sanctuary's orangutans from a canopy walkway. Honestly, the red apes here are just as cute as the ones at Sepilok (p77), and it's way less crowded as well. Plus, your money is still going towards a preservation organisation. There's different rates for all of the above activities depending on whether or not you're a guest at the hotel; for more information, email rrr@shangri-la.com or call 88-797888. The two-hour orangutan viewing occurs daily at 10am.

LOCAL KNOWLEDGE

A DETACHED SENSE OF FEAR

If you're out at night in Kota Belud and hear a strange noise, or happen to be either pregnant or a newborn infant, get inside. Because you may become the next victim of the *penanggalan*, Kota Belud's resident phantasm. The *penanggalan* ("detach"), known locally as the *balan-balan*, to Westerners is an odd monster: a mix of banshee, vampire and biology experiment. By day it appears to be a beautiful young woman; at night it is also a beautiful young woman, or at least the head of one. The rest of the 'body' is a trailing mass of intestines and other internal organs. The *balan-balan* is said to seek the scent of newborn flesh and the blood (and placentas) of pregnant women. There's a pretty great 2011 Malaysian horror movie on the subject called *Penanggal*, complete with flying heads, lots of screaming and folks getting eaten.

week (and a smaller version takes place on Wednesdays!). The most impressive site in Kota Belud is sadly an uncommon one these days: a procession of fully caparisoned Bajau horsemen from the nearby villages, decked out, along with their steeds, in vivid, multi-coloured satin 'armour'.

A *tamu* is not simply a market where villagers gather to sell their farm produce and to buy manufactured goods from traders; it's also a social occasion where news and stories are exchanged. These days tourists now often outnumber buffalo, and the horsemen have mostly moved away from the car park, though some do put on a show for visitors.

Visitors looking for tribal handicrafts and traditional clothing may find a prize here, but it's cheaply made stuff for tourists. Ironically, the best way to experience this commercial event is to come not expecting to buy anything – soak up the convivial, occasionally manic atmosphere, enjoy a good meal at the lovely food stalls and just potter about like Grandma at a Sunday flea market.

🛏 Sleeping & Eating

Most people visit Kota Belud as a day trip from KK, since you can make it there and back with plenty of time for the market.

Kota Belud is hardly a gastronome's delight, but tasty snacks can be picked up at the Sunday market. There are plenty of Chinese and halal coffee shops around the municipal offices.

TOP
CHOICE **Mañana**　　　　GUESTHOUSE **$$**
(📞014-679 2679, 014-679 3679; www.manana -borneo.com; hammock/r/ste from RM50/70/150) This fantastic property is in the little village of Kampung Pituru Laut, way out on the

coast. The name comes from a Canadian guest, who was so enchanted with the resort he kept putting off leaving till mañana...then mañana...then mañana... Owners Yan and Nani have situated the property on a private, boat-only-accesible beach that is basically a slice of heaven buttered with paradise. Simple, cleverly designed chalets look out onto clear water, hammocks sway in the ocean breeze, an on-site restaurant-bar serves hot food and cold beer, and the sunsets will blow your mind. Ask about diving trips to see what may be the world's largest brain coral. The owners prefer you book ahead so transport can be arranged; their suggested agent in KK is the excellent GogoSabah (p45).

Kota Belud Travelers' Lodge　　LODGE **$**
(📞088-977228; http://mykbtl.com; 6 Plaza Kong Guan; r without bathroom RM65, en suite RM85-115; ▣) A simple affair in the centre of town, it's about 200m southwest of the mosque in a shopping block (it's well marked, so finding it shouldn't be a problem). It's got the whole concrete-block-with-cosy-rooms vibe going that is oddly typical of interior Sabah hotels.

❶ Getting There & Away

MINIBUS & TAXI

Minivans and share taxis gather in front of Pasar Besar, the old market. Most of these serve the Kota Belud–KK route, (RM7 to RM10, two hours) or Kudat (RM10 to RM15, two hours), departing from 7am to 5pm. To get to Kinabalu National Park, take any minibus going to KK and get off at Tamparuli, about halfway (RM5, 30 minutes). There are several minivans from Tamparuli to Ranau every day until about 2pm; all pass the park entrance (RM5, one hour). To go all the way to Ranau costs RM13 (the trip takes just over an hour).

KUDAT

Despite being only a few hours from Kota Kinabalu, there's a dreamy, end-of-the-world feeling in Kudat. Maybe it's the drowsy quality of the air; Malaysian towns don't get much more laid-back and friendly than this. You can thank the local Rungus people. Filipinos too – there's loads of them around.

Kudat is a quiet port that rewards a bit of initiative. The town itself is fairly unremarkable; there is a large **Chinese temple** (admission free) by the main square and a **fish market** near the docks, but mainly this is a quiet place where it's nice to potter about, smile at people and be smiled at. It's the country that leads up to the tip of Borneo that you want to explore. There are miles and miles of beautiful beaches about, some of which are excellent for surfing, while others are good for watching lonely cattle and blood-red sunsets. The trick is finding these spots, as there's very little tourism infrastructure to speak of.

You can disappear down side roads that lead to the ocean and see what you find – we did and had a grand time, but we had our own wheels. We're purposely suggesting you do it yourself as there is such unreliable road signage here, yet not too many roads. Trust us when we say that with a little exploratory gusto you might find that mythical traveller pot of gold: the hidden, untouched beach. Swing by **New Way Car Rental & Souvenir Centre** (☎088 625868; 40 Jln Lo Thien Chok) if you want to explore the area under your own steam. Staff can also book your accommodation on Pulau Banggi.

Sleeping & Eating

TOP CHOICE **Tampat Do Aman** ECO-CAMP $
(☎013-880 8395; http://tampatdoaman.com; r from RM30; 📶) Tampat Do Aman means 'place of friends' in the local Rungus language. It's a fitting title; you'll be made to feel welcome as hell here by Howard Stanton and his Rungus wife. The couple are committed to creating sustainable tourism in the area, and work with the local Rungus community to preserve some of Kudat's lovely beaches and stretches of jungle. Howard will hook you up with bicycles and car rides out to some of the most isolated, lovely beaches in Sabah – ask to see the honeymooners' point, or for tips on snorkeling spots. Tampat Do Aman itself is a very rustic eco-camp, with fan-cooled basic thatch huts and longhouse, set in a supremely romantic spot between the jungle and the ocean. The staff provides nice home-cooked meals (and plenty of beer) on demand.

🍃 **Tip of Borneo Resort** RESORT $$
(Tommy's Place; ☎013-811 2315, 088-493468; http://tipofborneoresort.com/; r RM130-160; ❄📶) If you're not into the rustic camp atmoshere, head to Tommy's Place, the Tip of Borneo Resort. This is an excellent property of wonderful villas and chalets set up with sweeping views of the Kudat headlands. Staff are committed to preserving natural beauty and have engaged in projects to help sea turtles lay their eggs. You can look into diving, windsurfing and other activities here, and management is happy to direct you to awesome beaches.

TOP CHOICE **Hibiscus Riviera** VILLA $$$
(☎019-895 074; www.hibiscusvillaborneo.com; villas from US$800; ❄📶🏊) The Hibiscus looks like the place where Jay-Z and *GQ* magazine would throw the mother of all Southeast Asian parties. It's tasteful – dark-wood floors, indigenous art, scrubbed pebbles and an incredible infinity pool – yet unmistakably, impeccably upper class. In short, this is one of the finest top-end accommodation options in Sabah. From late December to early January the rate climbs to US$1100 a night (US$1030 without breakfast) and there is a minimum 3-night stay rule.

Ria Hotel HOTEL $$
(☎088-622794; http://riahotel.blogspot.com/; 3 Jln Marudu; r RM120-275; ❄@) If you have to stay in Kudat town, the Ria has clean, spacious, well-appointed rooms, nice bathrooms with hot showers, and little balconies. It's a short walk southwest of the bus station.

Getting There & Away

The bus station is in Kudat Plaza in the western part of town, very close to the Ria Hotel. Bus destinations include KK (RM25, three hours) and Kota Belud (RM15, 1½ hours). Minivans and jeeps also operate from here; a ride to KK in a full van will cost around RM45.

AROUND KUDAT

The area around Kudat includes many hidden coves, beaches and hill trails that are almost all tucked away down hidden or unmarked roads. You'll want to get in touch with the folks at Tampat Do Aman or Tip of Borneo Resort to find the best spots. You can attempt some of the side roads in a 2WD or motorbike, but be careful, especially if it's been raining (which doesn't happen often; this is the driest part of Sabah). Either way, make sure you take in one of the lovely tropical sunsets – Sabah's west coast is famous for 'em! The **Rungus longhouses** (Bavanggazo Rungus Longhouses/Maranjak Longhouse; ☑088-621673, 612846; per person per night from RM70) of Kampung Bavanggazo, 44km south of Kudat, are highly touted by Sabah Tourism, but were in a bit of a neglected state when we visited them.

TIP OF BORNEO

Sabah's northernmost headland, at the end of a wide bay some 40km from Kudat, is known as Tanjung Simpang Mengayu, or the Tip of Borneo. Magellan reputedly landed here for 42 days during his famous round-the-world voyage. Once a wild promontory, this windswept stretch where the cliffs meet the sea has been co-opted as a tourist attraction – there's a large, truncated globe monument dominating the viewpoint. A sign warns visitors not to climb down onto the rocks that form the mainland's actual tip, effectively guaranteeing that tourists will do exactly that. Seriously, please don't attempt to swim here; a Korean tourist drowned during our research.

There's no public transport, so you'll need to negotiate a taxi from Kudat (around RM90, including waiting time upon arrival) or drive yourself.

Offshore Islands

The real highlights of northwestern Sabah lie offshore. The first gem is Pulau Mantanani, perfect tropical islands lying about 40km northwest of Kota Belud. The second is Layang Layang, a diving mecca about 300km northwest of KK – it's basically just an airstrip built on a reef way out in the middle of the South China Sea. Famous for great visibility, seemingly endless wall dives and the occasional school of hammerheads, it's second only to Sipadan on Malaysia's list of top dive spots.

PULAU MANTANANI

Pulau Mantanani Besar (Big Mantanani Island) and **Pulau Mantanani Kecil** (Little Mantanani Island) are two little flecks of land fringed by bleach-blond sand and ringed by a halo of colourful coral, about 25km off the coast of northwest Sabah (about 40km northwest of Kota Belud).

Those on a budget – well, actually, anyone – should opt for the excellent **Mari Mari Backpackers Lodge** (☑088-260501; www.riverbug.asia; dm RM60, r RM80-175), operated by Riverbug. Guests are placed in raised stilt chalets pocketed around a white-sand beach. The huts are a modern take on the thatch-longhouse theme, and a well executed one at that. Diving and snorkelling activities feature high on the itinerary list, but this is also a lovely tropical escape if you just want to chill.

PULAU BANGGI

If you want to fall off the map, get out to Pulau Banggi, which lies some 40km northeast of Kudat. The Banggi people, known locally for their unusual tribal treehouses, are Sabah's smallest indigenous group, and speak a unique non-Bornean dialect. The island is a postcard-esque slice of sand, tropical trees and clear water, and is actually one of the largest offshore islands in all of Malaysia.

Accommodation is provided by a small government **resthouse** (r RM40) and the modest **Banggi Resort** (☑019-587 8078; r fan/air-con RM50/65, huts RM70; ✲), which can arrange boat trips and other activities. The small huts have kitchens and twin beds – make sure you request the charming treehouse hut. This place can get fully booked on weekends, so reserve in advance. At either location, ask staff about the trails that lead into the small jungle interior of the island.

Kudat Express (☑088-328113; one-way RM15) runs a ferry between Kudat and the main settlement on Pulau Banggi. It departs the pier (near the Shell station) at 9am and 2pm daily. In the reverse direction, it leaves Pulau Banggi daily at around 3pm.

LAYANG LAYANG

Some 300km northwest of Kota Kinabalu, Layang Layang is a tiny island that is surrounded by a coral atoll. It's an exclusive **dive location**, and is well known among scubaholics as part of the famous Borneo Banks. Thanks to its utter isolation, the reef here is healthy and diverse. Although it may not be quite as colourful as the reef at Sipadan, it's quite likely to be one of the most unspoilt bits of coral most divers have seen. There are plenty of reef fish and reef sharks, as well as a with a healthy population of rays.

Please note: there is *no decompression chamber* at Layang Layang, so don't press your luck while underwater. The resort only provides air – no nitrox. Trivia buffs may be pleased to know Layang Layang is the only one of the remote Spratly Islands that receives regular flights.

Layang Layang Island Resort (⬛in Kuala Lumpur 03-2170 2185; www.avillionlayanglayang. com; 6-day, 5-night all-inclusive package twin-share per person from US$1490; ✱ ✱) is the only game in town here and it's all about the diving. The five daily meals are scheduled around the dive times. The standard rooms are very comfortable, with air-con, TV, private verandahs and hot-water showers. The all-inclusive packages include accommodation, food, 12 boat dives and tank usage. Package rates for nondivers start at US$850. An extra night costs diver/nondiver $180/$125. Be warned, nondivers: besides a little snorkelling, there's nothing for you to do here but sunbathe.

The resort operates its own Antonov 26 aircraft, which flies every Tuesday, Thursday, Friday and Sunday between KK and Layang Layang. The flight over from KK in this bare-bones Russian prop plane is a big part of the adventure: it feels more like a military transport than a commercial airliner. The return flight costs US$285, which is not included in the accommodation-food-dive package.

EASTERN SABAH

Eastern Sabah takes nearly everything that is wonderful about the rest of Borneo and condenses it into one hard-hitting brew of an outdoor shot consisting of equal parts adventure, wildlife, undersea exploration and flat-out fun. Let's tick off some of the natural wonders that are packed into this relatively tiny corner of the island: the great ginger men – ie the orangutans – of Sepilok; pot-bellied, flop-nosed proboscis monkeys in Labuk Bay; the looming vine tunnels and muddy crocodile highway of the Sungai Kinabatangan; pygmy elephants and tree-top canopies that scratch in the sky in the Danum Valley and Tabin; plunging seawalls rainbow-spattered with tropical marine life in the Semporna Archipelago; a forest as old as human civilisation in the Maliau Basin.

Did we just pique your travel appetite? Yeah, we thought so. With easier transport links and improved infrastructure, it's easier than ever to hit up the east side of Sabah.

You'll be told, when you're here, that the only way around is via package tours, but trust us with a little prior planning and a bit of heart, you can explore this area independently and in-depth.

Sandakan

POP 480,000

Sabah's second city lacks the small cosmopolitan pulse that keeps KK throbbing; in contrast, Sandakan feels like a provincial city with provincial horizons, not to mention a grubby city centre. But Sandakan was once a major port of call, and as such it has played an important role in Borneo's past, as attested by religious relics, haunting cemeteries and stunning colonial mansions.

◉ Sights

Central Sandakan is light on 'must-see' attractions, although history buffs will appreciate the *Sandakan Heritage Trail* brochure available at the tourist office. The centre, where you'll find most hotels, banks and local transport, consists of a few blocks squashed between the waterfront and a steep escarpment from where you can look out over the bay (Teluk Sandakan). Warning: don't go to Sandakan Crocodile Park unless you like watching sadly neglected reptiles.

Chinese Cemetery   CEMETERY
Sandakan's massive Chinese Cemetery essentially takes up all of a valley that runs into the hills east of Sandakan. Gravesites are studded into the slopes, many shaped by *feng shui* principles so that the back of the grave backs into the solid angle of the earth, while the front often features a small artificial pool, reflecting the traditional Chinese belief that an ideal home has a mountain behind it and running water in front. As you wander further along the cemetery, the graves become older and more decrepit – many have been claimed by the jungle. You will also see some charnel houses that accommodate the important members of Sandakan's major Chinese clans. Across the road from the cemetery is a cremation ground for Hindus and Sikhs.

Japanese Cemetery   CEMETERY
Located beyond the grounds of the Chinese cemetery, this is a poignant piece of Sandakan's ethnic puzzle. The gravesite was founded in the 1890s by Kinoshita Kuni, known to the English as Okuni of South Seas

Sandakan

Sandakan

and to greater Sandakan as the successful madam-manager of the lucrative 'Brothel 8', once located on Lebuh Tiga. Today the cemetery is quite small, but at one time there were hundreds of buried dead, most of them prostitutes. A monument to the fallen Japa-nese soldiers of WWII was erected in the cemetery in 1989. To get here and to the Chinese cemetery, climb the shady Tangga Seribu to Jln Residensi Dr and turn right; there will be signs pointing the rest of the way to the cemetery.

Agnes Keith House   MUSEUM

(Map p72; ☑089-221140; Jln Istana; admission RM15; ☺9am-5pm) On the hill above town, overlooking Teluk Sandakan and the city itself, is Agnes Keith House, an old two-storey wooden villa now renovated as a museum. Keith was an American who came to Sandakan in the 1930s with her husband, then Conservator of Forests, and ended up writing several books about her experiences, including the famous *Land Below the Wind*. The house fell into dis repair during the 1990s, but Sabah Museum has since restored it as a faithful recreation of Keith's original abode.

The villa documents Sandakan in all its colonial splendour, with detailed displays on the lives of the Keiths. Most poignant are mementos of Agnes' imprisonment by the Japanese during WWII, when she had to try to care for her young son under gruelling conditions. There's some great vintage photographs, including a shot of Keith's husband standing with a dead elephant in full *Heart of Darkness* safari gear. The admission price includes entry to the various branches of the Sabah Museum in KK – now didn't we tell you to keep hold of your ticket? Also on the grounds is the English Tea House & Restaurant, conveniently ignoring Keith's American background and the fact that she found Sandakan too 'too British' when she first arrived.

To reach the museum, follow Jln Singapura from the city centre and turn right up the hill, or head up the Tangga Seribu (100 Steps) to Jln Istana and turn left. Just below the museum gardens is an **observation pavilion** built by the local Rotary Club, which offers more fine views.

Sandakan Memorial Park   HISTORIC SITE

(☺9am-5pm) This park marks the site of a Japanese POW camp and starting point for the infamous WWII 'death marches' to Ranau. Of the 1800 Australian and 600 British troops imprisoned here, the only survivors by July 1945 were six Australian escapees. Today the site of the POW camp has been converted into a quiet forest orchard and series of gardens.

Large, rusting machines testify to the camp's forced-labour program, and a pavilion at the park's centre includes accounts from survivors and photographs from personnel, inmates and liberators. In 2006 the original march route was officially reopened as a memorial trail – see www.sandakan -deathmarch.com for details.

To reach the park, take any Batu 8 (or higher-numbered) bus from the local bus station in the city centre (RM1.80); get off at the 'Taman Rimba' signpost and walk down Jln Rimba. A taxi from downtown costs about RM25 one way.

Puu Jih Shih Temple   TEMPLE

(Off Jln Leila) Architecturally, the Puu Jih Shih is one of the finer Chinese temples in Sabah: wrapped in the usual firework-colour display of reds, golds and twining dragons, festooned with lanterns that illuminate the grounds like a swarm of fat fireflies. As an added bonus, this large Buddhist temple is perched on a steep hill overlooking Teluk Sandakan, offering an extremely impressive view of the city. Take a bus to Tanah Merah and ask for directions; from where you depart the bus it's not a far walk, but it's a steep uphill one. A taxi here shouldn't cost more than RM6 one way, but don't be surprised if cabbies try to charge RM20 for a round-trip plus waiting at the temple.

St Michael's & All Angels Church   CHURCH

(Off Jln Puncak) This incongruous slice of the Home Counties is one of the few all-stone buildings in Malaysian Borneo and the former locus of colonial worship. In 1893, prison labourers lugged said stones across the jungle during the church's construction. Today, despite a little mouldering, the church very much looks like a displaced bit of the Cotswolds transplanted into the heart of Borneo. Although the church is officially off Jln Puncak, many people call the street 'Church Rd'.

Sam Sing Kung   TEMPLE

(Jln Padang) The Sam Sing Kung temple (also pronounced 'Sam Sing Gong') dates from 1887, making it the oldest building in Sandakan. The name means 'three saints' temple – in this case saints for general righteousness, fishermen and students (easy to see how the latter two would be important to Sandakan's education-oriented, dependent-on-the-sea Chinese community). The temple itself is a smallish, if attractive affair – a lovely example of a house of worship dedicated to the traditional Chinese Taoist pantheon.

Kampong Buli Sim Sim   VILLAGE

This traditional stilt village, located about 4km east of the town centre, is the original settlement Sandakan grew from. You'll likely be grinned at as you wander around the

THE SANDAKAN DEATH MARCHES

Sandakan was the site of a Japanese prisoner-of-war camp during WWII, and in September 1944 there were 1800 Australian and 600 British troops interned here. What is not widely known is that more Australians died here than during the building of the infamous Burma Railway.

Early in the war, food and conditions were bearable and the death rate stood at around three per month. However, as the Allies closed in, it became clear to the officers in command that they didn't have enough staff to guard against a rebellion in the camps. They decided to cut the prisoners' rations to weaken them, causing disease to spread and the death rate to rise.

It was also decided to move the prisoners inland – 250km through the jungle to Ranau, on a route originally cut by locals to hamper the Japanese invaders, passing mainly through uninhabited, inhospitable terrain. On 28 January 1945, 470 prisoners set off; 313 made it to Ranau. On the second march, 570 started from Sandakan; just 118 reached Ranau. The 537 prisoners on the third march were the last men in the camp.

Conditions on the marches were deplorable: most men had no boots, rations were less than minimal and many men fell by the wayside. The Japanese brutally disposed of any prisoners who couldn't walk. Once in Ranau, the surviving prisoners were put to work carrying 20kg sacks of rice over hilly country to Paginatan, 40km away. Disease, starvation and executions took a horrendous toll, and by the end of July 1945 there were no prisoners left in Ranau. The only survivors from the 2400 at Sandakan were six Australians who escaped, either from Ranau or during the marches.

As a final bitter irony, it emerged postwar that a rescue attempt had been planned for early 1945, but intelligence at the time had suggested there were no prisoners left at the camp.

wooden boards built over the water, as much an oddity to locals as their water village is to you. Have a stroll, be on the lookout for those budding entrepreneurs who have turned their homes into ad hoc souvenir shops, but please don't take pictures of people without asking permission. You can take a taxi here for no more than RM15.

☞ Tours

It is possible to visit many of the attractions around Sandakan independently, but if you want to stay at the river lodges on the Kinabatangan, you'll need to prebook accommodation. It's advisable to do so in Sandakan or in KK (p56). Sandakan also has plenty of general tour operators offering packages to Sepilok and the Gomantong Caves. Hotels in Sandakan and Sepilok are all capable of booking tours as well, as are many of the tour companies we list in KK. Borneo Express (p53), in KK, has an office in Sandakan, as does **Sandakan Car Rental** (☏019-823 7050, 016-815 0029; sandakancarrental.com; Bandar Maju Batu 1, Jln Utara).

Sabah Holidays SIGHTS
(☏089-225718; www.sabahholidays.com; ground fl, Sandakan Airport) Rents cars and minivans,

and can arrange tours and accommodation in Kota Belud, the Danum Valley and Maliau Basin.

**Sepilok Tropical
Wildlife Adventure** NATURE
(Map p72; ☏089-271077; www.stwadventure.com; 13 Jln Tiga) This midpriced tour specialist is connected to Sepilok Jungle Resort and Bilit Adventure Lodge on the Sungai Kinabatangan.

SI Tours NATURE
(Map p72; ☏089-213502; www.sitoursborneo.com; Lot 59, Block HS-5, Sandakan Harbour Square Phase 2) This full-service agency operates Abai Jungle Lodge and Kinabatangan Riverside Lodge.

Uncle Tan NATURE
(Map p78; ☏089-535784; www.uncletan.com; Batu 14) Tour menu includes its Sukau River Lodge on the Kinabatangan. Located in Sepilok.

Wildlife Expeditions NATURE
(Map p72; ☏089-219616; www.wildlife-expeditions.com; 9th fl, Wisma Khoo Siak Chiew, Lebuh Empat) Also has accommodation in Sukau. There's also a **KK office** (☏246000; Wisma Merdeka).

🛌 Sleeping

Sandakan doesn't bowl folk over in the lodging department, and budget options are sparse. That said, if you can shell out into RM80-and-above territory, there's some decent deals. If you're only passing through Sandakan to see the orangutans, it's better to stay at Sepilok itself, since the rehabilitation centre is only 25km from town.

Nak Hotel
HOTEL $$

(Map p72; ☎089-272988; www.nakhotel.com; Jln Pelabuhan Lama; s/d incl breakfast from RM85/118; ✳🐠) The Nak is a solid midrange hotel that's a fair steal if you're travelling as a couple or with friends, and nice value even if you're by yourself. The oldest dedicated hotel in town has a somewhat Soviet-chic exterior, but once you get inside rooms are quite attractive: nice monochromatic colour schemes with hints of East Asian and Borneo-inspired design flairs. This is a well put-together spot, which is no surprise given the hotel's kick-ass roof lounge, Balin (p76) – a must even if you aren't staying here.

Sea View Sandakan Budget & Backpackers Hotel
HOSTEL $

(Map p72; ☎089-221221; Lot 126, 1st fl, Jln Dua, Harbour Square 14; dm from RM30, r from RM50; ✳🐠) The name of this place is a little deceptive; you won't be getting many sea views per se (especially because it seems a new building is going up right on the waterfront). That said, this is an excellent little hostel, with clean, good value rooms, helpful staff and a friendly vibe.

Mark's Lodge
HOTEL $$

(☎089-210055; www.markslodge.com; Lot 1-7, Block 36, Bandar Indah; r from RM154; ✳🐠) The word 'boutique' is written in fogged glass across the front entrance – just in case you didn't get the memo. This business-class hotel, located at Batu 4 (Bandar Indah) is a solid option for a comfortable sleep. The rooms are all about the 'dark tropical wood floors plus white sheets' look, and it comes off quite well. It's a RM15 taxi ride into town.

Rose Guesthouse
GUESTHOUSE $

(Map p72; ☎089-223582; www.shsbnb.com; HS10, Harbour Square Complex; dm/d RM20/40, d with bathroom RM47; ✳🔞) This is no delicate rose with lacy table settings and Devonshire teas. Think more of a modern, somewhat cookie-cutter Sabah budget spot for crashing out. Service is friendly and personable, and fan

dorms are dirt cheap (but not dirty). Near the Alliance Bank.

Sandakan Backpackers
HOSTEL $

(Map p72; ☎089-221104; www.sandakanbackpackers.com; Lot 108, Block SH-11, Harbour Square Complex; dm/s/d/tr RM25/40/60/90; ✳🔞) This place is one of the most popular budget deals in town and a firm fixture on the Borneo backpacker trail. Clean, well-lit, affordable and a decent place to meet other citizens of Backpackistan.

Swiss-Inn Waterfront Sandakan
HOTEL $$

(Map p72; ☎089-240888; www.swissgarden.com; Harbour Square Complex; r from RM161; ✳🔞🏊) If you're in the mood for an essentially Western style waterfront resort, the Swiss Garden is where you want to be. Big rooms, standard chain-style upper-class hotel decor, big windows that look out onto the water – there's no surprises here, and we mean that in a good way. A lovely pool, spa and workout facilities are all on-site at this business-class option.

🍴 Eating

For an authentic Malay meal, head to the KFC in the waterfront Harbour Square Complex (but don't eat there!) – the restaurants surrounding it are cheap and flavourful. Most are standard Malay *kedai kopi*, with prices that rarely top RM6 per mains; all are open from roughly 9am to 9pm. **Habeeb Restaurant** (Map p72; Jln Tiga) is good for a cheap curry; it's actually part of a chain that serves good Indian Muslim food, so if you see other branches around town, consider them a solid bet.

New Market
FOOD STALLS $

(Map p72; Jln Pryor; dishes RM3-10; ⊗7am-2pm) Despite being located in what looks like a multistorey car park, this is the best spot in town for cheap eats and stall food. On the bottom floor you'll find the usual 'wet' and 'dry' markets, selling fish, sea cucumber, herbs, vegetables, meat and such. Farmers and fishermen rock up here from their fields and boats throughout the day, bringing fresh produce, bloody butchered meat and flopping denizens of the ocean. Upstairs you'll find strictly halal food stalls, with a mix of Chinese, Malay, Indonesian and Filipino stalls. Hours given for the food stalls above are a bit flexible, but by 3pm most are empty.

Sim Sim Seafood Restaurant SEAFOOD $
(Sim Sim 8; dishes RM5; ⊘8am-2pm) Located in the heart of the Sim Sim stilt village, this 'restaurant' is more of a dockside fishery, where the daily catch is unloaded and sorted and prepared for the immediate consumption of travellers like you (and a lot of locals). A cluster of red plastic patio furniture huddles in the corner – just grab a seat and point to your prey! Or ask a friendly regular for help ordering; there are lots of off-menu specialities determined by what's caught that day. Ask a cab to drop you off at 'Sim Sim Bridge 8' (they'll very likely know where you're going).

**English Tea House
& Restaurant** TEA HOUSE $$$
(Map p72; ☑089-222544; www.englishteahouse. org; 2002 Jln Istana; mains RM24-40, cocktails RM26.50; ⊘breakfast, lunch & dinner) It seems every place that suffered under colonialism likes to recreate the atmosphere of being a rich colonialist, the English Tea House being Sabah's contribution to the genre. Don your safari suit, wax that moustache and butter that scone, *sahib*. The manicured gardens are a particular joy, with wicker furniture and a small croquet lawn overlooking the bay, perfect for afternoon tea (RM17.25), a round of sunset Pimms or some ice coffee.

♟ Drinking

Bandar Indah, commonly known as Mile 4 or Batu 4, is a buzzing grid of two-storey shophouses and the playground of choice for locals and expats alike, packed with restaurants, bars, karaoke lounges and nightclubs. It comes alive at night in a way that makes central Sandakan seem deader than the morgue in a ghost town. Bars generally close around 1am or 2am, music venues slightly later.

TOP CHOICE **Balin** BAR
(Map p72; ☑089-272988; www.nakhotel.com; Nak Hotel, Jln Pelabuhan Lama; drinks from RM9, mains from RM15; ⊘lunch & dinner) Bringing a certain LA rooftop sexiness to Sandakan, Balin is your best bet for nightlife in the city centre. The three tiers of uberchill lounge space are accented by a factory's worth of pillows and some genuinely classy cocktails that any boutique 'mixologist' bar in London or New York would be justifiably jealous of.

ℹ Information

Internet
Cyber Café (3rd fl, Wisma Sandakan, Lebuh Empat; per hr RM3; ⊘9am 9pm)

Medical Services
Duchess of Kent Hospital (☑089-212111; http://hdok.moh.gov.my/; Mile 2, Jln Utara) Best private care in the area.

Money
HSBC (Lebuh Tiga)
Maybank (Lebuh Tiga) In addition to a full-service bank and ATM, a sidewalk currency-exchange window is open 9am to 5pm daily for changing cash and travellers cheques.
Standard Chartered Bank (Lebuh Tiga)
Wang Liau Chun Mii Moneychanger (23 Lebuh Tiga; ⊘8.30am-4.30pm) Cash only.

Post
Main post office (☑089-210594; Jln Leila)

Tourist Information
Tourist Information Centre (☑089-229751; Wisma Warisan; ⊘8am-12.30pm & 1.30-4.30pm Mon-Thu, 8-11.30am & 2-4.30pm Friday) Located opposite the municipal offices (known as MPS) and up the stairs from Lebuh Tiga. The staff dispenses advice on everything from regional attractions to local restaurants and can link travellers together for group excursions. One of the more helpful TICs in Sabah.

ℹ Getting There & Away

Air
Malaysia Airlines (☑1300-883 000; cnr Jln Pelabuhan Lama & Lebuh Dua & 1st fl, airport) has daily flights to/from KK and KL; its subsidiary, **MASwings**, located in the same office, offers one daily flight to/from Tawau and two to/from KK. **AirAsia** (☑089-222737; 1st & 2nd fl, Airport) operates two daily direct flights to/from KL and KK.

Bus & Minivan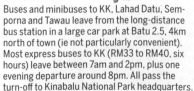
Buses and minibuses to KK, Lahad Datu, Semporna and Tawau leave from the long-distance bus station in a large car park at Batu 2.5, 4km north of town (ie not particularly convenient). Most express buses to KK (RM33 to RM40, six hours) leave between 7am and 2pm, plus one evening departure around 8pm. All pass the turn-off to Kinabalu National Park headquarters.

Buses depart regularly for Lahad Datu (RM20, 2½ hours) and Tawau (RM40, 5½ hours) between 7am and 8am. There's also a bus to Semporna (RM33, 5½ hours) at 8am. If you miss it, head to Lahad Datu, then catch a frequent minivan to Semporna.

GETTING TO THE PHILIPPINES: SANDAKAN TO ZAMBOANGA

Getting to the border Sandakan is a good spot to grab a ferry to the southern Philippines. **Weesam Express** (☎089-212872; ground fl, Hotel New Sabah, Jln Singapura) goes to Zamboanga in the Philippines (1st/2nd class RM260/280) on Tuesday and Friday, leaving Sandakan harbour at 6am and arriving in Zamboanga at 7.30pm the same day. There are ostensibly ferries to Jolo (1st/2nd class RM240/260) and Bongao (1st/2nd class RM220/240), but these weren't running at time of research due to political unrest on those islands. Travellers we spoke to said you didn't need an onward ticket to enter the Philippines, and the Filipino government says otherwise, it's wise to have one just in case.

At the border Once you get to the Philippines, the Filipino government requires you to provide evidence of an onward ticket to enter the country. From Zamboanga you can grab buses to the rest of Mindanao or ferries to the Sulu Archipelago, assuming the security situation in those islands has calmed down.

Minivans depart throughout the morning from Batu 2.5 for Ranau (RM26, four hours) and Lahad Datu (some of those continuing to Tawau). Minivans for Sukau (RM15) leave from a lot behind Centre Point Mall in town.

❶ Getting Around

To/From the Airport

The airport is 11km from the city centre. Batu 7 Airport bus (RM1.80) stops on the main road about 500m from the terminal. A coupon taxi to the town centre costs RM35; going the other way, around RM28.

Bus & Minivan

Buses run from 6am to 6pm on the main road to the north, Jln Utara, designated by how far from town they go, ie Batu 8. Fares range from RM1 to RM4.

Local minivans wait behind Centre Point Mall; fares cost from RM2. Use for the harbour area.

To reach the long-distance bus station, catch a local bus (RM1.50) from the stand at the waterfront; it takes about 20 minutes. The same bus leaves when full from the bus station for the city centre.

Taxi

Short journeys around town should cost RM10; it's about RM15 to Bandar Indah and RM40 to RM50 to Sepilok depending on your bargaining skills. A taxi from the long-distance bus station to town (or vice versa) will probably run RM20; you may be able to argue drivers down to the local fare of RM10.

Sepilok

The orangutan is the associative species of Sabah, despite the fact that the living space of the beast shrinks annually. The most reliable place to see this primate is the little hamlet of Sepilok, which sees almost as many visitors as the granite spires of Mt Kinabalu. Sepilok's Orang-Utan Rehabilitation Centre (SORC) is the most popular place on earth to see Asia's great ginger ape in its native habitat. Those who have time to stick around will also uncover several scenic nature walks, sanctuaries for the adorable sun bear and elusive proboscis monkey, and a couple of great places to call home for a night or two.

⊙ Sights & Activities

Sepilok Orang-Utan Rehabilitation Centre (SORC)   ANIMAL SANCTUARY
(Map p78; ☎089-531180; soutan@po.jaring.my; Jln Sepilok; admission RM30, camera fee RM10; ☺9-11am & 2-3.30pm, walking trails 9am-4.15pm) One of only four orangutan sanctuaries in the world, this place occupies a corner of the **Kabili-Sepilok Forest Reserve** about 25km north of Sandakan. The centre was established in 1964; it now covers 40 sq km and has become one of Sabah's top tourist attractions, second only to Mt Kinabalu.

Orphaned and injured orangutans are brought to Sepilok to be rehabilitated to return to forest life. We have to stress: while thousands of people see orangutans during feeding time at Sepilok, there is a chance you won't. These are, after all, wild animals. On the bright side, there are two major feeding times a day, so if you miss them in the morning, you can always try again in the afternoon (or the next day).

Feedings are at 10am and 3pm and last 30 to 50 minutes. Schedules are posted at the **visitor reception centre**. Tickets are valid for one day, although you can see two feedings in the same day. The morning feed-

Sepilok

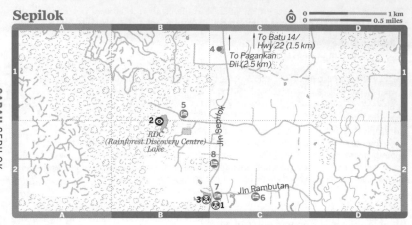

Sepilok

⦿ Sights
1 Borneo Sun Bear Conservation
 Centre...C2
2 Rainforest Discovery Centre
 (RDC)...B2
3 Sepilok Orang-Utan
 Rehabilitation Centre
 (SORC)...B2

✪ Activities, Courses & Tours
4 Uncle Tan C1

🛏 Sleeping
5 Sepilok B&B B1
6 Sepilok Forest Edge Resort C2
7 Sepilok Jungle Resort C2
8 Sepilok Nature Resort.......................C2

ing tends to be more tour-group heavy, so if you want a quieter experience, try the afternoon. Use the lockers for your valuables – orangutans and macaques have been known to relieve tourists of hats, bags, sunglasses, cameras, even clothing. It's especially important that you don't bring any containers of insect repellent into the reserve, as these are highly toxic to the apes and other wildlife. Spray yourself before entering.

Nature Education Centre
A worthwhile 20-minute video about Sepilok's work is shown five times daily (9am, 11am, noon, 2.10pm and 3.30pm) opposite reception in the auditorium here.

Walking Trails
If you want to explore the sanctuary further, several walking trails lead into the forest; register at the visitor reception centre to use them. Trails range in length from 250m to 4km, and different paths are open at different times of year. Guided night walks can be arranged through the centre or at the various lodges. There's also a 10km trail through mangrove forest to **Sepilok Bay**; this is quite a rewarding walk, and if you're especially fit you may be able to complete it between feeding times. A permit from the **Forestry Department** (☏089-660811, 089-213966; Jln Leila) is required in advance for this route. The department can also arrange basic overnight accommodation at the bay (RM100) or a boat back to Sandakan. Some travel or tour agencies can assist with the permit and other arrangements.

📷 Borneo Sun Bear Conservation Centre ANIMAL SANCTUARY
(BSBCC; Map p78; ☏089-534491; www.bsbcc.org. my; Jln Sepilok; RM30; ⊗9am-4pm) The sun bear is the smallest of the world's bear species, as well as one of the most threatened. Named for the splotch of yellow fur that spreads like a bright Rorschach across their chests, sun bears, while adorable, also have razor claws that they use to build their nests (which very much resemble orangutan nests). They are endangered thanks to the usual culprits of habitat loss and Chinese traditional medicine; the latter institution values the bears' bile. In China and Vietnam the beasts are strapped in tiny cages and hooked to IVs that pump bile from their gallbladders.

Thankfully this does not happen in Sabah, although the bears are still under enormous threat from habitat loss.

Set to open to the public in 2013, the BSBCC, at the time of research, cared for some 27 rescued sun bears. The pretty little beasts lumbered and played in open-air forest enclosures; visitors will be able to peek in on their activity from an expertly crafted walkway system. The BSBCC does good work, and is another activity option for tourists to consider when visiting Sepilok. Please note the centre's admissions and opening times may change, as it was not officially open at the time of writing.

Rainforest Discovery Centre (RDC)

NATURE RESERVE

(Map p78; ✆089-533780; www.forest.sabah.gov. my/rdc; adult/child RM10/5; ⊙8am-5pm) The RDC offers an engaging graduate-level education in tropical flora and fauna. Outside the exhibit hall – itself filled with displays that are easily accessible to children – a botanical garden presents varying samples of tropical plant life, the accompanying descriptions every bit as vibrant as the foliage. There's a gentle 1km lakeside walking trail, studded along the way with environmental education signage. A series of eight canopy towers connected by walkways give you a birds-eye view of the green rooftops of the trees, by far the most rewarding element of a trip here. Paddleboats (RM5) are available to ride around the inviting lake near the centre's entrance. You can also book night walks, which afford the chance to spot nocturnal animals like tarsiers and wild cats.

It's best to get there either at 8am or 4pm, as wildlife tends to hibernate during the sweltering hours in the middle of the day. A proper visit along the trails and towers takes around 1½ hours.

Labuk Bay Proboscis Monkey Sanctuary

SANCTUARY

(✆089-672133; www.proboscis.cc; admission RM 60, camera/video RM10/20) Proboscis monkeys *(Nasalis larvatus)* are an even more exclusive attraction than orangutans. After all, you can see orangutans in Sumatra but the proboscis is found only on Borneo, although if you take a close look at them, you'd swear you've spotted one in the corner at a dodgy bar. Named for their long bulbous noses, proboscis monkeys are potbellied and red-faced, and males are constantly, unmistakably...aroused. With the arrival of Europeans, Malays nicknamed the proboscis *monyet belanda* (Dutch monkey). Because of their diets, proboscis monkeys tend to have severe flatulence, another attractive element of this already most graceful of species. Jokes aside, the proboscis are oddly compelling, and one of nine totally protected species in Sabah.

THE WILD MAN OF BORNEO & HOW TO HELP HIM

The term 'orangutan' literally means 'man of the wild', or 'jungle man' – a testament to the local reverence for these great ginger apes. Traditionally orangutans were never hunted like other creatures in the rainforest; in fact, Borneo's indigenous people used to worship their skulls in the same fashion as they did the heads taken from enemy tribesmen. Orangutans are the only species of great ape found outside Africa. A mature male is an impressive, not to mention hairy, creature with an arm span of 2.25m, and can weigh up to 144kg. Dominant males also have distinctive wide cheek pads to reinforce their alpha status. It was once said that an orangutan could swing from tree to tree from one side of Borneo to the other without touching the ground. Sadly this is no longer the case, and hunting and habitat destruction continue to take their toll; it's estimated fewer than 15,000 specimens now exist in the wild.

If you'd like to get involved with the work of the Sepilok Orang-utan Rehabilitation Centre, contact **Sepilok Orang-Utan Appeal UK** (www.orangutan-appeal.org.uk) a UK-based charity. The Appeal's orangutan adoption scheme is a particular hit with visitors: for UK£30 a year you can sponsor a ginger bundle of fun and receive updates on its progress; see the Appeal's website for details. If you're really taken with the place, Sepilok has one of the most popular overseas volunteer programs in Malaysia. Apply through **Travellers Worldwide** (www.travellersworldwide.com); as of recently, the cost of an eight-week volunteer package, including accommodation, meals and a number of excursions, was UK£3345.

A local palm-plantation owner has created a private proboscis monkey sanctuary, attracting the floppy-conked locals with sugar-free pancakes at 11.40am and 4.30pm feedings. A third feeding at 2.30pm often occurs during a ranger-led hike deeper in the sanctuary. An estimated 300 wild monkeys live in the 6-sq-km reserve. Animals in the reserve generally steer clear of human contact, except for those mischievous macaques, who just love snacks and sun-hats. This is clearly more of a commercial affair than the feedings at the SORC; the proboscis monkeys are enticed onto the main viewing platform so tourists can get better pictures, which may put you off if you're looking for a more ecologically minded experience.

The sanctuary offers package trips. A half-day visit costs RM160, including transfers from Sandakan (RM150 from Sepilok). Overnight trips with meals and a night walk start at RM250. Food and accommodation are provided at the **Nipah Lodge**, on the edge of the oil-palm plantations that surround the sanctuary; the lodge is quite comfortable, a collection of chalets that are simply adorned, airy and inviting in a tropical-chic way. Guests can also venture out on mangrove treks into the surrounding jungle, night treks with guides, and are often invited to give basic English lessons at a nearby village schoolhouse.

Independent travel here is difficult unless you have your own vehicle, as Teluk Labuk (Labuk Bay) sits 15km down a rough dirt track off the main highway. If you're staying here, Nipah Lodge will handle all transfers; otherwise your lodging in Sepilok will be able to arrange transport for around RM120. You can also look for minivans and taxis in the car park of SORC; travellers who want to go to Teluk Labuk should be able to negotiate shared taxis and vans to the proboscis feeding for around RM150 (round-trip from Teluk Labuk back to your Sepilok lodging).

🛏 Sleeping & Eating

If you came to Sandakan for the orangutans of Sepilok, do yourself a favour and stay near the apes. The lodging here tends to have more character than Sandakan spots. Most accommodation options are scattered along Jln Sepilok, the 2.5km-long access road to the rehabilitation centre.

TOP
CHOICE **Paganakan Dii** BOUTIQUE HOTEL $$
(☑089-532005; www.paganakandii.com; dm/chalet RM30/150; 🅿) There are some places that reinvent what budget-to-midrange accommodation is capable of, and Paganakan Dii falls firmly into this vaunted category of hotel. This welcoming and quiet retreat sits deep within a deer preserve, just past a public park. Chic design details made from recycled materials, crisp white linens, smooth wooden chalets, views into a jungle seemingly sliced out of Eden and friendly staff will have you thinking the owners surely left a zero off the price tag. Overall, staying here is a great reason to get stuck in Sepilok. Transfers to the Sepilok Rehabilitation Centre are included in the price. The ridge chalets are some of the best value for money chalets in Sabah, especially seeing as they can be split between three to four people. Book early.

Sepilok Forest Edge Resort RESORT $$
(Map p78; ☑089-533190, 089-533245; www.sepilokforestedge.com; Jln Rambutan, Sepilok Mile 14; dm/d/chalets from RM40/80/220; 🅿🅿) This fine resort grew out of the excellent Labuk B&B, which is still technically part of the Forest Edge property. Serviceable dorm and double rooms are located in a pretty longhouse, but it's the chalets that are the property's pièce de résistance. The comfortable cabins are peppered across an obsessively maintained acreage (think golf course). There's a relaxing tropical pool/jacuzzi on the grounds as well, which is reserved for chalet guests (or backpackers willing to drop an extra RM8).

Sepilok Nature Resort RESORT $$$
(Map p78; ☑089-674999, 089-673999; http://sepilok.com; r from RM280; 🅿@) This is as luxurious as Sepilok gets – the full five-star tropical treatment. Run by the very exclusive Pulau Sipadan Resort & Tours, these rattan-accented chalets are exquisitely decked out and have private verandahs overlooking scrumptious gardens and a shaded lagoon. The on-site restaurant cooks the best Western food in Sepilok (not that there's a lot of competition).

Sepilok B&B B&B $
(Map p78; ☑089-532288, 019-833 0901; www.sepilokbednbreakfast.com; Jln Arboretum; dm/r RM45/60) This unpretentious option has a palpable summer-camp vibe. That goes for the large crowds who stay here and the

decor of the place, which runs towards stark, simple yet cosy. Crooked picnic tables and varnished lounge chairs offer backpackers plenty of room to chill out after a sweaty day of orangutanning under the equatorial sun. Located opposite the Rainforest Discovery Centre (RDC).

Uncle Tan   GUESTHOUSE $
(📞016-824 4749, 089-535784; www.uncletan.com; dm/tw incl all meals RM48/100, plus RM50 per extra sharing; ❄️🏠) The Uncle Tan empire is one of the oldest backpacker/adventure travel outfits in Sabah. Now they've set up shop in the heart of Sepilok with a couple of decent thatch-roofed gazebos and a stack of backpacker shacks.

Sepilok Jungle Resort   RESORT $$
(Map p78; 📞089-533031; www.sepilokjungleresort. com; dm RM28, r RM105-220; ❄️@🏊) Everyone seems to stay here but it's hard to see why. Well, no, it's not – this is a big stop on the package-tour path. Some rooms are a bit drab: cheap carpeting and bedspreads and musty windows. Renovated rooms are a better deal – the sort of clean, if institutional hotel room you'd expect at home (but in a jungle).

Most accommodation in the area serves breakfast, and some offer guests three-meal packages. The **SORC cafeteria** (meals from RM5; 🕐7am-4pm) vends sandwiches, noodle bowls, rice plates, snacks and beverages, though they are known for running out of items during the tourist rush. **Mah Fung Enterprise** (🕐Mon-Sat), across from the turn-off to the RDC, sells cold drinks, snacks, sunscreen and insect repellent. There's also a small hut with a blue fence at Batu 14 serving snacks and cold drinks.

ℹ️ Information

Sepilok is located at 'Batu 14' – 14 miles (23km) from Sandakan. The street connecting the highway to the centre is lined with various accommodation (except Paganakan Dii, which is located on the other side of the road).

It's best to get money in Sandakan, but an ATM had been installed in a Petronas station on the road between Sandakan and Sepilok. The next-closest ATM is in Sandakan Airport. Money can be changed at upmarket sleeping spots for a hefty change fee.

ℹ️ Getting There & Away

Bus
Bus 14 from Sandakan (RM3) departs hourly from the city centre. If coming from KK, board a Sandakan-bound bus and ask the driver to let you off at 'Batu 14'. You will pay the full fare, even though Sandakan is 23km away.

Taxi
If you are coming directly from Sandakan, a taxi should cost no more than RM45 (either from the airport or the city centre). Taxi 'pirates', as they're known, wait at Batu 14 to give tourists a ride into Sepilok. It's RM3 per person for a lift. Travellers spending the night can arrange a lift with their accommodation if they book ahead of time. Walking to the SORC is also an option – it's only 2.5km down the road.

Minivan
You can usually organise a pick-up (in a shared minivan from the Kinabatangan operators) from Sepilok after the morning feeding if you are planning to head to Sungai Kinabatangan in the afternoon.

Sandakan Archipelago

While everyone knows about the Semporna Archipelago, it seems hardly anyone wants to visit the Sandakan Archipelago, off the coast of its namesake port. What gives? Don't like fluffy specks of emerald sprouting like orchids out of the Sulu Sea, or seabound rock walls, or tales of POW derring-do?

Although it's highly promoted by Sabah Tourism, we cannot recommend Turtle Islands National Park at this time. The trip to watch green sea turtles lay eggs is, at best, ill-managed, and at worst a circus. On any one night dozens of gawping tourists cluster round a single laying turtle; this seems to have the effect of scaring some of the reptiles off. Allowing visitors to handle baby turtles before releasing them is highly dubious. The illegal turtle egg trade is certainly alive in Sandakan: we have personally seen turtle eggs for sale within the city's markets, and while this activity is technically illegal, vendors weren't shy about approaching us. That's the sort of adventure on offer in the Sandakan Archipelago.

PULAU LANKAYAN
Pulau Lankayan isn't just photogenic; it's your desktop screen saver. Water isn't supposed to get this clear, nor sand this squeaky clean. A spattering of jungle, a few swaying palms...sigh. No wonder so many lovers come here for their honeymoons, which are often (but not necessarily) accompanied by dive expeditions at **Lankayan Island Resort** (📞088-238113, 089-673999; lankayan-island.com;

Batu 6; r RM3350/RM2728), the one accommodation option on Lankayan. There are a couple dozen cabins dotted along the sand where the jungle meets the sea, decked out in flowing light linens and deep tropical hardwood accents. Transfers from Sandakan are included in your accommodation.

Sungai Kinabatangan

The Kinabatangan River is Sabah's longest: 560km of water so chocolatey brown it would pose a serious safety risk to Augustus Gloop. It coils like the serpents that swim its length far into the Borneo interior. Riverine forest creeps alongside the water, swarming with wildlife that flee ever-encroaching palm-oil plantations. Lodges are set up all along the banks, while homestay programs pop up with the frequency of local monkeys. Dozens of tin boats putter along the shores offering tourists the opportunity to have a close encounter with a rhinoceros hornbill or perhaps a doe-eyed orangutan.

◉ Sights

Gomantong Caves   CAVES
(☑089-230189; www.sabah.gov.my/jhl; adult/child RM30/15, camera/video RM30/50; ⊙8am-noon & 2-4.30pm) Sarawak's Mulu and Niah caverns may be more famous, but for our ringgit, we think the Gomantong Caves give them a run for their money: a massive crack in a mountain, a cathedral-like grand inner chamber formed of limestone, spot-speckled with tubes of golden sunlight and a veritable small hill of bat shit, cockroaches and scorpions. The Gomantong Caves are disgusting, yes, but they're also magnificent.

The forested area around the caves conceals plenty of wildlife and a few good walks – we spotted a wild orangutan out here, which local staff said was rare but not unheard of (sadly, that's because increased logging is pushing the primates into protected areas like this). The most accessible of the caves is a 10-minute walk along the main trail near the information centre. Head past the living quarters of the nest collectors to get to the main cave, **Simud Hitam** (Black Cave). Venture into the main chamber and keep walking counter-clockwise on the raised platform, which hovers over a steaming soup of bat crap and a chittering, chitinous army of roaches, centipedes and scorpions. The same lovely mix coats the walkway's handrails, so try not to grip

them when you (inevitably) slip on the river o' guano. A 45-minute uphill trek beyond the park office leads to **Simud Putih** (White Cave), containing a greater abundance of prized white swiftlets nests. Both trails are steep and require some sweaty rock climbing.

The majority of visitors to Gomantong come as part of an add-on to their Kinabatangan tour package. It is possible to visit the caves under one's own steam, though, usually by private vehicle. The turn-off is located along the road connecting Sukau to the main highway and is quite well signposted. Minivans plying the route between Sandakan and Sukau (RM17) can drop you off at the junction, but you'll have to walk the additional 5km to the park office.

Bukit Belanda   HILL
Bukit Belanda – Dutch Hill – is a 420m hill located behind the village of Bilit. The land is owned by the citizens of Bilit, who, despite pressures from logging companies, have not opened the hill to the timber industry, preferring to maintain it as a haven for wildlife. You can hike to the top in an hour if you're fit, where you'll be rewarded by lovely views of Sungai Kinabatangan and, if you're lucky, glimpses of local wildlife (at the very least, you're sure to hear the shrieks of local primates.) It's best to make this trek early in the morning for purposes of both catching the sunrise and avoiding the heat of the day. There's no official infrastructure when it comes to visiting the hill; just ask someone in your lodge or Bilit itself to guide you to the beginning of the ascent path.

Batu Tulug   CAVES
(☑089-565145; http://museum.sabah.gov.my; admission RM15; ⊙9am-5pm, closed Fri) On the road from Sandakan to Lahad Datu you can catch a glimpse of Agop Batu Tulug, a jutting knife of white limestone slicing out of the jungle. This hill, located above the village of Batu Putih, is studded with caves that house the ancestors of both local Chinese and the Orang Sungai (People of the River). Because the Kinabatangan has a habit of frequently flooding, the final resting place of the dead has traditionally been located in cave complexes (a practice that has eroded thanks to Christianity and Islam). Heavy wooden coffins – it must have been an awful effort lugging them up the sheer rocks – are interred in the Batu Tulug caves with spears, knives, gongs, bells and Chinese curios. Some coffins

WORTH A TRIP

PULAU BERHALA

Berhala is supremely serene, an exemplar of a rare genre: a lovely tropical island hardly touched by tourists. Sandstone cliffs rise above the Sulu Sea, hemming in quiet patches of dusty, sandy prettiness. The vibe is so sleepy it's narcoleptic, an atmosphere accentuated by a quiet water village inhabited by fishing families, loads of migrating birds (their presence is heaviest in October and November) and...well, OK. There's not a lot else, except some very big rocks.

But oh what rocks. Rock climbers grade the formations here F5a – F6b, which is jargon for a mix of slow sloping walls and vertical cliff faces. Fieldskills Adventures (p45) in Kota Kinabalu runs 2-day/1-night rock-climbing trips out here for RM500 per person.

Berhala was a leper colony during the colonial period, and the Japanese used the island as a civilian internment centre and POW camp during WWII. Agnes Newton Keith was kept here awhile, as was a group of Australian POWs who managed to escape the island by boat and sail to Tawi-Tawi in the Philippines.

are carved with relatively simple geometric patterns, others in beautiful animal designs. This trove of artefacts makes the hill one of the most important archaeological sites in Sabah. **Sabah Museums** runs the site and has built wooden staircases that snake up the 40m hill. There are two main caves to explore, but if you climb the stairs to the top, you'll be rewarded with a nice view of the surrounding jungle and the Kinabatangan River. An interpretive information centre is also located on the site.

The easiest way to get here is to include the caves in your package tour of the Kinabatangan. If you've got your own vehicle, look for signs indicating the turn-off to Batuh Putih or Muzium Batu Tulug on the Sandakan–Lahad Datu road. The village is south of Sukau Junction, about 1½ hours from Sandakan and 45 minutes from Lahad Datu. GPS coordinates are N5024.935' E117056.548'.

Kinabatangan Orang-utan Conservation Project (KOCP)   RESEARCH CENTRE

(☑088-413293; www.hutan.org.my) Inside Sukau village is this conservation camp dedicated to studying and protecting Sabah's most iconic animal ambassador. The project is run in partnership with HUTAN, a French NGO, which also works with villagers to establish environmental-education programs, reforestation initiatives and an elephant-conservation project in the Sukau-Bilit area. This is not a tourist-oriented outfit like the Sepilok sanctuary, and as such is not open to casual visitors, but it may be worth contacting it as staff may be willing to hire out guides should you want to go searching for wild orangutans.

🏃 Activities

Wildlife River Boat Cruises   BOAT TOUR

Wildlife is the number-one reason to visit Sabah, and a cruise down the Kinabatangan is often a highlight for visitors to the state. In the late afternoon and early morning, binocular-toting enthusiasts have a chance of spotting nest-building orangutans, nosy proboscis monkeys, basking monitor lizards and hyper long-tailed macaques. That said, there is such a preponderance of operators out here that boats tend to cluster around the wildlife, which kind of ruins the sense of wild exposure. Also, the reason so many animals are here is depressing: the expansion of palm oil plantations has driven local wildlife to the riverbank. They simply have nowhere else to live.

Mammals can be seen all year, moving around in small groups while travelling through plantations. Colourful birds are a huge draw: all eight varieties of Borneo's hornbills, plus brightly coloured pittas, kingfishers and, if you're lucky, a Storm's stork or the bizarre Oriental darter all nest in the forests hugging the Kinabatangan. Avian wildlife is more numerous and varied during rainier months (usually October to late March), which coincides with northern-hemisphere migrations. Though friendly for birds, the wet season isn't accommodating for humans. Flooding has been a problem of late and a couple of lodges will sometimes shut their doors when conditions are severe.

The success rate of animal-spotting largely depends on luck and the local knowledge of your guide – don't be afraid to ask hard questions about the specifics of your trip before you sign up. Elephants and other larger

THE BUSINESS OF BIRD NESTS

The Gomantong Caves are Sabah's most famous source of swiftlet nests, used for the most revered, rare, luck-and-'strength'-inducing dish of the traditional Chinese culinary oeuvre: the eponymous birds-nest soup. Wait, you ask, people *want* to eat bird nest? Well, it's not twigs and stones folk want to devour: swiftlets make their nests out of their own dried spit, which is the main ingredient in the soup. When added to soup broth, the swiftlet spit dissolves and becomes gelatinous. Wait, you ask, people *want* to eat bird vomit? Well, yes. Very much so.

There are two types of soup-worthy bird nests: black and white. Black are a mix of twigs and spit, while the white nests are purely made from the birds' saliva. The white nests are significantly more valuable and Gomantong's got a relatively large amount of them. A kilogram of white swiftlet spit can bring in over US$4000, making nest-grabbing a popular profession despite the perilous task of shimmying up bamboo poles.

In the last few years visiting has been restricted due to dwindling bird populations (cash-hungry locals were taking the nests before the newborn birds had enough time to mature). Today, the caves operate on a four-month cycle, with closings at the beginning of the term to discourage nest hunters. It's worth asking around before planning your visit – often the caves are empty or off-limits to visitors. The four-month cycles are strictly enforced to encourage a more sustainable practice of harvesting.

---

animals come and go, as herds often break up to get through the palm plantations.

River tours should always be included in lodge package rates. If you prefer to explore independently, contact local homestay programs, which will be able to hook you up with a boat operator. Or ask about renting a boat in Sukau – everyone in the village is connected to the tourism industry either directly or through family and friends, and someone will be able to find you a captain. Another option: just before the entrance to Sukau village is a yellow sign that says 'Di sini ada boat servis' (Boat service here); different river pilots hang out here throughout the day. Whatever way you choose to find a boat and a guide, expect to pay at least RM100 for a two-hour river cruise on a boat that can hold up to six people (ie you can split the cost with friends).

Some of the villages you see along the river are inhabited by Filipino migrants who are stateless citizens, unrecognised by both Malaysia and the Philippines.

Trekking
TREKKING

Depending on the location of your lodge, some companies offer short treks (one to three hours) through the jungle. Night hikes are some of the best fun to be had on the Kinabatangan – there's something magical about being plunged into the intense, cavern-like darkness of the jungle at night. Headlamps should be carried in your hand, rather than worn on your head – bats tend to be attracted to light sources and may fly into them; they also secrete an enzyme causing localised paralysis (it's temporary but can muck up your typinghshshenfnvnwurj – just kidding. Seriously, it's temporary).

🛏 Sleeping & Eating

You'll need to book at river lodges in advance. In Kinabatangan lingo, a 'three-day, two-night' stint usually involves the following: arrive in the afternoon on day one for a cruise at dusk, two boat rides (or a boat-hike combo) on day two, and an early morning departure on day three after breakfast and a sunrise cruise. When booking a trip, ask about pick-up and drop-off prices – this is usually extra.

SUKAU

Sukau means 'tall tree' in the local dialect, and the name is quite fitting. The tiny town sits on the river among the skyscraping branches of a shaded thicket, across from massive stone cliffs that are quite attractive, seemingly lifted from a Chinese silk-scroll painting.

Last Frontier Resort
RESORT $$$

(☎016-676 5922; www.thelastfrontierresort.com; 3-day, 2-night package RM550; ❄@☎) Getting to the Last Frontier is a good first step towards better cardiac health: the only hilltop lodge in the Kinabatangan region sits high, high up (538 steps!) on a hill overlooking the flood plains. Sadly, a Sherpa is not included in the rates. What you do get is excellent fusion cuisine in the on-site **Monkey Cup Cafe** (this place is owned by a Belgian Malaysian couple – anyone want *frites mit/avec nasi lemak?*), gorgeous views of the river, well-crafted, simple chalets and a host of trekking options.

Sukau Rainforest Lodge   LODGE $$$
(☏088-438300; www.sukau.com; 3-day, 2-night package RM1/50; ❄🌐) The Rainforest Lodge participates in tree-planting projects aimed at reviving degraded portions of riverine forest, aims to reduce use of plastics and is pioneering the use of quiet electric motors on its river cruises (which utilise boats made of recycled materials). All this is well and good, but the sleeping experience is lovely as well: swish but unpretentious longhouses dotted into the jungle, situated around a lovely common space stuffed with gongs, tiki torches and *bubu* (local fish traps), welcome guests after their riverine adventures. Don't miss the 440m annotated boardwalk in the back that winds through the canopy.

Kinabatangan Riverside Lodge   LODGE $$$
(☏089-213502; www.sitours.com; 2-day, 1-night package per two people US$315; ❄🌐) Come here to fall gently asleep in a series of luxury chalets, adrift in simple white sheets and polished wood floors, all connected by a series of shady raised walkways through the jungle. A looping nature trail is out the back and an adorable dining area abounds with stuffed monkeys, faux foliage and traditional instruments. It's managed by SI Tours, which charges in US$.

Barefoot Sukau Lodge   LODGE $
(☏089-237525; www.barefootsukau.com; r RM250; 🌐) Smiling staff direct you to rooms that are small but covered with thick coats of white paint. Just outside Barefoot's cute waterfront cafe is a series of slate-grey cliffs mottled with jungle, creeper and vines.

Sukau Greenview B&B   B&B $
(☏013-869 6922, 089-565266; http://sukaugreenviewbnb.zxq.net/; 2-day, 1-night package from RM330) This pleasant option offers rooms with twin-size beds in a small cottage-style lodge. It's basic (the floors are made from particleboard) for the price.

BILIT
Bilit is a teeny-weeny village that is primarily full of friendly locals and homestays. River lodges are located on both the Bilit side of the Kinabatangan River and the opposite bank. There's a jetty from which boats depart to lodges on the other side of the river, and across the street is a small yard where you can park a car if you drove; the family that owns the house charges RM20 a day for the privilege. A small banana orchard acts as a magnet for pygmy elephants, which a) are popular with tourists and b) have a bad habit of trampling and eating local crops.

Nature Lodge Kinabatangan   LODGE $$
(☏088-230534, 013-863 6263; www.naturelodgekinabatangan.com; 3-day, 2-night package dm/chalet RM380/415) Located just around the river bend from Bilit, this charming jungle retreat is a decent choice for backpacker budgets. The campus of bungalows is divided into two sections: the Civet Wing caters to penny-pinchers with dorm-style huts, while the spiffed-up Agamid Wing offers higher-end twin-bed chalets. Neither sleeping experience will blow you away: mattresses are thin and the rooms get dank after the rains, so don't expect luxury. The activity schedule, on the other hand, is fantastic: the three-day, two-night packages include three boat tours, three guided hikes *and* all meals, which is as good value as you'll find in these parts.

Bilit Rainforest Lodge   LODGE $$$
(☏088-448409; http://bilitrainforestlodge.com; 2-day, 1-night accommodation only RM420; ❄🌐) One of the more luxurious sleeping spots along the Kinabatangan, this snazzy option caters to an international clientele with huge bungalows, modern bathrooms and generous amounts of gushing air-con. Common areas are plucked from luxury travel magazine pictorial spreads, and the outdoor bar is especially lovely for nighttime drinks. Unlike many lodges we mention, Bilit charges based off the activites you chose; the above rate is for rooms only. Adding two boat tours and three meals a day increases the rate by RM310 a day. A huge array of package tours is available; see the website for more details.

Bilit Adventure Lodge   LODGE $$$
(☏089-271077; www.stwadventure.com; 2-day, 1-night package from RM665, with air-con RM740; ❄) This lodge allows you to adventure in (overpriced) style, or at least sleep as such, in a collection of 24 chalets, some fan-cooled and some with air-con, all decorated in safari style with wooden accents and big fluffy beds.

Myne Resort   RESORT $$$
(☎089-216093; www.myne.com.my; 2-day, 1-night package from RM1055; ❄❂🖥) The newest up-market option on the river consists of over a dozen dark-toned chalets wedged into a dual ridgeline that overlooks a sweeping bend of the Kinabatangan. With fresh smooth sheets, comfy air-con and an enormous deck area for snacking and drinking, this is a solid upper-tier choice that tends to be popular with tour groups from Europe and China.

Kinabatangan Jungle Camp   LODGE $$
(☎013-540 5333, 019-843 5017, 089-533190; www.kinabatangan-jungle-camp.com; 2-day, 1-night package RM550) This earth-friendly retreat caters to a niche market of birders and serious nature junkies; facilities are functional, with the focus emphasising quality wildlife-spotting over soft, comfortable digs. Packages include three meals, two boat rides, guiding and transfers. The owners also run the Labuk B&B in Sepilok, and four out of five travellers opt for a Kinabatangan-Sepilok combo tour.

DON'T MISS

HOMESTAYS ON THE KINABATANGAN

Homestay programs are popping up with increasing frequency in Sukau, Bilit and other villages, giving tourists a chance to stay with local Orang Sungai – 'people of the river' – and inject money almost directly into local economies. Please note the contacts we provide are for local homestay program coordinators who will place you with individual families.

Our favourite homestay in the region is in the village of Abai. The villagers love hosting guests and, to the degree they can, chatting with you and generally forming cross-cultural bonds (the levels of English are admittedly not great). Expect to be asked to participate in the local village volleyball matches! This homestay is best arranged through Adventure Alternative Borneo (p45) in Kota Kinabalu, which maintains direct contact with the villagers.

In Sukau, **Bali Kito Homestay** (☎089-568472, 013-869 9026; http://sukauhomestay.com; 3-day, 2-night package for four RM650, one night with two meals RM50) can connect you with several different families and, for additional fees, hook you up with cultural programs, fishing trips, opportunities to work on traditional farms, treks, wildlife cruises and other fun. A special walk-in rate of RM30 is also available if you just rock up to the village (meals are RM10 each). A four-person three-day, two-night package that includes meals, four river cruises, transport to and from Sandakan and a visit to the Gomantong Caves runs to RM650 per person, but different packages can be arranged for smaller groups.

In tiny Bilit, we often wondered which houses *weren't* homestays. Contact the exceptionally helpful **Bilit Village Homestay** (☎013-891 3078, 019-537 0843, 019-853 4997; http://bilithomestay.wordpress.com; r from RM55). This outfit offers package deals that are much the same experience as what you would find in Sukau. Three-day, two-night rates, which include river cruises and trekking, run RM360 per person.

Near Batu Pulih (the village adjacent to the Batu Tulug caves), **Mescot/Miso Walai Homestay** (☎012-889 5379, 019-582 5214, 089-551070; www.mescot.org; r RM70) is one of the oldest, best-run community ecotourism initiatives in the area. By dint of its location, this homestay also happens to be outside the tourist crush in Sukau and Bilit, so your chances of spotting wildlife are a bit better.

When staying in a homestay, it is important to act as a guest in someone's home as opposed to a tourist on holiday. Privacy will be reduced, and you may be expected to help with chores, cooking, cleaning etc (this depends on the family you stay with). Men and women should dress modestly and couples will want to avoid overt displays of affection, which locals tend to frown on. English may not be widely spoken, especially at newer homestays, although you'll be impressed at the multilingual abilities of kids who have grown accustomed to meeting travellers from around the world! The experience is a different one, one which many visitors absolutely love, but it's certainly not everyone's cup of tea. That said, we strongly encourage giving homestays a shot if you haven't done so before.

Proboscis Lodge Bukit Melapi LODGE $$
(☑088-240584; http://www.sdclodges.com; 2-day, 1-night package lw share per person RM330; ☀) The Proboscis is a study in subdued, simple luxury. The management has created a sociable ambience with its large bar area and comfy tree-stump seating. Wooden bungalows, strewn along a shrubby hill, have oxidised copper-top roofs that clink when it rains. The two-day, one-night packages include three meals, one river cruise and a pick-up from the Lapit jetty.

UPRIVER

Abai Jungle Lodge LODGE $$$
(☑089-213502, 013-883 5841; www.sitoursborneo. com; 2-day, 1-night packages from US$290) Managed by SI Tours (p74) (the same company that runs Kinabatangan Riverside Lodge), Abai Jungle Lodge sits 37km upstream from Sukau just as the river emerges from the secondary forest. This is a great option for the adventurous – isolated and ecologically minded, Abai also manages to feel quite comfortably luxurious. The woodsy exterior pavilions are good for strolling after crashing in your cosy private room. Eco-conscious attempts are being made to increase sustainability: rainwater is collected in cisterns above the chalets, which run on low-emitting diesel engine generators.

Uncle Tan's Jungle Camp LODGE $$
(☑016-824 4749, 089-535784; www.uncletan.com; 2-day, 1-night packages from RM320 3-day 2-night packages from RM420) Uncle Tan was one of the earliest guides and environmentalists working along the Kinabatangan. Although he died in 2002, his legacy lives on in the form of this lodge, a descendant of his original backpacker mecca. This camp isn't for everyone; some travellers may be put out by the spartan conditions, which are basic (running water is the concession to luxury). Others may embrace the roughing-it attitude, especially as the drop in creature comforts is offset by experienced staff members who are skilled at finding wildlife.

❶ Getting There & Away

Transfers are usually arranged with your lodging as part of your package, but you can save by arriving independently. Arrange transport from any of the drop-off points with your tour operator or with a local minivan. Don't get on Birantihanti buses – they stop anytime someone wants to get on or off, which could quadruple travelling time.

Bus & Minivan

From KK, board a Tawau- or Lahad Datu–bound bus and ask the driver to let you off at 'Sukau Junction', also known as 'Meeting Point' – the turn-off road to reach Sukau. If you are on a Sandakan-bound bus, make sure your driver remembers to stop at the Tawau-Sandakan junction – it's called 'Batu 32' or 'Checkpoint' (sometimes it's known as Sandakan Mile 32).

From Sepilok or Sandakan, expect to pay around RM20 to reach 'Batu 32', and around RM30 if you're on a Sandakan–Tawau bus and want to alight at 'Meeting Point'.

A minivan ride to 'Meeting Point' from Lahad Datu costs RM20. When buying your bus tickets remember to tell the vendor where you want to get off so you don't get overcharged.

Car

If you are driving, note that the Shell petrol station on the highway at Sukau Junction (at the turn-off to Sukau) is the last place to fill up before arriving at the river. The road to Sukau is pretty smooth, but as you get closer to Bilit you'll start running into some dirt patches. It is possible to get to Bilit via 2WD – just drive carefully, especially if it's been raining.

Lahad Datu

POP 220,000

Lahad Datu is where a lot of Eastern Sabah is heading: a company town where the company is palm oil plantations.

The locals are lovely and as proud of their home as folks are anywhere else in the world, but there's no real reason to stop here except to arrange a visit to the Danum Valley or Tabin Wildlife Reserve. **Borneo Nature Tours** (☑089-880207; www.borneonaturetours. com; Lot 20, Block 3, Fajar Centre), which runs the Borneo Rainforest Lodge (BRL), and the **Danum Valley Field Centre** (☑088-326300, 089-881092; rmilzah@gmail.com; Block 3, Fajar Centre) have offices next to each other in the upper part of town – known as Taman Fajr, or Fajar Centre. There is a difference between the two Danum options (and yes, these are your only two options). Most people are here to book a stay in the Danum Valley Field Centre, as those who can afford to stay with Borneo Nature Tours aren't likely to book at the last minute and will probably arrange lodging earlier (either in KK or overseas). Because the Field Centre is exactly that – a research centre that doesn't cater to tourists – its office can be slow about responding to emails or phone calls asking for lodging. Sometimes it is best to show up in person and politely request to speak with someone about sleeping arrangements. Otherwise, contact Rose John Kidi at rmilzah@gmail.com, or ☑088-326300, or else contact Patricia Mobilik or Mahdah Aripin (☑089-881688, 089-0881092; danum@care2.com).

Around the block, you'll find the booking office of Tabin Wildlife Holidays (p90), a secondary forest sanctuary on the other side of Lahad Datu. As this office is a tourism outfit, it is much better about responding to emails; nonetheless, you'll likely pass through Lahad Datu on your way to Tabin.

🛏 Sleeping & Eating

Hotel De Leon   HOTEL $$
(☑089-881222; www.hoteldeleon.com.my; Darvel Bay Commercial Centre; s/d from RM168/178; ❄🖥📶) A good midrange option with business-class standard, fresh, air-conditioned rooms. Perfect for those needing a night of comfort after the bush. Wi-fi is only available in common areas.

Full Wah   HOTEL $
(☑089-884100; Jln Anggerik; s/d from RM40/60; ❄) If you're on a tight budget, we recommend Full Wah. While located in a *very* dowdy building, the interior rooms are exceedingly mediocre, in a good way – clean, characterless carpets and bedding. This is as opposed to mildew ceilings and mouldy bathrooms, which seem the unfortunate norm in Lahad Datu's cheaper accommodation.

MultiBake   BAKERY $
(cakes from RM1.80; ⊙8am-10pm; 📶) Malaysia's franchised patisserie is located in Fajar Centre (it has free wi-fi too).

Dovist   RESTAURANT $
(mains from RM5; ⊙lunch & dinner) Around the corner from the Danum booking offices; a respectable spot for a more substantial meal. It's worth stopping by one of the convenience stores in Fajar Centre to stock up on a couple of snacks before your trip into the Danum Valley.

ⓘ Getting There & Away
Air
MASwings (☑1800-883000, outside Malaysia 03-7843 3000) currently operates four daily flights to Lahad Datu from KK. The airport is in the upper part of town near Fajar Centre. You must take the first flight of the day (departing KK at 6:25am) if you don't want a one-day layover in town before heading to the Danum Valley.

Bus
Express buses on the KK–Tawau route stop at the Shell station (Taman Fajr) near the Danum Valley office in the upper part of town. Other buses and minivans leave from a vacant lot near Tabin Lodge in the lower part of town. There are frequent departures for Sandakan (RM35, 2½ hours), Sukau (RM23, two hours), Semporna (RM25 to RM30, two hours) and Tawau (RM25 to RM35, 2½ hours). Charter vehicles and 4WDs wait in an adjacent lot; these guys are difficult to hire after sunset.

Danum Valley Conservation Area

Flowing like a series of dark, mossy ripples over some 440 sq km of central Sabah, the Danum Valley is a humid, cackling, cawing mass of lowland dipterocarp arboreal amazement. The forest here is thick – so thick that it has never been (to the best knowledge of anyone living) settled permanently. By humans, that is. Oh, there's life here of another sort in abundance: orangutans, tarsiers, sambar deer, bearded pigs, flying squirrels, proboscis monkeys, gibbons and the pygmy elephant (to name a few), watered by Sungai Segama and shaded by 70m-high old-growth canopy and 1093m-high Mt Danum.

This pristine rainforest is currently under the protection of **Yayasan Sabah** (Sabah Foundation; www.ysnet.org.my), a semigovernmental organisation tasked with both protecting and utilising the forest resources of Sabah. They say that at any given time, there are over a hundred scientists doing research in the Danum Valley. Tourists are less frequent visitors, but they are here, and you should count yourself lucky if you join their ranks. That said, to come here you either need a lot of cash or persistence, as the only two places to stay are a very luxurious resort or a budget-priced research centre where the main priority is accommodating scientists as opposed to, well, you. See the website of the **South East Asia Rainforest Research** (www.searrp.org) for more information on research occurring in the valley.

⊙ Sights & Activities
Both the Borneo Rainforest Lodge (BRL) and the Danum Valley Field Centre offer a variety of jungle-related activities. Only the BRL has official nature guides, whereas the Field Centre offers park rangers.

Trekking

The main activities at the BRL and the Danum Valley Field Centre are walking on more than 50km of marked, meandering trails.

At the BRL, take advantage of the well-trained guides who can point out things you would have never seen on your own. The **Coffincliff Trail** is a good way to start your exploration and get your bearings. It climbs 3km to a cliff where the remains of some Kadazan–Dusun coffins can be seen (although the provenance of the coffins is unclear). After reaching an eye-popping panoramic viewpoint 100m up the way, you can either return the way you've come or detour around the back of the peak to descend via scenic **Fairy Falls** and **Serpent Falls**, a pair of 15m falls that are good for a quick dip.

The **Danum Trail, Elephant Trail** and **Segama Trails** all follow various sections of Danum Valley and are mostly flat trails offering good chances for wildlife spotting. All can be done in an hour or two. The **Hornbill Trail** and **East Trail** have a few hills, but are still relatively easy, with similarly good chances for wildlife sightings. Finally, if you just need a quick breath of fresh air after a meal, the **Nature Trail** is a short plankwalk near the lodge that allows you to walk into the forest unmolested by leeches.

There are heaps of fantastic trails weaving around the Field Centre – you must bring a ranger along if you aren't a scientist (note that a guide is better than a ranger though, as rangers are not trained to work with tourists). About a two-hour hike away are the **Tembaling Falls**, a cool slice of tropical Edenic beauty. A more strenuous, four-hour trek gets you to the immensely rewarding **Sungai Purut** falls, a series of seven-tiered pools that are fed by waters that drop down 20m from the nearby mountains.

Birdwatching

Danum Valley is very popular with birdwatchers from around the world, who come here to see a whole variety of Southeast Asian rainforest species, including the great argus pheasant, the crested fireback pheasant, the blue-headed pitta, the Bornean bristlehead and several species of hornbill, among many others. If you're serious about birding, it may be best to stay at the Borneo Rainforest Lodge. The canopy walkway here is ideal for birdwatching, and some of the guides are particularly knowledgeable about birds; attempts are made to match birders

up with these pros. The access road to BRL is also a good spot for birding, as is, frankly, your porch.

Canopy Walkway

As you'll probably know, most of the action in a tropical rainforest happens up in the forest canopy, which can be frustrating for earthbound humans. The BRL's 107m-long, 27m-high canopy walkway gives mere mortals a means of transcending the surly bonds of earth. The swinging bridges traverse a nice section of forest, with several fine *mengaris* and *majau* trees on either side. Birdwatchers often come here at dawn in hopes of checking a few species off their master list. Even if you're not a keen birder, it's worth rolling out of bed early to see the sun come up over the forest from the canopy walkway – when there's a bit of mist around, the effect is quite magical. It's located on the access road, a 10-minute walk from the lodge. You need to be a guest at the BRL to access the walkway.

Night Drives

This is one of the surest ways to see some of the valley's 'night shift', but driving in the forest hardly gets a gold star for eco-friendliness; sensitive souls might empathise with that 'caught-in-the-headlights' feeling. Expect to see one or two species of giant flying squirrels, sambar deer, civets, porcupines and possibly even leopard cats; lucky sightings could include elephants, slow loris and clouded leopards (if you spot those, boy are you ever lucky).

Night drives leave the BRL most evenings; the best trips are the extended night drives, which depart at about 8.30pm and return at 1am or 2am. Things you'll be glad you brought: light waterproof jacket, camera with flash, binoculars and a powerful torch. Drives can be arranged at the Field Centre as well, although you'll probably have to arrange the vehicle one day in advance.

🛏 Sleeping & Eating

There are two lodging options in the Danum Valley, and you absolutely must have accommodation arranged with one of them before you visit – no dropping in. If price is paramount go for the Field Centre. Wildlife fanatics who value professionally trained guides should pick the BRL. The people at Sabah Tourism will try to point you towards the BRL and are reluctant to recommend the Field Centre. Bear in mind: Danum is a jungle, and you may spend your entire time without spotting wildlife, which is one of the main complaints readers have sent us after staying in the following spots.

Borneo Rainforest Lodge
RESORT $$$

(BRL; ☑088-267637, 089-880207; www.borneonaturetours.com; d standard/deluxe 3-day, 2-night package RM2390/2690 per person) Borneo Rainforest Lodge is a class act deep within the buzzing haze of Sabah's remaining old-growth forest. Want the experience of staying in an uber-luxurious chalet while keeping an eye peeled for an adorable tarsier? You're in luck. Go for the deluxe if you can; they have private jacuzzis on the wooden verandahs that overlook the quiet ravine – romantic as hell. Honeymooners should go for Kempas D11 – this room has a secluded jacuzzi in its own wooden pagoda. Meals are taken on a beautiful terrace also fronting the river. We were pretty impressed with the assortment of dishes at the buffet – especially since it all had to be lugged in by 4WD. The BRL's only downfall is its marketing strategy. Yes, the lodge is lovely and the outdoor jacuzzis in the superior rooms are undoubtedly lavish, but this isn't a five-star resort. And how could it be, surrounded by relentlessly encroaching jungle? We're impressed, though, that this much luxury exists so deep in the rainforest. Guests who temper their expectations will adore the ambience and find plenty of creature comforts at their fingertips (no air-con though). It's best to book online or in KK.

Danum Valley Field Centre
LODGE $$

(DVFC; ☑088-326300, 088-881688; rmilzah@gmail.com; resthouse r & board from RM180, camping RM30; ☀) An outpost for scientists and researchers, the field centre also welcomes tourists. Accommodation at the centre is organised into four categories: hostel, resthouse, VIP and camping. We recommend the resthouse rooms, which are located at arm's length from the canteen (the only place to eat). These rooms are basic but clean, sporting ceiling fans and twin beds. Towels are provided for the cold-water showers. The simple hostel is about a seven-minute walk from the canteen, and the barracks-style rooms are separated by gender. If you want to camp, you can lay your sleeping kit (no tent needed) out on the walkways – bug spray recommended! All buildings at the field centre run on generated power, which shuts off between midnight and 7am. There

are no professionally trained guides at the centre – only rangers who can show you the trails. You might luck out and find a friendly researcher who will point you in the direction of a few cool things, but some of the scientists (especially the birders) value their privacy (and can you blame them?). There is a kitchen on the campus, however it is reserved for the research assistants. Tourists take their meals in the cafeteria-style canteen (vegie friendly).

❶ Getting There & Away

Bus & Car

The Danum Valley is only accessible by authorised private vehicle. Borneo Rainforest Lodge guests depart from the lodge office in Lahad Datu at 9am, arriving by lunchtime. If you do not want to spend the night in Lahad Datu, it is recommended you take the 6:25am MASwings flight from KK. If you've prebooked, the driver will wait should your flight be delayed.

Tourists staying at the Danum Valley Field Centre must board one of two jungle-bound vans that leave the booking office in Lahad Datu at 3.30pm on Mondays, Wednesdays and Fridays. Transport is RM100 per person each way (this may increase by the time you read this). Vans return to Lahad Datu from the Field Centre at 8.30am on the same days.

Tabin Wildlife Reserve

Tabin's patch of jungle is essentially the downmarket alternative to the Danum Valley. The 1205-sq-km reserve consists mainly of lowland dipterocarp forest with mangrove areas – most of it is technically secondary forest, but that doesn't seem to trouble the wildlife or visitors. The stars here are the elephants and primates – gibbons, red-leaf monkeys and macaques, plus a lot of orangutans. Rescued orangs from Sepilok are actually released here, so you've got a pretty good chance of spotting some hairy red primates in the wild. Birdlife is abundant, and there's a herd of the endangered Sumatran rhino, though you're unlikely to see them.

The park is managed by **Tabin Wildlife Holidays** (☑088-267266; www.tabinwildlife.com.my; Lot 11-1, Block A, Damai Point; 2-day, 1-night package from RM1150), which runs the on-site **Tabin Wildlife Resort**, a pretty retreat with a clutch of upscale chalets. Fair warning: the chalets are attractive, but they're overpriced for what you get. Five trails snake out into the jungle from in front of the resort. Try the Elephant Trail (800m) if you're interested in belching mud pits. **The Gibbon Trail** (2.8km) leads to the pretty **Lipa Waterfall**.

Tabin can be accessed with a rental vehicle (4WD is a must), but most folks arrange transport with Tabin Wildlife. There are several entrances to the reserve; the easiest one to navigate to is near the junction of Ladan Tungju and Ladang Premai (it's 15km from Lahad Datu Airport to Ladang Kajai).

Semporna

POP 142,000

Most travellers, upon reaching Semporna, turn into little kids on a long car trip: 'But how much *longer* till we get there', with 'there' being Sipadan. Semporna-the-town is the mainland stopping point before Semporna-the-archipelago and all your diving/snorkelling fantasies. Unless you're lucky enough to get here early in the morning, there's a good chance you'll be sticking around overnight. Semporna's fine for an evening of carousing at a bar before donning your fins or checking out the *pasar ikan* (fish markets) and water villages; past that, enjoy your sleep. Not much longer, kids.

Sights & Activities

'Diving' or (rarer) 'snorkelling' is the answer every tourist gives when someone asks them why they're in Semporna. Scuba is the town's lifeline, and there's no shortage of places to sign up for it. Operators are clustered around the 'Semporna Seafront', while other companies have offices in KK. Due to the high volume of interest, it is best to do your homework and book ahead – diving at Sipadan is limited to 120 persons per day.

Sleeping

If you have to overnight in Semporna, your options are limited – but not dire. If you've already signed up with a scuba operator ask them about sleeping discounts (and don't be shy about trying to finagle a good deal, especially if you're sticking around for a while).

Sipadan Inn   HOTEL $
(Map p92; ☑089-781766; www.sipadaninn-hotel. com; Block D, Lot No. 19-24, Semporna Seafront; s/d from RM84/95) If you're on a budget, this is one of the better spots in Semporna. The bright white rooms are military clean, without a speck of dust, and it's a stone's throw from most of the dive centres.

Seafest Hotel   HOTEL $$
(Map p92; ☑089-782333, www.seafesthotel. com; Jln Kastam; r RM90-260; ☀) The jauntily dubbed Seafest is six storeys of bay-view, business-class comfort at the far end of the 'Semporna Seafront' neighbourhood. It's affiliated with Seafest fishery, so check the restaurant's catch of the day. Don't be shy about asking for discounts, and note suites aren't really worth the extra ringgit.

Dragon Inn   HOTEL $
(Rumah Rehat Naga; Map p92; ☑089-781099; www. dragoninnfloating.com.my; 1 Jln Kastam; dm RM20, r incl breakfast from RM80; ☀@) The owners of Dragon figured 'Tourists want stilt houses built over the water and tiki tropical decor' and ran with that theme for several miles. It's a bit tacky, but in an endearing way, and the more upmarket rooms are actually attractive, with dark flooring and island chic decor. The water the Inn stands over is green slop, but the staff is so friendly and eager to please, we forgive this minor trespass.

Scuba Junkie Dive Lodge   HOSTEL $
(Map p92; ☑089-785372; www.scuba-junkie. com; Lot 36, Block B, Semporna Seafront; dm/r RM50/120; ☀@) A sociable, clean and basic spot offering 50% discounts for divers who book through Scuba Junkie. There's an adjacent bar (open from 4pm till the last guest passes out) that gets kicking with the dive instructor set come night.

Borneo Global
Sipadan BackPackers   HOSTEL $
(Map p92; ☑089-785088; www.borneotourstravel. com; Jln Causeway; dm/tr/f incl breakfast RM20/70/100; ☀) Near the Seafest (on the seafront – say that three times fast), this dullish spot is cheap and cheerful. There are posters of fish, to remind you of why you came to Semporna, we guess.

Eating

Various *kedai kopi* line the 'Semporna Seafront', while restaurants at the Seafest Hotel complex offer Chinese seafood. If you want to go native, sample the *nasi lemak* or *korchung* (rice dumplings) – Semporna is well known for these two dishes.

Anjung Paghalian Café   SEAFOOD $
(Map p92; Jln Kastam; mains RM3-5; ☺5pm-10pm) Beside the Tun Sakaran Marine Park entrance sign, this indoor-outdoor place on a pier features fish, prawn, chicken, squid and venison sold by portions (for two or

Semporna

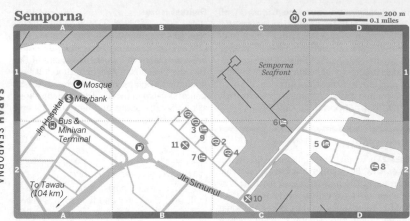

more people) and cooked in your choice of up to 12 different styles. It also has standard Malay hawker stalls and even one which serves burgers.

Mabul Steak House STEAKHOUSE **$$**
(Map p92; ☎089-781785; Semporna Seafront; mains from RM11; ☺noon-11pm) This easygoing balcony restaurant's large and glacial 'ice-blended juices' are a soothing antidote for sucking bottled air. For further chilling, there's a leather couch and overstuffed chairs around a huge TV showing movies or sport. Malaysian standards are done well, and the signature steaks are a surprisingly mouthwatering treat after long days of diving.

ℹ Information

If you're arriving in Semporna under your own steam, leave the bus and minivan drop-off area and head towards the mosque's spiking minaret. This is the way to the waterfront. Follow the grid of concrete streets to the right until you reach 'Semporna Seafront' – a collection of buildings decked out in primary colours that starkly contrast with the charmless pastels throughout the rest of town. This neighbourhood is home to the diving outfitters, each stacked one next to the other in a competitive clump. Sleeping and eating options crowd around here, too.

Decompression Chamber (☎089-783100) The closest **decompression chamber** is at the naval base in Semporna.

Maybank (☎089-784852; Jln Jakarullah) Expect small lines and the occasional beggar, especially in the evening.

ℹ Getting There & Away

Air

Flights to Tawau from KK and KL land at Tawau Airport, roughly 28km from town. A private taxi from Tawau Airport to Semporna costs RM90, while Tawau–Semporna buses (RM15) will stop at the airport if you ask the driver nicely. Buses that do not stop at the airport will let you off at Mile 28, where you will have to walk a few (unshaded) kilometres to the terminal. Remember that flying less than 24 hours after diving can cause serious health issues, even death.

Bus

The 'terminal' hovers around the Milimewa supermarket not too far from the mosque's looming minaret. All buses run from early morning until 4pm (except Kota Kinabalu) and leave when full.

Kota Kinabalu	(RM65, nine hours) leaves at around 7am or 7pm.
Lahad Datu	(RM25 to RM30, 2½ hours)
Sandakan	(RM35 to RM40, 5½ hours)
Tawau	(RM15, 1½ hours)

Semporna Archipelago

Take the word 'blue' and mentally turn it over through all of its possibilities. From the deepest, richest shades to the light robin's egg shade of the sky to kelp-like aqua. This is the rippled waterscape of the Semporna Archipelago, broken up with pebbles of white sand and swaying palms and the rainbow-coloured boats of copper-skinned Sea Gypsies. But no one comes this way for islands, such as it were – rather it is the blue, the ocean and everything beneath it, that appeals, because this is first and foremost a diving destination, one of the best in the world.

◉ Sights & Activities

Maybe the name Semporna doesn't ring a bell – that's because the key word here is 'Sipadan'. Located 36km off Sabah's southeast coast, Sipadan (also called 'Pulau Sipadan') is the shining star in the archipelago's constellation of shimmering islands. The elliptical islet sits atop a stunning submerged pinnacle and world famous near-vertical walls. This underwater beacon is a veritable way station for virtually all types of sea life, from fluttering coral to school-bus-sized whale sharks. Sea turtles and reef sharks are a given during any dive, and luckier scubaholics may spot mantas, eagle rays, octopus, scalloped hammerheads and monitor lizards that could double as Godzilla.

Roughly a dozen delineated dive sites orbit the island – the most famous being the aptly named Barracuda Point, where streamers of barracuda collide to form impenetrable walls of undulating fish. Reef sharks seem attracted to the strong current here and almost always swing by to say hello. South Point sits at exactly the opposite end of the island from Barracuda Point and usually hosts the large pelagics (manta magnet!). The west side of the island features technicolour walls that tumble down to an impossibly deep 2000m – words can't do the sight of this justice. The walls are best appreciated from out in the blue on a clear afternoon. The east coast tends to be slightly less popular, but that's a relative statement – turtles and sharks are still inevitable.

Although Sipadan outshines the neighbouring sites, there are other reefs in the marine park that are well worth exploring. The macro-diving around Mabul (or 'Pulau Mabul') is world-famous. In fact, the term 'muck diving' was invented here. The submerged sites around Kapalai, Mataking and Sibuan are also of note.

While it is possible to rock up and chance upon an operator willing to take you to Sipadan the following day, we strongly suggest that you book in advance. There are travellers and operators who say we are being too cautious with this advice, but your holiday is likely limited, and frankly, better safe than sorry. The downside to prebooking, of course, is that you can't visit each dive centre's storefront to suss out which one you like best, but Johnny come-latelies might be forced to wait a few weeks before something opens up.

SNORKELLING IN SEMPORNA

Many nondivers wonder if they should visit Semporna. We give a qualified 'yes'. The diving here is obviously the main draw, as there are no real beaches to speak of (besides some small patches of sand). But if you like snorkelling, there's some incentive to come out this way. Snorkelling is not the obsessive hobby that diving is – people don't plan their holidays around it the way they do with diving. But if you're travelling in a group or as a couple where some dive and some don't, the Semporna islands are a lot of fun; dive and snorkelling trips are timed so groups leave and come back at similar times, so you won't feel isolated from each other. If you're on your own and only want to snorkel, it's still pretty great, but not as world class as the diving experience, and a bit pricey relative to the rest of Malaysia – snorkel trips cost around RM150, and you also have to factor in the relatively high cost of accommodation here and the price of getting out to the islands. Then again, you still have a good chance of seeing sting rays, sea turtles and all sorts of other macro-marine wildlife while in the midst of a tropical archipelago, so really, who's complaining?

DON'T MISS

REGATTA LEPA

The big annual festival of local Bajau Sea Gypsies is the Regatta Lepa. (A *lepa* is a type of small boat, so the title somewhat redundantly means 'Boat regatta'.) Traditionally, the Bajau only set foot on mainland Borneo once a year; for the rest of the time they live on small islets or their boats. Today the Bajau go to Semporna and other towns more frequently for supplies, but the old cycle of annual return is still celebrated and marked by the regatta *lepa*. For visitors, the highlight of the festival is the *lepa*-decorating contest held between Bajau families. Their already rainbow-coloured boats are further decked out in streamers, flags (known as *tapi*), bunting, ceremonial umbrellas (which symbolise protection from the omnipresent sun and rain that beats down on the ocean) and *sambulayang*, gorgeously decorated sails passed down within Bajau clans. On each boat you can see a smaller, rectangular *lamak kapis* sail and the larger *lamak bua'an* sail, shaped to resemble the maw of a fish. Violin, cymbal and drum music, plus 'sea sports' competitions like duck catching and boat tug-of-war, punctuate the entire affair. It's a hell of a show. The regatta occurs in mid-April; check etawau.com for details, and don't miss the show if you're in town at this time of year.

The government issues 120 passes (RM40) to Sipadan each day (this number includes divers, snorkellers and day trippers). Bizarre rules and red tape, like having certain gender ratios, make the permit process even more frustrating. Each dive company is issued a predetermined number of passes per day depending on the size of its operation and the general demand for permits. Each operator has a unique way of 'awarding' tickets – some companies place their divers in a permit lottery, others promise a day at Sipadan after a day (or two) of diving at Mabul and Kapalai. No matter which operator you choose, you will likely be required to do a non-Sipadan intro dive unless you are a Divemaster who has logged a dive in the last six months. Permits to Sipadan are issued by day (and not by dive) so make sure you are getting at least three dives in your package.

A three-dive day trip costs between RM250 and RM500 (some operators include park fees, others do not – make sure to ask), and equipment rental (full gear) comes to about RM50 or RM60 per day. Cameras (around RM100 per day) and dive computers (around RM80 per day) are also available for rent at most dive centres. Top-end resorts on Mabul and Kapalai offer all-inclusive package holidays (plus a fee for equipment rental).

Although most of the diving in the area is 'fun diving', Open Water certifications are available, and advanced coursework is popular for those wanting to take things to the next level. The only problem with getting your Open Water certification here is that

all other dive sites may pale in comparison! Diving at Sipadan is geared towards divers with an Advanced Open Water certificate (currents and thermoclines can be strong), but Open Water divers should not have any problems (they just can't go as deep as advanced divers). A three-day Open Water course will set you back at least RM950. Advanced Open Water courses (two days) cost the same, and Divemaster certification runs for around RM2500.

Several dive operators are based at their respective resorts, while others have shopfronts and offices in Semporna and/or KK. Please note we have listed the following alphabetically, not in order of preference – we simply didn't have the time to go diving with every outfitter in the islands. No matter where your desired operator is located, it is *highly* recommended you contact them in advance. The following dive operators are among the growing list of companies in the area:

Big John Scuba　　　　　　　　DIVING
(Map p92; www.smiffystravels.com/bjsuba2.htm) 'Big John' is a local guy who loves Sabah, Semporna and diving. He specialises in macro photography and muck diving and while he is an instructor, he separates his students from his diving groups. Has an office by the Dragon Inn.

Billabong Scuba　　　　　　　　DIVING
(Map p92; ☎089-781866; www.billabongscuba.com; Lot 28, Block E, Semporna Seafront) Accommodation can be arranged at a rickety 'homestay' on Mabul.

Blue Sea Divers

DIVING

(Map p92; ☏781 322; www.blueseadivers-sabah. com; Semporna Seafront) Reputable day-trip operator in Semporna.

Borneo Divers

DIVING

(☏088-222226; www.borneodivers.info; 9th fl, Menara Jubili, 53 Jln Gaya, Kota Kinabalu) The original operators in the area, Borneo Divers unveiled Sipadan to an awestruck Jacques Cousteau. It has maintained its high standards throughout the years, offering knowledgeable guides and comfy quarters. The office is located in Kota Kinabalu. There is a comely resort on Mabul. Recommended.

Scuba Junkie

DIVING

(Map p92; ☏089-785372; www.scuba-junkie.com; Lot 36, Block B, Semporna Seafront) Popular with the young backpacker crowd.

Scuba Jeff

DIVING

(☏019-5855125, 017-8690218; www.scubajeffsipadan.com) Jeff, a friendly local bloke, runs his adventures out of the local fishing village in Mabul. Good option for the budget crowd.

Seahorse Sipadan

DIVING

(☏012-279 7657, 016-835 5388, 089-782289; www.seahorse-sipadanscuba.com) Backpacker-oriented outfit that runs a hostel on Mabul.

Seaventures

DIVING

(☏088-261669; www.seaventuresdive.com; 4th fl, Wisma Sabah) Highly regarded outfit that will put you up in an ocean platform off the coast of Mabul. Offices in KK.

Sipadan Scuba

DIVING

(Map p92; ☏089-784788, 089-919128; www. sipadanscuba.com; Lot 23, Block D, Semporna Seafront) Twenty years of Borneo experience and an international staff makes Sipadan Scuba a reliable, recommended choice.

Sipadan Water Village

DIVING

(Map p92; ☏089-784227, 010-932 5783, 089-751777, 089-950023; www.swvresort.com; Jln Kastam) A private operator based at the Mabul resort with the same name.

SMART

DIVING

(☏088-486389; www.sipadan-mabul.com.my) The dive centre operating at Sipadan-Mabul Resort and Mabul Water Bungalow; both are located on Mabul. Also has offices in KK.

Uncle Chang's

DIVING

(Borneo Jungle River Island Tours; Map p92; ☏089-786988, 017-895 0002, 089-781002; www. ucsipadan.com/; 36 Semporna Seafront) Offers diving and snorkelling day trips, plus stays at its lodge on Mabul (RM90 per person).

🛏 Sleeping & Eating

From opulent bungalows to ragtag sea shanties, the marine park offers a wide variety of accommodation catering to all budgets. Sleeping spots are sprinkled across the archipelago with the majority of options clustered on Mabul (Sipadan's closest neighbour). No one is allowed to stay on Sipadan. Note that prices rise in August and September. Nondivers are charged at different rates than divers.

At almost all of the places listed below, you are tied to a set schedule of three to five meals broken up by roughly three diving (or snorkelling) trips per day. Meals are included; drinks are always extra, although tea and coffee are often gratis. If you feel the need to let loose at night, there are occasional parties at Uncle Tan's or Scuba Junkie on Mabul. High-end resorts have their own bars and restaurants; you may be able to eat and drink here if you're staying in a budget spot and the man at the gate is in a good mood, but you'll pay for it.

Divers and snorkellers can also opt to stay in the town of Semporna. That means slightly better bang for your buck, but no fiery equatorial sunsets. Perhaps more pertinently, it takes at least 30 minutes, and usually a bit longer, to get to dive sites from Semporna town.

Every one of the accommodation options listed below can arrange diving trips, including certification courses and trips to Sipadan.

SINGAMATA

Not an island at all, but rather a floating village built onto a sandbar about 30 minutes from Semporna, **Singamata** (☏089-784828; www.singamata.com; 3-day, 2-night diving/non-diving RM720/500) is a pretty assemblage of stilt chalets and decks with its own pool full of giant fish (which you can snorkel amid). If you feel like dipping into the water, you can literally just step out of your room (annoyingly, rubbish from Semporna sometimes still floats into the vicinity). Rooms are basic but pretty and breezy. You may feel isolated out here, but if you need an escape, this is a lovely option.

MABUL

Mabul is the main accommodation centre in the islands. This little speck is blessed with one very small white-sand beach, fantastically blue waters and two small settlements: a camp of Bajau Sea Gypsies and a Malaysian water village of stilt houses built over the seashore, where most of the island's budget accommodation is clustered.

It's worth having a walk around the island, which should take you all of an hour or two. Behind the resorts are generators and barracks-style housing for resort staff. The locals are eager for your business; there's little shops in the villages that sell candy, crisps, cigarettes and other little incidentals. Plus watching the sunset bleed over stilt houses, as the Bajau set cooking fires in their houseboats, is mind-blowingly romantic, and a bit unexpected in a place that's so marketed towards diving.

Mabul Beach Resort   RESORT $$

(☏089-785372; www.scuba-junkie.com; dm RM95, r RM225-375; ❋☎) Owned and operated by Scuba Junkie, this spot is all the rage with the flashpacker crowd. Chalets with en suite bathrooms, porches and polished wood floors make for some posh digs priced (relatively) within the top of the budget range. Note the room prices are for single occupancy – rooms all have two beds, and are cheaper if rented out by two people.

Mabul Water Bungalow   RESORT $$$

(☏088-486389; www.mabulwaterbungalows.com; 3-day, 2-night dive package from US$1016, nondivers US$606; ❋☎) Travellers in Asia tend to love crystal-clear water and temples. These two concepts come together with a heaping dash of amazing at Mabul Water Bungalows, a gorgeously executed series of chalets-cum-Balinese shrines built over the Celebes Sea. This is easily the best upmarket option on Mabul. Rooms are effortlessly opulent, and the resort's only suite, the Bougain Villa (ha!), features a trickling waterfall in the bathroom, its own private dock and glass floors revealing the starfish-strewn sea floor.

Borneo Divers Mabul Resort   RESORT $$$

(☏088-222226; www.borneodivers.net; per person twin/single RM1148/765; ❋@☎) The oldest dive centre in the region offers lodging in a horseshoe of semidetached mahogany bungalows with bright-yellow window frames. Open-air pavilions with gauzy netting punctuate the perfectly manicured grounds. Wi-fi is available in the dining room.

Scuba Jeff   LODGE $

(☏019-5855125, 017-8690218; www.scubajeff sipadan.com; r RM80; ☎) Jeff is a very friendly dude who maintains this large stilt house in the Malay fishing village. While his place is a little tatty, it reminds us of the fun of backpacking – staying in a flophouse and meeting random folk on a budget (including quite a few backpacking Malays).

Sipadan Adventures   HOMESTAY $

(☏012-822 9984; www.sipadanadventures.com; dm/r per person RM70/90) Clean, remodelled rooms and a focus on budget travel make for a fun diving joint. Staff will help arrange dive trips for you and the owners cook up some mean fish.

Uncle Chang's   GUESTHOUSE $

(☏089-781002, 017-895 002, 089-786988; www. ucsipadan.com; per person dm/d RM70/90, per person d with air-con & bathroom RM100; ❋) A Sipadan backpacking stalwart catering to the like-named dive operator, Chang's is a fun, sociable spot that periodically throws kicking little parties. The air-con rooms, clocking in at RM90, are good value for money.

Seaventures Dive Resort   RESORT $$$

(☏088-261669; www.seaventuresdive.com; 4-day, 3-night dive package from RM2160; ❋) This oil rig (no, really) sits just off Mabul's silky shoreline. There are two schools of thought on Seaventures' aesthetic impressions: 'A worthy attempt at giving tourists a unique accommodation option,' and 'That thing? Forget it.' Honestly, we're not sure where we fall in this debate, but its diving staff comes very highly recommended.

Billabong   GUESTHOUSE $

(☏089-781866; www.billabongscuba.com; per person r with fan/air-con RM70/120) Chill with fishermen, watch the sunset over the plankboards and set out for some diving adventures with associated Billabong Scuba at this homestay.

Sipadan-Mabul Resort   RESORT $$$

(SMART; ☏088-486389; www.sipadan-mabul.com. my; 7-day, 6-night dive package from US$1570, nondivers US$1186; ❋☎❋) Even though the summer-camp styling suits the tropical landscape, the prices here are out of whack. Long-stays get the hard sell. If you feel like splurging why not go all the way and snag a room at SMART's sister property, Mabul Water Bungalow (p96)? Wi-fi is available in the dining area.

Sipadan Water Village Resort
RESORT $$$

(☎089-751777; www.swvresort.com; 4-day, 3-night package from RM4100; ✳@) Outmoded design details (although when were wooden tarantula ornaments ever in style?) quickly set the tone here – this resort-on-stilts doesn't pull off 'graceful elegance' quite like Mabul Water Bungalow next door, despite the idyllic location. If you decide that this is the spot for you, then go for the 'grand deluxe' bungalows

Seahorse Sipadan
GUESTHOUSE $

(☎016-8355388, 089-782289; www.seahorse-sipadanscuba.com; dm/r from RM80/90) Basic digs for budget backpackers.

KAPALAI
Although commonly referred to as an island, Kapalai is more like a large sandbar sitting slightly under the ocean surface. From afar, the one hotel, **Kapalai Resort** (☎088-316011/3; http://sipadan-kapalai.com/; 63 Gaya Street, Kota Kinabalu; 4-day, 3-night package from RM2790; ✳@) looks like it's sitting on palm trunks in the middle of the sea. The resort designers went for a Sea Gypsy theme and tacked on an opulent twist, making the sea cabins out of shiny lacquered wood.

MATAKING
Mataking is also essentially a sandbar, two little patches of green bookending a dusty tadpole tail of white sand. **Mataking Island Resort** (☎089-786045, 089-770022; www.mataking.com; Jln Kastam; 3-day, 2-night package for divers/nondivers from RM2470/2110; ✳@) is the only accommodation here. This is an impeccably luxurious escape full of dark-wood chalets and gossamer sheets. This sandy getaway has some really beautiful diving – an artificial reef and sunken boats provide a haven for plenty of sea life – and has set up a novel 'underwater post office' at a local shipwreck site.

POM POM
Pom Pom needs no cheerleading – this stunning, secluded haven sits deep within the Tun Sakaran Marine Park, about one hour by boat from Semporna. **Sipadan Pom Pom Island Resort** (☎089-781918; pompomisland.com; 3-day, 2-night package RM1600-2000; ✳@) runs the only operation on the island. The poshest rooms are built over the water, while reed-and-thatch bungalows offer sea views from spacious balconies. The cheapest rooms are set back in a 'garden' area, but are still basically a hop from the ocean.

ROACH REEFS
This network of artificial reefs was once the private underwater playground for a wealthy businessman, but today **Roach Reefs Resort** (☎089-779332; www.roachreefsresort.com; 2-day, 1-night package for divers/nondivers per person US$185/148; ✳@) has opened its doors to tourists. You'll stay in simple shacks (a little *too* simple, frankly; we wouldn't mind a little more flash at these prices) plunked in a man-made spit of sand, shaded under coconut trees. Keep in mind boat transfers here come from Tawau, as opposed to Semporna.

❶ Information
The Semporna Islands are loosely divided into two geographical sections: the northern islands (protected as **Tun Sakaran Marine Park**) and the southern islands. Both areas have desirable diving – Sipadan is located in the southern region, as is Mabul and Kapalai. Mataking and Sibuan belong to the northern area. If you are based in Semporna you'll have a greater chance of diving both areas, although most people are happy to stick with Sipadan and its neighbours.

Consider stocking up on supplies (sunscreen, insect repellent etc) before making your way into the archipelago. Top-end resorts have small convenience stores with inflated prices. ATMs are nonexistent, but high-end resorts accept credit cards (Visa and MasterCard). Mabul has a small police station near the village mosque, as well as shack shops selling basic foodstuffs and a small pharmacy. Internet is of the wi-fi variety; most resorts now offer it, but service tends to be spotty.

The closest decompression chamber (p92) is at the Semporna Naval Base.

❶ Getting There & Around
Boat
With the exception of Roach Reefs, all transport to the marine park goes through Semporna. Your accommodation will arrange any transport needs from Semporna or Tawau Airport (sometimes included, sometimes for an extra fee - ask!), which will most likely depart in the morning. That means if you arrive in Semporna in the afternoon, you will be required to spend the night in town.

Tawau
POP 380,200
Ever been to an after-work happy hour and met a co-worker who is nice, courteous, polite, pleasant and agonisingly boring? Then you've met Tawau. There's nothing

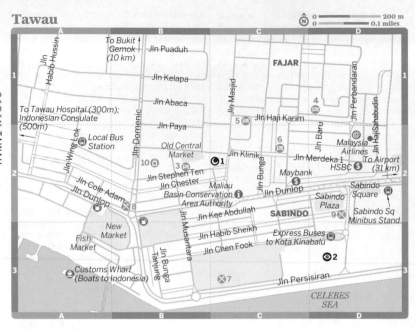

Tawau

◉ Sights
1 Mosque...C2
2 Public Library.....................................D3

🛏 Sleeping
3 Hotel Soon Yee B2
4 Kingston Executive Hotel...................D1
5 Monaco Hotel......................................C1
6 Shervinton Executive Hotel C2

✴ Eating
7 Hawker Seafood C3
8 Restoran Azura...................................B2
Restoran Azura.........................(see 9)
9 Sabindo Hawker Centre....................D2

🛍 Shopping
10 Servay Department Store..................B2

particularly *bad* we can write about this town, but (forgive us the pun) there's not a lot of 'wow' in Tawau either. This may be one of Sabah's larger cities, and it's the state's major border crossing to Indonesia – Kalimantan is just to the south. Apart from that? Not much. But if you're heading to Semporna or the Maliau Basin, there's a good chance you'll be passing through. And hey

– the people *are* friendly, the food is decent and the lodging is a pretty good deal. Just don't expect much past this and you'll likely leave satisfied after eating the great scoop of vanilla ice cream that is Tawau.

Tawau is the only crossing point with Kalimantan where foreigners can get a visa to enter Indonesia.

◉ Sights

Bukit Gemok Forest Reserve NATURE RESERVE (adult/child RM5/1) Located 10km from Tawau town centre, this reserve is a gem, and the best option for those who need to while away a day here. Developed in the early 1990s, the jungle is filled with chattering monkeys, and has become popular with trekkers, Hash House Harriers runners and tour groups – many consider it to be far better than the trails around Poring Hot Springs. The most popular trail is a demanding one-hour (if you're fit!) jaunt up **Lim Man Kui Quarry Hill**, a slate-grey knife of rock. It's a huff to make it to the top, but the stunning views from the top are worth it, as is your casual disbelief at the middle-aged Chinese fitness nuts who *jog* up this track on a regular basis.

Within the reserve, a 231m **canopy walkway** offers lovely views of the surrounding countryside and Tawau itself.

Be on the lookout for the relatively enormous (15cm) seeds of the gourd *Alsomitra macrocarpa*; the seeds are flattened into aerodynamic pancakes and regularly glide hundreds of metres through the forest; they're fairly breathtaking to watch in flight. A taxi to the park costs RM30 – make sure your driver either waits for you or is willing to come back and pick you up, as there's little public transport out this way.

🛏 Sleeping

Splurge for a midrange option if you're stopping through. They cater to local businessmen and are excellent value – miles beyond anything you can get in KK. Jalan Bunga and Haji Karim are packed with options. Budget digs tend to be pretty dire.

Shervinton Executive Hotel   HOTEL $$
(Map p98; ☎770000; www.shervintonhotel.com; Jln Bunga; r/ste from RM98/200; ❉🛜) The Shervinton is the brightest, most well-lit and freshest option in the city centre. An on-site spa, salon and gym facility (there's even a bakery!) make this a surprisingly luxurious option.

Monaco Hotel   HOTEL $
(Map p98; ☎769911/2/3; Jln Haji Karim; r from RM80; ❉) It's not the Riviera – there's no oversized sunglasses or suave men in tuxedos playing baccarat in this version of Monaco. Instead: an exterior painted a shade of yellow that may make your eyes bleed, offset by quite lovely interior rooms done up like the Holiday Inn, Malaysia-style.

Kingston Executive Hotel   HOTEL $$
(Map p98; ☎702288; 4581-4590 Jln Haji Karim; d RM80-100; ❉@) The title of this hotel may seem ambitious, but this 'executive' is nonetheless quite excellent value-for-money. It's a cheering attempt at emulating boutique quirk, an odd experience in sedate Tawau. Some rooms have duvets made from *kain songket* (traditional Malay handwoven fabric with gold threads).

Hotel Soon Yee   HOTEL $
(Map p98; ☎772447; 1362 Jln Stephen Tan; r RM30-35; ❉) Soon Yee is a backpacker standard. There are no phones, no hot water, but there is lots of camaraderie and character. Cheaper fan-cooled rooms have shared bathrooms.

🍴 Eating

Locals love splurging on the buffet lunch at the Belmont Marco Polo which, for RM18 (RM33 on weekends), is a steal considering the variety of tasty bites. The interior courtyard around the Kingston Hotel has a few local haunts serving up tasty dishes, and there's cheap Chinese *kedai kopi* along Jalan Bunga; most open around 7am and close

---

TAWAU TREATS

Thanks to Tawau's proximity to Indonesia and large population of Indonesians, Filipinos, Bajau and Hakka Chinese, the town has developed some worthwhile culinary specialities. All of the following can be found in almost any of Tawau's *kedai kopi* (coffee shops) and in the Sabindo Hawker Centre:

Mee Jawa Javanese-style noodles, the Javanese take on Asia's ubiquitous noodle soup. This version comes with a yellowish broth swimming with bean sprouts, groundnuts, bean curd, fish balls, the occasional prawn and sometimes (interestingly), sweet potato, plus the usual garlic, shallots, chillies and shrimp paste.

Gado gado A deliciously simple Indonesian speciality: vegetable salad with prawn crackers and peanut sauce. The glory of *gado* is the variations of the standard recipe – every cook and hawker puts a different spin on it.

Nasi Kuning Rice cooked with coconut milk and turmeric, hence the English translation of the name: 'yellow rice'. In Tawau, it is often wrapped and served in a banana leaf with deep-fried fish and eaten on special occasions.

Soto Makassar Oh yes! Soto (also spelled 'coto' and pronounced 'cho-to') Makassar is buffalo/beef soup from Southern Sulawesi, Indonesia. The dark broth is made incredibly rich by the addition of buffalo/cow blood, and enriched by a plethora of some 40 spices, plus beef heart, liver, tripe and brain. If you have a weak stomach, ignore those ingredients and trust us: this stuff is *delicious*, like liquid essence of beef spiced with all the wonderful herbs and spices of Southeast Asia.

around 10pm. You may notice severe posters around town with pictures of mutilated fish that say *Bom ikan*. *Bom ikan* means 'bomb(ed) fish,' a reference to fish that have been harvested from dynamited coral reefs. The posters warn of the illegality of possessing or selling 'bombed fish'.

Self-caterers should try the **Servay Department Store** (Map p98; Jln Musantara) across from the Old Central Market, for everything from picnic lunches to DVDs of dubious authenticity.

Sabindo Hawker Centre　　　HAWKER $
(Map p98; Jln Waterfront; dishes from RM5; ☺11am-10pm) Located along the Tawau waterfront, Sabindo is the place to come for impeccably fresh street stall food, which, as is often the case in Asia, is the tastiest stuff around. Prices run the gamut from cheap-as-chips soup stalls to Chinese seafood emporiums.

Restoran Azura　　　　INDIAN $
(Map p98; ☎012-863 9934; Jln Dunlop; dishes RM3-6; ☺8am-9pm) Recommended for its tasty South Indian food and snicker-worthy menu, Azura serves up a killer fish-head curry and sundry 'tits-bits'. The noodles are pretty good too. There's another branch at the Sabindo Hawker Centre (Map p98).

ℹ Information

Banks
HSBC (Jln Perbandaran) ATM.
Maybank (☎762333; Jln Dunlop)

Internet Access
City Internet Zone (☎760016; 37 Kompleks Fajar, Jln Perbandaran; per hr RM2-3; ☺9am-midnight)

Tourist Information
Maliau Basin Conservation Area Authority (☎759214; maliaubasin@gmail.com; 2nd fl, UMNO Building; Jln Dunlop) Can provide information on and help arrange visits to the Maliau Basin.

ℹ Getting There & Away

Air
Malaysia Airlines (☎089-761293; Jln Haji Sahabudin) and **AirAsia** (☎089-761946; Jln Bunga) have daily direct flights to KK and KL. **MASwings** (☎1300-883 000) flies to Sandakan twice daily, the afternoon flight continuing to KK.

Bus & Minivan
Kota Kinabalu Daily express buses for KK (RM65, nine hours) leave from behind the Sabindo area in a large dusty lot at 8am and 8pm (not in between).
Sandakan Departs hourly from Sabindo Sq (RM35 to RM40, five hours, 7am to 2pm), one block on a diagonal from the KK terminus, behind the purple Yassin Curry House sign.

GETTING TO INDONESIA: TAWAU TO TARAKAN

Getting to the border Tawau is the only crossing point with Kalimantan where foreigners can get a visa to enter Indonesia. The local Indonesian consulate is known for being fast and efficient – many travellers are in and out in an hour. The consulate is in Wisma Fuji, on Jln Sinn Onn. You can flag down a taxi (RM10) or take a bus from the central bus station (RM0.80). These buses leave every 30 minutes – as the touts swarm around you, say 'Indonesia consulate' and they'll point you to the right vehicle. Ask the driver to drop you off in front of the consulate; to get back, just stand by the road and flag a bus or minibus down to return to the city centre for a similar fare.

Visa applications are processed between 9:30am to 2pm Monday to Friday. You technically need to either provide proof of onward travel or a credit card, which consulate staff will make a copy of. A 60-day tourist visa will run RM170 and require two passport photos. Bank on spending at least one night in town before shipping off to Indonesia, given the ferry departure schedule, and bring extra cash to the consulate, as there are no ATMs nearby.

Ferry companies Tawindo Express and Indomaya Express make the three- to four-hour trip to Tarakan (RM140; 11.30am Monday, Wednesday and Friday, 10.30am Tuesday, Thursday and Saturday) and the one-hour trip to Nunukan (RM65; 10am and 3pm daily except Sunday). We recommend showing up at least 60 minutes before departure to get a ticket; less than that is cutting it fine. A taxi ride to the ferry terminal costs RM5.

At the border Blue minivans in Tarakan can get you around the city for Rp3000; expect to pay around Rp20,000 to get to the airport.

That's also the spot for frequent minivans to the following:

Semporna (RM15, two hours)
Lahad Datu (RM15, three hours)

ℹ Getting Around

TO/FROM THE AIRPORT

The airport is 28km from town along the main highway to Semporna and Sandakan. A shuttle bus (RM15) to the local bus station in Tawau's centre leaves six times daily. A taxi costs RM45.

Tawau Hills Park

Hemmed in by agriculture and human habitation, this small reserve has forested hills rising dramatically from the surrounding plain. The **park** (admission RM10) is intended to protect the water catchment for settlements in the area, but not before most of the accessible rainforest had been logged. Much of the remaining forest clings to steep-sided ridges that rise to 1310m Gunung Magdalena.

If getting into the Maliau Basin or Danum Valley feels like too much of an effort, consider Tawau Hills a user-friendly alternative. The forest here may not be as primevally awesome, but it's still impressively thick jungle, and the trails are quite easy on your feet. On a clear day the Tawau Hills Park's peaks make a fine sight.

The first trail leads along the Sungai Tawau (chattering with birds like a Disney movie when we attempted it) for 2.5km to **Bukit Gelas Falls** that, when not swarmed with school groups and tourists, is perfectly picturesque. Another track leads 3.2km to a group of 11 **hot springs** that are frankly as impressive as anything you'll see in Poring; locals believe the *ubat kulit* (skin medication) water has medicinal properties. If the above doesn't appeal, you can always take a quick 30-minute walk to **Bombalai Hill** (530m) to the south – the views from here are also quite rewarding.

There's accommodation at **Tawau Hills Park** (Taman Bukit Tawau; ☏089-918827/768719, 019-800 9607; camping/dm/chalet RM5/20/200). Rates are lower on weekdays. Both dorms and chalets are utilitarian, and there's not much reason to stay here unless you can't stomach a night somewhere else. If you want to camp, you'll need to bring all of your own equipment.

Tawau Hills is 28km northwest of Tawau. A taxi will cost about RM30 to RM40.

Maliau Basin Conservation Area

In the minds of most travellers, and certainly the entire marketing division of Malaysia's tourism board, Sabah is associated with wild adventure. But while there are many wild stretches of Sabah, this state has also been heavily impacted by logging, oil palm and, on a smaller scale, suburban sprawl.

This pocket of truly untouched, Eden-as-God-made-it wilderness remains. Hemmed in by mountains, separated by distance and altitude and expanse, the Maliau Basin Conservation Area (MBCA), known very appropriately as 'Sabah's Lost World', is...well, something special.

The basin is exactly that – a bowl-shaped depression of rainforest that was unnoticed by the world until a pilot almost crashed into the walls that hem it off in 1947. Run by the Sabah Foundation, this is the single best place in Borneo to experience old-growth tropical rainforest. More than that, it is one of the world's great reserves of biodiversity, a dense knot of almost unbelievable genetic richness. A visit to the basin is always a poignant affair, as you'll share the road with a parade of logging trucks hauling trees out of the forest at an astonishing rate.

Unbelievably, there is no known record of human beings entering the basin until the early 1980s (although it is possible that indigenous peoples entered the basin before that time). It is only recently that the area has been opened up to a limited number of adventurous travellers. Getting here requires time and resources, and officially a lot of money, although there may be ways around the latter.

◉ Sights & Activities

The trek through the Maliau Basin will likely be the most memorable hike of your Borneo experience. The density of the old-growth forest is striking, and as it is more remote than the Danum Valley, the preserved wildlife is even better. That said: you are in the jungle, and wildlife is not easy to spot. You may walk away without seeing anything but some of Borneo's most ancient trees, which isn't so bad, really.

Several treks are possible in the basin, ranging from short nature walks around **Agathis Camp** to the multiday slog to the rim of the basin via **Strike Ridge Camp**. The vast majority of visitors to the basin under-

INDEPENDENT EXPEDITIONS TO THE MALIAU BASIN

Private tour operators or employees of Sabah Tourism will tell you it is not possible to visit the Maliau basin without a prior tour arrangement, but we have found this is not necessarily true. With that said, you'll probably need at least RM1000 (and a fair bit of elbow grease) to make the following plan work, so this isn't an entirely budget proposal:

It's best to first contact the **Maliau Basin Conservation Area Authority** (☏089-759214; maliaubasin@gmail.com; 2nd fl, UMNO Building, Jln Dunlop) in Tawau. You may need to show up to the office in person, as this is not a tourism body accustomed to dealing with visitors. You can also try driving to the park entrance from Tawau (2½ hours) or KK (at least five hours); a 2WD Proton can make the trip with cautious driving, while a motorbike would be dodgy but doable.

To get into the park you need to pay an administration fee (RM60), a vehicle entry fee (RM5 per vehicle), and if you stay overnight, a conservation fee (RM50). If you plan to hike (and what else are you going to do?) you *must* hire a guide, which costs RM200 per day. The different camps in the basin cost RM180 to RM205 per person per night for a room; some offer dorm beds for RM70, and you can camp in your own tent for RM30. Meals can be taken in the guesthouses for RM40/50/60 per person for breakfast/lunch/dinner. You can also arrange meals while trekking; this requires a porter and costs RM70/100/130 for breakfast/lunch/dinner.

We have talked with travellers who were able to arrange all of the above at the park entrance without even stopping by the Tawau office. Our sense is this scenario will not be possible if a flood of travellers starts pounding on the basin's gates, so you may still want to check with the Tawau office before coming all the way out here. Ideally, if you're not buying the package tour, we advise prearranging your tour with the office in Tawau.

take a three-day, two-night loop through the southern section of the basin that we'll call the Maliau Loop. This brilliant route takes in wide swaths of diverse rainforest and four of the basin's waterfalls: **Takob Falls**, **Giluk Falls**, **Maliau Falls** and **Ginseng Falls**.

Do not attempt the trek unless you are in excellent shape (in fact, Borneo Nature Tours will require a letter from a doctor testifying to your ability to undertake the trek). Your tour operator will supply a guide and porters to carry your food. You'll be in charge of your day pack, camera, leech socks, walking clothes and dry kit for the evening.

A **canopy walkway** stretches near the Basin study centre, and it is pretty astounding to walk its length amid rainforest canopy that has never felt a human cut.

🛏 Sleeping

Accommodation in the Maliau is in the form of simple camps, which range from basic bunkhouses to wood-frame two-storey huts with private bedrooms. None of the camps are luxurious, but after a day on the trail fighting leeches, they'll seem like paradise.

There are two ways to get here. **Borneo Nature Tours** (☏088-267637; www.borneonaturetours.com; Lot 10, ground fl, Block D, Kompleks Sadong Jaya) and affiliated agents offer a five-day, four-night all-inclusive tour of the Maliau for RM5220 per person for two to three people (this can go as low as RM4360 per person for a group of 10 to 15). The package is purposefully cost prohibitive to eliminate those who aren't the most die-hard nature fans.

The other way is via your own steam and initiative. This method is not anywhere as easy as booking a tour, and it's not dirt cheap either, but it's a bit more affordable.

ⓘ Information

The Maliau Basin is located in the southern part of central Sabah, just north of the logging road that connects Tawau with Keningau.

The basin is part of the Yayasan Sabah Forest Management Area, a vast swath of forest in southeastern Sabah under the management of **Yayasan Sabah** (www.ysnet.org.my), a semi-governmental body tasked with both developing and protecting the natural resources of Sabah.

The **MBCA security gate** is just off the Tawau–Keningau Rd. From the gate, it's a very rough 25km journey to the **Maliau Basin Studies Centre**, for researchers, and about 20km to **Agathis Camp**, the base camp for most visitors to the basin.

ℹ️ Getting There & Away

There is no reliable public transport to the park, so you either need to drive yourself or arrange transport. Borneo Nature Tours will handle all transport if you book through them.

Minibus

Minibuses occasionally ply the route bringing loggers to their camps, but this isn't a regular service and cannot be relied upon.

Car & Motorbike

Although the road here is not paved, there is gravel all along the route, and the basin can even be reached by motorbike. Drive carefully and take some jerry cans of petrol. A small shop at Batu 41, 15km from the park entrance, sells expensive petrol, but we can't guarantee its hours. Once at the security gate to the park, you'll have to take a dirt track to Agathis Camp. Rangers may transfer you if you're worried about driving your car.

Van

If you've prearranged with the Maliau Basin Conservation Area Authority in Tawau, that office may get a minivan to take you to the park entrance for RM650. In the park, rangers can arrange vans to take you back to Tawau or Keningau (closer to KK) for a similar price.

SOUTHWESTERN SABAH

The Crocker Range is the backbone of southwestern Sabah, separating coastal lowlands from the wild tracts of jungle in the east. Honey-tinged beaches scallop the shores from KK down to the border, passing the turbid rivers of the Beaufort Division. Offshore you'll find Pulau Tiga, forever etched in the collective consciousness as the genesis site for the eponymous reality show *Survivor,* and Pulau Labuan, centre of the region's oil industry and the transfer point for ferries heading onto Sarawak and Brunei.

The Interior

Sabah's interior constitutes some of the wildest territory in the state, and the best place for accessing this largely unexplored hinterland is via the southwest part of the state.

The landscape is dominated by the Crocker Range, which rises near Tenom in the south and runs north to Mt Kinabalu. The range forms a formidable barrier to the interior of the state and dominates the eastern skyline from Kota Kinabalu down to Sipitang. Once across the Crocker Range, you descend into the green valley of the Sungai Pegalan that runs from Keningau in the south and to Ranau in the north. The heart of the Pegalan Valley is the small town of Tambunan, around which you'll find a few low-key attractions.

CROCKER RANGE NATIONAL PARK

Much of the Crocker Range has been gazetted as Crocker Range National Park. The main means of accessing this landscape by foot is via the Salt Trail (Salt Trails; ☎088-553500; www.sabahparks.org.my/eng/crocker_range_park/salt_trail.asp), a series of four treks that trace the path of traditional trade routes across the mountains. At their shortest the trails can be completed in half a day; the longest route, the Inobong-Terian-Buayan-Kionop-Tikolod trail, takes three days to finish (if you're fit!). At the time of writing the tourism infrastructure around the salt trails was quite minimal, making this an excellent adventure for DIY trekkers who want to get off Sabah's package tourism trail. You'll need to get in touch with Crocker Range National Park to organise guides.

Even if you're not trekking, the Crocker Range and Pegalan Valley make a nice jaunt into rural Sabah for those with rental vehicles. As you make your way over the range between KK and Tambunan, you'll be treated to brilliant views back to the South China Sea and onward to Mt Trus Madi.

TAMBUNAN

Nestled among the green curves of the Crocker Hills, Tambunan, a small agricultural service town about 81km from KK, is the first settlement you'll come to in the range. The region was the last stronghold of Mat Salleh, who became a folk hero for rebelling against the British in the late 19th century. Sadly, Salleh later blew his reputation by negotiating a truce, which so outraged his own people that he was forced to flee to the Tambunan plain, where he was eventually killed.

👁 Sights

Tambunan Rafflesia Reserve NATURE RESERVE (☎088-898500; admission RM5; ⊙8am-3pm) Near the top of the Crocker Range, next to the main highway 20km from Tambunan, is this park devoted to the world's largest flower. The Rafflesia is a parasitic plant that grows hidden within the stems of jungle vines until it bursts into bloom, at which point it eerily resembles the monster plant from *Little Shop of Horrors*. The large bulbous flowers can be up to 1m in diameter. The 12 or so species of Rafflesia here are found only in Borneo and Sumatra; several species are unique to Sabah, but as they only bloom for a few days it's hard to predict when you'll be able to see one. Rangers can guide you into the jungle reserve for the day for RM100. Keningau-bound buses will stop here if you ask the driver to let you off, but getting back to Tambunan will require hitching on the highway. A round-trip taxi from Tambunan costs RM100, which includes waiting time.

🛏 Sleeping

Tambunan Village Resort Centre RESORT $$
(TVRC; ☎087-774076; http://tvrc.tripod.com; 24 Jln TVRC; r & chalets RM60-110; ❄) The main accommodation game is this quirky resort, located some 2km from the tiny town centre. The staff at the centre can help arrange trips up Mt Trus Madi. If you're driving here from KK, the centre is just south of the Shell station on the main road.

❶ Getting There & Away

BUS & MINIVAN

Regular minivans ply the roads between Tambunan and KK (RM15, 1½ hours), Ranau (RM15, two hours), Keningau (RM10, one hour) and Tenom (RM15, two hours). KK–Tenom express buses also pass through, though you may have to ask them to stop. The minivan shelter is in the middle of Tambunan town. Minivans to KK pass the entrance to the Rafflesia reserve; you'll usually be charged for the whole trip to KK.

MT TRUS MADI

About 20km southeast of Tambunan town is the dramatic **Mt Trus Madi**, Sabah's second-highest peak, rising to 2642m. Although logging concessions encircle the mount, the upper slopes and peak are wild and jungle-clad and classified as forest reserve. Ascents are possible, however it's more challenging than Mt Kinabalu, and more difficult to arrange. Independent trekkers must be well equipped and bring their own provisions up the mountain. It is possible to go by 4WD (RM500) up to about 1500m, from where it is a five- to seven-hour climb to the top. There are places to camp halfway up the mountain and on the summit. Before setting off, you are strongly advised to hire a guide (RM200) or at least get maps and assistance from the Tambunan Village Resort Centre or **Forestry Department** (Jabatan Perhutanan; ☎089-660811,

087-774691) in Tambunan. Bring winter clothes, as it gets cold towards the peak, and be prepared for a long, muddy slog.

You can get here on your own, but it's far easier to organise with a tour company. **Tropical Mountain Holidays** (☎013-545 7643, 013-549 2730; http://www.tropicalmountainholidaysmalaysia.com), based in KK, specializes in Trus Madi ascents. Their 2-day, 1-night climb up the mountain, which includes transfer from KK, runs US$300 per person, which is close to what you'll pay if you hire guides and your own vehicle to get out here.

KENINGAU

If you have a bent for the bucolic, you'll probably want to skip Keningau – this busy service town has a touch of urban sprawl about it, and most visitors only pass through to pick up transport, use an ATM or stock up on supplies. As far as attractions go, you might check out **Taipaek-gung**, a colourful Chinese temple in the middle of town, and the large **tamu** (market) held every Thursday.

For a sleepover, try **Hotel Juta** (☎087-337888; www.sabah.com.my/juta; Lg Milimewa 2; standard/superior d from RM175; ❄), which towers over the busy town centre. It's convenient to transport, banking and shopping needs, and rooms are nicely appointed in the Western-businessman style. There is a restaurant on the premises. Shabbier options include the nearby **Crown Hotel** (☎087-338555; Lg Milimewa; standard/superior d from RM40).

There are eight daily express buses to/from KK (RM15, 2½ hours) and four to/from Tenom (RM8, one hour). These buses stop at the Bumiputra Express stop on the main road across from the Shell station. Minivans and share taxis operate from several places in town, including a stop just north of the express bus stop; they all leave when full. There are services to/from KK (RM44, 2½ hours), Ranau (RM25, three hours) and Tenom (RM10, one hour).

TENOM

This sleepy little town at the southern end of the Crocker Range has seen better days but still manages to be more attractive than traffic-choked Keningau. Tenom was closely involved in uprisings against the British in 1915, led by the famous Murut chief Ontoros Antonom, and there's a **memorial** to the tribe's fallen warriors off the main road. Most people pass through Tenom on their way to the nearby Sabah Agricultural Park.

If you somehow get stuck in town, spend the night at **Orchid Hotel** (☑087-737600; Jln Tun Mustapha; s/d RM40/50; ﷽) Rooms are clean and well kept and good value for money. There are cheaper hotels in the vicinity, but they're all a bit musty.

Minivans operate from the *padang* (field) in front of the Hotel Sri Perdana. Destinations include Keningau (RM10, one hour) and KK (RM42, two to four hours depending on stops). There are also regular services to Tambunan (RM15, two hours). Taxis congregate at a rank on the west side of the *padang*.

SABAH AGRICULTURAL PARK

Heaven on earth for horticulturists: the vast **Sabah Agricultural Park** (Taman Pertanian Sabah; ☑087-737952; www.sabah.net.my/agripark; adult/child RM25/10; ◷9am-4.30pm Tue-Sun), about 15km northeast of Tenom, is run by the Department of Agriculture and covers about 6 sq km. Originally set up as an orchid centre, the park has expanded to become a major research facility, tourist attraction and offbeat campsite (RM10), building up superb collections of rare plants such as hoyas, and developing new techniques for use in agriculture, agroforestry and domestic cultivation.

Flower gardens and nature paths abound and a minizoo lets you get up close and personal with some farm animals and deer. Exploring by bicycle would be a good idea, but the fleet of rental bikes here has just about rusted to the point of immobility; if they've replaced them by the time you arrive, rentals cost RM3. There is a free 'train' (it's actually more like a bus) that does a 1½-hour loop of the park, leaving from outside the reception hourly from 9.30am to 3.30pm. If you're truly taken with the park, there's a bare bones on-site **hostel** (dm RM25), which is sometimes taken up by visiting school groups.

Take a minivan from Tenom heading to Lagud Seberang (RM5). Services run throughout the morning, but dry up in the late afternoon. Tell the driver you're going to Taman Pertanian. The park entrance is about 1km off the main road. A taxi from Tenom will cost around RM90.

SAPULOT & BATU PUNGGUL

Perhaps even more so than the Maliau Basin, this is as remote as it gets in Sabah. Not far from the Kalimantan border, **Batu Punggul** is a jungle-topped limestone outcrop riddled with caves, towering nearly 200m above Sungai Sapulot. This is deep in Murut country and the stone formation was one of several sites sacred to these people. Batu Punggul and the adjacent Batu Tinahas are traditionally believed to be longhouses that gradually transformed into stone. The view from the upper reaches of Batu Punggul may be the best in Sabah – in every direction is deep jungle, knife-like limestone outcrops and, if you are lucky, swinging orangutans. It can be difficult and expensive to get here, but this is a beautiful part of Sabah that few tourists visit, and it offers a chance to rub shoulders with the jungle Murut. It is almost impossible to get out here on your own, as there is virtually no tourism infrastructure and English is almost nonexistent, but even the most independent traveller will likely enjoy booking through Orou Sapulot.

TOP CHOICE **Orou Sapulot** CULTURAL (☑016-311 0056; www.orousapulot.com/; 3-day/2-night around per person RM750) Orou ('sun' in Murut) Sapulot is an excellent means of accessing the deepest areas of Sabah's interior. Run by Silas Gunting, a descendant of the local Murut who is now a successful KK businessman, Orou is one of the more innovative eco-tourism projects in the state, and offers what may be the best package tour in Sabah.

The trip encompasses the **Romol Eco Village**, a modern longhouse homestay where visitors live with the Murut; the **Pungiton** ('bat' in Murut) Caves, an extensive cavern system that resembles a bat-shit-laced cheese wheel, complete with rushing underground rivers and enormous underground chambers plucked from a cathedral; an **eco-camp** by Pungiton located on the banks of a heavenly river; a trip to the crystalline **Kabulungou** waterfalls, and finally, a river trip to Batu Pungull, along a chocolate-brown river hemmed in by primary rainforest. You will get the chance to swim in this river, and let us tell you: swimming through virgin jungle is as Edenic as life gets.

All the while, Orou is doing good work. It is common in Sabah for poorer indigenous communities to sell their lands to palm oil and timber companies; the liquid assets they gain are usually spent within a few years. By employing local Murut and encouraging their families to keep their lands and preserve them for eco-tourism purposes, Orou is trying to stave off the worst ecological and economic impacts of this trend while providing a sustainable income for the communities of Sabah's interior.

The above prices are estimated rates that take in all of the activities mentioned above. To offset costs, Orou prefers groups of travellers, but single travellers or small groups are encouraged as well; you will likely be folded into a larger group. In KK, Sticky Rice and Adventure Alternative Borneo (p45) are Orou Sapulot's preferred booking agencies.

Beaufort Division

This shield-shaped peninsula, popping out from Sabah's southwestern coast, is a marshy plain marked with curling rivers and fringed by golden dunes. Tourists with tight travel schedules should consider doing a wildlife river cruise at Klias or Garama if they don't have time to reach Sungai Kinabatangan. Yes, the Kinabatangan is better, but packs of proboscis monkeys can still be spotted here and it's only a day trip from KK. You can book trips to Beaufort, Weston and the Klias and Garama rivers in any KK travel agency.

BEAUFORT

Born as a timber town, Beaufort has reinvented itself with the proliferation of palm-oil plantations. A suitable pit stop for tourists travelling between Sabah and Sarawak, this sleepy township is the gateway to white-water rapids on the **Sungai Padas** and the monkey-filled Klias and Garama areas. The Sungai Padas divides Beaufort into two sections: the aptly named Old Town with its weathered structures, and New Town, a collection of modern shophouses on flood-phobic stilts.

◉ Sights & Activities

Memorial Stone   MEMORIAL
(Jln Tugu) There's a small monument to Private Thomas Leslie Starcevich, an Australian WWII veteran. In 1945, Starcevich single-handedly overwhelmed a Japanese machine-gun position, for which he received the Victoria Cross, the British military's highest decoration. The stone is at the bottom of a small embankment and is marked by brown signs and an arch.

RAFTING

White-water rafting enthusiasts can book a river trip with **Riverbug** (☑088-260501; www.riverbug.asia; Wisma Sabah, Jln Fuad Stephen), the premier operator in the area. Scuba Junkie, which runs a very popular dive centre in Semporna has an affiliated river-rafting outfit here called, appropriately, **River Junkie** (☑019-6012145; www.river-junkie.com; Wisma Sabah, Jln Fuad Stephen), which comes highly recommended by travellers. Day trips organised out of KK cost around RM200 to RM400 per person, depending on what package you choose. The cheapest options involve leisurely boat tours and proboscis monkey spotting; more expensive tours include white-water rafting expeditions and side trips to sites like the Mari Mari Cultural Village (Riverbug also offers a combo paintball day!). All trips include transfers by van, and normally require 24 hours' advance notice. Tourists who seek more serene waters can ride the rapids of Sungai Kiulu (bookable through the aforementioned operators), which is located near Mt Kinabalu and calm enough to be popular with families.

🛏 Sleeping

There's really no need to spend the night in Beaufort, but if you must, then try the **MelDe Hotel** (☑087-222266; 9-20 Lo Chung Park, Jln Lo Chung; s/d/ste from RM70/80/90; ❄) The rooms are a bit crusty in the corners, but it's passable for a night's sleep while in transit. Go for a room on one of the upper floors – they have windows. The Chinese restaurant under the inn is very popular with locals. MelDe is located in Old Town. If you're stopping in town for a bite, make sure you try a pomelo (football-sized citrus fruit) and local *mee Beaufort* (Beaufort noodles) – both are locally famous.

❶ Getting There & Away

BUS

Express buses operate from near the old train station at the south end of Jln Masjid (the ticket booth is opposite the station). There are departures at 9am, 1pm, 2.15pm and 5pm for KK (RM10, 1½ hours). There are departures at 9.10am, 10.30am, 1.45pm and 6.20pm for Sipitang (RM5, 1½ hours). The KK to Lawas express bus passes through Beaufort at around 3pm; the trip from Beaufort to Lawas costs RM15 and takes 1¾ hours.

MINIVANS

Minivans operate from a stop across from the mosque, at the north end of Jln Masjid. There are frequent departures for KK (RM10, two hours), and less-frequent departures for Sipitang (RM12, 1½ hours), Lawas (RM15, 1¾ hours) and Kuala Penyu (RM8, until around 2.30pm, one hour). To Menumbok (for Labuan) there are plenty of minivans until early afternoon (RM10, one hour).

TAXIS

Taxis depart from the stand outside the old train station, at the south end of Jln Masjid. Charter rates include: KK (RM70), Kuala Penyu (RM55), Sipitang (RM35), Menumbok (RM50) and Lawas (RM100).

KUALA PENYU

Tiny Kuala Penyu, at the northern tip of the peninsula, is the jumping-off point for Pulau Tiga if you are not accessing 'Survivor Island' via the new boat service from KK. From KK, minivans leave from behind Wawasan Plaza (RM10 to RM15, two hours). From Beaufort minivans to Kuala Penyu (RM10) leave throughout the morning, but return services tail off very early in the afternoon, so you may have to negotiate a taxi or local lift back. A minivan to/from Menumbok costs RM65 per vehicle.

TEMPURUNG

Tempurung Seaside Lodge (☏088-773066; http://www.borneotempurung.com/; 3 Putatan Point; 2-day, 1-night package from RM310), set along the quiet coastal waters of the South China Sea, is a good spot for hermits who seek a pinch of style. The main lodge was originally built as a vacation home, but friends convinced the owners that it would be a crime not to share the lovely property with the world. Rooms are scattered between several chalet-style bungalows accented with patches of jungle thatch. The packages include fantastic meals. Nightly rates are also available.

Borneo Express (☏in KK 012-830 7722, in Limbang 085-211 384, in Miri 012-823 7722) runs buses from KK (departing from Wawasan) at 6.45am, 10am and 12.30pm daily. Ask the driver to let you off at the junction with the large Kuala Penyu sign. The bus will turn left (south) to head towards Menumbok; you want to go right (north) in the direction of Kuala Penyu. If you arranged accommodation in advance, the lodge van can pick you up here (it's too far to walk). Buses pass the junction at 9.30am and 3.30pm heading back to KK. If you're driving, take a right at the junction and keep an eye out for the turn-off on the left side of the road just before Kuala Penyu. We suggest calling the lodge for directions. A charter taxi from Beaufort will cost about RM50.

KLIAS

The tea-brown Sungai Klias looks somewhat similar to the mighty Kinabatangan, offering short-stay visitors a chance to spend an evening in the jungle cavorting with saucy primates. There are several companies offering two-hour river cruises. We recommend Borneo Authentic (p46), the first operator to set up shop in the region. Trips include a large buffet dinner and a short night walk to view the swarms of fireflies that light up the evening sky like Christmas lights. Cruises start at dusk (around 5pm), when the sweltering heat starts to burn off and animals emerge for some post-siesta prowling.

There is no accommodation in Klias, although Borneo Authentic can set you up with one of its comfy rooms at the Tempurung Seaside Lodge nearby. Tourists can make their own way to the row of private jetties 20km west of Beaufort, however, most trip takers usually sign up for a hassle-free day trip from KK (which ends up being cheaper since you're sharing transport).

GARAMA

Narrower than the river in Klias, the Sungai Garama is another popular spot for the popular river-cruise day trips from KK. Chances of seeing fireflies are slim, but Garama is just as good as Klias (if not better) when it comes to primate life. Gangs of proboscis monkeys and long-tailed macaques scurry around the surrounding floodplain offering eager tourists plenty of photo fodder.

Like Klias, the tours here start at around 5pm (with KK departures at 2pm), and after a couple of hours along the river, guests chat about the evening's sightings over a buffet dinner before returning to KK. There are several operators offering Garama river tours; we prefer **Only in Borneo** (☏088-260506; www.oibtours.com; package tour RM190), an offshoot of Traverse Tours. It has a facility along the shores of Sungai Garama and offers an overnight option in prim dorms or double rooms.

It is technically possible to reach Garama with one's own vehicle, but the network of unmarked roads can be tricky and frustrating. We recommend leaving early in the morning from KK if you want to get here on your own steam.

WESTON

The little village of Weston – a couple of shacks clustered around a gold-domed mosque – is the jumping-off point for a gentle yet jungly patch of wetlands that is equal parts serene and overgrown. The area was bombed beyond recognition during WWII, but recent conservation efforts have welcomed groups of curious proboscis monkeys into the tidal marshlands, which are shaded by towering nipa palms and copses of spider-like mangroves. As the tide rolls in and out, entire swaths of jungle are submerged and revealed. Monkeys, monitor lizards, otters and mud skippers flash through the aquatic undergrowth, and as the sun sets, clouds of flying foxes (ie *big* bats) flap in with the darkness.

◎ Sights

Weston Wetland (☎016-813 4300, 013-881 3233; http://westonwetland.blogspot.com/) operates a variety of package tours including river-cruise day trips and sleepovers at its swamp-side longhouse (all-inclusive two-day, one-night package RM250). The dorm facilities are rustic at best, but the quality of the firefly show here is extremely high. Note that the folk at Weston Wetland insist you prebook before visiting.

While you're here, you can ask folk at the lodge to take you to **Che Hwa Schoolhouse**, the oldest wooden school building in Borneo and a fine example of antiquarian Chinese architecture.

MENUMBOK

The tiny hamlet of Menumbok is where you can catch car ferries to the Serasa Ferry Terminal in Muara, 25km northeast of Bandar Seri Begawan (Brunei), and to Pulau Labuan (adult/car RM5/40, departures every hour from 10.30am-3.30pm).

On land, a charter taxi from Beaufort costs RM60, minivans from Kuala Penyu cost RM50 per vehicle. There is a direct bus service connecting Menumbok to KK.

Pulau Tiga National Park

Outwit, outplay and outlast your fellow travellers on what is known throughout the world as 'Survivor Island'. The name Pulau Tiga actually means 'three islands' – the scrubby islet is part of a small chain created during an eruption of mud volcanoes in the late 1890s. Over 100 years later, in 2001, the island had its 15 minutes of fame when it played host to the smash-hit reality TV series *Survivor*. TV junkies still stop by for a look-see, although the 'tribal council' was destroyed in a storm and the debris was cleared after it turned into a home for venomous snakes. Whatever your viewing preferences, it's still a great place for relaxing on the beach, hiking in the forest and taking a cooling dip in burping mud pits at the centre of the island.

◎ Sights & Activities

Pulau Kalampunian Damit ('day-mit,' not 'dammit, I'm on snake island') is little more than a large rock covered in dense vegetation but is famous for the sea snakes that come ashore to mate, hence the island's nickname, **Snake Island**. Sounds like the tourism destination of the 21st century, right? On any one day up to 150 snakes can be present, curled up under boulders, among roots and in tree hollows. It's a fascinating phenomenon, made doubly enigmatic by the fact that the snakes are never seen on nearby Pulau Tiga. Pulau Tiga Resort runs boat trips to the island (RM40 per person), with a stop en route for snorkelling for RM30 extra. You can also dive off the island for RM100 per dive, or RM150 for a fun dive for those with no scuba experience; it's not the best diving in Borneo, but then again, you're in Borneo, so there's plenty of rainbow-coloured fish to peep at.

⌂ Sleeping

Pulau Tiga Resort   RESORT $$
(☎088-240584; www.pulau-tiga.com; 2-day, 1-night package from Kuala Penyu per person RM305-360, from KK RM455-510; ❄) Built to house the production crew for the *Survivor* series (Jeff Probst stayed in cabin E), this compound has been turned into a lovely seaside resort. Accommodation is available in dorm-style 'longhouse' rooms (three beds in each), while more luxurious private cabins have double beds and plenty of air-con. The beach-facing grounds offer amazing views of the sunset, while a detailed map is available for those that want to track down the beach where the Pagong Tribe lived (called Pagong Pagong Beach). There's currently only one staff member who was working here when *Survivor* was being filmed, but the most unpopular guest at the resort is still sent to Snake Island after dinner (joke!).

Sabah Parks CAMPING $

(☏088-211881; www.sabahparks.org.my; Lot 1-3, Block K, Kompleks Sinsuran, Jln Tun Fuad Stephens; r from RM75) Sabah Parks runs more basic lodging (ie block houses) on the island for less affluent survivalists. It's right next door to Pulau Tiga Resort, about 10m from where 'Tribal Council' was once held (sadly, tiki torches no longer line the way). Facilities here are limited and there's no restaurant, though a cooking area is provided.

ℹ Getting There & Away

Boat

From Kuala Penyu the boat ride takes about 20 minutes. Boats leave at 10am and 3pm. Most visitors to Pulau Tiga come as part of a package, in which case transport is included in the price. You can try showing up in Kuala Penyu and asking if you can board one of the day's boats out to the island (we don't recommend this option as priority is given to resort guests with bookings). For Sabah Parks' lodgings try to hop a ride with the Pulau Tiga Resort boat – chartering your own craft costs RM600 at least.

Pulau Labuan

POP 95,500

If you've ever wondered what a cross between a duty-free airport mall and a tropical island would look like, may we recommend the federal district of Pulau Labuan. Some call this Sabah's version of Vegas, and in the sense that Labuan offers both duty-free sin and tacky family fun, we kinda agree. By the way, everything here *is* duty free, because politically, Labuan is governed directly from KL. As such, a lot of the booze you consume and cigarettes you smoke in Sabah and Sarawak is illegally smuggled from Labuan.

The sultan of Brunei ceded Labuan to the British in 1846 and it remained part of the Empire for 115 years. The only interruption came during WWII, when the Japanese held the island for three years. Significantly, it was on Labuan that the Japanese forces in North Borneo surrendered at the end of the war, and the officers responsible for the death marches from Sandakan were tried here.

Bandar Labuan is the main town and the transit point for ferries linking Kota Kinabalu and Brunei.

◉ Sights & Activities

BANDAR LABUAN

Labuan's main settlement is light on character but has a couple of passable attractions.

FREE **Labuan Museum** MUSEUM

(Map p110; ☏414135; 364 Jln Dewan; admission free; ◷9am-5pm) This museum on Jln Dewan takes a glossy, if slightly superficial, look at the island's history and culture, from colonial days, through WWII, to the establishment of Labuan as an independent federal territory. The most interesting displays are those on the different ethnic groups here, including a diorama of a traditional Chinese tea ceremony (the participants, however, look strangely Western).

FREE **Labuan Marine Museum** MUSEUM

(Map p110; ☏425927/414462; Jln Tanjung Purun; admission free; ◷9am-6pm) On the coast just east of the centre, the Labuan International Sea Sports Complex houses a decent little museum with a good shell collection and displays of marine life found in the area. Don't forget to head upstairs where you'll find a 42ft-long skeleton of an Indian fin whale. The real highlight, however, and a guaranteed hit with the kids, is the 'touch pool' opposite reception. This has to be the only shark-petting zoo we've ever seen (fret not: the sharks are less than a metre long).

DIVING

Labuan is famous for its **wreck diving**, with no fewer than four major shipwrecks off the coast (two from WWII and two from the 1980s). The only dive outfit operating here is **Borneo Star Dives** (☏087-429278; stardivers2005@yahoo.com; International Seasports Complex; dive packages from RM438), which does island-hopping tours and can take you out to all four sites. Note that only the 'Cement Wreck' is suitable for novice divers; the 'Blue Water Wreck' (in our opinion, the most impressive of the bunch) requires advanced open-water certification, and the 'American' and 'Australian' wrecks are only recommended for certified wreck divers.

Bandar Labuan

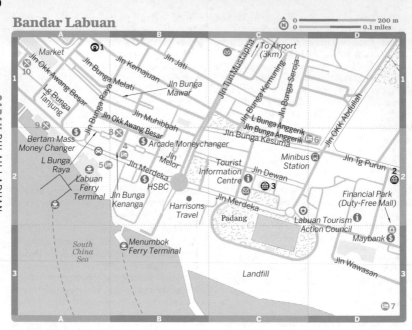

Bandar Labuan

◎ Sights
1. Chinese Temple A1
2. Labuan Marine Museum D2
3. Labuan Museum C2

🛏 Sleeping
4. ASV Backpackers B2
5. Grand Dorsett Labuan A2
6. Mariner Hotel D2
7. Waterfront Labuan Financial
   Hotel D3

✗ Eating
8. Choice Restaurant B2
9. Port View Restaurant A1
10. Restoran Selera Farizah A1

AROUND PULAU LABUAN
**WWII Memorial
(Labuan War Cemetery)** CEMETERY
A dignified expanse of lawn with row upon
row of headstones dedicated to the nearly
4000 Commonwealth servicemen, mostly
Australian and British, who lost their lives
in Borneo during WWII. The cemetery is
near the golf course, about 2km east of town
along Jln OKK Abdullah. A **Peace Park** on
the west of the island at Layang Layangan

commemorates the place of Japanese sur-
render and has a Japanese war memorial.

Labuan Bird Park WILDLIFE RESERVE
(☎463544; adult/child/under 5 RM3/1/free;
⊙10am-5pm, closed Fri) This pretty park offers
refuge to a wide range of species in three
geodesic domes, and a swath of rainforest –
the birds look a little bored, but healthy. The
park is located at the north end of the island
on Jln Tanjung Kubong.

Chimney LANDMARK
Believed to be part of an old coal-mining
station, this is the only historical monument of its kind in Malaysia, and has good
views along the coast. It's at the northeast
tip of the island, best accessed by minibus
or taxi.

Labuan Marine Park PARK
Pulau Kuraman, Pulau Rusukan Kecil and
Pulau Rusukan Besar are uninhabited islands lying southwest of Labuan that are
now protected by the federal government.
The beaches are pristine, but dynamite fishing has destroyed much of the coral. You can
hire boats from the jetty at the Labuan International Sea Sports Complex to explore the
marine park. A day's charter costs around
RM600 per group of six people.

Thanks to financial deregulation Labuan is now the home of some major offshore bank accounts, so you may also want to be on the lookout for men in sunglasses with big briefcases, although we suggest not taking pictures of them.

If you want to dive here, enquire at Borneo Star Dives (p109).

🛏 Sleeping

 Labuan Homestay Programme HOMESTAY $
(✆422622; www.labuantourism.com; 1/2 days incl full board RM65/140) This excellent service matches visitors with a friendly local in one of three villages around the island: Patau Patau 2, Kampong Sungai Labu and Kampong Bukit Kuda. Some of the homes are just as grand as one of the international-class hotels on the waterfront! If you want to be near Bandar Labuan, ask for accommodation at Patau Patau 2 – it's a charming stilt village out on the bay. Stay a bit longer and learn how to make *ambuyat,* also known as 'gluey sago porridge' and Brunei's favourite dish.

If you want to enrol in the program, book online at least a few days in advance.

Grand Dorsett Labuan HOTEL $$$
(Map p110; ✆422000; www.granddorsett.com/labuan; 462 Jln Merdeka; r from RM475; 🅿@🛜🌊) The Grand Dorsett (once a link in the Sheraton chain) has everything you would expect from an international hotel, with five-star rooms, good restaurants and a pub hosting live bands. Weekend rates go down to as low as RM230.

Waterfront Labuan Financial Hotel HOTEL $$
(Map p110; ✆418111; leslbn@tm.net.my; 1 Jln Wawasan; r RM250-580, ste RM580-2150; 🅿🌊) Not just for merchant bankers – this is a large, luxurious leisure hotel which practically feels like a mall, with full facilities and a small marina attached. The rooms are spacious and have a corporate appeal, and some have great sea views. There's a huge outdoor pool and a restaurant.

Mariner Hotel HOTEL $$
(Map p110; ✆418822; mhlabuan@streamyx.com; 468 Jln Tanjung Purun; r from RM110; 🅿@) Pitched at the low-end business-class market, this smart block offers good facilities for the price. Rooms come with fridges, laminate floors and neat, spacious bathrooms.

ASV Backpackers HOSTEL $
(Map p110; ✆413728; asvjau@yahoo.com; Lot U0101, Jln Merdeka; r with shared bathroom RM35; 🅿) No backpacker spots got ANY in its a respectable league – it manages to be cheap while more functionally clean and comfortable than most of the dingy midrangers around town. Shame there's not more, y'know, backpackers in Labuan.

🍴 Eating

Choice Restaurant INDIAN $$
(Map p110; ✆418086; 104 Jln OKK Awang Besar; dishes RM3-10; ⏱8am-10pm) Forget false modesty, the Choice simply proclaims 'We are the best', and this seems to be corroborated by the popularity of the authentic Indian meals with the authentic Indian residents who turn out for *roti,* fish-head curry and *sambal.*

Port View Restaurant SEAFOOD $$
(Map p110; ✆422999; Jln Merdeka; dishes RM15-30; ⏱lunch & dinner) An outpost of the successful Chinese seafood franchise in KK, this waterfront restaurant has air-con indoor seating and outdoor seating that affords a nice view, over Labuan's busy harbour.

Restoran Selera Farizah COFFEE SHOP $
(Map p110; Lg Bunga Tanjung; meals from RM3; ⏱8am-10pm) If you prefer a Muslim *kedai kopi,* you could try this place, which serves *roti,* curries and *nasi campur,* accompanied by pro-wrestling videos.

ℹ Information

Banks
HSBC (✆087-422610; 189 Jln Merdeka)
Maybank (✆087-443888; Financial Park) ATM.

Tourist Information
Labuan Tourism Action Council (✆087-422622; ground fl, Labuan International Sea Sports Complex; ⏱8am-1pm & 2-5pm Mon-Fri) Located about 1km east of the town centre, this is the most useful information office in town. It stocks the excellent *Fly Drive Labuan Island & Town Map of Labuan.*

Tourist Information Centre (✆087-423445; www.labuantourism.com.my; cnr Jln Dewan & Jln Berjaya; ⏱8am-5pm Mon-Fri, 9am-3pm Sat) Tourism Malaysia office. Less useful than Labuan Tourism Action Council.

Harrisons Travel (✆087-408096; www.harrisonstravel.com.my; 1 Jln Merdeka) Handy and reputable travel agency.

GETTING TO BRUNEI: BANDAR LABUAN TO BANDAR SERI BEGAWAN

Getting to the border Ferries to Brunei depart Bandar Labuan daily at 1:30pm, arriving in Brunei's Serasa Ferry Terminal about an hour later. The entire trip for an adult/child costs RM60/38. Aim to show up at the ferry terminal around 12.30pm.

At the border Most visitors are granted a visa on arrival for free, although Australians must pay a fee (see p471 for more information).

Moving on The Serasa Ferry Terminal is 20km northeast of BSB. From here, shuttles can take you to central Bandar Seri Begawan for B$2 (40 minutes). The terminal is linked by ferry with Pulau Labuan, from where boats go to Menumbok in Sabah.

See p465 for details on doing the trip in the opposite direction.

ℹ Getting There & Away

Air

Malaysia Airlines (☎1300-883000; www .malaysiaairlines.com.my) has flights to/from KK (45 minutes) and KL (2½ hours), which are usually booked full of oil prospectors. **AirAsia** (☎480401; www.airasia.com) currently flies to KL only.

Boat

Kota Kinabalu Passenger ferries (1st/economy class RM41/31, 3¼ hours) depart KK for Labuan from Monday to Saturday at 8am, and 1:30pm (3pm Sundays). In the opposite direction, they depart Labuan for KK from Monday to Saturday at 8am and 1pm, and 10:30am and 3pm on Sundays.

Sarawak There are daily speedboats to Limbang (2 hours, RM31) and Lawas (2 hours, 15 minutes, RM34) in Sarawak's Limbang Division.

ℹ Getting Around

Minibus

Labuan has a good minibus network. Minibuses leave regularly, albeit more frequently before sunset, from the parking lot off Jln Tun Mustapha. Fares range from 50 sen for a short trip to RM2.50 for a trip to the top of the island.

Taxi

Taxis are plentiful and there's a stand opposite the local ferry terminal. The base rate is RM10 for short journeys, with most destinations costing around RM15.

Borneo

Wildlife »
Diving »
Culture »

Iban warrior, Sarawak

PETER GUTTMAN/CORBIS ©

Wildlife

Borneo's lush rainforests teem with mammals, birds, amphibians, reptiles and insects, many of them found nowhere else on earth. Most fauna wisely shun the limelight, but in certain places, at the right time of day or in the right season, visitors can glimpse jungle animals in their natural habitats.

Borneo's most charismatic creature is the orangutan, the world's largest tree-dwelling animal, whose human-like form and eerily familiar habits captivate their distant, guidebook-toting cousins. Another primate with extraordinary treetop agility is the proboscis monkey, instantly recognisable by one of evolution's more unexpected adaptations, the male's long, floppy nose. Sabah is also home to about a thousand pygmy elephants.

The island's many colourful birds include eight species of hornbill, but to see them you'll probably have to get up at dawn or linger in the jungle at dusk. The most spectacular is the rhinoceros hornbill, instantly identifiable by some truly impressive avian bling, a red and yellow casque.

TOP WILDLIFE SPOTS

Sungai Kinabatangan (p82) Home to an astonishing variety of wildlife, including wild orangutans and pygmy elephants.

Semenggoh Nature Reserve (p149) Semi-wild orangutans frolic in the jungle canopy just 20 minutes from Kuching.

Bako National Park (p142) The park's coves and trails are one of the best places to spot proboscis monkeys.

Sepilok Orang-Utan Rehabilitation Centre (p77) Semiwild orangutans swing by to dine on fruit.

Gunung Mulu National Park (p180) Discover astonishing stick insects on a ranger-led night walk.

Clockwise from top left
1. Young orangutan, Tanjung Puting National Park (p251)
2. Orchid, Rainforest Discovery Centre (p79) 3. Male wreathed hornbill, Lok Kawi Wildlife Park (p43)
4. Pitcher plant, Maliau Basin (p101)

Diving

The waters off northeastern Borneo are as rich in weird and wonderful species as the island's terrestrial habitats. Somewhat wetter and considerably saltier than Borneo's rainforests, these celebrated reefs shelter a mind-boggling variety of corals, fish and marine mammals, offering some of the finest scuba diving in the world.

Borneo's most spectacular reefs fringe a number of tiny islands off the northeast coast. Amid thriving coral – sea fans can grow to 3km – and a wealth of sponges, divers often encounter shimmering schools of jacks, bumphead parrotfish and barracudas, and find themselves making the acquaintance of green turtles, dolphins, manta rays and several species of shark. Visibility can reach an incredible 30m to 50m, making the area's famed drop-offs – up to 2000m deep! – a truly breathtaking sight. If you've dreamed of experiencing the extraordinary biodiversity and astonishingly vivid hues of the 'Coral Triangle', Borneo offers some great options for your next underwater adventure.

TOP DIVE SITES

Pulau Sipadan (p93) Legendary for its deep wall dives, Sipadan is a favoured hang-out of turtles, sharks and open-ocean fish.

Layang Layang (p70) A deep-ocean island famed for its pristine coral and 2000m drop-off.

Pulau Mantanani (p70) These isolated, coral-ringed islands are prime habitat for dugongs (sea cows).

Mabul (p93) 'Muck dives' often turn up eels, crabs, squid, octopus and frogfish.

Pulau Derawan & Derawan Archipelago (p240 and p239) The area boasts a fantastic assortment of colourful reef fish.

Clockwise from top left
1. Spectacular coral reef, Sipadan 2. Snorkelling at the beach, Sipadan-Mabul region 3. Colourful mandarinfish 4. Diving in the reefs, Sipadan-Mabul region

Culture

Cultural diversity comes naturally to Borneo, where civilisations, languages, religions and culinary traditions have been meeting and mixing for thousands of years. From sophisticated cities with chic urban amenities to remote Dayak longhouses on the upland tributaries of mighty rivers, the island's cultural vibrancy never fails to amaze.

Borneo's indigenous peoples, often known as Dayaks, still joke about their headhunting past, but today many are working to integrate ancient lifestyles based on sustainability and mutual responsibility with the demands and opportunities of modern life. The best way to experience a slice of Dayak tradition is to visit a longhouse.

Many Muslim Malays live in picturesque *kampung* (villages) built on stilts over a river or estuary. Halal meals, including a delicious selection of barbecue meat, grilled fish and scrumptious rice and noodle dishes, are available in open-air markets.

Significant Chinese communities are found in many cities and towns. Each dialect group has its own dragon-adorned temples, community festivities and distinctive culinary traditions.

TOP CULTURAL ATTRACTIONS

Kuching (p124) Borneo's most stylish city is a 'salad bowl' of Chinese, Malay, Dayak, Indian and Western culture.

Kelabit Highlands (p186) The area's famously welcoming people are happy to share their traditions – and their delicious cuisine.

Batang Ai Region (p158) Home to some of Sarawak's most traditional Iban longhouses.

Pegunungan Meratus (Meratus Mountains; p263) Shamans still play an important role in this remote area.

Bandar Seri Begawan (p198) Brunei's Malay traditions live on in the sultanate's water villages and markets.

Clockwise from top left

1. Omar Ali Saifuddien Mosque (p198), Bandar Seri Begawan 2. Dayak woman in traditional dress, Kalimantan 3. Indonesian women at a mosque 4. Tua Pek Kong Temple (p159), Sibu

Vegetables and chillies at Satok Weekend Market (p131), Kuching's biggest and liveliest market

Sarawak

Why Go?

Sarawak makes access to Borneo's natural wonders and cultural riches a breeze. From Kuching, the island's most sophisticated and dynamic city, pristine rainforests – where you can spot orang-utans, proboscis monkeys, killer crocodiles and the world's largest flower, the Rafflesia – can be visited on day trips, with plenty of time in the evening for a delicious meal and a drink in a chic bar. More adventurous travellers can take a 'flying coffin' riverboat up the Batang Rejang, 'the Amazon of Borneo', to seek out remote longhouses, or fly to the spectacular bat caves and extraordinary rock formations of Gunung Mulu National Park, a Unesco World Heritage site. Everywhere you go, you'll encounter the warmth, unforced friendliness and sense of humour that make the people of Malaysia's most culturally diverse state such delightful hosts.

Best Places to Eat

- » Dyak (p134)
- » Top Spot Food Court (p134)
- » Jambu (p134)
- » Summit Cafe (p177)

Best Places to Stay

- » Batik Boutique Hotel (p132)
- » Dillenia Guesthouse (p175)
- » Threehouse B&B (p132)
- » Retreat (p155)

When to Go
Kuching

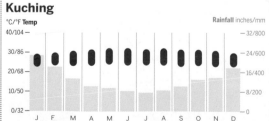

Jul Dayak bands and international artists jam at Kuching's Rainforest World Music Festival.

Jul–Sep It's tourist high season so book flights and treks early.

Nov–Jan Rough seas can make coastal boat travel difficult or impossible.

Sarawak Highlights

1 Watching semi-wild orang-utans swing through the canopy at **Semenggoh Nature Reserve** (p149)

2 Seeing the elusive Rafflesia, the world's largest flower, at **Gunung Gading National Park** (p155)

3 Strolling the Waterfront Promenade in **Kuching** (p124)

4 Spotting endangered proboscis monkeys in **Bako National Park** (p142) or **Kuching Wetlands National Park** (p148)

5 Watching the jungle glide by as you make your way into the very heart of Borneo along

To Pulau Labuan

Bandar Seri Begawan

Merapok

Lawas

Limbang

BRUNEI

Kuala Belait

Seria

Bangar

Kuala Baram

Medamit

SABAH

Miri

Miri Airport

Headhunter's Trail

Limbang Division

Long Semado

Marudi

Gunung Mulu (2377m)

Lambir Hills National Park

Long Terawan

Gunung Mulu National Park

Batu Lawi

Ba Kelalan

Niah National Park

Beluru

Long Seridan

Gunung Murud (2423m)

Long Bawan

Batu Niah

Long Teru

Pulong Tau National Park

Batu Niah Junction

Long Lama

Kelabit Highlands

Long Miri

Bario

Ramudu

Long Lellang

Tama Abu Range

Similajau National Park

Sungai Tinjar

Bintulu Airport

Simpang Bakun (Bakun Junction)

Dulit Range

Long Akah

Lio Matoh

Bintulu

Tubau

Bukit Seludong (1371m)

Long Banga

Batang Kemena

Sungai Asap Longhouses

Sungai Baram

Bukit Semalong (1281m)

Lumut Range

Batang Belaga

Belaga

Bakun Dam

Murum Dam

Sangan

Batang Tatau

Bukit Robertson (1710m)

Sungai Linau

KALIMANTAN

INDONESIA

Batang Rejang

Batang Rejang

Pelagus Rapids

Sungai Mujong

Batang Balui

Long Jawi

Hose Range

Rejang

Kapit

Batang Baleh

Interwau

Sungai Mengiong

Batang Baleh

the **Batang Rejang** (p163), 'Borneo's Amazon'

6 Experiencing longhouse life and Kelabit hospitality in the **Kelabit Highlands** (p186)

7 Ascending to the summit of Gunung Mulu, the highest peak in Borneo's best nature park, or going spelunking in **Gunung Mulu National Park** (p183)

8 Entering a netherworld of stalactites and bats in the caves of **Niah National Park** (p171)

History

After a century of rule by the White Rajahs and four years of Japanese occupation, Sarawak became a British Crown colony in 1946. At Westminster's urging, the territory joined the Malay Peninsula, Sabah and Singapore to form Malaysia in 1963 (Singapore withdrew two years later). At about the same time, neighbouring Indonesia, under the leftist leadership of President Soekarno, laid claim to all of Borneo, including Sarawak, launching a military campaign known as the Konfrontasi (1962–66). Tens of thousands of troops from the UK, Australia and New Zealand were deployed to secure Sarawak's border with Kalimantan.

Since 1981 Sarawak's chief minister has been Abdul Taib Mahmud, who has frequently been accused of corruption, most recently in a 2012 report by the Bruno Manser Fund (www.bmf.ch/en), a Swiss NGO. Entitled 'The Taib Timber Mafia', the dossier identifies Taib as Malaysia's richest man, with a personal fortune estimated at US$15 billion, and accuses him of abusing his office to award timber and other resource concessions to family and friends. In the state assembly elections of 2011, Taib's political coalition, the Barisan Nasional (BN), retained its two thirds majority but is under pressure in the run-up to Malaysia's 2013 federal elections.

KUCHING

POP 600,000

Borneo's most stylish and sophisticated city brings together a kaleidoscope of cultures, crafts and cuisines. The bustling streets – some very modern, others with a colonial vibe – amply reward visitors with a penchant for aimless ambling. Chinese temples decorated with dragons abut shophouses from the time of the White Rajahs, a South Indian mosque is a five-minute walk from stalls selling half-a-dozen Asian cuisines, and a landscaped riverfront park attracts families out for a stroll and a quick bite.

Kuching's other huge asset is its day trip proximity to a dozen first-rate nature sites.

◉ Sights

The main attraction here is the city itself. Leave plenty of time to wander aimlessly and soak up the relaxed vibe and charming cityscapes of areas such as Jln Carpenter (Old Chinatown), Jln India, Jln Padungan (New Chinatown) and the Waterfront Promenade.

Sarawak's excellent museums are free.

WATERFRONT PROMENADE

The **south bank** (Map p126; along Main Bazaar & Jln Gambier; river cruises RM20) of Sungai Sarawak, from the Indian Mosque east to the Hotel Grand Margherita Kuching, has been turned into a watery promenade, with paved walkways, lawns, flowerbeds, a children's playground, cafes and food stalls. It's a fine place for a stroll any time a cool breeze blows off the river, especially at sunset. In the evening the waterfront is ablaze with colourful fairy lights and full of couples and families eating snacks as trans-river *tambang* (small passenger ferries) glide past with their glowing lanterns. The loveliest panoramas are from the bend in the river across from the Hilton. Several companies offer **river cruises** (RM20). The water level is kept constant by a downstream barrage.

The promenade affords great views across the river to the white, crenellated towers and manicured gardens of the Astana; hilltop Fort Margherita, also white and crenellated; and, between the two, the Sarawak State Assembly, with its dramatic, golden pointy roof.

Chinese History Museum   MUSEUM
(Map p126; cnr Main Bazaar & Jln Wayang; ⊘9am-4.45pm Mon-Fri, 10am-4pm Sat, Sun & holidays) Housed in the century-old Chinese Court building, the Chinese History Museum provides an excellent introduction to the nine Chinese communities – each with its own dialect, cuisine and temples – who began settling in Sarawak around 1830. Highlights of the evocative new exhibits, inaugurated in 2011, include ceramics, musical instruments, historic photos and some fearsome dragon and lion dance costumes. The entrance is on the river side of the building.

Square Tower   HISTORIC BUILDING
(Map p126) Along with Fort Margherita, the Square Tower, built in 1879, once guarded the lazy river against marauders. Over the past century, the structure – still emblazoned with Sarawak's Brooke-era coat-of-arms – has served as a prison, a mess and a dance hall; it now houses an art gallery. Nearby Jln Gambier is named after a vine used for tanning and dyeing.

Old Court House Complex   HISTORIC BUILDING
(Map p126; btwn Jln Tun Abang Haji Openg & Jln Barrack) The Old Court House, now officially

called the Sarawak Tourism Complex, was built in the late 1800s to serve as the city's administrative centre. Today, this ensemble of airy, colonnaded structures - well worth a wander – is home to the very helpful Visitors Information Centre and the National Park Booking Office. Out front, across the street from the Square Tower, stands the **Brooke Memorial**, erected in 1924 to honour Charles Brooke.

OLD CHINATOWN

Jalan Carpenter   STREET

(Map p126) Lined with evocative, colonial-era shophouses and home to several vibrantly coloured Chinese temples, Jln Carpenter – the heart of Kuching's Old Chinatown – stretches from ornamental **Harmony Arch** (Map p126; cnr Jln Tun Abang Haji Openg & Jln Carpenter) eastward to **Hong San Si Temple** (Map p126; cnr Jln Wayang & Jln Carpenter; ☺6am-6pm), with its roofline of tiled dragons. Established sometime before 1848 (and extensively restored in 2004), it is also known by its Hokkien name, Say Ong Kong.

There is a big celebration here in April, with a long procession of floats, lion and dragon dancers, and other groups winding their way through town following the altar of Kong Teck Choon Ong (the deity at the temple).

Hiang Thian Siang Temple   TEMPLE

(Sang Ti Miao Temple; Map p126; btwn 12 & 14 Jln Carpenter) Near the Harmony Arch end of the street, this temple, rebuilt shortly after the fire of 1884, serves the Teochew congregation as a shrine to Shang Di (the Emperor of Heaven).

The temple's most interesting celebration is the Hungry Ghost Festival, held on the 15th day of the seventh lunar month (mid-August or early September). The Chinese believe that the gates of hell swing open for the entirety of the month and the spirits of the dead are free to roam the earth. On the 15th day, offerings of food, prayer, incense and paper money are made to appease the spirits. A priest blesses the offerings and promptly burns an enormous effigy of the Hell King in a dramatic bonfire.

Directly across Jln Carpenter from the temple, you can dine on excellent Teochew Chinese dishes at Yang Choon Tai Hawker Centre (p135).

Hin Ho Bio   TEMPLE

(Map p126; 36 Jln Carpenter; ☺6am-5pm) One of Kuching's hidden gems is tucked away on the roof of the Kuching Hainan Association.

Mount the staircase to the top floor (there are clean bathrooms on the 1st floor) and you soon get to a vivid little Chinese shrine, Hin Ho Bio (temple of the Queen of Heaven), with rooftop views of the area.

Sarawak Textile Museum   MUSEUM

(Muzium Tekstil Sarawak; Map p126; Jln Tun Abang Haji Openg; ☺9am-4.45pm Mon-Fri, 10am-4pm Sat, Sun & holidays) Housed in a 'colonial Baroque'-style building constructed in 1909, this museum displays some superb examples of traditional Sarawakian textiles, including Malay *songket* (gold brocade cloth), as well as the hats, mats, belts, basketwork, beadwork, silverwork, barkwork, bangles and ceremonial headdresses created by the Iban, Bidayuh, Penan and other Dayak groups. Dioramas recreate the sartorial exuberance of Orang Ulu, Malay, Chinese and Indian weddings. Explanatory panels shed light on materials and techniques.

The historic old **General Post Office**, an impressive, Corinthian-colonnaded structure built in 1931, is across the street.

JALAN INDIA AREA

Indian Mosque   MOSQUE

(Map p126; Indian Mosque Lane; ☺6am-8.30pm except during prayers) Turn off Jln India (between Nos 37 and 39A) or waterfront Jln Gambier (between Nos 24 and 25A) onto tiny Indian Mosque Lane (Lg Sempit) and you enter another world. At the Jln Gambier end, shops sell spices in bulk (orange-yellow turmeric, greenish-yellow coriander, reddish-orange chilli powder) – the aromas are overwhelming and exhilarating! Further along, hole-in-the-wall hat shops sell the white crocheted caps (RM10) worn by men who have performed the hajj to Mecca; *songkok* (RM25), the black velvet hats worn by Malay men on formal occasions; and colourful headscarves for Muslim women.

About midway between the two thoroughfares, entirely surrounded by houses and shops, stands Kuching's oldest mosque, a modest structure built of *belian* (ironwood) in 1863 by Muslim traders from Tamil Nadu. Painted turquoise and notable for its simplicity, it is an island of peace and cooling shade in the middle of Kuching's commercial hullabaloo.

Jalan India   STREET

(Map p126; Jln India) Once Kuching's main shopping area for imported textiles, brassware and household goods, pedestrianised Jln India – essentially the western continuation

SARAWAK KUCHING

SARAWAK KUCHING

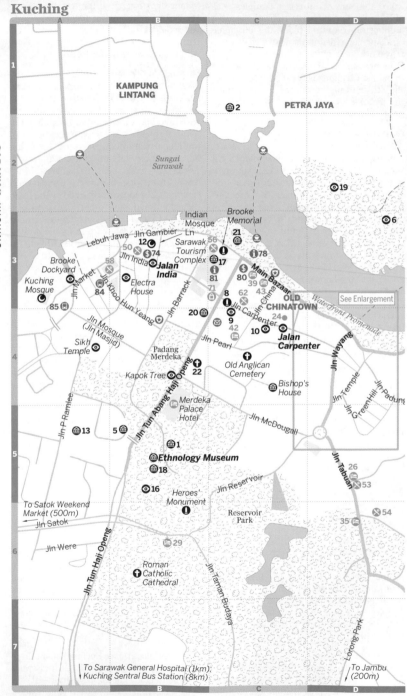

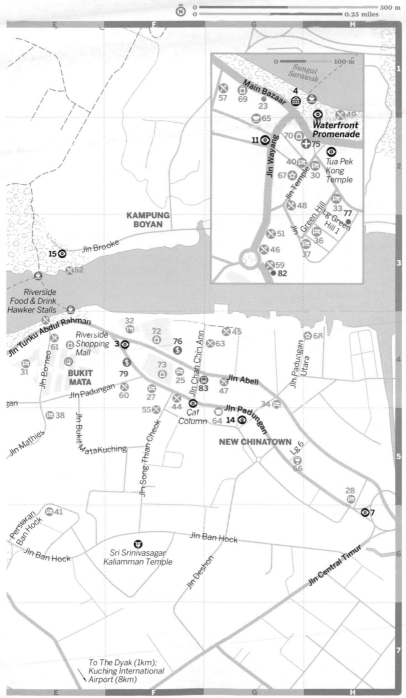

Kuching

of Jln Carpenter – remains an exuberant commercial thoroughfare. The shops along the eastern section are mostly Chinese-owned; those to the west are run by Indian Muslims with roots in Tamil Nadu. This is *the* place in Kuching to come for cheap textiles.

Sarawak Museum　　　　　MUSEUM
(Map p126; www.museum.sarawak.gov.my; Jln Tun Abang Haji Openg; ◔9am-4.45pm Mon-Fri, 10am-4pm Sat, Sun & holidays) Established in 1891, this excellent museum has a first-rate collection of cultural artefacts and is a must-visit for anyone interested in Borneo's peoples, cultures and habitats.

Ethnology Museum　　　　MUSEUM
(Map p126; ◔9am-4.45pm Mon-Fri, 10am-4pm Sat, Sun & holidays) At the top of the hill, on the western side of Jln Tun Abang Haji Openg, the Ethnology Museum (the Old Building) –

guarded by two colonial cannons – spotlights Borneo's incredibly rich indigenous cultures. Upstairs, it has superb exhibits on indigenous crafts, including masks, spears, basketry, musical instruments and a Bidayuh door charm for keeping evil spirits at bay; information on native customs such as tattooing and the infamous *palang* penis piercing; and long-houses, including a full-size Iban longhouse and scale models for other groups.

Downstairs is an old-fashioned natural-history museum whose highlight – remembered with horror by generations of Kuching children – is a hairball taken from the stomach of a man-eating crocodile, accompanied by the following explanation: 'human dental plate found attached to the hairball'. And if this isn't enough to put you off taking a dip in a muddy estuary, the 'watch found inside stomach' (the croc's stomach, of course) surely will – unless you'd like your smartphone to feature in a future exhibit!

Museum Garden   GARDENS
(Map p126, ◷9am-4.45pm Mon-Fri, 10am-4pm Sat, Sun & holidays) The landscaped Museum Garden stretches south from the Ethnology Museum, leading past flowers and fountains to a white-and-gold column called the **Heroes' Monument**.

The cast-iron, open-air pavilion behind the museum houses the **Akuarium** (Aquarium; Map p126; ◷9am-6pm), run by the city, on a shoestring budget, for educational purposes. It houses fish tanks (it's nice to see local fish that aren't laid out on ice, ready to be grilled, fried or baked) as well as turtles.

Art Museum   MUSEUM
(Map p126; ◷9am-4.45pm Mon-Fri, 10am-4pm Sat, Sun & holidays) Down the driveway from

the Ethnology Museum, the Art Museum (Muzium Seni) features sculpture and paintings inspired by Dayak motifs and traditions and by Borneo's flora, fauna and landscapes. May be closed at lunchtime.

Dewan Tun Abdul Razak   MUSEUM
(Map p126; ◷9am-4.45pm Mon-Fri, 10am-4pm Sat, Sun & holidays) Linked to the Ethnology Museum by a footbridge decorated with Orang Ulu motifs, Dewan Tun Abdul Razak (the New Building) has fine permanent exhibits on Sarawak's fascinating history, from the Brunei sultanate through to the Brooke era; prehistoric archaeology, including important finds from the Niah Caves; Chinese ceramics; and colourful Dayak crafts and costumes.

Islamic Museum   MUSEUM
(Map p126; Jln P Ramlee; ◷9am-4.45pm Mon-Fri, 10am-4pm Sat, Sun & holidays) Directly behind

Dewan Tun Abdul Razak, this museum offers a pretty good introduction to Malay-Muslim culture and its long ties with the Muslim heartland far to the west. Displays range from Bornean-Malay architecture, musical instruments and wood carvings to Arabic calligraphy and astrolabes of the sort that helped Arab mariners travel this far east.

NEW CHINATOWN

Jalan Padungan   STREET

(Map p126; Jln Padungan) Built starting in the 1920s, initially with money from the rubber boom, Kuching's liveliest commercial thoroughfare – pronounced pah-*doong*-ahn – is lined with Chinese-owned businesses and noodle shops. In recent years, the area has attracted a growing number of trendy cafes, bars and restaurants. Covered arcades make it a fine place for a rainy-day stroll. It stretches for 1.5km from Jln Tunku Abdul Rahman to the Great Cat of Kuching.

Tun Jugah Foundation   MUSEUM

(Map p126; 4th fl, Tun Jugah Tower, 18 Jln Tunku Abdul Rahman; ⊘9am-noon & 1-4.30pm Mon-Fri) Has excellent exhibits on Iban *ikat* and *sungkit* weaving, as well as beadwork. Iban woman come here to make traditional textiles using hand looms.

NORTH BANK OF THE RIVER

To get to Sungai Sarawak's northern bank, take a *tambang* (river ferry; 50 sen) from one of the docks along the Waterfront Promenade.

Kampung Boyan   NEIGHBOURHOOD

(Map p126) This sedate, old-time Malay *kampung* (village), filled with joyously colourful houses and a profusion of flowering plants, is a world away from the glitz and bustle of downtown Kuching, to which it's connected by boat (there's talk of building a pedestrian bridge). The waterfront area has two roofed hawker centres as well as other Malay-style eateries.

Fort Margherita   HISTORIC SITE

(Map p126; Kampung Boyan; ⊘9am-4.30pm) Built by Charles Brooke in 1879 and named after his wife, Ranee Margaret, this hilltop fortress long protected Kuching against surprise attacks by pirates. It did so exclusively as a remarkably successful deterrent: troops stationed here never fired a shot in anger.

Inspired by an English Renaissance castle, whitewashed Fort Margherita manages to feel both medieval-European and tropical. A steep spiral staircase leads up three flights of stairs to the crenellated roof, a great place to take in panoramic views of the river and get a feel for the lie of the city.

To get there from Kampung Boyan, follow the signs up the hill for 500m.

Astana   HISTORIC BUILDING

(Map p126; Petra Jaya; ⊘closed to public) Built by Charles Brooke in 1869, the Astana (Bahasa Sarawak for 'palace') – conveniently labelled in giant white letters – and its manicured gardens still serve as the home of the governor of Sarawak. The best views are actually from the south (city centre) bank of the river, so it's not really worth taking a *tambang* across.

To walk from the Astana to Fort Margherita, you have to circle a long way north, around the Sarawak State Assembly.

Sarawak State Assembly   NOTABLE BUILDING

(Map p126; Dewan Undangan Negeri, north bank of Sungai Sarawak, Petra Jaya; ⊘closed to public) Inaugurated in 2009, the iconic home of Sarawak's State Assembly is an imposing structure whose soaring golden roof is said to resemble either a *payung* (umbrella) or a *terendak* (Melanau sunhat). The best views are from Jln Bishopsgate and the Waterfront Promenade.

ELSEWHERE IN KUCHING

St Thomas's Cathedral   CHURCH

(Map p126; http://kuching.anglican.org; ⊘6am-6pm Mon-Sat, to 7pm Sun) Facing Padang Merdeka (Independence Sq), with its huge and ancient **kapok tree**, Kuching's Anglican cathedral (1954) has a mid-20th-century look and, inside, a bright red barrel-vaulted ceiling. The main gate is usually closed, so enter from Jln McDougall, named after Kuching's first Anglican bishop, who arrived here in 1848.

At the top of the hill, on the other side of the new Parish Centre (opened in 2012) from the cathedral, stands the **Bishop's House**. Kuching's oldest building, it was constructed in 1849 - with admirable solidity - by a German shipwright.

Tucked away in a corner of the Anglican compound, behind the Verger's Quarters, is the **Old Anglican Cemetery**, a number of whose tombs – there are just a few dozen – go back to the 1840s. Some are finely carved in granite while others are just weathered wooden planks; several belong to infants.

Cat Statues KITSCH

It's just a coincidence that in Bahasa Malaysia, Kuching means 'cat' (spelled 'kucing'), but the city fathers have milked the homonym for everything it's worth, branding Sarawak's capital as the 'Cat City' and erecting a number of marvellously kitschy cat statues to beautify the urban landscape.

The **Cat Fountain** (Map p126; Jln Tunku Abdul Rahman) is an ensemble of polychrome cats who pose and preen opposite the Hotel Grand Margherita Kuching. On the roundabout at the corner of Jln Padungan and Jln Chan Chin Ann, the **Cat Column** features four cats around the bottom and four Rafflesia flowers near the top – the latter are just below the cat-adorned shield of the South Kuching municipality. And the **Great Cat of Kuching** (Map p126; Jln Padungan), a 2½m-high white pussycat with blue eyes and wire whiskers, is perched at the eastern end of Jln Padungan, on a traffic island just outside the Chinese ceremonial gate.

FREE **Cat Museum** MUSEUM
(www.dbku.sarawak.gov.my; Jln Semariang, Bukit Siol; admission free, camera/video RM3/5; ☺9am-5pm) A veritable shrine to feline kitsch, this homage to the city's name features hundreds of entertaining, surprising and bizarre *kucing* (cat) figurines – some the size of a cow, others tiny, ubercute and very Japanese – alongside learned presentations on 'Cats in Malay Society' and 'Cats in Chinese Art'. The cafeteria, used by council workers, is quite good.

Kuching North City Hall NOTABLE BUILDING

Situated 8km (by road) north of the city centre is the hilltop Kuching North City Hall (known by its Malay abbreviation, DBKU), a landmark prestige project – some say it looks like a UFO – inaugurated in 1993. Buses K5 and K15 (RM1.50, about hourly) link the Saujana Bus Station with the bottom of the hill. A taxi from the centre costs RM20 to RM25. If you're going to the Santubong Peninsula by car, you can stop here on the way.

🏃 Activities

Satok Weekend Market MARKET

(Pasar Minggu; Jln Satok; ☺about noon-10pm Sat & 6am-1pm or 2pm Sun) Kuching's biggest and liveliest market begins around midday on Saturday, when rural folk, some from area longhouses, arrive with their fruits, vegies, fish and spices. The air is heady with the aromas of fresh coriander, ginger, herbs and jungle ferns, which are displayed among piles of bananas (10 kinds!), mangoes, custard apples and obscure jungle fruits. If you smell something overpoweringly sweet and sickly from November to February, chances are it's durian. Vendors are friendly and many are happy to tell you about their wares, which are often divided into quantities worth RM1 or RM2.

At research time, the market was situated on Jln Satok about 1km west of the Sarawak Museum – from the centre, walk south on Jln Tun Abang Haji Openg and turn east at Jln Satok (under the flyover). But there were plans – bitterly opposed by vendors – to move (some would say exile) it across the river to a complex about 2km further west.

Hash House Harriers FUN RUNS

Kuching's various Hash House Harriers (HHH) chapters hold about half-a-dozen one- to two-hour runs, over meadow and dale (and through thick jungle), each week. For details, ask around or visit www.kuchingcityhash.com, the website of the Saturday afternoon run. Visitors are welcome to join the fun.

Kuching Bike Hash CYCLING

(www.kbh.doturf.com) Bashers (bicycle hashes) gather every second Sunday afternoon to ride 17km to 25km. Visitors are welcome. Cycling has become hugely popular with outdoorsy Sarawakians in recent years.

🍴 Courses

Bumbu Cooking School DAYAK COOKING

(Map p126; ☎012-897 2297, 019-879 1050; http://bumbucookingclass.weebly.com; 57 Jln Carpenter; per person RM150, without market visit RM120; ☺approx 8am or 9am-1pm & 2-6.30pm daily) Raised in a Bidayuh village, Joseph teaches the secrets of cooking with fresh, organic ingredients from the rainforest. At the market you'll learn how to spot top-quality, jungle ferns; back in the kitchen you'll prepare this crunchy delicacy, along with a main dish and a dessert that's served in a *pandan*-leaf basket you weave yourself. A bit pricey but gets great reviews. Maximum 10 participants.

☞ Tours

Telang Usan Travel & Tours TOUR

(Map p126; ☎082-236945; www.telangusan.com; Telang Usan Hotel, Persiaran Ban Hock) A well-regarded, veteran agency based in the Telang Usan Hotel. Audry, currently president of the Sarawak Tourism Federation, speaks English and French.

Rainforest Kayaking
TOUR

(Borneo Trek & Kayak Adventure; ☎082-240571, 013-804 8338; www.rainforestkayaking.com) Specialises in river trips.

Borneo à la Carte
TOUR

(☎082-236857; www.borneoalacarte.com) A Kuching-based agency offering innovative, tailor-made trips, mainly for a French-speaking clientele, to indigenous communities other agencies don't cover. Amélie, the owner, is known for having very reasonable prices and sharing receipts equitably with local communities.

Borneo Experiences
TOUR

(Map p126; ☎082-421346; www.borneoexperiences.com; ground fl, Jln Temple; ☺10am-7pm Mon-Sat, may also open Sun) Singgahsana Lodge's (p132) new travel agency. Destinations include a remote Bidayuh 'village in the clouds' and an Iban longhouse in the Batang Ai area (one/two nights per person RM688/888). Also offers cycling tours. Gets excellent reviews.

Borneo Adventure
TOUR

(Map p126; ☎082-245175; www.borneoadventure.com; 55 Main Bazaar) Award-winning company that sets the standard for high-end Borneo tours and is the leader in cooperative projects benefiting Sarawak's indigenous peoples. Known for its outstanding guides.

Adventure Alternative Borneo
TOUR

(☎Danny Voon 016-810 5614; borneo@adventure alternative.com) Offers sustainable trips that combine 'culture, nature and adventure'. Can help you design and coordinate an itinerary for independent travel to remote areas.

★★ Festivals & Events

Rainforest World Music Festival
MUSIC

(www.rwmf.net; 1-/3-day pass RM110/300, child RM55/150; ☺2nd weekend in Jul) This three-day musical extravaganza brings together Dayak bands with international artists. Held in the Sarawak Cultural Village. Accommodation gets booked out well in advance.

Kuching Festival Fair
FOOD

(Jln Padungan; ☺5-11pm for 2 or 3 weeks late Jul-Aug) Scores of food stalls serve the specialities of the various Chinese dialect groups, Nonya desserts and beer. Held next to Kuching South City Hall (MBKS Building), about 2km southeast of the Hilton.

Chinese New Year
CELEBRATION

(☺late Jan or early Feb) The main festivities are along Jln Padungan.

Mooncake Festival
STREET FAIR

(☺Sep or early Oct) Musical performances and food stalls selling Chinese food, drink and, of course, mooncakes take over Jln Carpenter.

🛏 Sleeping

Kuching's accommodation options range from international-standard suites with high-rise views to windowless, musty cells deep inside converted Chinese shophouses. Many of the guesthouses – a great place to meet other travellers – are on or near Jln Carpenter (Old Chinatown), while the top-end spots are clustered a bit to the east in Kuching's high-rise district, on or near Jln Tunku Abdul Rahman. Cheap Chinese hotels can be found on or just off Jln Padungan and on the *lorong* (alleys) coming off L-shaped Jln Green Hill.

The majority of guesthouse rooms under RM50 have shared bathrooms; prices almost always include a very simple breakfast of the toast-and-jam variety. Rates at some guesthouses rise in July (especially during the Rainforest World Music Festival), or from June to September.

TOP CHOICE Batik Boutique Hotel
BOUTIQUE HOTEL $$

(Map p126; ☎082-422845; www.batikboutique hotel.com; 38 Jln Padungan; d incl breakfast RM250; 🅰🛜) A superb location, classy design and a super-friendly staff make this a top mid-range choice. The 15 spacious rooms, six with balconies, are sleek and elegant, and even come with iPod docks.

TOP CHOICE Threehouse B&B
GUESTHOUSE $

(Map p126; ☎082-423499; www.threehousebnb.com; 51 Upper China St; dm/d RM20/60; 🅰🛜) A spotless, family-friendly guesthouse in a great Old Chinatown location, with a warm and hugely welcoming vibe – everything a guesthouse should be! All nine rooms have shared bathrooms. Amenities include a common room with TV, DVDs and books, and a kitchen. Laundry costs RM8 per load, including drying.

TOP CHOICE Singgahsana Lodge
GUESTHOUSE $

(Map p126; ☎082-429277; www.singgahsana.com; 1 Jln Temple; dm RM30, d with shared/private bathroom RM88/98; 🅰🛜) Setting the Kuching standard for backpacker digs, this hugely popular guesthouse, decked out with stylish Dayak crafts, has an unbeatable location and a great chill-out lobby. Prices aren't low and the rooms, though colourful, are far from luxurious, but breakfast at the rooftop bar is included. The shared bathrooms are spotless. Laundry costs RM6.50 per kilo.

Telang Usan Hotel
HOTEL **$$**

(Map p120; ☏082-415588; www.telangusan.com; Persiaran Ban Hock; s/d from RM100/120) A famously welcoming hotel with gleaming tile hallways and 66 very clean rooms that come with freshly plumped pillows and crisply turned-back sheets. The decor is Kenyah and Kayan. Situated down the hill behind the Pullman Hotel, to which it's linked via an often-muddy track. Has an excellent restaurant. Outstanding value.

Lime Tree Hotel
HOTEL **$$**

(Map p126; ☏082-414600; www.limetreehotel.com.my; Lot 317, Jln Abell; d/family ste RM160/390; ❀@☞) Dashes of lime green – a pillow, a bar of soap, a staff member's tie, the lobby's Cafe Sublime – accent every room of this well-run semi-boutique hotel. The 55 rooms are sleek and minimalist and offer good value. The rooftop lounge has lovely river views. Situated just a block from lively Jln Padungan.

Ranee
BOUTIQUE HOTEL **$$$**

(Map p126; ☏082-258833; www.theranee.com; 6 & 7 Main Bazaar; d RM380-650, ste RM1000; ❀☞) Opened in 2012, this chic riverfront property – in an old shophouse that was completely rebuilt after a fire – has an urban resort feel. The 24 rooms are graced by high ceilings, floors made of rare merbau hardwood, and huge bathrooms with cool, indirect lighting.

Hilton Kuching Hotel
HOTEL **$$**

(Map p126; ☏082-233888; www.hilton.com; cnr Jln Tunku Abdul Rahman & Jln Borneo; s/d RM348/371; ❀@☞☰) The landmark Hilton has 315 spacious, international-standard rooms, in shades of cream, beige and maroon, with flat-screen consoles, LED reading lights and glass-topped work desks. Amenities include two business centres, a spa and a 24hr fitness centre. Wi-fi costs an outrageous RM55 for 24 hours.

Hotel Grand Margherita Kuching
HOTEL **$$**

(Map p126; ☏082-423111; www.grandmargherita.com.my; Jln Tunku Abdul Rahman; d incl breakfast RM275; ❀@☞☰) On a fine piece of riverfront real estate, this place will spoil you with a bright, modern lobby, 288 very comfortable rooms and amenities such as a fitness centre, a river-view swimming pool and a new spa. Wi-fi costs just RM5 for 24 hours.

Pullman Kuching
HOTEL **$$**

(Map p126; ☏082-222888; www.pullmankuching.com; 1A Jln Mathies, Bukit Mata; d from RM273; ❀@☞☰) Opened in 2010, the Accor-affiliated Pullman has a soaring white lobby and 389 rooms – in subdued tones of aquamarine, brown, white and green – spread over 23 floors. The focus is on business travellers.

Lodge 121
GUESTHOUSE **$**

(Map p126; ☏082-420121; www.lodge121.com; Lot 121, 1st fl, Jln Tabuan; d/tr RM99/129, dm/s/d/tr/q with shared bathroom RM24/49/69/89/119; ❀@☞) Polished concrete abounds at this mod charmer, whose owners have transformed a commercial space into a sleek, spotless and low-key hang-out for flashpackers. The carpeted, 10-bed dorm room, with mattresses on the floor, is in the garret. All 22 rooms – five with attached bath – either have windows to the outside or wood-slat openings to a hallway.

Nomad Borneo B&B
GUESTHOUSE **$$**

(Map p126; ☏082-237831; www.borneobnb.com; 3 Jln Green Hill; dm/s/d/f RM20/50/75/100; ❀@☞) There's a buzzing backpacker vibe at this Iban-run favourite – guests often hang out in the lounge area with the friendly management. Of the 17 rooms, 10 have windows (the others make do with exhaust fans). Dorm rooms have either four or eight beds. Laundry costs RM8 per load.

Fairview Guesthouse
GUESTHOUSE **$**

(Map p126; ☏013-816 4560, 082-240017; www.thefairview.com.my; 6 Jln Taman Budaya; s/d/f incl breakfast RM50/70/150; ❀@) An oldie but a goodie, this nine-room garden villa, a bit out of the city centre, scores big points with visiting researchers for its unpretentious atmosphere and friendly owners, who run great tailor-made tours.

B&B Inn
GUESTHOUSE **$**

(Map p126; ☏082-237366; bnbswk@streamyx.com; 30-I Jln Tabuan; dm RM16, s/d/tr with shared bathroom RM25/35/45, d RM70; ❀@☞) Clean and low-key, this establishment has a lived-in, old-fashioned feel and a dozen of the cheapest decent rooms in town. Air-con costs RM5 extra a day. Women and men have separate dorm rooms. A few rooms lack windows. If the street door is padlocked, ring the bell.

Beds
GUESTHOUSE **$**

(Map p126; ☏082-424229; www.bedsguesthouse.com; 229 Jln Padungan; dm/s/d RM30/50/70;

SARAWAK KUCHING

✳@⌐) In the heart of Kuching's New China-town, this spotless guesthouse has attracted a loyal following thanks to comfy couches in the lobby, a kitchen you can cook in and 12 clean rooms with shared bathrooms, nine with windows. Dorm rooms have metal-framed bunks of generous proportions. A load of laundry, including drying, costs just RM5.

Harbour View Hotel
HOTEL $$

(Map p126; ☑082-274666; www.harbourview.com. my; Jln Temple; s/d/f RM130/155/200; ✳@⌐) If it's modern comforts you're after, this 243-room tower, 13 storeys high, is one of Kuching's best bargains, offering full Western facilities for a thoroughly Southeast Asian price.

Wo Jia Lodge
GUESTHOUSE $

(Map p126; ☑082-251776; www.wojialodge. com; 17 Main Bazaar; dm/s/d/tr with air-con RM20/40/52/75, s/d with fan RM38/48; ✳@⌐) A friendly, central spot to lay your head. The 18 gleaming rooms (five with windows, the rest with exhaust fans to the hallway) contain beds and nothing else. In an old Chinese shophouse – the lobby still has the original hardwood floors.

John's Place
GUESTHOUSE $

(Map p126; ☑082-258329; 5 Jln Green Hill; d RM55-60, tr RM80; ✳@⌐) Hidden away in a commercial building, John's is a neat but rather unexciting spot to grab some Zs. Has 13 simple, practical rooms of medium size with spring mattresses – and without musty odours. The cheaper doubles look out onto the hallway.

Mandarin Hotel
HOTEL $

(Map p126; ☑082-418269; Lorong Green Hill 3; d/ tr from RM55/75; ✳⌐) This old-time Chinese hotel is head and shoulders above half-a-dozen similarly priced joints nearby. The 20 decent, no-frills rooms come with windows (no mustiness!), snow-white walls, 1960s Linoleum desks, 1970s-style window-unit air-con and a time-warp vibe.

Abell Hotel
HOTEL $$

(Map p126; ☑082-239449; www.abellhotel.com; 22 Jln Tunku Abdul Rahman; s/d from RM111/175; ✳@⌐) Opened in 2011, this nonsmoking hotel helps solve Kuching's shortage of good tourist-class hotels. The 80 rooms are stylish but not luxurious; the cheapest look out on an ersatz airwell. The name – like that of the street outside – is pronounced like the word 'able'.

✗ Eating

Kuching is the best place in Malaysian Borneo to work your way through the entire range of Sarawak-style cooking. At hawker centres, you can pick and choose from a variety of Chinese and Malay stalls, each specialising in a particular culinary tradition or dish. Jln Padungan, home to some of the city's best noodle houses, is undergoing something of a restaurant, cafe and bar boom.

If you'd like to start a good-natured argument, ask a group of locals where Kuching's best Sarawak laksa (a deliciously spicy, tangy noodle soup) is served.

⌐TOP CHOICE Dyak
DAYAK $$$

(☑082-234068; Jln Mendu & Jln Simpang Tiga; mains RM18-30; ◔noon-11pm, last order 9.30pm) Kuching's most important culinary event of the last few years was the opening of this elegant restaurant, the first to treat Dayak home cooking as true cuisine. The chef, classically trained in the Western tradition, takes traditional recipes, many of them Iban (a few are Kelabit, Kayan or Bidayuh), and fresh, organic jungle vegies to create mouthwatering dishes unlike anything else you've ever tasted. Vegetarian dishes, made without lard, are available upon request. Staff are happy to explain the origin of each dish. It's a good idea to reserve ahead on Thursday, Friday and Saturday nights. Dyak is situated 2km southeast of Old Chinatown. A taxi from the city centre – worth every cent – costs RM12.

⌐TOP CHOICE Top Spot Food Court
SEAFOOD $$

(Map p126; Jln Padungan; fish per kg RM35-70, vegetable dishes RM8-12; ◔noon-11pm) A perennial favourite among local foodies, this neon-lit courtyard and its half-a-dozen humming seafooderies sits, rather improbably, on the roof of a concrete parking garage – look for the giant backlit lobster sign. Grilled white pomfret is a particular delicacy. Ling Loong Seafood and the Bukit Mata Seafood Centre are particularly good.

⌐TOP CHOICE Jambu
MEDITERRANEAN $$$

(☑082-235292; www.jamburestaurant.com; 32 Jln Crookshank; mains RM28-55; ◔6-10.30pm, closed Mon) Once the venue for elegant colonial parties (check out the photos on the way to the bar), this 1920s mansion – with teak floors and soaring ceilings – is the best place in town for a romantic meal. Some of the tastiest dishes are Mediterranean-inflected. It has a stylish lounge-bar that serves tapas. Named for the *jambu air* (water apple) tree in the yard. Situated 1.5km south of the centre.

Junk ITALIAN $$$
(Map p126; ☑082-259450; 80 Jln Wayang; mains RM20-50; ◷6-11pm, closed Tue; ☎) Filled to the brim with antiques, this complex of chic dining rooms (three) and bars (two) – housed in three 1920s shophouses – is a favourite among Malaysian celebs. The Red Room is amply supplied with pillows and provocatively decorated with risqué pop art. Pasta and lasagne cost RM24 to RM45, pizzas are RM25 to RM39.

Chong Choon Cafe LAKSA $
(Map p126; Lot 121, Section 3, Jln Abell; mains RM4-5; ◷7am-11.30am or noon, closed Tue) You'd never guess it from the picnic tables cooled by a fleet of overhead helicopter fans, but this unassuming, tile-floored cafe serves some of Kuching's most famously excellent Sarawak laksa.

Lyn's Thandoori Restaurant INDIAN $$
(Map p126; Lot 267, Jln Song Thian Cheok; mains RM16-25; ◷9am-10pm Mon-Sat, 5-10pm Sun; ☎☑) This North Indian place, a Kuching fixture since 1994, sports a huge menu featuring tandoori chicken (of course!) as well as delicious mutton, fish and vegie options (almost 50 of them, including 22 types of *paneer*), all made with top-quality ingredients. Situated 300m due north of one of Kuching's three Hindu temples.

Tribal Scoops DAYAK $
(Map p126; Block H, Jln Borneo; mains RM4.50-10; ◷10.30am-9.30pm Mon-Sat; ☎) A convivial little slice of the Kelabit Highlands in downtown Kuching, this unpretentious restaurant is a huge hit with Kelabit students with a hankering for some home cooking. Specialities include *labo senutuq* (shredded beef cooked with wild ginger and dried chilli) and *ab'eng* (shredded river fish). Dishes are prepared without MSG or – because it didn't exist in the highlands in the old days – shrimp paste. A buffet lunch (RM16.50) is available from 11.30am to 2.30pm except Sunday. Situated across the street from the main entrance to the Hilton.

Open-Air Market LAKSA $
(Map p126; Jln Khoo Hun Yeang; mains from RM3-4.50; ◷6am or 7am-5pm, some stalls to midnight) Cheap, tasty dishes to look for include

superb laksa (available from about 7am to 4pm), Chinese-style *mee sapi* (beef noodle soup), red *kolo mee* (noodles with sweet barbecue sauce), tomato *kueh tiaw* (another fried rice-noodle dish) and shaved ice desserts (ask for 'ABC' at stall 17). An ideal spot for breakfast before boarding the bus to Bako National Park. Has two sections separated by a minivan parking area. The yellow tower was once used as a fire lookout.

Bla Bla Bla FUSION $$
(Map p126; ☑082-233944; 27 Jln Tabuan; most mains RM24-45; ◷6-11.30pm, closed Tue) Innovative, chic and stylish, Bla Bla Bla serves Chinese-inspired fusion dishes that – like the decor, the koi ponds and the Balinese Buddha – range from traditional to far-out. Specialities include *midin* (jungle fern) salad, cashew-nut prawns, ostrich meat stuffed with mozzarella, 'coffee chicken' and homemade cheesecake. The generous portions are designed to be shared.

Kok Boon Café LAKSA $
(Map p126; 30 J Jln Tabuan; mains RM3.50-5; ◷laksa served 6.30am-1.30pm or 2pm) The three noodle stalls at this ordinary-looking, open-air corner eatery serve the usual Foochow and Hokkien noodle dishes, but it's the scrumptious Sarawak laksa that makes this place special for breakfast or an early lunch.

James Brooke Bistro & Cafe WESTERN $$
(Map p126; Waterfront Promenade opposite Jln Temple; mains RM10-39; ◷10am-11pm) Gets consistently good reviews both for the cuisine and the lovely river views. Local dishes such as Sarawak laksa and their own invention, wild Borneo laksa, are quite reasonably priced. The beef stroganoff has a following.

Yang Choon Tai Hawker Centre CHINESE $
(Map p126; 23 Jln Carpenter; mains RM4-8; ◷24hr) Six food stalls, run by members of the Teochew Chinese community, serve up an eclectic assortment of native bites, including rice porridge with pork (3am to 9am), *kolo mee* (flash-boiled egg noodles; available from 6am to 2pm) and super fish soup (3pm to 10pm).

Green Hill Corner LAKSA $
(Map p126; cnr Jln Temple & Jln Green Hill; meals RM3-6; ◷7am-11pm) Hugely popular with locals. Half-a-dozen stalls here crank out porridge, laksa, chicken rice and noodle dishes. The stall run by twin brothers serves superb beef noodle soup (RM4).

Benson Seafood　　　　　　SEAFOOD $$
(Map p126; Jln Chan Chin Ann; 'small' mains RM10-20; ☺11am-11pm Tue-Sun, 4-11pm Mon) In a gritty riverfront area that may become chic in five or 10 years, this open-air pavilion, its big round tables covered with red tablecloths and surrounded by red plastic chairs, serves fresh Chinese-style fish and seafood and Sarawak classics such as *midin* stir-fried with *belacan* (shrimp paste). From the northern end of Jln Chan Chin Ann, turn right along the riverfront for half a block.

Sin Wei Tong Café　　　　　VEGETARIAN $
(Map p126; 9 Jln Temple; mains RM3-4.50; ☺6am-3.30pm; 🥢) Does cheap, tasty vegie versions of Chinese favourites such as *kueh chap* and chicken rice.

Zhun San Yen Vegetarian
Food Centre　　　　　　　VEGETARIAN $
(Map p126; Jln Chan Chin Ann; mains per 100g RM1.70; ☺8am-2pm & 5-8pm Mon-Fri, from 9am Sat; 🥢) Serves Taiwanese- and Malaysian Chinese-style vegie meals (eg curries), made with soy or gluten, that are as healthy as they are delicious. Buffet style. Remarkably inexpensive.

21 Bistro　　　　　　　　　FUSION $$
(Map p126; 64 Jln Padungan; mains RM10-48; ☺4pm-2am or later Mon-Sat, food until 11pm) This chic, sophisticated restaurant-cum-bar, popular with young professionals, made quite a splash when it opened in 2012. Serves excellent Western, Asian & fusion dishes, including pasta, grilled meats and fish (snapper is a speciality). As for the soundtrack, early evening jazz makes way for chill-out music later on.

Magna Carta　　　　　　　ITALIAN $$
(Map p126; Sarawak Tourism Complex, Jln Tun Abang Haji Openg; mains RM15-28; ☺10.30am-midnight) For great Brooke-era atmosphere, you can choose between the breezy verandah, with garden views, and the interior, whose decor is a mash-up of medieval England and

19th-century Straits Chinese. Good options include pasta, pizza with exquisitely thin crust (RM22), homemade bread and freshly squeezed orange juice. Across the patio, **Magenta** (Map p126; mains RM26-58; ☺5-11pm), under the same management, has a larger selection of meat and seafood dishes.

Lok Lok　　　　　　　　　　MALAY $
(Map p126; 7D Jln Ban Hock; mains RM5; ☺6pm-3am) This hugely popular nocturnal eatery specialises in *lok lok*, skewers (eg of fish, prawn, cuttlefish or bean curd; RM1.50 to RM2 each) that are either boiled or deep fried and eaten with sweet, sweet-and-sour, *belacan* or satay sauce. Also serves *rojak* and traditional mains such as curry chicken. Ideal for a late – or late-late – meal.

Kampung Boyan Hawker Centres　MALAY $
(Map p126; Jln Tunku Abdul Rahman; meals RM4.80-16, hawker centres mains RM3-4; ☺evening, hawker centres 11am-midnight) What could be better than a romantic evening stroll along the river accompanied by a bite to eat? Or you can take a ferry across the river to Kampung Boyan, whose new promenade has two tent-roofed hawker centres.

Jubilee Restaurant　　　　　INDIAN $
(Map p126; 49 Jln India; ☺6.30am-5.30pm or 6pm) A fixture in the heart of Kuching's Indian Muslim district since 1974. Halal specialities include *nasi briyani* [sic] (rice with chicken, beef or lamb; RM6 to RM7) and *roti canai* (flatbread with egg and/or cheese; RM1 to RM2.60). The cook hails from Madras.

Self-Catering

Ting & Ting　　　　　　　SUPERMARKET $
(Map p126; 30A Jln Tabuan; ☺9am-9pm, closed Sun & holidays) An impressive selection of wine (from Australia, California, Chile and France), Western-style snack food, chocolate, toiletries and nappies (diapers).

Everrise Supermarket　　　SUPERMARKET $
(Map p126; Jln Tunku Abdul Rahman; ☺9.30am-9.30pm) On the lower floor of the Sarawak Plaza shopping mall.

 Drinking

Cosmopolitan Kuching has a clutch of spirited drinking spots. Just for the record, Fort Margherita does not serve cocktails.

Jln Padungan hosts a growing selection of cool places to drink – many would not be out of place in Melbourne, London or San Francisco.

LAKSA LUCK

Borneo's luckiest visitors start the day with a breakfast of Sarawak laksa, a tangy noodle soup made with coconut milk, lemon grass, sour tamarind and fiery *sambal belacan* (shrimp-paste sauce), with fresh calamansi lime juice squeezed on top. Unbelievably *lazat* ('delicious' in Bahasa Malaysia)!

KEK LAPIS - COLOURFUL LAYER CAKES

The people of Kuching – from all communities – love to add a dash of colour to festivities, so it comes as no surprise to see stalls selling *kek lapis* (striped layer cakes) sprouting up around town (eg along Main Bazaar and the Waterfront Promenade) during festivals, including Hari Raya (Ramadan).

Kek lapis is made with wheat flour, egg, prodigious quantities of either butter or margarine, and flavourings such as melon, blueberry or – a local favourite – *pandan* leaves. Since *kek lapis* are prepared one layer at a time and each layer – there can be 30 or more – takes five or six minutes to bake, a single cake can take up to five hours from start to finish.

Over 40 flavours of *kek lapis* (with butter RM20, with margarine RM10) are available year-round – to satisfy demand from Peninsular Malaysians – at **Maria Kek Lapis** (Map p126; ☑252734; http://22.com.my/mariakeklapissarawak; ◷8am-5pm). Free tastes are on offer. Cakes stay fresh for one or two weeks at room temperature and up to a month in the fridge.

Junk BAR
(Map p126; 80 Jln Wayang; ◷4pm-1.30am, closed Tue) Kuching's most stylish hang-out is more than a restaurant – it also has two bars: Junk Bar, tucked away on the side, and the Backstage Bar, lit by red Chinese lanterns and chock full of old radios and musical instruments.

Ruai BAR
(Map p126; 7F Jln An Hock; ◷5pm-1am or 2am) This Iban-owned bar has a laid-back cool and welcoming spirit all its own. Decorated with old photos and Orang Ulu art (and, inexplicably, several Mexican sombreros), it serves as an urban *ruai* (the covered verandah of an Iban longhouse) for aficionados – local and expat - of vigorous outdoor activities such as caving, trekking and Hash House Harriers social runs. A great place to meet people. Starts to pick up after about 9pm.

Black Bean Coffee & Tea Company CAFE
(Map p126; Jln Carpenter; drinks RM3-4.80; ◷9am-6pm Mon-Sat; ☎) The aroma of freshly ground coffee assaults the senses at this tiny shop, believed by many to purvey Kuching's finest brews. Specialities, roasted daily, include Arabica, Liberica and Robusta coffees grown in Java, Sumatra and, of course, Sarawak. Also serves oolong and green teas from Taiwan. Has just three tables. Decaf not available.

Zeus Sports Bar BAR
(Map p126; cnr Jln Padungan & Lorong 6; ◷4pm-2am, closed Tue) Local rock bands strut their stuff from 9pm to 1am on Friday and 6.30pm to 10.30pm on Saturday (after that there's footy on the telly). The upstairs lounge is popular with the golfers. Owned by a personable golf aficionado – and, yes, although he's Iban, his first name is Polish.

Bing CAFE
(Map p126; 84 Jln Padungan; coffee RM5.50-14; ◷10am-midnight, to 1am Fri & Sat; ☎) Kuching's tropical-chic answer to Starbucks, this uberstylish, dimly lit coffee shop serves a dozen varieties of hot and iced Illy coffee.

☆ Entertainment

Kuching's after-dark charms range from the sedate (eating well) to the romantic (strolling along the Waterfront Promenade) to the loud and thumping (dancing the night away at a disco).

Terminal One Lounge CLUB
(Map p126; http://t1lounge.com; Jln Padungan Utara, River end; admission free for women and Sun-Tue for men, men Wed-Sat RM35; ◷4pm-2am or 3am) Kuching's most popular dance club and a magnet for celebrities both local and Peninsular, T1 is a genuine, pumping disco, complete with batteries of flashing, spinning coloured lights. Attracts a well-off crowd, mainly over 25 or 30, often in couples or groups. Things really get going at 10.30pm or 11pm and hit their peak after midnight. The dress code for men bans short pants, singlets (tank tops), flip-flops and sandals. Serves finger food.

Star Cineplex CINEMA
(Map p126; www.starcineplex.com.my; 9th fl, multi-coloured parking garage, Jln Temple; tickets RM5-9; ◷1st/last screenings at about noon/midnight) For a couple of hours of escapism – ideal on a rainy day – courtesy of Hollywood or the cinema industries of eastern Asia. Most films

are English; the rest have English subtitles. The elevator/lift is directly across Jln Temple from the Wong Eye Clinic & Surgery.

 Shopping

If it's traditional Borneo arts and crafts you're after, then you've come to the right place – Kuching is the best shopping spot on the island for collectors and cultural enthusiasts. Don't expect many bargains, but don't be afraid to negotiate either – there's plenty to choose from, and the quality varies as much as the price. Dubiously 'aged' items are common, so be sure to spend some time browsing to familiarise yourself with prices and range.

For insights into Sarawak's varied and rich handicrafts traditions, stop by the Sarawak Museum, the Textile Museum and the Tun Jugah Foundation and check out the website of the Kuching-based NGO **Crafthub** (www.crafthub.com.my), where you can download copies of *Crafts*, a quarterly magazine published for the Sarawak Craft Council.

Most of Kuching's shops are closed on Sunday.

Main Bazaar HANDICRAFTS
(Map p126; Main Bazaar; ⊘some shops closed Sun) The row of old shophouses facing the Waterfront Promenade is chock full of handicrafts shops, some outfitted like art galleries, others with more of a 'garage sale' appeal, yet others (especially along the Main Bazaar's western section) stocking little more than kitschy-cute cat souvenirs. Handmade items worth seeing (if not purchasing), many from the highlands of Kalimantan, include hand-woven textiles and baskets, masks, drums, brass gongs, statues (up to 2m high!), beaded headdresses, swords, spears, painted shields and cannons from Brunei. At many places, staff enjoy explaining the origin and use of each item.

UD Siburan Jaya FOOD
(Map p126; 66 Main Bazaar; ⊘8.30am-9pm Mon-Sat, 9.30-5pm Sun) Has an excellent selection of Sarawakian specialities such as pepper (black and white), laksa paste, *sambal*, Bario rice and even tax-paid *tuak* (Dayak rice wine).

Fabriko CLOTHING
(Map p126; 56 Main Bazaar; ⊘9am-5pm Mon-Sat) This fine little boutique has a well-chosen selection of made-in-Sarawak fabrics and clothing in both traditional and modern

Orang Ulu-inspired designs, including silk sarongs and men's batik shirts.

Nelson's Gallery ART
(Map p126; 54 Main Bazaar; ⊘9am-5pm) Upstairs, artist Narong Daun patiently creates vibrant, jungle-themed batik paintings on silk.

Fantasy Sarawak CLOTHING
(Map p126; 70 Main Bazaar; ⊘10am-7pm) Has Sarawak's classiest collection of T-shirts.

Sarawak Craft Council HANDICRAFTS
(Map p126; cnr Jln Tun Abang Haji Openg & Jln India; ⊘9am-4.30pm Mon-Fri) Run by a nonprofit government agency, this two-storey shop has a pretty good selection of Malay, Bidayuh, Iban and Orang Ulu handicrafts – check out the cowboy hats made entirely of bark and the conical *terendak* (Melanau hats). Housed in the Round Tower, constructed in 1886 and used by the dreaded Kempeitai (Japanese military police) during the occupation, which is why some locals believe it's haunted.

Tanoti WEAVING
(56 Jln Tabuan; ⊘8am-6pm, closed public holidays) Using the supplementary weft technique (in which designs are woven into the fabric as it's made), a dozen women hand-weave silk shawls (RM400 to RM2000), wedding veils and the like. Designs at this not-for-profit studio are both Bornean-traditional and modern.

Yusan Padan Gallery ART
(Map p126; Sarakraf, Waterfront Promenade; ⊘9.30am-4.30pm Mon-Sat) Sells crafts and fine art by Dayak artisans and artists. Occupies the historic Square Tower.

Mohamed Yahia & Sons BOOKS
(Map p126; ☏082-416928; Basement, Sarawak Plaza, Jln Tunku Abdul Rahman; ⊘10am-9pm) Specialises in English-language books on Borneo, including the four-volume *Encyclopaedia of Iban Studies*. Also carries Sarawak maps and guidebooks.

Popular Book Co BOOKS
(Map p126; Level 3, Tun Jugah Shopping Centre, 18 Jln Tunku Abdul Rahman; ⊘10am-9.30pm) A capacious modern bookshop with a big selection of English titles, including works by local authors, and guidebooks.

 Information

Kuching has Indonesian and Bruneian consulates and honorary consuls representing Australia and the UK.

Dangers & Annoyances

There have recently been incidents of bag snatching from tourists (mainly women) by motorbike-mounted miscreants. Exercise reasonable caution when walking along deserted stretches of road (eg Jln Reservoir and Jln Tabuan), especially after dark.

Emergency
Police, Ambulance & Fire (☑999)

Internet Access
Cyber City (Ground fl, Block D, Taman Sri Sarawak; 1st/2nd hr RM4/3; ☺10am-11pm Mon-Sat, 11am-11pm Sun & holidays) Hidden away behind the Riverside Complex shopping mall on Jln Tunku Abdul Rahman – to get there, exit the mall on the '2nd floor' and walk up the hill.

Laundry

Most hotels have pricey laundry services with per-piece rates, but some guesthouses let you do your washing for just RM5 to RM8 per load, including drying.

Mr Clean (Map p126; ☑082-246424; Lorong Green Hill 1; per kg RM8, 4hr service RM12; ☺8am-6pm Mon-Sat, to 3pm Sun & holidays) A central, reliable place to have your clothes washed.

Medical Services

Kuching has some first-rate but affordable medical facilities – some of the doctors are UK- and US-certified – so it's no surprise that 'medical tourism', especially from Indonesia, is on the rise. For minor ailments, guesthouses and hotels can refer you to a general practitioner, who may be willing to make a house call.

Klinik Chan (Map p126; ☑082-240307; 98 Main Bazaar; ☺8am-noon & 2-5pm Mon-Fri, 9am-noon Sat, Sun & holidays) Conveniently central. A consultation for a minor ailment costs RM30 to RM35.

Normah Medical Specialist Centre (☑082-440055, emergency 311 999; www.normah. com.my; Jln Tun Abdul Rahman, Petra Jaya; ☺emergency 24hr, clinics 8.30am-4.30pm Mon-Fri, to 1pm Sat) Considered Kuching's best private hospital by many expats. Has a 24-hour ambulance. Situated north of the river, about 6km by road from the centre. Served by the same buses as Bako National Park.

Sarawak General Hospital (Hospital Umum Sarawak; ☑082-276666; http://hus.moh. gov.my/v3; Jln Hospital; ☺24hr) Kuching's large public hospital has modern facilities and remarkably reasonable rates but is often overcrowded. Situated about 2km south of the centre along Jln Tun Abang Haji Openg. To get there, take bus 2, K6, K8, K9 or K18.

Timberland Medical Centre (☑082-234466, emergency 234 991; www.timberlandmedical. com, Jln Rock, Mile 2-1/2; ☺emergency 24hr) A private hospital with highly qualified staff. Has a 24-hour ambulance. Situated 5km south of the centre along Jln Tun Abang Haji Openg and Jln Rock.

Money

The majority of Kuching's banks and ATMs are on or near the Oat Fountain on Jln Tunku Abdul Rahman. If you need to change cash or travellers cheques, money changers are a better bet than banks, which often aren't keen on handling cash (especially banknotes with certain serial numbers – go figure!) – and US\$100 bills.

KK Abdul Majid & Sons (Map p126; 45 Jln India; ☺9am-6pm Mon-Sat, 9am-3pm Sun) A licensed money changer dealing in cash only.

Maybank (Map p126; Jln Tunku Abdul Rahman; ☺9.15am-4.30pm Mon-Thu, to 4pm Fri) Has an ATM. Situated on the corner near KFC.

Mohamed Yahia & Sons (Map p126; Basement, Sarawak Plaza, Jln Tunku Abdul Rahman; ☺10am-9pm) No commission, good rates and accepts over 30 currencies (including US\$100 bills), as well as travellers cheques in US dollars, euros, Australian dollars and pounds sterling. Situated inside the bookshop.

United Overseas Bank (Map p126; 2 Main Bazaar; ☺9.30am-4.30pm Mon-Fri) Has a 24-hour ATM around the corner on Jln Tun Abang Haji Obeng.

Police
Central Police Station (Balai Polis Sentral; ☑082-244444; 2 Jln Khoo Hun Yeang; ☺24hr) In a blue-and-white building constructed in 1931.

Tourist Police (☑082-250522; Waterfront Promenade; ☺8am-midnight) Most of the officers speak English. The pavilion is across the street from 96 Main Bazaar.

Post
Main Post Office (Jln Tun Abang Haji Openg; ☺8am-4.30pm Mon-Sat, closed 1st Sat of month)

Tourist Information
National Park Booking Office (Map p126; ☑082-248088; www.sarawakforestry.com; Sarawak Tourism Complex, Jln Tun Abang Haji Openg; ☺8am-5pm Mon-Fri) Sells brochures on each of Sarawak's national parks and can supply the latest news flash on Rafflesia sightings. Telephone enquiries are not only welcomed but patiently answered. Bookings for accommodation at Bako, Gunung Gading and Kubah National Parks and the Matang Wildlife Centre can be made in person, by phone or via http://ebooking.com.my. Situated next door to the Visitors Information Centre.

Visa Department (Bahagian Visa; ☑082-245661; www.imi.gov.my; 2nd fl, Bangunan Sultan Iskandar, Kompleks Pejabat Persekutuan, cnr Jln Tun Razak & Jln Simpang Tiga; ◐8am-5pm Mon-Thu, 8-11.45am & 2.15-5pm Fri) Situated in a 17-storey federal office building about 3km south of the centre (along Jln Tabuan). Served by City Public Link buses K8 or K11, which run every half-hour or so. A taxi from the centre costs RM15.

Visitors Information Centre (Map p126; ☑082-410942, 082-410944; www.sarawaktourism.com; Jln Tun Abang Haji Openg, Sarawak Tourism Complex; ◐8am-5pm Mon-Fri) Located in the atmospheric old courthouse complex, this office has helpful and well-informed staff, lots of brochures (including the useful *Kuching Visitors Guide*) and oodles of practical information (eg bus schedules), much of it on bulletin boards.

Sarawak Tourism Federation (Map p126; ☑082-240620; www.stf.org.my; Waterfront Promenade; ◐8am-5pm Mon-Fri, closed public holidays) This is mainly an administrative office for local tourism professionals but Priscilla is happy to help travellers with questions.

❶ Getting There & Away

As more and more Sarawakians have acquired their own wheels, public bus networks – especially short-haul routes in the Kuching area – have withered. For complicated political reasons, some services have been 'replaced' by unregulated and chaotic minibuses, which have irregular times, lack fixed stops and are basically useless for tourists.

The only way to get to many nature sites in Western Sarawak is to hire a taxi or join a tour. The exceptions are Bako National Park, Semenggoh Nature Reserve, Kubah National Park, Matang Wildlife Centre and, somewhat less conveniently, the Wind Cave and the Fairy Cave.

Air

Kuching International Airport, 12km south of the city centre, has direct air links with Singapore, Johor Bahru (the Malaysian city across the causeway from Singapore), Kuala Lumpur (KL), Penang, Kota Kinabalu (KK), Bandar Seri Begawan (BSB) and Pontianak.

MASwings, a subsidiary of Malaysia Airlines, is basically Malaysian Borneo's very own domestic airline. Flights link its hubs in Miri and Kuching with 14 destinations around Sarawak, including the lowland cities of Sibu, Bintulu, Limbang and Lawas and the upland destinations of Gunung Mulu National Park, Bario and Ba Kelalan.

The airport has three departure halls: 'Domestic Departures' for flights within Sarawak; 'Domestic Departures (Outside Sarawak)' for travel to other parts of Malaysia; and 'International Departures'.

Inside the terminal, there's a **Tourist Information Centre** (Arrival level, Kuching International Airport; ◐9am-10pm) next to the luggage carrousels and customs. Foreign currency can be exchanged at the **CIMB Bank counter** (Arrival level, Kuching International Airport; ◐7.30am-7.30pm) but rates are poor. Places with **free wi-fi** include Starbucks and McDonald's. Among the **ATMs** there is one in front of McDonald's. To buy a Celcom SIM Card, head to the **Blue Cube kiosk** (Departure level). For ticketing issues, drop by the **Malaysian Airlines & MASwings office** (Departure level, Kuching International Airport; ◐5am-8pm).

Those overweight kilos can be shipped to airports around Malaysia at the **Excess Baggage counter** (☑014-287 3330; Next to Departure Hall B, Kuching International Airport; ◐7.30am-8.30pm). One kilo costs RM3.50 to Sibu, Bintulu and Miri and RM6.50 to RM8.50 to KL (minimum weight: 10kg).

Boat

Ekspress Bahagia (☑in Kuching 016-889 3013, 082-412246, in Sibu 016-800 5891, 319-228) runs a daily express ferry from Kuching's Express Wharf, 6km east of the centre, to Sibu. Departures are at 8.30am from Kuching and at 11.30am from Sibu (RM45, five hours). It's a good idea to book a day ahead. A taxi from town to the wharf costs RM25.

Bus

Every half-hour or so from about 6am to 6.30pm, various buses run by City Public Link (eg K9) and STC (eg 3A, 4B, 6 and 2) link central Kuching's Saujana Bus Station with the Regional Express Bus Terminal. Saujana's ticket windows can point you to the next departure. A taxi from the city centre costs RM28 to RM30.

KUCHING SENTRAL This massive **bus terminal-cum-shopping mall** (cnr Jln Penrissen & Jln Airport), opened in 2012, handles almost all of Kuching's medium- and all long-haul routes. Situated about 10km south of the centre, it's also known as Six-and-a-Half-Mile Bus Station. Amenities include electronic departure boards and cafes offering wi-fi. Book your ticket at a company counter, then pay at counter 2 or 3 (marked 'Cashier/Boarding Pass'). Before boarding, show your tickets to the staff at the Check-In desk.

TO CENTRAL SARAWAK From 6.30am to 10.30pm, a dozen different companies send buses at least hourly along Sarawak's northern coast to Miri (RM80, 14½ hours), with stops at Sibu (RM50, 7½ hours), Bintulu (RM70, 11½ hours), Batu Niah Junction (jumping-off point for Niah National Park) and Lambir Hills National Park. Bus Asia, for instance, has nine departures a day, the first at 7.30am, the last at 10pm; unlike its competitors, the company has a **city centre office** (Map p126; ☑082-411111; cnr Jln Abell & Jln Chan Chin Ann; ◐6am to 10pm) and, from Monday to Saturday, runs shuttle buses out to Kuching Sentral. Luxurious 'VIP buses', eg those run by **Asia Star** (☑1300-888 287; http://asiastar.my), have just three seats across (28 in total), and some come with on-board toilets, and yet cost a mere RM10 to RM20 more than regular coaches. To get to Brunei, Limbang or Sabah, you have to change buses in Miri.

TO WESTERN SARAWAK Buses to the Semenggoh Wildlife Centre, Bako National Park, Kubah National Park and the Matang Wildlife Sanctuary stop at or near Saujana Bus Station. Buses to Lundu (including the Wind Cave and Fairy Cave) use Kuching Sentral.

Taxi

For some destinations, the only transport option – other than taking a tour – is chartering a taxi through your hotel or guesthouse or via a company such as Kuching City Radio Taxi (p142). Hiring a red-and-yellow cab for an eight-hour day should cost about RM250, with the price depending in part on distance; unofficial taxis may charge less. If you'd like your driver to wait at your destination and then take you back to town, count on paying about RM20 per hour of wait time.

Listed below is a sample of one-way taxi fares from Kuching (prices are 50% higher at night):

Destination	Fare
Annah Rais Longhouse	at least RM80
Bako Bazaar (Bako National Park)	RM40
Express Wharf (ferry to Sibu)	RM25
Fairy Cave	RM40 (including Wind Cave and three hours wait time: RM170)
Kubah National Park	RM50
Matang Wildlife Centre	RM60
Santubong Peninsula Resorts	RM50
Sarawak Cultural Village	RM50
Semenggoh Nature Reserve	RM40 (round-trip including one hour wait time RM90 to RM100)
Wind Cave	RM40

ⓘ Getting Around

Almost all of Kuching's attractions are within easy walking distance of each other so taxis or buses are only really needed to reach the airport, Kuching Sentral (the long-haul bus terminal), the Express Wharf for the ferry to Sibu and the Cat Museum.

To/From the Airport

The price of a red-and-yellow taxi into Kuching is fixed at RM26, including luggage; a larger *teksi eksekutiv* (executive taxi), painted blue, costs RM35. Coupons are sold inside the terminal next to the car-rental counters.

Boat

Bow-steered wooden boats known as *tambang*, powered by an outboard motor, shuttle passengers back and forth across Sungai Sarawak, linking jetties along the Waterfront Promenade with destinations such as Kampung Boyan (for Fort Margherita) and the Astana. The fare for Sarawak's cheapest cruise is 50 sen (more from 10pm to 6am); pay as you disembark. If a *tambang* isn't tied up when you arrive at a dock, just wait and one will usually materialise fairly soon.

Bus

Saujana Bus Station (Map p126; Jln Masjid) handles local and short-haul routes. Situated in the city centre on the dead-end street that links Jln Market with the Kuching Mosque. Three companies use the Saujana Bus Station:

City Public Link (☑082-239178) Has a proper ticket counter with posted schedules. Line numbers start with K. Urban services run from 6.30am or 7am to about 5.30pm. Buses K3 and K10 go to Kuching Sentral (the long-distance bus station) several times an hour.

Sarawak Transport Company (STC; ☑082-233579) The ticket window is in an old shipping container. Buses 2 and 3A go to Kuching Sentral (2A) about three times an hour. Bus 2 to Kuching's Sarawak General Hospital and Bau is run in conjunction with **Bau Transport Company**.

Bicycle

On Jln Carpenter, basic bicycle shops can be found at Nos 83, 88 and 96. Borneo Experiences (p132) can rent out bicycles for RM30 per day.

Car

Not many tourists rent cars in Sarawak. The reasons: road signage is not great; even the best road maps are a useless 1:900,000 scale; and picking up a vehicle in one city and dropping it off in another incurs hefty fees. That said, having your own car can be unbelievably convenient.

Before driving off, make sure the car you've been assigned – some companies rent out vehicles that have seen better days – is in good shape mechanically and has all the requisite safety equipment (eg seat belts).

Half-a-dozen car-rental agencies have desks in the arrivals hall of Kuching Airport, including:

Ami Car Rental (☑082-427441, 082-579679; www.amicarrental.com)

Flexi Car Rental (☑082-452200, 082-335282, emergency 24hr 019-886 5282; www.flexicarrental.com)

SARAWAK KUCHING

Golden System (☑082-333609, 082-611359; www.goldencar.com.my) We've had good reports on this outfit.

Hertz (☑082-450740; www.hertz.com) Backed by an international reputation.

Motorbike

Renting a motorbike can be a great way to visit Kuching-area sights – provided you know how to ride, your rain gear is up to scratch and you manage to find your way despite the poor signage. Borneo Experiences (p132) have motorbikes for daily rent: RM40 for 100cc and RM50 for 125cc.

An Hui Motor (Map p126; ☑016-886 3328, 082-412419; 29 Jln Tabuan; ⊗8am-6pm Mon-Sat, 8am-noon Sun) A motorbike repair shop that charges RM30 per day for a Vespa-like Suzuki RG (110cc) or RGV (120cc) and RM40 for a 125cc scooter (including helmet), plus a deposit of RM100. Insurance covers the bike but not the driver and may be valid only within a 60km radius of Kuching, so check before you head to Sematan, Lundu or Annah Rais. Situated next to Ting & Ting supermarket.

Taxi

Kuching now has two kinds of taxis: the traditional red-and-yellow kind; and the larger, more comfortable – and pricier – executive taxis (*teksi eksekutiv*), which are painted blue.

Taxis can be hailed on the street, found at taxi ranks (of which the city centre has quite a few, eg at larger hotels) or ordered by phone 24 hours a day from:

ABC Radio Call Service (☑016-861 1611, 082-611611)

Kuching City Radio Taxi (☑082-348898, 082-480000)

T&T Radio Call Taxi (☑016-888 2255, 082-343343)

All Kuching taxis - except those on the flat-fare run to/from the airport (RM26) – are required to use meters; overcharging is not common so taking a taxi is only rarely an unpleasant experience. Flag fall is RM10; after the first 3km (or, in traffic, nine minutes of stop-and-go) the price is RM1.20 per km or for each three minutes. There's a RM2 charge to summon a cab by phone. Fares go up by 50% from midnight to 6am. One-way taxi fares from central Kuching:

Cat Museum (North Kuching)	RM20 to RM25
Indonesian consulate	RM25 to RM30
Kuching Sentral	(long-distance bus terminal) RM28 to RM30
Visa Department	RM15

WESTERN SARAWAK

From Tanjung Datu National Park at Sarawak's far western tip to Bako National Park northeast of Kuching, and inland to Annah Rais Longhouse and the Batang Ai Region, western Sarawak offers a dazzling array of natural sights and indigenous cultures. Most places listed below are within day trip or overnight distance of Kuching.

Bako National Park

Occupying a jagged peninsula jutting into the South China Sea, Sarawak's oldest **national park** (☑at Bako Bazaar 082-431336, at park HQ 082-478011; www.sarawakforestry.com; adult RM20; ⊗park office 8am-5pm) is just 37km northeast of downtown Kuching but feels like it's worlds away. It's one of the best places in Sarawak to see rainforest animals in their native habitats.

The coast of the 27-sq-km peninsula has lovely pocket beaches tucked into secret bays interspersed with wind-sculpted cliffs, forested bluffs and stretches of brilliant mangrove swamp. The interior of the park is home to streams, waterfalls and a range of distinct ecosystems, including classic lowland rainforest (mixed dipterocarp forest) and *kerangas* (heath forest). Hiking trails cross the sandstone plateau that forms the peninsula's backbone and connect with some of the main beaches, all of which can be reached by boat from park HQ.

Bako is notable for its incredible biodiversity, which includes almost every vegetation type in Borneo and encompasses everything from terrestrial orchids and pitcher plants to long-tailed macaques and bearded pigs. The stars of the show are the proboscis monkeys – this is one of the best places in Borneo to observe these endemics up close.

Bako is an easy day trip from Kuching, but it would be a shame to rush it – we recommend staying a night or two to really enjoy the wild beauty of the place. Getting to Bako by public transport is easy.

◎ Sights & Activities

Interpretation Centre   MUSEUM

Offers an old-fashioned introduction to the park's seven distinct ecosystems and an exposé of the co-dependent relationship between nepenthes (pitcher plants) and ants. There are plans to move the centre to the new HQ building.

Around Kuching

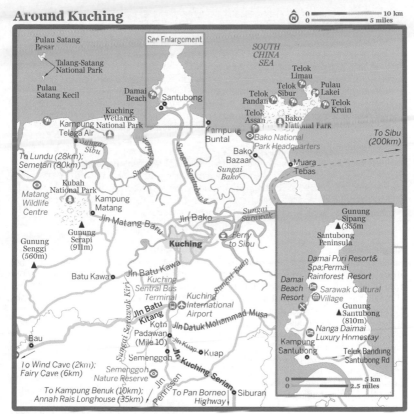

Wildlife Watching

Scientists estimate that Bako is home to 37 species of mammal, including silver-leaf monkeys, palm squirrels and nocturnal creatures such as the mouse deer, civet and colugo (flying lemur); 24 reptile species, among them the common water monitor, which can reach a length of over 1m; and about 190 kinds of bird, some of them migratory.

Jungle creatures are easiest to spot shortly after sunrise and right before sunset, so for any real wildlife watching you'll have to stay over. Surprisingly, the area around park HQ is a particularly good place to see animals, including reddish-brown proboscis monkeys, whose pot-bellied stomachs are filled with bacteria that help them derive nutrients from almost-indigestible vegetation. You often hear them as they crash through the branches long before seeing a flash of fur – or a male's pendulous nose flopping as he munches on tender young leaves.

Proboscis monkeys, who show little fear of, or interest in, humans, can often be found: on branches above the park's visitors chalets; around the mangrove boardwalk between the jetty and park HQ; in the trees along the Telok Assam Beach near park HQ; along the Telok Paku Trail, where they forage in the trees lining the cliff; and along the Telok Delima Trail.

The muddy floors of mangrove forests are home to an assortment of peculiar creatures, including hermit crabs, fiddler crabs and mudskippers (fish that spend much of their time skipping around atop the tidal mud under mangrove trees).

The Bornean bearded pigs that hang around near the cafeteria and chalets with their piglets are a big hit with kids. Not long ago a tourist guide was overheard commenting, 'at the longhouse they would be on the grill already!'

CHEEKY MACAQUES

That sign at Bako National Park's campground – 'Naughty monkeys around – watch out!' – is not a joke. The long-tailed macaques that hang about the park HQ are great to watch, but they are mischievous and cunning – an attitude fostered by tourists who insist on offering them food. The monkeys (and some tourists) are opportunists, and they will make running leaps at anything potentially edible they think they can carry off. Keep your room's doors and windows closed, zip your bags and do not leave valuables, food or drink – or anything in a plastic bag (known by macaques as the preferred human repositories for edibles) – unattended, especially on the beaches or on the chalet verandahs.

It's wise to leave the monkeys in peace – the males can be aggressive, and once you've seen a macaque tear open a drink can with his teeth you'll be happy that you didn't mess with them. Rangers advise against looking a macaque in the eye (he'll think you're about to attack) or screaming (if he knows you're scared, he'll be more aggressive). Recently, especially aggressive large males have been tranquillised, captured and released far, far away. Monkeys are not a problem after dark.

Jungle Walks

Bako's 17 trails are suitable for all levels of fitness and motivation, with routes ranging from short strolls to strenuous all-day treks to the far (ie eastern) end of the peninsula. It's easy to find your way around because trails are colour-coded and clearly marked with stripes of paint. Plan your route before starting out and aim to be back at Telok Assam before dark, ie by about 6pm at the latest. It's possible to hire a boat to one of the far beaches and then hike back, or to hike to one of the beaches and arrange for a boat to meet you there.

Park staff are happy to help you plan your visit, provide updates on trail conditions and tides, help with boat hire and provision you with a B&W map that has details on each of the park's hiking options. A billboard near the Education Centre lists conservative time estimates for each trail. Even if you know your route, let staff know where you'll be going so that they can inscribe you in the Guest Movement Register Book; sign back in when you return.

Take adequate water and be prepared for intense sun (with a sun hat and sunscreen) as the *kerangas* (distinctive vegetation zone of Borneo), has precious little shade for long stretches. Sun-sensitive folks might consider lightweight long-sleeve shirts and trousers. Mozzie repellent is a good idea as well.

A note on trail names: *bukit* means hill, *tanjung* means point, *telok* means bay, *pantai* means beach and *ulu* means upriver or interior.

Lintang Trail   HIKING

If you have only one day in Bako, try to get an early start and take the Lintang Trail (5.8km, 3½ to four hours round-trip). It traverses a range of vegetation and climbs the sandstone escarpment up to the *kerangas,* where you'll find some grand views and many pitcher plants (especially along the trail's northeastern segment).

Telok Limau Trail   HIKING

Bako's longest trail goes to Telok Limau, 13km from park HQ (8½ hours one-way), where there's a nice beach and a designated camping area. Consider hoofing it one way and taking a boat the other (RM164 for up to five people). Cellphone coverage is often available from the slopes above the beach but don't count on being able to coordinate with your boatman by mobile.

Swimming

At Bako, it's easy to combine rainforest tramping, which quickly gets hot and sweaty, with a refreshing dip in the South China Sea.

Stinging jellyfish can sometimes be a nuisance, especially in April and May. Also to be avoided, especially around Telok Paku: stingrays, whose stabs can be quite painful. To keep away the sandflies on the beach, use mozzie repellent.

The muddy, tannin-stained waters of Bako's rivers shelter crocodiles, so forget about taking a dip. A few years ago a schoolboy was eaten by a croc a bit upriver from Bako Bazaar; his body was never found.

Telok Assam Beach BEACH

Swimming is allowed at the beach near park HQ but the water can be muddy. In the distance (to the west) you can see the wild east coast of the Santubong Peninsula.

Telok Pandan Beaches BEACH

The gorgeous beach at **Telok Pandan Kecil**, a 2.6km walk from park HQ, is surrounded by spectacularly colourful sandstone formations. Pitcher plants can be seen on the trail down to the beach. Around the point (to the northwest) is the famous **Bako Sea Stack**, an islet that looks like a cobra rearing its head. To get close enough for a photo, though, you'll have to hire a boat.

As you move east, the next beach you come to is **Telok Pandan Besar**, a quiet, attractive stretch of sand accessible only by boat. Hiring a boat at park HQ costs RM40/80 one-way/return.

Telok Sibur Beach BEACH

The rarely visited beach at Telok Sibur is accessible on foot (it's 5.5km from park HQ) but hard to reach as the descent is steep and you have to make your way through a mangrove swamp. Before heading out, check the tidal schedule with park staff to make sure the river won't be too deep to cross, either going or returning. A boat from park HQ costs RM105/210 one-way/return.

Telok Limau Beach BEACH

At the park's northeastern tip, Telok Limau is 13km on foot from park HQ. A boat to/from Telok Limau and the nearby island of **Pulau Lakei**, which has a white-sand beach and the grave of a Malay warrior, costs RM164 one-way.

Telok Kruin Beach BEACH

At the peninsula's far eastern tip, this bay is 12km on foot from park HQ; a boat ride all the way around Telok Limau costs RM250 one-way.

Nightwalk WILDLIFE WATCHING

(per person RM10; ☺8pm) The best way to see creatures that are out and about at night – we're talking spiders, fireflies, cicadas, frogs, anemones, owls and the like – is to take a night-time walk led by a park ranger trained in spotting creatures that city slickers would walk right by. Reviewed by one traveller as 'awesome', Bako's 1½- to two-hour night treks, when available, are not to be missed. Bring a torch (flashlight).

 Tours

Park HQ does not have enough permanent staff to accompany individual visitors, so if you'd like to hike with a guide, enquire at the boat terminal in Bako Bazaar or, better yet, ask the National Park Booking Office in Kuching for the phone numbers of approved guides. The park is very strict about allowing only certified guides (unlicensed guides and the groups they're with are forced to leave). Kuching travel agencies charge about RM230 per person for a tour, including the boat ride.

Sleeping

Bako has developed a reputation for less-than-adequate accommodation but by the time you read this, the new hostel should be open and at least some of the chalets upgraded. There's a RM10 key deposit. Unlocked storage is available at park reception free of charge.

In-park accommodation often fills up, especially from June to October, so if you'd like to stay over book ahead:

» Online via http://ebooking.com.my
» By email (npbooking@sarawaknet.gov.my)
» By phone or in person through the National Park Booking Office in Kuching
» By phoning the park (only after 5pm Monday to Friday and on weekends and holidays)

Some travel agencies reserve blocks of rooms that they release a week ahead if their packages remain unsold, and individual travellers also sometimes cancel, so week-before and last-minute vacancies are far from unknown.

Forest Hostel HOSTEL $

(dm RM15.90, 4-bed r RM42) The new hostel, made of concrete, will have a private bathroom in each simply-furnished, three-bed room. Bring your own towel and a top sheet (bottom sheets are provided).

Forest Lodge Type 5 CHALET $$

(3-bed r RM106, 2-room chalet RM159) Each two-room (six-bed) chalet, two of which are being upgraded, has one bathroom and one fridge. Fan-equipped.

Forest Lodge Type 6 CHALET $

(d RM53, 2-room chalet RM79.50) Each rustic, two-bed room has a wood-plank floor, private bathroom, fridge and fan.

Camping

CAMPGROUND $

(per person RM5) Because of 'naughty monkeys', tents can be set up at park HQ's fenced-in camping zone only after 6pm and must be taken down during the day. You can also pitch your tent in the park's far eastern reaches at Sibur, Kruin and Limau Beaches and on Pulau Lakei.

✗ Eating

Cooking is not allowed in park accommodation. The canteen charges RM0.50 for boiling water to prepare instant noodles. The nearest grocery is in Bako Bazaar.

Canteen

CAFETERIA $

(3-dish buffet meal approx RM8.50; ☺7.30am-10pm) The new cafeteria, designed to be macaque-proof, serves a varied and tasty selection of fried rice, chicken, fish, hot dogs and cooked vegies. Buffet meals are available from 11.30am to 2pm and 6.30pm to 8pm.

❶ Getting There & Away

Getting to the park by public transport is a cinch. First take one of the hourly buses from Kuching to Bako Bazaar, then hop on a motorboat to Telok Assam jetty, about 400m along a wooden boardwalk from park HQ.

Park HQ and some other parts of the park have (low-power) mobile-phone coverage, ideal for coordinating your boat ride back to Bako Bazaar. At HQ, Celcom customers may have to head to the beach to get reception.

Boat

Motorboat hire (Bako Bazaar dock; ☺8am-4pm) from Bako Bazaar dock, where visitors pay their park entry fee, to park HQ costs RM94 return; the journey takes about 20 minutes. Each vessel can carry up to five people; assemble a quintet to optimise cost-sharing. If you don't plan to return at the same time as your boat-mates, the fee for the return leg (RM47) may have to be split among a smaller number of passengers. If you link up with other travellers at the park and share a boat back to Bako Bazaar, your return voucher – valid whether you come back the same day or overnight at the park – is theoretically reimbursable. Changing your return time is easy: just phone your boatman's mobile phone (it's a good idea to note his boat number as well).

Most day trippers try to get back to Bako Bazaar by 4.15pm to catch the 4.30pm bus to Kuching (the 5.30pm bus is not 100% reliable). Note: buses have been known to leave a few minutes before their scheduled departure time.

When the tide is low, boats may not be able to approach the jetty at Telok Assam so you

may have to wade ashore. Boatmen may insist on an early afternoon return time to beat a late afternoon low tide – but bold outboard jockeys have been known to make the trip back to Bako Bazaar even at the lowest of tides.

From late November to February or March, the sea is often rough.

Bus

Bright red bus 1 (RM3.50) leaves from 6 Jln Khoo Hun Yeang in Kuching (in front of Toko Minuman Jumbo buffet restaurant), right across the street from the food stalls of the Open-Air Market. Departures from Kuching are every hour on the hour 7am to 5pm, and from Bako Bazaar every hour on the half-hour from 6.30am to (usually) 5.30pm. If you miss the last bus, ask around the village for a minibus or private car (RM40) to Kuching.

In Kuching, bus 1 also picks up passengers at stops along the waterfront, on the river side of the street; motion to the driver to stop. These include bus shelters on Jln Gambier across the street from the Brooke Memorial; across the street from 15 Main Bazaar, next to the Chinese Museum; on Jln Tunku Abdul Rahman next to the 7-Eleven in the Riverside Suites; and on Jln Abell in front of Alliance Bank, a block northwest of the Lime Tree Hotel.

Taxi

A cab from Kuching to Bako Bazaar (45 minutes) costs RM40.

Santubong Peninsula

Like Bako National Park 8km to the east, the Santubong Peninsula (also known as Damai) is a 10km-long finger of land jutting out into the South China Sea. The main drawcards are the longhouses of the Sarawak Cultural Village, some beaches, jungle walks, a golf course and a great seafood restaurant in the fishing village of Kampung Buntal. Santubong is the best place in Sarawak for a lazy, pampered beach holiday.

◉ Sights & Activities

Sarawak Cultural Village ECO-MUSEUM
(SCV; ☏082-846411; www.scv.com.my; adult/child 6-12yr RM60/30, cultural show 45 minutes; 11.30am & 4pm; ☺9am-5.15pm, last entry 4pm) This living museum is centred on seven traditional dwellings: three Dayak longhouses (including a Bidayuh headhouse with skulls and the only Melanau tallhouse left in Sarawak), a Penan hut, a Malay townhouse (the only place you have to remove your shoes) and a

Chinese farmhouse. It may sound contrived and even hokey but the SCV is held in high esteem by locals for its role in keeping their cultures and traditions alive.

The dwellings are (supposed to be) staffed by members of the ethnic group they represent – except the Penan dwelling, that is, whose emissaries, true to their nomadic tradition, went walkabout. Signage, however, is poor, so if you don't ask questions of the 'locals' – who demonstrate crafts and cookie-making – the subtle differences in architecture, cuisine, dress and music between the various groups may not be apparent. At the Penan hut you can try a blowpipe (RM1 for three darts), while the Malay townhouse offers top spinning (three spins for RM1).

Twice a day, the **cultural show** showcases traditional music and dance. The lively Melanau entry involves whirling women and clacking bamboo poles, while the Orang Ulu dance (spoiler alert!) includes four women, several balloons and a blowpipe hunter.

It may be possible to book workshops (RM5 per person per hour) in handicrafts (eg bead-making), music and dance – contact the SCV in advance. If you're planning to get married, you can choose to tie the knot here with a colourful Iban, Bidayuh, Orang Ulu or Malay ceremony.

Hotels and tour agencies in Kuching offer packages (per person RM125), but it's easy enough to get out here by shuttle bus. The SCV is a short walk from both the Damai Beach Resort and the Permai Rainforest Resort.

Permai Rainforest Resort   BEACH

(☎082-846490; www.permairainforest.com; Damai Beach; adult/child RM5/2) The day rate at this bungalow complex is a real bargain. In addition to a safe, fine-sand beach with changing facilities, a variety of leisure and adventure activities are on offer, including a high-ropes course (per person RM60), a perfectly vertical climbing wall (RM48), sea kayaking (RM80 for three hours) and mountain biking (RM10 per hour). Great for tweens and teens.

Damai Beach Resort   BEACH

(www.damaibeachresort.com; Teluk Bandung, Santubong) Access to the hotel's lovely beach costs just RM2. For RM119 two adults and two children can have daytime (10am to 6pm) room access and can use the resort's wealth of facilities, including the pool.

Damai Central Beach   BEACH

A free beach with places to eat, situated across the parking lot from the Sarawak Cultural Village. From 10am to 7pm, amenities include showers (RM2), towel rental (RM5) and lockers (RM3).

Jungle Walks   HIKING

Several trails take you into the jungle interior of the peninsula, declared a national park in 2007. One, a challenging route with red trail markings, ascends towering **Gunung Santubong** (880m); the last bit is pretty steep, with steps and rope ladders, so it takes about three hours up and two hours down. A few recent climbers have gotten lost and stranded after dark so whatever happens start heading down by about 2pm. The peak – which some people want to make accessible by cable car – features in a variety of local ghost stories related to a princess captured by a prince.

Another trail, an easy-to-moderate circular walk (3km, two hours) with blue markings, passes by a pretty **waterfall**.

These trails can be picked up at two points along the main road to the beach resorts: at Bukit Puteri and, about 2km north, at Green Paradise Seafood, which tries to charge entry fees, a procedure currently being investigated by the government.

The east side of the peninsula – the coast you can see from Bako National Park – is wild and undeveloped, with a profusion of wildlife. Ask locals about how to get there on foot from the Permai Rainforest Resort and the main road to Kuching, or you can hire a boat in Kampung Buntal.

☞ Tours

Coastal areas west and east of the Santubong Peninsula are home to a wide variety of wildlife. Oft-spotted species include endangered Irrawaddy dolphins (known locally as *pesut*), proboscis monkeys, estuarine crocodiles and all manner of birds.

Resorts on the peninsula, and guesthouses and tour agencies in Kuching, can make arrangements, or you can contact:

CPH Travel   BOAT

(☎in Kuching 082-243708; www.cphtravel.com.my; Damai Puri Resort & Spa) Offers boat trips, including cruises through the Kuching Wetlands National Park.

Mr Ehwan bin Ibrahim BOAT
(📞019-878 5088; Kampung Buntal) A local boatman who offers three-hour dolphin-and-mangrove tours (per person for two/four people RM180/155) and four- or five-hour fishing trips that include a swimming stop at remote Polycarp Beach (RM500 for two people).

🛌 Sleeping

Many resorts allow children to stay in parents' rooms for no extra charge. Kampung Santubong has about 15 homestays. It's possible to camp at the Permai Rainforest Resort.

Permai Rainforest Resort BUNGALOW $$
(📞082-846490, 082-846487; www.permairain forest.com; Damai Beach; 6-bed longhouse RM260, 6-bed cabin RM305, 2-bed tree house RM300, camping per person RM15; @🛜) This lushly forested bungalow complex, on a beach-adjacent hillside, hosts macaques and silver-leaf monkeys in addition to paying guests. Accommodation ranges from rustic, simply furnished cabins to air-con wooden bungalows towering 6m off the ground. Offers plenty of outdoor activities. Prices drop from Sunday to Thursday.

Damai Beach Resort RESORT $$$
(📞082-846999; www.damaibeachresort.com; Teluk Bandung, Santubong; d incl breakfast from RM440; ❄@🛜🏊) A great getaway for families, this 252-room beach resort has enough activities and amenities to make you feel like you're on a cruise ship (in a good way), including boat excursions, sea kayaking (RM15 to RM20 per hour) and even an 18-hole **golf course** (www.damaigolf.com) designed by Arnold Palmer.

Nanga Damai Luxury Homestay B&B $$
(📞019-887 1017; www.nangadamai.com; Jln Sultan Tengah, Santubong; d incl breakfast RM100-160; ❄@🏊) The lovely living room, cosy chill-out verandah, 8m kidney-shaped pool and bright, comfortable rooms (six in total) make it easy to meet the two-night minimum stay. Not suitable for children under 16. The Kuching-Santubong shuttles pass by here.

Santubong Homestay HOMESTAY $
(📞013-895 1245, 082-846773; niesa0619@gmail. com; House 207, Kampung Santubong; per person RM30, with lunch RM40, with lunch & dinner RM40) Sauji and Mariah rent out three rooms in their home, one with attached bath. Homey and tranquil. Great value.

🍴 Eating

All the resorts have restaurants. At the Sarawak Cultural Village, the **restaurant** (meal RM7-10) serves a buffet of Sarawakian dishes.

TOP
CHOICE **Lim Hock Ann Seafood** SEAFOOD $$
(Kampung Buntal; mains RM8-20, fish per kg RM39-85; ⏱11am-2pm & 5-10pm, closed Mon lunch) A sprawling, open-air shed on stilts with a wide-plank floor and a tin roof, this classic Chinese-style seafood restaurant is in Kampung Buntal, a fishers' village 11km southeast of the SCV (on the east coast of the base of the peninsula). The fresh, locally landed fish is superb.

Damai Central HAWKER $
Across the parking lot from the Sarawak Cultural Village, this attractive new complex has several restaurants, a 7-Eleven and a food court (mains RM5 to RM8).

❶ Getting There & Away

Minibus
Kuching is linked to the Santubong Peninsula (45 minutes) by the slow K15 bus (RM4) from Saujana Bus Station and minibuses operated by two companies:

Setia Kawan (📞019-825 1619; adult/child under 12yr RM10/5) Has departures from Kuching's waterfront every two hours from 7.15am to 10pm; stops include the Singgahsana Lodge (p132), which can take bookings; the Harbour View Hotel; and the Hilton, whose concierge is the go-to guy. Minibuses set off from the peninsula's Permai Rainforest Resort depart between 9am and 9pm.

Damai Beach Resort (📞082-380970, 082-846999) Has departures from Kuching's Grand Margherita Hotel and Riverside Majestic Hotel four times a day between 10.15am and 6.15pm; if possible, book a day ahead. The last run back to Kuching leaves the Damai Beach Resort at 5.15pm.

Taxi
A cab from Kuching to the SCV or the resorts costs RM50 to RM60 (RM70 from the airport).

Kuching Wetlands National Park

The only way to see the majestic mangroves of 66-sq-km Kuching Wetlands National Park is – as you would expect – by boat. Situated about 15km northwest of Kuching (as the crow flies), the park doesn't have a HQ complex, just low-lying islands and saline waterways lined with salt-resistant trees that provide food and shelter to proboscis monkeys, silver-leaf monkeys and fireflies (above the water line); estuarine crocodiles and amphibious fish called mudskippers (at the water line); and countless varieties of fish and prawns (below the water line). Nearby open water is one of the finest places in Sarawak to spot snub-nosed Irrawaddy dolphins.

The morning (about 9am) is the best time to see the dolphins, while late-afternoon cruises are optimal for sighting a flash of reddish-brown fur as proboscis monkeys leap from tree to tree in search of the tenderest, tastiest young leaves. Sunset on the water is magical – and unbelievably romantic, especially if your guide points out an *api-api* tree (a 'firefly tree', surrounded by swirling green points of light). After dark, by holding a torch up at eye level, you can often spot the reflections of animalian eyes, including – if you're lucky – a crocodile, its reptilian brain wholly focused on biting, drowning and then devouring its next warm-blooded victim.

☞ Tours

Packages include transfers from and to your hotel. Boats usually set sail from the Sarawak Boat Club or Telaga Air.

CPH Travel Boat   BOAT
(☑in Kuching 082-243708; www.cphtravel.com. my) Has a near-monopoly on boats heading to the wetlands. Offers a mangrove and Irrawaddy dolphin sighting cruise (RM140 per person) at 8.30am and a wildlife cruise (RM160) at 4.30pm.

Semenggoh Nature Reserve

One of the best places in the world to see semi-wild orang-utans in their natural jungle habitat, swinging from trees and scurrying up vines, the **Semenggoh Wildlife Centre** (☑082-618325; www.sarawakforestry.com; ⊗8am-5pm), can be visited on a half-day trip from Kuching or combined with visit to Annah Rais Longhouse and/or Kampung Benuk.

Situated within the 6.8-sq-km Semenggoh Nature Reserve, the centre is home to 25 orang-utans: 11 who were rescued from captivity or orphaned and their 14 Semenggoh-born offspring, some mere babes-in-arms

who spend their days hanging onto their mother's shaggy chests. Four of the tree-dwelling creatures are completely wild (ie find all their own food), but the rest often swing by (literally) park HQ to dine on bananas, coconuts, eggs and – though they don't know it – medications. There's no guarantee that any orang-utans, the world's largest tree-dwelling animal, will show up, but even in fruiting season (late November or December to February or March) the chances are excellent. Semenggoh is noticeably less touristy (and much cheaper) than Sepilok Orang-utan Rehabilitation Centre in Sabah.

Hour-long feedings, in the rainforest a few hundred metres from park HQ, run from 9am to 10am and from 3pm to 4pm. When the feeding session looks like it's over, rangers sometimes try to shoo away visitors (especially groups, whose guides are in any case eager to get back to Kuching), but orang-utans often turn up at park HQ, so don't rush off straightaway if everything seems quiet.

For safety reasons, visitors are asked to stay at least 5m from the orang-utans – the animals can be unpredictable – and are advised to keep a tight grip on their backpacks, water bottles and cameras because orang-utans have been known to snatch things in search of something yummy. To avoid annoying – or even angering – the orang-utans, do not point at them with anything that looks like a gun (eg a walking stick); do not scream or make sudden movements; and, when you take pictures, do not use flash.

Semenggoh Nature Reserve has two beautiful trails that pass through primary rainforest: the **Masing Trail** (Main Trail; red trail markings; 30 minutes), which links the HQ with the highway; and the **Brooke's Pool Trail** (yellow and red trail markings), a 2km loop from HQ. At research time both were closed because of attacks on staff and visitors by two particularly aggressive orang-utans, Ritchie and Delima ('Hot Mama'), whom rangers guess were mistreated in captivity. When the trails reopen, it should be possible to hire a guide at the Information Centre for RM30 per hour (for up to 10 people). Tickets are valid for the whole day so it's possible to come for the morning feeding, visit a longhouse, and then see the afternoon feeding as well. Note: there's nowhere in the park to buy food.

❶ Getting There & Away

Two bus companies provide reliable public transport from Kuching's Saujana Bus Station to the park gate, which is 1.3km down the hill from park HQ (RM3, 45 minutes):

City Public Link – bus K6 departs from Kuching at 7.15am, 10.15am, 1pm and 3.30pm, and from Semenggoh (spelled 'Semenggok' on bus schedules) at about 8.30am, 11.15am, 2.15pm and 4.30pm.

Sarawak Transport Company – bus 6 has Kuching departures at 7am and 1pm; buses back pass by Semenggoh at about 9.45am and 3.45pm.

A taxi from Kuching costs RM45 one-way or RM90 to RM100 return, including one hour of wait time. Tours are organised by Kuching guesthouses and tour agencies.

Kampung Benuk

This quiet, flowery **Bidayuh village** (adult RM6), where the loudest sound is often the crowing of a cock, attracted lots of tourist back when the road ended here. These days, it gets relatively few visitors, despite being a pleasant place to spend a few hours.

The traditional, 32-door **longhouse** (Lg 5), with bouncy bamboo common areas, is still home to a few families, though most of the villagers now live in attractive modern houses. In the **barok** (ritual hall), you can see about a dozen headhunted skulls, bone-white but tinged with green, hanging from the rafters; pick up the key at the reception office. And at the end of the lane, about 100m beyond the *barok*, the widow of the village shaman runs a **mini-museum** (donation requested; ⊙9am-5pm Mon-Sat) filled with all sorts of interesting bric-a-brac, including ceramic rice jars, monkey skulls, blow-dart pipes and two WWII helmets, one British, the other Japanese.

🛏 Sleeping

Kurakura Homestay   HOMESTAY $$
(☑012-892 0051; www.kurakura.asia; per person incl meals RM160) Run by Norwegian-born Lars and his Bidayuh wife Liza, this superfriendly, sustainable jungle homestay occupies a wooden house built in 2008 on land that once belonged to her grandfather. Activities include kayaking and trekking (RM165 for an all-day outing). Situated 20 minutes to 40 minutes by boat from the village of Kampung Semadang. Rates include transport to and from Kuching or the Kuching Airport.

Annah Rais Longhouse

Although this Bidayuh longhouse has been on the tourist circuit for decades, it's still an excellent place to get a sense of what a longhouse is and what longhouse life is like.

The 500 residents of **Annah Rais** (adult/student RM8/4) are as keen as the rest of us to enjoy the comforts of modern life – they do love their mobile phones and 3G internet access – but they've made a conscious decision to preserve their traditional architecture and the social interaction it engenders. They've also decided that welcoming modern tourists is a good way to earn a living without moving to the city, something most young people end up doing.

◉ Sights & Activities

Longhouse Veranda   NOTABLE BUILDING
Once you pay your entry fee (in an eight-sided wooden pavilion next to the parking lot), you're free to explore Annah Rais' three longhouses (Kupo Saba, Kupo Terekan and, across the river, Kupo Sijo) with a guide or on your own.

The most important feature of a Bidayuh longhouse is the *awah*, a long, covered common verandah – with a springy bamboo floor – that's used for economic activities, socialising and celebrations. Along one side, a long row of doors – Annah Rais has a total of 97 – leads to each family's private *bilik* (apartment). Paralleling the *awah*, opposite the long row of doors, is the *tanju*, an open-air verandah.

Headhouse   NOTABLE BUILDING
Whereas the Iban traditionally hung hunted heads outside each family's *bilik*, the Bidayuh grouped theirs together in the community's *panggah* or *baruk* (communal meeting hall). The heads are no longer believed to protect the village – these days the people of Annah Rais are almost all Anglican (the Bidayuh of Kalimantan are mainly Catholic) – but about a dozen smoke-blackened human skulls still have pride of place in the headhouse, suspended over an 18th-century Dutch cannon. It is said that in some longhouses, a few old people still remember the name of each of the heads.

🛏 Sleeping

Annah Rais is a peaceful, verdant spot to chill out. Half-a-dozen families run homestays with shared bathrooms, either in one of the three longhouses or in an adjacent detached house. Standard rates, agreed upon by the community, are RM98 per person for accommodation and delicious Bidayuh board, and RM298 per person – a bit much, perhaps – for a package that includes activities such as trekking, rafting, fishing, (mock) blowgun hunting, soaking in a natural hot spring and a dance performance.

Emily & John Ahwang   HOMESTAY $$
(☏Emily 010 977 8114, John 016-855 2195; http://22. com.my/homestay) Emily and John, both of whom speak fluent English, love to welcome guests to their spotless, modern, two-storey home, built right into the longhouse.

Akam Ganja   HOMESTAY $$
(☏010-984 3821; winniejagig@gmail.com) It's a pleasure to be hosted by Akam, a retired forestry official, and his wife Winnie, an English teacher, at their comfortable detached house on the riverbank.

❶ Getting There & Away

Annah Rais is about 40km south of Kuching. A taxi from Kuching costs RM80 one-way.

A variety of Kuching guesthouses and tour agencies offer four-hour tours to Annah Rais (per person RM115, including Semenggoh Nature Reserve RM140).

Kubah National Park

Mixed dipterocarp forest, among the lushest and most threatened habitats in Borneo, is front and centre at this 22-sq-km national park (☏082-845033; www.sarawakforestry.com; admission incl Matang Wildlife Centre RM20; ⊙8am-5pm), which more than lives up to its clunky motto, 'the home of palms and frogs'. Scientists have found here an amazing 98 species of palm, out of 213 species known to live in Sarawak; and they have identified 61 species of frog and toad (www.frogsofborneo.org), out of Borneo's more than 190 species. In 2012 researchers identified what they believe to be a new species of frog, adding it to a list that includes the aptly-named (but oddly shaped) horned frog and a flying frog that can glide from tree to tree thanks to the webbing between its toes. Kubah's jungles are also home to a wide variety of orchids – and seven semi-wild orang-utans.

Kubah's trails are much more shaded than those at Bako National Park, making the park ideal for the sun-averse. And when you're hot and sweaty from walking, you can cool off under a crystal-clear waterfall.

◎ Sights & Activities

Rainforest Trails   HIKING
When you pay your entry fee, you'll receive a hand-coloured schematic map of the park's four interconnected trails (two other trails were closed as of mid-2012). They're well-marked so a guide isn't necessary. The park has about half-a-dozen rain shelters – keep an eye out for them so you'll know where to run in case of a downpour.

The **Selang Trail** (40 minutes to 60 minutes; trail-marked in yellow), linking the **Main Trail** (trail-marked in white) with the short segment of the **Rayu Trail** that's still open, passes by the **Selang Viewpoint**. Offshore you can see the turtle sanctuary of Pulau Satang.

The concrete-paved **Summit Road** (closed to non-official traffic), also known as the **Gunung Serapi Summit Trail**, runs along the park's southeastern edge from park HQ right up to the top of Kubah's highest peak, **Gunung Serapi** (911m), which holds aloft a TV and telecom tower; on foot, it's 3½ hours up and a bit less coming down. As you ascend, notice that the mix of trees and plants (including pitcher plants and ferns) changes with the elevation. The summit is often

SARAWAK KUBAH NATIONAL PARK

GETTING TO INDONESIA: KUCHING TO PONTIANAK

Getting to the border A variety of bus companies ply the route between Kuching's Kuching Sentral bus terminal (and other cities along the Sarawak coast) and the west Kalimantan city of Pontianak (economy RM60, 1st class RM80, seven/10 hours via the new/old road), passing through the Tebedu-Entikong crossing 80km south of Kuching.

At the border Travellers from 64 countries can get a one-month Indonesian visa on arrival at the road crossing between Tededu (Malaysia) and Entikong (Indonesia), the only official land border between Sarawak and Kalimantan.

Moving on Pontianak is linked to other parts of Indonesia and to Singapore by airlines such as Batavia Air (www.batavia-air.com).

shrouded in mist but near the top there's a viewing platform. When it's clear, there are stupendous views all the way from Tanjung Datu National Park on the Indonesian border (to the northwest) to Gunung Santubong and Kuching (to the east).

The **Waterfall Trail** (3km or 1½ hours from HQ one-way; trail-marked from the Summit Road in blue) passes by wild durian trees and *belian* trees, otherwise known as 'ironwood' (*Eusideroxylon zwageri*). This incredibly durable – and valuable, and thus endangered – tropical hardwood was traditionally used in longhouse construction. As you would expect, this trail ends at a waterfall and a natural swimming pool.

Some visitors combine the Selang Trail and the Waterfall Trail to create a circuit that takes four to six hours. It is no longer possible to walk to the Matang Wildlife Centre because of the risks posed by semiwild orang-utans.

Natural Frog Pond　　　WILDLIFE RESERVE
Situated 300m above sea level and about a half-hour's walk from park HQ, this artificial pool provides a breeding ground for numerous frog species. The delicate amphibians are especially active an hour or so after sunset (from about 8pm to 11pm), particularly when it's raining hard (during the day most prefer to hide in a hole in a tree), so the only way to see them is to overnight at the park. Bring a good flashlight. It may be possible to hire a ranger as a guide.

Palmetum　　　GARDENS
A labelled palm garden near park HQ, on the Main Trail.

⊨ Sleeping

Kubah is a lovely spot to kick back and relax. The attractive chalets, which have a total of 74 beds, can be booked online through http://ebooking.com.my, by email (npbooking@sarawaknet.gov.my), through the National Park Booking Office in Kuching, or by calling the park office. There's usually space, even on weekends, except on public and school holidays. A **camping ground** (per person RM5) is being constructed.

Forest Lodge Type 4　　　CHALET **$$**
(6-bed chalet RM225; ✿) These bi-level, all-wood chalets come with a balcony, a sitting room, a shower with enough room for two, a two-bed room and a four-bed room.

Forest Lodge Type 5　　　CHALET **$**
(10-bed chalet RM150) Has a living room with couch and chairs, a dining table with a lazy Susan, and three bedrooms with a total of 10 beds. Fan-cooled.

Forest Hostel　　　HOSTEL **$**
(dm RM15) Has 12 beds. Fan-cooled.

✕ Eating

All accommodation options come with fully equipped kitchens, including a fridge, toaster and burners. There are plans to open a canteen (cafeteria) in the new HQ building but as of press time there was nowhere to buy food so bring all you'll need.

ⓘ Getting There & Away

Kubah National Park is 25km northwest of Kuching. A taxi from Kuching costs RM50.

From Kuching's Saujana Bus Station, bus K21 to the Politeknik stops on the main road 400m from park HQ, next to the Kubah Family Park (RM4, one hour). Departures from Kuching are at 8am, 11am, 2pm and 4.30pm, and from the Politeknik, situated 2km beyond (ie north) of Kubah, at 6.30am, 9.30am, 12.30pm and 3.30pm.

MATANG WILDLIFE CENTRE

Situated at the western edge of Kubah National Park, the **Matang Wildlife Centre** (✆082-374869; www.sarawakforestry.com; admission incl Kubah National Park RM20; ⊗8am-5pm, last entry 3.30pm) has had remarkable success rehabilitating rainforest animals rescued from captivity, especially orang-utans and sun bears. The highly professional staff do their best to provide their abused charges with natural living conditions on a limited budget, but there's no denying that the centre looks like a low-budget zoo plopped down in the jungle. Because of the centre's unique role, it's home to endangered animals that you're unlikely to see anywhere else in Sarawak.

⊙ Sights & Activities

Interpretation Centre　　　VISITORS CENTRE
Most of the display panels illustrate orang-utan rehabilitation. Inside the new HQ building.

Rescued Animals　　　WILDLIFE RESERVE
Some of the creatures here were orphaned, some were confiscated and others were surrendered by the public. Unless they're needed as evidence in court, all are released as soon as possible – unless they lack survival skills, in which case returning them to

the wild would be a death sentence, either because they'll starve or because, having lost their fear of humans, they're liable to wander into a village and get eaten (Unless it's a Malay village, that is – Malays, as Muslims, do not consume most rainforest animals).

Among the most celebrated residents of Matang is Aman, one of the largest male orang-utans in the world. Known for his absolutely massive cheek pads, he hit the headlines in 2007 when he became the first of his species to undergo phacoemulsification (cataract surgery). The procedure ended 10 years of blindness, though it did nothing to restore his tongue, removed after he chomped into an electric cable, or his index finger, bitten off by a rival dominant male.

Matang is home to three bearcats (binturongs), two of them females, that are too old to be releases. This extraordinary tree-dwelling carnivore, whose closest genetic relative is the seal or walrus, can tuck away a fertilised egg for months and perhaps years, delaying pregnancy until sufficient fruit is available (the trick is called embryonic diapause).

Other animals that live here include two clouded leopards and nine of the happiest captive sun bears in the world. In horrific condition when brought here, they are undergoing a rehabilitation program that's the first of its kind anywhere.

One of Matang's rarest creatures is the false (Malayan) gharial, the most endangered of the 16 species of crocodile. Easily identifiable thanks to its long, thin snout, scientists estimate that only about 2500 are left in the wild.

Rare birds that live here include a buffy (Malay) fish owl, a changeable (crested) hawk-eagle, a white-bellied sea eagle and a confiscated mallard duck (an exotic in these parts!) who's taken to following around a lesser adjutant stork, thinking perhaps that it's his mother.

Many of the centre's caged animals are fed from 9am to 10am.

Trails HIKING

The **Animal Enclosure Trail** (8.30am-3.30pm) takes visitors through the jungle past animals' enclosures and cages. The 15-minute **Special Trail**, where you can see pitcher plants, is wheelchair accessible. If they've got time, rangers are happy to guide visitors around.

The Pitcher Nature Trail and the Rayu Trail to Kubah National Park are closed because of the risk of attacks by semi-wild orang-utans.

Volunteering VOLUNTEERING

(2/4 weeks incl food & lodging US$2048/2984) For details on paid volunteering – nothing glamorous: we're talking hard physical labour – contact the **Great Orangutan Project** (www.orangutanproject.com) or, at the park, **Leo Biddle** (☑013-845 6531). In keeping with best practice, volunteers have zero direct contact with orang-utans because proximity to people (except a handful of trained staff) will set back their rehabilitation by habituating them to humans.

🛏 Sleeping

You can stay in a longhouse-style **Forest Hostel** (4-bed room RM40) with fan and attached bathroom, a spacious, two-room **Type 5 Forest Lodge** (chalet RM150; ❄) that sleeps eight, or a **campground** (per person RM5) equipped with open-air rain shelters (no need to bring a tent, just a mosquito net and sheets or a sleeping bag). Book accommodation by phone, online via http://ebooking.com.my or at the National Park Booking Office in Kuching.

🍴 Eating

At research time there was no place to buy food, so bring your own. Cooking is forbidden in park accommodation but an electric kettle, great for making instant noodles, is available on request.

❶ Getting There & Away

Matang is about 33km northwest of Kuching. By the new road, it is 8km from Kubah National Park HQ. A taxi from Kuching costs RM60 one-way.

Bus K21 from Kuching's Saujana Bus Station to the Politeknik stops near the park entrance. Departures from Kuching are at 8am, 11am, 2pm and 4.30pm.

Bau & Environs

About 26km southwest of Kuching, the onetime gold-mining town of Bau is a good access point to two interesting cave systems and some Bidayuh villages.

WIND CAVE NATURE RESERVE

Situated 5km southwest of Bau, the **Wind Cave** (Gua Angin; ☑082-765472; admission RM5; ◷8.30am-4.30pm) is essentially a network of underground streams. Unlit boardwalks in the form of a figure eight run through the caves, allowing you to wander along the three main passages (total length: 560m) with chittering bats (both fruit- and insect-eating) swooping overhead.

Near HQ, 300m from the cave entrance, you can cool off with a refreshing swim in the waters of Sungai Sarawak Kanan; changing rooms are available.

Flashlights/torches are available for rent (RM3) – if you get a feeble one, ask to exchange it. No food is sold at the reserve itself, though there is a drinks stand.

ⓘ Getting There & Away

To get from Bau to the Wind Cave turn-off (a 1km walk from the cave), take Bus Transport Company (BTC) bus 3 or 3A – they depart about hourly from 7.40am to 5pm except from 1pm to 3pm.

A taxi from Kuching costs RM40 one-way, or RM170 return including the Fairy Cave and three hours of wait time. A tour from Kuching to both caves costs RM125 per person.

FAIRY CAVE

About 9km southwest of Bau, the **Fairy Cave** (Gua Pari Pari; admission free; ⊙24hr) – almost the size of a football pitch and as high as it is wide – is an extraordinary chamber whose entrance is 30m above the ground in the side of a cliff; access is by staircase. Outside, trees grow out of the sheer rock face at impossible angles. Inside, fanciful rock formations, covered with moss, give the cavern an otherworldly aspect, as do the thickets of ferns straining to suck in every photon they can.

Cliff faces near the Fairy Cave, many rated 6a to 7a according to the UK technical grading system, are popular with members of Kuching's friendly rock climbing community, especially on Saturday and Sunday. The sheer white cliff 300m back along the access road from the cave has three easy routes and about 15 wall routes with bolts. Nearest the cave is the Tiger Wall; nearby routes include the Orchid Wall and the Batman Wall. For information on guided rock climbing, contact **Outdoor Treks** (http://bikcloud.com/rock ropes.htm).

ⓘ Getting There & Away

To get from Bau to the Fairy Cave turn-off (a 1.5km walk from the cave), take BTC bus 3A, which runs five times a day.

From Kuching, a taxi to the Fairy Cave costs RM40 one-way, or RM170 return including the Wind Cave and three hours of wait time. A tour from Kuching to both caves costs about RM125 per person.

TRINGGUS & GUNUNG BENGOH

Inland from Bau, most of the population is Bidayuh. Unlike their distant relations on the eastern side of the Bengoh (Bungo) Range – that is, in the area around Padawan and Annah Rais – the Bau Bidayuh have never lived in longhouses. The area's Bidayuh speak a number of distinct dialects.

Tour agencies in Kuching can arrange treks into the valleys around **Gunung Bengoh** (966m) – including the fabled **Hidden Valley** (aka Lost World) – either from the Bau side or the Padawan side. Kuching's Borneo Experiences (p132), for instance, runs treks to the remote and very traditional Bidayuh longhouse community of **Semban**, where a few old ladies still sport brass ankle bracelets. A three-day, two-night trip, including transport, food and a guide, costs RM700/600 per person in a group of two/five.

Tringgus Bong, the furthest-inland of the three Bidayuh hamlets known collectively as Tringgus, has a delightful **home-stay** (per person incl food RM60) in House 392; for details, call **Baon** (☎012-882 9489). At the confluence of two burbling streams, facing a hillside pineapple patch and reached by a traditional wood-and-bamboo bridge, this paradisiacal corner of Borneo is a great place to get away from it all. The nearest Indonesian village, across the border in Kalimantan, is just two or three hours away on foot.

Two vans link Bau with Tringgus (RM4) four times a day until the early afternoon – for details, call **Baon** (☎012-882 9489) or **Bayin** (☎014-579 7814).

SEEING MOUNTAINS FROM THE INSIDE

Many of Sarawak's limestone hills are as filled with holes as a Swiss cheese. Boardwalks let you stroll around inside the Wind Cave, the Fairy Cave and the caverns of Niah National Park and Gunung Mulu National Park, but to get off the beaten track you need an experienced guide – someone like UK-born James, who runs **Kuching Caving** (☎012-886 2347; www.kuchingcaving.com). He knows more than almost anyone about the 467 cave entrances that have been found within two hours of Kuching, the longest of which is 11km. For an all-day caving trip, prices start at RM200 per person (minimum four).

❶ Getting There & Away

Bau is 43km southwest of Kuching. The town is linked to Kuching's Saujana Bus Station (RM4.50, 1½ hours) by City Public Link bus B2 (hourly) and also by bus 3 (every 40 minutes), run jointly by Bau Transport Company (BTC) and Sarawak Transport Company (STC).

Lundu

The quiet town of Lundu, an overgrown fishing village about 33km west of Kuching, is the gateway to Gunung Gading National Park.

The road north out of town leads not only to Gunung Gading National Park but also to two beaches that are popular with Kuchingites on weekends and holidays. Romantic, coconut palm-fringed **Pantai Pandan**, 11km north of Lundu, is one of Sarawak's nicest beaches (despite the sandflies), with a gentle gradient that's perfect for kids. A few beachfront huts sell eats and drinks. Camping is possible. **Pantai Siar**, 8km north of Lundu, is home to several small resorts that appeal mainly to the domestic market.

Otto Steinmayer, an American-born literature professor who lives in – and loves – Lundu, has an interesting website, www.ikanlundu.com.

🛏 Sleeping

TOP CHOICE Retreat
RESORT $$
(☎082-453027; www.sbeu.org.my; Pantai Siar; Sun Fri/Sat chalet from RM158/248; ❉🛜⊠) Owned by the Sarawak Bank Employees Union, this is the ideal place to mix chilling on the beach with workers' solidarity. The grassy, family-friendly campus has 38 comfortable rooms, including 21 chalets, and gets enthusiastic reviews from travellers. Day use of the pool costs RM15/5 for adults/children; the beach itself is free. Situated 8km from Lundu.

Lundu Gading Hotel
HOTEL $
(☎082-735199; 174 Lundu Bazaar; d RM60; ❉) Few hotels have less style sense than Lundu's only hostelry, whose 10 rooms sport blue-tile floors, brightly coloured towels, big windows and peeling ceilings. Situated diagonally across the street from the RHB Bank.

🍴 Eating

Happy Seafood Centre
SEAFOOD $
(mains from RM4.50; ⊘7am-8pm) A very informal, open-air eatery with surprisingly good fish. Facing the bus station.

Fruit & Vegie Market
HAWKER CENTRE $
(mains RM4; ⊘8am-5pm) Chinese and Malay dishes are available upstairs. Situated across the grassy triangular square from the bus station.

Malay Night Market
FOOD STALLS $
(⊘5-10pm) Supposed to move from the Fruit & Vegie Market to the riverfront.

❶ Getting There & Away

Buses run by the Sarawak Transport Company (STC) link Kuching Sentral long-haul bus station (counter 20) with Lundu (RM12, 1½ hours); departures in both directions are at 8am, 11am, 2pm and 4pm.

At the Lundu bus station, it's possible to hire a private car (RM5 per person) to take you to Gunung Gading National Park or Sematan.

Gunung Gading National Park

The best place in Sarawak to see the world's largest flower, the renowned Rafflesia, **Gunung Gading National Park** (☎082-735144; www.sarawakforestry.com; adult RM20; ⊘8am-5pm) makes a fine day trip from Kuching. Its old-growth rainforest covers the slopes of four mountains *(gunung)* – Gading, Lundu, Perigi and Sebuloh – traversed by well-marked walking trails that are great for day hikes. The park is an excellent spot to experience the incredible biodiversity of lowland mixed dipterocarp forest, so named because it is dominated by a family of trees, the Dipterocarpaceae, whose members are particularly valuable for timber and thus especially vulnerable to clear-cutting.

The star attraction at 41-sq-km Gunung Gading is the *Rafflesia tuan-mudae*, a species that's endemic to Sarawak. Up to 75cm in diameter, they flower pretty much year-round but unpredictably, so to see one you'll need some luck. To find out if a Rafflesia is in bloom – something that happens here with human knowledge only about 25 times a year – and how long it will stay that way (never more than five days), contact the park or call or visit the National Park Booking Office in Kuching.

◎ Sights & Activities

A variety of well-marked, often steep trails lead through the lush jungle. Park signs give *one-way* hike times. Except when instructed otherwise by a ranger, keep to the trails to avoid crushing Rafflesia buds underfoot.

Don't count on seeing many animals as most species found here are nocturnal and wisely prefer the park's upper reaches, safely away from nearby villages.

Since these hikes must be done in one day (camping is permitted only at park HQ), you might want to arrive the day before to facilitate an early morning start.

Rafflesia Loop Trail
WALKING
(RM30 per hour for a group of up to 10) This 620m-long trail, which begins 50m down the slope from park HQ, goes through a stretch of forest that Rafflesias find especially convivial. Since most of the blooms are off the path, finding them requires hiring a ranger.

Hiking Circuit
HIKING
For views of the South China Sea, you can follow a circuit that incorporates the **Viewpoint Trail** (follow the red-and-yellow stripes painted on trees), the **Lintang Trail** (red stripes) and the **Reservoir Trail** (a cement stairway).

Gunung Gading
HIKING
Trekking up Gunung Gading (906m; trail-marked in red and yellow after Waterfall 7) takes seven to eight hours return, but don't expect panoramic views – the summit is thickly forested so you'll see mainly the bottom of the rainforest canopy. Somewhere atop the mountain are the ruins of a British army camp used during the Konfrontasi. At **Batu Berkubu** (10 to 12 hours return; trail-marked in red and blue), you can see a communist hideout from the same period.

Waterfalls
SWIMMING
Three lovely cascades are easily accessible along the **Main Trail** (market in red and white). You can take a dip at **Waterfall 1**, **Waterfall 7** (1.5km from park HQ) and the **swimming hole**, fed by a crystal-clear mountain stream, at the beginning of the Rafflesia Loop Trail.

🛏 Sleeping & Eating
The busiest times are weekends, school holidays and when a Rafflesia is blooming. Bookings can be made online via http://ebooking.com.my, or by phone or in person through the National Park Booking Office in Kuching. Nearby Lundu has one hotel.

The **hostel** (dm/r RM15/40) has four fan rooms, each with four beds, and shared bathroom facilities. Each of the two three-bedroom **Forest Lodges** (RM150; ✸) sleeps up to six people. **Camping** (per person RM5) is possible at the park HQ, a bathroom-equipped site.

A canteen (cafeteria) is supposed to open soon inside the new park HQ building. Cooking is permitted in the chalets and the hostel. Another culinary option: driving or strolling about 2.5km to Lundu.

❶ Getting There & Away
Gunung Gading National Park is 85km northwest of Kuching.

Four public buses a day link Kuching Sentral long-distance bus station with Lundu, but from there you'll either have to walk north 2.5km to the park, or hire an unofficial taxi (about RM5 per person).

A tour from Kuching costs about RM230 per person including lunch (minimum two people) – for a group, that's much more than chartering a taxi for the day (about RM250).

Sematan

The quiet fishing town of Sematan, Sarawak's westernmost town, serves as the gateway to Tanjung Datu National Park. The nearby Indonesian border – yes, those forested mountains are in Kalimantan – is not (yet) open to tourists.

◉ Sights & Activities
A grassy north-south **promenade** lines the waterfront, where a concrete **pier** affords wonderful views of the mouth of the river, its sand banks and the very blue, very clear South China Sea. The deserted beaches of **Telok Pugu**, a narrow spit of land across the mouth of the Sematan River from Sematan's jetty, can be reached by boat (RM30 return).

At the northern end of the row of stores facing the waterfront, check out the shop called **Teck Huat** (shops 1, 2 & 3), which hasn't changed in over a century. Built of *belian*, it still has wooden shutters instead of windows.

The sands of shallow **Pantai Sematan**, clean and lined with coconut palms, stretch along the coast northwest of town. It is home to several resorts that fill up with Kuchingites on the weekends.

🛏 Sleeping
Sematan Hotel
HOTEL $
(📞013-828 1068, 082-711162; 162 Sematan Bazaar; d RM50; ✸) The nine very basic rooms, all upstairs, have tile floors and rudimentary

furnishings. Bathrooms are attached but lack hot water. Situated 150m inland from the six columns on the waterfront. If no one's around, look for the owner in the Seaview Cafe across the street.

ℹ️ Getting There & Away

Sematan is 107km northwest of Kuching, 25km northwest of Lundu and 30km (by sea) from Tanjung Datu National Park.

Buses link Kuching's Regional Express Bus Terminal with Lundu but from there you'll have to catch a ride with locals or hire an unofficial taxi (about RM30 one-way) at the bus station.

Tanjung Datu National Park

Occupying a remote, rugged peninsula at Sarawak's far northwestern tip, this 14-sq-km **national park** (www.sarawakforestry.com; adult RM20) features endangered mixed dipterocarp rainforest, jungle trails that hear few footfalls, crystal-clear seas, unspoilt coral reefs and near-pristine white-sand beaches on which endangered turtles occasionally lay their eggs. Few visitors make the effort and brave the expense to travel out here, but those who do often come away absolutely enchanted.

The park has four trails, including the **Telok Melano Trail** from the Malay fishing village of Telok Melano (a demanding 2.7km), linked to Sematan by boat; and the **Belian Trail**, which goes to the summit of 542m-high **Gunung Melano** (2km, one hour) and affords breathtaking views of the coastlines of Indonesia and Malaysia. To spot nocturnal animals, you can take a night walk on your own or with a ranger (it's good form to tip him RM20).

Snorkelling (but not scuba diving) is allowed in certain areas; details are available at park HQ. Bring your own equipment, including water shoes (the coral can be sharp).

Celcom and Digi (but not Maxis) cellphone signals can be picked up about 15 minutes' walk from park HQ, along the beach.

Recent travellers report encountering giant stinging bees.

🛏️ Sleeping & Eating

Park HQ offers four basic **guest rooms** (d/tr RM40/55) with electricity from 6pm to midnight and four open-sided, electricity-less **shelters** (per person RM15), each with space for three people. Blankets, sheets and mozzie nets are available for RM15. There's no way to book ahead – just show up.

For details on **homestays** (per person incl board RM70 to RM80) in Telok Melano, a steep, 2½-hour walk from park HQ, contact the National Park Booking Office in Kuching or ask around at the Sematan jetty.

Visitors must bring their own food. Cooking equipment can be rented for RM10 a day; cooking gas costs RM5.

ℹ️ Getting There & Away

The only way to get to Tanjung Datu National Park or the nearby village of Telok Melano, both about 30km northwest of Sematan, is by boat (one to 1½ hours). Weather and waves permitting, locals often (but not necessarily every day) pile into a motorboat and head from Telok Melano to Sematan early in the morning, returning in the early afternoon (around 2pm or 3pm). If you join them, expect to pay RM30 to RM40 per person one-way. Sea conditions are generally good from February or March or October. The rest of the year (especially December), the sea can be rough, so much so that on some days boats don't run. Walking to Telok Melano – the only other way to get there – takes a full day.

Motorboats with room for five to eight people, either for a day trip (RM450 return) or an overnight (RM500 return), can be hired at the Sematan jetty for travel either to the park or to Telok Melano. To find a boatman, ask around the jetty or call or email **Eric Yap** at the **Fairview Guesthouse** (☎013-801 1561; www.thefairview.com.my; Kuching).

You can also arrange trips through the **Fisheries Development Authority** (Persatuan Nelayan Kawasan Sematan/Lundu; ☎082-711152; for Rosdin Mawi deenazy@yahoo.com.my; Jln Bauxite, Sematan; ⊗8am-5pm Mon-Fri). From the jetty, walk 100m south and a bit inland; the office is upstairs.

Talang-Satang National Park

Sarawak's first **marine park** (www.sarawakforestry.com), established in 1999 to protect four species of marine turtle, consists of the coastline and waters around four islands: the two **Pulau Satang**, known as *besar* (big) and *kecil* (small), which are 16km west of the Santubong Peninsula; and, 45km to the northwest, the two **Pulau Talang-Talang**, also *besar* and *kecil*, situated 8km due north of Sematan Beach.

Once every four or five years, female marine turtles swim vast distances – sometimes thousands of kilometres – to lay their eggs on the exact same beach where they themselves hatched. Of every 20 turtles that come ashore in Sarawak to lay eggs, 19 do so on a beach in 19.4-sq-km Talang-Satang National Park. But of the 10,000 eggs a female turtle may lay over the course of her life, which can last 100 years, only one in a thousand is likely to survive into adulthood. To increase these odds, park staff patrol the beaches every night during the egg-laying season (mainly June and July, with fewer in August and a handful in April, May and September) and either transfer the eggs to guarded hatcheries or post guards to watch over them *in situ*.

Snorkelling and diving are permitted but only within certain designated areas, and divers must be accompanied by an approved guide.

PULAU SATANG

While the national park's conservation area is managed by Sarawak Forestry, the islands themselves are the property of a family from Telaga Air – their 999-year lease, granted by the last White Rajah, Charles Vyner Brooke, expires in the year 2945. About 100 cousins now share ownership, but day-to-day management has devolved to Abol Hassan Johari, a retired accountant who lives in Telaga Air and is much more interested in conservation and research than in tourists. His family retains customary rights to the turtles' eggs but these are 'sold' to the state government and the money donated to an orphanage.

The larger of the two islands, 1-sq-km **Pulau Satang Besar**, has a fine beach and a small wooden shelter. Lucky overnight visitors can sometimes watch fragile eggs being moved from the beach to a hatchery and, possibly, witness baby turtles being released into the wild.

Abol's resolutely non-commercial approach to the island, and the exigencies of conservation, mean that while you can theoretically overnight on Pulau Satang Besar, which is 14km northwest of Telaga Air, you probably can't as green turtles, hawksbill turtles, olive ridley turtles, leatherback turtles, researchers and students (in that order) are given priority.

PULAU TALANG-TALANG

The two Pulau Talang-Talang, accessible from Sematan or as a stop on the boat trip from Sematan to Tanjung Datu National Park, can be visited only during the day. You're allowed to land but swimming is forbidden within the core protected zone (anywhere within a 2km radius of the islands' highest point).

With the park's **Sea Turtle Volunteer Programme** (4 days & 3 nights RM2850; ⊗Jun-Sep), paying volunteers can stay on Pulau Talang-Talang Besar and help the staff of the Turtle Conservation Station patrol beaches, transfer eggs to the hatchery and even release hatchlings. For details, contact the National Park Booking Office in Kuching; booking is through Kuching-based tour agents such as Borneo Adventure (p132).

❶ Getting There & Away

The easiest way to visit the islands is to book a tour with a Kuching-based agency or to contact Eric Yap at Kuching's **Fairview Guesthouse** (☑082-240017; www.fairview.my), who has connections up and down the coast.

Day-trip charters (RM400 per person) to Pulau Satang can be arranged through tour agencies. Boats usually set out from the coastal villages of Telaga Air, 10km northeast (as the crow flies) from Kubah National Park.

If you hire a boat to get from Sematan to Telok Melano or Tanjung Datu National Park (RM450 return), you can arrange with the boatman to stop at Pulau Talang-Talang for an additional fee of RM10 per person. Hiring a boat for a day trip from Sematan costs RM250.

BATANG AI REGION

Ask anyone in Kuching where to find old-time longhouses – that is, those least impacted by modern life – and the answer is almost always the same: Batang Ai, many of whose settlements can only be reached by boat. This remote region, about 250km (4½ hours by road) southeast of Kuching, is not really visitable without a guide, but if you're genuinely interested in encountering Iban culture, the money and effort to get out here will be richly rewarded.

Managed with the help of an Iban community cooperative, the 240-sq-km **Batang Ai National Park** (www.sarawakforestry.com) is part of a vast contiguous area of protected rainforest that includes the Batang Ai Reservoir (24 sq km), Sarawak's Lanjak Entimau Wildlife Sanctuary (1688 sq km) and, across the border in West Kalimantan, Betung Kerihun National Park (8000 sq km). The park's dipterocarp rainforests have the highest density of wild orang-utans in central

Borneo (sightings are not guaranteed but are not rare either), and are also home to gibbons (more often heard than seen), langurs and hornbills.

Trips to the Batang Ai region can be booked in Kuching, either through a tour operator or with a freelance guide.

CENTRAL SARAWAK

Stretching from Sibu, on the lower Batang Rejang, upriver to Kapit and Bintulu and northeastward along the coast to Bintulu and Miri, Sarawak's midsection offers some great river journeys, fine national parks and modern urban conveniences.

Sibu

POP 255,000

Gateway to the Batang Rejang, Sibu has grown rich from trade with Sarawak's interior since the time of James Brooke. These days, although the 'swan city' does not rival Kuching in terms of charm, it's not a bad place to spend a day or two before or after a boat trip to the wild interior.

Situated 60km upriver from the open sea, Sibu is Sarawak's most Chinese city. Many of the two-thirds of locals who trace their roots to China are descendents of migrants who came from Foochow (Fujian or Fuzhou) province in the early years of the 20th century. The city was twice destroyed by fire, in 1889 and 1928. Much of Sibu's modern-day wealth can be traced to the timber trade.

◎ Sights

Strolling around the city centre (roughly, the area bounded by Tua Pek Kong Temple, Wisma Sanyan, Sibu Gateway and the Li Hua Hotel) is a good way to get a feel for Sibu's fast-beating commercial pulse. Drop by the tourist office for a brochure covering the new **Sibu Heritage Trail**.

Features of architectural interest include the old **shophouses** around the Visitors Information Centre, eg along Jln Tukang Besi, and the old **Rex Cinema** (Map p160; Jln Ramin), where art deco meets shophouse functionality.

Tua Pek Kong Temple   TEMPLE

(Map p160; Jln Temple; ◎6.30am-8pm) Established sometime before 1871 and damaged by Allied bombs in 1945, this colourful riverfront temple incorporates both a Taoist hall

on the ground floor, and a Chinese Buddhist sanctuary on the 1st floor. For a brilliant view over the town and up and down the muddy Batang Rejang, climb the seven-storey **Kuan Yin Pagoda**, built in 1987; the best time is sunset when a wheeling swirl of swiftlets buzzes the tower at eye level. Ask English-speaking Mrs Lee, at the ground-floor desk, for the key; as you ascend, don't forget to lock the gate behind you.

Sibu Heritage Centre   MUSEUM

(Map p160; Jln Central; ◎9am-5pm, closed Mon & public holidays) Housed in a gorgeously airy municipal complex built in 1960, this excellent museum explores the captivating history of Sarawak and Sibu. Panels, rich in evocative photographs, take a look at the various Chinese dialect groups, Sarawak's communist insurgency (1965-90), Sibu's Christian (including Methodist) traditions, and even local opposition to Sarawak's incorporation into Malaysia in 1963. Don't miss the photo of a 1940s street dentist – it's painful just to look at.

Rejang Esplanade   PARK

(Map p160; Jln Maju; ◎24hr) One of Sibu's 22 community parks – most donated by Chinese clan associations – this pleasant strip of riverfront grass affords views of the wide, muddy river and its motley procession of fishing boats, tugs, timber-laden barges and 'flying coffin' express boats.

Lau King Howe Memorial Museum   MUSEUM

(Jln Pulau; ◎9am-5pm, closed Mon) One glance at this medical museum's exhibits and you'll be glad saving your life never required the application of early-20th-century drills, saws and stainless-steel clamps – or the use of a ferocious gadget called a 'urological retractor'. Another highlight: an exhibit on the evolution of local nurses' uniforms that some visitors may find kinky. Situated about 500m northwest of Wisma Sanyan.

Bawang Assan Longhouse
Village   LONGHOUSE

An Iban village one hour downstream from Sibu (by road the trip takes just 40 minutes), Bawang Assan has nine 'hybrid' longhouses (ie longhouses that combine traditional and 21st-century elements). To stay here without going through a Sibu-based tour company, contact the **Bawang Assan Homestay Programme** (☑014-582 8105; http://ibanlonghouse stay.blogspot.com; per person incl 3 meals RM110); ask for Marcathy Gindau, who can often be

Sibu

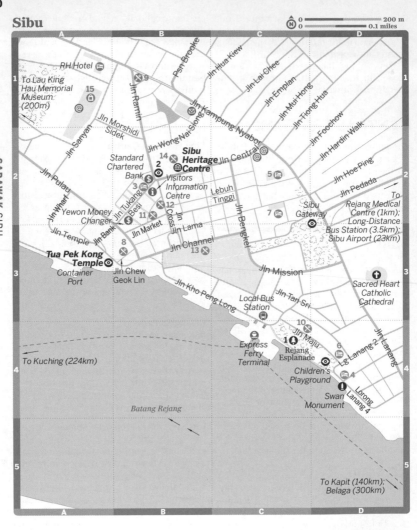

found in Sibu at the **Lehdo Inn** (Map p160; ☎084-331894; 21 Jln Tukang Besi). To arrange transport by van, call **Mr Broken** (☎019-836 1134).

👉 Tours

Two well-regarded Sibu-based travel agencies offer tours of the city and visits to sights both upriver and down.

Greatown Travel   TOUR
(☎084-211243, 084-219243; www.greatowntravel. com; No 6, 1st fl, Lg Chew Siik Hiong 1A) Offers longhouse stays (eg at Bawang Assan and in the Kapit area), visits to the 'Melanau heartland' around Mukah, and various other trips lasting three to six days. Staff are happy to tailor-make bespoke itineraries. Its office is about 1km northeast of the centre along Jln Pedada.

Great Holiday Travel   TOUR
(☎084-348196; www.ghtborneo.com; No 23, 1st fl, Pusat Pedada, Jln Pedada) Based out near the long-distance bus station, this outfit can organise half-day walking tours of Sibu, a day trip or overnight to Bawang Assan Longhouse Village, and two-day trips up to the Kapit area. Reasonably priced.

Sibu

⭐ Festivals

Borneo Cultural Festival   CULTURE
(⏰10 days in early Jul) Brings to town music, dance, cultural performances and food representing Central Sarawak's Chinese, Malay-Melanau and Dayak traditions.

🛏 Sleeping

Sibu has dozens of hotels. Some of the ultra-budget places (ie those charging less than RM35 a room) are of a very low standard and double as brothels. Not long ago some Japanese tourists were bitten by rats while staying in one local dive!

TOP CHOICE Li Hua Hotel   HOTEL $$
(Map p160; ☎084-324000; www.lihua.com.my; cnr Jln Maju & Lg Lanang 2; s/d/ste from RM50/65/150; ❄@🛜) Sibu's best-value hotel has 68 spotless, tile-floor rooms spread out over nine storeys and staff that are both highly professional and friendly. Lift-equipped. Especially convenient if you're arriving or leaving by boat. Book by phone or email.

Tanahmas Hotel   HOTEL $$
(Map p160; ☎084-333188; www.tanahmas.com.my; Jln Kampung Nyabor; s/d RM250/270; ❄@🛜🏊) As comfortable as it is central, with 114 spacious rooms. Amenities include a small fitness centre and an open-air pool, both on the 3rd floor.

Premier Hotel   HOTEL $$
(Map p160; ☎084-323222; www.premierh.com.my; Jln Kampung Nyabor; s/d from RM209/244; ❄🛜) Offers 189 really nice, comfortable rooms in prime downtown location. About what you'd expect for this price – think 3½ stars. Four of the 10 floors are nonsmoking.

River Park Hotel   HOTEL $
(Map p160; ☎016-578 2820; siewling1983@hotmail.com; 51-53 Jln Maju; d/tr/q from RM68/95/110; ❄🛜) A well-run, 30-room hotel in a convenient riverside location. A decent option if the Li Hua Hotel is full.

🍴 Eating

Sibu is famous for Foochow-style Chinese dishes such as *kam pua mee* (thin noodle strands soaked in pork fat and served with a side of roast pork), the city's signature dish, and *kompia* (sesame-flecked mini-bagels filled with pork).

TOP CHOICE Sibu Central Market   MARKET $
(Pasar Sentral Sibu; Map p160; RM2.50-5; ⏰food stalls 3am midnight) Malaysia's largest fruit and vegie market has more than 1000 stalls. Upstairs, Chinese-, Malay- and a few Iban-owned food stalls serve up local specialities, including porridge (available early in the morning and at night), *kam pua mee* (available at most of the noodle shops, but some of the best is on offer at evening-only Stall 102) and *kompia* (check out Stall 17 and Stall FL12, which faces Stall 91; both are open from 7am to 5pm). Most of the noodle stalls close around noon. Got questions? Head to Stall 98 and ask for Noriza.

SWANS

While Kuching's mascot is, famously, the cat, Sibu's is the swan, an 'ancient Chinese symbol of good fortune and health, an auspicious omen for a community living in harmony, peace and goodwill'. Keep an eye out for swan statues as you wander around town.

Café Café FUSION $$
(Map p160; 10 Jln Chew Geok Lin; mains RM10-38, set weekday lunch RM10-15; ☺noon-4pm & 6-11.30pm, closed Mon; ☑) Chic enough to create a buzz in Kuching (or Melbourne), Café Café serves outstanding fusion fare, including Nonya-style chicken, amid decor that mixes Balinese, Chinese and Western elements. Vegetarian dishes are available upon request.

Islamic Nyonya Kafé PERANAKAN $$
(Map p160; 141 Jln Kampung Nyabor; mains RM8-18; ☺10am-11pm; ☜☑) Serves the deliciously spicy dishes of the Straits Chinese, including *ayam halia* (ginger chicken) and *kari kambing* (mutton curry). 'Islamic' means it's halal. Has great lunch deals (RM5.90 to RM9.90) from 11am to 2pm.

New Capitol Restaurant CHINESE $$
(Map p160; 46 Jln Kampung Nyabor; mains RM10-30; ☺11am-2pm & 5-9pm) A classy, old-school Chinese restaurant. Among foochow specialities are sea cucumber soup (RM15), bean curd oyster soup (RM8) and duck with red fermented rice (RM30).

Night Market FOOD STALLS $
(Pasar Malam; Jln Market; ☺5pm-midnight) **Chinese stalls** (Map p160), selling pork and rice, steamed buns etc, are at the western end of the lot, while **Malay stalls** (Map p160) (with superb satay and scrumptious barbecue chicken) are to the northeast. Also has a few Iban-run places.

Kopitiam CAFE $
(Map p160; mains RM3.30-6; ☺6am-4pm) Several old-time *kopitiam* (coffee shops) can be found along Jln Maju, between the Express Ferry Terminal and the Li Hua Hotel. In the morning, locals gather to dine on Foochow specialities, read Chinese newspapers and chat – a typical Sarawakian scene.

Vegetarian Food Stall VEGETARIAN $
(Map p160; Jln Central; mains RM3.50; ☺7.30am-2.30pm Mon-Sat; ☑) In the small hawker centre on the ground floor of the Sibu Heritage Centre.

☕ Drinking

Much of what passes for nightlife in Sibu involves cover versions of Western hits and scantily clad young women.

Queen BAR
(Map p160; 12 Jln Chew Geok Lin; beer from RM10, cocktails RM22-38; ☺4pm-12.30am, closed Mon) Decked out like a Victorian sitting room, this chic, dimly lit bar features plush couches and overstuffed wing chairs in black and burgundy velvet. Stop by from 9pm to 11.30pm for live guitar and/or keyboard music. Food can be ordered from Café Café next door.

🛍 Shopping

Public Book Store BOOKS
(Map p160; Level 4, Wisma Sanyan, 1 Jln Sanyan; ☺9am-9pm) The best bookstore in town, with a decent selection of English books. The mall, Wisma Sanyan, is owned by the Sanyan Group, a vast and politically well-connected timber company.

ℹ Information

Email Centre (ground fl, Sarawak House Complex, cnr Jln Central & Jln Kampung Nyabor; per hr RM4; ☺9.30am-9pm Mon-Sat, to 3pm Sun) Internet access. The entrance is on the building's northern side.

ibrowse Netcafé (Shop 4.21, Level 4, Wisma Sanyan, 1 Jln Sanyan; per hr RM3; ☺9.30am-9.30pm) Internet access.

Main Post Office (Jln Kampung Nyabor; ☺8am-4pm Mon-Fri, to 3.30pm Sat) Changes cash.

Rejang Medical Centre (☎084-330733; www.rejang.com.my; 29 Jln Pedada) Used by most expats and tourists. Has 24-hour emergency services, including an ambulance. Situated about 1km northeast of the Sibu Gateway.

Sibu General Hospital (☎084-343333; http://hsibu.moh.gov.my; Jln Ulu Oya, Km 5-1/2) Situated 8km east of the centre, towards the airport.

Visitors Information Centre (☎084-340980; www.sarawaktourism.com; 32 Jln Tukang Besi; ☺8am-5pm Mon-Fri, closed public holidays) Well worth a stop. Has a friendly and informative staff (ask for Jessie), plenty of maps, bus and ferry schedules, and brochures on travel around Sarawak.

Yewon Money Changer (8 Jln Tukang Besi; ☺8.30am or 9am-5pm Mon-Sat) Changes cash. Look for the gold-on-red sign.

ℹ Getting There & Away

Air

MASwings (www.maswings.com.my) has inexpensive services to Kuching, Bintulu, Miri and Kota Kinabalu (KK). **Malaysia Airlines** (www.malaysiaairlines.com) flies to Kuala Lumpur (KL), and **AirAsia** (www.airasia.com) flies to Kuching (40 minutes), KL and Johor Bahru (across the causeway from Singapore).

Boat

At the entrance to the **Express Ferry Terminal** (Jln Kho Peng Long, Terminal Penumpang Sibu, 🛜), ferry company booths indicate departure times using large clocks. Be on board 15 minutes before departure time – boats have been known to set sail early.

TO KAPIT & BELAGA

'Flying coffin' express boats head up the Batang Rejang to Kapit (RM20 to RM30, 140km, 2½ to three hours) once or twice an hour from 5.45am to 2.30pm. Water levels at the Pelagus Rapids permitting (for details, call Mr Wong at 013-806 1333), one boat a day, departing at 5.45am, goes all the way to Belaga, 155km upriver from Kapit (RM55, 11 hours).

TO KUCHING

Unless you fly, the quickest way to get from Sibu to Kuching is by boat. **Ekspress Bahagia** (📞 in Kuching 016-889 3013, 082-412246, in Sibu 016-800 5891, 084-319228) runs a daily express ferry to/from Kuching's Express Wharf (RM45, five hours) that passes through an Amazonian dystopia of abandoned sawmills and rust-bucket tramp steamers. Departures are 11.30am from Sibu and at 8.30am from Kuching. It's a good idea to book a day ahead.

Bus

Sibu's **long-distance bus station** (Jln Pahlawan) is about 3.5km northeast of the centre along Jln Pedada. A variety of companies send buses to Kuching (RM50 to RM60, seven to eight hours, regular departures between 6.15am and 4am), Miri (RM50, 6½ hours, roughly hourly from 6am to 3.30pm) and Bintulu (RM25, 3¼ hours, roughly hourly from 6am to 3.30pm).

ℹ Getting Around

To/From the Airport

Sibu Airport is 23km east of the city centre; a taxi costs RM35.

From the local bus station, the Panduan Hemat bus to Sibu Jaya passes by the airport junction (RM2.70, every hour or two from 6am to 7.15pm), which is five minutes on foot from the terminal.

Bus

To get from the local bus station (in front of the Express Ferry Terminal) to the long-distance bus station, take Lanang Bus 20 or 21 (RM1.20, 15 minutes, once or twice an hour 6.30am to 5.15pm).

Taxi

Taxis can be ordered 24 hours a day at 084-320773 or 084-311286. Taking a taxi from the city centre to the long-distance bus station costs RM13.

Batang Rejang

A trip up the tan, churning waters of 640km-long Batang Rejang (Rejang River) – the 'Amazon of Borneo' – is one of Southeast Asia's great river journeys. Express ferries barrel through the currents, eddies and whirlpools, the pilots expertly dodging angular black boulders half-hidden in the roiling waters. Though the area is no longer the jungle-lined wilderness it was in the days before Malaysian independence, it retains a frontier, *ulu-ulu* (upriver, ie back-of-the-beyond) vibe, especially in towns and longhouses accessible only by boat.

To get a sense of the extent of logging and oil palm monoculture, check out Google Earth.

LONGHOUSE VISITS

Many of the indigenous people of the Batang Rejang basin, both Iban and members of Orang Ulu groups such as the Kenyah, Kayan, Lahanan, Punan and Sekapan, still live in longhouses. While most aren't as traditional as travellers may envision, visiting one can be a great way to interact with some of Borneo's indigenous people.

Based on geography, Kapit and Belaga *should* be good bases from which to set out to explore longhouses along the upper Batang Rejang and its tributaries. Unfortunately, we've been hearing about two sorts of difficulties faced by some recent travellers:

Visiting longhouses without an invitation or a guide is becoming more complicated as traditional Dayak norms, according to which visitors are always welcome, are giving way to more 'modern' (ie commercial) ideas.

Some area tour guides and van drivers demand inflated prices and/or provide services that aren't up to standard. For instance, visitors may be dropped off at a longhouse with nothing to do and no way to communicate with the residents until they're picked up the next day.

In short, it can sometimes be difficult to find a guide who has good local knowledge and contacts, speaks English and charges reasonable prices. Some travellers report being invited by locals to their longhouses – but that's not something you can count on. One good option is to make arrangements through one of the tour agencies based in Sibu. For up-to-date feedback from other travellers, check out Lonely Planet's Thorn Tree forum (www.lonelyplanet.com).

ℹ Getting Around

Pretty much the only transport arteries into and around the Batang Rejang region are rivers. A road from Kapit to Kanowit (already connected to Sarawak's highway network) is being built and a rough logging road already connects Bintulu with Belaga, so come before easy land access changes this part of Borneo forever.

Boats can navigate the perilous Pelagus Rapids, between Kapit and Belaga, only when the water level is high enough – these days, determined mainly by how much water is released from the Bakun Dam. In an attempt to make navigation safer and less subject to fluctuating water levels, the government has recently been attaching explosive charges to some of the boulders that create the Pelagus Rapids and blowing them to smithereens.

Express river boats – nicknamed 'flying coffins' because of their shape, not their safety record – run by half-a-dozen companies head up the broad, muddy Batang Rejang from Sibu with goods and luggage strapped precariously to the roof. If you opt to ride up top for the view (not that we recommend it...), hang on tight! The passenger cabins tend to be air-conditioned to near-arctic frigidity.

From Sibu, boats to Kapit (140km, 2½ to three hours) leave once or twice an hour from 5.45am to 2.30pm; from Kapit, boats heading down to Sibu depart between 6.40am and 3.15pm. If you travel 2nd or 3rd class (RM20), boarding is likely to involve inching your way along a narrow, rail-less exterior gangway; 1st- (RM30) and business-class (RM25) passengers board near the prow.

If the water level at the Pelagus Rapids (32km upriver from Kapit) is high enough (for the latest low-down, call Mr Wong in Sibu on 013-806 1333 or Daniel Levoh in Belaga at 013-848 6351), one 77-seat **express boat** (📞013-806 1333) a day goes all the way to Belaga, 155km upriver from Kapit, stopping at various longhouses along the way. Heading upriver, departures are at 5.45am from Sibu (RM55, 11 hours) and 9.30am from Kapit (RM35, 4½ hours). Coming downriver, the boat leaves Belaga at about 7.30am. When the river is too low, the only way to get to Belaga is overland via Bintulu!

KAPIT
POP 14,000

The main upriver settlement on the Batang Rejang, Kapit is a bustling trading and transport centre dating back to the days of the White Rajahs. A number of nearby longhouses can be visited by road or river but the pickings are thin when it comes to finding a good local guide.

Fans of Redmond O'Hanlon's *Into the Heart of Borneo* may remember Kapit as the starting point of the author's jungle adventures.

◉ Sights & Activities

Fort Sylvia   MUSEUM

(Map p166; Jln Kubu; ⊘10am-noon & 2-5pm, closed Mon & public holidays) Built by Charles Brooke in 1880 to take control of the Upper Rejang and to keep the peace, this wooden fort – built of *belian* – was renamed in 1925 to honour Ranee Sylvia, wife of Charles Vyner Brooke. On the facade, lines mark the high-water marks of historic floods, one of which crested at an incredible 19m above normal. Inside, the exhibits offer a pretty good intro to the traditional lifestyles of the Batang Rejang Dayaks and include evocative photos of the colonial era. A worthwhile stop before you head to a longhouse.

UPPER REJANG TRAVEL PERMITS

Theoretically, a free, two-week permit is required for all travel:

» Along the Batang Rejang to points upriver from the Pelagus Rapids (32km upstream from Kapit).

» Up the Batang Baleh, which flows into the Batang Rejang 9km upriver from Kapit.

In fact, we've never heard of anyone having their permit checked, and the whole arrangement seems to be a bureaucratic holdover from the time when the government sought to limit foreign activists' access to Dayak communities threatened by logging or the controversial Bakun Dam. Permits are not required, even in theory, if you travel to Belaga overland from Bintulu.

Permits are issued in Kapit at the **Resident's Office** (📞084-796230; www.kapitro. sarawak.gov.my; 9th fl, Kompleks Kerajaan Negeri Bahagian Kapit, Jln Bleteh; ⊘8am-1pm & 2-5pm Mon-Thu, 8-11.45am & 2.15-5pm Fri), in a nine-storey building 2km west of the centre. To get there, take a van (RM1.50) from the southeast corner of Pasar Teresang. To get back to town, ask the lobby guards for help catching a ride (offer to pay the driver).

Waterfront
PORT

(Map p166) Kapit's waterfront is lined with ferries, barges, longboats and floating docks, all swarming with people. Porters carry impossibly heavy or unwieldy loads – we've seen 15 egg crates stacked in a swaying pile – up the steep steps from the wharfs.

Pasar Teresang
MARKET

(Map p166; ☺5.30am-6pm) Some of the goods unloaded at the waterfront end up in this colourful covered market. It's a chatty, noisy hive of grass-roots commerce, with a galaxy of unfamiliar edibles that grow in the jungle, as well as handicrafts. Orang Ulu people sell fried treats and steamed buns.

☞ Tours

LONGHOUSE TOURS

Longhouses, many of them quite modern and some accessible by road (river travel is both slower and pricier than going by minibus), can be found along the Batang Baleh, which conflows with the Batang Rejang 9km upstream from Kapit, and the Sungai Sut, a tributary of the Batang Baleh. Longhouses along these rivers tend to be more traditional (ie still have hunted heads on display) than their counterparts along the mainline Batang Rejang.

The problem is finding a good guide. Tours run by **Alice Chua** (☎019-859 3126; atta_kpt@yahoo.com), Kapit's only licensed guide, are pricey and, frankly, do not get rave reviews. You could also ask at your hotel for recommendations. A few lucky travellers get invitations from locals!

According to the Kapit Resident's Office, the license of one local guide has been revoked for cause. Despite this, he continues to approach visitors, some of whom have made complaints. Because licensed guides are rare in Kapit, and quite a few of Sarawak's unlicensed guides are competent and knowledgeable, it can be difficult to gauge a guide's suitability at first encounter. We advise that you talk to other travellers and local hotel owners as to which operators are recommended or best avoided.

VISITING LONGHOUSES ON YOUR OWN

A few communities around Kapit are accustomed to independent travellers, charging RM10 or RM15 for a day visit or RM50 per person if you overnight, including the preparation of food that you bring along. The headman may also expect a tip. Some people recommend bringing sweets or school supplies for the children. There may not be much to do at a longhouse, especially if there aren't any English speakers around.

Longhouses you may consider visiting:

» **Rumah Bundong** One of the area's few remaining traditional Iban longhouses. Situated on Sungai Kapit a 45-minute (10km) drive from Kapit.

» **Rumah Jandok** A traditional longhouse on Sungai Yong with quite a few English speakers, situated down the Batang Rejang from Kapit.

» **Nanga Mujong** This Iban longhouse, site of a school and a clinic, is served by a road that ends on the opposite bank of the Batang Baleh, from where boats ferry residents across.

» **Rumah Penghulu Jampi** An Iban longhouse at the final express-boat stop on the Batang Baleh.

» **Rumah Lulut Tisa** This longhouse has an official homestay. To get there, take the road to Rumah Masam, whence it's another 1½ hours by boat.

We've heard reports that a local minibus cooperative is charging outrageous rates (RM180 one-way!) for land transport to nearby longhouses. A better bet might be to join the locals on one of the service-taxi minivans that hang out around Kapit Town Square (at the corner of Jln Teo Chow Beng and Jln Chua Leong Kee) and at Pasar Teresang (on Jln Teo Chow Beng).

To get to longhouses accessible only by river, head to **Jeti RC Kubu** (Jln Temenggong Koh), the jetty facing Fort Sylvia, and negotiate for a longboat. These can be expensive – imagine how much fuel the outboard slurps as the boat powers its way upstream.

⚒ Festivals & Events

Baleh-Kapit Raft Safari
RAFT RACE

A challenging, two-day race recreating the experience of Iban and Orang Ulu people rafting downstream to bring their jungle produce to Kapit. Often held in April. For details, check with the Resident's Office in Kapit or Sibu's Visitors Information Centre.

🛏 Sleeping

New Rejang Inn
HOTEL $

(Map p166; ☎084-796600; 104 Jln Teo Chow Beng; d RM68; ✳🌐) A welcoming and well-run hotel whose 15 immaculate, good-sized rooms come with comfortable mattresses, hot water, TV, phone and mini-fridge. The best-value accommodation in town.

Kapit

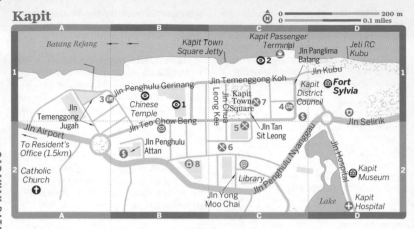

Kapit

◎ Top Sights
Fort Sylvia D1

◎ Sights
1 Pasar Teresang B1
2 Waterfront C1

🛏 Sleeping
3 Hiap Chiong Hotel A1
4 New Rejang Inn C1

✖ Eating
5 Famous Bakery C2
Gelanggang Kenyalang .... (see 8)
6 Night Market C2
7 Soon Kit Café C1

🏬 Shopping
8 Sula Perengka Kapit B2

Hiap Chiong Hotel
HOTEL **$**
(Map p166; ☎084-796314; 33 Jln Temenggong Jugah; d RM45-50; 🖥) The 15 rooms have dinged-up, outdated furniture but are clean and have tiny flat-screen TVs.

✖ Eating & Drinking

Soon Kit Café
CHINESE **$**
(Map p166; 13 Jln Tan Sit Liong; mains RM2.70-6; ⊙5.30am-5pm) An old-time *kopitiam* with laksa (RM4) in the morning and delicious chicken rice (RM5).

Gelanggang Kenyalang
FOOD COURT **$**
(Map p166; off Jln Penghulu Nyanggau; mains from RM3.20; ⊙6am-btwn 4pm & 7pm) A food court with Malay and Chinese favourites,

including breakfast yummies like laksa and *roti canai*.

Night Market
FOOD STALLS **$**
(Map p166; Taman Selera Empurau; mains RM2.50-5; ⊙5pm-11pm or midnight) An excellent place for satay or barbecue chicken. Situated a block up the slope from Kapit Town Square.

Famous Bakery
BAKERY **$**
(Map p166; 22 Jln Teo Chow Beng; pastries RM1-3.40; ⊙6am-6pm) Fresh Chinese and (approximately) Western-style pastries, cakes, mini-pizzas and other easy-to-pack day trip picnic fare.

🛍 Shopping

Sula Perengka Kapit
HANDICRAFTS
(Map p166; off Jln Penghulu Nyanggau; ⊙8am-4pm Mon-Sat, 8am-noon Sun) A tiny, Iban-owned handicrafts place (Shop 21) upstairs at the Gelanggang Kenyalang food court.

❶ Information
Kapit Hospital (☎084-796333; Jln Hospital; ⊙24hr) Three ambulances and half-a-dozen doctors.

❶ Getting There & Away

BOAT
Express boats to Sibu (RM20 to RM30, 2½ to three hours, once or twice an hour) depart between 6.40am and 3.15pm from the **Kapit Passenger Terminal** (Jln Panglima Balang; 🖥), which has wi-fi that attracts whatever the river equivalent of road warriors is, and a nice verandah cafe with breezy river views.

Water levels permitting (for details, call Daniel Levoh in Belaga at 013-848 6351), an express boat heads upriver to Belaga (RM35, 4½ hours) from the **Kapit Town Square jetty** (two blocks downriver from the Kapit Passenger Terminal) once a day at about 9.30am.

One express boat a day heads up the Batang Baleh, going as far as the Iban longhouse of Rumah Penghulu Jampi. It departs from Kapit at about 10am and from Rumah Penghulu Jampi at 12.30pm.

VAN

A small road network around Kapit, unconnected to the outside world, links the town to a number of longhouses. Vans that ply these byways congregate at Kapit Town Square.

BELAGA
POP 2500

By the time you pull into Belaga after the long cruise up the Batang Rejang, you may feel like you've arrived in the very heart of Borneo – in reality, you're only about 100km (as the crow flies) from the coast. There's not much to do here except soak up the frontier vibe, but nearby rivers are home to quite a few Kayan/Kenyah and Orang Ulu longhouses.

☉ Sights

To get a feel for the pace of local life, wander among the two-storey shophouses of the compact, mostly Chinese **town centre**, or stroll through the manicured **park** – outfitted with basketball and tennis courts – between Main Bazaar and the river. Along the riverfront, a wooden bridge leads downstream to **Kampung Melayu Belaga**, Belaga's Malay quarter, whose wooden homes are built on stilts. Although there's 24-hour electricity (provided by a generator – Belaga is not yet connected to the Bakun Dam grid), pretty much everything closes by 7pm.

☂ Activities
LONGHOUSE VISITS

The main reason travellers visit Belaga is to venture up a jungle stream in search of hidden longhouses and secret waterfalls. Possible destinations include (listed alphabetically):

» **Dong Daah** – a Kayan longhouse 10 minutes upriver by boat from Belaga

» **Lirong Amo** – a Kayan longhouse about half-an-hour's walk from Belaga

» **Long Liten** – a huge, old Kejaman longhouse a ways upriver

» **Long Segaham** – a Kejaman longhouse situated upriver

» **Sekapan Panjang** – a traditional, all-wood Sekapan longhouse half-an-hour downstream by boat from Belaga

» **Sihan** – a Penan settlement a two-hour walk from the other bank of the Batang Rejang

Before you can share shots of *tuak* with smiling locals, however, you need to find a guide. A good package should include a boat ride, jungle trekking, a waterfall swim, a night walk and activities such as cooking and fruit harvesting.

Daniel Levoh   TOUR
(☎013-848 6351, 086-461997; daniellevoh@hotmail.com; Jln Teh Ah Kiong) A Kayan former teacher and school headmaster, Daniel is friendly and knowledgeable. A daytrip costs RM150 to RM200 for two or three people, a three-day, two-night longhouse visit costs RM600 to RM750 for a group of three. Daniel can also arrange private transport around Belaga and Bintulu.

Hamdani   TOUR
(☎019-886 5770) For a group of four, Hamdani charges RM75 per person for a day trip and RM115 per person for an overnight stay.

Hasbi Awang   TOUR
(☎013-842 9767; freeland_blg@yahoo.com; 4 Main Bazaar, Belaga B&B) A day trip to two longhouses costs RM80 per person, an overnight trip is RM200 per person.

☆ Events

Belaga Rainforest Challenge   TRIBAL EVENT
(☉Aug or Sep of even-numbered years) The three- or four-day event combines a 12km jungle run with boat races and traditional music and dance performances. Intended for area tribes but tourists are welcome.

☷ Sleeping

Belaga's accommodation is of the cheap and shabby variety.

Daniel Levoh's Guesthouse   GUESTHOUSE $
(☎013-848 6351, 086-461997; daniellevoh@hotmail.com; Jln Teh Ah Kiong; dm RM15, d/tr RM30/35; ☏) The four simple rooms, each named after one of the owners' children, the chill-out balcony and the bathrooms are all on the 2nd floor. Owner Daniel Levoh, a retired teacher and one-time guide, is happy to share stories of Kayan longhouse life. Situated two blocks behind Main Bazaar.

Belaga Hotel   HOTEL $
(☎086-461244; 14 Main Bazaar; d RM30-35; ❄) A convenient location makes up for the less-than-perfect standards at this veteran doss

house. The air-con – available in all but two of the 15 beat-up rooms – works, which is more than can be said for some of the plumbing.

Belaga B&B HOTEL $
(📱013-842 9767; Main Bazaar; r RM20-25; 🌐) Has seven very basic rooms, some with air-con, and shared bathroom facilities. Owned by Hasbi, a long-time longhouse guide.

✖ Eating

Simple cafes serving Chinese and Malay dishes are sprinkled around the town centre, including Main Bazaar.

Kafeteria Mesra Murni MALAY $
(Jln Temenggong Matu; dishes RM3.50-6; ⊗7am-7pm) This family-run Malay restaurant has the only riverfront dining in town. Almost adjacent Crystal Cafe, owned by an Iban-Kenyah family, is also good for a simple meal.

ℹ Information

The new BSM Bank branch has an ATM but it's often (or should we say usually) on the fritz. The medical clinic has one doctor. Several places to stay offer wi-fi.

ℹ Getting There & Away

When the express boat is running, it's possible to visit Belaga without backtracking, cruising the Batang Rejang in one direction and taking the logging road to/from Bintulu in the other.

BOAT

If the water levels at the Pelagus Rapids (32km upriver from Kapit) are high enough, you can take an express boat to Kapit (RM35, 4½ hours) departing at about 7.30am. To find out if the boat is running, call tour guide Daniel Levoh (p167). When the river is too low, the only way to get out of Belaga is by 4WD to Bintulu.

LAND

A bone-jarring (and, in the rain, fiendishly slippery) logging road connects Belaga with Bintulu (160km). Part of the way the route follows the 125km-long paved road to the Bakun Dam.

4WD Toyota Land Cruisers link Belaga with Bintulu (RM50 per person, RM400 for the whole vehicle, four hours) on most days, with departures from Belaga at about 7.30am and from Bintulu in the early afternoon (between noon and 2pm). In Belaga, vehicles to Bintulu congregate in front of Belaga B&B at about 7am. To arrange a vehicle from Bintulu, call Daniel Levoh (p167).

If you're coming from Miri or Batu Niah Junction or heading up that way (ie northeast), you can arrange to be picked up or dropped off at Simpang Bakun (Bakun Junction), which is on the inland (old) highway 53km northeast of Bintulu and 159km southwest of Miri.

UPRIVER FROM BELAGA

About 40km upstream from Belaga, the Batang Rejang divides into several rivers, including the mighty Batang Balui, which wends and winds almost all the way up to the Kalimantan border. Just below this junction, the controversial Bakun Dam generates electricity and provides locals with a place to fish. Belaga-based guides can arrange visits to area longhouses.

One express boat a day links Belaga with Long Bangu (RM20, one hour), 2km downstream from the Bakun Dam. Departures are at about 3pm from Belaga and 6.15am from Rumah Apan.

Bintulu

POP 120,000

Thanks to huge offshore natural gas fields, Bintulu is Sarawak's most important centre for the production of LNG (liquefied natural gas) and fertiliser. The town, roughly midway between Sibu and Miri (about 200km from each), makes a good staging post for visits to Similajau National Park and for overland travel to Belaga.

⊙ Sights & Activities

Tua Pek Kong TEMPLE
(Map p170; Main Bazaar; ⊗dawn-dusk) This classic Chinese temple adds vibrant colours to the rather drab city centre. Follow the cock-a-doodle-doos to the park around back, where young, impressively plumed **fighting cocks** (Map p170) – kept tethered to avoid strife – strut and crow.

Taman Tumbina GARDENS, ZOO
(www.tumbina.com.my; Jln Tun Abdul Razak; adult RM2; ⊗8am-5pm) This 57-hectare park includes an orchid garden, a butterfly house and lots of flamingos. The name is a contraction of the first syllables of two Malay words, *tumbuhan* (plant) and *binatang* (animal). Situated about 5km north of Bintulu Town (RM15 by taxi).

✱ Festivals

Borneo International Kite Festival KITES
(www.borneokite.com) An annual event, usually held over four or five days in September, that brings fanciful and extravagant kites from around the world to the old airport.

🛏 Sleeping

There are quite a few hotels, some on the dodgy side, on and near Jln Keppel, its southern continuation, Jln Abang Galau, and parallel on Jln Masjid.

Kintown Inn
HOTEL $

(Map p170; ☑086-333666; 93 Jln Keppel; s/d RM80/86; ❄️🛜) The 50 carpeted rooms are smallish but bright, with good views from the upper floors. Delivers the best value for your buck in town.

Riverfront Inn
HOTEL $$

(Map p170; ☑086-333111; riverfrontinn@hotmail.com; 256 Taman Sri Dagang; d with window RM104; ❄️🛜) A long-standing favourite with business and leisure visitors alike, the Riverfront is low-key but has a touch of class. Try to get a deluxe room (RM110) overlooking the river – the view is pure Borneo.

✖️ Eating & Drinking

Local nightlife, such as it is, consists mainly of single men hanging out along Jln Masjid.

Ban Kee Café
SEAFOOD $$

(Map p170; off Jln Abang Galau; mains RM6-15; ⊙6am-midnight; ☑) An indoor-outdoor Chinese seafood specialist with fresh fish (per kg RM40 to RM80) and seafood and, for breakfast, noodles and laksa (RM3.50).

Popular Corner Food Centre
HAWKER $

(Map p170; 50 BDA Shahida Commercial Centre; mains RM3-8; ⊙6am-10pm) Eight stalls sell laksa (morning only), rice porridge, dim sum and fresh Hong Kong-style seafood.

Night Market
FOOD STALLS $

(Map p170; off Jln Abang Galau; mains RM2.50-5; ⊙4-10pm or 11pm) A good place to snack track for fresh fruit and Malay favourites such as satay.

Pasar Utama
FOOD STALLS $

(Map p170; New Market; Main Bazaar; mains RM3-5; ⊙7am-5pm) Malay and Chinese food stalls fill the upper floor of this blue-coloured, figure-eight-shaped fruit and vegie market.

Chef
BAKERY $

(Map p170; 92 Jln Abang Galau; cakes from RM1; ⊙8.30am-9pm) Makes Chinese-inflected halal baked goods, including buns with hot dogs baked inside (RM1.70) and surprisingly tasty Belgian chocolate cake (RM6.80). Ideal fare for a picnic lunch.

ℹ️ Information

Fi Wee Internet Centre (1st fl, 133 Jln Masjid; per hr RM2; ⊙9am-midnight) Has 27 internet computers at the top of a filthy staircase.

ℹ️ Getting There & Away

To arrange transport by 4WD Toyota Land Cruiser from Bintulu to Belaga (per person RM50, four hours) on some pretty rough logging roads, call Daniel Levoh (p167). Departures are generally in the early afternoon (between noon and 2pm).

Air

AirAsia (www.airasia.com) and **Malaysia Airlines** (www.malaysiaairlines.com) have direct flights to Kuching and Kuala Lumpur (KL). MASwings (www.maswings.com.my) can whisk you to Kota Kinabalu (KK), Miri, Sibu and Kuching.

Bus

The long-distance bus station is at Medan Jaya, 5km northeast of the centre (aka Bintulu Town); a taxi costs RM15. About a dozen companies have buses approximately hourly:

Kuching (RM60 to RM65, 10 hours) Via Sibu (RM20 to RM25, four hours), from 6.45am to midnight.

Miri (RM20 to RM25, four hours) Via Niah Junction (RM12 to RM15, 2-3/4 hours), from 6am to 11.15pm.

ℹ️ Getting Around

To/From the Airport

There is no public transport to/from the airport, which is 23km from the centre by road. A taxi costs RM35.

Similajau National Park

An easy 30km northeast of Bintulu, Similajau National Park (☑by satellite phone 086-489003, office in Bintulu 086-313726; www.sarawakforestry.com; admission RM20; ⊙park office 8am-1pm & 2-5pm Sat-Thu, 8-11.45am & 2.15-5pm Fri) is a fine little coastal park with golden-sand beaches, good walking trails and simple accommodation. Occupying a narrow, 30km-long strip along the South China Sea, its 90 sq km encompasses littoral habitats such as mangroves, *kerangas* (heath forest) and mixed dipterocarp forest, (classic lowland tropical rainforest). Four species of dolphin, including Irrawaddy, can sometimes be spotted out at sea, and green turtles occasionally trundle ashore to lay their eggs along Turtle Beach II and Golden Beach.

Bintuluans flock to Similajau (especially the beaches) on weekends and public holidays, but the park is gloriously deserted on weekdays.

Bintulu

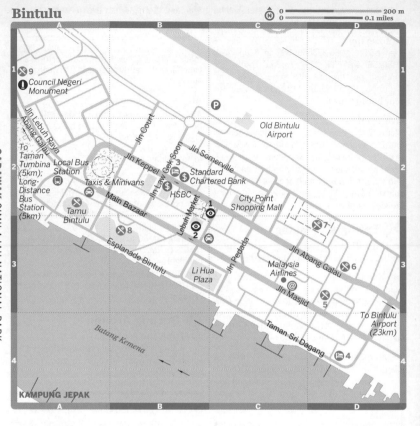

Bintulu

⊙ Sights
1 Fighting Cocks..C2
2 Tua Pek Kong B3

🛏 Sleeping
3 Kintown Inn...B2
4 Riverfront Inn D4

🍴 Eating
5 Ban Kee Café D3
6 Chef D3
7 Night Market..D3
8 Pasar Utama...B3
9 Popular Corner Food Centre A1

DANGERS & ANNOYANCES
Similajau's waterways are prime crocodile habitat so do not swim or wade in the rivers or near river mouths, and be careful when walking near riverbanks, especially early or late in the day.

Because of dangerous undertows, swimming is forbidden at the two Turtle Beaches and at Golden Beach.

⊙ Sights & Activities
The casuarina-lined beach at park HQ, strewn with driftwood but clean, is a great place to chill out and swim – but watch out for jellyfish (if you get stung, rangers can provide vinegar to alleviate the pain).

Similajau's gently undulating **Main Trail** (Coastal Trail) parallels the coast, starting across Sungai Likau from park HQ and ending at **Golden Beach** (10km, four hours one-way). En route it passes by rocky headlands, small bays, **Turtle Beach I** (6km, three hours) and Turtle Beach II (7.5km, 3½ hours). For a view back along the coast towards Bintulu and its natural gas installations, head to the **View Point** (1.3km from HQ, 40 minutes).

Right after you cross the suspension bridge next to park HQ, a plankwalk to your right follows the river upstream. Both the 600m **Education Trail** and its continuation, the 1.7km **Circular Trail** (which takes you back to a point near the bridge), pass through brilliant estuarine mangroves and mixed dipterocarp forest.

Similajau's trails are easy to follow and are clearly marked (in the case of the Main Trail, in red) so a guide isn't necessary, though it's possible to hire one for RM30 per hour (RM40 per hour for a **night walk**). A simple but useful trail map is available at park HQ. Bring plenty of drinking water.

HQ staff are happy to arrange travel in a national park-owned boat with space for up to five passengers. Sea conditions sometimes get rough after about noon. Among your cruising options:

Night River Cruise (RM150; ☉7-9pm) A great way to see crocs. Reserve during office hours.

Batu Mandi Tide Pools (RM150) The tidal pools around this low, rocky island can only be visited at low tide and when the sea is calm.

Turtle Beaches I and II (one-way/return RM180/230) Take the boat out there (it's a half-hour ride) and you can walk back.

Golden Beach (one-way/return RM220/280) Another option for a one-way walk.

🛏 Sleeping

Similajau's rustic overnight options, just 100m from the beach, are booked out months ahead on public holidays and sometimes fill up on weekends. To reserve, contact the park by phone, fax (086-489 002) or email (norhider@sarawakforestry.com). Bookings *cannot* be made through the national park offices in Kuching or Miri.

Renting a towel costs RM6.

Chalets   CHALET **$$**
(1/2 rooms RM106/159) Each of the six new chalets has two rooms, each of which has one queen bed, one twin bed and one fan.

Rest House   CHALET **$$**
(per night RM318; ❄) Sleeps four in air-con comfort.

Hostel   HOSTEL **$**
(per room RM42) Each room has four beds (bunks in the case of Hostel 3) and a wall fan. Hostels 1 and 2, built in 2011, have

attached bathrooms. Dorm beds are not available individually.

Campground   CAMPGROUND **$**
(per person RM5) Camping is only permitted next to park HQ. Showers are provided.

🍴 Eating

The park's **cafeteria** (Canteen; mains RM5-13; ☉7.30am-9pm; 🖫) serves noodle and rice dishes and can prepare packed lunches. Cooking is not allowed in the chalets or the hostel but there are designated sites for barbecuing. To prepare packaged noodles, you can borrow an electric kettle at the park office.

ℹ Getting There & Away

The HQ of Similajau National Park is about 30km northeast of Bintulu, 9km off the coastal road to Miri. Count on paying RM50 one-way to hire a **taxi** (☎086-332009) – or a 10-seat minibus – from Bintulu's Pasar Utama (Main Bazaar) (p169); from the airport, the cab ride costs about RM75.

To get back to Bintulu, you can pre-arrange a pick-up time or ask HQ staff to help you call for a taxi.

Niah National Park

The vast limestone caverns of 31-sq-km **Niah National Park** (☎085-737450, 085-737454; www.sarawakforestry.com; admission RM20; ☉park office 8am-5pm) are among Borneo's most famous and impressive natural attractions. At the heart of the park is the Great Cave, one of the largest caverns in the world.

Niah's caves have provided groundbreaking insights into human life on Borneo way back when the island was still connected to mainland Southeast Asia. In 1958 archaeologists led by Tom Harrisson discovered the 40,000-year-old skull of an anatomically modern human, the oldest remains of a *Homo sapiens* discovered anywhere in Southeast Asia.

Rock paintings and several small canoe-like coffins ('death ships') indicate that the site was used as a burial ground much more recently. Some of the artefacts found at Niah are on display at the Sarawak Museum in Kuching; others (a handful) are in the park's own museum.

Niah's caves accommodate a staggering number of bats and are an important nesting site for swiftlets, some of whose species supply the vital ingredient for bird's-nest soup. Traditionally, the Penan are custodians and collectors of the nests, while the Iban have the rights to the caves' other commodity, bat and bird guano, which is highly valued as fertiliser (no prizes for guessing who got first pick). During the harvesting season (August to March), nest collectors can be seen on towering bamboo structures wedged against the cave roof.

We've heard travellers say that if you've been (or will be going) to Gunung Mulu National Park, going to Niah might not be worth the effort – unless you're fascinated by human prehistory, of course.

◎ Sights & Activities

Niah Archaeology Museum   MUSEUM
(motor launch per person 7.30am-5.30pm RM1, 5.30-7.30pm RM1.50, after 7.30pm RM3 by pre-arrangement; ◎9am-4.30pm, closed Mon) Across the river from park HQ, this museum has rather old-fashioned displays on Niah's geology, ecology and prehistoric archaeology, including an original burial canoe that's at least 1200 years old, a reproduction of the Painted Cave, a case featuring swiftlets' nests, and a replica of the 40,000-year-old 'Deep Skull'.

To get to the museum from HQ, cross the Sungai Niah by motor launch.

If you don't have your own, torches/flashlights (RM5; make sure the one you get is working) – extremely useful if you want to go any distance into the caves – can be rented at the ferry terminal and the museum.

Great Cave & Painted Cave   CAVE
From the museum, a raised boardwalk leads 3.1km (3½ to four hours return) through swampy, old-growth rainforest to the mouth of the Great Cave, a vast cavern approximately 2km long, up to 250m across and up to 60m high. To make it back by nightfall, start your stroll by about 2pm.

As you walk, stop and stand silently every once in a while – you'll hear lots of birds and, if you're lucky, may hear or even see macaques, especially early in the morning or in the evening.

Just before the cave entrance, the boardwalk forks. The right fork leads to the cave, while the left fork goes to Rumah Patrick Libau, an Iban longhouse hamlet. Villagers usually sit at the junction selling cold drinks and souvenirs.

Inside the Great Cave, the trail splits to go around a massive central pillar, but both branches finish at the same point so

it's impossible to get lost if you stick to the boardwalk. The stairs and handrails are usually covered with dirt or guano, and can get very slippery in places. The rock formations are spectacular and ominous by turns, and as you slip in and out of the gloom you may find yourself thinking of Jules Verne's *Journey to the Centre of the Earth*. When the sun hits certain overhead vents, the cave is penetrated by dramatic rays of other-worldly light. When you're halfway through the dark passage known as **Gan Kira** (Moon Cave), try turning off your flashlight to enjoy the experience of pure, soupy blackness.

The **Painted Cave** is famed for its ancient drawings, in red hematite, depicting jungle animals, human figures and the souls of the dead being taken to the afterlife by boat. At research time it was closed for maintenance until further notice.

Bats & Swiftlets   FLYING CREATURES
At one time, some 470,000 bats and four million swiftlets called Niah home. There are no current figures, but the walls of the caves are no longer thick with bats and there are fewer bird's nests to harvest.

Several species of swiftlet nest on the cave walls. The most common by far is the glossy swiftlet, whose nest is made of vegetation and is therefore of no use in making soup. For obvious reasons, the species whose nests are edible (ie made of delicious salivary excretions) are far less abundant and can only be seen in the remotest corners of the cavern. Several types of bat also roost in the cave, but not in dense colonies, as at Gunung Mulu National Park.

The best time to see the cave's winged wildlife is at dusk (5.30pm to 6.45pm) during the 'changeover', when the swiftlets stream back to their nests and the bats come swirling out for the night's feeding. If you decide to stick around, let staff at the park HQ's Registration Counter know and make sure you either get back to the ferry by 7.30pm or coordinate a later pick-up time with the boatman.

Bukit Kasut   TRAIL
This 45-minute trail, part of it a boardwalk through freshwater swamp forest, goes from near the museum southward up to the summit of Bukit Kasut (205m). In the wet season, it can get muddy and treacherously slippery.

🛏 Sleeping & Eating

Park HQ has a decent **canteen** (Cafeteria; mains RM5-10; ⊙8am-10pm; 🖉). Cooking is prohibited in park accommodation but, except at the hostel, you can boil water to make instant noodles.

Batu Niah town, 4km from park HQ (3km if you walk), has a couple of basic hotels.

NIAH NATIONAL PARK

Bookings for park-run accommodation can be made at park HQ (in person or by phone) or through one of the **National Park Booking Offices** (🖉in Kuching 082-248088, in Miri 085-434184) – but *not* through Sarawak Forestry's website. Lodges and rooms often fill up on Chinese, Malay and public holidays.

Forest Lodges   CHALET $$
(1/2 rooms with fan RM106/159, with air-con RM159/239) The park has six rustic two-room chalets with attached bath; each room can sleep up to four.

Hostel   HOSTEL $
(r RM42) Each basic hostel room has space for up to four people.

Homestay   HOMESTAY $
(🖉019-805 2415; per person incl dinner & breakfast RM70) The Iban longhouse village of Rumah Patrick Libau, near the Great Cave, has an informal homestay program.

Campground   CAMPGROUND $
(per person RM5) Camping is permitted near park HQ.

BATU NIAH JUNCTION

If your bus arrives late or is leaving early, you might consider overnighting at Batu Niah Junction, a major transport hub 15km south of park HQ.

Hangar-like **Batu Niah Food Court Centre** (⊙24hr) has lots of Chinese and Malay food stalls and, in the little grocery to the left as you enter the hall, **internet access** (per hour RM3; ⊙24hr). Bathrooms are way in back, beyond the terrariums holding reptiles believed to bring good luck – people leave cash offerings for the ancient river turtle, on loan from a Chinese temple, and the albino snake. There are more food stalls and a fruit and vegie market across the highway.

TTL Motel   HOTEL $$
(🖉086-738377; d from RM80-118; ⊙reception 24hr; 🌣) This newish, 39-room low-rise complex is pricey for what you get, which is mostly convenience. All rooms have windows but some of the more expensive ones are a bit musty. To get there from Batu Niah Food Court Centre, go out the back door and hang a diagonal left.

❶ Getting There & Away

Niah National Park is about 115km southwest of Miri and 122km northeast of Bintulu. If you're pressed for time, it can be visited as a day trip from either city.

Park HQ is 15km north of Batu Niah Junction, a major transport hub on the inland (old) Miri–Bintulu highway. This makes getting to the park by public transport a wee bit tricky (but it's much harder to get to from the new coastal highway).

All long-haul buses linking Miri's Pujut Bus Terminal with Bintulu, Sibu and Kuching stop at Batu Niah Junction, but the only way to get from the junction to the park is to hire an unofficial taxi. The price should be RM30 (RM40 for a group of four) but you'll have to nose around the junction to find one. A good place to check: the bench in front of Shen Yang Trading, at the corner of Ngu's Garden Food Court. National park staff (or, after hours, park security personnel) can help arrange a car back to the junction.

From Batu Niah Junction, buses head to Miri (RM10 to RM12) from about 8am to 1am and to Bintulu (RM15, two hours) from about 8am to 10.30pm. Other well-served destinations include Sibu (RM30 to RM40, five to six hours) and Kuching (RM70 to RM80, 12 hours). Kiosks representing various companies can be found at both ends of the building directly across the highway from the Batu Niah Food Court Centre.

From Miri, a taxi to Niah costs RM150 one-way or RM300 return, including three hours of wait time.

Lambir Hills National Park

The 69-sq-km **Lambir Hills National Park** (🖉085-471609; www.sarawakforestry.com; admission RM10; ⊙park office 8am-5pm) shelters dozens of jungle waterfalls, plenty of cool pools where you can take a dip, and a bunch of great walking trails through mixed dipterocarp and *kerangas* forests. A perennial favourite among locals and an important centre of scientific research, Lambir Hills makes a great day or overnight trip out of the city.

The park encompasses a range of low sandstone hills with an extraordinary range of plants and animals – perhaps even, as noted in Sarawak Forestry's publications, 'the greatest level of plant biodiversity on the planet'. Studies of a 52-hectare research plot (closed to visitors) have found an amazing 1200 tree species! Fauna include clouded leopards, barking deer, pangolins, tarsiers, five varieties of civet, 10 bat species and 50 other kinds of mammals, though you are unlikely to see many of them around park HQ. Lambir Hills is also home to an unbelievable 237 species of bird, among them eight kinds of hornbill, and 24 species of frog – and more are being found all the time.

🏃 Activities

Lambir Hills' colour-coded trails branch off four primary routes and lead to 14 destinations – rangers, based in an ugly new HQ building opened in 2012, can supply you with a map and are happy to make suggestions. Make sure you get back to park HQ before 5pm – unless you're heading out for a night walk, that is, in which case you need to coordinate with park staff. Hiring a guide (optional) costs RM20 per hour for up to five people.

From HQ, the **Main Trail** follows a small river, Sungai Liam, past two attractive waterfalls to the 25m-high **Latak Waterfall** (1km, 15 minutes to 20 minutes one-way), which has a picnic area, changing rooms and a refreshing, sandy pool suitable for swimming. It can get pretty crowded on weekends and holidays.

You're likely to enjoy more natural tranquillity along the path to **Tengkorong Waterfall**, a somewhat strenuous 6km walk (one-way) from park HQ.

Another trail, steep in places, goes to the summit of **Bukit Lambir** (465m; 7km one-way from HQ), which affords fine views. Keep an eye out for changes in the vegetation, including wild orchids, as the elevation rises.

🛏 Sleeping & Eating

The park has 13 reasonably comfortable, two-room **chalets** (1/2 rooms with fan RM50/75, with air-con RM100/150); the old ones are wooden, the four new ones are made of concrete. Fan rooms have two beds, while air-con rooms have three. If you get in before 2pm (check-in time), bags can be left at the camp office. **Camping** (per person RM5) is permitted near the park HQ. Individual dorm beds are not available.

Book by calling the park or through Miri's National Park Booking Office; on-line booking is not yet possible. Chalets are sometimes booked out on weekends and during school holidays.

A small **canteen** (Cafeteria; mains RM4-6; ⏰8am or 8.30am-5pm or later) serves fried rice and noodles. Cooking facilities are not available but you can rent an electric kettle (RM5) to boil water for instant noodles.

🛈 Getting There & Away

Park HQ is 32km south of Miri on the inland (old) highway to Bintulu. All the buses that link Miri's Pujut Bus Terminal with Bintulu, Sibu and Kuching pass by here (RM10 from Miri) – just ask the driver to stop. Local buses from Miri to 'Lambir' go to the village of Lambir on the coast, not to the park.

A taxi from Miri costs RM60 one-way (RM120 return, including two hours of wait time).

Miri

POP 295,000

The dynamic oil town of Miri is busy and modern – not much about it is Borneo – but there's plenty of money sloshing around so the eating is good, the broad avenues are brightly lit and there's plenty to do when it's raining. The city's friendly guesthouses are a good place to meet other travellers. The population is about 40% Dayak (mainly Iban), 30% Chinese and 18% Malay.

Miri serves as a major transport hub, so if you're travelling to/from Brunei, Sabah, the Kelabit Highlands or the national parks of Gunung Mulu, Niah or Lambir Hills, chances are you'll pass this way.

◉ Sights

Miri is not big on historical sites – it was pretty much destroyed during WWII – but it's not an unattractive city. A walk around the centre is a good way to get a feel for the local vibe – streets worth a wander include (from north to south) Jln North Yu Seng, Jln South Yu Seng, Jln Maju and Jln High Street.

Miri City Fan　　　　　　　　　　　PARK
(Jln Kipas; ⏰24hr) Decked out in coloured lights at night, this 10.4-hectare park's Chinese- and Malay-style gardens and ponds are great for a stroll. Also boasts a beautiful, new library, an indoor stadium and an Olympic-sized swimming pool (RM1).

Canada Hill　　　　　　　　HILL, MUSEUM
(Bukit Kanada, Bukit Tenaga) The low ridge 2km southeast of the town centre was the site of Malaysia's first oil well, the **Grand Old Lady**, drilled in 1910. Appropriately, the old

derrick stands right outside the **Petroleum Museum** (Jln Canada Hill; ⊙9am-4.30pm, closed Fri), whose interactive exhibits, some designed for kids, are a good, pro-Big Oil introduction to the hugely lucrative industry that has so enriched Miri (and Malaysia's federal government).

The hill itself is a popular exercise spot, and it's worth driving up here at sunset (it's a bit far to walk) for the views across town to the South China Sea.

Saberkas Weekend Market MARKET
(⊙3pm Fri-evening Saturday, daily during Ramadan) One of the most colourful and friendly markets in Sarawak. Vendors are more than happy to answer questions about their colourful products, which include tropical fruits and vegies, barbecue chicken, satay, grilled stingray and handicrafts. Situated about 3km northeast of the centre near the Boulevard Commercial Centre, Miri's newest shopping mall. Served by buses 1, 1A, 31, 42, 62, 63, 66 and 68.

San Ching Tian Temple TEMPLE
(Jln Krokop 9) Said to be the largest Taoist temple in Southeast Asia. Built in 2000, the design features intricate dragon reliefs brought over from China. A huge new Chinese temple is being built right nearby. Situated about 1km northwest of the Saberkas Weekend Market. Served by bus 44.

🏃 Activities

Sandflies can be a pesky problem at Miri-area beaches.

Scuba Diving SCUBA DIVING
Although the waters off Miri are better known for drilling than diving, the area – much of it part of the **Miri-Sibuti Coral Reef Marine Park** (www.fri.gov.my/friswak/eprocoral.htm) – has some excellent 7m- to 30m-deep scuba sites, including old oil platforms teeming with fish and assorted trawler and freighter wrecks. Water visibility is at its best from March to September.

Red Monkey Divers (☎014-699 8296; www.redmonkeydivers.com; Jln Dato Abang Indeh, Gymkhana Club; ⊙10am-5pm Mon-Sat, closed Dec-Feb), based about 2km south of the Mega Hotel, is a professional outfit that offers PADI and BSAC diving courses.

Hash House Harriers RUNNING
(www.mirihhh.com) Visitors are welcome to join friendly locals and expats for runs, which begin at 5.15pm every Tuesday and at

4.30pm on the first Saturday of the month. For details, ask the owners of the Ming Café (p178), who are enthusiastic hashers.

Megalanes East Bowling Alley BOWLING
(Map p176; 3rd fl, Bintang Plaza, Jln Miri Pujut; per game RM3.80-5.90, shoes RM2; ⊙10am-midnight) The 24 lanes are a great escape on a rainy day.

👉 Tours

Miri-based companies offering trekking in northeastern Sarawak include:

Borneo Jungle Safari TREKKING
(☑085-422595; www.borneojunglesafari.com; Lot 1396, 1st fl, Centre Point Commercial Centre II, Jln Kubu) Runs the Ba Kelalan Apple Lodge Homestay up in Ba Kelalan.

Borneo Tropical Adventure TREKKING
(Map p176; ☑085-419337; www.borneotropicaladventures.com; Lot 906, Shop 12, ground fl, Soon Hup Tower, Jln Merbau) Runs the Benarat Inn at Gunung Mulu National Park.

✨ Festivals

Borneo Jazz Festival JAZZ
(www.jazzborneo.com; Jln Temenggong Datuk Oyong Lawai; ⊙weekend in mid-May) Features an eclectic assemblage of international talent. Formerly known as the Miri International Jazz Festival.

🛏 Sleeping

Miri has some of Sarawak's best backpackers' guesthouses.

If you're on a tight budget, choose your bed carefully – at the cheapie dives catering to oil-rig roustabouts (eg on and east of Jln South Yu Seng), many of the dreary rooms are windowless and musty, and Miri's brothel business booms at some of the shadier bottom-end digs.

⭐ TOP CHOICE **Dillenia Guesthouse** GUESTHOUSE **$$**
(Map p176; ☑085-434204; https://sites.google.com/site/dilleniaguesthouse; 1st fl, 846 Jln Sida; dm/s/d/q incl breakfast RM30/50/80/110; ✳@🛜) This super-welcoming guesthouse, with 11 rooms and lots of nice little touches (eg plants in the bathrooms), lives up to its motto, 'a home away from home'. Incredibly helpful Mrs Lee is an artesian well of useful travel information and tips – and leech socks. All rooms have shared bathrooms. Served by local bus 42.

Miri

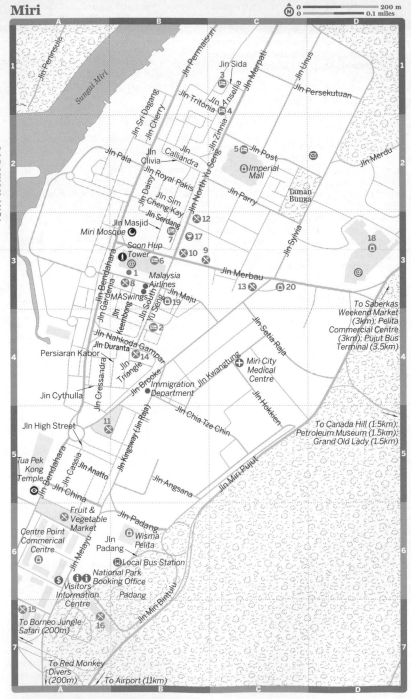

Miri

SARAWAK MIRI

Minda Guesthouse
GUESTHOUSE $

(Map p176; ☎085-411422; www.mindaguesthouse.com; 1st & 2nd fl, Lot 637, Jln North Yu Seng; dm per person incl breakfast RM20, d RM50-60; ❄@🛜) In the heart of Miri's dining and drinking district, this comfy establishment offers 13 clean rooms with colourful bedclothes, a small kitchen, a DVD lounge, unlimited tea and coffee and a great rooftop sundeck. Dorm rooms are pretty packed, with eight or 12 beds. Two rooms come with private bath. Light sleepers be warned: the nightclub across the street pumps out music until 2am.

Highlands Backpackers
GUESTHOUSE $

(Map p176; ☎085-422327; www.highlandsmiri.com; 2nd fl, Lot 839, Jln Merpati; dm/d RM22/50; ❄@🛜) Miri's original guesthouse, in new digs since mid-2012, offers 15 rooms (52 beds), two-thirds of them with windows; a lounge with satellite TV; and inexpensive laundry (RM8 per load, including drying). The dorm rooms have six to 14 beds. The affable owner, a Twin Otter pilot from New Zealand everyone calls Captain David, sometimes drops by. Served by local bus 42.

Imperial Hotel
HOTEL $$

(Map p176; ☎085-431133; www.imperialhotel.com.my; Jln Post; d from RM200; ❄🛜☲) The city centre's poshest hotel boasts 23 floors, 266 rooms, business and fitness centres, a sauna and a swimming pool.

Mega Hotel
HOTEL $$

(Map p176; ☎085-432432; www.megahotel.com.my; 907 Jln Merbau; r from RM195; ❄@🛜☲) Don't judge a hotel by its tasteless exterior or tacky lobby – the 288 rooms here, spread over 16 storeys, are comfortable and very spacious, if a bit old-fashioned. Amenities include a fitness centre (7th floor) and a 30m pool with town views and a jacuzzi (4th floor).

Apollo Hotel
HOTEL $

(Map p176; ☎085-433077; fax 085-419 964; 4 Jln South Yu Seng; s/d/tr from RM65/75/85; ❄) An old-fashioned but well-maintained Chinese cheapie. Very central. The 18 rooms are simple and spotless. Reception is around behind the Apollo Seafood Centre.

Miri Trail Guesthouse
AIRPORT HOTEL $

(☎012-8040806, 017-850 3666; www.miritrailguesthouse.com; Airport Commercial Centre, Jln Airport; dm/d incl breakfast RM25/55, day use RM15/30; ❄@🛜) A basic crash pad with six rooms, most without windows. Bathrooms are shared. Situated across the road from the airport (above the MASwings office), so if you're transiting through Miri you can rest here overnight or during the day.

✖ Eating

🔝 Summit Cafe
DAYAK $

(Map p176; Centre Point Commercial Centre, Jln Melayu; mains from RM3; ☺6am-early afternoon Mon-Sat) If you've never tried Kelabit cuisine, this place will open up whole new worlds for your tastebuds. Try the colourful array of 'jungle food' – *canko manis* (forest ferns), *dure'* (fried jungle leaf), minced tapioca leaves, and (sometimes) wild boar. The best selection is available before 11.30am – once the food runs out they close! Gets rave reviews.

Meng Chai Seafood
SEAFOOD $$

(Map p176; 11a Jln Merbau; fish per kg RM25-80; ⊗4.30pm-midnight) Discerning locals crowd this first-rate eatery, housed in two and very unassuming adjacent buildings. Specialities include barbecued garlic fish, *kampung*-raised chicken and *midin* fern. Seawater tanks hold live clams and prawns. Does not serve pork.

Rainforest Cafe
CHINESE $$

(Map p176; 49 Jln Brooke; mains from RM10; ⊗10am-2pm & 5-11.30pm) Often packed with local families, this breezy, open-air eatery specialises in Chinese-style dishes such as 'braised rainforest bean curd', 'crispy roasted chicken' and 'pork leg Philippine style'.

Muara Restoran
INDONESIAN $$

(Map p176; Jln North Yu Seng; mains RM7-15; ⊗11am-4am) Expat Indonesian oil workers in bright yellow overalls flock to this tin-roofed shed for *lalapan* (tofu, tempeh, meat, spinach-like greens, raw cucumber and rice, eaten with spicy *sambal belacan*). Great for a late-late meal.

Ming Café
ASIAN, WESTERN $$

(Map p176; www.mingcafe.com.my; cnr Jln North Yu Seng & Jln Merbau; mains RM5-25; ⊗10am-2am) Take your pick of Chinese, Malay, buffet-style Indian (from RM5) and Western food at this ever-busy corner eatery. Fresh fruit juice and shakes cost RM6 to RM8.50. The bar stocks two dozen bottled beers and has six beers on tap, including Guinness. Happy hangout of the Hash House Harriers.

Khan's Restaurant Islamic
INDIAN $

(Map p176; 229 Jln Maju; mains RM4-8; ⊗6.30am-8.30pm; ✈) This simple canteen is one of Miri's best North Indian eateries, whipping up tasty treats like mouth-watering chicken vindaloo (RM12) and seven vegie mains (RM4).

Miri Central Market
HAWKER $

(Map p176; Jln Brooke, Pasar Pusat Miri; mains RM2.50-4; ⊗7am-midnight) Especially popular Chinese food purveyors here include Stall 5, which serves up chicken curry rice in the morning, and Stall 6, known for its chicken porridge (available in the evening).

Tamu Muhibbah
MARKET

(Map p176; Jln Padang; ⊗2am-6pm or 7pm) Fruits and vegies, some straight from the jungle, are sold at stalls owned by Chinese, Malay, Iban and Orang Ulu.

Sin Liang Supermarket
SUPERMARKET $

(Map p176; Jln Duranta; ⊗8.30am-9pm) Well stocked with munchies, toiletries and Aussie wines.

Drinking

Barcelona
BAR

(Map p176; Jln North Yu Seng; draught beer RM8-12; ⊗4pm-2am, happy hour 4-9pm) More equatorial than Iberian, this place has a relaxed, upscale vibe and a big screen for footy. Seating is open-air at wooden tables. Liquid specialities range from Spanish and Australian wines to mojitos (RM15) and sex on the beach (RM20), not something you often find in Malaysia. Serves tapas and some Western dishes. The bar next door, World-Club Station, hosts a rockin' Filipino band from 10pm to 2am daily except Monday.

Pelita Commercial Centre
BAR DISTRICT

(cnr Jln Miri Pujut & Jln Sehati) If you're keen on a pub crawl, consider catching a cab to this warren of small streets lined with pubs, cafes, restaurants and dodgy karaoke places

---

ECO-LODGE

Looking for great place to hang out and be mellow, surrounded by tropical fruit trees? **TreeTops Lodge** (☑085-472172; www.treetops-borneo.com; Kampung Siwa Jaya; d/q incl breakfast RM120/180, with fan & shared bathroom RM80; ▓🎧), run by Mike (a retired British pilot) and his Sarawakian wife Esther, has eight, beautifully maintained rooms – four of them quite basic – set in a lovely, calming garden. When you're not lounging on the beach (2km away), you can fish for tilapia in the pond or go hiking. A light lunch costs RM7, and dinner is RM22.

TreeTops is 15km southwest of Miri along the coastal (new) road to Bintulu. From Miri's local bus terminal, take bus 13 (RM4, every 1½ to two hours from 5.50am to 6.30pm) to the end of the line, whence it's a 2km walk. From the airport, a blue taxi costs about RM75. TreeTops is not far from the western reaches of Lambir Hills National Park but getting to park HQ involves a 40km drive (transport available).

3km north of the centre. Don't mess with the local toughs.

Shopping

Miri Handicraft Centre   HANDICRAFTS
(Map p176; cnr Jln Brooke & Jln Merbau; ⊙8am-5.30pm) Thirteen stalls, rented from the city, sell colourful bags, baskets, sarongs, textiles etc made by Iban, Kelabit, Kenyah/Kayan, Lun Bawang, Chinese and Malay artisans. Stall No 7 has some fine Kelabit beadwork from Bario.

Borneo Arts   HANDICRAFTS
(Map p176; Jln South Yu Seng; ⊙9am-9pm) Dayak handicrafts and souvenirs.

Popular Book Store   BOOKS
(Map p176; 2nd fl, Bintang Plaza, Jln Miri Pujut; ⊙10am-10pm) A mega-bookshop with a huge selection of English books, and Lonely Planet titles in English and Chinese.

Bintang Plaza   SHOPPING CENTRE
(Map p176; Jln Miri Pujut; ⊙10am-10pm) A modern, multistorey, air-con mall that could *almost* be in Singapore. The 3rd floor is full of shops specialising in computers and cameras.

① Information

For local low-down, some great tips and an outline of local history, see Miri's unofficial website, www.miriresortcity.com.

ATMs can be found at the airport and are sprinkled all over the city centre.

It's a good idea to stock up on medicines and first-aid supplies before heading inland to Gunung Mulu National Park or the Kelabit Highlands.

Internet Access
Internet Shop (1st fl, Shop 1-04, Soon Hup Tower, cnr Jln Bendahara & Jln Merbau; per hr RM2; ⊙8am-8pm) Popular with zombified teenage gamers.

IT Cyber Station (3rd fl, western end, Bintang Plaza, Jln Miri Pujut; per hr RM2.50; ⊙10am-10pm) Has 72 computers.

Laundry
If you drop off your clothes at **EcoLaundry** (☑016-878 9908, 085-414266; 638 Jln North Yu Seng; per kg RM5; ⊙7am-7pm Mon-Sat, to 5pm Sun) before flying up to Gunung Mulu National Park or the Kelabit Highlands, you'll save luggage weight and have clean undies when you return! Offers free pickup at guesthouses and hotels.

Medical Services
Colombia Asia Hospital (☑085-437755; http://columbiaasia.com/miri; Jln Bulan Sabit, ⊙24hr) A 35-bed private hospital, used by many expats, with a 24-hour accident and emergency ward and a 24-hour ambulance. Situated 4km northeast of the Mega Hotel.

Miri City Medical Centre (☑085-426622; www.mcmcmiri.com; 916-920 Jln Hokkien) Has an ambulance, a 24-hour accident and emergency department and various private clinics. Accepts direct payment for in-patient care from certain insurance companies. Conveniently located in the city centre.

Post
Main Post Office (Jln Post; ⊙8am-4pm Mon-Fri, to 2.30pm Sat)

Tourist Information
National Park Booking Office (☑085-434184; www.sarawakforestry.com; 452 Jln Melayu; ⊙8am-5pm Mon-Fri) Inside the Visitors Information Centre. Has details on Sarawak's national parks and can book beds and rooms at Niah and Lambir Hills (but not at Gunung Mulu or Similajau).

Visitors Information Centre (☑085-434181; www.sarawaktourism.com; 452 Jln Melayu; ⊙8am-5pm Mon-Fri, 9am-3pm Sat, Sun & public holidays) The helpful staff can provide city maps, information on accommodation and a list of licensed guides. Situated in a little park.

Visas
Immigration Department (Jabatan Imigresen; ☑085-442117; www.imi.gov.my; 2nd fl, Yulan Plaza, cnr Jln Kingsway & Jln Brooke; ⊙8am-5pm Mon-Thu, 8-11.45am & 2.15-5pm Fri) For visa extensions.

① Getting There & Away

Miri is 212km northeast of Bintulu and 36km southwest of the Brunei border.

Air
AirAsia (www.airasia.com) can get you to Kuching, Kota Kinabalu (KK), Kuala Lumpur (KL), Johor Bahru (across the causeway from Singapore) and Singapore, while **Malaysia Airlines** (www.malaysiaairlines.com) flies to KL.

Miri is the main hub of the Malaysia Airlines subsidiary **MASwings** (www.maswings.com. my), whose inexpensive flights serve destinations such as Gunung Mulu National Park, Bario and Ba Kelalan (in the Kelabit Highlands), Kuching, Sibu, Bintulu, Marudi, Limbang, Lawas, Pulau Labuan and KK.

Miri's **airport** (Jln Airport) has a separate check-in area for MASwings' 'Rural Air Service' routes, eg to Gunung Mulu National Park and Bario. If you're flying on a Twin Otter, you'll be asked to weigh yourself on a giant scale while holding your carry-on.

Free wi-fi is available at Starbuck's, on the check-in level. In the departure area (beyond security), the Coffee Bean & Tea Leaf also has wi-fi; the password is posted next to the cash register.

Bus & Van

Long-distance buses use the Pujut Bus Terminal, about 4km northeast of the centre.

Once or twice an hour, buses head to Kuching (RM80, 12 to 14 hours, departures from 6am to 10pm) via the inland (old) Miri–Bintulu highway, with stops at Lambir Hills National Park, Batu Niah Junction (access point for Niah National Park; RM10 to RM12, 1½ hours), Bintulu (RM20 to RM27, 3½ hours) and Sibu (RM40 to RM50, seven to eight hours). This route is highly competitive so it pays to shop around. Taking a spacious 'VIP bus', with just three seats across, is like flying 1st class! Companies include **Bintang Jaya** (☎085-432178, 085-438301), **Bus Asia** (Biaramas; ☎414999, hotline 082-411111; http://mybus.com.my) and **Miri Transport Company** (MTC; ☎085-438161; www.mtcmiri.com).

Bintang Jaya also has services northeast to Limbang (RM45, four hours), Lawas (RM75, six hours) and KK (RM90, 10 hours). Buses leave Miri at 8.30am; departures from KK are at 7am. **Borneo Bus** (☎010-967 6648) serves the same destinations, except on Wednesday, at 7.45am; departures from KK are also at 7.45am. Bus Asia has a bus to Limbang at 2pm. Be aware that with all these companies, getting off in Brunei is not allowed.

ⓘ Getting Around

To/From the Airport

A red-and-yellow **taxi** (☎013-838 1000; ⊗24hr) from the airport to the city centre (15 minutes, in traffic 25 minutes) costs RM22 (RM33 from 11.45pm to 6am); a *kupon teksi* (taxi coupon) can be purchased at the **taxi desk** (⊗7am-11pm) just outside the baggage-claim area (next to the car-rental desks). If you're heading from town to the airport, the fare is RM20. Spacious blue 'executive taxis' charge RM30.

Bus 28 links the local bus station with the airport (RM2.60) every 1½ hours or so; last departures are at 5.20pm (from the airport) and 6.30pm (from the local bus station). At the airport, the stop is on the Arrivals Island in front of the terminal (look for an upright reading 'Bas').

Bus

Local bus transport is handled by three companies: Miri City Bus, Miri Transport Company (MTC) and Miri Belait Transport. The **local bus station** (Jln Padang), next to the Visitors Information Centre, has schedules posted. Fares start at RM1; most lines run from 7am to 6pm.

MTC buses 20 and 33A link the local bus station with Pujut Bus Terminal (RM1.60 to RM2.60, hourly until 6.30pm).

Car

Most of Miri's guesthouses are happy to organise private transport to area destinations such as Lambir Hills National Park (RM85 return) and Niah National Park (RM180 return).

The half-dozen car rental companies with desks at Miri Airport, just outside of baggage claim, include:

FT Car Rental (☎085-438415; www.ftcarrental.com)

Golden System Car Rental (☎085-613359; www.gocar.com.my)

Hertz (☎012-879 2979, 085-614740; www.hertz.com; ⊗8am-5pm, closed Sun & public holidays)

Kong Teck Car Rental (☎085-617767; www.kongteck.com.my)

Taxi

Taxi stations are sprinkled around the city centre. A short cab ride around downtown is RM10, while a ride from the centre to the Pujut Bus Terminal costs RM15. Taxis run by the **Miri Taxi Association** (☎085-432 277; ⊗24hr) can be summoned by phone 24 hours a day.

NORTHEASTERN SARAWAK

Gunung Mulu National Park

Also known as the **Gunung Mulu World Heritage Area** (☎085-792300; www.mulupark.com; adult/child for 5-day pass RM30/10; ⊗HQ office 8am-5pm), this park is one of the most majestic and thrilling nature destinations anywhere in Southeast Asia. No surprise, then, that Unesco declared it a World Heritage site in 2005.

Few national parks anywhere in the world pack so many natural marvels into such a small area. Home to **caves** (www.mulucaves.org) of mind-boggling proportions, otherworldly geological phenomena such as the Pinnacles, and brilliant old-growth tropical rainforest (the park has 17 different vegetation zones), this is truly one of the world's wonders.

Among the remarkable features in this 529-sq-km park are its two highest peaks, Gunung Mulu (2376m) and Gunung Api (1710m). In between are rugged karst

GETTING TO BRUNEI: MIRI TO BANDAR SERI BEGAWAN

Getting to the border The only company that's allowed to take passengers from Miri's Pujut Bus Terminal to destinations inside Brunei is **PHLS** (Jesselton Express; in Brunei +673-718-3838, +673-719-3835, +673-717-7755, in Miri 085-438301), which sends buses to Bandar Seri Begawan (BSB; RM40) via Kuala Belait (RM25) and Seria (RM25) at 8.15am and 3.45pm. Tickets are sold at the Bintang Jaya counter. Another option to BSB (RM50, 2¾ hours) is to take a **private van** (☑in BSB +673-887 7642, in Miri 016-873 2742) from Pujut Bus Terminal; hotel pickup can be arranged. For details, contact the Dillenia (p175) (Mrs Lee), Minda (p177) or Highlands (p177) guesthouses in Miri or Miri's Visitors Information Centre (p179).

At the border Border formalities are usually quick and for most nationalities Bruniean visas are free (see p213 for more details), but the process can slow down buses.

Moving on Brunei's Serasa Ferry Terminal, 20km northeast of BSB, is linked by ferry with Pulau Labuan, from where boats go to Menumbok in Sabah. Several buses a day go from BSB to Sarawak's Limbang Division and destinations in Sabah. If you're eventually headed overland to Sabah, make sure you have enough pages in your passport for 10 new chops (stamps).

See p208 for details on doing the trip in the opposite direction.

mountains, deep gorges with crystal-clear rivers, and a unique mosaic of habitats supporting fascinating and incredibly diverse wildlife. Mulu's most famous trekking attractions are the Pinnacles, a forest of razor-sharp limestone spires, and the so-called Headhunters' Trail, which follows an old tribal war path down to Limbang.

Some cave tours (especially the more difficult ones) and treks (especially the longer ones) are booked out well in advance.

The park's facilities are managed by Borsarmulu, a controversial private company partly owned by the sister of Sarawak's chief minister.

◉ Sights & Activities

When you register, park staff will give you a placemat-sized schematic map of the park on which you can plan out your daily activities. HQ staff are generally very helpful in planning itineraries and are happy to (try to) accommodate special needs and interests (eg for family-friendly activities).

All the plankwalks (eg to the entrance to the Deer Cave) are wheelchair-accessible but cave interiors are not.

The park's excellent website (www.mulupark.com) and the brochures available at park HQ have details on walks and boat trips not covered here.

Activities Without Guides

Visitors are not allowed to go inside any of the caves without a qualified guide, but you

can take a number of **jungle walks** unaccompanied so long as you inform the park office (or, when it's closed, someone across the path in the Park Security building). For instance, you can walk to the **Bat Observatory** near the entrance to the Deer Cave and to **Paku Waterfall** (3km one-way), where it's possible to swim.

Mulu Discovery Centre   MUSEUM
(⊙7.30am-9pm) Offers a fine introduction to the park as a 'biodiversity hotspot' and to its extraordinary geology. Situated in the new HQ building, between the park office and Café Mulu.

FREE **Tree Top Tower**   BIRDWATCHING
(admission free, key deposit RM50) Basically a 30m-high bird hide. The best time to spot our feathered friends is early in the morning (5am to 9am) or in the late afternoon and early evening (4pm to 8pm). Reserve a time slot and pick up the key at park HQ or, after 4.30pm, from Park Security (across the boardwalk from the park office). Situated about 500m from park HQ.

Guided Forest Walks

Nightwalk   WALKING
(Night Shift; per person RM10; ⊙7pm except if raining) The ideal first-night introduction to the park's nocturnal fauna, this 1½- to two-hour walk (the route varies) wends its way through alluvial forest. Creatures you're very likely to see – but only after the guide points them out – include tree frogs just

1cm long, enormous spiders, vine snakes that are a dead ringer for a vine wrapped around a branch, and stick insects (phasmids), extraordinary creatures up to 30cm long that look like they've been assembled from pencils and toothpicks. If you put your torch (bring one!) up to eye level and shine it into the foliage, the eyes of spiders and other creatures will reflect brightly back.

Don't wear insect repellent or you risk repelling some of the insects you're trying to see. Mosquitoes are not a problem.

If you order dinner at the Wild Mulu Café before heading out, you can pick it up when you return (make sure you're back before 9.30pm). Eateries outside the park stay open later.

You can take the nightwalk trail on your own, without a guide, either before 5pm (so that your scent, which scares away the wildlife, dissipates before the guided group comes through) or after 8pm. Make sure you inform either the park office or, when it's closed, someone in the Park Security pavilion. Between 5pm and 8pm, you can design your own nightwalk by taking trails the guided group isn't using.

Mulu Canopy Skywalk   WALKING

(per person RM35; ⊙departures every 1 or 2 hrs 7am-2pm) Climbing up into the rainforest canopy is the only way to see what a tropical rainforest is all about because most of the flora and fauna do their thing high up in the trees, not down on the ground, where less than 2% of the forest's total sunlight is available. Mulu's 480m-long skywalk, unforgettably anchored to a series of huge trees, has handy signage and is one of the best in Southeast Asia. Often gets booked out early – for a specific time slot, reserve as soon as you've got your flight.

Show Caves

Mulu's 'show caves' (the park's name for caves that can be visited without specialised training or equipment) are its most popular attraction and for good reason: they are, quite simply, awesome. All are accessible on guided walks from park HQ. Bring a powerful torch.

Deer Cave & Lang's Cave   CAVE

(per person RM20; ⊙departures at 2pm & 2.30pm) A lovely 3km walk (40 minutes to 60 minutes) through the rainforest along a plankwalk takes you to these adjacent caverns. The highlight here is not so much what's in the caves as what comes out of

them every evening around dusk (unless it's raining): millions of bats in spiralling, twirling clouds that look a bit like swarms of cartoon bees. It's an awe-inspiring sight. The bats' corkscrew trajectory is designed to foil the dinner plans of bat hawks perched on the surrounding cliffs. Count on getting back to park HQ at around 7pm.

The **Mulu Bat-Cam** (www.muluparkbat cams.com) – in fact, five infrared webcams – follows the lives of bats inside the Deer Cave. It's not internet live-streamed yet but you can see the feed at the **Bat Observatory**, next to the cave's grassy bat-viewing amphitheatre, as well as back at HQ in the park office.

The Deer Cave – over 2km in length and 174m high – is the world's largest cave passage open to the public. (It was considered the world's largest cave passage, full stop, until what may be an even larger one was discovered in Vietnam in 2009.) It is home to two million to three million bats belonging to 12 species (more than in any other single cave in the world) who cling to the roof in a seething black mass as they gear up for their evening prowl.

We're not sure who did the calculations or how, but it's said that the Deer Cave's bats devour 30 tonnes of mosquitoes every night. That's one reason why mosquito bites are almost unknown at Mulu.

If it's raining, the bats usually (but not always) stay home because echolocation (the way they find prey) is not very good at honing in on flying insects amid an onslaught of raindrops.

Wind Cave & Clearwater Cave   CAVE

(per person incl boat ride RM50; ⊙departures at 8.45am & 9.15am) Zipping along an upland jungle river in a flat-bottomed longboat is not a bad way to start the day! This tour takes about four hours, leaving time for another cave visit in the afternoon – or the afternoon flight to Miri.

The Wind Cave, named for the deliciously cool breezes that flow through it, has several chambers – including the cathedral-like King's Chamber – filled with phantasmagorical forests of stalactites and stalagmites. Clearwater Cave is vast – as of 2012, 225km of passages had been surveyed – of which only a tiny segment is open to casual visitors. As the name suggests, the highlight here is an underground clearwater river.

After visiting the caves, you can take a dip in the refreshingly cool waters of a sandy

GUIDES, RESERVATIONS & FEES

For almost all caves, walks and treks in **Gunung Mulu National Park** (☏085-792300; www.mulupark.com), visitors must be accompanied by a guide licensed by Sarawak Forestry, generally supplied either by the park or by an adventure tour agency (eg those based in Kuching, Miri or Limbang). Prices in this chapter are for tours booked directly through the park, as are the time frames for making reservations; agencies charge considerably more but also supply extras, such as meals, and can often offer more flexibility when it comes to advance booking.

If you've got your heart set on adventure caving, or on trekking to the Pinnacles or up to the summit of Gunung Mulu, advance reservations – by phone or email (enquiries@mulupark.com) – are a must. They're doubly important if you'll be coming in July, August or September, when some routes are booked out several months ahead, and are absolutely crucial if your travel dates are not flexible. If this is your situation, don't buy your air tickets until your trek or caving dates are confirmed.

Bookings are not a zero sum game: if the park has sufficient advance notice of your plans, they may be able to reassign guides to accommodate you. And if you can spend a week or two hanging out at the park (this usually means staying in a basic guesthouse outside the park's boundaries as in-park accommodation is in very short supply), trekking and caving slots do sometimes open up.

The park's own trekking and caving guides are well trained and speak good English but there are only about 15 of them. Park administrators have been working to improve the quality of the guides but this process has excluded – and thus angered – some locals who used to earn a living as (semi-qualified) park guides.

Some travellers hire freelance guides unattached to a tour agency, eg from a nearby village. Despite being licensed by Sarawak Forestry (they wouldn't be allowed to operate in the park if they weren't), such guides' nature knowledge and English skills vary widely, from excellent to barely sufficient. In addition, they may lack state-of-the-art safety training and equipment (eg two-way radios, which the park supplies to all of its own guides) and, perhaps most importantly, are unlikely to have proper insurance, a factor that could be crucial if a helicopter evacuation is necessary.

A caving group must consist of at least four participants (including the guide) so that if someone is injured, one person can stay with them and the other two can head out of the cave together to seek help.

Park prices for caving and treks are now on a straight per-person basis (minimum three people).

swimming hole so don't forget your swimsuit; changing facilities are available. It's no longer possible to walk back to park HQ.

Tours begin with a stop at the riverside village of Batu Bungan, set up by the government as part of a campaign to discourage the nomadic lifestyle of the Penan. Locals sell trinkets and handicrafts.

Fast Lane   CAVE
(per person incl boat RM55; ☉1.30pm) This route through Lagang Cave has gotten rave reviews since it opened in 2010 thanks to its extraordinary stalactites and stalagmites. Keep an eye out for 'moonmilk', a fibrous mineral formation – known to scientists as Lublinite – created when bacteria break down calcite, the main component of limestone. Don't touch it – it's very fragile!

Getting to the cave requires a one-hour walk; the entire visit takes three or four hours. Groups are limited to eight people.

Adventure Caves

Cave routes that require special equipment and a degree of caving (spelunking) experience are known here as 'adventure caves'. Rosters for the eight half- or all-day options fill up early so reserve well ahead. Groups are limited to eight participants. Heavy rains can cause caves to flood.

Caving routes are graded beginner, intermediate and advanced; guides determine each visitors' suitability based on their previous caving experience. If you have no background in spelunking, you will be required to do an intermediate route (Racer Cave) before moving on to an advanced one.

Minimum ages are 12 for intermediate and 16 for advanced. The park office has details on 'family adventure caving', ie a section of Lagang Cave that's suitable for the entire family. Fees include a helmet and a headlamp; bring closed shoes, a first-aid kit and clothes you won't mind getting dirty in.

Keep in mind that adventure caving is not for everyone, and halfway into a cave passage is not the best time to discover that you suffer from claustrophobia, fear the dark or simply don't like slithering in the mud with all sorts of unknown creepy crawlies.

Sarawak Chamber   ADVANCED CAVING

(per person RM225; ⊘departure at 7am) Measuring an incredible 700m long, 400m wide and 70m high, this chamber – discovered in 1981 – has been called the world's largest enclosed space. Don't count on seeing much, though – ordinary lights are no match for the ocean of black emptiness, big enough to park 10 A380s lined up nose to tail. This circuit is very demanding – getting to the cave and back involves six hours of trekking (three hours each way) and moving around inside the cave requires some use of fixed ropes. The whole route takes 10 to 15 hours.

Clearwater Connection   ADVANCED CAVING

(per person RM170) This 4.8km, four- to eight-hour circuit starts at Wind Cave and heads into the wilds of the vast Clearwater Cave system. There's a good bit of scrambling and the route includes a 1.5km river section.

Lagang Cave   INTERMEDIATE CAVING

(per person RM95) Lots of stalagmites, stalactites and boulders, plus an ancient river bed. No climbing. Takes two to four hours.

Racer Cave   INTERMEDIATE CAVING

(per person RM95; ⊘departure at 9am) Has some rope-assisted sections that require a bit of upper-body strength. Named after the non-dangerous cave racer snake, which dines mainly on bats. Takes two to four hours.

Trekking & Climbing

Mulu offers some of the best and most accessible jungle trekking in Borneo. The forest here is in excellent condition and there are routes for every level of fitness and skill.

Expect rain, leeches, slippery and treacherous conditions, and a very hot workout – carry lots of water. Guides are required for overnights, except for the Headhunters' Trail. Book well ahead. Don't even think of taking one of these treks if you've got asthma, or heart or knee problems.

Bring a first-aid kit and a torch/flashlight.

The Pinnacles   TREKKING

(per person RM325) The Pinnacles are an incredible formation of 45m-high stone spires protruding from the forested flanks of Gunung Api. Getting there involves a boat ride (you can stop off at Wind Cave and Clearwater Cave for a fee of RM20) and, between two overnights at Camp 5, an unrelentingly steep 2.4km ascent; the final section – much more gruelling than anything on Mt Kinabalu – involves some serious clambering and some rope and ladder work. Coming down is just as taxing so when you stagger into Camp 5, a swim in the cool, clear river may look pretty enticing. The trail passes through some gorgeous jungle.

Bring shoes that will give you traction on sharp and slippery rocks, bedding (many people find that a sarong is warm enough at Camp 5) and enough food (eg instant noodles) for six meals. Cooking equipment and gas stoves are available at Camp 5, home – recent climbers report – to lots of stinging bees.

Gunung Mulu Summit   TREKKING

(per person RM385, with a porter RM475) The climb to the summit of Gunung Mulu (2376m) – described recently by one satisfied ascendee as 'gruelling' and, near the top, 'treacherous' – is a classic Borneo adventure. If you're very fit and looking for real adventure, this 24km trek may be for you.

Bring proper hiking shoes, a sleeping bag (Camp 4 can get quite chilly), a sleeping pad (unless you don't mind sleeping on wooden boards), rain gear (some groups end up having rain the whole way) and enough food for four days. The camps along the way have very basic cooking equipment, including a gas stove. Bring water-purification tablets if you're leery of drinking the rainwater collected at shelters en route. Near the summit you may spend much of your time inside clouds; a fleece jacket is the best way to ward off the damp and cold. Recent trekkers report having been visited by rats at Camp 3 and by squirrels who were 'keen on noodles' at Camp 4. The trip takes four days and three nights.

Headhunters' Trail   TREKKING

The physically undemanding Headhunters' Trail is a backdoor route from Mulu to Limbang and can be done in either direction, although most people start at the park. The route is named after the Kayan war parties that used to make their way up the Sungai Melinau from the Baram area to the Melinau Gorge, then dragged their canoes overland to the Sungai Terikan to raid the peoples of the Limbang region.

Starting in Limbang, it's possible travel up to the park without a guide, hiring transport (a vehicle and then a boat) as you go. The journey takes two days and one night. If you're on your own, don't forget to contact the park to reserve sleeping space at Camp 5.

Heading down to Limbang, getting from Kuala Terikan (11km on foot from park HQ) or nearby Lubang Cina, both uninhabited, to Medamit (linked by road with Limbang) is possible only if you arrange in advance to be met by a boatman or a guide. Mr Lim of Limbang-based **Borneo Touch Ecotour** (☎013-844 3861; www.walk2mulu.com) can organise a boat and a van in either direction for RM500 for up to five people, and also offers well-reviewed tour packages.

🛏 Sleeping

Accommodation options range from longhouse-style luxury to extremely basic digs. MASwings uses 68-seat turboprops for the Miri–Mulu route, so depending on how long people stay, there may end up being more seats on the planes than there are places to stay inside the park.

Camping is no longer permitted at park HQ but you can pitch a tent at some of the guesthouses just outside the park (across the bridge from HQ). Elsewhere in the park, the only places you can sleep out – and then only if you have reservations (space is limited) – are Camp 5 (tents prohibited) and several huts along the Gunung Mulu Summit trail.

INSIDE THE NATIONAL PARK

Park HQ, a lovely spot set amid semi-wild jungle, has 24-hour electricity, tap water that's safe to drink and a total of 88 beds. All private rooms have attached bathrooms. Prices (except for Camp 5) include a delicious breakfast.

If you'll be travelling from July to September, staff recommend booking in-park beds before purchasing plane tickets – just call (☎085-792300) or email (enquiries@mulupark.com). Reservations cannot be made through Sarawak Forestry.

Rooms can be cancelled up to 48 hours ahead without penalty, which is why space

sometimes opens up late in the game; phone for last-minute availability.

Garden Bungalows   BUNGALOW $$
(s/d/tr incl breakfast RM200/230/250; ❀) Opened in 2011, these eight spacious units come with verandahs.

Chalets   CHALET $$
(s/d/tr/q incl breakfast RM170/180/215/250; ❀) Each of the two chalets has two rooms and a huge living room.

Longhouse Rooms   GUESTHOUSE $$
(s/d/tr/q incl breakfast RM170/180/215/250; ❀) There are eight of these, four in each of two wooden buildings.

Hostel   HOSTEL $
(dm incl breakfast RM40) All 20 beds are in a clean, spacious dormitory-style room with ceiling fans. Lockers are available for a RM20 deposit.

Camp 5   CAMPGROUND $
(per person including boat ride RM160) An open-air sleeping platform with mats, cooking facilities (including cooking gas) and bathrooms. Space is limited (to 50 people) so only hikers who are heading up to the Pinnacles or down the Headhunters' Trail can stay here. Reserve ahead and pay at the park office. It's warm enough here without a sleeping bag (a sarong will do).

OUTSIDE THE NATIONAL PARK

Several ultra-budget places, unaffiliated with the park, are located just across the bridge from park HQ, along the banks of the Melinau River. Reservations are not necessary so if you don't mind very basic digs, you can fly up without worrying about room availability.

For those on a generous budget, the Mulu Marriott Resort & Spa is also almost never full.

Contact Miri-based **Borneo Tropical Adventure** (☎085-419337; www.borneotropicaladventures.com) for details on staying at the mid-range Benarat Inn.

Mulu Marriott Resort & Spa   RESORT $$$
(☎085-792388; www.marriott.com; ❀@☎☎) Situated 3km from park HQ, this 100-room, all-wood complex is finally getting the major make-over it's badly needed for years.

Mulu River Lodge   HOSTEL $
(Edward Nyipa Homestay; ☎012-852 7471; dm incl breakfast RM35) Has 30 beds, most in a giant,

non-bunk dorm room equipped with clean showers and toilets at one end. Electricity flows from 5pm to 11.30pm. This is the only guesthouse outside the park with a proper septic system.

Mulu Homestay GUESTHOUSE $
(☑for Betty 012-875 3517; beds RM15, campsites per person RM5) Has 30 beds (more are being added), electricity from 6pm to 9pm and very personable owners.

Melinau Homestay GUESTHOUSE $
(MC; ☑for Diang 012-871 1372; dm RM20) Has seven extremely basic rooms, river-water bucket showers and flickering electricity from 6pm to 10pm. This is the third guesthouse along the river from the bridge.

✗ Eating

A handful of tiny shops sell a very limited selection of food items, eg instant noodles. Most food is flown in, which partly explains why prices are significantly higher than on the coast (eg RM6 for a large bottle of water).

Inexpensive curries, fried rice and noodle dishes are available at several places across the bridge from park HQ.

Cooking is not allowed at any park accommodation except Camps 1, 3, 4 and 5.

Café Mulu ASIAN, WESTERN $$
(mains RM7.40-17; ◷7.30am-9.30pm, last orders 9pm) The Berawan women who work here make great breakfasts (free if you're staying in the park, RM15.90 otherwise) and a few Western items, but the standouts are local dishes such as the spectacular Mulu laksa. A beer or a glass of wine, supremely relaxing after a day's hiking, costs RM9.60. Staff are happy to prepare packed lunches (RM18).

ℹ Information

For sums over RM100, the park accepts Visa and MasterCard (but not American Express). Cash and travellers cheques can be exchanged at the Mulu Marriott Resort & Spa. There are no ATMs at the park.

The shop at park HQ has an excruciatingly slow **internet computer** (RM5 per hour; RM10 per hour if you're staying outside the park) but it's usually out-of-service. There's another **internet-enabled computer** (RM35 per hour) at the Mulu Marriott Resort & Spa, which is supposed to have wi-fi in the lobby.

The **clinic** in the nearby village of Batu Bungan is now staffed by a doctor and has a dispensary (small pharmacy).

ℹ Getting There & Away

Air

MASwings (www.maswings.com.my) flies 68-seat ATR 72-500 turboprops from/to Miri and Kuching. Departures from Miri are at 9.20am and 1.50pm and from Mulu at 10.10am and 2.40pm, with onward flights to Kota Kinabalu (KK) and other destinations.

ℹ Getting Around

Park HQ is a walkable 1.5km from the airport and 3km from Mulu Marriott Resort & Spa. Vans run by **Melinau Transportation** (☑for Diang 012-871 1372) and other companies meets incoming flights at the airport; transport to park HQ and the adjacent guesthouses costs RM5 per person. Oversized tuk-tuks shuttle guests between park HQ and Mulu Marriott Resort & Spa (RM6 per person one-way).

It's possible to hire local longboats for excursions to destinations such as the government-built Penan longhouse village of Long Iman (RM60 per person return, minimum three people), 40 minutes away by river.

Kelabit Highlands

Nestled in Sarawak's northeastern corner, the upland rainforests of the Kelabit (keh-*lah*-bit) Highlands are sandwiched between Gunung Mulu National Park and the Indonesian state of East Kalimantan. The main activity here, other than enjoying the clean, cool air, is trekking from longhouse to longhouse on mountain trails. Unfortunately, logging roads – ostensibly for 'selective' logging – are encroaching and some of the Highlands' primary forests have already succumbed to the chainsaw.

The area is home to the Kelabits, an Orang Ulu (inland Dayak) group who number only about 6500 worldwide and who inspire awe throughout Sarawak for their unparalleled ability to wrangle government investments and subsidies. For an excellent 'profile' of the Kelabits by Dr Poline Bala, a Bario-born anthropologist, see www.unimas.my/ebario/community.html. There's more information on Bario and the Kelabits, some of it out-of-date, at www.kelabit.net and on Facebook – see www.kelabit.org.

BARIO
POP 800

The 'capital' of the Highlands, Bario consists of about a dozen 'villages' – each with its own church – spread over a beautiful valley, much (though less and less) of it given over to growing the renowned local rice. Some of the appeal lies in the mountain climate (the valley is 1500m above sea level) and splendid isolation (the only access is by air and torturous 4WD track), but above all it's the unforced hospitality of the Kelabit people that will quickly win you over. An amazing number of travellers find themselves extending their stays in Bario by days, weeks or even years. Do yourself a favour and get stuck here for a while!

Before the Konfrontasi, Bario consisted of only one small longhouse, but in 1963 residents of longhouses near the frontier fled raids by Indonesian troops and settled here for safety.

Except for a few places powered by a small hydroelectric dam and by photovoltaic cells (a large solar farm is planned), Bario has electricity – provided by private generators – only in the evening. It's hard to imagine life in hyper-social Bario without the mobile phone, a technology unknown in these parts until 2009.

◎ Sights & Activities

The Bario area offers plenty of opportunities for jungle exploration even if you're not a hardcore trekker. Guides can arrange activities such as **fishing**, **bird-watching** and **kayaking** (🖉for Stu 019-807 1640; per boat RM60).

The forests around Bario are a great place to spot pitcher plants, butterflies and even hornbills – and are an exceptional venue for tiger leeches to spot you. Most guesthouses are happy to pack picnic lunches.

Bario Asal Longhouse   LONGHOUSE

This all-wood, 22-door longhouse has the traditional Kelabit layout. On the *dapur* (enclosed front verandah) each family has a hearth, while on the other side of the family units is the *tawa'*, a wide back verandah – essentially an enclosed hall over 100m long – used for weddings, funerals and celebrations and decorated with historic family photos.

A few of the older residents still have earlobes that hang almost down to their shoulders, created by a lifetime of wearing heavy brass earrings. If you'd like a picture, it's good form to chat with them a bit (they may offer you something to drink) and only then to ask if they'd be willing to be photographed. Afterwards you might want to leave a small tip (RM5 or RM10).

Bario Asal has 24-hour electricity (evenings only during dry spells) thanks to a micro-hydro project salvaged from a larger government-funded project that functioned for just 45 minutes after it was switched on in 1999 (it had been designed to operate on a much larger river).

Tom Harrisson Monument   MEMORIAL

Shaped like a *sapé* (a traditional stringed instrument), this stainless-steel monument, dedicated in 2010, commemorates the March 1945 parachute drop into Bario by British and Australian commandos under the command of British Major Tom Harrisson. Their goal – achieved with great success – was to enlist the help of locals to fight the Japanese, whose cruelty had made them hugely unpopular. For the life story of this colourful and controversial character, see *The Most Offending Soul Alive*, a biography by Judith M Heimann. Harrisson's widow lived in Bario until her death in 2011.

The monument is a short walk up the slope from the Bario Asal Longhouse, on the site of Tom's one-time garden (his post-war house was about 100m from here, where the local cemetery now is).

Junglebluesdream Art Gallery   ART GALLERY

(http://junglebluesdream.weebly.com; ⊙daylight hours) Many of artist Stephen Baya's paintings have traditional Kelabit motifs. In April 2013 his colourful illustrations of the Kelabit legend of Tuked Rini were to feature at the Museum of Archaeology and Anthropology in Cambridge, England (and in a children's book).

Prayer Mountain   TREKKING

From the Bario Asal Longhouse, it's a steep, slippery ascent (two hours) up to the summit of Prayer Mountain, which has a cross that was erected in 1973, thickets of pitcher plants and amazing views of the Bario Valley and of the mixed Penan and Kelabit hamlet of Arur Dalan, with its three defunct wind turbines. Two-thirds of the way up is what may be the world's least pretentious church.

⛏ Sleeping

Bario's various component villages are home to lots of guesthouses where you can meet English-speaking locals and dine on delicious Kelabit cuisine (accommodation prices almost always include board). Some of the most relaxing establishments are a bit out of town (up to 5km). Air-con is not necessary up in Bario but hot water – alas, not yet an option – will some day be

SARAWAK KELABIT HIGHLANDS

a nice treat. Almost all rooms have shared bathroom facilities. If you're on a very tight budget, enquire about renting a bed without board.

No need to book ahead – available rooms outstrip the space available on flights, and guesthouse owners meet incoming flights at the airport. The places below are listed alphabetically.

Bario Airport Homestay GUESTHOUSE $
(☑013-835 9009; barioairporthomestay@gmail. com; beds RM20, per person incl board RM80; ☜) Five rooms right across the road from the airport terminal. Run by Joanna, the airport's personable dynamo of an operations manager.

Bario Asal Lembaa Longhouse HOMESTAY $
(☑for Jenette 014-590 7500, for Peter 014-893 1139; jenetteulun@yahoo.com; beds RM20, per person incl 3 meals RM60; ☜) Run as a cooperative by the entire longhouse. Some local families let out rooms, while others do the cooking. A great way to experience longhouse living. Transport from the airport costs RM10 per person each way.

De Plateau Lodge HOMESTAY $
(☑019-855 9458; deplateau@gmail.com; per person incl meals RM80; ☜) Situated about 2km east of the centre (bear left at the fork), this two-storey wooden chalet has seven rooms (including one triple) and a homey living room. It is owned by Douglas, a former guide. Recent visitors have missed flights due to transport confusion so make sure your needs are clear.

Gem's Lodge GUESTHOUSE $
(☑013-828 0507; gems_lodge@yahoo.com; per person incl meals RM70) Situated 5km southeast of town (bear right at the fork) five minutes from the longhouse village of Pa' Umor. Managed by Jaman, one of Bario's nicest and most experienced guides, this

place is tranquillity incarnate, with eight pleasant rooms, a cosy common area, river swimming and solar power. Transport to/ from the airport by 4WD costs RM25 per person.

Junglebluesdream GUESTHOUSE $
(☑019-884 9892; http://junglebluesdream.weebly. com; per person incl board RM80; ☜) Owned by artist and one-time guide Stephen Baya, a Bario native, and his friendly Danish wife Tine, this super-welcoming lodge (and art gallery) has four mural-decorated rooms, good-quality beds and quilts, and fantastic Kelabit food. Guests can consult Stephen's extraordinary hand-drawn town and trekking maps. Organises kayaking excursions.

Libal Paradise GUESTHOUSE $
(☑019-807 1640; per person RM65, dm without board RM25; ☜) Surrounded by a verdant fruit and vegie garden where you can pick your own pineapples, this sustainably-run farm – an idyllic spot to chill – is run by a local woman, Dorkas Parir, and her Canadian husband Stu, who runs kayaking trips. Solar collectors power 24-hour LED lighting. Kitchen facilities are available. To get there from the airport terminal, walk eastward along the road that parallels the runway.

Nancy & Harriss GUESTHOUSE $
(Hill View Lodge; ☑013-850 5850, 019-858 5850; nancyharriss@yahoo.com; dm RM30; per person incl board RM70) Run by a former guide whose grandmother was once married to Tom Harrisson, this rambling place has seven guest rooms, a lovely verandah, a library-equipped lounge and endearingly tacky floor coverings. Situated 250m along a dirt track south of the main road; the turn-off is just east of Kaludai. Prices include airport transfer.

THE 'EBARIO MODEL'

Bario has produced some remarkable leaders, including local councillor John Tarawe, CEO of the award-winning internet initiative **eBario** (www.unimas.my/ebario and www .ebario.org), who is much sought after around the world by groups (eg the UNDP) that are interested in 'community mobilisation' among indigenous groups. His efforts to plug the Highlands into the internet (even in remote villages he'd like the children to grow up 'IT savvy') and establish a hugely popular community radio station, **Radio Tauh** (94MHz FM; ☺7.30-9am or 10am & 7-9pm or 10pm Mon-Sat), have been so groundbreaking that NGOs on distant continents are adopting the 'eBario model'.

THE PENAN

The Kelabit Highlands are home not only to the Kelabits but also the Penan, an indigenous group that was nomadic – surviving almost exclusively on hunting and gathering – until quite recently and has fared much less well than other indigenous groups in modern Malaysia. The Penan are often looked down upon, and discriminated against, by other Orang Ulu groups. Around Bario, if you see barefoot people wearing ragged clothes who drop their gaze when you approach, you can be sure they're Penan. Kelabits have intermarried with Chinese, Westerners, Malays and other Orang Ulu groups for several generations but the first Kelabit-Penan marriage took place only recently.

Since independence, the Sarawak state government has often sold off rainforest lands to well-connected logging companies and then evicted the Penan and other Dayak groups with minimal or no compensation. The Swiss rainforest and human-rights advocate **Bruno Manser** (www.bmf.ch) spent years living with the Penan and agitating to protect their human and civil rights. He disappeared near Bario in May 2000 and is presumed dead – many people, in the Kelabit Highlands and abroad, suspect he was murdered.

Ngimat Ayu's House　　GUESTHOUSE **$**
(☑013-840 6187; engimat_scott@yahoo.com; per person incl board RM95) This brown, two-storey place, run by the impressive but personable son of the Kelabits' former *pemancha* (paramount chief), has seven rooms and a chill-out verandah with rice-field views. Situated on a slope 200m east of the yellow public library. Rates include transport from and to the airport.

✖ Eating

Most guesthouses offer full board – almost always delicious Kelabit cuisine – but Bario also has several modest eateries. **Pasar Bario**, the town's yellow-painted commercial centre, is home to half-a-dozen basic **cafes** (mains RM4; ⊘7am-10pm, closed Sun morning) selling mainly generic fried noodle and rice dishes, though Kelabit food can sometimes be special-ordered.

🍺 Drinking

Finding a beer in Bario can be a bit of a challenge. This is a very Evangelical town – you're as likely to hear Christian country as the sound of the *sapé* – so most establishments do not serve alcohol, and some of those that do keep it hidden. But what was it that Matthew once said? 'Ask, and it shall be given you; seek, and ye shall find'.

At Pasar Bario, don't go through the swinging doors of the Bario Saloon looking for a stiff drink – it's a unisex beauty salon!

Y2K　　BAR
(⊘7am-midnight or later) Local men quaff beer (RM4 to RM6) and play pool. Has karaoke in the evening (until 10pm).

Keludai　　BAR
(mains RM4; ⊘noon-1am or 2am) An all-wood saloon with beer (RM4), instant noodles, satellite TV and a pool table.

🛍 Shopping

Sinah Rang　　HANDICRAFTS
(Bario Asal Longhouse; ⊘daily) Sinah sells lovely Kelabit beadwork, all locally made, from her living room. This is a good place to pick up a *kabo'* (RM50 to RM100, depending on the quality of the beads), a beadwork pendant shaped like a little beer barrel that's worn around the neck by Kelabit men.

Y2K　　GENERAL STORE
(⊘7am-midnight or later) An old-fashioned, Old West-style general store that sells everything from SIM cards to something called Zam-Zam Hair Oil.

ℹ Information

There are no banks, ATMs or credit-card facilities anywhere in the Kelabit Highlands so bring plenty of small-denomination banknotes for accommodation, food and guides, plus some extra in case you get stranded. Commerce is limited to a few basic shops, some of them in Pasar Bario, Bario's bright yellow commercial centre.

The best Malaysian cell-phone company to have up here is Celcom (Maxis works at the airport and in parts of Bario; Digi is useless). The airport has wi-fi, as do several guesthouses.

Bario Telecentre (www.unimas.my/ebario; Gatuman Bario; per hr RM4; ⊘9.30-11.30am & 2-4pm, closed Sat afternoon & Sunday) Solar-powered internet access.

Klinik Kesihatan Bariio (☑085-796404; Airport Rd intersection; ⊘8am-1pm & 2-5pm Mon-Thu, 8-11.45am & 2.15-5pm Fri, emergency 24hr) Bario's innovative, ecologically sustainable rural health clinic, powered by solar energy, has one doctor, two paramedics, a dispensary (small pharmacy) and a helicopter on standby.

ℹ Getting There & Around

AIR

Bario Airport (☑for Joanna 013-835 9009, for Norman Peter 013-824 8006) is linked with Miri twice a day by Twin Otters operated by **MASwings** (www.maswings.com.my). Weather (especially high winds) not infrequently causes delays and cancellations. For flight updates or if you're having a problem making a flight out of Bario, just ring the friendly staff at the airport.

Twin Otters have strict weight limits, so much so that checked baggage is limited to 10kg, carry-ons to 5kg and passengers themselves are weighed on a giant scale when they check in. Enforcement is particularly strict on the way up because planes have to carry enough fuel to get back to Miri, and more cargo is flown into Bario than out. For the same reason, it's easier to find a seat from Bario to Miri than the other way around. Consider leaving some of your belongings in Miri at your hotel or guesthouse.

When you land in Bario, the first thing you should do is register for your flight out at the counter – your name will be inscribed in a crumpled old ledger. A schematic map of the Bario area is posted on a nearby wall.

The airport is about a 30-minute walk south of the shophouses but you're bound to be offered a lift on arrival. As you'll notice, the people of Bario treat the air link to Miri almost like their own private airline and absolutely love dropping by the wi-fi-equipped airport terminal to meet flights, hang out with arriving or departing friends, and surf the net.

CAR

The overland trip between Bario and Miri, possible only by 4WD (per person RM150), takes 12 hours at the very least and sometimes a lot more, the determining factors being the weather and the condition of the rough logging roads and their old wooden bridges. When things get ugly, vehicles travel in convoys so when one gets

stuck the others can push or winch it out. At press time, some sectors were being upgraded to make the route safer and more reliable.

A new road from Bario via Pa' Lungan to Ba Kelalan (already connected by road with Lawas) is under construction.

In Bario, 4WD vehicles can be hired for RM250 or RM300 a day including a driver and petrol; guesthouses can make arrangements.

BA KELALAN

Known for its rice, organic vegetables, apples and annual apple festival – and the general vibrancy of its farming sector – the Lun Bawang town of Ba Kelalan is a popular destination for treks from Bario.

Guesthouse options include the nice **Ba Kelalan Apple Lodge Homestay** (per person about RM70), run by **Borneo Jungle Safari** (☑013-286 5656, in Miri 085-422595; www.borneojunglesafari.com); the **Ba Kelalan Inn**, the only place in town that serves beer; and the **Green Valley Guesthouse** (per bed RM20).

ℹ Getting There & Away

The only way to get from Ba Kelalan to Bario is on foot (a road via Pa' Lungan is in the works). A rough, 125km logging road links Ba Kelalan with Lawas (per person RM70 to RM80 by 4WD, seven hours, daily).

It's possible to get from Ba Kelalan to Long Bawan in Kalimantan by motorbike.

MASwings (www.maswings.com.my) flies Twin Otters from Ba Kelalan to Lawas and Miri three times a week.

TREKKING IN THE KELABIT HIGHLANDS

The temperate highlands up along Sarawak's far eastern border with Indonesia offer some of the best jungle trekking in Borneo, taking in farming villages, rugged peaks and supremely remote Kenyah, Penan and Kelabit settlements. Most trails traverse a variety of primary and secondary forests, as well as an increasing number of logged areas. Treks from Bario range from easy overnight

---

BARIO SALT

If you're interested in the Kelabit's culinary traditions, you might want to walk out to Bario's **main tudtu** (literally 'salty sweet'; natural salt lick; overnight facilities planned), under an hour's walk from Pa' Umor, where mineral-rich saline water is put in giant vats over a roaring fire until all that's left is high-iodine salt that goes perfectly with local specialities such as deer and wild boar. This traditional production technique is beginning to die out, but in Bario you can still purchase salt made the old way – look for something that resembles a 20cm-long green Tootsie roll wrapped in a leaf (RM17 to RM20).

RICE & PINEAPPLES

Bario is famous throughout Malaysia for two things: Bario rice, whose grains are smaller and more aromatic than lowland varieties; and sweeter-than-sweet pineapples (RM2.50 in Bario) that are free of the pucker-inducing acidity of their coastal cousins. Outside of the Kelabit Highlands, 1kg of Bario rice can cost a whopping RM16 and Bario pineapples are usually unavailable at any price.

excursions to nearby longhouses to one-week slogs over the border into the wilds of Kalimantan.

While the Highlands are certainly cooler than Borneo's coastal regions, it's still hard work trekking up here (don't forget the altitude) and you should be in fairly good shape to consider a multiday trek. Be prepared to encounter leeches – many trails are literally crawling with them. Bring extra cell-phone and camera batteries as charging may not be possible.

The routes we list are intended to serve as a starting point. With so many trails in the area, there is ample scope for custom routes and creative planning.

MEGALITHS NEAR BARIO

Hidden deep in the jungle around Bario are scores of mysterious megaliths and other 'cultural sites'. For more information, ask your guide for a copy of the booklet *Stone Culture of the Northern Highlands of Sarawak, Malaysia* (RM20).

At research time, trails equipped with overnight shelters for megalith circuits lasting two to five days were being constructed. Overnight options include:

Pa' Umor Route   TREKKING

From Bario it's a 1½-hour walk – notorious for its legions of lecherous leeches – to **Pa' Umor**, where there's **longhouse accommodation** (☑for Jaman 013-828 0507, for Rian 013-812 8851). Continue on for 2km (50 minutes) and you come to a salt spring.

About 15 minutes from Pa' Umor is Arur Bilit Farm, home to **Batu Narit**, an impressive stone carving featuring a human in the spread-eagled position among its designs.

From the farm, use the log bridge to cross a small river (25 minutes) in order to reach **Batu Ipak**. According to local legend, this stone formation was created when an angry warrior named Upai Semering pulled out his parang (machete) and took a wrathful swing at the rock, cutting it in two. This circuit should take four or five hours – maybe a tad longer if your guide is a good storyteller.

Pa' Lungan Route   TREKKING

(homestays per person incl board RM70, **boat ride** up to 4 people RM250) A wide, muddy forest trail – used by water buffalos to pull sleighs carrying goods and, on occasion, medical evacuees – heads from Bario to **Pa' Lungan** (four hours). Unlike almost all the other Highland trails, this one is walkable without a guide as long as you have clear instructions. About halfway along you can stop at **Batu Arit**, a large stone featuring bird carvings and humanoid figures with heart-shaped faces.

From Pa' Lungan it's a two-minute walk to **Batu Ritung**, a 2m stone table (probably a burial site), although no one is quite sure as the site was created outside of living memory. Also near Pa' Lungan (15 minutes away) is **Perupun**, a huge pile of stones of a type assembled to bury the valuables of the dead who had no descendants to receive their belongings.

If you've got a bit more time, you could consider basing yourself for a day or two in Pa' Lungan, believed by many to produce the very best Bario rice. Longhouse homestays, including **Batu Ritung Lodge** (☑019-805 2119; baturitunglodge@yahoo.com), serve Kelabit-style dishes such as *pa'u* (fern) and *puluh* (bamboo shoots).

A scenic boat ride can be arranged to take you on the **Pa' Debpur** from a spot an hour's hike from Pa' Lungan back to Pa' Umor (in Kelabit, *pa'* means 'river').

BARIO TO BA KELALAN

The three- to four-day trek from Bario to Ba Kelalan covers a variety of mostly gentle terrain – some of it on the Indonesian side of the frontier – and gives a good overview of the Kelabit Highlands. An alternative route, the Kalimantan Loop, which takes five to seven days, goes deeper into Kalimantan, passing by Lembudud.

To avoid doubling back, you can trek from Bario to Ba Kelalan and then fly or take a 4WD down to the coast. Remember, though that you'll have to pay the guide for the two days it will take him to walk back to Bario.

HIRING A GUIDE: THE PRACTICALITIES

With very few exceptions, the only way to explore the Kelabit Highlands is to hire a local guide. Fortunately, this could hardly be easier. Any of the guesthouses in Bario can organise a wide variety of short walks and longer treks led by guides they know and rely on. Some of the best guides for longer treks live in Pa' Lungan, an easy walk from Bario. If you link up with other travellers in Bario or Miri, the cost of a guide can be shared.

Although there's a growing shortage of guides, in general it's no problem to just turn up in Bario and make arrangements after you arrive, especially if you don't mind hanging out for day or two in Bario. If you're in a hurry, though, or your trip coincides with the prime tourism months of July and August, consider making arrangements with your guesthouse in advance by email or phone.

The going rate for guides is RM100 per day for either a Bario-based day trip or a longer trek. Some itineraries involve either river trips (highly recommended if the water is high enough) or travel by 4WD – naturally, these significantly increase the cost. The going rate for a porter is RM80 to RM100 a day.

If you are connecting the dots between rural longhouses, expect to pay RM70 for a night's sleep plus three meals (you can opt out of lunch and save RM10 or RM15). Gifts are not obligatory but the people who live in remote longhouses are appreciative if, after you drink tea or coffee with them, you offer RM10 'to cover the costs' or 'to buy pens and paper for the children'.

If your route requires that you camp in the forest, expect to pay approximately RM120 per night; in addition, you may be asked to supply food, which is provided for both you and your guide when you stay in a longhouse. Equipment for jungle camping (eg a sleeping bag, hammock, mozzie net and bed roll) cannot be purchased in Bario so it's a good idea to bring your own, though Bario Asal Longhouse may be able to rent it out.

If you're trekking in one direction only (eg Bario to Ba Kelalan), you will be asked to continue paying the guiding fee while your guide returns home through the jungle (in this scenario, it would take them two days to trek from Ba Kelalan back to Bario).

Detailed topographical maps of Sarawak exist but it's nearly impossible to get hold of them. According to in-the-know locals, the government's calculation seems to be that activists will find it harder to fight for native land rights if they lack proper maps.

BATU LAWI

If you were sitting on the left side of the plane from Miri to Bario, you probably caught a glimpse of the two massive limestone spires known as Batu Lawi, the taller of which soars to 2040m. During WWII they were used as a landmark for parachute drops.

While an ascent of the higher of the two rock formations, known as the 'male peak', is only for expert technical rock climbers, ascending the lower 'female peak' – described by one veteran trekker as 'awe-inspiring' – is possible for fit trekkers without special skills. It's a tough, four- or five-day return trip from Bario. Be prepared to spend the second day passing through areas that have been impacted by logging. Only a handful of guides are experienced enough to tackle Batu Lawi – perhaps the best is Richard from Pa' Ukat.

GUNUNG MURUD

Sarawak's highest mountain (2442m), part of 598-sq-km **Pulong Tau National Park**, is just begging to be climbed, but very few visitors make the effort to put the trip together. This adventure is only for the fittest of the fit. **Borneo Touch Ecotour** (☑013-8443861; www.walk2mulu.com) offers four-day, three-night ascents for RM1500 per person (minimum four).

The mountain is linked by trails with both Ba Kelalan and Bario. From Bario, the more common starting point, a typical return trip takes six or seven days. You can also walk from Bario via Gunung Murud to Ba Kelalan (five days one-way), but as you approach Ba Kelalan you'll have to walk along a depressing logging road.

A rough logging road links the base of Gunung Murud with the lowland town of Lawas (five to eight hours by 4WD).

Limbang Division

Shaped like a crab claw, the Limbang Division slices Brunei in two and separates the diminutive sultanate from Sabah. Tourism is underdeveloped in these parts, but Bruneians love popping across the border to find shopping bargains, including cheap beer smuggled in from duty-free Pulau Labuan. As one local put it with just a hint of exaggeration, 'Los Angeles has Tijuana, BSB has Limbang'.

The area, snatched from the sultan of Brunei by Charles Brooke in 1890, is still claimed by Brunei.

LIMBANG

The bustling river port of Limbang (pronounced *lim*-bahng) is something of a backwater, but you may find yourself here before or after taking the Headhunters' Trail to/from Gunung Mulu National Park.

◉ Sights & Activities

Limbang's old town stretches inland from riverfront Jln Wong Tsap En (formerly Main Bazaar) and southward from 12-storey Purnama Hotel, a useful landmark.

Limbang Regional Museum　　MUSEUM
(www.museum.sarawak.gov.my; Jln Kubu; ⊗9am-4.30pm Tue-Sun) Features well-presented exhibits on the Limbang Division's archaeology, culture and crafts. Situated on the riverbank about 1km south of the Purnama Hotel, on the upper floor of a Charles Brooke fort built in 1897 and rebuilt (after a fire) in 1991.

Limbang Raid Memorial　　MEMORIAL
(Jln Wong Tsap En) Commemorates four members of the Sarawak Constabulary and five members of the UK's 42 Commando Royal Marines killed before and during the famous Limbang Raid on 12 December 1962, which retook the town from rebels of the pro-Indonesian North Kalimantan National Army. As one local put it, 'if the rebels win, we will be Indonesian, not Malaysian'. A trailer for a TV documentary about the raid, *Return to Limbang*, can be found on www.vimeo.com. The memorial is 400m south of the Purnama Hotel, on the riverfront across the street from the police station.

Public Library　　LIBRARY
(Perpustakaan Awam; 4th fl, Limbang Plaza Shopping Mall; ⊗9am-5pm Mon-Sat, closed public holidays) The library has an excellent collection of English-language books on Sarawak (on a shelf labelled 'Sarawakiana'). This is a great place to do air-conditioned research before an upcountry trek, especially on a rainy day. Free internet for up to an hour. Situated next to the Purnama Hotel.

☞ Tours

The following outfits run canoe trips in the Limpaki Wetlands, where you can often see proboscis monkeys, and can take you to the crash site of a **B-34 Liberator** shot down by the Japanese in 1944, and to the salty **Maritam Mud Spring** (aka the 'Mud Volcano'), 34km towards BSB.

Chua Eng Hin　　SIGHTSEEING, CANOEING
(☎019-814 5355; chualbg@streamyx.com) A well-known local personality with a passion for Limbang District's largely unknown charms.

Borneo Touch Ecotour　　CANOEING, TREKKING
(☎013-844 3861; www.walk2mulu.com; 1st fl, 2061 Rickett Commercial Bldg) Run by the dynamic Mr Lim (no, Limbang is not named for him), this local company offers highly recommended treks up or down the Headhunters'

CROSSING INTO INDONESIA

Thanks to long-standing cultural and personal ties across the Sarawak–Kalimantan frontier, drawn in colonial times by the British and the Dutch, a local trans-border initiative has made it possible for both Highland residents and tourists to cross from Ba Kelalan into Kalimantan to visit nearby settlements such as Long Bawan, Lembudud and Long Layu. All you need is a *pas lintas batas* (transboundary pass), issued locally according to an agreement signed between the Malaysian and Indonesian foreign ministries. Passports are not stamped and you must return to Sarawak within 14 days. To make arrangements, ask your guide or contact John Tarawe in Bario.

Malaysian ringgits are very popular in this remote part of Kalimantan but US dollars are not.

TREKKING IN THE PENAN HIGHLANDS

Community-based and sustainably managed, **Picnic with the Penan** (www.picnicwith thepenan.org) is a pioneering, non-profit tourism initiative that offers intrepid trekkers a rare chance to visit remote Penan villages in the *ulu-ulu* (back-of-the-beyond) Upper Baram area between the Highland airports of Long Lellang and Long Banga. Itineraries take at least five days and four nights. Booking is by email or through Highlands Back-packers (p177) in Miri.

Trail to/from Gunung Mulu National Park (RM950 per person for three days and two nights, including the Pinnacles; minimum four people).

🛏 Sleeping

East Asia Hotel HOTEL $
(☎085-215 600; cnr Jln Wong Tsap En & Jln Wayang; d old/new RM45/78; ✴🗢) A water-front hostelry with 33 clean and comfy rooms, eleven of them nicely remodelled; some have river views. Situated four short blocks south of the Purnama Hotel. Room deposit: RM100.

Purnama Hotel HOTEL $$
(☎085-216700; www.purnamalimbang.com; Jln Buangsiol; s/d from RM105/115; ✴🗢) En-sconced in Limbang's tallest building (12 storeys), this uninspiring hotel – orna-mented with rainbow-hued balconies – has 218 spacious but aesthetically challenged rooms that come with big views and small bathrooms.

🍴 Eating

Pusat Penjaja Medan Bangkita MARKET $
(Jln Bangkita; ⊙6am or 7am-5pm or 6pm) Bisayah, Lun Bawang and Iban women sell jungle ed-ibles, sausage-shaped Ba Kelalan salt and a dozen kinds of upland rice. The larger weekly *tamu* (market) takes place all-day Thursday and until noon on Friday. From the Purnama Hotel, go one long block inland.

Thien Hsing Vegetarian CHINESE $
(mains RM3-4; ⊙6.30am-2pm; 🥢) A very basic eatery serving vegie Chinese dishes. Situated on a back alley 3½ short blocks south of the Purnama Hotel, right behind Ling Brother Enterprise bike shop at 46 Jln Wayang.

Bangunan Tamu Limbang HAWKER $
(Jln Wong Tsap En; mains RM3.50-5; ⊙6.30am-5.30pm) Houses Limbang's main Malay market, with an upstairs hawker centre. Di-agonally opposite the Purnama Hotel.

Night Markets FOOD STALLS $
In the afternoon and evening, food-stall action shifts to the **Malay night market** (⊙5pm-midnight), on the riverfront 300m northwest of the Purnama Hotel; and to the **Chinese night market** (Jln Bangkita; ⊙2-10pm), a block northeast of the Purnama Hotel.

❶ Information

Limbang has several international ATMs.

Sun City Cybercafe (Jln Bangkita, 1st fl; per hr RM2.50; ⊙8.30am-midnight) A haven for gam-ers. One long block east of the Purnama Hotel, above the Cahaya Delima Cafe.

❶ Getting There & Around

The Sungai Pandaruan ferry between Limbang and Bangar (Brunei), a major bottleneck, should be replaced by a bridge in 2013.

AIR

MASwings (www.maswings.com.my) links Limbang's airport, 7km south of the centre, with Miri. A taxi into town costs RM18.

BOAT

Express ferries from Limbang's immigration hall to Pulau Labuan (RM30, two hours, 8am daily) are run by two companies on alternate days, **Lim Pertama** (☎012-865 3753) and **Royal Limbang** (☎013-882 3736). Departures from Pulau Labuan are at 1.30pm. Bookings can be made by SMS/text message.

BUS

There's a tiny bus station at the eastern end of Jln Wayang, two blocks inland from the river. **Biaramas/Bus Asia** (☎012-828 2042) sends a bus to Miri's Pujut Bus Terminal (RM45, four hours) every day at 9am. A spot in a seven-person van to Miri costs RM50, with departures at around 8.30am and 1pm. The cheapest way to Bandar Seri Begawan (BSB) is to take Syarikat Bus Limbang's 1pm bus to Kualah Lurah (RM5) and then a local Bruneian bus (B$1).

The only company that can drop you off in-side Brunei is **Jesselton Express** (PHLS; ☎in Brunei +673-718-3838, +673-717-7755, +673-719-3835, in KK 016-836 0009, in Limbang

016-855 0222, 085-212990), which has daily buses to BSB (RM20 or B$10) at 2pm or 3pm; and to Bangar, Lawas (RM30, 2 hours) and Kota Kimabalu (KK; RM50) at 9.30am. Heading to Limbang, a bus departs from BSB every day at 8am. Tickets are sold at **Wan Wan Cafe & Restaurant** (Jln Bangkita).

Bintang Jaya (016-859 4532) sends daily buses to Miri (RM45) at 1.45pm, and to Lawas (RM30) and KK (RM50) at 12.30pm. Tickets are sold at **Hock Chuong Hin Cafe** (Jln Bangkita).

TAXI & MINIBUS

Minibuses and red-and-yellow taxis hang out at the **Stesyen Teksi** (085-213781; Jln Wong Tsap En; 5am-6pm or later), on the waterfront a block south of the Purnama Hotel. If you're heading towards BSB, one-way travel to the Kuala Lurah crossing costs about RM60 (more after 7pm); cheap, frequent local buses can take you from there to BSB. If you're coming from BSB, taxis wait on the Malaysian side of the Kuala Lurah crossing.

Brunei

POP 410,000 / AREA 5765 SQ KM

Best Places to Eat

» Taman Selera (p205)

» Lim Ah Siaw Pork Market (p204)

» Pondok Sari Wangi (p204)

Best Places to Stay

» Ulu-Ulu Resort (p214)

» Brunei Hotel (p203)

» Pusat Belia (p203)

Why Go?

The small sultanate of Brunei almost looks like a geographic comma plunked between Sarawak and Sabah. It certainly forms a conceptual one, because unless you're a petroleum engineer, when folks ask 'Why go to Brunei?' the answer is usually the travel equivalent of a pause: transfer or stopover.

But there's more here than passport queues. This quiet *darussalam* (Arabic for 'abode of peace') has the largest oil-fields in Southeast Asia, and because oil generates money, Brunei hasn't turned its rainforests into palm plantations. Old-growth greenery abounds, especially in verdant Ulu Temburong National Park. Because booze is banned, the citizens of the capital, Bandar Seri Begawan (BSB), are mad for food and shopping.

This tranquil (sometimes somnolent) nation is the realisation of a particular vision: a strict, socially controlled religious state where happiness is found in pious worship and mass consumption. Visit and judge the results for yourself.

When to Go
Bandar Seri Begawan

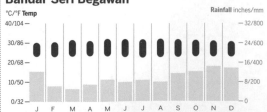

Oct–Dec The rainiest, if coolest, months of the year.

Jan–May February and March are the driest months. National Day is celebrated on 23 February.

Jun–Aug It's *hot*. The sultan's birthday (15 July) is marked with festivities around the country.

N

0   20 km
0   10 miles

SOUTH CHINA SEA

To Pulau Labuan (35km); Menumbok, Sabah (45km)

Brunei Bay

Pantai Muara

Pantai Meragang

Bukit Shahbandar (100m)

Empire Hotel **6**

Muara

Serasa

Pulau Muara Besar

To Lawas (Sarawak) (15km)

Jerudong Park Playground

Brunei International Airport

BANDAR SERI BEGAWAN

BRUNEI-MUARA

Pulau Selirong

Sundar

2 **3** **4**

5 **8**

Pantai Seri Kenangan

Tutong

Kampung Parit

Sungai Brunei

Limbang

Peradayan Forestry Reserve

TEMBURONG

Trusan

Pan Borneo Hwy

Sinaut

Kampung Abang

Limau Manis

Kuala Lurah

Bangar

Labu

Bukit Peradayan (410m)

Kampung Telisai

Seria

Oil & Gas Discovery Centre

Lumut

Forestry Museum

Kampung Sungai Liang

Layong

Lamunin

Trans Borneo Hwy

LIMBANG DIVISION

Sungai Temburong

Bukit Patoi (310m)

Sumbiling Eco Village **7**

Batang Duri

Kuala Belait

To Kuala Baram (20km); Miri (40km)

Kampung Badas

Sungai Belait

Kuala Balai

Sungai Liang Forest Recreation Park

Tasek Merimbun

Kampung Merimbun

TUTONG

Ulu Temburong National Park **1**

Bukit Belalong (913m)

Luagan Lalak Forest Reserve

Labi

Rampayoh

Mendaram Basar

Mendaram Kecil

Teraja

BELAIT

Kampung Sukang

Sungai Tutong

Sungai Limbang

LIMBANG DIVISION

Bukit Teraja (442m)

Kampung Melilas

Bukit Pagon (1850m)

Marudi

Gunung Mulu National Park

SARAWAK

MALAYSIA

Brunei Highlights

1 Climbing high into the rainforest canopy and swimming in a cool jungle river at **Ulu Temburong National Park** (p212)

2 Tearing along mangrove-lined waterways on a **speedboat** (p210) from BSB to Bangar

3 Taking a water taxi to the water village of **Kampung**

Ayer (p198) and then indulging in a boardwalk stroll

4 Walking along BSB's newly refurbished **waterfront promenade** (p198)

5 Visiting BSB's opulent **mosques** (p198)

6 Marvelling at the **Empire Hotel & Country Club** (p203),

a sparkling monument to world-class profligacy

7 Relaxing amid rural greenery at **Sumbiling Eco Village** (p212) in Temburong District

8 Gorging yourself on the culinary delights of the many restaurants of **BSB** (p204)

BANDAR SERI BEGAWAN

POP 100,000

Cities built on oil money tend to be flashy places, but with the exception of a palace you usually can't enter, a couple of enormous mosques and one wedding cake of a hotel, Bandar (as the capital is known, or just BSB) is a pretty understated place. Urban life pretty much revolves around malls, restaurants and, depending on your level of piety, illicit parties or Islam (and sometimes both). BSB does have a few museums and the biggest water village in the world, a little slice of vintage that speaks to the Bruneian love of cosiness and nostalgia.

BSB's city centre is on the north bank of Sungai Brunei at a spot – 12km upriver from Brunei Bay – that's easy to defend against seaborne attack and sheltered from both storms and tsunamis. During the Japanese occupation, the city centre – known until 1970 as Brunei Town – was severely damaged by Allied bombing.

◉ Sights & Activities

All of central BSB is within easy walking or sailing distance of the Omar Ali Saifuddien Mosque, but unless you don't mind walking for hours in the tropical sun, you'll have to make do with buses and taxis to get to sights east, north and west of downtown. Many malls and restaurants are in Gadong, located about 5km northwest of central BSB. There is a pleasant **promenade** along Jln McArthur, at the foot of Jln Sultan facing Kampung Ayer, which is a nice spot for an evening stroll.

CENTRAL BSB

Kampung Ayer   WATER VILLAGES

(Map p200) Home to an estimated 20,000 people, Kampung Ayer consists of 28 contiguous stilt villages – named after the crafts and occupations traditionally practised there – built along both (but especially the southern) banks of Sungai Brunei. A century ago, half of Brunei's population lived here, and even today many Bruneians – despite government inducements – still prefer the lifestyle of the water village to residency on dry land. If you look to the main roads on the opposite banks of the village you'll see luxury cars lined up on the shoulder of the road; many of these cars belong to water village residents. That said, Kampung Ayer is also home to a sizable population of undocumented immigrants that constitute Brunei's underclass.

Founded at least a thousand years ago, the village is considered the largest stilt settlement in the world and has its own schools, mosques, police stations and fire brigade. The houses, painted sun-bleached shades of green, blue, pink and yellow, have not been cutesified for tourists, so while it's far from squalid, be prepared for trash that, at low tide, carpets the intertidal mud under the banisterless boardwalks, some with missing planks. When Venetian scholar Antonio Pigafetta, who accompanied Ferdinand Magellan on his last voyage, visited Kampung Ayer in 1521, he dubbed it the 'Venice of the East', which is, as descriptions go, a bit ambitious.

A good place to start a visit – and get acquainted with Brunei's pre-oil culture – is the **Kampung Ayer Cultural & Tourism Gallery** (Map p200; ◉9am-5pm Sat-Thu, 9-11.30am & 2.30-5pm Fri), directly across the river from Sungai Kianggeh (the stream at the eastern edge of the city centre). Opened in 2009, this riverfront complex focuses on the history, lifestyle and crafts of the Kampung Ayer people and usually has a live handicrafts demonstration. Like many of the sultanate's public institutions, this one is overstaffed, yet somehow seems underserviced, leading to lots of people who spend much of their time just standing around. A square, glass-enclosed **viewing tower** offers panoramic views of the scene below.

Getting across the river from the city centre (ie the area next to and east of the Yayasan Complex) or the eastern bank of Sungai Kiangeh is a breeze. Just stand somewhere a water taxi – BSB's souped-up version of the gondola – can dock and flag an empty one down.

To visit the villages on the river's **north bank** (the same side as the city centre), follow the plankwalks that head southwest from Omar Ali Saifuddien Mosque, or those leading west (parallel to the river) from the Yayasan Complex, itself built on the site of a one-time water village.

Omar Ali Saifuddien Mosque   MOSQUE

(Map p200; Jln Stoney; ◉interior 8.30am-noon, 1.30-3pm & 4.30-5.30pm Sat-Wed, 4.30-5pm Fri, closed Thu, exterior compound 8am-8.30pm daily except prayer times) Built from 1954 to 1958, Masjid Omar Ali Saifuddien – named after the 28th sultan of Brunei (the late father of the current sultan) – is surrounded by an artificial lagoon that serves as a reflecting pool. The mosque is basically the happening

ⓘ RAMADAN ROAD RULES

Brunei is an extremely religious, majority-Muslim nation that takes Ramadan seriously. If you're visiting during the holiest month of the Islamic year, keep in mind that by around 3pm, most people – especially drivers – are tired or stressed or both thanks to the daily fast. It's a documented fact that many car accidents occur at this time, and it's an anecdotal observation that normally polite Bruneians can get downright testy around this time. Just be mindful when interacting with locals and careful if you're out on the roads during late afternoon at this time.

centre of city life in Bandar come evenings; folks come for prayer, then leave to eat or shop, which is sort of Brunei in a nutshell. The 44m minaret makes it the tallest building in central BSB, and woe betide anyone who tries to outdo it – apparently the nearby Islamic Bank of Brunei building originally exceeded this height and so had its top storey removed by order of the sultan.

This being Brunei, the interior is pretty lavish. The floor and walls are made from the finest Italian marble, the stained-glass windows and chandeliers were crafted in England, and the luxurious carpets were flown in from Saudi Arabia and Belgium. Jigsaw enthusiasts can admire the 3.5-million-piece Venetian mosaic inside the main dome.

The ceremonial stone boat sitting in the lagoon is a replica of a 16th-century *mahligai* (royal barge).

FREE **Royal Regalia Museum**　MUSEUM
(Map p200; Jln Sultan; ⊙9am-5pm Sun-Thu, 9-11.30am & 2.30-5pm Fri, 9.45am-5pm Sat, last entry 4.30pm) When called upon to present a gift to the sultan of Brunei, you must inevitably confront the question: what do you give a man who has everything? Here you'll see how various heads of state and royalty have solved this conundrum (hint: you'll never go wrong with priceless gold and jewels). We particularly like the mother of all beer mugs, given by Queen Elizabeth II.

Water-Taxi Cruise　BOAT TOUR
The best way to see BSB's water villages and the sultan's fabled palace, Istana Nurul

Iman, is from a water taxi, which can be chartered along the waterfront for about B$30 to B$40 (a bit of negotiating will occur, but at least you know the locals can't claim the petrol is expensive!). Finding a boat won't be a problem, as the boatmen will have spotted you before you spot them.

After you admire the palace's backyard, your boatman can take you further upriver to **Pulau Ranggu**, an island that's home to a large colony of proboscis monkeys. The best time to head out is late afternoon, as the monkeys are easiest to spot around sunset.

EAST OF CENTRAL BSB

Brunei Museum　MUSEUM
(☑224 4545; Jln Kota Batu; ⊙9am-5pm Sat-Thu, 9-11.30am & 2.30-5pm Fri, last entry 30 min before closing; Ⓟ) Brunei's national museum, officially opened by Queen Elizabeth II in 1972, is a decent place to blow an hour of your time. It definitely feels a little dated.

The oldest pieces are in the newest, most well-kept section of the museum: the **Islamic Art Gallery**, which displays ceramics from Iran and Central Asia and blown glass from Egypt and the Levant dating from the 9th and 10th centuries. Other highlights include illuminated manuscripts of the Koran, tiny Korans the size of a matchbox and gold jewellery.

The **Brunei Traditional Culture Gallery** spotlights Brunei's role in Southeast Asia's history, cultures and commerce, and has a section on Western trade and intervention in Brunei, starting with the arrival of the Spanish and Portuguese in the 1500s. There's some frankly creepy, life-sized depictions of Malay rituals like weddings, child-rearing and (ouch) circumcision, and a collection of Brunei's famous ceremonial cannons, known as *bedil,* some with barrels shaped like dragon heads.

The **Natural History Gallery** is a decent introduction to Borneo's extraordinary biodiversity. Quite a few of the stuffed animals look to be on their last, moulding legs.

At the time of our visit there was an entire **wing** devoted to oil and gas extraction, the technology behind it, the good it has done for Brunei and an extensive exhibit on the kingdom's long-term plan for its economy after the oil runs out. Just kidding about that last bit.

The Brunei Museum is 4.5km east of central BSB along the coastal road, on a bluff overlooking Sungai Brunei. To get here, take the Central Bus line or a taxi (around B$10 from the bus station).

BRUNEI BANDAR SERI BEGAWAN

Bandar Seri Begawan

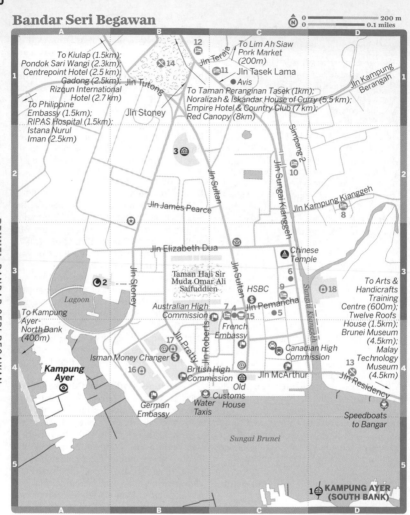

Malay Technology Museum MUSEUM
(Jln Kota Batu; ☉9am-5pm Sun-Thu, 9-11.30am &
2.30-5pm Fri, 9.45am-5pm Sat, last entry 30 min
before closing) Linked to the Brunei Museum
by a short path down the hill, this museum
has somewhat outdated displays on life in a
Malay water village (stilt architecture, boat
making, fishing techniques, handicrafts)
and a Murut (Lun Bawang) longhouse.

Twelve Roofs House MUSEUM
(Bubungan Dua Belas; ☑224 4545; Jln Residency;
☉9am-4.30pm Mon-Thu, 2:30am-4:30pm Fri, Sat
9am -11.30am; ℗) The one-time residence

of Britain's colonial-era high commission-
ers, said to be the sultanate's oldest extant
building, is now a museum dedicated to the
longstanding 'special relationship' between
Brunei and the UK. The evocative photos
include views of Brunei as it looked a century ago and many fine shots of Queen Elizabeth II. The swimming pool out the back
is rumoured to be haunted – during WWII
the Japanese executed people there. It was
unaccountably closed when we visited, so
you may want to call ahead.

The building is 1.5km southeast of Sungai
Kianggeh, towards the Brunei Museum, on

Bandar Seri Begawan

a hilltop dominating the river. To get here from the city centre, take the Central Bus line, a taxi or a water taxi.

NORTH & WEST OF CENTRAL BSB

Jame'Asr Hassanil Bolkiah Mosque MOSQUE
(Sultan Hassanal Bolkiah Hwy, Kampung Kiarong; ⊙8am-noon, 2-3pm & 5-6pm Mon-Wed & Sat, 5-6pm Fri, 10.30am-noon, 2-3pm & 5-6pm Sun, closed Thu; ℗) Built in 1992 to celebrate the 25th year of the current sultan's reign, Brunei's largest mosque and its four terrazzo-tiled minarets dominate the 'suburbs' of BSB. It's certainly a...noticeable building; because the sultan is his dynasty's 29th ruler, the complex is adorned with 29 golden domes. At night the mosque is lit up like a gold flame.

The interior is best described as jaw-droppingly over-the-top. The sheer volume in itself is amazing, not to mention the myriad woven rugs scattered across the men's prayer hall.

The mosque is about 3km northwest of the city centre towards Gadong. To get here, take buses 1 or 22 from the main bus terminal.

Istana Nurul Iman PALACE
(Jln Tutong) If you drink too much water before visiting Istana Nurul Iman (Palace of the Light of the Faith), the official residence of the sultan, never fear: the palace has 257 bathrooms. The 200,000-sq-m behemoth

boasts 1531 more rooms (that's 1788 in total) and is one of the largest habitations of any sort in the world – more than four times the size of the Palace of Versailles and three times larger than Buckingham Palace.

Designed by Filipino architect Leandro Locsin, the palace – 3km southwest of the centre of town – mixes Malay and Islamic elements with the sweep and oversized grandeur of an airport terminal. Nonetheless, it's relatively attractive from a distance or when illuminated in the evening.

Istana Nurul Iman is open to the public only during the three-day Hari Raya Aidil Fitri festivities at the end of Ramadan. The best way to check it out the other 362 days of the year, is to take a water-taxi cruise or to stop by the riverside pavilion at **Taman Persiaran Damuan**, a landscaped park 1.2km beyond the palace (when travelling from the city centre).

Taman Peranginan Tasek PARK
(Tasek Recreational Park; Jln Tasek Lama; ℗) BSB's tinier, dustier version of Central Park has greenery, picnic areas and peaceful walks to a small waterfall and a large reservoir. Locals come here to do t'ai chi (6am to 9am), jog (in the evening), use the exercise apparatus and admire the view. It's situated about 2km north of the city centre; to walk here turn east 400m north of the Terrace Hotel in the north of the city centre, otherwise catch a Northern Line bus.

JERUDONG

Jerudong Park Playground AMUSEMENT PARK

(Jerudong; admission free, under 5/over 5 rides B$8/10; ☉4-10.30pm Wed, Thu & Sun, 2-10pm Fri & Sat, closed Mon & Tue except during school holidays) In its heyday, this B$1 billion amusement park, a Prince Jefri project opened in 1994, was the pride of Brunei, and the only major modern amusement park in Southeast Asia. The concert hall hosted free shows by the likes of Whitney Houston and Michael Jackson, the latter to celebrate the sultan's 50th birthday, and the many rides included a giant roller coaster.

That attraction, along with most of the others, was sold off to repay debts, and today Jerudong is mostly a depressing lesson in hubris and economics: don't build something people don't want. Ostensibly 10 rides, including a merry-go-round and junior bumper cars, still operate. In our experience, this is not a sound assumption to make, so ask the person in front if any rides work before you buy a ride ticket. The park seems pretty busy on weekends, which is probably the best time to visit. The rumour is some party out there wants to convert the park into a smaller children's play area with basic rides and attractions, which sounds like a lovely idea.

There is no bus service to the park, which is near the coast about 20km northwest of BSB, so the only way to get here is by taxi (about B$35 from the centre) or private car.

MUARA'S BEACHES

Pantai Muara (Muara Beach), near the tip of the peninsula, is a popular weekend retreat. It's pretty, but like many beaches in Borneo it's littered with driftwood and other flotsam that comes in with the tide. Quiet during the week, it has food stalls, picnic tables and a children's playground.

About 4km west of Muara along the Muara–Tutong Hwy, **Pantai Meragang** (Crocodile Beach) is another stretch of pleasant seaside sand that's not quite as crowded as the others on weekends. There are a couple of food stalls that make this a good place for a picnic. We've never heard of crocodiles here, by the way.

The beaches are about 25km northeast of BSB around the cargo, ferry and naval port of Muara, the site of an Australian amphibious landing in April 1945. Muara's town centre is served by buses 37, 38 and 39 (B$1) from BSB city centre; bus 33 will take you from Muara town to Pantai Muara. Pantai Meragang is difficult to get to without your own transport.

☞ Tours

A number of local agencies offer tours of BSB and trips to nature sites around the sultanate, including Ulu Temburong National Park and the mangroves of Pulau Selirong, 45 minutes by boat from the city. Some also offer night safaris where you can spot proboscis monkeys, crocs and fireflies.

Borneo Guide TOUR

(Map p200; ☎718 7138, 876 6796, 242 6923; www. borneoguide.com; Unit 204, Kiaw Lian Building, Jln Pemancha; ☉9am-5pm Mon-Fri, 9am-1pm Sat) Excellent service, good prices and a variety of eco-programs around Brunei and Borneo. A day trip to Ulu Temburong National Park costs B$120 from BSB (7.30am to 4.30pm or 5pm). Two days and one night at the park, including food and activities, costs B$245 from BSB. The office also serves as a useful tourism information centre.

Intrepid Tours TOURS

(Map p200; ☎222 1685, 222 1686; www.bruneibay. net/intrepidtours/index.html; 1st fl (Unit 105), PGGMB Building, Jln Sungai Kianggeh) Has its

---

BLASTED, BLASTING BEDIL

One of the more interesting exhibits in the **Brunei Museum** – partly because it's one of the few pieces of displayed culture that is native solely to Brunei, as opposed to the surrounding Malay culturesphere – is a series of *bedil*, or cannons. It was not oil but these bronze-cast weapons that were once the source of the sultanate's wealth and power. The cannons of Brunei subjugated many of the smaller kingdoms of Borneo and extended the sultanate's power all the way to the Philippines. They were so common they became an expected dowry gift; perhaps rightly so – *bedil* are beautiful. All are decorated in a baroque fashion, and some are carved to resemble dragons and crocodiles, because let's face it: what's more terrifying than a cannon ball erupting from a crocodile's mouth?

DON'T MISS

MONKEY BUSINESS

Long-tailed macaques and their adorable offspring often frolic in the trees along the road that heads up the hill (towards the radio tower) from the intersection between the Terrace and Radisson Hotels – listen for the tell-tale rustle of branches as they prance from tree to tree. As ever, don't approach the monkeys, no matter how beguiling they are. The primates are somewhere nearby all day long – sneaking into someone's kitchen through an open window, perhaps – but are easiest to spot very early in the morning, in the late afternoon and around dusk.

own lodge near Batang Duri (on the way to Ulu Temburong National Park). Main office located about 9km northeast of central BSB.

Mona Florafauna Tours OUTDOORS, TOUR
(Map p200; ☎24hr 884 9110; jungle-dave.blogspot.com.au; 209 1st fl, Kiaw Lian Bldg, 140 Jln Pemancha; ⏲8.30am-5pm) Specialises in outdoor and wildlife tours, with friendly and personable service. Email or call in advance.

Freme Travel Services TOUR
(Map p200; ☎223 4277; www.freme.com; 4th fl, office 4.03B, Wisma Jaya, Jln Pemancha) A bit corporate, but has plenty of options, as befits one of Brunei's largest travel agencies.

Sleeping

Budget options are thin on the ground. Upscale places often offer big discounts online.

TOP CHOICE **Brunei Hotel** HOTEL $$
(Map p200; ☎224 4828; thebruneihotel.com; 95 Jln Pemancha; incl breakfast r B$91-220, ste B$242-440; ❄@📶) The best bang for your Brunei dollar in town, the Brunei is...hip. OK, it's not the W or anything, but there are clean lines, monochromatic colour schemes, geometric patterns and a general sense of ultramodern cool, which is pretty unexpected in the sultanate. There's a decent breakfast buffet thrown into the deal served in the downstairs **Choices Cafe**, and the staff are friendly, helpful, competent and eager; the latter quality was frankly unexpected and greatly appreciated.

Pusat Belia HOSTEL $
(Youth Centre; Map p200; ☎887 3066, 222 2900; Jln Sungai Kianggeh; dm B$10; ❄🏊) Gets rave reviews from backpackers despite the fact that couples can't stay together. The 28 spacious, strictly sex-segregated rooms, with four or 10 beds (all bunks), have functional furnishings, big windows, red cement floors and passable bathrooms. Situated at the southern end of the Youth Centre complex (behind the cylindrical staircase). Reception is supposed to be open from 7.45am to 4.30pm Monday to Thursday, and on call til 10pm otherwise, but staffing can be intermittent. If the office is locked, hang around and someone should find you. The adjacent swimming pool costs B$1. May fill up with government guests on holidays and for sports events.

Terrace Hotel HOTEL $$
(Map p200; ☎224 3554, 224 3555, 224 3556, 224 3557; www.terracebrunei.com; Jln Tasek Lama; d B$65-75; ❄@📶🏊) A classic tourist-class hotel whose 84 rooms are dowdy (think 1980s) but clean, and come with marble bathrooms. It also has a great little swimming pool. In a good location just 800m north of the waterfront, near a hawker centre.

Empire Hotel & Country Club RESORT $$$
(☎241 8888; www.theempirehotel.com; Muara-Tutong Hwy, Kampung Jerudong; r incl breakfast from B$400, villas B$1300-2900; ❄@📶🏊) Pharaonic (or perhaps Dubaian) in its proportions and opulence, this 523-room extravaganza was commissioned by Prince Jefri as lodging for guests of the royal family. To recoup some of the US$1.1 billion investment, the property was quickly transformed into an upscale resort. So what's it like inside? To paraphrase Dolly Parton, it takes a lot of money to look this cheap. Sorry, we're just not ones for yards of marble and columned everything. Anyways, now anyone with a thing for Las Vegas–style bling can hang out in the lobby and enjoy one of the US$500,000 lamps made of gold and Baccarat crystal (the other one in the Emperor Suite can be appreciated privately for around B$17,000 per night). Even the cheapest rooms (except the recently opened Ocean rooms) have remote-control everything, hand-woven carpets, gold-plated power points and enormous bathrooms

with marble floors, but the decor still somehow feels stodgy and unimaginative. But hey, worth a visit for the gilded spectacle; tea in the Lobby Lounge costs a mere B$5 a pot and the enormous pool complex outside is popular with expats and the wealthy. To get here, take bus 57 from the city centre or Gadong (runs two or three times a day; on the way back, book at the Transport desk), or a taxi (B$30 to B$35).

Radisson Hotel HOTEL $$$
(Map p200; ☏224 4272; www.radisson.com/brunei; Jln Tasek Lama; r from B$170; ﹡＠🄿🅆🅂） This Radisson chain hotel, plopped on the edge of the town centre, flies the flag for international standards. The sparkling lobby exudes comfort and wealth, as do the business-class rooms. Amenities include two pools (one for kids), a fitness centre, a spa and two restaurants. Free shuttle service to Gadong and downtown three times a day.

Jubilee Hotel HOTEL $$
(Map p200; ☏222 8070; www.jubileehotelbrunei.com; Jln Kampung Kianggeh; d B$70-95, f B$145; ﹡＠) The Jubilee's rooms aren't flash – they may remind you of your old aunt's seldom-used guest bedroom – but are liveable and clean. 'Superior' rooms come with kitchenettes.

Centrepoint Hotel HOTEL $$$
(☏243 0430; www.thecentrepointhotel.com; Abdul Razak Complex; r B$280-380, ste from B$550; 🅿﹡🅆） The Centrepoint is a flash business-class hotel located in trendy Gadong. The rooms are plush and decently luxurious in an executive kind of way. To get to Gadong, either hop in a taxi or you can take the Circle Line bus.

KH Soon Resthouse GUESTHOUSE $
(Map p200; ☏222 2052; khsoon-resthouse.tripod.com; 2nd fl, 140 Jln Pemancha; s/d B$35/39, with shared bathroom B$30/35; ﹡） This rather matter-of-fact guesthouse, in a converted commercial space with floors the colour of a man-o-war's decks, offers budget rates, huge but spartan rooms, and a supercentral location. An extra bed costs around B$17.

Rizqun International Hotel HOTEL $$$
(☏243 3000; www.rizquninternational.com; Abdul Razak Complex; r from B$320; ﹡） Another tourist hotel in the Gadong district, the Rizqun is much more sophisticated than you'd expect for something growing out of a shopping mall. Plenty of restaurants, friendly staff and business-class amenities on hand. To get here, take a taxi or Circle Line bus.

Eating

BSB is not exactly a city that screams sex, drugs and rock 'n' roll – the second part of that equation is illegal, the other two are definitely happening behind closed doors. So how do people have fun? *Makan* (eat). *Makan, makan, makan.* "Food and instagramming our food is Brunei's national pastime," says Thanis Lim, a food blogger who's website (cookiemonzters.blogspot.com) is the go-to spot for those into the Brunei food scene.

In the city centre, restaurants can be found along the waterfront and on Jln Sultan (south of Jln Pemancha). The big shopping malls, including those out in Gadong, have **food courts** everywhere. Find a spot that looks busy and chow down. All restaurants listed have air-conditioning except outdoor food stalls.

⌐TOP⌐CHOICE⌐ Pondok Sari Wangi
INDONESIAN, CHINESE $$
(☏244 5403; Block A, No.12-13, Abdul Razak Complex, Jln Gadong; mains B$5-$18; ◷10am-10pm; ☏) Located in Gadong, Pondok Sari Wangi is a beloved Bandar institution. The cuisine is Indonesian/Chinese, which means lots of gloriously rich, decadent, colourful grub like marinated 'smashed chicken', a fried fish with fiery *sambal*, sweet sauteed local greens and vegetables, mouth-watering satay with a heavily textured peanut sauce and the signature short ribs, braised to something like perfection. If you want to have some culinary indulgence on your trip, we recommend coming out here and ordering one of everything.

⌐TOP⌐CHOICE⌐ Lim Ah Siaw Pork Market
HAWKER $$
(☏222 3963; Jln Teraja; mains B$3.50-9; ◷6:30am-10pm) Lim Ah Siaw has great food, sure. Crispy braised pork knuckle, pork belly, pork buns, pork dumplings; it's seriously *Babe*'s hell. More so, because it is actually forbidden to raise pigs in Brunei, Lim Ah Siaw is the closest thing we found in Brunei to a speakeasy. Seriously. You kinda feel like a smuggler sneaking into this Chinese market-turned-restaurant. It also has the atmosphere of a Hong Kong gambling hall, which might take away from the food but certainly spices up the illicit zeitgeist.

Aminah Arif
AMBUYAT **$$**

(☏265 3036; Unit 2-3, Block B, Rahman Bldg, Spg 88, Kiulap; ambuyat for 2 B$16; ☺9am-10pm; ✐) Aminah Arif is synonymous with *ambuyat* (thick, starchy porridge), Brunei's signature dish. If you're up for trying a generous serving of wiggly white goo, this is a good spot to do so. Also serves rice and noodle dishes. Meals can be washed down with iced *kasturi ping* (calamansi lime juice; B$1.80). There are nine branches of Aminah Arif in town but this one seems the most popular.

Tamu Kianggeh
HAWKER **$**

(Map p200; Jln Sungai Kianggeh; mains from B$1; ☺5am-5pm) The food stalls here serve Brunei's cheapest meals, including *nasi katok* (plain rice, a piece of fried or curried chicken and *sambal*; B$1) and *nasi lemak* (rice cooked in coconut milk and served with chicken, beef or prawn, egg and cucumber slices; also B$1). In the market's northeast corner, a vegetarian-Chinese stall called **Tamu Chakoi** (stalls 49-51; ☺8.30am-noon, closed Mon; ✐) serves a variety of inexpensive fried pastries and noodle dishes. We like the stalls for their food; we love them because this is one of the few places in Brunei that feels a little chaotic and messy, which is a little refreshing.

Taman Selera
HAWKER **$**

(Map p200; cnr Jln Tasek Lama & Jln Stoney; mains B$1-3.50; ☺4pm-midnight) At this old-fashioned hawker centre, set in a shady park, diners eat excellent, cheap Malaysian dishes under colourful tarps and ceiling fans. Options include satay (four skewers for B$1), fried chicken, seafood, rice and noodle dishes, and iced drinks (B$1). Situated 1km north of the waterfront, across from the Terrace Hotel.

Pasar Malam Gadong
NIGHT MARKET **$**

(Jln Pasar Gadong; ☺4-10pm) Thanks to its authentic Brunei-style snacks and dishes, this is Brunei's most popular and beloved night market. Unfortunately, it's geared to car-driving locals who take the food away so there are almost no places to sit. Situated 3km northwest of the city centre and 200m across the river from The Mall shopping centre. Served by buses 1 and 22, but after about 7pm the only way back to town is by taxi (B$15, more after 8pm).

Noralizah & Iskandar
House of Curry
INDIAN **$**

(☏867 5781; Kompleks Awang Hj Ibrahim, Jln Berakas; mains B$3-7; ☺7am-8pm; ✐) It's all about the roti flatbreads at this spot, from flaky roti to deliciously oily paratha, stuffed with ground lamb and onions in a *murtabak*, or bananas and a dusting of sugar for a breakfast treat. Dip that deliciousness in one of several bowls of warming curry. Very popular with students looking for a cheap meal.

The restaurant is located near the airport. To get here you'll need to take a taxi ($B8-10 from the city centre) or a bus (Northern Lines 1 and 2 or the Central Line).

Kimchi
KOREAN **$**

(☏222 2233; Unit 19, Block B, Regent Sq; B$3-11; ☺11am-2:30pm & 6pm-10pm) Korean restaurants are pretty ubiquitous in BSB, and Kimchi, in Regent Sq west of the centre, is the best of the bunch. The titular *kimchi* (fermented cabbage) is delightfully smelly and spicy, rice cakes are drowned in a hot, rich sauce and the chicken wings...well, when are chicken wings a bad idea? The *bulgogi* (barbeque) is a lovely indulgence. Take a taxi or bus here (Central Line or the Northern Lines 1 and 2).

BRUNEI BANDAR SERI BEGAWAN

AMBUYAT – GUMMY, GLUEY & GLUTINOUS

Remember that kid in kindergarten who used to eat paste? Well, *ambuyat*, Brunei's unofficial national dish, comes pretty darn close. It's a gelatinous porridge-like goo made from the ground pith of the sago tree, which is ground to a powder and mixed with water, and eaten with a variety of flavourful sauces.

To eat *ambuyat*, you'll be given a special pair of chopsticks that's attached at the top (don't snap them in two!) to make it easier to twirl up the tenacious mucous. Once you've scooped up a bite-sized quantity, dunk it into the sauce. After your *ambuyat* is sufficiently drenched, place the glob of dripping, quivering, translucent mucilage in your mouth and swallow – don't chew, just let it glide down your throat.

The easiest way to try *ambuyat* is to stop by one of the nine branches of Aminah Arif in BSB.

Gerai Makan Jalan Residency HAWKER $
(Jalan Residency Food Court; Map p200; Jln Residency; mains B$2-5.50; ⊘4pm-midnight) Along the riverbank facing Kampung Ayer, this grouping of food stalls features satay (B$1 for four chicken or three lamb skewers), dozens of kinds of *mee goreng* and *nasi goreng*, and soups such as *soto* (noodle soup). The hours we give are not set in stone, and sometimes, some stalls are open 24 hours.

Red Canopy INTERNATIONAL $
(☑245 3879; Unit 11 Hassain Complex, Jln Delima; B$4-9; ⊘7am-11pm) Plunked by the airport, the Red Canopy serves up a tasty combination of Malay, Thai, Chinese and Western cuisine (not all at once, obviously). A Malay lunch buffet keeps customers satisfied by day; at night daily specials rotate in and out, from buttermilk chicken on Tuesdays to quail egg soup on Thursdays.

🍷 Drinking

The sale and public consumption of alcohol is officially banned in Brunei, but locals and expats may know of places (often Chinese restaurants) that discreetly serve beer to regulars, or establishments that let you bring your own.

Locals are fond of *air batu campur* ('ice mix'), usually called ABC, which brings together ice, little green noodles, grass jelly, sago pearls and red beans.

Coffee Bean & Tea Leaf CAFE
(Map p200; Mayapuri Bldg, 36 Jln Sultan; ⊘8am-midnight Sun-Wed, to 1.30am Thu-Sat; 🛜) The hangout of choice for folks who need to bang out some work on their laptops or just relax in air-conditioned frigidity. Serves hot and 'ice blended' beverages, hearty breakfasts, pastries (muffins, cakes, scones), gourmet sandwiches (B$6 to B$8) and pasta (B$4.80 to B$7.50).

De Royalle Café CAFE
(Mayapuri Bldg, 38 Jln Sultan; ⊘24hr; 🛜) Organised into two mini living rooms plus sidewalk tables, this always-open establishment has a supply of perusable English-language newspapers and serves up pastries, sandwiches (B$4 to B$11 – lox is the priciest) and, of course, fresh-brewed coffee. A fine place for a relaxed rendezvous with friends.

☆ Entertainment

Locals often head to Gadong for a night out, which in Brunei usually amounts to nothing more than dinner and perhaps a movie. Based on what you hear, you might conclude that the area is a seething nightlife zone or at least a fine collection of smart restaurants. Unfortunately, it's neither – just some air-con shopping malls and commercial streets.

🛍 Shopping

Shopping is Brunei's national sport. Locals bop through the shopping malls scouting out the best deals while bemoaning the fact that their micro-nation doesn't have as much variety as Singapore.

The country's only traffic jam occurs nightly in Gadong, about 3km northwest of the centre. The area features several air-conditioned bastions of commerce, including two huge malls, Centrepoint and The Mall.

Arts & Handicrafts
Training Centre CRAFT
(☑224-0676; Jln Kota Batu; ⊘8am-5pm Sat-Thu, 8-11.30am & 2-5pm Fri) Sells silverwork, carved wood items, ornamental brass cannons (from B$500) and ceremonial swords (about B$500), made by the centre's students and graduates, for much, much more than you'd pay in Sarawak or Kalimantan. Not bad for window-shopping, though – check out the *jong sarat* (hand-woven cloth made from gold and silver threads; B$400 to B$4000 for a 2m-long bolt). If you're serious about Bruneian artisanship, pick up the centre's *Directory of Handicraft Entrepreneurs* (B$4.80). The centre is on the river 600m east of Sungai Kianggeh.

Paul & Elizabeth Book Services BOOKS
(Map p200; ☑222-0958; 2nd fl, eastern bldg, Yayasan Complex, Jln Pretty; ⊘9.30am-9pm) This place stocks a few books on Brunei, a street map of the entire sultanate and a small range of English-language paperbacks, including some ancient LP guides! There's also an internet cafe (p207).

Hua Ho Department
Store DEPARTMENT STORE
(Map p200; ⊘10am-10pm) Don't miss four-level Hua Ho with its cache of traditional Bruneian sweets in the basement.

Tamu Kianggeh CRAFT
(Map p200; Jln Sungai Kianggeh) Woven crafts are sold along the river here, but prices are higher than in Malaysia.

ℹ Information

Emergency
Ambulance (📞991)
Fire Brigade (📞000)
Police (📞993)

Internet Access
Amin & Sayeed Cyber Cafe (1st fl, cnr Jln Sultan & Jln McArthur; per hr B$1; ⊙9am-midnight)

Paul & Elizabeth Cyber Cafe (2nd fl, eastern bldg, Yayasan Complex, Jln Pretty; per hr B$1; ⊙9am-9pm) Overlooks the central atrium in the eastern building of the Yayasan complex. Decent connections, bad soundtrack.

Medical Services
RIPAS Hospital (📞224 2424; www.moh.gov. bn/medhealthservices/ripas.htm; Jln Tutong; ⊙24hr) Brunei's main hospital, with fully equipped, modern facilities. Most of the senior staff are Western trained. Situated about 2km west of the centre (across the Edinburgh Bridge).

Jerudong Park Medical Centre (📞emergency 261 2461, 261 1433; www.jpmc.com.bn; Tutong-Muara Hwy; ⊙24hr) Private medical facility; high standards of care. Located about 27km northwest of the BSB centre, accessible by bus 55.

Money
Banks and international ATMs are sprinkled around the city centre, especially along Jln McArthur and Jln Sultan. The airport has ATMs, and you can change travellers cheques at larger hotels.

HSBC (cnr Jln Sultan & Jln Pemancha; ⊙8.45am-4pm Mon-Fri, to 11.30am Sat) Has a 24-hour ATM. You must have an HSBC account to change travellers cheques.

Isman Money Changer (ground fl, eastern bldg, Yayasan Complex, Jln Pretty; ⊙9.30am-7.30pm) Changes cash but not travellers cheques. Just off the central atrium.

Post
Main Post Office (cnr Jln Sultan & Jln Elizabeth Dua; ⊙8am-4.30pm Mon-Thu & Sat, 8-11am & 2-4pm Fri) Has a free internet computer. The Stamp Gallery displays some historic first-day covers and blow-ups of colonial-era stamps.

Tourist Information
Keep an eye out for the free **Borneo Insider's Guide** (BIG; www.borneoinsidersguide.com), a glossy magazine published four times a year.

For a mix of fresh news, business information and visitor tips about Brunei, check out www.brudirect.com.

Brunei Tourism (www.bruneitourism.travel), whose wonderful website has oodles of useful information, runs three tourist-information counters that can supply the only decent maps of the sultanate. One is at **Old Customs House**; one is in the arrival hall at the BSB Airport; and one at the Kampung Ayer Cultural & Tourism Gallery (p207), across the river from the city centre.

Airport (arrival hall; ⊙8am-noon & 1.30-5pm)

Brunei Tourism (⊙9am-5pm Sat-Thu, 9-11am & 2.30-5pm Fri) Across the river from the city centre.

ℹ Getting There & Away

Air
Brunei International Airport (📞233 1747, flight enquiries 233 6767; www.civil aviation. gov.bn) By the time you read this, flash new

---

GETTING TO SABAH: BANDAR SERI BEGAWAN TO BANDAR LABUAN

Getting to the border Travel by sea to Sabah is the easiest option, avoiding the hassles and delays of land borders – traffic at the Kuala Lurah crossing has been known to cause three-hour delays. Car ferries from Serasa Ferry Terminal in Muara, about 20km northeast of BSB, to the Malaysian federal territory of Pulau Labuan (1½ hours) are run by PKL Jaya Sendirian. If you have a car, get there at least an hour before sailing.

PKL Jaya Sendirian also operates a car-ferry service from the Serasa Ferry Terminal to the Sabah port of Menumbok (2½ hours), which is 152km by road from Kota Kinabalu. Adult/car B$35/90 from Muara, RM80/210 from Menumbok; departures at 10.30am from Muara, 4pm from Menumbok. A new ferry service on the Kimanis-1 boat was scheduled to begin three round-trip services between BSB and Menumbok via Labuan as of press time.

Three express buses a day (B$3, 40 minutes) link BSB direct with the ferry; departures from BSB's bus terminal (from the berth for bus 39) are at 6.30am, 11.30am and 2.15pm. To go by public transport, you can take a more convoluted trip via bus 37, 38 or 39 to Muara town (B$1 at least twice an hour); from there it's a short ride on bus 33 to the ferry.

At the border Most travellers to Malaysia are granted a 30- or 60-day visa on arrival.

Moving on From Bandar Labuan, daily ferries go to Kota Kinabalu (115km by sea). See p112 for details on doing the trip in the opposite direction.

GETTING TO SARAWAK: BANDAR SERI BEGAWAN TO MIRI

Getting to the border PHLS Express (☏771 668) links BSB with Miri (B$18 from BSB, RM40 from Miri, 3½ hours) via Seria and Kuala Belait (two hours) twice a day. Departures from BSB's PGGMB building (on Jln Sungai Kiangggeh just south of the Chinese Temple) are at approximately 7am and 1pm and from Miri's Pujut Bus Terminal at about 8am and 4pm. Tickets are sold on board. Travel between Miri and Seria or Kuala Belait costs B$12 or RM25.

Another option for travel between BSB and Miri is a 'private transfer' (RM60 per person) in a **seven-seater van** (☏016-807 2893, in Malaysia 013-833 2331) run by a father-son team. Departures from BSB are usually at 1pm or 2pm; departures from Miri are generally at 9am or 10am but may be earlier. It may also be possible to hitch a ride (RM50 per person, 3½ hours) with a **newspaper-delivery van** (☏in BSB 876 0136, in Miri before 4pm 012-878 0136). Departure from Miri is at 5.30am; be prepared for an hour's delay at customs.

At the border Most travellers to Malaysia are granted a 30 or 60 day visa on arrival.

Moving on The bus will leave you at Miri's Pujut Bus Terminal, a 4km taxi ride from the city centre.

See p181 for details on doing the trip in the opposite direction.

---

renovations are supposed to turn this small airport into a modern international hub.

TEMBURONG DISTRICT

The fastest way to get to Bangar is by speedboat (adult/senior B$6/5, 45 minutes, at least hourly from 6am to at least 4.30pm, until as late as 6pm on Sunday and holidays). The dock is on Jln Residency about 200m east of Sungai Kiangggeh.

Bus & Van

BSB's carbon monoxide–choked bus terminal is on the ground floor of a multistorey parking complex two blocks north of the waterfront. It is used by domestic lines, including those to Muara, Seria, Tutong and Kuala Lurah, and services to Pontianak in Kalimantan, but not to Sabah or Sarawak. Schematic signs next to each numbered berth show the route of each line.

For details on various bus and van options to Malaysia, contact KH Soon Resthouse (p204) in BSB or Miri's Visitors Information Centre (p179).

ⓘ Getting Around

To/From the Airport

The airport, about 8km north of central BSB, is linked to the city centre, including the bus terminal on Jln Cator, by buses 23, 24, 36 and 38.

A cab to/from the airport costs B$25-35; taxis are unmetered, so agree on a price before you get in. Some hotels offer airport pick-up.

Bus

Brunei's public bus system, run by a variety of companies, is rather chaotic, at least to the uninitiated, so getting around by public transport takes effort. Buses (B$1) operate daily from 6.30am to about 6.30pm (7pm on some lines);

after that, your options are taking a cab or hoofing it. If you're heading out of town and will need to catch a bus back, ask the driver if and when they're coming back and when the last bus back is.

Finding stops can be a challenge – some are marked by black-and-white-striped uprights or a shelter, others by a yellow triangle painted on the pavement, and yet others by no discernible symbol. Fortunately, numbers are prominently displayed on each 20- or 40-passenger bus.

The bus station lacks an information office or a ticket counter, and while the schematic wall map may make sense to BSB natives, it's a bit of a cipher to the uninitiated. Some tourist brochures include a schematic route map.

Jesselton Express (☏012-622 9722, 717 7755, 719 3835, in BSB 718 3838, in KK 016-836 0009) sends a bus to KK (B$45, eight to nine hours) via Limbang, Bangar, Lawas and various towns in Sabah daily at 8am. Make sure you have your passport ready if you're travelling overland to Sabah because you'll be stopping at a whopping eight checkpoints (thanks mainly to the outgrowth of Temburong District). As long as your ID is in order you'll be fine; the trip is tedious rather than dodgy.

Car

Brunei has Southeast Asia's cheapest petrol – gasoline is just B$0.53 a litre and diesel goes for only B$0.30! If you're driving a car (eg a rental) with Malaysian plates and are not a Brunei resident, you'll be taken to a special pump to pay more (this is to prevent smuggling).

Hiring a car is a good way to explore Brunei's hinterland. Prices start at about B$80 a day. Surcharges may apply if the car is taken into Sarawak. Most agencies will bring the car to your hotel and pick it up when you've finished, and drivers can also be arranged, though this could add B$100 to the daily cost. The main roads are in good condition, but some back roads require a 4WD.

I he following are among the rental companies (most of them local) with offices at the airport:

Avis (☑242- 6345, 876 0642; www.avis.com)
Hertz (☑245 2244, 872 6000; www.hertz.com)

Taxi

Taxis are a convenient way of exploring BSB – if you can find one, that is. There is no centralised taxi dispatcher and it's difficult or impossible to flag down a cab on the street. Hotels can provide drivers' cell-phone numbers. Most taxis have yellow tops; a few serving the airport are all white.

BSB's only proper taxi rank is two blocks north of the waterfront at the bus terminal on Jln Cator.

Some taxis use meters ($B3 for the first kilometre, and $B1 for every kilometre thereafter), although many drivers will just try to negotiate a fare with you. Fares go up by 50% after 10pm; the charge for an hour of wait time is B$30 to B$35. Sample day-time taxi fares from the city centre include the Brunei Museum (B$10), Gadong (B$15), the airport (B$30), the Serasa Ferry Terminal in Muara (B$35), the Empire Hotel & Country Club (B$35) and the Jerudong Park Playground (B$35 to B$40).

Water Taxi

If your destination is near the river, water taxis – the same little motorboats that ferry people to and from Kampung Ayer – are a good way of getting there. You can hail a water taxi anywhere on the waterfront a boat can dock, as well as along Venice-themed Sungai Kianggeh. Crossing straight across the river is supposed to cost B$0.50 per person; diagonal crossings cost more.

TUTONG & BELAIT DISTRICTS

Most travellers merely pass through the districts of Tutong and Belait, west of BSB, en route to Miri in Sarawak, but there are a few worthwhile attractions. Frequent buses link Kuala Belait, Seria and Tutong with BSB, but if you want to really see the sights the best way is to take a tour or rent a car.

Tutong

POP 20,000

About halfway between Seria and BSB, Tutong is the main town in central Brunei. The town itself is neat but unremarkable, but the area is famous in Brunei for two things:

pitcher plants and sand. Tutong has six species of pitcher plants and the locals cook a variety of dishes in their insect-catching sacs. Some of the sand near Tutong is so white that Bruneians will often take pictures with it while pretending it's snow (did we mention there's no booze here? Have your fun any way you can, Brunei). You can see *pasir putih* (white sand) in patches along the side of the Pan Borneo Hwy.

There's a great beach, **Pantai Seri Kenangan**, also known as Pantai Tutong, a couple of kilometres west of town, on Jln Kuala Tutong. Set on a spit of land, with the ocean on one side and the Sungai Tutong on the other, the casuarina-lined beach is arguably the best in Brunei. The royal family clearly agrees, as they have a surprisingly modest palace here for discreet getaways.

❶ Getting There & Away

The buses that link BSB with Seria stop in Tutong (B$3, one hour, every 30 to 60 minutes until 5pm).

Jalan Labi

A few kilometres after you enter Belait District (coming from Tutong and BSB), a road branches inland (south) to Labi and beyond, taking you through some prime forest areas. The easiest way into the interior of western Brunei, Jln Labi offers a chance to stop by Brunei's **Forestry Museum** (⊙8am-12:15pm & 1:30am-4:30pm, closed Fri & Sun) and see a number of Iban longhouses, which in these parts come complete with mod cons and parking lots.

About 40km south of the coastal road, Labi is a small Iban settlement with some fruit arbours. Further south, you come to the Iban longhouses of **Rampayoh**, **Mendaram Besar**, **Mendaram Kecil** and finally, at the end of the track, **Teraja**, where a local guide may be able to take you to a nearby waterfall.

Seria

POP 34,000

Spread out along the coast between Tutong and Kuala Belait, low-density Seria is home to many of Brunei Shell's major onshore installations. A Ghurkha infantry battalion of the British Army is stationed here, the UK's last remaining military base in eastern Asia. A big market is held on Friday until about 3pm.

⊙ Sights

Oil & Gas Discovery Centre   MUSEUM
(☑337 7200; www.bsp.com.bn/ogdc; off Jln Tengah; adult/teenager/senior B$5/2/3; ☺8:30am-5pm Mon-Sat, 9:30am-6pm Sun) Puts an 'edutainment' spin on the oil industry. Likely to appeal to young science buffs and Shell employees. About 700m northwest of the bus station.

Billionth Barrel Monument   MONUMENT
Commemorates (you guessed it) the billionth barrel of crude oil produced at the Seria field, a landmark reached in 1991. We really were hoping this monument would look like an actual oil barrel because, well, that'd be hilarious, but it's more like a bunch of blue noodles topped by the emblem of the sultanate. Which, come to think of it, is cool too. Out to sea, oil rigs producing the sultanate's second billion dot the horizon. Situated on the beach about 1km west of the Oil & Gas Discovery Centre.

⊨ Sleeping

Hotel Koperasi   HOTEL $$
(☑322 7586, 322 7589, 322 7592; hotel_seria@bru net.bn; Jln Sharif Ali; s/d B$72/88; ⊞⊛) Seria's only proper hotel, with 24 neat, if boring, rooms. Situated 150m northwest of the bus station.

ⓘ Getting There & Away

Frequent buses go southwest to Kuala Belait (B$1, three times an hour from 6.30am to 6.15pm) and northeast to BSB (B$6, 2½ hours, every 30 to 60 minutes until about 5pm) via Tutong.

Kuala Belait

POP 35,500

Almost on the Sarawak frontier, coastal Kuala Belait (KB) is a modern, sprawling company town – the company being Brunei Shell – of one-storey suburban villas interspersed with grasshopper-like pump jacks. Although there's a reasonable beach, most travellers just hustle through on their way to or from Miri.

⊨ Sleeping & Eating

In the town centre, restaurants can be found along Jln McKerron and, two short blocks east, on parallel Jln Pretty, KB's main commercial avenue. Locals recommend the roast duck.

Hotel Sentosa   HOTEL $$
(☑333 1345; www.bruneisentosahotel.com; 92-93 Jln McKerron; s/d B$98/103; ⊞@⊛) Clean, well-run, tourist-class accommodation right in the centre of town. Situated one block south of the bus station.

ⓘ Information

HSBC Bank (cnr Jln McKerron & Jln Dato Shahbandar) Has an international ATM. Situated diagonally opposite the bus station.

ⓘ Getting There & Away

The bus station (cnr Jlns McKerron & Dato Shahbandar) is smack in the town centre. Miri Belait (☑419 129) runs five daily buses to Miri (B$8/RM8), and PHLS Express (p208) (☑771 668) runs two more comfortable daily trips for similar prices. Purple minibuses go to Seria (B$1) three times an hour from 6.30am to 6.15pm.

TEMBURONG DISTRICT

This odd little exclave (that means a part of a country physically separated from the rest of the nation; feel free to take that to the next pub quiz night) is barely larger than Penang, but happens to contain one of the best preserved tracts of primary rainforest in all of Borneo. The main draw is the brilliant Ulu Temburong National Park, accessible only by longboat.

The speedboat ride from BSB out to Bangar, the district capital, is the most fun you can possibly have for B$6. You roar down Sungai Brunei, slap through the nipah-lined waterways and then tilt and weave through mangroves into the mouth of Sungai Temburong.

Want to get depressed? Go to Google Earth and look at the outline of Temburong District. It's easy to spot: at the Brunei frontier, Malaysia's logging roads – irregular gashes of eroded earth – and trashed hillsides give way to a smooth carpet of trackless, uninhabited virgin rainforest. Until not long ago, almost all of Borneo looked like this.

Bangar

Little Bangar, perched on the banks of Sungai Temburong, is the gateway to, and administrative centre of, Temburong District. It can be visited as a day trip from BSB if you catch an early speedboat, but you'll get more out of the town's easygoing pace if you stay over and explore the area, which has some fine primary rainforest and nine longhouses, not all of them very long.

🛏 Sleeping

Temburong District has a number of homestays used mainly by tour operators and locals with cars. In addition to the options listed below, there are also five or six guesthouses scattered around town. They're all acceptably clean and comfortable and otherwise nondescript.

Lukat Intan Guesthouse　　　GUESTHOUSE $$
(☑864 3766, 522 1078; lukutintan@hotmail.com; B$30-50; 🅿🌀) Run by a friendly older couple, Lukat offers spic and span rooms and personable service; you get breakfast with your stay and they're happy to give you free rides to the Bangar jetty.

**Rumah Persinggahan Kerajaan
Daerah Temburong**　　　GUESTHOUSE $
(☑522 1239; Jln Batang Duri; s/d/tr/q B$25/ 30/40/50, 4-person chalets B$80; 🌀🛜) Set around a grassy, L-shaped courtyard, this government-run guesthouse has friendly, helpful staff and six spacious but slightly fraying rooms with rather more bathtub rust and somewhat cooler hot water than many would deem ideal. Situated a few hundred metres west of the town centre, across the highway from the two mosques.

Youth Hostel　　　HOSTEL $
(Pusat Belia; ☑522 1694; www.bruneiyouth.org.bn; dm B$10; ⊘office staffed 7.30am-4.30pm, closed Fri & Sat) Part of a youth centre, this basic hostel sits in a fenced compound across the street from (west of) the Tourist Information Centre. Rooms, each with six beds (bunks), are clean and fan-cooled. If no one's around try phoning or looking helplessly at passers by – worked for us.

🍴 Eating

The **fruit and vegie market**, behind the row of shops next to the Tourist Information Centre, has an upstairs **food court** (⊘7am-10pm).

A handful of restaurants serving passable Malay and Chinese food can be found around the market, along and just in from the riverfront.

ℹ Information

3 in 1 Services (per hr B$1; ⊘7.45am-9.30pm, closed Sun) Internet access on the first floor of the building next to the market (across the pedestrian bridge from the hawker centre). The shop number is A1-3.

Bank Islam Brunei Darussalam (⊘8.45am-3.45pm Mon-Thu, 8.45-11am & 2.30-4pm Fri, 8.45-11.15am Sat) The only bank in town. Changes US dollars and pounds sterling but not Malaysian ringgits. The ATM did not take international cards at time of research, but staff said this may change soon. On the river 150m north of the bridge.

Hock Guan Minimarket Exchanges Malaysian ringgits for Brunei dollars. In the second row of shops from the Tourist Information Centre.

Jayamuhibah Shopping Mart Carries some over-the-counter medicines (Temburong District does not have a proper pharmacy). In the second row of shops from the Tourist Information Centre.

ℹ Getting There & Away

Boat

By far the fastest way to/from BSB is by speedboat (adult/senior B$6/5, 45 minutes, at least hourly from 6am to at least 4.30pm, until as late as 6pm on Sunday and holidays). Bangar's **ferry terminal**, Terminal Perahu Dan Penumpang, is on the western bank of the river just south of the red bridge.

Boats depart at a scheduled time or when they're full, whichever comes first. When you get to the ticket counters, check which company's boat will be the next to leave and then pay and add your name to the passenger manifest. Peakhour departures can be as frequent as every 15 minutes.

Bus

Buses run by **Jesselton** (☑719 3835, 717 7755, in BSB 718 3838) pick up passengers heading towards Limbang and BSB in the early afternoon; its bus to KK (B$25) and Lawas (B$10) passes through town at about 10am.

Taxi

Bangar doesn't have official taxis, but it's usually not too difficult to hire a car if you ask around under the rain awning in front of the ferry terminal. Drivers may not speak much English. Possible destinations include the Malaysian border towards Limbang (B$6), a distance of 4km; the town of Limbang (about B$40) and the Peradayan Forest Reserve (Bukit Patoi; about B$25 return).

Taxis do not wait on the Malaysian side of the border towards Limbang.

Pulau Selirong

At the northern tip of Temburong District, this 25-sq-km island is a sanctuary for mangroves and the fauna that live in them, including proboscis monkeys. The only way to visit is with a boat tour, which BSB tour operators can organise for around B$75. The trip across the open water of Brunei Bay takes about 45 minutes.

Batang Duri

Batang Duri, about 16km south of Bangar, is the jumping-off point for longboat rides to Ulu Temburong National Park. As you head south, the sealed road passes Malay settlements, then Murut (Lun Bawang) hamlets and finally a few partly modern Iban longhouses.

🛏 Sleeping

TOP CHOICE Sumbiling Eco Village
GUESTHOUSE $$

(☎242 6923, 876 6796; borneoguide.com/eco village; per person incl meals B$50; P @) If you're looking for Brunei's version of a jungle camp with basic amenities and a chilled-out atmosphere that encourages slipping into a green state of utterly relaxed Zen, come to Sumbiling. This ecofriendly rustic camp offers great Iban cuisine (served on simpur leaves) and plenty of outdoor activities, including visits to nearby Ulu Temburong National Park, jungle overnights, inner-tubing and a forest trek. The basic rooms have glassless windows and a fan attached to the ceiling to make sure air circulates inside the mozzie nets (nice touch). Also has a rain-protected camping area, organic composting and importantly, no handouts of single-use plastic bottes. Nearby is a five-door Iban longhouse with fierce, beautiful fighting cocks – each family's prized possessions – tethered outside. Prices do not include transport. Run by Borneo Guide (p202) in cooperation with the local community. Situated a few minutes downstream from Batang Duri.

Peradayan Forest Reserve

If you can't be bothered with the logistics or expense of a trip up to Ulu Temburong National Park, the Peradayan Forest Reserve is a good day-trip alternative. There's a 5km

(one-way) trek up to the jungle-cloaked peak of **Bukit Patoi** (310m); it may also be possible to continue on to **Bukit Peradayan** (410m). The trail, through pristine jungle, begins at the picnic tables and toilet block of **Taman Rekreasi Bukit Patoi** (Bukit Patoi Recreational Park), about 15km southeast of Bangar (towards Lawas). Bring lots of water and be prepared to turn back if the path, not always properly maintained along its entire length, becomes too overgrown to follow.

If you don't have your own transport, you can get here from Bangar by unofficial taxi (about B$30 return).

Ulu Temburong National Park

It's odd that in a country as manicured and regulated as Brunei, there's still a sizable chunk of true untamed wilderness. Therein lays the appeal of **Ulu Temburong National Park** (admission B$5), located in the heart of a 500-sq-km area of pristine rainforest covering most of southern Temburong. It's so untouched that only about 1 sq km of the park is accessible to tourists, who are only admitted as part of guided tour packages. To protect it for future generations, the rest is off-limits to everyone except scientists, who flock here from around the world. Permitted activities include a canopy walk, some short jungle walks, and swimming in the cool mountain waters of Sungai Temburong – so don't forget your swimsuit.

The forests of Ulu Temburong are teeming with life, including as many as 400 kinds of butterfly, but don't count on seeing many vertebrates. The best times to spot birds and animals, in the rainforest and along river banks, are around sunrise and sunset, but you're much more likely to hear hornbills and Bornean gibbons than to see them.

🏃 Activities

Longboat Trip
BOAT TOUR

One of the charms of Ulu Temburong National Park is that the only way to get there is by *temuai* (shallow-draft Iban longboat). The exhilarating trip, which takes 25 to 40 minutes from Batang Duri, is tough on the boats, which last just a few years, and challenging even for experienced skippers, who need a variety of skills to shoot the rapids – going upstream – in a manner reminiscent of a salmon: submerged boulders and logs have to be dodged, hanging vines must be evaded and the outboard must be taken out of the water at exactly the right moment. When it rains, the water level can quickly rise by up to 2m, but if the river is low you might have to get out and push.

Aluminium Walkway CANOPY WALK
The park's main attraction is a delicate aluminium walkway, secured by guy wires, that takes you through (or, more accurately, near) the jungle canopy, up to 60m above the forest floor. In primary rainforests, only limited vegetation can grow on the ground because so little light penetrates, but up in the canopy all manner of life proliferates. Unfortunately, there are no explanatory signs here and some guides don't have the background to explain the importance of the canopy ecosystem and point out the huge variety of organisms that can live on a single tree: orchids, bird's-nest ferns and other epiphytes; ants and myriad other insects; amphibians and snakes; and a huge selection of birds.

The views of nearby hills and valleys from the walkway are breathtaking, if you can get over the vertigo – the tower, built by Shell using oil-rig scaffolding technology, wobbles in the wind. Whatever you do, don't think of metal fatigue or lightning. If you'd like to share the experience with friends or loved ones back home and have a Malaysian cell phone, the tops of the towers are a good place to catch a cross-border signal.

The trail up to the canopy walk begins near the confluence of Sungais Belalong and Temburong. It's a short, steep, sweaty walk. If you stay overnight at the resort, you can do the canopy walk at sunrise, when birds and animals are most likely to be around.

Rivers & Waterfalls SWIMMING
Places to take a refreshing dip in the park's pure mountain waters include several rivers and waterfalls – your guide can point out the best spots.

At one small waterfall, just outside the boundaries of the national park, you can stand in a pool, and 2cm to 4cm long fish that look like tiny sharks will come up and nibble your feet, giving you a gentle, ticklish pedicure as they feast on the dry skin between your toes. To get there, head downriver from the Ulu-Ulu resort for about 500m – your guide can help find the creek you need to follow upstream for a few hundred metres.

🛏 Sleeping

TOP CHOICE **Ulu-Ulu Resort** LODGE **$$$**
(www.uluuluresort.com; per person from B$290; ❄) In Malay, *ulu* (as in Ulu Temburong) means 'upriver' and *ulu-ulu* means, essentially, 'back of beyond'. The park's only accommodation is an upscale riverside lodge, built entirely of hardwood, with some rooms thoughtfully built in the style of 1920s Malaysian-style chalets. It has a cinema for rainy evenings – after the canopy walk, Hitchcock's *Vertigo* might be an excellent choice. Prices include transport from BSB and board; activities tend to be expensive.

❶ Getting There & Away

For all intents and purposes, the only way to visit the park is by booking a tour; several BSB-based agencies (p202) organise tour groups and guides.

Kalimantan

POP 13,800,000

Why Go?

If jungle rivers get your blood running, then be prepared for rapids. Occupying three-quarters of Borneo, the world's third-largest island Kalimantan harbours a vast and legendary jungle cut by countless rivers, including two around 1000km in length. Within this primordial puzzle something extraordinary always lies around the next bend. You'll encounter exotic wildlife, such as the unforgettable orangutan, mysterious Dayak villages with only one foot in the modern world, and pure boating thrills. Adventure travellers of all levels can participate, from novices enjoying the romantic *klotok* (canoes) of Tanjung Puting to hardened trekkers shooting rapids on the landmark Cross-Borneo Trek. Divers will revel in the Derawan Archipelago, a world-class underwater destination. Cities here are mostly transit points, and foreigners exceedingly rare, but locals everywhere will greet you with a cheerful 'Hey Mistah!', making travel a tropical breeze.

Best Jungle River Journeys

» Sungai Bungan (p250)

» Sungai Mahakam (p228)

» Sungai Sekonyer (p251)

Best Places to Stay

» Nunukan Island Resort (p241)

» Wisma Alya (p264)

» Wehea Forest Lodge (p237)

» Hotel Gran Senyiur (p222)

When to Go
Pontianak

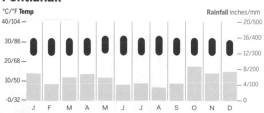

Jan–Feb Rough weather limits diving trips in the Derawan Archipelago.

Feb–Apr Blooming fruit brings orangutans into view.

Aug–Sep Dry season makes roads better, skies clearer.

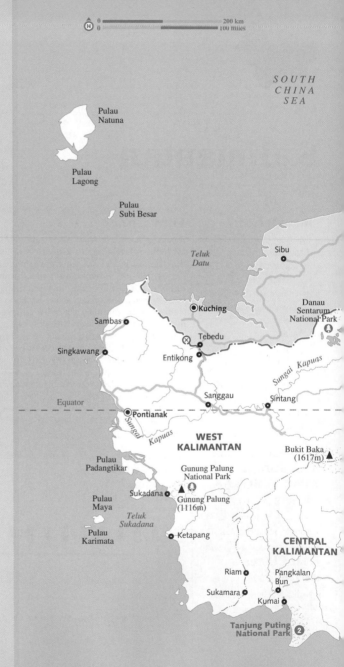

Kalimantan Highlights

1 Completing the landmark **Cross-Borneo Trek** (p219) – if you can

2 Meeting the orangutans of **Tanjung Puting National Park** (p251)

3 Travelling up **Sungai Mahakam** (p228) – and into the past

4 Living the (inexpensive) high life in **Balikpapan** (p220)

5 Exploring the **Derawan Archipelago** (p239), both under water and above

6 Settling into village life in lovely **Loksado** (p263)

7 Cruising **Sungai Kahayan** aboard the luxurious *Rahai'i Pangun* (p258)

8 Ascending the tower of the extraordinary **Islamic Centre of Samarinda** (p225)

9 Hiking unspoiled **Wehea Forest** (p237) – the Earth as it used to be

History & Culture

Separated from Southeast Asia's mainland 10,000 years ago by rising seas, Kalimantan was originally populated by the Dayaks, who still define its public image. The culture of this jungle people included headhunting, extensive tattooing, stretched earlobes, blowguns and longhouses – horizontal apartment buildings big enough to house an entire village. That culture has been slowly dismantled by the modern world, such that some elements, such as headhunting (thankfully), no longer exist, while others are in various stages of disappearing. Tribal identity persists, but many Dayaks have either abandoned their traditional folk religion, Kaharingan, or combined it with Christianity (or Islam).

In addition to the Dayaks, Kalimantan contains two other large ethnic groups, Chinese and Malay. The Chinese are the region's most successful merchants, having traded in Kalimantan since at least 300BC. They're responsible for the bright-red Confucian temples found in many port towns, and a profusion of Chinese restaurants, some of Kalimantan's best dining. The Malays are predominantly Muslim, a religion that arrived with the Melaka empire in the 15th century. Their most obvious presence is the grand mosques in major cities and towns, along with the call to prayer. Several palaces of Muslim sultans, who came to power after the Melaka fell to Portugal, can still be visited as well.

Since colonial times, Kalimantan has also been a destination for *transmigrasi*, the relocation of people from more densely populated areas of the archipelago. A sure sign is a small town of identical huts laid out in a grid. This and an influx of jobseekers from throughout Indonesia has led to some conflict, most notably a year-long struggle between Dayaks and Madurese (people from the island of Madura) in 2001, which killed 500 people, and a smaller conflict in 2010 between Dayaks and Bugis in Tarakan.

Most of the struggle in Kalimantan, however, has taken place over its bountiful natural resources, and involved foreign powers. Oil, rubber, spices, timber, coal, diamonds and gold have all been pawns on the board, causing many years of intrigue between British and Dutch colonial interests. During World War II oil and other resources made Borneo an early target for Japan, leading to a brutal occupation, in which some 21,000 people were murdered in West Kalimantan alone. In 1963, Indonesian President Soekarno led a failed attempt to take over all Borneo by staging attacks on the Malaysian north. According to Dayaks near the border 'over 1000 men fell to the dart'.

Today the struggle for Kalimantan's resources is more insidious. As one watches the endless series of enormous coal barges proceeding down rivers lined with tin-roof shacks, there is the constant sense of an ongoing plunder in which the local people benefit little, outmanoeuvered by a shadowy collection of foreign businessmen and local government officials overseen from Jakarta. Meanwhile, as palm-oil plantations spread across the landscape, the great Bornean jungle recedes, never to return. Numerous conservation groups are struggling to halt the social and environmental damage, and to save some remarkable wildlife. Best to visit soon.

Wildlife

Much of the same flora and fauna is found throughout Kalimantan. The region is best known for its orangutans, Asia's only great ape, and a most impressive sight, particularly given their endearing human qualities. These are best seen at rehabilitation centres, including Tanjung Puting and Orangutan Island on the Kahayan River. River cruising commonly reveals long-nosed proboscis monkeys (unique to Borneo), macaques, gibbons, crocodiles (including gharials), monitor lizards and pythons. Hornbills are commonly seen flying overhead, and are a spiritual symbol for many Dayaks; the upturned rooflines of local buildings mimic their wings. Forests harbour the rare clouded leopard, sun bear, giant moths and millipedes, and tarantulas. For divers, the Derawan Archipelago is renowned for its sea turtles, manta rays and large pelagic fish.

❶ Getting There & Away

The only entry points to Kalimantan that issue visas on arrival are Balikpapan's Sepinggan Airport, Pontianak's Supadio Airport and the Tebedu–Entikong land crossing between Kuching (Sarawak) and Pontianak. All other entries from outside Indonesia – by land, sea or air – require a visa issued in advance.

AIR There are no direct flights from Europe or the Americas to Kalimantan. The major cities are reached via Jakarta. See individual city sections for airline options.

For European travellers, a good strategy is to combine a round-trip ticket to Kuala Lumpur

THE CROSS-BORNEO TREK: A WORLD-CLASS ADVENTURE

Borneo offers one of the world's greatest, and most overlooked, adventure-travel routes. East and West Kalimantan are divided by the Muller mountain range, which also serves as the headwaters for Indonesia's two longest rivers *(sungai)*. Sungai Mahakam flows 930km to the east coast, by Samarinda, while Sungai Kapuas, the world's longest island river, snakes 1143km to the west coast, by Pontianak. Thus, by travelling up the Mahakam, hiking over the Muller Range, and travelling down the Kapuas (or vice versa) it is possible to cross the world's third-largest island from one side to the other, forming a single Cross-Borneo Trek. This three-part jungle-river extravaganza takes you into the very heart of Borneo, and out again, stitching together virtually everything Kalimantan has to offer, from wildlife to culture to pure adventure, including some absolutely thrilling boat rides. There are even international airports near either end, with visas available on arrival, making getting there and away a simple matter. Be forewarned, however: while the two river journeys are easily managed, the central trek of five days or more across the Muller Range is a significant undertaking, for serious jungle trekkers only. On the other hand, if you can't do the entire Cross-Borneo Trek, the first stage is great by itself.

Stage One: Sungai Mahakam (p228) The preferred cross-Borneo route begins in Balikpapan, the one cosmopolitan city in Kalimantan, where you can collect your visa and prepare yourself for what's ahead with an inexpensive five-star hotel room, a day at the beach, and some lively nightlife. From there you travel overland to Samarinda, whose great mosque stands like an exotic sentinel at the start of your upriver journey. After several days in a succession of boats, making side trips into lakes and marshes, spotting wildlife, and visiting small river towns, you'll finally arrive at Tiong Ohang, near the trailhead for stage two. Allow a full week.

Stage Two: The Muller Mountains (p235) You do this jungle trek for the same reason you climb Mt Everest: because it's there. Noted for its river fordings, hordes of leeches, and treacherous slopes, it requires the assistance of a professional guiding company, a critical decision. We recommend only two: De'Gigant Tours (p225) in Samarinda for east-west itineraries, and Kompakh (p249) in Putussibau for west-east crossings. If you walk steadily eight hours a day, you can make it across in five days, but seven is more comfortable and safer.

Stage Three: Sungai Kapuas (p250) This leg begins with a single day-long boat ride along the upper Kapuas and its tributary, Sungai Bungan, the latter being the most thrilling part of the entire journey. After reaching Putussibau, it's best to fly or drive to Pontianak the next morning, as boat travel down the lower Kapuas is unscheduled, meaning it can take several days to weeks. This makes the last stage only two days long.

The east-to-west itinerary above is preferable, as the Mahakam gets progressively wilder the further up you go – the perfect beginning – whereas the day-long boat trip downriver to Putussibau, from boiling rapids to a placid sunset arrival, is a fine ending. In contrast, the lack of public transport from Pontianak to Putussibau cuts the Kapuas journey in half, you miss the downriver sleigh ride on the Bungan, and the Muller trek is steeper and thus more difficult from the west.

In local terms, the Cross-Borneo Trek is a bit pricey due to transport costs, which increase the further you go into the interior. The total is around 22,000,000Rp per person for two people, 20,000,000Rp for three, and 17,000,000Rp for four. But the overall experience, while by no means easy, is a noteworthy achievement, something you'll remember for the rest of your life.

If you haven't had enough of Kalimantan, you can continue from Pontianak along the southern coast all the way back to Balikpapan, via Sukadana, Ketapang, Tanjung Puting, Pangkalan Bun, Palangka Raya, Banjarmasin and Loksado, forming a great circle. Once you've done this, you've done Kalimantan and will know it far better than the locals, who sadly cannot afford this luxury.

ℹ TRANSPORT SAFETY

Road washouts, river rapids, flash floods, weaving scooters, speeding Kijangs, overweight canoes, questionable airlines and a general lack of maintenance and safety equipment require an extra dose of caution when travelling in Kalimantan.

with a discount ticket from KL to Balikpapan on **AirAsia** (www.airasia.com), which also reaches KL from London. **Silk Air** (www.silkair.net) flies between Singapore and Balikpapan, but not inexpensively. **Batavia Air** (www.batavia-air.co.id) flies between Kuching (in Sarawak) and Pontianak.

BOAT Major ferry ports in Kalimantan include Balikpapan, Samarinda, Banjarmasin and Pontianak. **Pelni** (www.pelni.co.id) and other carriers connect to Jakarta, Semarang and Surabaya on Java, and Makassar, Pare Pare, and others on Sulawesi. At time of research the ferry from Tawau (Sabah) to Nunukan and Tarakan wasn't operational, but there was an alternative speedboat service.

BUS Air-con buses link Pontianak with Kuching (140,000Rp to 200,000Rp, nine hours), cities along Sarawak's central coast, and even Brunei (600,000Rp, 25 hours).

ℹ Getting Around

Kalimantan is both immense and undeveloped. River travel is as common as road travel, and transport options can form a complex picture. To assess your options locally it is often easiest to visit a travel agent, as the situation is ever-changing and many fares are unpublished.

Highways between major cities range from excellent to pockmarked, with the region from Muara Wahau to Berau being the worst. Many connections feature basic buses or air-con for a bit extra. A Kijang (4WD minivan) taxi can be chartered between cities; the front seat is best. Intracity journeys can be taken in a Colt, a small minibus, usually blue, green and orange, which operates on given routes. An *ojek* (motorcycle that takes passengers) means you are really going native – just wear a helmet.

River travel is done by a variety of craft, including *kapal biasa* (river ferry with second-storey accommodation), *klotok* (river boat with covered passenger cabins), longboats (a speedboat with passenger seats) and motorised canoes, including *ces*, the local longtail. *Tok-toks* are narrow open fishing boats that sound just like their name, and are used to reach offshore islands. Bring your earplugs.

Kalimantan's five regional provinces – East, North, West, Central and South – are political entities, but serve the traveller mainly as geographical coordinates.

EAST KALIMANTAN

Balikpapan

📞 0542 / POP 459,000

Kalimantan's only cosmopolitan city, Balikpapan is also the only one worthy of being considered a destination unto itself, particularly with children. The influx of oil money has had a tremendous impact here in recent years. At once both Western (with its heavy expat influence) and Asian, the city is clean and vibrant, with several enormous shopping areas and (for Kalimantan) some rare beaches. High-end hotels abound, at very reasonable prices, including some fabulous ones. And the nightlife surprises, from the heights of the world-class Skybar to the smoky depths of waterfront clubs. The city sprawls in all directions, but most of the action takes place in the centre, off Jl Sudirman: the place to stay. This main drag comes alive at night, flush with scooters and clothed in advertising. Overall the city makes a fine weekend break, and a great place to begin or end more adventurous travels.

◉ Sights

TOP CHOICE **Ruko Bandar**   NEIGHBOURHOOD
(Jl Sudirman) This excellent waterfront development offers everything you need for a night out and more, including above-par restaurants, hot nightclubs, and a dozen fun but easy-to-miss cafes (at the rear, facing the sea). Make this your first stop.

Kemala Beach   BEACH
(Jl Sudirman) A beach in Kalimantan! Yes, and it's clean, with good sand, plenty of adjacent bars and a laid-back vibe. If you need a break from the jungle, urban or natural, this is your best local option, although it gets hot at midday.

Masjid Agung At-Taqwa   MOSQUE
(Jl Sudirman) An impressive sight, this mosque is adorned with a complex sheath of Islamic geometrical patterns and lit up in multicoloured splendour at night.

👉 Tours

Indra GUIDE
(📞081 2585 9800; indrahadi91@yahoo.com) The first choice for Japanese tourists; his English is serviceable too.

Ahmad GUIDE
(📞0821 5180 8818; ahmad_tour74@yahoo.com) An experienced city and jungle guide with excellent English and organisational skills.

Balikpapan

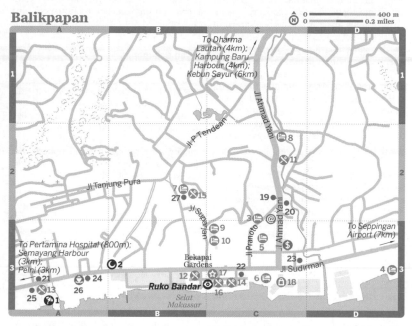

KALIMANTAN BALIKPAPAN

🛏 Sleeping

TOP CHOICE Hotel Gran Senyiur   HOTEL $$$

(☎080 0122 6677; http://gran.senyiurhotels.com; Jl ARS Muhammad 7; r incl breakfast from 780,000Rp; ❄🛜) Unique in Kalimantan, this expansive and genteel purveyor of old-world Asian luxury stands apart from the new breed of business hotel, all of which were designed by the same consultant. Fine woodwork warms spaces throughout, and rooms are both sumptuously appointed and reasonably priced. The classy junior suites, with their Dayak artefacts, are unbeaten anywhere. From the lobby lounge to the world-class Sky Bar, which adds a modern note to the roof, everything is upscale without being ostentatious.

TOP CHOICE Ibis Hotel   HOTEL $$

(☎820 821; www.ibishotels.com; Jl Suparjan 2; r Sat-Sun/Mon-Fri incl breakfast 300,000/499,000Rp; ❄🛜) Balikpapan's great steal, particularly on weekends. The cosy, design-conscious rooms are stylish and sophisticated, with bursts of bright colour and sexy space-station bathrooms. Best of all, guests are welcome to use the considerable amenities of the adjoining five-star Novotel. Basically, you're staying at the Novotel for a third of the price.

Hotel Pacific   HOTEL $$

(☎750 888; www.hotelpacificbalikpapan.com; Jl A Yani 33; d incl breakfast 435,000Rp; ❄🛜) An excellent midrange boutique hotel, dated in style but not in quality. The staff is friendly, the rooms comfy and the public spaces worth an extra star. Discounts on weekends.

Le Grandeur Balikpapan   HOTEL $$$

(☎420 155; www.legrandeurbalikpapan.com; Jl Sudirman; r 1,100,000Rp; ❄🛜🏊) If you're in town for a weekend getaway, you can't do much better than this luxury hotel, which offers a great beachfront location with all associated amenities (such as waterfront dining) and some classy touches (eg live jazz). When you're done with the sea, there's an elegant pool, too. Babysitting available. On Jl Sudirman about 2km east of Ruko Bandar.

Hotel Gajah Mada   HOTEL $$

(☎734 634; info@gajahmada-hotel.com; Jl Sudirman 328; s 206,000-400,000Rp; d 261,000-415,000Rp; ❄🏊) Rooms are concrete boxes, but freshly painted and spotless, with either en suite Western bathroom or mandi.

Novotel Balikpapan   HOTEL $$$

(☎820 820; www.novotel.com/asia; Jl Suparjan 2; r incl breakfast 990,000-1,200,000Rp; ❄🛜🏊) A world-class, family-friendly hotel, with an ubermodern interior and all amenities, including a patisserie, gym, numerous cafes, a spa and an excellent rooftop pool with panoramic views (45,000Rp to outsiders). Parents liberated by free kids club.

Aston Balikpapan   HOTEL $$

(☎733 999; www.astonbalikpapan.com; Jl Sudirman 7; r 700,000-888,000Rp; ❄🛜🏊) This new kid on the block wins the contemporary design award for its tropical lobby with gorgeous horizon pool facing the sea – the best in Kalimantan. The entry-level rooms don't have the same pizzazz, with plasticky doors and furniture, so pay up for the upper-storey deluxe rooms, where windows on both sides take you into the clouds. Third night free on weekends.

Aiqo Hotel   HOTEL $$

(☎750 288; www.aiqohotel.com; Jl Pranoto 9; r 248,000-298,000Rp; ❄🛜) A clean midmarket option with light-filled superior and deluxe corner rooms.

Hotel Citra Nusantara   LOSMEN $

(☎425 366; Jl Gajahmada 76; r with fan/air-con incl breakfast 140,000/250,000Rp; ❄🛜) Just off the main road, the shared mandi budget rooms in this losmen (budget guesthouse) are basic, though the higher ranks are surprisingly modern. Couples need proof of marriage.

🍴 Eating

TOP CHOICE Ocean's Resto   SEAFOOD $

(☎739 439; Ruko Bandar; mains from 18,000Rp; ⏰noon-3pm, 6-10pm) The anchor restaurant on the Ruko Bandar, this ocean-side seafood classic, with a reef's worth of iced fish to choose from, is always popular, both inside and out (so think about reserving). The tiny open-air curry house, upstairs and to the right before you enter, is a good place for appetisers.

TOP CHOICE Sky Bar/Sky Grill   SEAFOOD $$

(Jl ARS Muhammad, Hotel Gran Senyiur; mains from 55,000Rp; ⏰3-11pm) The Gran Senyiur Hotel has an awesome rooftop, combining glass-walled alfresco dining (mains 55,000Rp) and a sophisticated piano bar with panoramic city views. You pay for it, with the signature Cosmopolitan drink at 95,000Rp, but this is a world-class spot not to be missed.

WORTH A TRIP

AROUND BALIKPAPAN

There's a potpourri of sights around Balikpapan that make for an interesting full-day trip, but given transport, navigation, and reservation requirements, it is best to use a local tour guide. Indra (p221) will take two to three people to the following for 1,500,000Rp, including car, lunch, boat and admission fees:

KWPLH Sun Bear Sanctuary (http://en.beruangmadu.org) Home to several sun bears in their natural habitat. Catch the morning feeding at 9am (another is at 3pm).

Hanging Bridge (Bukit Bangkirai) Walk a rope bridge through the forest canopy, around 50m above ground, and enjoy great views.

Black River Canoe the mangrove forest of Balikpapan Bay in search of proboscis monkeys and bird life.

Samboja Lestari (☑0542-702 3600; www.orangutan.ord.id) Research centre focused on orangutan reintroduction, sun-bear protection, and reforestation.

Penangkaran Buaya Crocodile Farm This commercial venture won't win any ecotourism awards, but harbours some real brutes. There's a nice longhouse next door.

Beach House Restaurant The perfect end to the day.

Beach House Restaurant   INTERNATIONAL $
(Jl Mulawarman Km19; mains from 20,000Rp; ☺lunch & dinner) These rattan tables by the sea, set in a tropical park 6km past the airport, are a little slice of Bali. The diverse menu offers great sandwiches, steaks, burgers, pasta and pizza alongside Eastern specialities. The plush waterfront cabanas go fast.

Bondy   WESTERN $
(Jl Ahmad Yani; mains 30,000-50,000Rp; ☺10.30am-10pm) An expat oasis offering steaks, home-made ice cream, and choose-your-own seafood on ice, with alfresco dining.

Kemala Beach & Resto   INDONESIAN $
(Jl Sudirman, Pantai Polda; mains from 25,000Rp; ☺10am-10pm) Billowing white curtains beckon you to this unique open-air pavilion at the end of Kemala Beach, where a long line of food stalls covers the gamut of culinary options, and a large Balinese restaurant surrounds a freshwater pond. Choose your own fresh seafood here (the crab is excellent) and enjoy live music Saturday and Monday.

Zeus   ASIAN $
(Ruko Bandar; mains from 18,000Rp; ☺11am-3am) An excellent Asian dim sum restaurant with plenty of outdoor seating. Upstairs is a cool new lounge (beer 45,000Rp) that is easily missed: take the door to the right as you enter. A great place to hang out and talk if there's no live music.

De Cafe   FUSION $$
(Jl Sudirman; mains from 45,000Rp; ☺11am-2pm, 6-11pm; ☻) This cosy bakery-cafe offering a wide assortment of irresistible desserts is a welcome anomaly. Comfy sofas and wi-fi create a homey atmosphere, while the Asian fusion menu nods to Western tastes.

☆ Entertainment

TOP CHOICE Connexion   LIVE MUSIC
(Ruko Bandar) Don't let the cover charge (100,000Rp for bands) hold you back: this small club is an absolute blast, with the best bands brought in from around Indonesia and walkway dancers who keep the whole house shaking until the early hours. Whew!

🛍 Shopping

Shopping is concentrated at City Balcony and **Balikpapan Plaza** (cnr Jl Sudirman & Jln Ahmad Yani), two huge malls separated by a Hypermart (for groceries).

Pesar Kebun Sayur   SOUVENIRS
(☺9am-6pm) Market for local handicrafts, gemstones and souvenirs. Ten minutes by taxi west of the city centre.

ℹ Information

Aero Travel (☑443 350; jony_satriavi@yahoo.com; Jl Ahmad Yani 19) Organises specialist river trips up Sungai Mahakam. Also books flights and can help you get to Derawan Archipelago. Ask for English-speaking Jony.

Bayu Buana Travel (☎422 751; www.bayubua
natravel.com; Jl Ahmad Yani) Very helpful
English-speaking staff for flights, Sungai
Mahakam tours.

Haji La Tanrung Star Group (Jl Ahmad Yani
51; ☺7.30am-9pm) Moneychanger with several
branches.

Kantorimigrasi Kelas (☎421 175; Jl Sudirman
23) Immigration office.

Pertamina Hospital (☎734 020; www.rspb.
co.id; Jl Sudirman 1)

Speedy Internet (Jl Ahmad Yani 7; per hr
7000Rp) Air-con, moderately speedy and no
smoking.

ⓘ Getting There & Away
Air
Batavia Air (☎739 225; Jl Sudirman 15C)
Citilink (☎080 4108 0808; airport)
Garuda (☎422 301; Jl Sudirman 2, Adika Hotel
Bahtera)
Kalstar (☎737 473; Jl Marsaiswahyudi 12)
Lion Air (☎707 3761; airport)
Merpati (☎424 452; Jl Sudirman 32)

SilkAir (☎730 800; Jl ARS Muhammad 7, Hotel
Gran Senyiur)

Boat
Balikpapan has several ports along its gulf
coast. If arriving from Banjarmasin by bus you'll
take the ferry from Penajam to Kariangau Harbour. Further south lies Kampung Baru Harbour,
which serves Sulawesi. Semayang Harbour, at
the entrance to the gulf, is the main cargo and
passenger port.

Dharma Lautan (☎422 194; Kampung Baru
dock)
New Agung Sedayu (☎420 601; Jl Sudirman
28) Best source for all boat tickets.
Pelni (☎424 171; Jl Yos Sudarso 76)
Prima Vista (☎732 607; Jl Sudirman 138)

Bus
Buses to Samarinda leave from Batu Ampar bus
terminal at the north end of town. Buses to Banjarmasin leave from the terminal across the harbour. To get there take *angkot* (city minibus) 6 to
Jl Monginsidi and hop on a speedboat (10,000Rp
to 20,000Rp, 10 minutes) to the other side. If

TRANSPORT FROM BALIKPAPAN

Air

DESTINATION	COMPANY	COST (RP)	DURATION	FREQUENCY
Banjarmasin	Batavia Air, Sriwijaya Air	375,000	45min	daily
Berau	Batavia Air, Sriwijaya Air	550,000	1hr	daily
Jakarta	Lion Air, Sriwijaya Air, Batavia Air, Garuda, Citilink	625,000	2hr	daily
Jogjakarta	Garuda, Lion Air, Batavia Air, Sriwijaya Air	800,000	2hr	daily
Kuala Lumpur	AirAsia	440,000	2½hr	3-4 weekly
Makassar	Lion Air, Sriwijaya Air, Garuda, Merpati	550,000	1½hr	daily
Singapore	Silk Air	4,300,000	2½hr	Mon-Sat
Surabaya	Batavia Air, Sriwijaya Air, Lion Air, Garuda, Citilink	575,000	1hr	daily
Tarakan	Lion Air, Sriwijaya Air, Batavia Air	400,000	1hr	daily

Boat

DESTINATION	COMPANY	COST (RP)	DURATION (HR)	FREQUENCY
Makassar	Dharma Lautan, Prima Vista, Pelni	175,000	19-24	5 weekly
Pare Pare	Prima Vista	162,000	19	Mon, Tue
Surabaya	Dharma Lautan, Prima Vista	275,000	36	almost daily
Tarakan-Nunukan	Pelni	294,000	3	Sun, Mon, Wed

arriving, your bus ticket will automatically include a ferry across the harbour. However, since this can mean an hour wait, it may be better to get off at the ferry landing and take a speedboat.

❶ Getting Around

Taxis from the city centre cost 50,000Rp to Sepinggan Airport (30 minutes) and 15,000Rp to Batu Ampar bus terminal. Balikpapan Plaza is a focal point for *angkot* (3000Rp) and *ojek*s (from 10,000Rp).

Samarinda

📞 0541 / POP 726,000

Samarinda! The very name oozes exoticism, like some capital in the *Arabian Nights*. And happily, you will find some of that here in this sprawling riverfront city. The enormous mosque of the new Islamic Centre stands like a sentinel at the gates of the mighty Mahakam River, a most impressive sight, giving the city a welcome dash of Istanbul. But like many fairy-tale settings, there is also a jarring profusion of highs and lows, from a few quality hotels to the thousands of rusting tin-roofed shacks spread over the surrounding hills. Unlike Balikpapan, anything goes here, for better or worse, so take a taxi after 9pm.

◉ Sights

TOP CHOICE ⟩ Samarinda Islamic Centre   MOSQUE
(Jl Slamet Riyadi; tower admission 10,000Rp; ⊙mosque 8-10am & 4-6pm, tower 7am-6pm) The skyline of Samarinda is dominated by this new must-see complex containing an awe-inspiring mosque and adjacent tower. The latter is the highest point in the city, offering panoramic views up and down a great bend in the Mahakam. The muezzin's call at sunset is a captivating moment here.

Mesjid Siratal Mustaqim   MOSQUE
(Samarinda Seberang) A 400-year-old wooden mosque designed by a Dutchman, in colonial architectural style, with a unique wooden minaret. On the south side of the river near the boat landing.

Mesjid Raya Darussalam   MOSQUE
(Jl Niaga Selatan) A striking mosque with missile-like minarets.

☞ Tours

TOP CHOICE ⟩ De'Gigant Tours   ADVENTURE
(☏0812 584 6578, 700 0774; www.borneotour gigant.com; Jl Martadinata 21) De'Gigant is the

ℹ MOSQUE ATTIRE

You don't need to be Muslim or Confucian to admire the architecture of Samarinda's great buildings. Visitors are welcome. But when it comes to mosques, both men and women should wear plain, loose-fitting clothing, and remove hats and sunglasses upon entrance. Men can wear short-sleeve shirts, but women should be covered to the wrists and wear a headscarf. Men and women occupy different rooms in a mosque, so if you are in mixed company you will be separated during your visit; sometimes there are also separate entrances.

best tour company to deal with in Kalimantan, offering strong and trustworthy management, experienced guides and island-wide contacts. Its sharp Dutch owner, Lucas Zwaal, speaks English, German, Indonesian, Dayak, Kutai, Banjarese and Javanese. This is one of only two tour companies we recommend for the Cross-Borneo Trek (p219), and the best for an east-to-west itinerary, with expertise all the way up the Mahakam. For a memorable jungle trek or river cruise, start here.

🛏 Sleeping

Don't skimp here: budget digs are gloomy and upgrading to midrange options only adds a Western toilet to your concrete cube. However, top-end hotels can be good value, particularly on weekends, when many offer steep discounts. Rooms fill up accordingly, so reserve ahead on weekends.

TOP CHOICE ⟩ Hotel Mesra   HOTEL $$
(☏732 772; www.mesra.com/hotel; Jl Pahlawan 1; s/d incl breakfast 350,000/400,000Rp, d cottage 820,000Rp; ❋ 🛜 ☲) The Mesra is a welcome surprise, a true resort privately located on a hilltop in town and very reasonably priced, attracting families from near and far on weekends. Rooms have balconies overlooking the expansive grounds, which include two pools open to the public (30,000Rp), gardens, tennis courts, a spa and an excellent restaurant. The latter offers Western, Asian and Indonesian cuisine in an atmospheric traditional wooden building, if you don't mind the enormous *garuda* (mythical

Samarinda

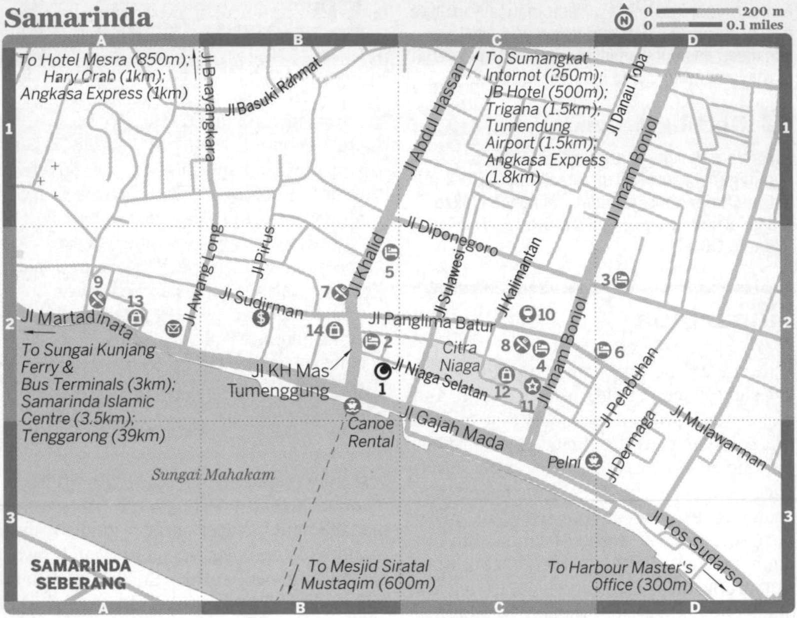

Samarinda

Sights

1 Mesjid Raya Darussalam B2

Sleeping

2 Aida B2
3 Aston Samarinda D2
4 Hotel Grand Jamrud 2 .... C2
5 Hotel MJ B2
6 Swiss-Belhotel D2

Eating

7 Hero Supermarket B2
8 Sari Pacific Restaurant C2
9 Teluk Lerong Restaurant & Café A2

Drinking

10 Déjà Vu Bar C2

Entertainment

11 Maximum C2

Shopping

12 Citra Niaga C2
13 Hendra Art Shop A2
14 Pasar Pagi B2

bird) staring down at you. Worth coming just for the breakfast (90,000Rp).

Aston Samarinda HOTEL **$$**
(☎732 600; www.astonsamarinda.com; Jl Pangeran Hidayatullah; r 760,000;) A bargain at this price, this brand-new, attractively designed hotel and convention centre sports a collonaded pool, comfy rooms that cross over from business to leisure, and if you can pull your eyes away from the huge flat-screen TVs, some grand views of the river. Fine dining and an in-house spa round out the luxury. Promo rate on Sunday and 10% online discount.

Swiss-Belhotel HOTEL **$$$**
(☎200 888; www.swissbelhotel.com; Jl Mulawarman 6; s 995,000-1,055,000Rp, d 1,055,000-1,710,000Rp;) This nicely decorated business hotel with its large glass lobby, pool and extensive buffet is new, and much cheaper than the published rates quoted here when you factor in the walk-in discount. All rooms numbered 18–face the river. Credit cards accepted.

Hotel MJ
HOTEL $$

(☑747 689; www.mjhotel.com; Jl Khalid 1; r incl breakfast 275,000 405,000Rp, ste incl breakfast 465,000-575,000Rp; ❄️🛜) Part of this hotel has been renovated to great effect, although the new rooms had not yet been priced at time of research. The cafe is bright and cheery and there is an excellent buffet. All rooms have air-con, en suites, TVs, comfortable beds, hot water and Dayak artwork. Ask about discounts.

Hotel Grand Jamrud 2
HOTEL $$

(☑731 233; Jl Panglima Batur 45; r incl breakfast 300,000-470,000Rp; ❄️🛜) Centrally located, with clean concrete cubes as rooms, this is a better choice than its sibling the Jamrud 1, but check rooms to avoid mould and view issues. The breakfast is OK, but the cafe looks out on a wall.

JB Hotel
HOTEL $$

(☑737 688; jbhotel_samarinda@yahoo.com; Jl Agus Salim 16; r 228,000-333,000Rp; ❄️🛜) A bit out of the way, JB is seemingly undecided whether it's art deco or Moorish kitsch. Air-con rooms are large and clean, but only deluxe rooms have hot water.

Alda
HOTEL $

(☑742 572; Jl KH Mas Tumenggung; d incl breakfast 180,000-240,000Rp, tr 255,000Rp; ❄️) The nondescript rooms here are cheap, but that's about it. The cheapest rooms have a fan and cold water; the rest air-con and hot water. They could all be cleaner.

🍴 Eating

Night cafes proliferate opposite Mesra Indah Mall, with tasty warungs (food stalls) and unpretentious seafood restaurants further up Jl Abdul Hassan.

TOP CHOICE Teluk Lerong
Restaurant & Café
INTERNATIONAL $

(Jl Martadinata; mains 20,000Rp; ⏱8am-1am Mon-Thu, to 2am Fri-Sun; 🛜) Perched above the busy riverside drive, this new and stylish cafe is a breath of fresh air in a city that sorely needs more like it. The open-air dining is atmospheric, if a bit loud, and the menu offers something for everyone, be it Chinese, pasta or steak.

TOP CHOICE Lipan Hill
Resto & Cafe
INTERNATIONAL $

(Jl Kusumo, Samarinda Sebarang; mains from 30,000Rp; ⏱breakfast, lunch & dinner) With a commanding location overlooking the Mahakam from its southern bank, about 2km south of the bridge, this is a refreshing spot, as it takes advantage of the city's greatest asset: its river views. The excellent food brings in the locals. Live music 10am to 11pm.

Hary Crab
SEAFOOD $$

(Jl Pahlawan 41; crab 75,000Rp; ⏱6-10pm) A unique local institution, these streetside outdoor benches are generally packed with people digging into some delicious crab. Wear your bib.

Sari Pacific Restaurant
INTERNATIONAL $

(Jl Panglima Batur; mains 33,000Rp; ⏱9am-10pm) Plush dining, with a menu featuring tenderloin and T-bone steaks as well as beef burgers. Perfect for a carb injection before the basic fare up the Mahakam, although portions are small. Live music daily.

Hero Supermarket
SUPERMARKET $

(Mesra Indah Mall) Good place to stock up on snacks before heading upriver.

🍷 Drinking

Déjà Vu Bar
BAR

(Jl Panglima Batur; ⏱10pm-2am) This complex contains a booming nightclub (admission 75,000Rp) with cocktail tables and lots of security and a separate, very classy dinner restaurant frequented by a hip and dressy crowd. The menu includes international cuisine plus a spectrum of cocktails. Yikes: a bottle of tequila is $150.

☆ Entertainment

Maximum
DISCO

(Jl Niaga Timur 21; ⏱8pm-close) In the Citra Niaga, this ear-splitter is the most popular dance club in the city. Go after midnight. Cover (50,000Rp) buys a free drink.

WORTH A TRIP

PAMPANG DAYAK CEREMONIES

Every Sunday at 2pm, Pampang, 25km west of Samarinda, has authentic Kenyah Dayak ceremonies at its longhouse, one of the last places to see traditional long ears. Offer a donation for taking photographs. Take a public minibus from Segiri terminal (10,000Rp, one hour), or charter a taxi or Kijang with other travellers (100,000Rp).

KALIMANTAN SAMARINDA

PROSTITUTION

Prostitution is integrated into Kalimantan society to a degree perhaps unmatched anywhere else in the world, and for reasons that have nothing to do with foreign tourists. Most hotel spas, massage centres, karaoke bars (with private rooms), nightclubs and pubs offer 'the extras'. In some cases the scale of these operations is truly audacious, with bars, karaoke and dance clubs united in huge multilevel entertainment complexes attached to five-star hotels. Apart from a growing focus on HIV, Kalimantan society as a whole turns a huge blind eye on this booming enterprise. Indeed, many Muslim-run hotels still demand that couples produce a marriage licence.

Shopping

TOP CHOICE **Hendra Art Shop** ANTIQUES
(☑734 949; hendra.art@gmail.com; ⊗9am-5pm) Carved bison skull, anyone? For curios, antiques, and other Borneo exotica, the two packed floors of this rare shop can't be beat. Before testing your haggling skills, ensure that what you are buying is authentic and can be removed from the country.

Citra Niaga MARKET
(@) Contains several souvenir shops offering beautiful batik sarongs and Dayak carvings. There's also a food court (mains 25,000Rp to 35,000Rp).

Pasar Pagi MARKET
(Morning Market; Jl Sudirman) A wonderfully chaotic morning market.

ⓘ Information

Angkasa Express (☑200 281; aexsri@telkom. net; Plaza Lembuswana) Air tickets.
Bank Central Asia (BCA; Jl Sudirman) For foreign exchange.
Main post office (cnr Jl Gajah Mada & Jl Awang Long)
Prima Tour & Travel (☑737 777; prima_sriol@ yahoo.co.id; Jl Khalid 1, Hotel MJ) Air tickets and cars.
Rumah Sakit Haji Darjad (☑732 698; Jl Dahlia) Modern, massive hospital. Off Jl Basuki Rahmat.
Sumangkat Internet (Jl Agus Salim 35; per hr 7000Rp; ⊗8am-midnight) Plus postal services and wartel (telephone office).

ⓘ Getting There & Away

Air
Kalstar (☑747 972; Jl Subroto 80, en route to airport) The only airline serving Samarinda. Most flights connect through Balikpapan.

Boat
Pelni (☑741 402; Jl Yos Sudarso 76) Mahakam ferries (*kapal biasa*) leave at 7am from Sungai Kunjang terminal (3km via *angkot*)

Pelni ferries leave from the main harbour on Jl Yos Sudarso. See the harbour master (Jl Yos Sudarso 2) for service to Pare Pare aboard *Queen Soya*.

Bus
Samarinda has multiple bus terminals:
Sungai Kunjang terminal For Kota Bangun (23,000Rp, three hours) and Balikpapan (27,000Rp, two hours).
Lempake terminal (north end of town) For Bontang (25,000Rp, three hours), Sangatta (20,000Rp, four hours) and Berau (150,000Rp, 16 hours).
Harapan Baru terminal (south bank of Sungai Makaham, *angkot* route G) For minibuses to Tenggarong (10,000Rp, one hour).
Segiri terminal (north end of Jl Pahlawan) For minibuses to Pampang (7000Rp, one hour).

A direct bus to Balikpapan Airport (50,000Rp) departs from the office of Prima Tour & Travel six times per day.

Car & Kijang
A Kijang seat is 300,000Rp to Kota Bangun, and 250,000Rp to Berau. Hiring a car and driver is 500,000Rp per day. A 4WD doubles the price. You can organise a car through Prima Tour & Travel.

ⓘ Getting Around

Minibuses, called *angkot* or taxis (3000Rp), converge at Pasar Pagi. Taxis from Tumendung Airport (3km) cost 35,000Rp. Alternatively, walk 100m to Jl Gatot Subroto, turn left and catch *angkot* B into town.

Cross-Mahakam ferries to Samarinda Seberang (5000Rp) leave from the end of Jl Tumenggung.

Sungai Mahakam

The second-largest river in Indonesia, the mighty Mahakam is at once a major highway, a cultural tour and a wildlife-spotting expedition. It is also the only major river with public transport all the way into the heart of Borneo, making its 930km length entirely accessible.

🏃 Activites

Travelling up this jungle river is a journey in the fullest sense of the word. One heads away from the industrial centre of Samarinda and slips deeper and deeper into the jungle, and into Borneo's past. A week later it is either time to start the difficult next stage of the Cross-Borneo Trek, or turn back. Along the way there is great variety, including the many boats that ply the river and local wildlife. Between Tanjung Isuy and Mancong our research trip encountered river otter, gold-ringed snake, python, proboscis monkey, macaque, kingfisher, monitor lizard, hornbill, stork, and an unidentified condor. There are many opportunities for exploration, from towns and longhouses to huge lakes, wetlands and other rivers. This is a place that rewards travellers with time on their hands and hence the ability to jump off the boat and wait for the next one, even if it means staying overnight.

As you continue upriver, tourist facilities recede – and what there is ain't great. On the other hand, the Mahakam is one of those places where you shouldn't worry too much about the details. Homestays materialise, 'my brother's boat' appears, closed stores open. Westerners in particular will be greeted with legendary hospitality. Transport gets increasingly expensive the further upriver you go, due to the cost of lugging fuel that far, but everything else is dirt cheap, so a little money goes a long way.

In summary, this is off-the-beaten-track travel of the highest order. Outside the summer season, you'll probably not see another foreigner your entire trip. There are few creature comforts, making health precautions particularly wise, but you also have the flexibility to turn back whenever you think you've seen enough (and the current downriver cuts the return journey in half). If you are comparing this with rivers elsewhere in Borneo, it is the defining experience.

STAGES OF TRAVEL

The Mahakam is ascended from Samarinda in different stages, each requiring its own form of transport, although there are also some personal choices to be made. Here is an ideal itinerary:

Stage one: Samarinda to Kota Bangun by land While Samarinda is where Mahakam journeys are arranged, it is not where they typically begin. Travellers usually go overland to Kota Bangun via Tenggarong, either by bus (20,000Rp, three hours) or by hiring a car (450,000Rp), as this stretch of river is highly developed. Otherwise it is an eight-hour journey from Samarinda by *kapal biasa*, which depart every morning at 7am.

TRANSPORT FROM SAMARINDA

Air

DESTINATION	COMPANY	COST (RP)	DURATION	FREQUENCY
Balikpapan	Kalstar	316,000	30min	2 daily
Berau	Kalstar	720,000	45min	3 daily
Nunukan	Kalstar	1,274,000	3hr	1 daily
Tarakan	Kalstar	983,000	2hr	1 daily

Boat

DESTINATION	COMPANY	COST (RP)	DURATION	FREQUENCY
Long Bagun (seasonal)		350,000	36hr	daily
Long Iram		120,000	18hr	daily
Melak		100,000	16hr	daily
Pare Pare	Pelni	250,000	22hr	2 weekly
Surabaya	Pelni	381,000	3 days	monthly
Tenggarong		20,000	2hr	daily

Stage two: Kota Bagun to Muara Pahu by ces This wonderful section of rivers, lakes and marshes, which is full of wildlife, requires a *ces* to explore. Otherwise you can stay on the main river and take the *kapal biasa*, but you are really missing out. *Kapal biasa* head upriver every morning at 9am.

Stage three: Muara Pahu to Long Bagun by kapal biasa A fulfilling stretch of riverboat travel, with an overnight stay on the boat.

Stage four: Long Bagun to Tiong Ohang by longboat The most exhilirating part of the entire journey. Ever shot rapids upstream in a 400 horsepower speedboat?

Note that *kapal biasa* reach Long Bagun, 523km from Samarinda (350,000Rp, 36 hours), when water levels permit. Otherwise they stop in Tering, 409km upstream (155,000Rp, 18 hours). From here on, transport gets expensive, with charter rates of 100,000Rp per hour for a *ces* and 1,000,000Rp per hour for a speedboat. Be prepared to haggle, and remember that the larger the group, the cheaper the individual cost to charter a boat.

GUIDES

If you do not speak Bahasa, you will need a guide, as English becomes harder to find the further upriver you go. You can get by on the *kapal biasa* without it, but step ashore and you're lost. If you buy a tour package a guide

will be provided, and costs defined ahead of time. If not, you'll have to hire a guide yourself. Some travellers do so as they move along the lower river, but it is better to take the time to find a suitable guide in Samarinda, where they are relatively plentiful, rather than having this requirement hanging over your head. A short interview is essential to confirm any guide's language skills.

Guide fees generally range from 150,000Rp to 200,000Rp per day, with the best getting 250,000Rp. The client is responsible for a guide's expenses as well, but be clear about what this entails ahead of time. Usually the client picks up the guide's meals, which are inexpensive. Guides can generally arrange their own local accommodation, too, which is relatively cheap or even free. Transport can be very expensive, especially beyond Long Bagun, but guides can often get the price of their own ticket reduced. In general, the best guides will look out for their client's financial interests, leading to savings that actually defray their fee. But be aware that, while you are with them for one journey, they deal with the same locals all the time.

The following recommended guides speak English:

Ahmad GUIDE
(☏0821 5180 8818; ahmad_tour74@yahoo.com) An experienced cross-Borneo guide with excellent organisational skills.

Abdullah GUIDE
(☏0813 4727-2817; doe21@yahoo.com) Friendly and resourceful.

Suriyadi GUIDE
(☏081 6450 8263) Speaks German.

Rustam GUIDE
(☏081 2585 4915, 735 641)

Jaelani GUIDE
(☏0813-4633 8343)

THE HOT ROD OF THE MAHAKAM

Need a *ces* (motorised canoe with long propellor shaft) to explore the waters beyond Kota Bangun? Cheerful **Udin** (☏0812 5311 1357) has the perfect ride. Powerful, gaily painted and comfortable, with a cushion seat below and a canopy overhead, this colourful canoe is as cool as river travel gets. Udin also knows how to slow down for wildlife, navigate the narrowest paths and keep you dry. A full day's itinerary – Kota Bangun, Muara Muntai, Jantur, Tanjung Isuy, Mancong, and back to Tanjung Isuy – is 1,500,000Rp for the entire boat, drinks included. Seats six comfortably.

TENGGARONG
☏0541 / POP 75,000

Tenggarong is an important destination, but also a heartbreaker. Once the capital of the mighty Kutai sultanate, it made a recent attempt to recreate that past grandeur, and failed mightily. Several years ago the local regent and his cohorts, flush with mining profits, made a massive investment in the city's infrastructure. The development focused on turning Pulau Kumala, the city's river island, into a huge tourist attraction,

CHARIOTS OF THE MAHAKAM

You'll need several different types of boat to go the length of the Mahakam. Here are the principal varieties:

Kapal Biasa These bi-level riverboats ply the lower Mahakam, from Samarinda to Long Bagun. The open lower deck holds cargo, the kitchen (meals 20,000Rp) and basic bathrooms (visualise a hole in the deck). The closed upper deck is the sleeping area, a floating hostel where 60 people or so bed down, side by side, on simple mattresses (provided). If you're making an overnight journey, head directly upstairs to stake a claim. The atmosphere is very congenial; everyone else is used to this madness. The secret treasure is the balcony at the front, directly over the captain, which provides an awesome elevated viewing platform. As the boat chugs upstream and kilometres of jungle pass by, you can sit there serenely for hours on end in shaded comfort, munching on strange fruit from the last stop. There is only room for five people or so, though, so let one be you, as it truly makes the voyage.

Longboats Long speedboats with a canvas top and rows of seating for passengers, these powerful craft, with 400 horsepower behind them, are necessary for handling the rapids in the upper river. If you sit up front, you'll bounce around a lot but it's worth it, as visibility is better. While sitting in the middle is smoother, you'll end up in a blue haze, as everyone smokes like a chimney. Expensive, but a hell of a ride.

Ces What else can we say? This is one romantic way to travel. These narrow wooden canoes are powered by a lawnmower engine, attached to a propeller via a long stalk – the same longtails seen elsewhere in Asia. They are also surprisingly stylish, with upturned snouts, raked sterns, occasional cabanas and colourful paint jobs. Best of all, they provide access to the narrowest and shallowest stretches on the river, including some vast marshes. All things considered, there is nothing, *nothing* like exploring the jungle on a beautiful day in one of these, a private journey fit for a sultan. Sit on the cushioned hull in shaded comfort, eagerly awaiting the next source of amazement. Just bring your earplugs.

River travel! The joy of Kalimantan.

with a hotel, restaurants, amusement park and sky tower. It also included the construction of a large suspension bridge across the Mahakam, dubbed 'Indonesia's Golden Gate'. Today Pulau Kumala lies unfinished and bankrupt, its history plagued by a massive corruption scandal. Far worse, in 2011 the bridge suddenly collapsed into the river, killing 36 people. The result is a setting worthy of Greek drama. The waterfront is framed by a massive statue of a *lembuswana*, a mythical winged horse with an elephant's trunk, which perches at the end of Pulau Kumala; and by the enormous, twisted remains of the collapsed bridge, its fallen roadway spearing the Mahakam.

◉ Sights

TOP CHOICE Keraton/Mulawarman
Museum   MUSEUM
(Jl Diponegoro; admission 5000Rp; ◷9am-4pm, closed Mon & Fri) The former sultan's palace *(keraton)* is known for its excellent museum, which ranges widely across culture, natural history and industry, and has Eng-

lish signage. However, it is the building itself that is the star attraction. The sparkling white exterior, with its strong parallel lines, is a futurist vision worthy of Shangri-La, and reminiscent of Frank Lloyd Wright. Built by the Dutch in 1937, this is a significant work of architecture that has fallen off the world's radar screen; further information is difficult to come by. Nearby you'll find the sultan's cemetery, a souvenir market and an ATM.

Pulau Kumala   ISLAND
While the future of this island amusement park is uncertain, a boat trip and stroll to the huge *lembuswana* at the tip is a worthwhile outing. Boats (per person 20,000Rp) leave 100m from Keraton.

✵ Festivals & Events

Erau Festival   CULTURAL
In late September thousands of Dayaks hold a vast intertribal party punctuated by traditional dances, ceremonies and other events that is not to be missed. Ask at hotels for schedule.

Sleeping & Eating

Grand Elty Singgasana Hotel HOTEL $$
(☎664 703; Jl Pahlawan 1; r 589,000-697,000Rp;
❄) The only comfortable hotel anywhere nearby, this one ultimately maddens, as its beautiful hillside location, attractive villa courtyard and quality rooms are consistently marred by peeling paint, broken walkways, a malfunctioning website and clueless staff. The silver lining: a prime candidate for price negotiation.

Hotel Anda Dua HOTEL $
(☎0821 5684 9766; Jl Sudirman 65; r 120,000-170,000Rp; ❄) This wooden lodge has fan-cooled rooms with shared *mandi* and, out the back, comfortable air-con rooms with private bathroom and breakfast.

Rumah Makan Tepian Pandan INDONESIAN $
(Jl Diponegoro 23; mains 15,000Rp; ⊙breakfast, lunch & dinner) A relaxed, open-air restaurant serving Indonesian cuisine, with superb river views.

ⓘ Getting There & Away
The *kapal biasa* dock is 2km north of town, with *angkot* (2500Rp) service to the centre. *Ojeks* cost 10,000Rp. Boats depart for Samarinda at 7am daily (20,000Rp, two hours) and Kota Bangun at 9am daily (50,000Rp, six hours).

Petugas bus terminal is 5km south of town, also with *angkot* service to the centre (5000Rp). Buses depart hourly from 9am to 4pm for both Samarinda (10,000Rp) and Kota Bangun (23,000Rp).

There is no regular car service from Tenggarong. Kijang can be chartered for 150,000Rp for the first hour, 100,000Rp thereafter.

KOTA BANGUN
This busy town and transport hub is where upriver journeys generally begin. You can hire a *ces* from here to take you through a complex of rivers, lakes and marshes interspersed with villages. You'll cross lakes with wide-open skies, twist and turn through wetland channels, pass through forests of silver-barked trees, lunch at riverside *warungs*, and generally breeze along, pausing for the odd monkey or some of the last few Irrawaddy dolphins. Don't miss it.

Sleeping

Losmen Muzirat LOSMEN $
(☎081 2553 2287; Jl Mesjid Raya 46; r 40,000Rp) Colourfully painted, with simple, fan-cooled rooms and shared *mandi*. Pay up for light. There's a decent verandah to watch spectacular sunsets, nearby *warungs* and, further down the road, an internet cafe and ATM.

ⓘ Getting There & Around
A *ces* from Kota Bangun takes 1½ hours to Muara Muntai (250,000Rp), just over two hours to Jantur (325,000Rp), three hours to Tanjung Isuy (500,000Rp) and 6½ hours to Mancong (900,000Rp).

MUARA MUNTAI
This riverside town is remarkable for its massive boardwalk, more than 2km long, which serves as the main street. After sitting in a *ces* for hours, it's the perfect spot to stretch your legs and hunt for a snack.

Sleeping

Penginapan Srimuntai LOSMEN $
(☎0853 4963 0030; s/d 50,000/100,000Rp) Nice wide hallways and cleaner rooms elevate this one above the competition.

Penginapan Adi Guna LOSMEN $
(☎0853 4963 0030; r 50,000Rp) Basic fan-cooled rooms and large, shared *mandi*. There's free coffee and tea and a welcome breeze on the balcony.

MAHAKAM BY HOUSEBOAT

There is no better way to cruise the rivers of Kalimantan than by houseboat. The *Budi Sejati* is a rare opportunity to do this on the Mahakam. The 18m, two-storey craft, a larger version of the *klotok* seen in Tanjung Puting, has a kitchen, toilet and shower, a crew of two, an air-conditioned stateroom and, best of all, your own private shaded balcony at the front of the upper deck, the perfect viewing platform. Add an English-speaking guide, a cook and all provisions, and you are off on your own private river expedition – in first class. The highly varied itinerary includes river villages, wildlife, culture and more. For a four-day trip, the cost per person is 7,676,000Rp for two or three people; 6,144,000Rp for four or five; 5,268,000Rp for six to eight people; and 4,428,000Rp for nine to 12, all expenses included. For more information contact De'Gigant Tours (p225).

ℹ Getting There & Away

Get here from Samarinda by *kapal biasa* (70,000Rp, 10 hours) or bus to Kota Bangun (23,000Rp, three hours) and *ces* from there (250,000Rp, two hours).

JANTUR

Jantur is the most interesting river town on the Mahakam, partly because of its location, where the river enters a huge lake (Lake Jempang) bordered by wetlands, partly because it is built on stilts, with two huge boardwalks connecting each side of the river; and partly because it is missing from every map. The latter is particularly surprising, as this is no small village. As you enter, it just keeps on going.

The town was founded by Banjarese from Negara, which has a similar topography, and the brightly painted houses reflect this. A big, commanding yellow mosque, with its bright aluminum dome, sits proudly upon the river, an impressive sight as you emerge from the forest. Unfortunately there's no accommodation, but if you can arrange a homestay, do so. The friendly people hardly ever see tourists, making for some great exchanges, while the surrounding area is unique on the river, a vast wetlands savannah with a huge sky, like the Everglades. In any case, be sure to get out and stroll the boardwalk, which is also a stroll through village life; your camera will be clicking every few seconds. One example is the storks at the end of people's docks, which are used as guard animals. If they start squawking, someone is pinching your dried fish!

TANJUNG ISUY

Tanjung Isuy is the first Dayak village as you head upriver. You're equally likely to hear a shaman chanting as a mobile phone chirruping, as modern culture is only skin deep.

🛏 Sleeping

Louu Taman Jamrout   LONGHOUSE $
(Jl Indonesia Australia; r per person 60,000Rp) This longhouse is part craft centre, part hostel and part stage. Travellers can commission a Dayak dance for 500,000Rp. Weavings are available at reasonable prices. Rooms are boxlike and clean, with warm showers in shared bathrooms, and share a lively communal dinner table.

Losmen Wisata   LOSMEN $
(Jl Indonesia Australia; s/d 35,000/50,000Rp) About 500m from the jetty, offers rooms with double beds and mosquito nets off a

---

THE LAST IRRAWADDY DOLPHINS

The freshwater Irrawaddy dolphin (*pesut*) was common all along Sungai Mahakam until the 1980s. Today there are around 90 left. They can generally be seen near Muara Pahu and, more frequently, en route to Muara Muntai from Muara Kaman. If you have a particular interest in seeing them, contact Budiono or Danielle Kreb at yk.rasi@gmail.com.

---

central dining area. The airy common space has wall-to-wall windows for superior views.

ℹ Getting There & Away

Tanjung Isuy is not on the *kapal biasa* route from Samarinda. Chartering a *ces* from Muara Muntai (250,000Rp, 1½ to two hours) is the easiest way to get here. A public *ces* to Muara Muntai leaves daily in the early morning (from 75,000Rp, depending on number of passengers). You can charter a *ces* direct to Kota Bangun (500,000Rp, three hours), then catch a bus and be in Samarinda or Balikpapan that night. In dry season, Tanjung Isuy is 30 minutes by *kijang* or *ojek* from Mancong.

MANCONG

For optimum jungle drama Mancong is best reached by boat on the Ohong river, meandering past monitor lizards, sapphire-hued kingfishers, bulb-nosed proboscis monkeys and marauding macaques. The journey beneath towering banyan trees, their roots foraging like witches' fingers in the dark river, is as much a part of the experience as your arrival.

🛏 Sleeping

Mancong Longhouse   LONGHOUSE $
(Mancong; per person 50,000Rp) This exquisitely restored 1930s longhouse (no bedding, food or electricity), surrounded by wood-carved sentinels, is the centrepiece of the village. As in Tanjung Isuy, the locals oblige with welcome dances, available on request for 500,000Rp, and there's an interesting souvenir shop.

ℹ Getting There & Away

To visit Mancong charter a *ces* from Tanjung Isuy (500,000Rp return, about three to four hours each way) early in the morning. In the dry season, it's possible to travel to/from Tanjung Isuy by *ojek* (100,000Rp, 30 minutes).

MUARA PAHU

Lining one side of a big curve in the Mahakam, this town is known mainly for its proximity to the Irrawaddy dolphin. There's an extensive boardwalk, a good place for a stroll where you can also find warungs.

🛏 Sleeping

Pension Anna LOSMEN $
(s/d 50,000/100,000Rp) Two identical well-lit rooms in the front of a private home, near the bridge.

❶ Getting There & Around

You can charter *ces* around Muara Pahu for from one hour to all day (150,000Rp to 600,000Rp). It's also possible to combine dolphin-watching with transport to Maura Muntai or Tanjung Isuy (400,000Rp) via Sungai Baroh, an area rich with birds and monkeys, or to Melak (500,000Rp). Trained boatmen go slow for wildlife viewing, so travel times vary. *Kapal biasa* to/from Samarinda (80,000Rp, 12 hours) pass by in the early evening.

MELAK

Unlike other towns on the river, Melak is not defined by its waterfront. As you walk up the landing into town, and keep going, you could be anywhere in roadside Kalimantan, meaning generally unpleasant sprawl. This is primarily a coal-mining town, with a rough-and-ready aspect. From Dayak funeral rights to cockfights, you never know what you might run into. But there are a few souvenir shops, an ATM on Jl Tendean, and an internet cafe.

Sights around Melak include an orchid garden and some longhouses, but they require renting a car, the road is terrible and the sights themselves underwhelming. Best to continue on when transport allows.

🛏 Sleeping & Eating

You can find some decent seafood here, but the hotels are particularly unpleasant and very much alike – musty concrete boxes without a drop of character that we might not otherwise list. They are all near one another so, if you must, walk around and choose the least painful option. A much better idea: take this opportunity for a homestay on the river. It's roughing it in a different way, but it's cooler, prettier, cheaper, and far more educational.

Hotel Monita HOTEL $
(📞081 154 7316; Jl Dr Sutomo 76; r incl breakfast 150,000-330,000Rp; ❄) The best concrete box in town, but about 2km from the port. Often full with mining clients so book ahead.

Hotel Flamboyan HOTEL $
(📞0812 5323 1994; Jl A Yani; r with fan/air-con 80,000/130,000Rp; ❄) Offers private *mandi* with Western toilets, but definitely not flamboyant.

Penginapan Rahmat Abadi LOSMEN $
(📞0813 5023 2282; Jl Tendean; r 50,000Rp) Close to the pier, with fan-only rooms and shared bathrooms.

Ketapang INDONESIAN $
(Jl A Yani; mains 30,000Rp; ☉6-9pm) The town's most popular restaurant, with sizzling fried prawns, chicken and fish dishes. Opposite the boat landing.

Rumah Makan Jawah Indah SEAFOOD $
(Jl A Yani; mains 25,000-35,000Rp; ☉7am-9pm; 📶) Clean and cool seafood joint by the river.

FLOATING HOMESTAY

Mahakam river towns often contain floating houses, and the bank opposite Melak is lined with them. These are very basic homemade huts constructed on logs pulled from the river, logs which must be replaced every five years or so. In this unique environment, people go about living lives that are as recognisable as they are different. Children jump into the river to bathe before putting on their school uniforms. Their school bus is a canoe. Satellite dishes sit on top of roofs made from cast-off lumber. A homestay in this environment is very basic, as it involves sleeping on a mat and using the river outhouse, like everyone else. But at the same time it is a window on life that only opens this way. Sitting outside your floating house with a cup of coffee, watching river traffic at sunset, is a lasting memory.

Murni (📞no English 0813 5042 8447; Melak; r incl dinner & breakfast per person 50,000Rp), a *ces* taxi driver, offers a homestay in his floating house directly across from the harbour, with free pick up and return. Additional sightseeing trips are 200,000Rp.

ℹ Information

Ruma Pelangi (per hr 5000Rp; ⊗8am-10pm)
To find this Internet cafe, from the harbour turn left at intersection and go another 50m.

ℹ Getting There & Away

Boats leave for Samarinda daily between 11am and 2pm (120,000Rp, 15 hours, 325km). To/from Tanjung Isuy, charter a *ces* (600,000Rp, four hours). The *kapal biasa* to Tering departs at 2am (160,000Rp, five hours). A *ces* will cost 500,000Rp to 800,000Rp, depending on your negotiating skills. The daily bus to Samarinda (100,000Rp, nine hours) is a very uncomfortable ride.

TERING

A planned community deep in gold-mining country, Tering (140,000Rp, 24 hours from Samarinda) is sometimes the last stop for *kapal biasa*, depending on the water level. It's really two settlements straddling the river: **Tering Lama**, a Bahau Dayak village on the northern bank, and **Tering Baru**, a Malay village where the *kapal biasa* docks. The latter is an ordered grid of cottages that can be circumnavigated on foot in 15 minutes, but you'll want to pause at the highlight, a magnificent wooden **church** with intricate painted pillars and a bell tower supported by totem poles. A speedboat to Long Bagun is 300,000Rp per person.

LONG BAGUN
⎹🛏 Sleeping

[TOP CHOICE] **Penginapan Polewall**   LOSMEN $
(⌨081 350 538 997; r 50,000Rp) This mountain lodge with traditional furnishings is a breath of fresh air after the concrete boxes downriver. In fact, it is the best hotel on the Upper Mahakam. Rooms are small, and bathrooms shared, but a nice breeze on the porch keeps you outside, and there are warungs nearby. Turn right after you get off the boat.

TIONG OHANG

Divided by the Mahakam, Tiong Ohang is united by its creaking pedestrian suspension bridge, offering scenic views of the surrounding hills. This is the last stop before starting the second stage in the Cross-Borneo Trek, the hike across the Muller Range. Guides/porters are assembled here, although this should be done by a tour company. The trailhead is two hours upriver by *ces* (1,000,000Rp). In the past the Muller trek began another three hours further on, at scenic **Long Apari**, but the added expense, which is considerable this far upriver, now makes this impractical.

DON'T MISS

THE WAY TO BORNEO'S HEART

From Long Bagun you embark upon the most thrilling ride on the Mahakam, the longboat to **Tiong Ohang** (800,000Rp, four hours). You'll need to wait until the boat has enough passengers, or pay more. This serpentine adventure takes you through some spectacular gorges, with scenic waterfalls, ancient volcanic peaks and plenty of rapids to keep you bouncing around as the powerful boat strains against the current. Somewhere along this ride, surrounded by lush and dense primary growth forest, comes the uncanny realisation that you've entered the heart of Borneo.

Around four hours into the trip you'll pass **Data Dawai**, which has the only airport upriver from Samarinda. **Susi Air** (⌨0542 764 416; www.susiair.com; Jl Pupuk Raya 33) flies charters here from Samarinda on Sunday, Wednesday and Friday (800,000Rp), although this schedule is undoubtedly dynamic.

⎹🛏 Sleeping

Putra Apari   LOSMEN $
(r 60,000Rp) The only accommodation in town, and surprisingly hospitable. Typical losmen rooms have no fan and shared *mandi*, but a nice porch with a cross-breeze overlooks the main street. Small shops and warungs nearby.

The Muller Mountains

The second stage of the larger Cross-Borneo Trek (p219), the journey from Tiong Ohang across the Muller Mountains to Tanjung Lokan (or vice versa) is a very different experience from what precedes it. This is neither a cultural tour nor a wildlife-spotting expedition. In fact, views of any kind are scarce. This is a jungle trek, and a very difficult one, whose primary purpose is to get to the other side. It can also be dangerous if you are not prepared. The trailside grave of a Dutchman who died in 2011 after hitting his head in a fall reinforces this fact.

The trek requires five days of walking steadily eight hours a day. Most people do it in seven days or more. There are several bare campsites along the way, but otherwise you're following a narrow path – if that – through a green maze, with the occasional need for the *mandau* (machete). You are also constantly crossing the same river switchbacks. In the beginning the fords are ankle deep, but as you get further downstream they become chest high. The mountains themselves are an anticlimax, as a pass makes crossing over them far easier than you'd expect. The leeches are not to be underestimated, however. Even with the proper protection, it is difficult to keep them out. The walk from breakfast to lunch will typically yield 20-or so small travellers on your shoes. They pose no danger, apart from slightly itchy bites, but they are high on the disgusting index, particularly after they have gorged themselves on your blood, at which point they are the length of a thumb.

The journey should be organised by a tour company such as De' Gigant Tours (p225) in Samarinda or Kompakh (p249) in Putussibau, who will send a guide with you upriver. In turn, this guide will arrange for local porters and guides near the trailhead (eg Tiong Ohang). One of the more interesting parts of the journey is watching these forest people trek, sometimes walking barefoot. Armed with *sumpit* (blowgun) and spear, and carrying homemade rattan packs, they move through difficult undergrowth as if on a footpath, hopping from wet stone to mossy rock with the sure-footedness of a mountain goat. Campsites are put up with the clever use of sticks and machete, without any modern gear except for a tarp. Cooking is done over an open fire.

All things considered, the experience hasn't changed much since George Muller first crossed his namesake range in 1825. While that first trek ended with the locals cutting off Muller's head, the primary risk today is breaking a leg or merely twisting an ankle so far from outside help. To that end, heed all the precautions, and ensure that your tour company will as well, prior to departure.

The Muller Trek is a horizontal Everest. You tackle it for the same reasons you climb. And when you succeed, it is both a lifetime memory and a noteworthy achievement. Very few Westerners have crossed from one side of Borneo to the other. But with the proper precautions in place, it is now entirely possible to do so.

Kutai National Park

This park is a disappointment. The only reason to come here is if you want to see a wild orangutan and have no chance to do so anywhere else. The park's once-vast acreage, long the target of natural-resource exploitation, has now dwindled to 10km of trails,

---

MULLER TREK SAFETY REQUIREMENTS

» Choose a professional local tour company. Do not even think of organising this yourself.

» Wear proper shoes. When it rains in the forest, the trail changes dramatically. What was a walk across leaves on solid ground becomes a slog across leaves on mud. In these conditions the locals wear a rubber version of a football cleat, with six spikes. Real football cleats would do fine, although you will have to wear them wet, as you cannot afford to take your shoes off and put them on again at every ford.

» Wear gloves to protect your hands from thorns.

» Wear proper leech protection. The only full solution here is a pair of spandex pants, such as cyclists wear. Otherwise expect many leech bites.

» Be firm about setting the pace at which you walk. Local guides and porters are not always aware of the difference between their skill level and your own. It is also in their interest to get across and back as soon as possible. Be sure to spread walking hours evenly among the days of the journey.

» Do not trek at night. Locals have no problem with this, but it greatly magnifies the risk, particularly if it is raining.

» Ensure that someone in your party has first-aid training and a first-aid kit.

» Bring 10 days' worth of food. If there is a problem midway, you'll need enough to last until someone walks to the nearest village and returns with help.

helping to concentrate its wildlife, so sightings are nearly assured (particularly if you call ahead, so the ranger can find one). The best time is April to August, when fruit is on the trees.

Access is gained by entering a foul river next to a sewage treatment facility, with a huge pipe pumping wastewater directly into it. You then follow this upstream in a canoe for half an hour until you reach Camp Kakap, the park's lodge, located on an otherwise attractive bend. Do not attempt this at night, even if asked to do so: the combination of an overloaded canoe with gunwales inches from the waterline, large logs hurtling downstream and no flotation devices, is a recipe for disaster. The lodge is rundown and basic, with bare rooms and a communal squat toilet. The trails need maintenance too. The picture is completed by the local gas exploration crews cutting through the forest in their grey jumpsuits.

To get here, take a bus from Samarinda to Sangatta (30,000Rp, three hours) and a taxi to Kantordesa Kabo Jaya (Kabo) where one of the rangers, **Udin** (☑081 3464 17675) or **Mr Supliani** (☑081 3463 48803), will meet you. Be sure to call ahead so they can organise your permit. The boat ride is 300,000Rp return. Park permits are 15,000Rp. Half-day treks cost 100,000Rp, full-day treks 200,000Rp.

Wehea Forest

Compared to Kutai, Wehea is an extraordinary breath of fresh air. This is the rainforest as you imagined it to be, in all its primordial glory. From atop its lone watchtower, you look over misty mountains that take you back to another Earth. The forest is home to many of Borneo's most interesting species, including the clouded leopard, sun bear, Storm's stork, grizzled langur, Bornean gibbon and orangutan. To date, 82 mammal species have been documented, of which 22 are vulnerable or endangered. Having said that, this is raw rainforest with few trails, making wildlife spotting difficult, and a good local guide essential.

Surprisingly, there is an excellent wooden lodge built by WWF, beautifully situated on a rushing river bend, with a generator, space for 20 people in private rooms, and a waterfall. The sounds of the forest and the river are priceless here. It takes some doing to arrange a stay, however, as the lodge is not permanently staffed. On the other hand, that's why the forest exists in such a pristine state and why it is such a great opportunity to visit now, as an incongruous helicopter pad attests: the US embassy flies in VIPs from Jakarta.

Wehea is not a national park, but a 38,000-hectare forest protected by *adat* (traditional law), a different conservation model spearheaded by Ledjie Taq, leader of the Wehea Dayak. The forest is patrolled by *petkuq mehuey* (forest guardians), a cadre of 35 to 40 rangers who keep it free from illegal activities such as poaching and logging. Their cause is assisted by Integrated Conservation (www.integratedconservation.org), a small and highly dedicated NGO run by Brent Loken and Sheryl Gruber, who have placed 75 photo traps on various wildlife trails to document the forest's biodiversity. See the results on the website.

So how do you visit? There are two ways. At time of research Integrated Conservation was nearing completion of a new conservation centre in the small village of Nehas Liah Bing, which will serve as the gateway to the forest. It is the first new longhouse to be built in many years, with modern facilities such as solar power and internet access, and three guest rooms. The centre will provide information on the forest, register visitors and arrange visits, including transport, food, lodging and guides drawn from the *petkuq mehuey*. Prices are still being established, but advance enquires may be made by email (info@integratedconservation.org).

Getting to Nehas Liah Bing is no small feat, however. First you must get to Muara Wahau, either by driving up from Sangatta by 4WD, or taking the bus (150,000Rp, three times daily). Either way it is six or seven hours on a notoriously bad road, one of the worst in Kalimantan. However, this *Top Gear* adventure has its rewards, at least in a 4WD, and the last two hours are very scenic. In Muara Wahau you can overnight in basic **Hotel Aldi** (☑0819 9915 7970; Muara Wahau; r 50,000rP-150,000Rp), which offers clean rooms with en suite *mandi*. To get to Nehas Liah Bing, take the main road from here to Berau, but keep straight when it curves to the right. Turn right on a small dirt road exactly 2km later, just past a post office (*kantor pos*). Continue on for 200m and follow the road as it curves to the left. After another 300m you'll see the Wehea Conservation Center (also referred to locally as the 'kantor

PM') on your left. At least one day's advance notice of your arrival is key to avoid delays. Centre staff can also arrange a day trip to two interesting limestone caves at Kombeng and Gua Maria (250,000Rp-400,000Rp).

Once your visit is arranged, you must still get to the forest. This requires a 2½-hour drive from Nehas Liah Bing down remote logging roads, which may be impassable during the wet season (during our research trip a flash flood came in the car doors). This last leg creates a welcome sense of separation from the world, heightening your anticipation. You. are really heading into the wild.

The other way to access Wehea Forest is to purchase a package tour from De'Gigant Tours (p225), the only regular provider of this itinerary. A four-day all-inclusive trip for two or three people, including round-trip transport from Balikpapan, is 6,372,000Rp. Compare rates, access and expertise with the above alternative. De'Gigant frequently bundles Wehea with a trip to the Derawan Archipelago, combining jungle and reef in one itinerary. This involves coming down to Wehea from Berau, avoiding the drive from Sangatta.

Berau

☎0554 / POP 52,000

Berau's new international airport has made this flat riverside town the first stop en route to the Derawan Archipelago. Another reason to come here is not readily apparent.

Sights

Museum Batiwakkal MUSEUM
(Gunung Tabur Kraton; admission by donation; ⏲8am-5.30pm Tue-Thu, 8am-1pm Sat & Sun) An eclectic collection of sultan-obilia.

Sleeping & Eating

Berau is saturated with overpriced concrete-box hotel rooms. There is little escape. Even worse, the rooms are often full, taken by mining workers. Best to move on if possible.

Hotel Sederhana HOTEL $$
(☎21353; Jl P Antasari 471; r incl breakfast 280,000-365,000Rp; ❄📶) The deluxe rooms here are the best in town, but nothing to write home about. Some renovations were under way at time of research.

Hotel Berau Plaza HOTEL $$
(☎23111; Jl P Antasari; r incl breakfast 297,000-440,000Rp; ❄) Rooms here are clean and have high ceilings, Western en suites, TV and air-con, but are crippled by lack of light. VIP1 rooms are best.

Hotel Kartika HOTEL $
(☎21379; Jl P Antasari; r 140,000-200,000Rp; ❄) Cheap but rough: these concrete cubes are dark and badly need paint.

De Bunda Cafe BAKERY $
(☎21305; Jl Antasari 5; dessert 5000Rp; ⏲7am-8pm) Chocolate and sponge cakes, iced coffees, fruit shakes and fresh spring rolls. Watch the morning rush hour alfresco from under an umbrella.

Sari Ponti Restaurant CHINESE $
(Jl Durian II 35; mains from 20,000Rp; ⏲8am-9pm) The local Chinese favourite: clean, well-lit, attentive staff, reliable food.

Warung Asri INDONESIAN $
(Jl A Yani; mains 15,000-20,000Rp; ⏲7am-9pm) Overlooking the riverfront, this friendly nook does classic warung fare well. Good choice for lunch.

Entertainment

BP Club CLUB
(Jl Isa; ⏲7pm-2am) The most popular nightclub in the city.

Information

Arabic Net (Jl Niaga I; per hr 5000Rp; ⏲6am-5pm) Private cubicles.

BNI Bank (Jl Maulana) Foreign exchange.

THM Travel (☎21238; Jl Niaga II) English-speaking staff help with flights and transport in the Derawan Archipelago.

Getting There & Away

See Getting There & Around in the Derawan Archipelago section for information on reaching Berau from there.

Air

Batavia Air (☎26777; Hotel Derawan Indah, Jl Panglima Batur 396)

Kalstar (☎21007; Jl Maulana 45)

Sriwijaya Air (☎202 8777; Jl Pemuda 50)

Trigana (☎202 7885; Jl Tendean 572)

Bus & Kijang

The **bus terminal** (Jln H Isa) is just south of the market on *angkot* routes. Buses to Tanjung Batu (50,000Rp, two hours) drop you off at the dock,

Berau

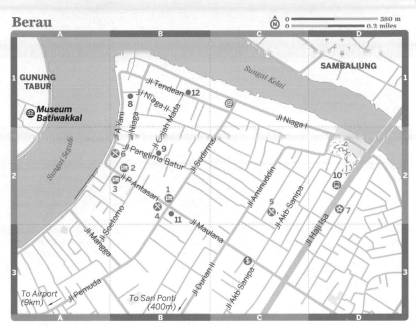

from where you pick up a speedboat to Derawan Island.

Kijang gather across from the terminal and demand a minimum of four passengers. Buy multiple seats to leave faster. Destinations include Tanjung Batu (60,000Rp, two hours), Tanjung Selor (70,000Rp, 2½ hours) and Samarinda (250,000Rp, 14 to 18 hours).

ℹ Getting Around

Taxis to the airport (9km) cost 50,000Rp. *Angkot* cost 3000Rp. River crossings by canoe cost 3000Rp; charters cost 50,000Rp per hour.

Derawan Archipelago

Occupying a large area of ocean east of Berau, the Derawan Archipelago consists of 31 named islands, of which the most significant to travellers are Derawan, Maratua, Sangalaki, Kakaban, Nabucco and Nunukan. This archipelago is unique in Kalimantan. It offers the chance to explore some classic tropical isles, including a huge atoll, and enjoy some of the best scuba diving there is. It's also very hard to get around (although it can be done), so it pays to think through your itinerary very carefully and give yourself plenty of time. Seas are rough in January and February, limiting diving.

Berau

◎ Top Sights

    Museum Batiwakkal A1

⬚ Sleeping

    1 Hotel Berau Plaza B2
    2 Hotel Kartika B2
    3 Hotel Sederhana B2

✕ Eating

    4 De Bunda Cafe B2
    5 Sari Ponti Restaurant C2
    6 Warung Asri B2

✪ Entertainment

    7 BP Club D2

ℹ Information

    8 THM Travel B1

ℹ Transport

    9 Batavia Air....................................... B2
    10 Bus Terminal D2
    11 Kalstar B2
    12 Trigana B1

ℹ Getting There & Around

There is no regularly scheduled public transport in the Derawan Archipelago. Chartered speedboats for Pulau Derawan leave from the dock at

FLIGHTS FROM BERAU

DESTINATION	COMPANY	COST (RP)	DURATION	FREQUENCY
Balikpapan	Trigana, Sriwijaya Air, Batavia Air	500,000	45min	5 daily
Banjarmasin	Trigana	811,000	2hr	daily
Nunukan	Kalstar	740,000	1hr	daily
Pangkalan Bun	Trigana	175,000	5½hr	Mon, Thu, Sat
Samarinda	Kalstar	635,000	45min	3 daily
Solo	Trigana	203,000	4hr	daily
Surabaya	Sriwijaya Air, Batavia Air	860,000	3hr	daily
Tarakan	Kalstar	378,000	30min	daily

Tanjung Batu, a coastal town two hours' drive from Berau. The 20-minute ride is 250,000Rp for the boat, which seats five. Ask to be dropped off near your hotel. Chartering to other islands is expensive for an individual traveller, but of course decreases when divided among a group. A four-hour return trip from Derawan to Sangalaki and Kakaban is 1,500,000Rp. From Tanjung Batu to Nabucco costs 3,250,000Rp return. Enquire about specifics at the speedboat dock, and take your driver's mobile phone number for future reference.

Nabucco Island Resort operates a fast shuttle from the centre of Berau to Nabucco (1,450,000Rp return, three hours), departing on Wednesdays and Saturdays, returning Tuesdays and Fridays. Depending on the tide, this boat can also drop off passengers at Derawan, midway to the mainland. This is the quickest way to get to the outer islands. Call for reservations.

The cheapest, and slowest, way to get between islands is by *tok-tok*, a local open fishing boat with a noisy little engine. You can arrange this in any village, just aware of the time involved, as you may be bobbing around in the sun for hours (eg Berau to Maratua is eight hours). Having said that, it is a fun way to get between nearby islands, like Nabucco and Maratua (50,000Rp).

At time of research an airport was under construction on Maratua, projected to open in 2014. This will make the outer islands much more accessible. So go now.

PULAU DERAWAN

The closest and best known of the islands, Derawan is also overbuilt and increasingly dirty. With a sandy main street lined with budget restaurants and hotels, it has long been a backpacker magnet, and this is part of its attraction. There are fascinating, amiable people wandering the streets, many of whom have been travelling for months or even years, providing many opportunities to swap stories over a few beers. Another attraction is the excellent new Derawan Dive Lodge (not to be confused with Derawan Dive Resort, which has seen better days). However, tourism has definitely taken hold and the local reef is degraded; if you're looking for more idyllic surroundings, consider Maratua. Beware of stingrays when walking at low tide.

🏃 Activities

Derawan Dive Lodge   DIVING

(☎0878 4646 2413; www.derawandivelodge.com; ❄) The best dive centre on the island is clearly this brand-new operation, with two fast dive boats reaching Maratua, Sangalaki and Kakaban. A full day diving Derawan (up to three dives) is US$115; a dive trip to Maratua, Kakaban and Sangalaki is US$165. Lodging packages available.

🛏 Sleeping & Eating

TOP CHOICE **Derawan Dive Lodge**   HOTEL $$$

(☎0878 4646 2413; www.derawandivelodge.com; s/d incl breakfast US$80/95) This is the only upscale place to stay on Pulau Derawan, and very well done. Located on the edge of town, it has its own private beach and 10 comfortable, individually designed rooms, with a cosy outdoor cafe. If you want to combine a dive holiday with some island life, this is your top choice in the archipelago. Full board US$20, airport transfer US$50.

TOP CHOICE **Pelangi Guesthouse**   LOSMEN $$

(☎0813 4780 7078; r 200,000-300,000Rp; ❄) Derawan has many losmen built out on docks, but this is the best one, offering colourful en suite rooms with private verandahs over the sea, a basic cafe/restaurant, and sea turtles for free.

Lestari I
LOSMEN $

(☎0813 4722 9636; Pulau Derawan; r 75,000-150,000Rp; ❄) Imagine a longhouse on a pier and you have this pleasant losmen, with colourful verandahs, some with air-con. The owner will take you to neighbouring islands for 700,000Rp.

April's Restaurant
INDONESIAN $

(☎0813 5058 2483; mains 25,000Rp; ⏱7am-8pm) Wedged between Danakan and Lestari 1, guacamole-green April's dishes up reliable Indonesian favourites.

If Pelangi is full, there are three similar waterfront losmen nearby: **Sari** (☎0813 4653 8448; r incl breakfast with fan/air-con 175,000/225,000Rp) has sizeable adjoining rooms and nice end units; **Dira** (☎0813 4795 5950; r with fan/air-con 150,000/200,000Rp) has a restaurant overlooking the water; **Danakan** (☎086 8121 6143; r with fan/air-con 150,000/250,000Rp; ❄) has large baths but suffers from a rough entrance.

PULAU MARATUA

Maratua is an enormous U-shaped atoll almost completely untouched by tourism. There are two fishing villages at opposite ends with a pleasant surprise in between: a nicely paved path through the jungle some 15km in length. The tidy village of **Bohesilian**, directly across from Nabucco Island, is the best base, with tightly packed cottages on the edge of the jungle, pleasant sea views, a little market, cheerful residents and several homestays. **Senterbung**, near the pier, offers a front room with double bed for 200,000Rp, including three meals, but look at a few and decide. **Bohebekut**, the village at the other end of the trail, is poorer and the beach is dirty.

For backpackers with time on their hands, Maratua is a slice of heaven. Hire a scooter for a day (150,000Rp) and explore to your heart's content, passing over bridges between islets, heading down long jetties and swimming in the lagoon. Like Kakaban, there is a stingless freshwater jellyfish pond, although it's difficult to reach. The island's striking dorsal ridge is also begging for exploration. Add a special someone and a visit here could easily stretch into days...

NABUCCO & NUNUKAN ISLAND RESORTS

These two small islets in the mouth of the Maratua atoll are owned by Extra Divers, a German dive resort operator with eight properties worldwide. As such, the upscale clientele is about 80% German and Austrian, although the managers speak English. Both islands are run by the same professional couple, Rainer and Evelyne, each well schooled in hospitality. Some visitors split their time between islands: an excellent idea.

🛏 Sleeping

TOP CHOICE **Nunukan Island Resort**
RESORT $$$

(☎0542 594 655; www.nunukanislandresort.com; r per person incl full board s/d €127/190) This island is surprisingly different from its sister. The resort is built on the blackened remains of a reef that resembles a razor-sharp lava field. All common areas are up on stilts, with boardwalks between them, a design that is uniquely attractive. The private beachfront bungalows are very luxurious, with four-poster platform beds and inventive showers with one-way windows on the sea. The reclining sofa on the large porch will hold you for hours, particularly when the stars are out. There is also a small spa with a dipping pool perfectly situated at the base of a long walkway leading to another islet, yet to be developed. A dive is €32.

TOP CHOICE **Nabucco Island Resort**
RESORT $$$

(☎0542 593 635; www.nabuccoislandresort.com; r per person incl full board s/d €127/190; ❄)

KALIMANTAN DERAWAN ARCHIPELAGO

DERAWAN DIVING HIGHLIGHTS

Pulau Sangalaki Famous for its manta rays, which are present throughout the year. Sea turtles also abound.

Pulau Kakaban Big pelagic fish and a cave dive offshore; a rare lake full of nonstinging jellyfish inland.

Pulau Maratua Known for 'the channel' frequented by big pelagic fish, eagle rays and huge schools of barracuda. Occasional thresher sharks.

Pulau Derawan Small creatures draw photographers: ghostpipe fish, frogfish, harlequin shrimp, jawfish, blue-ring octopus.

When you get off the dock at Nabucco, the sign says 'Welcome to Paradise' and this charming little island really does fit the bill. Located in the Maratua lagoon, it has interesting views in all directions and well-kept parklike grounds with swaying palms, boardwalks and white beaches, all of which can be circumnavigated in 10 minutes. The large, varnished duplex bungalows come with mosquito nets and each one faces the sea, with shared porches. The Asian fusion food is outstanding. Almost everyone is here for the diving, but a snorkeller would fit right in. Dives are €41 each, and courses are available.

PULAU KAKABAN & PULAU SANGALAKI

These two undeveloped islands beyond Maratua are begging for exploration. Pulau Sangalaki is pretty and unspoiled, all forest and deserted beaches, with a sea-turtle nursery (www.turtle-foundation.org) open to visitors. Pulau Kakaban is known for its freshwater lake full of non-stinging jellyfish. Travellers speak highly of the eerie experience of swimming among them.

NORTH KALIMANTAN

☑0551

North Kalimantan is a brand-new province carved out of the top of East Kalimantan. It includes the island of Nunukan (not to be confused with the one in the Derawan Archipelago), Sembakung, Bulungan, Tanjung Selor, Tarakan, Krayan, Kayan Mentarang and the Apokayan. This area includes some of the most pristine forests on Borneo, making it one of the last frontiers for hardcore jungle trekking. Only a handful of people have crossed the vast jungle of Kayan Mentarang.

The most common reason for travellers to pass through North Kalimantan is on their way to or from Malaysian Borneo. At time of research the direct ferry from Tawau (Sabah) to Tarakan wasn't operating, but there is a speedboat service from Tawau to Tarakan (140,000Rp, four hours) via Nunukan (two hours) where you switch boats. The boat leaves Tawau at noon, but show up an hour early to clear immigration and ensure a seat. Save five ringgits for the terminal fee. The quicker but more expensive route is the daily MASwings flight from Tawau to Tarakan (550,000Rp-800,000Rp).

To get from Tarakan to Berau/Derawan Archipelago, take an early morning boat to Tanjung Selor (80,000Rp) and then a car from the harbour (55,000Rp to 75,000Rp). For air tickets see **Angkasa Express** (☑30288; fax 24848; Jln Yos Sudarso, Hotel Tarakan Plaza) or **Derawan Travel** (☑35599; fax 35799; Jln Mulawarman 21, Hotel Paradise). The **immigration office** (☑21242; Jln Sumatra) has information on visas. If you need to stay over, **Hotel Bungamuda** (☑21349; Jl Yos Sudarso 7, Tarakan; r 55,000-132,000Rp; ✴✱) is a good budget option, while **Swiss-Belhotel Tarakan** (☑21133; www.swiss-belhotel. com; Jln Mulawarman 15; r incl breakfast 440,000-594,000Rp; ✴) is an upscale bargain.

WEST KALIMANTAN

Pontianak

☑0561 / POP 550,000

Standing astride the equator, Pontianak is a gateway to all points of the compass: Putussibau (east), Singkawang (north), Sukadana (south) and Natuna (west). Commerce keeps things buzzing, but the city is otherwise a grey jumble, brightened only by some inexpensive luxury hotels and lukewarm sights.

◉ Sights

Taman Alun Kapuas   PARK
(Jl Rahadi Usman) This riverside park swells with families, hawkers and food stalls at night.

Istana Kadriyah   MUSEUM
(admission by donation; ☺8.30am-4pm) If you're up for an outing that will show you a bit of the town, the leaking palace of Pontianak's first sultan, now a half-hearted museum, lies on the east bank of Sungai Kapuas next to his mosque, **Mesjid Abdurrahman**. Get there by canoe taxi (2500Rp) from the foot of Jl Mahakam.

Vihara Bodhisatva Karaniya Metta TEMPLE
(Jl Sultan Muhammad) KalBar's oldest Chinese temple (1679) is a sensory feast.

Museum Provinsi Kalimantan Barat   MUSEUM
(West Kalimantan Provincial Museum; Jl A Yani; admission 1000Rp; ☺8am-2.30pm Tue-Thu, 8-11am & 1-2.30pm Fri, 8am-2pm Sat-Sun, closed Mon) A nice succinct overview of local culture, with English placards, including a longhouse,

NATUNA ARCHIPELAGO

If you're up for some real off-the-beaten track exploration, you'd be hard-pressed to find a better opportunity than this. Located northwest of Kalimantan, the Natuna Archipelago contains 272 islands, of which Pulau Natuna is the largest. They include some spectacular landscapes of towering volcanic domes, white sandy beaches and colourful coral reefs. **Orion Expeditions** (www.orionexpeditions.com), a high-end speciality cruise line, has visited the islands several times in recent years: a very good sign. The archipelago is not part of West Kalimantan but in the newly formed Riau Islands province, which includes the Anambas Archipelago and Batam.

Trigana has recently begun air service from Pontianak to Pulau Natuna. Flights leave twice weekly (754,000Rp). Start with a room in Natuna's **Central Hotel** (📞0819 9120 1133; r 200,000-350,000Rp) where owner Yuli speaks English. Simple fishing boats can be hired to move between islands. The rest is up to you.

shop and restaurant (mains 15,000Rp to 35,000Rp). Take a red or pink *opelet* (intracity minibus) south along Jl Yani.

Patung Khatulistiwa   MONUMENT
(Equator Monument; Jl Khatulistiwa; ⊙8.30am-4.30pm, closed Mon) If you desire to stand astride the equator, here's your formal chance. You may even get a certificate signed by the governor. Cross the river by ferry or bus and take Jl Khatulistiwa 1.6km northwest. The monument is roadside.

☞ Tours

Times Tours & Travel   TRAVEL AGENCY
(📞770 259; Jl Komyos Sudarso 6) Organises tours to Kapuas Hulu and beyond. Owner Iwan speaks excellent English and is super-responsive and very efficient. Call before visiting.

Borneo Access Adventurer   TRAVEL AGENCY
(📞081 2576 8066; www.borneoaccessadventurer.com; Jl Tanjung Harapan Gang HD Usman 46) West Borneo Tour Guide Association chairman Alex Afdhal knows the landscape and means well. Clarify your tour expectations with him.

🛏 Sleeping

TOP CHOICE Hotel Santika   HOTEL $$
(📞733 777; www.santika.com; Jl Diponegoro 46; r incl breakfast 360,000Rp; ✴@🛜🏊) If you can wangle one of its steep discounts (around 40% – included in price quoted here), this contemporary business-leisure hotel is the best value in Kalimantan. The spacious rooms are very comfy, staff is as friendly as can be, the breakfast buffet excellent, and the public spaces top-notch, including a winning

spa. The nearby rooftop terrace, with pool and running water, offers an attractive setting for relatively inexpensive meals (if it's not raining). Tight budget? Splurge.

TOP CHOICE Aston Pontianak   HOTEL $$
(📞761 118; Jl Gajah Mada 21; r incl breakfast 518,000-658,000Rp) This island of luxury has all the amenities one needs to recover from a jungle trek, although the prices are higher than the competition's (ask for discounts). In the rooms, wood, leather and glass combine to form a sophisticated decor; the executive rooms are particularly superb. Beyond lies a big open lobby with glass elevator, and a swanky bar. The breakfast buffet with Western menu is enough to last you through the day. And the enormous RiverX entertainment complex will definitely perk you up at night.

Hosanna Inn   HOTEL $
(📞735 052; www.hosannainn.com; Jl Pahlawan 224/2; s/d incl breakfast 98,000/138,000Rp; ✴🛜) The city has no standout budget rooms, but the best are here, particularly room 205, which has windows and access to a public balcony. Room 307 is similar but has no balcony. The spiral staircase will test your tolerance for Bintang (an Indonesian beer).

Kartika Hotel   HOTEL $$
(📞734 401; fax 738 457; Jl Rahadi Usman 2; r incl breakfast 288,000-432,000Rp; ✴🛜) The quiet riverside location sets this hotel apart. The standard doubles are the best, particularly those on the river, as the more expensive the room, the worse value they are. The Panorama Restaurant is a plus; the fish farm in front is a question mark.

Pontianak

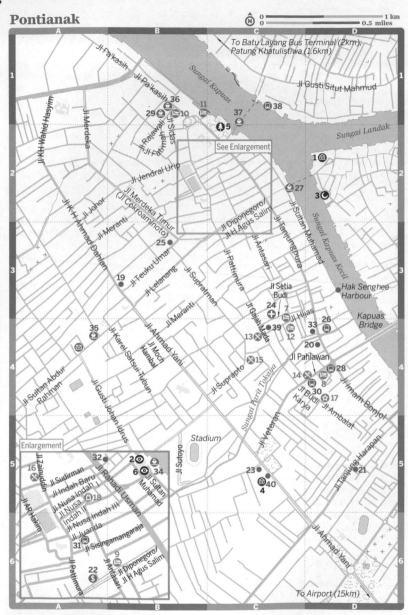

To Batu Layang Bus Terminal (2km);
Patung Khatulistiwa (1.6km)

Mess Hijas — HOTEL **$**

(📞081 256 960 03; Jl Hijas 106; s & d 75,000-
150,000Rp; ❄) Hidden behind a scooter dealer,
this hotel surprises with attractive wooden
design elements (in some rooms), hot water
and air-con. Find one with a window.

Hotel Surya — HOTEL **$**

(📞734 337; Jl Sidas 11A; r incl breakfast 150,000Rp;
❄@) Clean, basic concrete boxes with air-
con and private bathroom (squat toilet and
mandi).

Pontianak

KALIMANTAN PONTIANAK

✕ Eating

Warungs and stalls abound along Jl Diponegoro/H Agus Salim, Jl Pattimura, Jl Hijas and Jl Setia Budi. At night, new stalls sprout, particularly along Jl Gajah Mada.

 General Chef　　　CHINESE $
(cnr Jl Gajah Mada & Jl Pahlawan; mains from 20,000Rp; ☺10am-10pm) Conveniently located at the intersection of Gajah Mada and Pahlawan, this newcomer has raised the bar on local cuisine. Service is quick and efficient, the food creative and sophisticated, and the overall presentation excellent. Ever tried jellyfish?

TOP CHOICE **Somay Bandung**　　　INDONESIAN $
(Jl Zainuddin 15; mains 9000-16,000Rp; ☺lunch & dinner) Mobbed at lunch for the national version of *siomay* (steamed dough, potatoes, tofu, and cabbage drowned in peanut sauce), this restaurant has a great dose of local atmosphere, with benches arrayed beneath a large awning.

Café Corner　　　CAFE $
(Jl Gajah Mada; mains 20,000Rp; ☺7am-1am) This popular cafe on the corner of a city block is an excellent place to hang out, with coffee flowing from morning to night and, after jungle adventures, a refreshing dose of beer and European football. It's 150m north of Jl Suprapto intersection.

Restoran Hawaii　　　CHINESE $
(Jl Suprapto 16; mains 20,000-60,000Rp; ☺9.30am-9.30pm) Local Chinese-cuisine legend in a large banquet hall.

Panorama Restaurant　　　SEAFOOD $
(Jl Rahadi Usman; mains from 25,000Rp; ☺7am-11pm) Unique for its riverfront setting, this chicken and seafood spot in the Kartika Hotel is popular with local families.

☆ Entertainment

TOP CHOICE **Café Tisya**　　　LIVE MUSIC
(Jl Budi Karya; ☺7pm-2am) A fun and gentle nightspot occupying the open corner of a

city block, this is where you go to have a few Bintangs, enjoy some live music and meet the locals, from university students to an entire ship's crew.

🛍 Shopping

For general souvenirs, visit the crafts shops lining Jl Pattimura.

 Borneo Art Shop ANTIQUES
(☎0813 5227 7796; Jl Nusa Indah I; ☺9am-5pm) The name is misleading: come here to enter the world of exotic curios from around Borneo.

ℹ Information

Antya Tour (☎733 688; Jl Teuku Umar 62) Kijang and car-rental specialist.

Aria Tour (☎577 868; Jl Imam Bonjol, near Hotel Garuda) Good for airline tickets.

Haji Tunrung Star (Jl Diponegoro 155) Foreign-exchange broker.

Immigration Office (☎765 576)

Klinik Kharitas Bhakti (☎734 373; Jl Siam 153; ☺7.30am-9pm) Medical centre.

Main post office (Jl Sultan Abdur Rahman 49; ☺7.30am-9.30pm Mon-Sat, 8am-2pm Sun) Poste restante.

ℹ Getting There & Away

Air

Batavia Air (☎734 488; Jl Cokroaminoto 278A)

Garuda (☎734 986; Jl Rahadi Usman No 8A)

IAT (Indonesia Air Transport; ☎ext 212 Jakarta 021 8087 0668; airport)

Kalstar (☎739 090; Jl Tanjungpura 429)

Lion Air (☎706 661 11; airport)

MASwings (☎603 7843 3000 Malaysia; airport)

Sriwijaya Air (☎768 777; Jl Gajah Mada 70)

Trigana (☎749 090; Megamall, Jl Ahmad Yani)

Boat

Boats to Java leave from the main harbour on Jl Pak Kasih, north of the Kartika Hotel. Ferry companies:

Dharma Lautan Utama (☎765 021; Jl Pak Kasih 42F)

Pelni (☎748 124; www.pelni.co.id; Jl Sultan Abdur Rahman 12)

Prima Vista (☎761 145; Jl Pak Kasih 90B)

The jetboat to Ketapang leaves from Hak Senghee Harbour on Jl Barito; air-con class is worth the extra fare. If no one is present, call **Bahari Express** (☎760 820) or **Poly Express** (☎741 536).

Longboats (☎Dedek for reservations 9.30am boat 0856 5440 9299, Jony for reservations 8.30am boat 0813 4598 2328, Surya for reservations 9.30am boat 0813 5213 4440) to Sukadana leave from behind the **Kapuas Indah Building** at 8.30am and 9.30am.

There are no scheduled passenger boats upriver to Putussibau, but travel agents may be able to find a speedboat going to Sanggau. If time is not an issue, try finding passage by *bandung*, a combination freighter and general store that can take several days to a month for the 800km journey. Price negotiable.

Bus

It is wise to consult a travel agent regarding the complex landscape of bus and Kijang options.

WORTH A TRIP

VILLA BUKIT MAS, SINGKAWANG

The **Villa Bukit Mas** (☎0562 333 5666; Singkawang; s/d 560,000/600,000Rp) is a sophisticated hotel and restaurant complex that sits on top of a hill overlooking the city of Singkawang, three hours north of Pontianak. With excellent rooms, fine dining, swimming and panoramic views, this establishment reaches surprising heights of quality as well as altitude. The rooms at the very top are the best in the city, with wooden floors, private porches and a refined seclusion. The restaurant has grand open-air seating and specialises in *shabu shabu* (59,000Rp for four), a Japanese fondue. Reserve ahead for weekends.

Meanwhile, the largely Chinese city below feels at times like Shanghai circa 1930. There are some classic shophouses, a vibrant street market (Jl Diponegoro), rickshaws and Chinese temples. A new fairy-tale mosque – Mesjid Raya – has arisen, too, dressed in green. The people hardly ever see tourists, so Western visitors will encounter many new friends, none of whom speak any English at all. This is travel at its most authentic, with the past in the valley below and the future growing atop the surrounding hills. Buses leave for Singkawang daily from Pontianak (35,000Rp). A **taxi** (☎0821 4876 9999) direct from Pontianak Airport is 120,000Rp.

TRANSPORT FROM PONTIANAK

Air

DESTINATION	COMPANY	COST (RP)	DURATION	FREQUENCY
Jakarta	Sriwijaya Air, Garuda, Lion Air, Batavia Air	650,000	1½hr	daily
Ketapang	Kalstar, IAT	365,000-509,000		
Kuching	MASwings	765,000	45min	daily
Kuching	Batavia Air	765,000-980,000	45min	Tue, Thu, Sun
Natuna	Trigana	754,000	1½hr	Wed, Fri
Pangkalan Bun	Kalstar	450,000-720,000	1½hr	daily
Putussibau	Kalstar	814,000	1hr	daily
Singapore	Batavia Air	1,500,000	1½hr	Mon, Fri
Sintang	Kalstar, IAT	476,000-700,000	45min	3 weekly
Yogyakarta	Batavia Air	1,100,000	1½hr	daily

Boat

DESTINATION	COMPANY	COST (RP)	DURATION (HR)	FREQUENCY
Jakarta	Pelni, Prima Vista	170,000	36	weekly
Ketapang (jetboat)	Bahari Express, Poly Express	170,000	8	daily
Natuna	Pelni	140,000	28	weekly
Semarang	Pelni, Prima Vista, Dharma Lautan	216,000	40	weekly
Sukadana (longboat)		175,000	4	daily 8am/9am
Surabaya	Pelni	259,000	44	weekly

Bus

DESTINATION	COST (RP)	DURATION (HR)	FREQUENCY
Brunei	600,000	25	daily 7am, 9pm
Entikong	60,000	9	daily
Kuching	170,000-240,000	9	daily 7am, 9pm
Putussibau	200,000-300,000	16-18	daily
Sambas	45,000	5	daily
Sanggau	53,000	6	daily
Singkawang	35,000	3	daily

For Singkawang, Sambas, Sanggau and the Entikong border crossing use the Batu Layang bus terminal north of town. For air-con express buses to Kuching see **Bintang Jaya** (☑659 7402; Jl Tanjungpura 310A) and the companies on Jl Sisingamangaraja. **Damri** (☑744 859; Jl Pahlawan 226/3) also serves Brunei. Buses to Putussibau via Sintang leave from the Kapuas Indah Building.

Car

Travel agencies can arrange a car with driver for 450,000Rp per day.

🛈 Getting Around

Airport taxis cost 90,000Rp to town (15km). *Opelet* (2500Rp) routes converge around Jl Sisingamangaraja. Becaks (bicycle rickshaws) are available, but a dying breed. Taxis are unmetered and scarce. Some hotels have Kijangs standing by; fares for these 'hotel taxis' start at 10,000Rp.

Sukadana

☏ 0534 / POP 15,000

After Pontianak, Sukadana is a most welcome surprise, all the more so because few people seem to know about it. Half the fun is just getting there, via a wonderful four-hour river trip by longboat from Pontianak. After travelling down the Kapuas, all bets are off as to what the route actually is, as no published map reflects it. You enter a tributary which eventually broadens into a lake, **Warah Kubu**, full of attractive jungle-covered hills and various islands. Along the way you stop for lunch at a scenic riverside warung serving world-class fried chicken. Then you're back in the region known as **Teluk Air**, which contains a vast and largely uninhabited mangrove swamp. Finally you reach a broad bay on the South China Sea and skirt the coastline, passing **Batu Daya**, where a vertical wall of rock soars in the distance. Sukadana is hidden in a fold of this coastline. As you round a corner, its major landmark, the Makhota Kayong, appears suddenly, making you wonder how a huge hotel built on pilings over the water can exist this far from anywhere. You then enter a horseshoe-shaped bay with an attractive beach surrounded by rolling hills of green jungle. Add nearby Gunung Palung National Park and some offshore islands to explore, and you have the makings for an excellent getaway. The new BNI ATM adds the final essential element (accessible 8am to 3pm Monday to Friday, but knock and, reportedly, the 24-hour guard will let you in any time).

⊙ Sights

TOP CHOICE **Pulau Datok Beach**   BEACH

This is a well-kept town beach that feels far more exotic, as it is encircled by jungle hills and looks out on some alluring islands. There are two basic restaurants and a cart that sells fresh sugar cane (10am to 5pm Saturday and Sunday). More private beaches lie further along the coast; ask locally.

Juanta Island   ISLAND

There are several islands near Sukadana to explore, some with attractive beaches, of which Juanta is the most popular. A round trip costs around 350,000Rp for a slow boat, 600,000Rp for a speedboat; enquire at Sukadana Harbour.

🛏 Sleeping & Eating

Sukadana has one very interesting hotel and several budget digs of the concrete-box variety. For meals, the Mahkota and Anugrah

---

GUNUNG PALUNG: A PARK THAT'S HARD TO LOVE

With a large population of resident orangutans and diverse other wildlife, Gunung Palung National Park has a lot of potential that is sadly being squandered by poor management and rampant illegal logging (you may even hear chainsaws). The three tour companies that once provided entry have been whittled down to one, **Nasalis Tour and Travel** (☏ 0534 772 2701; http://gunungpalung.net; Jl Gajah Mada 24, Ketapang), which now controls the park for its own economic benefit, including some expensive tour packages that require at least one overnight stay. The company is a for-profit enterprise run by park administrators; outside guides are charged the tourist rate. The prices of these packages further include a transfer from Ketapang. Travellers who enter from Sukadana, which is much closer, report that a second price list appears when this important distinction is raised. Note Sukadana is vastly preferable to Ketapang as a gateway to the park. The latter adds to transport costs, has no tourism value of its own, and cuts out the wonderful longboat trip from Pontianak.

The easiest and least expensive package is a two-day, one-night return trip to Lubuk Baji. The posted price from Ketapang – 1,910,000Rp for two people, including a guide, meals and accommodation in a basic jungle lodge – drops to 1,350,000Rp from Sukadana. The trip entails a fairly gentle two-hour hike in and out. Once they get past park management, travellers enjoy this experience. Other options include homestays, canoeing and visiting the small **Cabang Panti** (http://people.bu.edu/orang) orangutan research station. For more information visit the **park office** (Jl Tangjungpura 41, ⊗8am-4pm Mon-Fri) in Sukadana or consult the Nasalis website; there is no separate park website, as there is no separate park...

(Jl Bhayangkara) hotels have decent restaurants, but **Satay** (Jl. Sungai Mengkuang), across from the ASRI clinic, is the local favourite.

TOP CHOICE **Mahkota Kayong Hotel** HOTEL $$
(☏772 2777; www.mahkotakayonghotel.com; Jl Irama Laut; r/ste 350,000/700,000Rp; ❄) This grand anomaly has an amusing personality all its own. Built on piles over the water, in a lovely if remote situation, it dwarfs the rest of the town's accommodation, but empties when its convention market dries up, leaving the staff in a situation comedy. The rooms are a bit pricey and beaten up by the sea air – do negotiate – but you come here for an interesting story, not an ironed duvet. Or hot water.

Penginapan Family LOSMEN $
(Jl Tanjungpura Sukadana; r with fan 50,000Rp, d/tw 175,000/200,000Rp) Definitely the nicest people you could ever rent a room from, this family provides free bikes to guests, solving your local transport problem and proving the name is no exaggeration.

ⓘ Getting There & Around

Longboats (☏Darwin for reservations 9.30am boat 0852 5207 6070, Indira for reservations 9.30am boat 0813 5207 0117, Untung for reservations 8.30am boat 0812 5613 3570) to Pontianak depart Sukadana harbour twice each morning (one-way 175,000Rp; ⊙departs 8.30am & 9.30am). The journey takes four hours. Sukadana can also be reached by bus or car from Ketapang, which has an airport, but the longboat trip is not to be missed. Tanjung Puting is reached by flying from Ketapang to Pangkalan Bun.

Sukadana is spread out, requiring transport. If you can't wangle a bike from Penginapan Family, the ASRI clinic can help you find a scooter. Otherwise don't be afraid to stick out your thumb.

Sungai Kapuas

Indonesia's longest river, Sungai Kapuas begins in the foothills of the Muller Range and snakes 1143km to the sea. Unlike the Mahakam, however, there is no *kapal biasa* to make your way upstream from Pontianak, nor are the views as good, as the forests of the lower Kapuas have been heavily logged and developed. Buses have replaced boats as the primary means of transport all the way to Putussibau, via unremarkable Sintang. Thus, for the traveller the primary area of interest lies upriver, in the area known as

ASRI TO THE RESCUE

Admirable **ASRI** (Alam Sehat Lestari; ☏0813 5246 6704; www.alamsehatlestari. org; Jl Sungai Mengkuang), an NGO based in Sukadana, is applying a unique lever against the logging in Gunung Palung: those communities who opt to conserve the forest are given access to affordable health and dental care. Patients are offered long-term payment options and allowed to use compost, handicrafts and organic vegetables to barter. Interested in participating? Six-week volunteer opportunities are available for medical and dental professionals, conservationists, engineers and other skilled tradespeople.

Kapuas Hulu (upper Kapuas), half of which is now a protected area.

PUTUSSIBAU
This lively river port town is the last stop for airlines and long-distance buses, the last ATMs and the launch point for excursions into the forests of Kapuas Hulu. There's a lively morning market along Jl Yani.

⌖ Tours

TOP CHOICE **Kompakh** ADVENTURE
(☏085 6500 2101; www.kompakh.org; Jl Kenanga Komp. Ruko Pemda 3D) This unique organisation should be your first stop upon entering Putussibau. A WWF ecotourism initiative, the folks here know everything about Kapuas Hulu and can arrange all sorts of tours, including Danau Sentarum National Park, longhouse visits, river cruising and jungle treks. This is one of two organisations in Kalimantan qualified to offer the Cross-Borneo Trek. Manager Hermas (hrmaring@yahoo.com) speaks fluent English – unique among guides in Putussibau.

🛏 Sleeping

TOP CHOICE **Mess Pemda** HOTEL $
(☏21010; Jl Merdeka 11; r 137,000-165,000Rp; ❄) Called 'Wisma Uncak Kapuas' by its sign outside, this government hostel offers surprisingly nice rooms, each with air-con, TV, Western toilet and *mandi,* arrayed around the central living area of a large single-level house. The well-lit rooms in front are best. Like it or not, there is no better value in

KALIMANTAN SUNGAI KAPUAS

Putussibau. From Jl A Yani, turn left on Jl Dahar and make two rights to Jl Merdeka.

Sanjaya Hotel
HOTEL $$

(☑21653; Jl Yos Sudarso 129; r incl breakfast 100,000-375,000Rp; ❄) The few deluxe rooms here, which line a refreshing hallway of contemporary design, are the only somewhat upmarket accommodation in town. However, the economy rooms are unlit tombs.

Aman Sentosa Hotel
HOTEL $

(☑21691; Jl Diponegoro 14; r 70,000-200,000Rp; ❄) It was once Putussibau's best hotel but now Aman Sentosa's rooms are battered from years of neglect and its car park has turned into a scrapyard.

✖ Eating & Drinking

Pandung Meranti
INDONESIAN $

(Jl Yos Sudarso; mains 12,000-15,000Rp) A big, blue, open warehouse full of polished wooden tables, this restaurant has both personality and excellent food, including barbecued chicken. Half the menu is given over to imaginative drinks, including killer milkshakes from tasty cappuccino to wacky avocado flavour. On a hot day, you could easily polish off several. In fact...

Pondok Fajar
PADANG $

(Jl Yos Sudarso; mains 5000-30,000Rp; ⊘6am-11pm) This Padang place packs 'em in for its buffet.

TOP CHOICE Cafetenda
CAFE

(milkshake 3000Rp; ⊘8am-3am) This new cafe near the bridge, located next to a ruined temple, has large, simple tables spread around a riverside park, making it a uniquely popular place to hang out, at all hours.

❶ Information

For internet access try popular Rifki Cafe on Jl Komyos Sudarso.

❶ Getting There & Around

Putussibau Airport is only served by **Kalstar** (☑0821 5202 2213), which has a daily flight to Pontianak at 1.15pm. Taxis from the airport (10km) cost 35,000Rp, if you can find one; *ojeks* cost 20,000Rp.

The local bus terminal is on Jl Diponegoro, near the market. Buses leave daily for Sintang at 6.30am (120,000Rp, 10 hours), from where you can connect to the Entikong border, and for Pontianak at 10am, noon and 2pm (economy/aircon 175,000/200,000Rp, 16 hours).

River boats use the pier on Sungai Kapuas east of the bridge. From Jl Merdeka, take any street south to the waterfront.

The only way to get around Putussibau is to hire a scooter (100,000Rp per day), as *angot* have gone away.

TANJUNG LOKAN & SUNGAI BUNGAN

For those coming across the Muller Range on the Cross-Borneo Trek, the first stop in Kapuas Hulu is the village of Tanjung Lokan, a small group of huts with a basic lodge (50,000Rp) located on Sungai Bungan, a tributary of the Kapuas. From here it is possible to travel all the way to Putussibau in one extraordinary seven-hour journey. But beware: while undoubtedly a welcome sight after several days walking in the jungle, this village is infamous for its fickle memory. Promises to numerous trekking companies have been made and never kept, sometimes within a half-hour period, and trekkers have been charged exorbitant rates for downriver passage. During our visit in May 2012 the local chief and his advisors agreed to price the trip to Putussibau at 1,000,000Rp per seat, up to 4,000,000Rp per fully chartered boat, with guides travelling free. This was set out in writing in the chief's logbook with all his advisors present. Travellers should reference this agreement if necessary.

WORTH A TRIP

DANAU SENTARUM NATIONAL PARK

If you have two days or more, this 132,000-hectare seasonal wetland area, which resembles the lakes area of the Mahakam, is begging for exploration. Surrounded by attractive mountains, it offers numerous islands, some intriguing villages, wildlife (including the red arowana, a trophy aquarium fish) and interesting boat journeys. Reach the park via minibus from Putussibau to **Lanjak** (85,000Rp, 3½ hours), where you can rent a boat and see the islands. Don't miss the newly renovated field station on **Pulau Tekaneng**, which has six rooms with shared baths (100,000Rp with meals), or the village of **Meli-au**, at the southern end of the lake, where you can find a basic homestay in a longhouse. For more information contact Kompakh (p249).

The canoe trip downriver is one you will never forget. It begins by tackling Sungai Bungan, the most thrilling stretch of water in Kalimantan. As the river picks up pace, you pass through roaring gorges knifing through the jungle – a beautiful setting. The canoe is crewed bow and stern with amazing skill, with the stern operator using the engine and steering at the bow done with a paddle. In this way you hurtle downstream, twisting and turning to avoid the rocks in your path. At one point the canoe must be slowly lowered downstream by rope. When Sungai Bungan meets the Kapuas the rapids die off and the rest of the journey is a pleasant cruise through the jungle until Putussibau. If you make this journey in the opposite direction, it takes twice as long due to the current, and costs twice as much.

WORTH A TRIP

BOBO

About three hours walk from Tanjung Lokan is an astonishing vertical shaft of rock thrusting skyward out of the jungle for hundreds of metres. Known as Bobo, it has never been climbed, locals say. A recent *National Geographic* expedition, the first to investigate the area, discovered the remains of a 5000-year-old settlement strewn with artefacts nearby. A good circuit and investigation would probably require a day, and can be combined with the Muller trek, which passes nearby. This is raw exploration, of a kind increasingly difficult to find.

CENTRAL KALIMANTAN

Tanjung Puting National Park

Tanjung Puting offers a safe and comfortable jungle river cruise, open to anyone, that brings you up close and personal with Borneo's great ape, the orangutan. This winning combination, part *African Queen* and part *National Geographic*, has made it the most popular tourist destination in Kalimantan, with many people flying in and out on their way to Bali or Borobudur. Cruises go up Sungai Sekonyer, in one corner of the huge 4150-sq-km park, and past three orangutan feeding stations, where you come ashore and watch the 'people of the forest' emerge from hiding – an amazing moment.

Just as amazing, the park is largely the result of a single remarkable woman. Dr Biruté Galdikas is a member of Leakey's Angels, a trio of young women trained by famous naturalist Louis Leakey to study the world's great primates in the wild. For Diane Fossey it was the gorilla, for Jane Goodall the chimpanzee, and for Galdikas the orangutan. In 1971 the young primatologist arrived at Tanjung Puting by canoe and soon established Camp Leakey, where she still lives at certain times of year. Here she made such seminal discoveries as the orangutan's eight-year birth cycle, which makes the species highly vulnerable to extinction. A very personal approach to 'her' orangutans has lost her some supporters in the academic

establishment, but the fact remains that the 6000 wild orangutans living in Tanjung Puting today form the single largest population in the world.

The park serves as an orangutan rehabilitation centre, where orphaned or formerly captive individuals are trained to live in the wild. Part of that process is daily hour-long feedings at jungle platforms, open to visitors. Females arrive with their clinging young to feed on a pile of bananas, which they peel with their lips. If you're lucky, they'll scatter before a large male, with his enormous cheek pads and powerful body – a most impressive sight. The highlight is spotting the current alpha male, Tom, but since males range widely, this is hit or miss. Wild orangutans can also be seen along the river, particularly at low tide, when they come to eat palm fruit, and around Camp Leakey, where they like to sit on the boardwalk. While some may appear deceptively tame, do not attempt to touch or feed them, or to get between a mother and child, as certain apes are prone to bag-snatching and occasionally biting visitors.

The other significant reason for Tanjung Puting's popularity, which should not be underestimated, is the *klotok*. The Sekonyer is navigated on your own private riverboat, a romantic form of travel that leaves you feeling like a rajah. These two-storey, 8m to 10m wooden craft come with captain, mate and cook, and serve as both home and viewing platform. During the day you sit up top on an open deck, surveying the jungle with binoculars in one hand and a drink in the other,

KALIMANTAN TANJUNG PUTING NATIONAL PARK

as the boat chugs along its narrow channel. Come twilight you moor on the edge of the jungle, listening to its primordial sounds as the cook makes a fine dinner. Later you retire to your own mattress and mosquito net, with stars twinkling overhead. Believe us when we say that you could get used to this life, particularly when its price is so reasonable. And that is why you won't be alone, especially in July and August, when feeding stations get very crowded. But, apart from seeing other rajahs passing by, this is still an authentic experience, as our own research trip confirmed, when a rare clouded leopard swam right in front of the boat in broad daylight. More common sights include macaques, pot-bellied proboscis monkeys, darting kingfishers, majestic hornbills and – if you're lucky – toothy gharials, a remarkable crocodile best seen at low tide, and the reason why you should avoid swimming (a visitor was eaten at Camp Leakey a decade ago).

Tanjung Puting is best visited during the dry season (May to September). The park's 200 varieties of wild orchid bloom mainly from January to March, but the abundance of March fruit may lure orangutans away from feeding platforms. At any time, bring rain protection and insect repellent. For an even more luxurious jungle cruise, consider the *Rahai'i Pangun* (p258) in Palangka Raya.

◉ Sights & Activities

The Sekonyer River is opposite the port of Kumai, where you meet your *klotok*. It is largely muddy due to upstream mining operations, although it eventually forks into a more natural, tea-coloured tributary that leads to Camp Leakey. The upriver journey contains several noteworthy stops (listed here in order):

Tanjung Harapan   WILDLIFE
(Tanjung Harapan; ⊘feeding 3pm daily) Feeding station with small interpretation centre.

Sekonyer Village   VILLAGE
A small village that arose around Tanjung Harapan but has since been relocated across the river. There's a small shop and lodging.

Pasalat   FOREST
(Pasalat camp) A reforestation camp where native saplings are being reintroduced after fire damage. Popular for birding. The 800m forest boardwalk will be excellent once repairs are made; otherwise be careful.

Pondok Tanggui   WILDLIFE
(Pondok Tangui; ⊘feeding 9am daily) Feeding station.

Camp Leakey   WILDLIFE
(Camp Leakey; ⊘feeding 2pm daily) Feeding station. Good for birds.

You won't necessarily see everything in this order, as you may choose to see some of these on the return trip.

The ideal journey is three days and two nights, giving you ample time to see everything. If you only have one day, you should take a speedboat from Kumai. A *klotok* can reach Camp Leakey in 4½ hours, making a return trip possible in one day if you leave at 6am, but this is not recommended.

During the dry season, there is an overnight trek from Pondok Tanggui to Pasalat (1,500,000Rp all inclusive). This is a unique chance to see nocturnal wildlife and can be combined with a boat trip. Your guide can arrange this, or enquire at Flora Homestay (p254) in Sekonyer Village.

ORANGUTANS

Adult male orangutans are said to be eight times stronger than a human. Semi-solitary in nature, they undergo vicious battles to ascend to alpha status, often losing teeth and fingers in the process. Tom, the present alpha at Camp Leakey, deposed his predecessor after a long reign, exiling him to the jungle. A male's cheek pads grow with his accession to dominance and wither after he is demoted. Mothers rear their young for seven years – the longest nursery time in the animal kingdom. During this intimate period they teach them everything they need to know to thrive in the jungle, from how to climb through the canopy by brachiation (travelling from branch to branch) to the medicinal qualities of plants, which nuts are poisonous, which critters they should avoid and how to mentally map the forest. Rehabilitation of orphans involves as close an approximation to this as possible.

☞ Tours

You have the choice of hiring a *klotok* (and guide) yourself, or having a tour operator do it for you. The former is cheaper, the latter easier.

Tour Companies

TOP CHOICE Borneo Wisata

Permai Tours   ADVENTURE

(☑ 081 2500 0508; www.borneowisata.com) The best tour company in the area. Diligent owner Harry Purwanto knows every *klotok*, captain and guide and can help you organise the best trip from all available choices.

☑ Borneo Orangutan

Adventure Tour   ADVENTURE

(☑ 0062-852 745 600; www.orangutantravel.com) Run by the excellent Ahmad Yani, the first official guide in the area.

Klotok Hire

The cost of hiring a klotok varies. The sizes range from small (two to four passengers, 400,000Rp to 450,000Rp per day) to large (eight to 10 passengers, 650,000Rp to 700,000Rp per day), including captain, mate and fuel. Cooks and food are an additional 100,000Rp per person per day. If you stay overnight you'll be charged for two full days so bargain if you want to come back early.

When you factor in permits and fees, the total cost for a three-day, two-night guided trip for two people is about 3,295,000Rp, a very reasonable price with seasonal fluctuations (expect a premium in summer). Note that not all boats have generators, necessary for showers. Some recommended boats:

Kingfisher   BOAT TOUR

(☑ Harry 081 2500 0508; harnavia@yahoo.com; Tanjung Puting) For small parties of two to four people, you can't do better than *Kingfisher*, the first *klotok* at Tanjung Puting. The attentive crew know exactly what they are doing, the food is excellent and the boat spotless.

Harapan Mina   BOAT TOUR

(☑ Muslian 0813 4961 7210) Freshly painted, clean, with a good crew and a quiet engine, this is a larger boat handling six to eight people.

Queen Ratu   BOAT TOUR

(☑ Yatno 081 2507 8490; garudaratu@yahoo.com) The best *klotok* choice for large parties (sleeps 10).

ℹ KLOTOK RENTAL COSTS

The cost of renting a *klotok* can be confusing, given the number of factors that go into it. Here is the breakdown for a typical three-day, two-night trip:

Boat 425,000Rp per day x 3 days = 1,275,000Rp

Cook & Food 100,000Rp per person x 2 people x 3 days = 600,000Rp

Guide 200,000Rp per day x 3 days = 600,000Rp

Registration 120,000Rp per person per day x 2 people x 3 days = 720,000Rp

Camera (one-time fee) = 50,000Rp

Boat Parking (one-time fee) = 50,000Rp

TOTAL 3,295,000Rp

Guides

It is not mandatory to hire a guide, but recommended, as it facilitates a smooth trip. Guides purchase food, set your itinerary, communicate with your *klotok* driver, take you trekking, spot animals and tell you about the park. They can also help you find a boat. To acquire a licence each guide has to speak basic English and undergo survival training and wildlife knowledge. Fees range from 150,000Rp to 250,000Rp per day.

Some recommended guides:

Erwin   GUIDE

(☑ 0858 6666 0159; erwinvanjava@gmail.com) Intelligent, well-read and good company, Erwin knows the park inside out, and shows interesting photos of local wildlife on his cell phone.

Andy Arysad   GUIDE

(☑ 0813 5295 0891; andijaka01@gmail.com) The park's most experienced guide.

Ancis Banderas   GUIDE

(☑ 0813 4920 5251; ecotourism.820@gmail.com) Excellent English, passionate about nature, points out much along the way.

🛏 Sleeping & Eating

If you're looking to stay outside the park (typically before or after your cruise), see Kumai or Pangkalan Bun reviews; the latter offers the only upscale accommodation in the area. If you wish to stay on terra firma inside the park, you can do that in two locations:

Rimba Lodge
HOTEL **$$$**

(☑0532 671 0589; www.ecolodgesindonesia.com; r incl breakfast 585,000-1,485,000Rp; ✴) This riverside lodge set in the jungle has the right ambience, with comfortable en suite cabanas, warm showers and traditional decor. Its restaurant (mains 50,000Rp, set menus 150,000Rp; open 7am to 9pm) serves Chinese and Indonesian food. Book via an agent and get 20% off.

Flora Homestay
HOMESTAY **$$**

(☑0812 516 4727; r 450,000Rp) Offers three basic en suite rooms with fans. Located at the entrance to Tanjung Harapan village. A speedboat here from Kumai is 150,000Rp.

❶ Information

Contact the following organisations for additional information about the region's orangutans, conservation efforts and volunteer opportunities:

Friends of the National Parks Foundation (FNPF; www.fnpf.org) Rescue and relocation of orangutans.

Orangutan Foundation International (OFI; www.orangutan.org; 4201 Wilshire Blvd, ste 407, Los Angeles, CA, USA 90010) Founded by Biruté Galdikas, runs the park's feeding stations.

Orangutan Foundation UK (www.orangutan. org.uk; 7 Kent Tce, London, NW1 4RP) Major UK organisation with focus on saving orangutan habitat.

❶ Getting There & Around

Tanjung Puting is typically reached via a flight to nearby Pangkalan Bun and a taxi to Kumai (120,000Rp, 20 minutes). Visitors should register at Pangkalan Bun police station upon arrival. Bring photocopies of your passport and visa (airport taxi drivers know the steps). This can also be organised by your guide. Once in Kumai, the next stop is the **PHKA office** (National Parks Office; fax 23832; Jln HM Rafi'l Km 1.5; ⊙8am-2pm Mon-Thu, 8am-11am Fri, 8am-1pm Sat) located portside. Registration costs 120,000Rp per day per person, 50,000Rp per trip for a klotok parking permit (30,000Rp per speedboat) and 50,000Rp per trip for a camera licence. Provide a copy of your police letter from Pangkalan Bun and another photocopy of your passport. When the park office is closed, it may be possible to arrange entry at the first feeding station, Tanjung Harapan. Ask your boat captain or guide.

Speedboats from Kumai cost 500,000Rp per day, and take about two hours to reach Camp Leakey, but this is pure transport, not wildlife spotting. Canoes are a quieter alternative for exploring Sungai Sekonyer's shallow tributaries, and can be rented at Sekonyer Village store for 50,000Rp per day.

Kumai
☑0532 / POP 23,000

The port of departure for Tanjung Puting National Park, Kumai is also known for its bird-nest business, which fills the town with screeching warehouses. A handful of guesthouses and warungs line the main street, Jl Idris. Backpackers sometimes meet here to share the price of a klotok. There's an ATM near the harbour.

🛏 Sleeping & Eating

TOP CHOICE Losmen Aloha
LOSMEN **$**

(☑61210; Jl HM Idris 465; s/d 40,000/60,000Rp) Across from the harbour, Caribbean-hued Aloha has a restaurant with chequered tables and local fare downstairs, and rooms above with shared bathrooms and a nice porch for hanging out. The street-facing rooms with windows are best.

Losmen Permata Hijau
LOSMEN **$**

(☑61325; Jl HM Idris; r with fan/air-con 70,000/100,000Rp; ✴) These budget rooms are good value for the price, with clean shared bathrooms, if you don't mind a lack of windows.

Mentari Hotel
HOTEL **$**

(☑no phone; Jl Gerliya 98; r incl breakfast 125,000Rp; ✴) Basic concrete boxes, although they do have windows and air-con. Only one has hot water.

❶ Getting There & Away

Reach Kumai by minibus from Pangkalan Bun (1000Rp, 20 minutes). Taxis from Pangkalan Bun airport to Kumai cost 150,000Rp.

Ferries run by **Pelni** (☑24420; Jln HM Idris), opposite the market, and **Dharma Lautan Utama** (☑081 3483 33444, 61008; Jln Gerliya 265) connect Kumai with Semarang (155,000Rp, 28 hours) once or twice weekly, and Surabaya (160,000Rp, 26 hours) almost daily. Tickets available at Aloha Travel, part of Losmen Aloha.

Aloha also sells bus tickets to Banjarmasin (economy/air-con 125,000/165,000Rp, 14 hours) via Sampit (economy/air-con 60,000/75,000Rp, six hours) and Palangka

Raya (economy/air-con 80,000/120,000Rp, 10 hours). The bus departs daily at 4pm.

Pangkalan Bun

📞0532 / POP 250,000

Pangkalan Bun is another transit city, with an airport, some hotels and very few ways to spend your time. But if you want something better than backpacker digs before or after visiting Tanjung Puting, you'll find it here.

◎ Sights & Activities

Pangkalan Bun Park   PARK

The town's tidy park, visible from the riverfront along JL Antasari, is crowned by the former sultan's home, **Istana Kuning** (Yellow Palace; ◔8am-2pm Mon-Thu, 8am-1pm Fri, 8-11am Sat, closed Sun). This large and mostly empty wooden building was built in 1806 and rebuilt in 1990 after a deranged woman burned it to the ground. It's not yellow, but was originally draped in yellow fabric.

TOP
CHOICE **Hotel Avila Pool**   SWIMMING

(JI Diponegoro 81; admission 25,000Rp) Blink blink – can it be? This fabulous Mediterranean-style hotel pool with adjoining restaurant is a lifesaver on a scorching hot day. It's 1km east of town.

Sungai Arot   BOAT TOUR

You can wave to almost any boat on the river and take an educational circuit around the ramshackle waterfront for 50,000Rp.

🛏 Sleeping & Eating

TOP
CHOICE **Yayorin Homestay**   HOMESTAY $$

(📞29057; www.yayorin.org; JI Bhayangkara, Km 1; r incl breakfast 300,000Rp; ❄) A unique woodland setting with a working fishpond sets these charming cottage rooms apart. Yayorin is a local NGO working to preserve Kalimantan's forests. About 4km east of town.

TOP
CHOICE **Swiss-Belinn**   HOTEL $$

(📞27888; www.swiss-belhotel.com; JI Ahmad Yani Km2; r incl breakfast 650,000-850,000Rp; ❄) Easily the top business hotel in the city, this new three-star is also your only upscale choice. It's a bit austere, but there's a pool and in-house spa to warm things up, plus a decent restaurant. Follow Jl Yani east 2km from town.

Hotel Bahagia   HOTEL $

(📞21226; JI P Antasari 100; r 85,000-245,000Rp; ❄🛜) A great option for Tanjung Puting backpackers if you can't find a closer room in Kumai. Upper-floor economy rooms 201, 206, and 210 have streetside windows and a

Pangkalan Bun

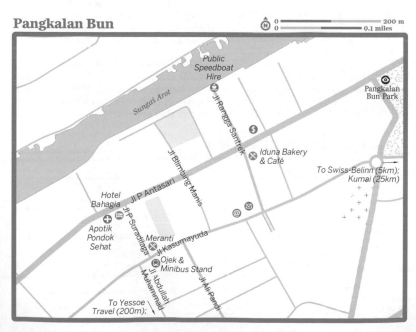

common porch; other rooms are more up-scale.

Hotel Andika HOTEL $
(☑21218; Jl Hasanudin 20A; r incl breakfast 70,000-110,000Rp; ❋) Rooms here are more interest-ing than the usual concrete box – all have windows facing a verdant courtyard. A new addition nearing completion promises even better options. Midway down Jl Hasanudin.

TOP CHOICE **Iduna Bakery & Café** WESTERN $
(☑24007; Jl Rangga Santrek 5; mains 15,000-32,000Rp; ☺9am-9pm) A sophisticated sur-prise, uniting a warm and trendy cafe with a tasty bakery (closes at 5pm).

Pranaban Fish Restaurant SEAFOOD $
(Jl Hasanudin; mains from 40,000Rp; ☺8am-10pm) Down the road from Kalstar this semi-alfresco resto is a real gem renowned by locals and expats for its grilled and fried *bakar* (fish), chicken and duck. Low-key, friendly vibe.

ℹ Information

Many businesses close late in the afternoon and reopen after dark.

Apotik Pondok Sehat (☑21276; Jl P Antasari 86) Well-stocked pharmacy with doctor's offices.

BNI Bank (Jl P Antasari) Exchanges travellers cheques and cash.

Pahala Internet Café (Jl Kasumayuda; per hr 5000Rp) Quick connection, no smoking and cool.

Post office (Jl Kasumayuda 29)

Yessoe Travel (☑21276; Jl Kasumayuda) Books air tickets and runs buses, which leave from its other office on the outskirts of town.

ℹ Getting There & Away

There are no longer any flights connecting Pang-kalan Bun and Palangka Raya. The best option is to fly from Pangkalan Bun to Sampit, then take a Kijang (75,000Rp, buy two front seats if pos-sible) to Palangka Raya. Reserve a car (☑0852 4920 5991, English shaky) ahead. Otherwise it is a brutal 15-hour bus trip, although you could get off in Sampit if you can't take any more.

Buses are run by Yessoe Travel, depart-ing from its office for Sampit (60,000Rp to 85,000Rp, six hours) and Banjarmasin (125,000Rp to 195,000Rp, 16 to 18 hours).

ℹ Getting Around

Taxis to/from the airport (5km) cost 50,000Rp. *Opelet* around town cost 10,000Rp. Minibuses to Kumai (20,000Rp, 20 minutes) and *ojeks* leave from the roundabout at the end of Jl Kasumayu-da. Taxis to Kumai cost 150,000Rp.

Palangka Raya
☑0536 / POP 213,000

Originally envisioned by President Soekarno as a new capital city for Indonesia – and even for a pan-Asian city state – Palangka Raya was built from scratch beginning in 1957. It shows in the streets, which are clearly laid out to plan, giving the city wide boulevards and a refreshing orderliness. While Soekarno's dream died, the city has a few surprises in store, including Kalimantan's only high-end jungle river cruise, a new luxury hotel, some trendy cafes and a bright spot of nightlife.

◎ Sights & Activities

Pasar Malam MARKET
The food stalls around Jl Halmahera and Jl Jawa run all day, but the maze of shops here comes alive at night.

FLIGHTS FROM PANGKALAN BUN

DESTINATION	COMPANY	COST (RP)	DURATION	FREQUENCY
Banjar	Kalstar, Trigana	1,200,000	1½hr	Mon, Thu, Sat
Jakarta	Kalstar	1,100,000	1hr	daily
Ketapang	Kalstar, Trigana	700,000	30min	daily
Pontianak	Kalstar, Trigana	920,000	1½hr	Sun, Mon, Wed, Thu, Sat
Sampit	Kalstar	550,000	30min	daily
Semarang	Trigana/IAT	955,000	1hr	daily
Solo	Trigana/IAT	665,000	2hr	Wed & Sun
Surabaya	Trigana	1,000,000	1hr	daily
Yogyakarta	IAT	665,000	1½hr	Fri, Sat, Sun, Mon

Palangka Raya

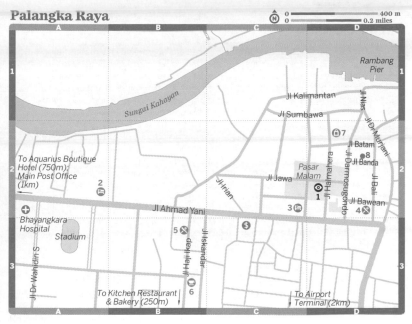

Borneo Orangutan Survival Foundation ZOO

(☎330 8414; www.orangutan.or.id; Jl Tjinik Riwut Km29; admission by donation; ⊙9am-3pm Sat & Sun) This is one of several conservation efforts run by the Borneo Orangutan Survival Foundation. Normally a dozen or so orangutans (and some sun bears) are visible through floor-to-ceiling windows in this sophisticated facility simulating the forest floor. Hire an *ojek*, or use taxi route A to Jl Tjinik Riwut Km8 station and take a minibus.

Tours

TOP CHOICE Kalimantan Tour Destinations BOAT TOUR

(☎322 2099; www.wowborneo.com; Jl Milono Km 1; ⊙9am-5pm Mon-Fri, 9am-3pm Sat) This eco-award-winning business, run by savvy Australian entrepreneur Gaye Thavisin, operates deluxe river cruises aboard the romantic *Rahai'i Pangun* (p258). A second boat, the *Spirit of Borneo,* is being refurbished. Homestays and local tours can also be arranged. Head south on Jl Milono (taxi route E) to the office.

Palangka Raya

Sleeping

TOP CHOICE Aquarius Boutique Hotel HOTEL $$

(☎324 2121; www.aquariusboutiquehotel.com; Jl Imam Bonjol 5; d 600,000-850,000Rp; ❄☎☎) Rooms here are some of the best in the city (be sure to ask for discounts) and the facilities excellent, including a rooftop pool and fitness centre. The superb entertainment

DON'T MISS

RAHAI'I PANGUN

Unique in Kalimantan, **Rahai'i Pangun** is owned and operated by Kalimantan Tour Destinations (p257). It is the ultimate jungle river cruiser, a 19m traditional wooden boat built from tropical hardwoods, that navigates the Kahayan and Rungan rivers in high style, like a huge mahogany royal barge. It has a broad, split-level upper deck with cosy rattan couches, and comfy staterooms below, including two double cabins with shared bathroom, two twins and one triple. A favourite of Jakarta embassies, the boat docks either in Palangka Raya or the ramshackle port town of Tangkiling, some 30km west. Short and long cruises are available, offering an itinerary similar to Tanjung Puting only more varied, including village visits with longhouses and dance performances, exploring lakes by canoe, and a rubber plantation. You won't get an arm's length from an orangutan, but you'll see lots of them, particularly as you circle Orangutan Island, a rehabilitation centre in the middle of the Kahayan run by the Borneo Orangutan Survival Foundation (p257).

Weekend cruises of two nights/three days cost 5,181,000Rp per person for a double or twin cabin; longer four-day, three-night cruises are 7,058,000Rp per person. Special rates are offered to travellers turning up just prior to cruise departures, provided there is availability.

complex makes it unique. Avoid the 5th- and 6th-floor rooms due to noise. It's 500m from the central traffic circle.

TOP CHOICE Swiss-Belhotel HOTEL $$
(☏081 1528 433; www.swiss-belhotel.com; Jl Tjilik Km5; s 555,000-685,000Rp, d 620,000-750,000Rp; ❇⊛) This extensive new luxury property, a successful combination of business and resort hotel, raises the local bar, although not without minor growing pains. There is a vast marble lobby, an excellent buffet breakfast with Western choices, and comfy rooms with glass showers, ranging from entry-level standards to the 5,000,000Rp Presidential Suite. It feels a bit like an architect's model, but management is wise and the price is right (ask about discounts). Located 5km from the central traffic circle on Jl Tjilik.

Hotel Dian Wisata HOTEL $
(☏322 1241; Jl A Yani 68; r incl breakfast 120,000-220,000Rp; ❇) The interesting design of this hotel, with its central well-lit atrium and colourful stairwell, leading down into subterranean rooms, separates it from the boring concrete boxes that define its competition. Easy access to buses.

Hotel Sakura HOTEL $$
(☏322 1680; Jl A Yani 87; r incl breakfast 250,000-425,000Rp; ❇) This hotel's tranquil courtyard offers a welcome respite from the city. The best rooms have courtyard windows; some come with rare two-person tubs. Overall good value.

✗ Eating & Drinking

Kitchen Restaurant & Bakery INTERNATIONAL $
(Jl Haji Ikap; mains from 20,000Rp; ⊙6am-9pm) A welcome example of eclectic thinking, this two-storey restaurant with its own waterfall is known for having the only pizza in town, part of a broad Western-Asian menu featuring Thai, Chinese and Indonesian dishes in big portions. Live music at night.

Family CHINESE $
(☏322 9560; Jl Bawean 16; mains 20,000-25,000Rp; ⊙8am-9.30pm) The best Chinese food in the city, with a standard menu. Known for its *ikan jelawat* (90,000Rp), a river fish cooked many ways. Serves beer (35,000Rp).

Warung Makan Bu Leman INDONESIAN $
(Jl Haji Ikap; mains from 20,000Rp; ⊙7am-4pm) Open-air dining around small communal tables makes this convivial local favourite very popular; the chicken soup does the rest.

TOP CHOICE Bistro de Garage CAFE
(Jl Haji Ikap 22; coffee 7500Rp; ⊙10am-midnight; ⊛) A rare find, this trendy cafe is located in a colourfully painted house, garage included. It offers free wi-fi, basic food (spaghetti, desserts), outdoor seating and live music.

☆ Entertainment

If you're looking for night life in Palangka Raya, the entertainment complex at the Aquarius Boutique Hotel (p257) is the only game in town, and no slacker. **Blu Music Hall** (☺8pm-1am) is a small but atmospheric blues bar that surprises with its sophistication. The adjacent **Vino Club** (☺10pm-?am) is a cosy state-of-the-art DJ club that doubles as the city's major performance venue. **Luna Karaoke** (☺2pm-3am) is the third, more local leg in the stool. A tall Bintang will run you 75,000Rp at any of these places. Overall this complex is where the city's style-conscious young professionals come to hang out, representing a new wave of urban life. Find it 500m along Jl Bonjol from central traffic circle.

Shopping

Souvenir shops are located along Jl Batam.

Information

Bank Mandiri (Jl A Yani; ☺8am-3pm Mon-Fri) Currency exchange.

Bhayangkara Hospital (☏322 1520; Jl A Yani)

Kevin Maulana Tours (☏323 4735; ptkevin_maulana@yahoo.com; Jl Milono Km1.5) Friendly KM can sort out air tickets, taxi charters and Kijang. Head south on Jl Milono (taxi route E).

Main post office (Jl Imam Bonjol; ☺7.30am-2.15pm) On taxi route D. West side of town, 500m south of main traffic circle.

Sumerta Sari Travel (☏322 1033; Jalan Cilik Riwut Km1)

Yessoe Travel (☏322 1436; Jl Banda 7)

❶ Getting There & Away

AIR Garuda, Lion Air, Sriwijaya Air, and Batavia Air fly daily to Jakarta (400,000Rp, 1½ hours) and Surabaya (425,000Rp, one hour). You'll find all the airline offices at the airport, which is only 2km from the eastern end of Jl Yani.

BUS Morning and evening buses depart from **Milono bus terminal** (☏3227 7765; Bundaran Burung, Jl Milono Km4.5) 5km on taxi route E. Yessoe Travel also runs buses at comparable fares from its in-town terminal just north of the market area. It is not clear when the new bus terminal, 10km south of the city centre, will be operational, if ever.

KIJANG Yessoe Travel serves Banjarmasin (90,000Rp, five hours). Sumerta Sari Travel

serves Sampit (70,000Rp, five hours) and Pangkalan Bun (145,000, 10 hours).

❶ Getting Around

Yellow minibuses ('taxis', 3000Rp) ply major thoroughfares. Airport service (6km, 15 minutes) costs 60,000Rp. Becak congregate on Jl A Yani around the petrol station near Jl Halmahera.

SOUTH KALIMANTAN

Banjarmasin

☏0511 / POP 611,000

Banjarmasin has been called the Venice of the East, a jaw-dropping exaggeration. Sadly, this enormous city, which lies at the confluence of several rivers, sprawls in all directions but offers very little for its size. It is best known for the boat trip to its floating markets, an experience both interesting and discomfiting, as it passes through great poverty. You may benefit from moving outside your comfort zone, but don't come expecting St Mark's Sq.

◉ Sights

Mesjid Raya Sabilal Muhtadin   MOSQUE (Jl Sudirman) This massive mosque resembles a landed spaceship. During Ramadan, the famous **Pasar Wadai** (Cake Fair) runs along the adjacent riverfront.

☞ Tours

Floating Market & Canal Tour CULTURAL TOUR (tour incl guide 200,000Rp; ☺5.30am-9.30am) You can see most of what Banjarmasin has to offer in a single journey. This begins by catching a dawn boat under Jembatan Dewi (Dewi Bridge) to the floating markets, where canoes full of wares mill about in search of a buyer. It takes an hour or so to get there via canals lined with ramshackle homes (many of which are collapsing into the water), each with its own outhouse. Along the way hordes of children will wave at you

---

BUSES FROM PALANGKA RAYA

DESTINATION	COST (RP)	DURATION (HR)	FREQUENCY
Banjarmasin	45,000	5	2am daily
Pangkalan Bun	80,000-150,000	10	7am & 4pm daily
Sampit	50,000-75,000	5	7am & 4pm daily

and try to swim out to your boat through the fetid water. While their smiles are the enduring image, passing through them in a sightseeing boat elevates the foreign tourist to a privileged status that can be profoundly discomfiting. Having said that, a floating market is interesting to see – there are two to choose from and either will do. Here you can sample a variety of exotic fruits as the river world comes to life.

A worthwhile stop on the return trip is **Pulau Kembang** (tour from 100,000Rp), where macaques walk the boardwalk. Another is gaily painted **Masjid Sultan Suriansyah**, one of the first mosques in Kalimantan, now beautifully restored.

Guides

You'll need a guide (who will secure a boat as well) to explain what you're seeing on the floating markets tour. Tour guides in Banjarmasin typically range up into the Meratus Mountains, too (see Loksado section for more trekking guides), although this interesting area demands more than a day trip.

Joe Yas   GUIDE
(☑0812 5182 8311; joyas64@gmail.com) A trekking expert who also gives city tours.

Sarkani Gambi   GUIDE
(☑0813 5187 7858; kani286@yahoo.com) Friendly Sarkani runs tours for large foreign groups as well as customised trips for individuals.

Muhammad Yusuf   GUIDE
(☑0813 4732 5958; yusuf_guidekalimantan@yahoo.co.id) Yusuf is friendly, energetic and professional.

Mulyadi Yasin   GUIDE
(☑0813 5193 6200; yadi_yasin@yahoo.co.id) Professional guide with extensive experience in Banjarmasin and the Meratus.

🛏 Sleeping

Book ahead on weekends.

TOP CHOICE Swiss-Belhotel Borneo   HOTEL $$
(☑327 1111; www.swiss-belhotel.com; Jl Pangeran Antasari 86A; s/d incl breakfast 650,000/700,000Rp; ❉◐❄) Unlike other Swiss-Bels, this one eschews modern business decor in favour of a traditional boutique feel, to include a Banjar roof and the warm use of wood throughout. Prices quoted are after the standard discount. Junior suite 201 (1,590,000Rp) is exceptionally nice, a corner room with both city and river views. The ho-

tel restaurant is also a top-choice listing, and there's live jazz from 8pm to 11pm.

Hotel Victoria Riverview   HOTEL $$
(☑336 0255; hotel_victoria48@yahoo.com; Jl Lambung Mangkurat 48; r incl breakfast 425,000-750,000Rp; ❉◐❄) The riverside location makes this hotel stand out. Interestingly, certain 'classic' rooms (eg 323) have a better view than more expensive ones. The show-stealer is the Victoria Suite (1,200,000Rp), one of the most stylish rooms in Kalimantan, with such touches as a flat-screen TV embedded in a glass wall, and a waterfront verandah. The coffee shop is nicely situated too, although the breakfast doesn't equal the view. Ask about discounts.

Hotel Perdana   HOTEL $
(☑335 2376; hotelperdana@plasa.com; Jl Katamso 8; r 100,000-160,000Rp; ❉) Popular with tourists, this excellent budget choice features 40 Caribbean-hued rooms around an inner atrium, many of them with air-con and en suites. There's no hot water, but staff speak English so at least they will understand your complaint.

Hotel SAS   HOTEL $
(☑335 3054; Jl Kacapiring Besar 2; r incl breakfast 204,000-259,000Rp; ❉) Standard double rooms here have attractive rattan floors and bamboo beds. Good value for the price.

✖ Eating & Drinking

TOP CHOICE Jukung   INTERNATIONAL $
(Swiss-Belhotel Borneo, Jl Pangeran Antasari 86A; mains from 25,000Rp; ⊙breakfast, lunch & dinner) Real burgers! Plus a nice setting in the Swiss-Belhotel, a great variety of Asian and Western dishes and live music makes this a very pleasant dinner spot.

Cendrawasih   SEAFOOD $
(Jl Pangeran Samudera; mains from 20,000Rp; ⊙9am-10pm) Delve deeper into Banjar cuisine at this renowned spot. Pick fish, seafood or chicken to cook on the outside grill and enjoy it inside with a cornucopia of sauces.

Rumah Makan Abdullah   INDONESIAN $
(Jl Ahmad Yani Km1; mains 18,000-25,000Rp; ⊙10am-midnight) Locals say the *nasi kuning* (saffron rice) at this unassuming place is Banjarmasin's best.

Rumah Makan Jayakarta   CHINESE $$
(Jl Haryono MT 7; mains 50,000-65,000Rp; ⊙11am-1.30pm & 5-11pm) All-day Chinese cafe selling

Central Banjarmasin

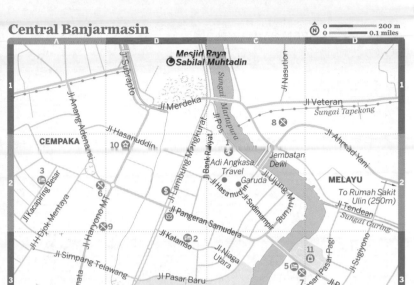

kepitang (crab), *ikan* (fish), *kodok* (frogs) and excellent *ayam* (chicken). Food is cooked on the outside range and beer is sold.

TOP CHOICE Sante   BAR

(Mercure Hotel, Jl Ahmad Yani 98; ◷noon-11pm) This colourful pool bar at the Mercure Hotel is a great place for happy hour (4pm to 5pm) and beyond.

☆ Entertainment

TOP CHOICE Dynasty   DJ, KARAOKE

(Hotel Aria Barito, Jl Haryono; admission male/female 50,000/25,000Rp) This vast new entertainment complex with disco, bar, and karaoke packs them in.

🛍 Shopping

Mitra Plaza has ATMs, fast-food outlets and Western-style shops in an air-con environment. Interesting Dayak handicrafts are sold opposite, along Jl Pangeran Antasari.

❶ Information

Adi Angkasa Travel (☑436 6100; Jl Hasanudin 27) Flight bookings via a few members of staff who speak English.
BNI Bank (Bank Negara Indonesia; Jl Lambung Mangkurat)

Central Banjarmasin

Family Tour & Travel (☑326 8923; familytourtravel@yahoo.com; Jl A Yani Km4.5, Komp Aspol Bina Brata 1E; ◷closed Sun) Books flights and buses to Pangkalan Bun as well as Balikpapan. Speak to owner Sam.

TRANSPORT FROM BANJARMASIN

Air

DESTINATION	COMPANY	COST (RP)	DURATION	FREQUENCY
Balikpapan	Sriwijaya Air, Trigana	325,000	45min	2 daily
Jakarta	Garuda, Sriwijaya Air, Lion Air, Batavia Air	500,000	1hr	10 daily
Pangkalan Bun	Kalstar, Trigana	450,000	1hr	1-2 daily
Solo	Trigana	450,000	1hr	daily
Surabaya	Sriwijaya Air, Lion Air, Batavia Air	270,000	1hr	7 daily
Yogyakarta	Lion Air	480,000	1hr	daily

Boat

DESTINATION	COMPANY	COST (RP)	DURATION (HR)	FREQUENCY
Semarang	Pelni	395,000	24	Mon & Fri
Surabaya	Dharma Lautan	160,000	18-24	3-5 weekly

Bus

DESTINATION	COST (RP)	DURATION (HR)	FREQUENCY
Balikpapan	115,000-170,000	1	several daily
Kandangan	45,000	3	several daily
Negara	50,000	4	several daily
Palangka Raya	40,000	6	several daily
Pangkalan Bun	110,000	20	several daily
Samarinda	140,000-195,000	13	several daily

Main post office (cnr Jl Pangeran Samudera & Jl Lambung Mangkurat)
Rumah Sakit Ulin (Jl A Yani Km2) Medical centre.

❶ Getting There & Away

Air
Batavia Air (☑327 4110; Jl A Yani Km4 221B)
Garuda (☑335 9065; Jl Hasanudin 31)
Lion Air (☑470 5277; airport)
Sriwijaya Air (☑327 2377; Jl A Yani Km2.5)

Boat
Ferries depart from Trisakti Pinisi Harbour (3km).
Dharma Lautan Utama (☑441 4833; Jl Yos Sudarso 8)
Pelni (☑335 3077; Jl Martadinata 10)

Bus
The main bus terminal is at Jl A Yani Km6, southeast of the city centre.

❶ Getting Around

Angkot routes (3000Rp) fan out from terminals at Jl Pangeran Samudera circle in the city core and Antasari Centre to the east. Becak and *ojeks* for hire gather around market areas. Taxis to/from Syamsuddin Noor Airport (26km) cost 100,000Rp.

Kandangan

 0517 / POP 45,000

While almost completely untouristed, Kandangan is one of the more attractive towns in Kalimantan: tidy and well planned, with two interesting budget hotels, a bustling market (with a huge new building under construction) and numerous restaurants. It is also the gateway to lovely Loksado. This is a perfect place to chill out and meet locals, particularly for budget travellers, but reserve ahead as rooms are few.

📖 Sleeping & Eating

TOP CHOICE **Wisma Duta** HOTEL $

(☎21073; Jl Permuda 9; r fan/air-con 90,000/ 100,000Rp; 🌬) Charm at last: a converted country home with the feel of a Chinese temple makes this unassuming hotel a rare and welcome find. Rattan walls are a nice touch.

Hotel Mutia HOTEL $

(☎21270; Jl Suprapto; r incl breakfast 175,000-250,000Rp, 🌬🖥) Formerly a private home, this interesting wooden building has large public spaces and basic box rooms.

The Kandangan bus terminal doubles as a food court, and is lined with enough warungs to keep you well fed for days. ATM nearby.

ℹ Getting There and Around

Colts run frequently to/from Banjarmasin's Km6 terminal (40,000Rp, 4½ hours) until midafternoon. Buses for Balikpapan and Samarinda (125,000Rp to 165,000Rp, 14 hours) leave 10 times per day from Kandangan terminal. Pick-up trucks located on Muara Bilui will take you to Loksado (50,000Rp, 1½ hours). Becak will run you around town for 20,000Rp per half hour.

Negara

Northwest of Kandangan, the riverside town of Negara is the gateway to a vast wetland ranch where water buffalo swim from their elevated corrals at sunrise in search of grazing areas and are herded back at dusk by cowboys in canoes – an interesting sight if you're there in late afternoon. The town is a memorable sight too, with its huge mosque and brilliant dome rising across the bridge as you enter. Surprisingly, there is no hotel. Rent a boat across the street to see the swimming cattle (200,000Rp).

To get here from Kandangan take a public minibus (7000Rp, one hour), shared Japanese sedan with four people (15,000Rp per person, charter 60,000Rp), or *ojek* (40,000Rp).

Loksado

Loksado is an absolutely charming hamlet of gingerbread cottages flanking a rushing stream, Sungai Amandit, with a pedestrian suspension bridge. Set amidst beautiful mountain scenery, it stands apart from the rest of Kalimantan's tropical jungle, a feeling reinforced by the wonderful drive in, which curves through green hills until you reach the end of the road, 40km from Kandangan (great by motorcycle!). You'll find the best backpacker pad in Kalimantan here, as well as a vibrant Wednesday market, and numerous hiking trails for exploring Pegunungan Meratus, a 2500-sq-km mountain range spotted with Dayak villages. If you're looking for a place to hang out indefinitely, you can't beat this combination.

🚶 Activities

Mountain Trekking HIKING

There are innumerable hiking trails in the Meratus combining forest, villages, rivers, suspension bridges and longhouse visits. However, deforestation has taken its toll; it's a good five hours' walk to get to primary

---

FROM BANJARMASIN TO KANDANGAN

The road from Banjarmasin to Kandangan isn't pretty, but contains three interesting stops accessible by Colt minibus:

Cempaka Diamond Fields (🕙Sat-Thu) Twenty wooden prospecting rigs spread over a large field of sand reveal diamond mining in its most basic form. At the huge roundabout just past Banjarbaru, switch to a green taxi to Alur (2000Rp) and walk 1km from the main road.

Museum Lambung Mangkurat (☎051 1477 2453; Jl A Yani 36; admission 5000Rp; 🕙8.30am-3pm Sun-Thu, 8.30-11am Fri, 8.30am-2pm Sat) An above-average museum of local arts – textiles, ceramics, sculpture – both contemporary and antique, housed in several interlinked buildings in Banjarbaru (Km30).

Penggosokkan Intan (Diamond Polishing; 🕙9am-4pm Sat-Thu) Watch diamonds from the nearby mines being polished. You can also shop for precious stones if you know what you are doing. Ask the Colt driver to let you off here (1km from Banjarbaru roundabout).

forest these days. The best one-day trek is from Loksado to Bali Haritai (four to six hours, depending on the route), which includes some waterfalls. For first timers, this is an excellent introduction to jungle trekking, with a moderate change in altitude, areas of dense foliage, and a few leeches for company. Multiday itineraries top out (literally) at the summit of Mt Besar (1901m), the tallest peak in the Meratus range (seven days). Be sure to be prepared for your particular route, and don't be afraid to rein in your guide if the pace or terrain is beyond your skill level. For advice on advanced jungle trekking, see p236.

Bamboo Rafting   RAFTING

It's fun to be poled downriver on a narrow bamboo raft, particularly when negotiating mild rapids. Ask your guide or hotelier for local providers; 90 minutes (250,000Rp) should suffice.

Muara Tanuhi Hot Springs   HOT SPRINGS

(admission 3000Rp) These hot springs located in the Tanuhi resort, 2km west of Loksado, are the perfect ending to a long trek, although the resort itself is in disrepair.

Tours

To trek safely, hire an English-speaking guide. Some recommended English-speakers (see also p253):

Shady   GUIDE

(☑0813 4954 5994; borneowanderer@yahoo.com) A young and enthusiastic guide from Kandangan with extensive trekking experience and a great sense of humour.

Amat   GUIDE

(☑0813 4876 6573) A personable Dayak and long-standing Loksado resident with complete knowledge of the area.

Sleeping

Wisma Alya   LOSMEN $

(☑0821 5330 8276; r 150,000Rp) Backpacker heaven! This two-storey cabin with rough-hewn wooden walls (the green house as you enter town) has five identical rooms, four upstairs accessed via a steep ladder and one down. They're bare as can be, with a floor mattress and small window, but the entire building is perched on rushing Sungai Amandit, with an overhanging balcony affording great views of the mountains. The shared *mandi* is large, clean and powered by mountain water. Laundry and *ojeks* are on offer, and the market is across the street. A sense of serenity sinks deeply into you here, ensuring a great night's sleep.

Amandit River Lodge   LODGE $

(☑0813 4826 3467; r 200,000Rp) It's too bad this lodge lies 3km from town, because it has a stunning location, with the river winding in front and a dramatic piton rising behind. If you have your own transport, though, the simple en suite rooms with Western toilets are good value. Open by appointment, so call ahead and speak with the resident caretaker.

Wisma Loksado   HOTEL $

(☑0852 5154 4398; r 220,000Rp) If you want an en suite room in Loksado, you can come here, but you will end up in a concrete box, missing the point of Loksado entirely. At the end of the suspension bridge.

ⓘ Getting There & Around

Pick-up trucks leave Kandangan terminal for Loksado (50,000Rp, 1½ hours) in the afternoon and leave Loksado for Kandangan early in the morning.

Understand Borneo

population per sq km

BORNEO   USA   UK

👤 ≈ 30 people

Borneo Today

Politics & Economics

Nothing rankles with Borneans more than corrupt politicians who line their pockets at the expense of the public purse, the island's dwindling rainforests, and indigenous land rights. On the internet you can find bloggers' accounts of back-room deals, especially with logging companies and palm-oil conglomerates, in all parts of the island.

Sabahans are well aware that while their state was Malaysia's second-richest in the 1970s, it is now the country's poorest. A major reason, they claim, is that all but 5% of Sabah's (and Sarawak's) oil revenue flows into federal coffers. Residents of both states are wise to the wonders that petrol dollars have done for neighbouring Brunei.

Sentiment on these issues is likely to bolster support for candidates running against the Barisan Nasional, in power since independence and at the time of writing. According to polls in the lead-up to Malaysia's 13th general election (in the first half of 2013), younger voters are in an increasingly anti-establishment mood and receptive to the opposition People's Alliance.

For progovernment news, read Sarawak's daily newspapers. For opposition opinion, check out the following:

» www.sarawak report.org

» www.horn billunleashed .wordpress.com

» www.moc sarawak.word press.com

» www.radio freesarawak.org

» www.bmf.ch/en

Ethnic Preferences

Following the race riots of 1969, the Malaysian government implemented a policy of 'affirmative action' (ie positive discrimination) to give the majority Malays a more equitable share of the economic pie. The result was a range of subsidies and preferences designed to benefit a category of people called *bumiputra* ('sons of the soil') that encompasses Malays and, in Sabah and Sarawak, indigenous groups (Dayaks) – that is, virtually everyone except the Chinese (and, on the mainland, Indians). Some Dayaks jokingly refer to themselves as 'third-class *bumiputra*' because while they are supposed to be among the beneficiaries of affirmative action, most advantages seem to accrue to Malays.

Courtesy Call

When you arrive at a Dayak longhouse, etiquette requires that you present yourself to the headman straight away. When you say 'take me to your leader', you may feel like an alien in a 1950s sci-fi flick!

It's Rude to Point

Pointing with your index finger, especially towards anything sacred, is a no-no. If you must indicate something in a particular direction, do as the locals do and use your thumb, joined to your closed palm.

Leech Etiquette

If you pluck off a leech, don't just flick it onto the ground, where it might rebound to attack your friends. Follow jungle best practice and chop it in two with your *parang* (Dayak machete).

belief systems
(% of population)

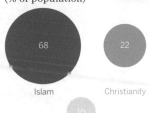

68 — Islam
22 — Christianity
10 — Other

if Borneo were 100 people

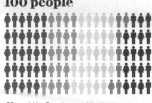

29 would be Dayak
19 would be Banjarese
14 would be Malay
12 would be Javanese
7 would be Chinese
10 would be other

As a result of these policies, ethnic Chinese have found themselves facing quotas and discrimination in housing, higher education and public-sector jobs. Critics say the system has created incentives in which individual merit counts less than your background, that wealthy Malays game the system at the expense of the poor Malays it was intended to help, and that Malaysia's global competitiveness is being sapped. Some Chinese have become frustrated and alienated, causing a brain drain the country can ill afford. Reform, however, has not been on political parties' pre-election agendas because entrenched Malay interest groups oppose reforms with populist passion.

In Brunei, the government offers financial incentives to convert to Islam. The Baha'i Faith is banned.

Inter-Ethnic Relations

Relations between the dozens of ethnic groups in Sarawak and Sabah tend to be more relaxed and open than in Peninsular Malaysia, but the states are not quite the multicultural paradise portrayed in Tourism Malaysia's 'Malaysia – Truly Asia!' campaign. Malays form the majority in a country based on *ketuanan Melayu* (Malay supremacy), but they are a minority in Sabah and Sarawak; ethnic Chinese wonder about their place in a society that often treats them as outsiders, generations after their ancestors put down roots; members of indigenous groups (Dayaks) juggle tribal identity and religious affiliation (the majority are Christian) in a Muslim-majority society that knows little about them.

Marriages are common between Dayak groups that hunted each other's heads just a few generations back, and between Dayaks and Chinese. Some Dayak parents, seeking the best education for their children, send them to academically rigorous Chinese schools where they learn Mandarin, further blurring cultural lines. There are fewer intermarriages with Malays, in part because a non-Muslim must convert to Islam to marry a Muslim.

1Malaysia

The campaign for Malaysian national unity and ethnic harmony, '1Malaysia', is supposed to promote eight values: perseverance, a culture of excellence, acceptance, loyalty, education, humility, integrity and meritocracy.

MIB

Melayu Islam Beraja (MIB; Malay Islamic Monarchy) is the 'national philosophy' of Brunei. It emphasises Malay language, culture and customs, Islamic laws and values, and the legitimacy of the sultan.

Headhunting

Don't be taken aback if your Dayak hosts make self-deprecating jokes about headhunting. Most Dayaks accept matter-of-factly that taking heads used to be part of their culture – and are glad colonial authorities put an end to the practice.

History

Considering Borneo's relatively remote location, it comes as no surprise that the island has rarely served as a major commercial or cultural crossroads. But neither has it been isolated from Asia's trade routes and religious currents. India and China have influenced and inspired Borneo's peoples for some 2000 years, and since the 15th century the island has been a meeting point of Islam and Christianity. For several centuries, Borneo was buffeted by the epic rivalries between Dayak tribes and among the European powers.

Borneo Becomes an Island

Borneo was connected to mainland Southeast Asia – as part of a land mass known as Sundaland – from 2.5 million years ago until some 10,000 years ago, when global deglaciation turned it back into an island. Archaeological evidence suggests that human beings arrived in Sarawak – overland – at least 40,000 years ago. More migrants arrived about 3000 years ago, probably from southern China, mixing with earlier inhabitants to form some of Borneo's indigenous groups.

Traders from India and China began stopping by Borneo – as a sideshow to their bilateral commerce – around the 1st century AD, introducing Hinduism and Buddhism. From about AD 500, Chinese traders started settling along Borneo's coasts. It is believed that the influence of the Sumatra-based kingdom of Srivijaya (7th to 13th centuries) extended to Borneo. During this time, Brunei emerged as a centre for trade with China; some historians believe that the first Muslims to visit Borneo came from China in the 10th century.

The Arrival of Islam & the European Powers

Islam was brought to present-day Peninsular Malaysia, including Melaka, by traders from South India in the early 15th century. Over time, diplomacy, often cemented by marriage, oriented Borneo's coastal sultanates towards Melaka and Islam.

Archaeological finds in western Borneo include glass beads made in the Roman Empire.

TRADE

TIMELINE	2.5 million BC	8000 BC	1st century AD
	Borneo is attached to mainland Southeast Asia, affording plants, insects, animals and eventually people easy migration routes.	Rising sea levels at the end of the last ice age submerge much of the Sundaland continental plate, transforming Borneo into the world's third-largest island.	Chinese and Indian traders detour to Borneo. By AD 500, Chinese are settling in coastal present-day West Kalimantan.

In the late 15th century, Europeans began to seek a direct role in the rich Asian trade. Christopher Columbus famously failed to reach India by sailing west, but Portugal's Vasco da Gama found the way around Africa in 1498. In 1511 Portugal conquered Melaka in its bid to control the lucrative spice trade. As a result, Muslim merchants moved much of their custom to Borneo's sultanates, and Brunei succeeded Melaka as the regional Islamic trading centre.

The British and Dutch began sparring over Borneo in the 17th century, extending a regional rivalry that began in Java and spread to the Malay Peninsula. The Anglo-Dutch Treaty of 1824 carved the region into spheres of commercial, political and linguistic influence that would turn into national boundaries in the 20th century. The Dutch got what became Indonesia, while Britain got the Malay Peninsula and Singapore. At the time, neither seemed much interested in Borneo.

Brunei: Empire in Decline

Under Sultan Bolkiah in the 16th century, Brunei was Borneo's most powerful kingdom, its influence extending from Kuching all the way to the island of Luzon, now in the Philippines. In subsequent centuries, however, facing internal strife, rebellions and piracy, Brunei's rulers repeatedly turned to foreigners, including the Spanish, for help. In exchange for assistance in suppressing an uprising in 1701, Brunei ceded Sabah to the Sultan of Sulu (an archipelago between Borneo and Mindanao). That cession is the basis for ongoing Philippine claims to Sabah.

Brunei's decline in the late 18th century led Sarawak to assert its independence, emboldened by a flourishing trade in antimony (*sarawak* in old Malay). In 1839 Brunei's sultan dispatched his uncle Rajah Muda Hashim, but he failed to quell the separatists. Seeing a chance to be rid of Bruneian rule, the rebels looked south for Dutch aid.

Sarawak's White Rajahs

In a case of impeccable timing, James Brooke, the independently wealthy, India-born (and possibly gay) son of a British magistrate, moored his armed schooner at Kuching. Rajah Muda offered to make the Englishman the rajah of Sungai Sarawak if he helped suppress the worsening revolt. Brooke, confident London would support any move to counter Dutch influence, accepted the deal. Backed by superior firepower, he quashed the rebellion and held a reluctant Rajah Muda to his word. In 1841 Sarawak became Brooke's personal fiefdom. The White Rajahs would rule Sarawak for the next 100 years.

Unlike British colonial administrators, Brooke and his successors included tribal leaders in their ruling council and respected local customs (except headhunting). They battled pirates (a policy that boosted trade),

The Venetian explorer Antonio Pigafetta, who sailed with Ferdinand Magellan on his last voyage, visited Brunei in 1521 and dubbed Kampung Ayer water village the 'Venice of the East'.

While maritime kingdoms and seafaring Europeans were vying for control of coastal Borneo, indigenous groups were developing their own societies deep in the rainforest. We know little about their history due to the lack of written records.

HISTORY

600s–1200s	1445	1511	1610
Sumatra's Hindu-Buddhist Srivijaya kingdom dominates Southeast Asia's sea trade. Under Srivijaya, ethnic Malays immigrate to Borneo.	Islam becomes the state religion of Melaka, Srivijaya's successor as Southeast Asia's trading power. Merchants spread a predominantly tolerant, mild form of Sunni Islam that accommodates existing traditions.	Portugal conquers Melaka in a bid to control the spice trade. Brunei succeeds Melaka as Southeast Asia's leading Islamic kingdom and trading centre.	The Dutch build a diamond-trading post in Sambas, West Kalimantan, beginning more than 300 years of Dutch interest in Kalimantan and its natural resources.

were disinclined towards European immigration, and discouraged European companies from destroying native jungle to create rubber plantations. They also invited Chinese, many from Fujian and Guandong, to work in Sarawak as miners, farmers and traders. Despite a bloody rebellion by Hakka immigrants in 1857, Chinese came to dominate Sarawak's economy.

When James Brooke died in 1868, he was succeeded by his nephew, Charles Johnson, who changed his surname to Brooke. During his long reign, which lasted until his death in 1917, Charles Brooke extended the borders of his kingdom (at the expense of the sultan of Brunei), developed Sarawak's economy and slashed government debt.

In 1917 Charles Vyner Brooke, son of Charles Brooke, ascended to the throne of Sarawak. A veteran of government service, he professionalised Sarawak's administration, preparing it for a modern form of rule.

> In Borneo's interior, tribal wars are believed to have been frequent for centuries, with long-standing rivalries pitting some groups, such as the Kenyah and Iban, against each other.

Brunei's Continuing Decline

In 1865, 15 years after Brunei and the United States signed a Treaty of Peace, Friendship, Commerce and Navigation, Brunei's ailing sultan leased Sabah to – of all people – the American consul in Brunei, Claude Lee Moses. His rights eventually passed to an Englishman, Alfred Dent, who also received Sulu's blessing. In 1881, with London's support, Dent formed the British North Borneo Company (later called the North Borneo Chartered Company) to administer the territory. Once again, Britain managed to bag a slice of Borneo on the cheap.

In 1888 the prospect of further territorial losses led the Sultanate of Brunei, tiny and in danger of becoming even tinier, to become a British protectorate. But British 'protection' did not prevent Brunei from losing Limbang to Sarawak in 1890, absurdly chopping the sultanate into two discontiguous parts (Brunei still claims the Limbang area). Ironically, Brunei's colonial status in the 19th century paved the way for its transformation into Borneo's only independent country a century later.

> As part of the resistance to Japan's occupation, Australian commandos encouraged a headhunting revival, offering 'ten bob a nob' for Japanese heads. Many of the skulls now displayed in Dayak longhouses are thought to be Japanese.

The Dutch in Kalimantan

The British presence along Borneo's northern coast spurred the Dutch to beef up their presence in Kalimantan. Dutch commercial exploitation, begun in the very late 1500s, reached its peak at the end of the 19th century with thriving rubber, pepper, copra, tin, coal and coffee exports, plus oil drilling in East Kalimantan. This assertiveness sparked disputes with indigenous groups, culminating in 1859 in a four-year war between the Dutch and the Banjarmasin sultanate; resistance continued until 1905.

World War II

Imperial Japan, in need of Borneo's natural resources to power its war machine, seized Sarawak's Miri oilfields on 16 December 1941; other targets in the poorly defended region quickly fell. The retreating British

1824

The Anglo-Dutch Treaty divides the region into spheres of influence. The Dutch are granted Kalimantan but are preoccupied with Sumatra and Java.

1841

After helping the sultan of Brunei's emissary suppress an uprising, Englishman James Brooke becomes first White Rajah of Sarawak.

POPPER FOTO/GETTY IMAGES ©

1881

The British North Borneo Company is established in Sandakan to administer Sabah. It is the state's governing authority until Sabah and Sarawak become Crown colonies after WWII.

» Sir James Brooke

sabotaged oil rigs and other key petroleum installations but the Japanese soon had the oil flowing again.

As elsewhere in Asia, the Japanese occupation of Borneo unleashed local nationalist sentiments, but at the same time Japanese forces acquired a reputation for brutality. At Mandor (about 90km north of Pontianak in West Kalimantan), 21,037 people – sultans, intellectuals and common people, all accused of plotting against Japanese rule – were murdered. In Sabah, the infamous labour camp at Sandakan's Agricultural Experimental Station housed Allied captives from across Southeast Asia. Of the 2434 Australian and British POWs incarcerated there, only six survived the war.

In 1944 a primarily British and Australian force parachuted into Bario in the Kelabit Highlands and allied with indigenous Kelabits against the Japanese. In 1945, Australian troops landed in East Kalimantan, fighting bloody battles in Tarakan and Balikpapan. But Japanese forces in Borneo surrendered only after the atomic bombings of Hiroshima and Nagasaki.

Colonisation & Decolonisation

After the war, which left many of Borneo's cities in ruins (mainly from Allied bombing), the North Borneo Chartered Company ceded authority over what is now Sabah to the British Crown. In Sarawak, the White Rajah returned briefly under Australian military administration but, overwhelmed by the cost of rebuilding, transferred sovereignty to the British government.

Local opposition to Sarawak's transformation from an independent kingdom into a Crown colony was widespread. Those demanding continued rule by the White Rajahs encompassed not only Anthony Brooke, Charles Vyner Brooke's nephew and heir apparent, but also many indigenous Sarawakians. The White Rajahs may have been of British stock, but after three generations many did not consider them outsiders but an integral part of Sarawak's cultural and ethnic patchwork.

In 1949, after a four-year war, the Dutch – facing tremendous international pressure, including an American threat to cut off postwar reconstruction aid – withdrew from the Dutch East Indies. Indonesia, including Kalimantan, which had remained on the sidelines during the conflict, gained independence.

Later that year, Sarawak's second colonial governor, Duncan Stewart, was stabbed to death in Sibu. Secret British documents uncovered in 2012 indicate that the assassins, hanged in Kuching in 1950, were not partisans of Anthony Brooke, as long suspected, but rather were seeking an Indonesian takeover of Sarawak. Anthony Brooke, after spending his life as a self-appointed ambassador of peace, died in New Zealand in 2011 at the age of 98.

WAR

HISTORY

Allied bombing raids against Japanese targets in 1945 left Sandakan in ruins, so authorities moved Sabah's capital to Jesselton, now Kota Kinabalu.

1888	1929	1941–45	1946
Once Southeast Asia's pre-eminent Islamic trading centre, Brunei – what's left of it – slumps into British arms as a protectorate.	Commercial quantities of oil are discovered in Brunei, 30 years after the sultanate's first oil well is drilled.	Imperial Japan occupies Borneo. Early resistance by local Chinese is brutally repressed. Nascent nationalists greet the Japanese as liberators, but the occupiers' cruelty turns opinion.	As British colonial rule is about to end in India, the third White Rajah and the North Borneo Chartered Company cede rule of Sarawak and Sabah to Westminster.

Malaysian Independence

When the Federation of Malaya, consisting of the states of Peninsular Malaysia, was granted independence in 1957, Sarawak, British North Borneo (Sabah) and Brunei remained under British rule.

In 1962 the British proposed incorporating their Bornean territories into Malaya. At the last minute, Brunei pulled out of the deal, as the sultan (and, one suspects, Shell Oil) didn't want to see the revenue from its vast oil reserves channelled to the peninsula. In September 1963 Malaysia – made up of the Malay Peninsula, Singapore, Sabah and Sarawak – achieved *merdeka* (ie independence; Singapore withdrew in 1965).

Konfrontasi & Transmigrasi

In the early 1960s, Indonesia's increasingly radicalised, left-leaning President Soekarno laid claim to all of Borneo. His response to the incorporation of northern Borneo into Malaysia was an undeclared war dubbed the Konfrontasi (literally, 'confrontation'; 1962–66), to which Indonesians were rallied with the bellicose slogan *ganyang Malaysia* (smash Malaysia). Soviet-equipped Indonesian armed forces crossed into Sabah and Sarawak from Kalimantan. At the height of the conflict, 50,000 troops from Britain, Australia and New Zealand patrolled Sabah and Sarawak's borders with Indonesia. Hundreds of soldiers and civilians on both sides were killed. When Soekarno's successor, President Soeharto (in office 1967–98), came to power, he quickly quieted tensions.

Soeharto also expanded the *transmigrasi* (transmigration) policies initiated by the Dutch in the 1930s, which moved millions of people from densely populated islands such as Java, Bali and Madura to more remote areas, including Kalimantan. From 1996 to 2001, hundreds of Madurese migrants were killed in attacks by Dayaks, joined at times by local Malays and Chinese. The conflict made international headlines because of the many reported cases of headhunting. Long-term, the most insidious effect of *transmigrasi* has been to marginalise Kalimantan's indigenous communities.

The name 'Borneo', introduced by the Spaniards, is a mispronunciation of 'Brunei' (or, according to another theory, of *buah nyiur*, Malay for coconut). In both Bahasa Malaysia and Bahasa Indonesia the entire island is called Kalimantan.

Bruneian Independence

Brunei achieved self-government, except in matters of defence and foreign affairs, in 1971. In 1984 Sultan Haji Hassanal Bolkiah reluctantly led his country to complete independence from Britain. A graduate of the Royal Military Academy Sandhurst, he continues to maintain very close political and military ties with the UK.

1963	1967	1984	2000
Sarawak and Sabah join Malaya and Singapore to create Malaysia. Their role: to maintain a non-Chinese majority. Indonesia claims all of Borneo and declares Konfrontasi against Malaysia.	Brunei sultan Omar Ali Saifuddien abdicates in favour of his eldest son, Hassanal Bolkiah, who remains in power to this day.	Brunei achieves full independence but continues close ties with Great Britain. The last British military base in eastern Asia, home to a Gurkha battalion, is at Seria.	Abu Sayyaf Islamic separatists from the southern Philippines kidnap 21 people on Sabah's resort island of Sipadan. Libya pays a ransom to free them.

Peoples & Cultures

Borneo's indigenous peoples, known collectively as Dayaks, belong to scores of different tribal groups that speak about 140 languages and dialects. Some live on the coast, others along the remote upland tributaries of great rivers. A few generations ago, some tribes still practised headhunting; today, many Dayaks are well integrated into 21st-century economic life, and it's not unusual to meet university professors, lawyers, government officials and airline pilots who grew up in longhouses.

Among the ancestors of today's Dayaks were migrants from southern China who came to Borneo about 3000 years ago, bringing with them elements of the Dongson culture, including irrigated rice cultivation, buffalo-sacrifice rituals and *ikat* (fabric patterned by tie-dying the yarn before weaving). These newcomers mixed with native groups – people like the cave dwellers of Niah – and eventually developed into more than 200 distinct tribes.

Stranger in the Forest tells the extraordinary tale of Eric Hansen's solo trek across Borneo and his encounters with various Dayak groups, including the Penan.

Who's a Dayak?

Not all of Borneo's indigenous tribes refer to themselves as Dayaks, but the term usefully groups together peoples who have a great deal in common – and not just from an outsider's point of view.

Traceable back to about 1840, the term 'Dayak' (or 'Dyak') gained currency thanks to its use by colonial authorities. It appears to be derived from the last two syllables of 'Bidayuh', itself an exonym (a name originally used by outsiders). As a result, while contemporary Iban in Sarawak think of, and refer to, themselves as Iban (although this term is also an exonym), when they talk about Dayaks they are likely to be referring to the Bidayuh. However, shared cultural practices, values and political, economic and environmental interests – and several generations of Christian faith and inter-group marriages – make it a no-brainer for different groups to work together. The only term that embraces everyone is 'Dayak'.

None of Sabah's indigenous ethnicities are particularly keen on using the term 'Dayak', preferring instead to see themselves as Kadazan, Dusun, Rungus, Murut etc. Not so in Kalimantan, where native groups have rallied around the Dayak banner and the term has become a focus for political unity across tribal lines.

For the purposes of affirmative action (positive discrimination) in Malaysia, Dayaks, like Malays, are considered *bumiputra* ('sons of the soil'; ie people considered indigenous under Malaysian law).

Indigenous non-Malays, mainly Iban and Kelabit, account for less than 10% of Brunei's population.

Sabah

More than 30 indigenous groups make Sabah a medley of traditions and cultures. The state's largest ethnic group, known as the Kadazan–Dusun,

THE PENAN

The least integrated – and most economically disadvantaged – aboriginal group in Sarawak and Brunei is the Penan, traditionally nomadic hunter-gatherers known for never taking more than they require from the jungle – and for never having engaged in headhunting. Because of their distinct culture and lifestyle, some people do not consider the Penan to be Dayaks.

Christian missionaries and the Sarawak government have long pressured the Penan to settle in longhouses, and today many live sedentary lives in northern Sarawak's Baram, Belaga and Limbang districts; only a few hundred are believed to remain true nomads. Settled Penan may plant rice, but they continue to rely on the jungle for medicine and food, including sago from palm trees and game that they hunt with blowpipes.

With their lands and way of life under severe threat from timber concessions and dams, the Penan have long engaged in civil-disobedience campaigns that have included blocking logging roads. While many sympathisers – such as the celebrated Bruno Manser (www.brunomanser.ch), an environmental activist who disappeared near Bario in 2000 – seek to protect the Penan's unique way of life, Malaysian authorities insist that they should be assimilated into mainstream society, whether they like it or not.

make up 18% of the population. Mainly Roman Catholic, the Kadazan and the Dusun share a common language and have similar customs, though the former originally lived mainly in the state's western coastal areas and river deltas, while the latter inhabited the interior highlands.

The Murut (3.2% of the population) traditionally lived in the south-western hills bordering Kalimantan and Brunei, growing hill-rice and hunting with spears and blowpipes. Soldiers for Brunei's sultans, they were the last group in Sabah to abandon headhunting.

Sarawak

Dayak culture and lifestyles are probably easiest to observe and experience in Sarawak, where Dayaks make up about 48% of the population.

About 29% of Sarawakians are Iban, descended from groups that migrated from West Kalimantan's Sungai Kapuas starting five to eight centuries ago. Also known as Sea Dayaks for their exploits as pirates, the Iban are traditionally rice growers and longhouse dwellers. A reluctance to renounce headhunting enhanced their ferocious reputation.

The Bidayuh (8% of the population), once known as Land Dayaks, live mainly in the hills south and southwest of Kuching, near the Kalimantan border. Their ancestors are thought to have migrated from the Sungkong area of what is now West Kalimantan many centuries ago. As with many Dayak groups, identities and traditions are very local, and adjacent villages sometimes speak dialects so distinct that people find it easier to communicate in English or Malay. Few Bidayuh still live in longhouses.

Upland groups, such as the Kelabit, Kayan and Kenyah – that is, almost everyone except the Bidayuh, the Iban and the coastal-dwelling Melanau – are often grouped together under the term Orang Ulu (upriver peoples). The Kenyah and Kayan are known for their elaborately decorated longhouses and the *kalong* motif, with its sinuous, intertwined creepers and vines.

DAYAKS

Up the Notched-Log Ladder is Sydwell Mouw Flynn's memoir of her parents' missionary work among Sarawak's Dayaks from 1933 to 1950, and her return to the land where she was raised half a century later.

Kalimantan

In Indonesian Borneo, the terms Dayak and Dayakism imply pan-Dayak political and ethnic solidarity.

In Central Kalimantan, the largest indigenous group is the Ngaju Dayak, who live along major rivers and do more fishing than hunting.

The Ot Danum Dayaks, who live further upriver, raise fruit, collect natural rubber and make dugout canoes that they sell to downriver tribes.

Along East Kalimantan's Sungai Mahakam, the Kutai are the main indigenous group in the lower reaches, hosting the annual Erau Festival at their capital Tenggarong.

The Kayan and the closely related Kenyah are found in the Apo Kayan Highlands, as well as in Sarawak and Brunei. They are known for building the most elaborately decorated longhouses and for having a strict social hierarchy.

The unique Punan cave dwellers live between the headwaters of the Mahakam and Kapuas rivers, spanning East and West Kalimantan. Today, most have given up troglodytic living.

West Kalimantan is home to a large population of Bidayuh, most of whom are Catholic (in Sarawak, quite a few of the Bidayuh are Anglican). Many identify strongly with the locality they're from – for instance, Bidayuh from Terebung refer to themselves as 'Dayak Terebung'.

The Longhouse

One of the most distinctive features of Dayak life is the longhouse (*rumah batang* or *rumah panjai*), which is essentially an entire village under one seemingly interminable roof. Longhouses take a variety of shapes and styles, but all are raised above the damp jungle floor on hardwood stilts and most are built on or near river banks. For reasons of geography, traditional Dayak societies did not develop a government structure beyond that of the longhouse.

The focus of longhouse life is the covered common verandah, known as a *ruai* to the Iban and an *awah* to the Bidayuh; the Kelabits have two, a *tawa'* for celebrations and a *dapur* for cooking (other groups use other terms). Residents use these communal spaces to socialise, engage in economic activities, cook and eat meals, and hold communal celebrations.

One wall of the verandah, which can be up to 250m long, is pierced by doors to individual family *bilik* (apartments), where there's space for sleeping and storage. If you ask about the size of a longhouse, you will usually be told how many doors, ie family units, it has. Traditional Iban courtship, known as *ngayap*, involved surreptitious night-time liaisons in the young woman's room.

Like the rest of us, Dayaks love their mod cons, so longhouses where people actually live fuse age-old forms with modern conveniences – the resulting mash-up frequently mixes traditional materials (bamboo slat floors) with highly functional features, such as corrugated iron, linoleum, satellite dishes and, out the front, a car park. The new longhouses built by the government for resettled Dayak villages usually follow the old floor-plan but use unremarkable modern construction techniques.

Most young Dayaks move away from the longhouse for greener pastures, seeking higher education and good jobs in the cities. But almost all keep close ties to their home longhouse, returning for major family and community celebrations. Some families that choose to remain in the longhouse community build a private house nearby, in part to escape the fire hazard inherent in living in a flammable structure with so many other people.

Dayak Religions

Traditional Dayak animism, which varies from tribe to tribe, focuses on the spirits associated with virtually all places and things. In Kalimantan it is known collectively as Kaharingan.

Carvings, totems, tattoos and other objects (including, in earlier times, headhunted skulls) are used to keep bad spirits at bay, attract good spirits and soothe spirits that may be upset. Totems at entrances to villages and

Some Dayak societies, such as the Iban and Bidayuh, are remarkably egalitarian, while others, such as the Kayan, used to have a strict social hierarchy – now somewhat blurred – with classes of nobles (*maren*), aristocrats (*hipuy*), commoners (*panyin*) and slaves (*dipen*).

PEOPLES & CULTURES

IBAN

The Iban traditionally kept headhunted skulls outside the head-taker's family apartment, on the longhouse verandah (*ruai*), while the Bidayuh exhibited theirs in a communal headhouse (*baruk or panggah*).

TRIBAL BODY ART

Elongated Ears

The most striking fashion feature of many older Dayak women (and, in some groups such as the Kelabit, men) is their elongated, pierced earlobes, stretched over the years by the weight of heavy gold or brass rings. Young people rarely follow this custom, and older Dayaks sometimes trim their ear lobes as a sign of having converted to Christianity.

Iban Tattoos

According to Iban tattoo master Ernesto Umpie (www.borneoheadhunter.com), *bejalai* can loosely be defined as a journey, or a voyage of discovery. With each life skill mastered, an Iban warrior-to-be would add a tattoo to their body, creating a biographical constellation of swirling designs.

At around the age of 10 or 11, a young Iban would get their first tattoo, a *bungai terung* (eggplant flower) drawn on each shoulder. The design, created using soot mixed with fermented sugarcane juice and hand-tapped bamboo or bone needles, commemorated the beginning of one's journey as a man (women were known to get them as well). The squiggly centre of the flower symbolised new life and represented the intestines of a tadpole, visible through their translucent skin. The plant's petals were a reminder that patience is a virtue, and that only a patient man can truly learn life's lessons.

Further attainments – for instance, mastering boatbuilding, hunting, shamanism and even traditional dancing – brought more ink, including the popular crab design, which symbolised strength and evoked the strong legs and hard shell of the crafty sideways walkers. Traditionally, the Iban believed that when drawn with magical ink, the design could act like the shell of a crab, protecting bearers from the blade of a machete.

The bravest travellers received the coveted throat tattoo as they evolved into a *bujang berani* (brave bachelor). The design – a fish body that morphs into a double-headed dragon – wanders up from the soft spot at the centre of the clavicle, known as the 'life point' to the Iban.

Through all this, elaborate rules had to be followed. For instance, only men who had taken a head were permitted to tattoo the tops of their hands. Also, every animal inked inward must have something to eat – dragons were always depicted with a small lizard near their mouths – because if the creature was left hungry it would feed on the bearer's soul.

When the warriors returned to their village, the tattoos were a bit like passport stamps, tracing borders crossed and frontiers explored. A large collection of blueish-black 'merit badges' greatly increased one's desirability as a bachelor and, it was believed, enabled a soul to shine brightly in the afterlife.

These days, after decades of decline, tattooing is making something of a comeback. In urban areas, some young Iban get tattoos to commemorate achievements such as travelling abroad or completing their military service or a university degree. Sometimes the tattoos are eclectic, combining designs from tribes that once warred with each other with modern motifs inspired by Eminem and Lady Gaga.

The Infamous Palang

If you thought tribal body art stopped at tattoos, you are very wrong. However, unlike the ubiquitous skin ink, you probably won't come head to head, so to speak, with a *palang*.

The *palang*, a long-standing Dayak tradition, is a horizontal rod of metal or bone that pierces the penis, mimicking the natural genitalia of the Sumatran rhino. As times change, this type of procedure is becoming less common, but many villages still have an appointed piercer, who uses the traditional method: a bamboo vice in a cold river. The real macho men opt for some seriously extreme adornments, from multiple *palang* to deliberate scarification of the penis. Some men will even sew beads into their foreskins to make their nether regions resemble the giant Rafflesia flower.

The impetus behind these self-inflicted 'works of art' is actually to enhance a woman's pleasure rather than personal adornment. Among some communities these radical procedures were once just as important as lopping off heads.

longhouses are markers for spirits. The hornbill is considered a powerful spirit and is honoured in dance and ceremony; its feathers are treasured. Black is widely considered a godly colour, so it features in traditional outfits. In some tribes, women have special roles – for instance, a female priest, called a *bobohizan,* presides over many key Kadazan–Dusun traditional rituals in Sabah.

Ancestor worship plays a large part in Kaharingan. After death, Dayaks join their ancestors in the spirit world. For some groups, spirits may reside in a particular mountain or other natural shrine. Burial customs include elaborately carved mausoleums, memorial monoliths and interment in ceramic jars.

Most Dayaks now belong to mainstream Protestant groups (eg the Anglican Church), evangelical denominations (especially the Borneo Evangelical Church, also known as the SIB) and the Roman Catholic Church. Some evangelicals insist on purging all vestiges of previous beliefs, but in most instances Christianity overlays older cultural practices. Very few Dayaks still follow traditional religious practices.

Festivities such as Gawai Dayak, the harvest festival in Sarawak, are usually considered to be an expression of Dayak culture rather than of pre-Christian religious beliefs.

Land of the Headhunters

Headhunting *(ngayau)* has been relegated to the realm of tourist brochures, T-shirts and Dayaks' self-deprecating witticisms, but for over 500 years it was an important element of Borneo's indigenous culture.

Many of the rites, rituals and beliefs surrounding this gruesome tradition remain shrouded in mystery but one aspect was unchanging: the act of taking heads was always treated with the utmost seriousness. Warriors would go out on two types of expeditions: *kayo bala,* a group raid involving several warriors; and *kayo anak,* performed by a *bujung berani* (lone brave). The takers of heads often bore no personal animosity to their victims.

In the upper regions of the Batang Rejang, the *kayo anak* was a common method of wooing a prospective bride. The most valuable heads were those belonging to women and children because only the savviest and stealthiest warrior could ambush a child or woman as they bathed or picked berries. Such heads were usually hidden away from marauders near the longhouse hearth.

After a successful hunt, the warrior would wander the jungle, wrestling with the taken spirit rather than letting down his guard for a nap. In the morning, he would return to his longhouse where the head would be smoked and strung up for the others to see and honour. Heads were worshipped and revered, and food offerings were not uncommon. A longhouse with many heads was feared and respected by the neighbouring clans.

The tradition began its gradual decline in 1841 when James Brooke, at the behest of Brunei's sultan, started quashing the hunt for heads, in part to attract foreign traders, who had understandably tended to keep their distance from Borneo's shores. A nasty skirmish involving a knife-wielding pirate and a Chinese merchant's noodle gave Brooke the opportunity to show the Dayaks that he meant business – he promptly executed the criminal.

Headhunting, to the extent that it continued, flew under the government's radar until WWII, when British commandos found the practice useful for the war effort – so long as the victims were Japanese. Many of the heads that now adorn longhouses date from this period.

These days, sensationalised accounts of inter-ethnic conflict in Indonesian Borneo often describe the violence as latter-day headhunting.

The White Rajahs of Sarawak allowed the Dayaks to live according to their age-old traditions and beliefs except in one area, headhunting, which they made great efforts to suppress.

PEOPLES & CULTURES

HEADHUNTING

If press descriptions are to be believed, the last '*tête* offensive' (so to speak) took place in Kalimantan in the early years of the 21st century, when migrants from the island of Madura who settled, or were resettled by the Indonesian government, in Dayak and Malay areas, were the victims.

As Borneo's indigenous people embraced Christianity and rejected traditional animistic superstitions, many longhouses dismantled their dangling skulls. Though if you ask around, you'll quickly learn that the heads haven't actually been tossed away – that would just be bad luck!

Native Land Rights

When a tract of forest is cut down for timber or to make way for a dam or oil-palm plantation, animals are not the only ones who lose their homes – Borneo's forest-dwelling indigenous peoples are also displaced.

The Penan have been especially hard hit by logging and forced relocations. In Sarawak, the government has tried to quash Penan protests – ongoing in 2012 – and often responds to any sign of civil disobedience with arrests. Legal challenges to the government's refusal to recognise traditional land tenure are continuing.

In Kalimantan, migrants from other parts of Indonesia have encroached upon the Dayaks' traditional lands, producing a sometimes violent backlash.

Visiting a Longhouse

According to longstanding Dayak tradition, anyone who shows up at a longhouse must be welcomed and given accommodation. Since almost all longhouses were, until quite recently, a considerable jungle trek or longboat ride from the nearest human settlement, this custom made a great deal of sense.

Generations of jungle travellers knew the routine: upon arrival they would present themselves to the headman (*ketua kaum* in Malay, *tuai rumah* in Iban and *maren uma* in Kayan), who would arrange for very basic sleeping quarters. But in the last decade or two, as transport has become easier and tourist numbers have soared, this tradition has come under strain, and these days turning up at a longhouse unannounced may be an unwelcome imposition on longhouse residents – in short, bad manners.

The upshot is that in many areas of Borneo, the days when anyone could turn up unexpectedly at a longhouse and stay the night are largely over. And even if you make your own way to a longhouse that's happy to have you, you are likely to face significant communication and cultural barriers. Interacting spontaneously with locals isn't always easy, as the elders usually don't speak English, and the younger people are often out working the fields or have moved to the city to pursue careers.

Finding a Guide

Hiring a guide who can coordinate your visit with longhouse residents and make introductions will help you avoid language and cultural barriers.

When considering a tour operator or freelance guide, it's best to keep an open mind about the itinerary but do not hesitate to be upfront about preferences and concerns. Do you require a certain level of sleeping comfort? Do you have any dietary restrictions? How important is it that you be able to communicate with your hosts in English? Will you be disappointed if you see a satellite dish dangling off the side of the longhouse's cellphone tower? Do you want to be the only traveller around, or would you prefer to share the experience with others? Finding the right guide – and, through them, the right longhouse – can mean the difference between spending a sleepless night with other sweaty, bored tourists, or having a spirited evening (double entendre intended) swapping smiles, stories and shots of *tuak* with the locals.

Dayak slash-and-burn (swidden) agriculture is sometimes blamed for deforestation and forest fires, but in fact indigenous farmers are responsible for only a minuscule fraction of the island's habitat loss.

TRADITIONS

At the Sarawak Cultural Village near Kuching, you can visit four Dayak longhouses – including the only remaining Melanau longhouse – constructed using just traditional materials and techniques. No tin roofs or satellite dishes!

GIFTS

Gift giving has become rather controversial over the last few years, with locals, tourists and tour operators offering a wide variety of advice on the subject. Longhouse communities do not traditionally require gifts from guests; in fact, some say that the tradition of gift giving actually began when travellers started visiting.

To avoid any awkward cultural miscommunications, your best bet is to ask your guide. Longhouses set far off the beaten track may appreciate bulk bags of rice or sugar, while communities that are a bit more in touch with the modern world might appreciate items such as pencils, school supplies or fishing line. Some travellers bring something edible that can be shared over glasses of *tuak*. Any way you do it, gifts are never a must, nor are they expected.

Many tourists prefer contributing to the longhouse economy by hiring locals for a longboat trip or buying one of the craft items offered for sale.

If you are visiting independently, it's polite to bring a small gift for the family of the person who invited you.

Sarawak has plenty of tour operators and guides eager to take you (and your money) on Borneo's ultimate cultural adventure. From Kuching, it's easy to arrange day trips and overnights to Annah Rais Longhouse. For something off the beaten track, Kuching-based tour agencies and guides can take you to the remote Sri Aman Division, to rivers such as the Batang Skrang, Batang Lemanak and Batang Ai. The upper Batang Rejang has lots of longhouses but we've been hearing tales of dubious guiding activity in Kapit (we've also heard from travellers who've had a great time there and in Belaga). Trekkers interested in walking from longhouse to longhouse in the Kelabit Highlands should head to Bario and plan their adventure from there.

There are a number of reliable tour agencies available. The Sarawak Tourism Board (www.sarawaktourism.com) has an online listing of about 100 licensed 'travel service providers'. Some of the best guides work for tour operators, which saves them from having to go through the rigmarole of getting their own STB licence. Some freelance guides are friendly and knowledgeable but, alas, some are not – ask your fellow travellers for recommendations. In any case, it can be hard to hold an unlicensed guide accountable if something goes wrong.

What to Expect

When you arrive at a longhouse, don't be surprised to find that it wouldn't make a very good film set for a period drama about headhunters. The Dayaks have moved – for the most part willingly – into the 21st century and so have their dwellings. Remember, though, that a longhouse, more than being a building, is a way of life embodying a communal lifestyle and a very real sense of mutual reliance and responsibility. It is this spirit, rather than the physical building, that makes a visit special.

Every longhouse is led by a headman. Depending on the tribe, he (or in a handful of cases she) may be appointed by his predecessor or elected; either way, heredity often plays a key role in selection. In many areas, longhouses are known by the name of the headman, so if you know the name of your destination you'll already know the name of the chief.

Depending on the various goings-on at the longhouse you're visiting, you may or may not spend time with the headman, although he will usually 'show face' as it is impolite for him not to do so. Your guide will usually be the one showing you where to sleep, which is likely to be on the longhouse verandah, in a resident's living room, or in a specially built hut next door to the longhouse.

LAND RIGHTS

The Borneo Project's documentary *Rumah Nor*, about an Iban community's fight for its land, can be viewed online at www .borneoproject .org (under 'Our Work').

GAWAI DAYAK

In Sarawak and Brunei, the main pan-Dayak event of the year is Gawai Dayak (literally, 'Dayak festival'). Coinciding with the rice harvest of some groups, it brings Dayak singles and families who live in the city back to their ancestral longhouses for round after round of socialising, eating, singing, dancing and the consumption of *tuak* (rice wine). As one ebullient host recently scolded, proffering *tuak* in bamboo cups, 'too much talking, no drinking, cannot!'

Many Dayak communities also hold community events, such as dance performances, sports competitions and beauty contests, to which many revellers (especially women) wear brightly coloured traditional costumes, including headdresses, bangles and beads.

Ceremonies marking the rice harvest are age old, but Gawai Dayak, as a festival celebrated simultaneously by once-rival Dayak tribes all across Sarawak, was introduced by the state government and only dates from the late 1950s. The festival officially begins on the night of 31 May and lasts for two days (1 and 2 June are public holidays in Sarawak), but in some areas (eg around Bau), kid-friendly village-level events take place on other dates between mid-May and the end of June.

Gawai Dayak festivities in longhouses and villages are invitation only, but thanks to Dayak traditions of hospitality, Western visitors are often welcome to join in the fun.

Do your best to engage with the inhabitants of any community you are allowed to enter, rather than just wandering around snapping photographs. A good guide can act as a translator when you strike up conversations, and he or she will keep you abreast of any cultural norms – like when and where to take off your shoes – so you won't have to worry too much about saying or doing the wrong thing.

Eat, Drink & Be Merry

If you are travelling with your own guide, he or she will be in charge of organising your meals – whether it's a separately prepared repast or a feast with some of the longhouse residents.

The Iban, in particular, like to honour their guests by offering meat on special occasions. Vegetarians and vegans should be clear about their dietary restrictions as vegetable dishes are often served in a chicken sauce. Meals will be plentiful no matter what, though it is not considered rude or disrespectful to bring your own food, too. Two important things to remember when eating with longhouse residents: don't put your feet near the food (which is always served in a communal fashion); and don't step over anyone's plate if you need to excuse yourself from the eating area.

Many Dayaks take their Christian faith very seriously, so much so that some communities have banned alcohol – including *tuak* (rice wine) – entirely.

After dinner, when the generators start clicking off, it may be time to hunker down with the evening's bottle of bootleg spirits: *tuak*. The ceremonial shot glass will be passed from person to person amid chit-chat and belly laughter. Drink the shot when it's your turn (you won't really have a choice) and pass the glass along. *Tuak* may taste mild but some types are pretty potent, and you can expect a stunning hangover the next day. When you reach your limit, simply press the rim of the glass with your finger like you're pushing an eject button. If you don't want to drink, you can claim a medical condition – but make sure you don't get caught sneaking a sip later on! Smiles, big hand gestures and dirty jokes go a long way, even in your native language (and it'll all be second nature when you're nice and lubricated).

Dayak ceremonies feature a variety of traditional dances. Accepting an invitation to join the dance and making a fool of yourself are sure crowd pleasers.

The Cuisines of Borneo

Eating in Borneo is never boring. Southeast Asia's main trade, immigration and colonisation routes are right nearby, which is why the island's cuisines include dishes from various provinces of southern China, the Malay parts of both mainland and island Southeast Asia, and even southern India – in addition to delicious indigenous (Dayak) dishes, based on ingredients that grow wild in the rainforest.

Throughout Borneo, *nasi* (rice) and *mee* (noodles) are the staples, and one or the other makes an appearance at almost every meal, including breakfast. Rice is eaten steamed, as *nasi goreng* (fried with other ingredients) and boiled as *bubur* (sweet or savoury porridge very popular for breakfast), or glutinous varieties are steamed and moulded into tubes or cubes and often wrapped with leaves. Noodles, in a variety of widths and thicknesses, can be made from wheat (with or without egg), rice or mung beans, and are served boiled in soup *(soto or sup)* – a Chinese favourite for breakfast – or fried *(mee goreng)* with other ingredients.

In some parts of Borneo, people get their carbs not from rice or noodles but from starch extracted from the pith of the sago tree. In Brunei it is served in an unbelievably gooey form known as *ambuyat*.

Dayak Cuisines

Borneo's indigenous peoples are remarkably diverse, expressing themselves with a rich variety of languages, traditions and artistic forms. But when it comes to cooking, they all turn to pretty much the same uniquely Bornean selection of leaves, flowers, fruits, roots, vines, ferns, fish and meats that the rainforest shares with all who know its edible secrets.

Each Dayak tribe has its own ideas about the best way to combine, season and prepare the natural bounty of the forest. Some dishes are tangy, others bitter or surprisingly spicy, and yet others characterised by peaty, jungly flavours unknown in other Asian culinary traditions. Many dishes are cooked or served in leaves (eg *daun isip*, used by the Kelabits) that add delicate flavours in addition to serving as ecofriendly packaging and plates.

Because some ingredients, such as ferns, are so perishable, they have to be eaten within a day of being picked and exporting them – even to Peninsular Malaysia – is virtually impossible. As a result, the only way to

---

BAMBOO CHICKEN

In many parts of Borneo, a perennial Dayak favourite is bamboo chicken (*asam siok* in Bidayuh, *pansoh manok* in Iban). To make it, rice, marinated chicken and spices, such as lemon grass, garlic, ginger and chillies are stuffed into a length of bamboo, which is then sealed with turmeric leaves. The resulting cylinder is then cooked near (but not too near) an open fire, thereby infusing the dish with the delicate aromas of bamboo and turmeric, sealing in the spices, and ensuring that the meat emerges deliciously tender.

WHERE TO SAMPLE BORNEO'S CUISINE

The best way to become familiar with the incredible variety of ingredients used by Bornean cooks is to visit a market (*tamu* or *pasar* – the latter term shares Persian origins with the English word 'bazaar') or, in Kalimantan's Banjarmasin, to head to the floating market. Some markets feature fresh, organic jungle products collected and brought to town by Dayak villagers – keep an eye out for *midin* and *paku* ferns and exotic fruits. In larger markets along the coast, you may spot literally scores of varieties of fish. Sellers are often happy to tell you about their wares (or at least show them to you), and sometimes offer samples. One stall owner we know once let a tourist taste every one of the 10 varieties of local banana piled up on his market table!

In Malaysian Borneo, most wet markets have a hawker centre (food stall section) upstairs. Because of Muslim dietary (halal) rules, Chinese stalls (which serve pork) and Malay stalls are often in separate areas. Night markets (*pasar malam*) open up only in the evening. During Ramadan most Malay food stalls are closed during daylight hours.

Other places to sample Borneo's incredible variety of dishes are no-frills cafes, sometimes with several vendors, known as *kopitiam* in Malay-inflected Hokkien Chinese and *kedai kopi* in Bahasa Malaysia (both names mean 'coffee shop'). Some traditional *kopitiam* open very early in the morning and stop selling food by the early afternoon. Also look out for food carts. These are known in Kalimantan as *kaki lima* (five legs): two for the proprietor, three for the cart.

experience the mouth-watering, eye-opening and tongue-tickling world of Dayak cuisine is to come to Borneo.

But even on the island, sampling Dayak cuisine – naturally organic and MSG-free – is rarely as easy as walking up to a hawker centre. There are a handful of restaurants in cities such as Kuching and Miri – of special note is the Dyak (p134), a pioneering gourmet establishment in Kuching – but otherwise the only way to savour indigenous dishes is to dine at a longhouse or be invited to dinner by a Dayak family.

Rice

A dozen or more varieties of Borneo-grown rice can be found in the markets, often in clear plastic sacks that let you see the colour, size and shape of the grains. Dayak groups traditionally grow rice using swidden (slash-and-burn) techniques.

Hill paddy, grown by upland villagers mainly for their own use, is generally unpolished and unprocessed. Red rice is generically known as *beras merah* (in Iban and Bahasa Malaysia), but other varieties of Bornean rice are white, light brown, dark brown and even reddish orange. Bario rice (from the cool Kelabit Highlands), Borneo's most prestigious rice variety, is famous for its small grains and delicate taste and aroma.

Glutinous rice (*pulut* in Iban and Bidayuh) is sometimes combined with coconut milk (*santan*), vegetable oil and a bit of salt and cooked in a length of bamboo lined with a banana leaf to produce *lemang*.

Ingredients

Ingredients you're likely to encounter in Dayak cooking – some are also used by Borneo's Malays and Chinese:

Bamboo shoots (*puluh* in Kelabit) Made from very young bamboo and often grown in people's gardens; in the Kelabit Highlands, *puluh* are sliced thin, boiled and then stir-fried with salt, pepper and small local fish.

Bitter beans (*petai*) Bright green beans that grow in long pods; they appear in dishes such as *petai gulai kechala* (stir-fried with wild ginger flowers, onions and anchovies).

Cassava leaves (*pucuk ubi* in Iban) Young leaves are often stir-fried (eg with chicken, or with anchovies, garlic and onions) and eaten with rice.

Chicken (*ayam* in Bahasa Malaysia) The tastiest kind comes from the *kampung* (villages) rather than large-scale commercial producers.

Chili paste (*bua' ladah* in Kelabit) Extremely hot, this condiment is made with chilli peppers, ginger, onion, garlic and salt.

Daun bungkang A leaf that grows on a fruit tree and, like bay leaves, is used to add flavour.

Doray (in Kelabit) A dark green goop that tastes a bit like spinach, made by boiling a leaf that grows along river banks with salt; said to be rich in vitamins and especially healthy for children, who eat it with rice or porridge.

Eggplant (*terung* in Iban and Bahasa; *brinjal* in Malaysian English) Bornean eggplants, which are the size of a peach, are often planted together with the hill rice and harvested before the rice stalks mature.

Fish (*ikan* in Bahasa Malaysia) Small fish grow in paddy fields, larger fish are caught in streams and rivers and in the sea.

Ginger flower (*bungai kechala* or *tepus*; *busak luduh* in Kelabit) Grows wild along river banks, has a lemony flavour and tastes a bit like artichoke heart; often chopped into very fine slivers, boiled and then fast-sautéed with onions.

Hot chilli (*cili*) Hot peppers used by all the various tribes.

Lemon grass (*sorai* in Bidayuh) The Bornean variety, which grows in the jungle, is more herbal and less sharp than the Thai variety.

Midin ferns These wild fiddlehead ferns (so called because their curled-up tips resemble the scroll of a violin or cello) were once eaten mainly by the rural poor, who collected the young fronds in forest clearings. Recently, though, they have been rediscovered by foodies and are hugely popular among Dayak, Malay and Chinese cooks. Tasty and nutritious, they're often lightly stir-fried to preserve their crunch. *Midin* ferns grow wild in dryer areas of the forest and in peat, and are now produced commercially on a small scale.

Paku ferns A type of fiddlehead fern that grows wild in moist parts of the forest

Pumpkin (*bua' lecak* in Kelabit) – bright orange on the outside and, when cooked, soft and creamy inside. Can be stir-fried, steamed or puréed to make cream of pumpkin soup.

Salt In upland Borneo, mineral-rich saline spring water is boiled in huge vats to produce high-iodine salt; it's sold in markets in leaf-wrapped 'sausages.

Tempoyak Preserved durian; the Bidayuh recipe (there are also Malay versions) calls for mixing deseeded durian pulp with coarse sugar, leaving it to ferment for a day or two, and then draining off the juices.

Tumeric leaves (*umiet* in Bidayuh) Used to wrap fish for steaming so that the flavour infuses the fish, or to seal the bamboo tube used to make bamboo chicken; contains minute quantities of cyanide, which the Dayaks remove by shredding the leaves and washing them before pounding them into a pulp

Venison (*payo* in Kelabit) Deer are still hunted in the forest in places like the Kelabit Highlands; after the animal is killed, the meat is immediately smoked (to preserve it) and then brought back to the village, where it is pounded (to soften it), boiled and finally stir-fried, often with lemon grass, ginger and onion. Before refrigeration, smoked meat was hung above the family hearth, where it would remain edible for months.

Tuak

When Dayaks get together for a celebration or to entertain visitors, festivities are traditionally lubricated with *tuak* (rice wine). Almost always home brewed, it comes in two main versions: *tuak laki* (gentlemen's *tuak*), which packs an alcoholic punch of 18% or more; and *tuak induk* (ladies' *tuak*), which is sweeter and has somewhat less alcohol. *Tuak*

THE CUISINES OF BORNEO

DURIAN

People either adore or are utterly disgusted by Southeast Asia's most notorious fruit, the flamboyantly odiferous durian. Hotels and airlines often post drawings of the spiky fruit slashed by a horizontal red bar to remind durian lovers to indulge elsewhere.

(known as *burak* to the Kelabits) is made from glutinous rice, sugar, yeast and water that are fermented for somewhere between two weeks and two or three months (the longer the better). Some versions are infused with fruits or wild herbs.

Each Dayak group has traditions associated with drinking *tuak*. Before drinking a bamboo cup of the potent liquid, bottoms-up style, the Bidayuh say 'tra-tra-tra-tra-ooooh-ah', with a rising tone on the 'ooooh' and a falling tone on the 'ah', while the Orang Ulu say something that sounds like 'ooh-weh-weh-weh-weeeeeeh aah-ah-ah'. To make the merry-making merrier, the Iban, at their festivities, send around a *sadong*, whose role is to *sadong* (pour) shots of *tuak* and cajole everyone to imbibe. The catch is that every time he asks someone to drink, they have the right to demand that he do so as well, with predictably mirthful results.

Other wines you may encounter at Dayak festivals include sugarcane wine *(tuak tobuh* in Bidayuh), which tastes a bit like port. To make it, sugarcane juice is boiled (to increase the concentration) and then fermented with a kind of bark the Bidayuh call *kohong*. Palm sap wine (*tuak tumbang* in Bidayuh, *ijok* in Iban), yellow in colour, is slightly fizzy, with a fruity flavour.

In Kuching, the Dyak restaurant serves unbelievably delicious *tuak* ice cream.

Malay Cuisine

Thanks to the spice trade, Malay cooking has absorbed ingredients and cooking methods from a variety of culinary traditions, including those of India, China and mainland Southeast Asia. Malay dishes are often made with hot chillies, ginger, galangal (a relative of ginger), lemon grass, garlic, shallots, turmeric leaves and, to add a rich, creamy feel, coconut milk.

Some of the Malay dishes and condiments widely available in Borneo:

Belacan Fermented shrimp paste

Bubur Rice porridge; often eaten for breakfast

Ikan bilis Tiny dried anchovies

Kangkung belacan Water spinach quick fried in a wok with *belacan*

Kari ayam Chicken curry; one of many Malay *kari* (curry) dishes

Mee goreng Malay-style fried noodles; usually made with wheat-and-egg noodles

Mee sapi Noodles with beef, either served in a hearty broth or with a light gravy

> Sarawak is famous all over Malaysia for its intricate and colourful *kek lapis* (striped layer cakes), available in Kuching along the Main Bazaar.

SARAWAK LAKSA

Tangy, chewy, spicy, crunchy and thoroughly lip smacking, Sarawak laksa is a supremely satisfying way to begin the day. It's the dish Sarawakians most often crave when they're away from Borneo

Sarawak laksa brings a hot, tangy broth – made with a paste of chilli, garlic, shallots, peanuts, galangal (a relative of ginger), candlenuts and lemon grass – together with *bee hoon* (vermicelli noodles) and an array of tasty toppings with toothsome textures: bean sprouts, omelette strips, chicken slices, shrimp and chopped cilantro (coriander). Diners squeeze calamansi lime on top and decide how much fiery *sambal belacan* they can handle.

Most purveyors of Sarawak laksa are, like *bee hoon*, of Chinese origin, but in the finest Malaysian tradition, this pungent dish brings together a variety of culinary influences, including classic Nonya (Peranakan) ingredients such as *sambal belacan* and coconut milk. Sarawak laksa, which does not contain curry, shares little more than its name with the 'laksa' dishes popular in Peninsular Malaysia and Singapore.

Nasi campur Rice served with a selection of side dishes, sometimes buffet-style (pricing is by weight); known as *nasi padang* in Indonesia

Nasi goreng Malay-style fried rice is distinguished from Chinese fried rice by the frequent presence of *belacan* (shrimp paste) and by the absence of pork

Nasi lemak White rice cooked in coconut milk and served with side dishes such as salted fish or egg; Malaysia's unofficial national dish, it's popular for breakfast

Pulut Glutinous rice

Rendang Spicy beef or chicken stew made with coconut milk

Roti canai Grill-fried Indian-style bread, often with a savoury or sweet filling; popular for breakfast

Sambal Any of a wide variety of spicy condiments or sauces made with hot chillies

Sambal belacan Ubiquitous condiment made with *belacan* (shrimp paste), hot chillies, *limau kasturi* (calamansi lime), sugar and sometimes other ingredients

Satay Skewers of *ayam* (chicken), *kambing* (goat, also used for lamb and mutton) and occasionally *ikan* (fish), *cumi* (squid) or *udang* (shrimp) grilled over an open fire and served with peanut sauce

Soto ayam Chicken soup made with rice vermicelli

Malay food is always halal – that is, it follows Muslim dietary rules: no pork or porcine derivatives, no products from animals that were hunted, and no alcohol.

THE CUISINES OF BORNEO

Chinese Cuisines

The ancestors of Borneo's ethnic Chinese population migrated from a variety of provinces in southern China (Kuching's Chinese History Museum spotlights nine different dialect groups). Their distinct culinary traditions – Hokkien, Teochow, Foochow, Hakka etc – are alive and well to this day, especially in the cities and larger towns of Sarawak and Sabah and in Singkawang (West Kalimantan), where many of the food stalls and restaurants are run by Chinese.

Near the coast, keep an eye out for Chinese fish and seafood restaurants that display the day's catch either alive, swimming in tanks, or laid out neatly on ice. Diners point to the creature they'd like to eat and specify the mode of preparation; the charge is by weight.

The flavours in Chinese cuisine tend to be muted compared to Malay cooking, and it has fewer complex spice combinations – the taste of the primary ingredients is usually foremost. Another defining aspect of Chinese food is its heavy reliance on pork and lard, both assiduously avoided by the Malays, though these days some Chinese eateries have deporkified in order to receive halal certification.

Chinese food stalls often serve up the following dishes:

Marriages between Malays and Straits Chinese resulted in a delicious fusion cuisine, known as Nonya or Peranakan, that mixes Chinese recipes and Malay spices. It can be a bit hard to find in Borneo but is well worth trying if you get a chance.

Bee hoon Rice vermicelli (very thin rice noodles)

Bubur Rice porridge (congee), often garnished with minced chicken or pork; popular for breakfast

Chicken rice White rice cooked with chicken stock and served with slices of chicken breast, *sambal* and cucumber slices

Fish ball soup Fish balls and stuffed tofu in a broth that's often made from pig bones; usually made with *tang hoon* (mung bean noodles)

Kam pua mee Foochow-style thin noodle soaked in pork fat and served with a side of roast pork; Sibu's signature dish

Kueh chap Tasty soup made with various spare piggy parts

Kolo mee Wheat noodles tossed in a mixture of oil and light soy sauce and garnished with barbecued pork and vegetables; a speciality of the Kuching area

Kueh teow Wide, flat rice noodles, served stir-fried or in soup

Lok-lok Deep-fried or boiled skewers of fish, bean curd etc that are eaten with sweet, sweet-and-sour or satay sauce, or with *belacan*

Lui char Traditional Hakka soup, bitter in taste, made of finely chopped herbs and vegetables; served with rice and roasted peanuts

Mee goreng When this Bahasa Malaysia term appears on a Chinese food stall, it's referring to Chinese-style fried noodles

Mee sua Wheat vermicelli; served by the Foochows with chicken and mushrooms in a large bowl of broth laced with Chinese wine

Vegetarian Cuisine

The Chinese and Indians have venerable vegetarian traditions, and all of Borneo's gastronomies include plenty of dishes made with vegetables such as *daun ubi* (cassava leaves), *cangkok manis* (a dark green leafy vegetable often fried with eggs), *sayur manis* (often called 'Sabah veg') and *kangkong* (water spinach or convolvulus). Soy beans (*dao* or *tau*) are widely available, often in the form of *tauhu* (bean curd) or tempe (fermented whole beans). Chinese establishments may be able to whip up *cap cai* (mixed vegetables), and you can always order a soup without meat, fish or seafood. At Malay places, the rice part of *nasi lemak* and *nasi campur* is obviously vegie, though some of the side dishes they're served with are not.

That's the good news. The bad news is that unless you specify otherwise, Malay-style stir-fried vegetables are often made with *belacan* (fermented shrimp paste), and Chinese stalls usually make their soup stock with animal bones, and slip into all sorts of dishes small quantities of pork (minced or ground) or lard. These ingredients may also make an unnoticed appearance in Dayak dishes.

If you're vegetarian, say: '*Saya hanya makan sayuran*' (I only eat vegetables). If you're a vegan, you may want to take it a step further: '*Saya tidak makan yang di perbuat dari susu, telur, ikan atau daging*' (I don't eat dairy products, eggs, fish or meat).

ABC

For a cooling dessert, try ABC (*ais batu campur*), also known as *ais kacang*, a hillock of shaved ice garnished with red beans, palm seeds, grass jelly, sweet corn and lurid-coloured syrups.

The Land & Environmental Issues

Borneo is one of the most geologically complex and biologically diverse places on the planet. Situated at the convergence of three great tectonic plates, the island owes much of its astounding biological range to the fact that as recently as 10,000 years ago it was connected to mainland Southeast Asia.

Within the lifetimes of many people alive today, almost the entirety of Borneo's land mass was covered with old-growth forests. Today, the rainforests of Borneo, a biodiversity hot spot of global importance, are critically imperilled – a quick look at Google Earth (compare Brunei's pristine Temburong District with adjacent parts of Sarawak) will illustrate what has been wrought over the last few decades. Fortunately, vast areas of the interior of Kalimantan are still relatively untouched, presenting humanity with one last opportunity to preserve Borneo's incredible natural riches.

The Land

At 740,330 sq km, Borneo is the third-largest island in the world (after Greenland and New Guinea). It is about one-third larger than France, and almost exactly the same size as Texas.

Bisected by the equator, Borneo is remarkably flat, with over 50% of the landscape less than 150m above sea level. Lowland areas tend to be swampy, with serpentine rivers and poor drainage. Malaysia's longest river is the Batang Rejang (563km) in Sarawak, while Indonesia's three longest rivers are all in Kalimantan: Sungai Kapuas (1143km), Sungai Mahakam (980km) and Sungai Barito (890km).

Mountains dominate much of the centre of the island, running on a diagonal axis from Mt Kinabalu in the northeast, southwestward into West Kalimantan. Unlike many islands in Indonesia and the Philippines, Borneo does not have any active volcanoes because it is part of a very stable continental shelf.

For an excellent, colourful introduction to Borneo's environment, check out *Wild Borneo* by Nick Garbutt.

COLONIALISM & CONSERVATION

Borders established in the 19th century ended up having a profound impact on the fate of Borneo's rainforests in the 21st century. Vast areas of forest land pried away from the sultan of Brunei by the White Rajahs and the British North Borneo Company ended up being clear-cut in the decades after Malaysian independence, whereas the vast majority of the territory that the sultan managed to retain is now pristine and protected wilderness.

Extensive deposits of limestone in northern Borneo show where ancient coral reefs were buried under thousands of metres of sediment, then lifted to form ranges of hills and mountains. In some areas, water has dissolved the limestone to form vast caves. Sarawak's Gunung Mulu National Park is one of the world's premier limestone landscapes, boasting towering rock pinnacles and the world's second-largest cave chamber. Niah National Park is also famous for its huge caves.

Borneo's most celebrated peak is 4095m Mt Kinabalu in Sabah, the highest mountain between the Himalayas and New Guinea and arguably the epicentre of Borneo's fabulous biodiversity. This colossal dome of granite, forced through the earth's crust as molten rock 10 to 15 million years ago, continues to rise about 5mm a year. Despite its location just north of the equator, Mt Kinabalu was high enough to be exquisitely sculpted by glaciers during the ice ages.

> Borneo has two Unesco World Heritage sites: Gunung Mulu National Park in Sarawak and Kinabalu National Park in Sabah.

Habitats

Borneo has dozens of highly specialised ecosystems. Following are the main ones you're likely to encounter.

Coral Reef

Borneo's fabled coral reefs are part of the 'Coral Triangle', a fantastically rich portion of the South China Sea that's home to 75% of the world's coral species and over 3000 types of marine fish. Reefs are in the best shape along the northeast coast of Borneo, where the water is clear and free of sediment. The islands of Sipadan in Sabah and Derawan in East Kalimantan have the greatest concentrations of reefs. Other protected areas include Tun Sakaran Marine Park in Sabah and Talang-Satang National Park in Sarawak.

Kerangas (Heath Forest)

Sandy soils that are highly acidic and drain quickly support a highly specialised habitat known as *kerangas,* an Iban word meaning 'land that cannot grow rice'. This forest type is composed of small, densely packed trees that seldom exceed 20m in height. Due to difficult growing conditions, plants of the *kerangas* have developed extraordinary ways to protect their leaves from the blazing sun and acquire needed minerals. Some, for example, obtain nutrients by providing a home for ant colonies that, like tiny pizza-delivery people, bring food to the plant.

The *kerangas* is home to the world's greatest diversity of pitcher plants *(Nepenthes),* which trap insects in chambers containing enzyme-rich fluids and then digest them.

Borneo's remaining *kerangas* is increasingly restricted to protected coastal areas like Sarawak's Bako National Park and remote mountain tops like those in Sabah's Maliau Basin Conservation Area.

> Borneo lies within what is known as the 'ever-wet zone' – it gets at least 60mm of rain every month of the year, with rainfall in most months averaging about 200mm.

Lowland Dipterocarp Forest

Found up to an altitude of about 900m or 1000m, Borneo's lowland forests are dominated by trees belonging to the dipterocarp family. More than 150 species of these magnificent trees, which can reach a height of 60m, anchor Borneo's most ecologically important ecosystem, the lowland dipterocarp forest, which has more species of flora than any other rainforest habitat in the world – a single hectare may shelter 240 different plant species!

Most trees in lowland dipterocarp forests synchronise their flowering and fruiting to coincide with the El Niño–induced dry weather that usually occurs every four years or so. With so many fruits available during the same six-week period, seed predators – gorge themselves though they

RAINFALL

may – are unable to devour them all, so enough are able to germinate. In recent years however, this pattern, first described by Prof Lisa M Curran of Yale, seems to have been disrupted.

Of the countless animals found in a dipterocarp forest, few are as flamboyantly well adapted as the many types of gliding animals. In addition to birds and bats, there are frogs, lizards, snakes, squirrels and lemurs that 'fly' between trees.

Dipterocarps, including Borneo's 155 endemic species, produce some of most valuable tropical hardwoods, which is why this type of forest is particularly endangered. Some fine patches can be found in national parks, including Sarawak's Niah National Park and Sabah's Danum Valley Conservation Area.

Montane Forest

On mountains above 900m, dipterocarp forest gives way to a magical world of stunted oaks, myrtle and laurel trees. Cloud-drenched and dripping, montane forest – often with a canopy height of just 10m – is full of ferns, rhododendrons, lichens and thick moss. It also provides a home for a stunning cornucopia of orchids.

Visitors from around the world travel to the lower reaches of Sabah's montane forests in the hope of seeing the world's largest flower, the legendary Rafflesia (p296).

Mangrove

Flourishing in a tidal world where land meets sea, mangroves have developed extraordinary ways to deal with an ever-changing mix of salt and fresh water, all the while anchored happily in suffocating mud. Not only do these remarkable trees fix the loose coastal soil, they also protect against erosion and even tsunamis.

Uncounted marine organisms and nearly every commercially important seafood species find sanctuary and nursery sites among mangrove roots. The forests' more endearing species include the proboscis monkey and the mudskipper, a fish that spends much of its time on almost-dry land, skipping along the muddy shore in search of food.

Mangroves once ringed virtually the entire island, especially around river deltas, but are increasingly limited to places like Sarawak's Bako National Park and Kuching Wetlands National Park, and Brunei's Temburong District.

Peat Forest

Peat forests form in areas near the coast and along rivers where dead plant matter, too waterlogged to decompose, accumulates in the form of peat, thereby sequestering enormous quantities of carbon. When peat land is drained or burnt – for instance, to establish oil-palm plantations – vast quantities of carbon are released into the atmosphere. In addition, dry peat is combustible, and if it catches fire can burn unchecked, underground, for months, releasing yet more carbon, popping up in unexpected locations (eg inside protected areas), and carpeting vast areas of Southeast Asia with haze.

Environmental Issues

Borneo is a land in ecological crisis. If used sustainably, the vast forests of Borneo could provide valuable resources for countless generations. When the forest is logged and fragmented, however, the entire ecosystem falls apart: soils become degraded, peat dries out and may catch fire, rivers silt up, plants and animals disappear, and indigenous human communities lose their sources of sustenance, both physical and spiritual.

The rainforests of Borneo are exposed to twice as much sunlight as temperate forests, but just 2% penetrates all the way to the forest floor. That's why so much jungle biodiversity is up in the canopy.

There is no record of any human entering Sabah's Maliau Basin until the 1980s.

ISOLATION

BORNEO'S NATIONAL PARKS & NATURE RESERVES

Borneo's national parks and nature reserves protect some of the island's most luxuriant and ecologically important habitats. Many are easy to get to, and some offer convenient overnight accommodation.

Sabah

Sabah's national parks (www.sabahparks.org) and conservation areas (www.searrp.org) are among the main reasons tourists visit the state. Almost 18% of Sabah's land has been gazetted as protected.

PARK	SIZE	FEATURES	PAGE
Crocker Range National Park	139 sq km	Huge swath of forested escarpment overlooking the coast; no facilities	p103
Danum Valley Conservation Area	438 sq km	Pristine old-growth rainforest with a superabundance of wildlife; run by the Sabah Foundation and visited mostly by scientists	p88
Kinabalu National Park	754 sq km	Mountain trekking up Mt Kinabalu (4095m), forest walks at HQ and Mesilau, and the hot springs at Poring; Sabah's most popular national park and Unesco World Heritage site	p56
Maliau Basin Conservation Area	588 sq km	Pocket of truly untouched wilderness protected by mountains, altitude and sheer remoteness; run by the Sabah Foundation	p101
Pulau Tiga National Park	15 sq km	Three islands 50km southwest of KK: one formed by volcanic mud eruptions, one famous for sea snakes and the other virtually washed away by wave action	p108
Tabin Wildlife Reserve	1205 sq km	Lowland dipterocarp forest and mangroves, much of it technically secondary, that shelters elephants and primates; managed by both the Forestry and Wildlife Departments	p90
Tawau Hills Park	28 sq km	Forested volcanic hills, waterfalls and hot springs	p101
Tun Sakaran Marine Park	325 sq km	Some of the best reef-dive sites in the world in the Semporna Archipelago	p93
Tunku Abdul Rahman National Park	49 sq km	Grouping of five islands, one quite large, a few kilometres from KK; beaches, snorkelling and hiking	p54
Turtle Islands National Park	17 sq km	Three tiny islands 40km north of Sandakan that are nesting grounds of sea turtles; because of management problems we recommend not visiting	p81

Brunei

Brunei has one major national park and several forest reserves. Almost 30% of Brunei's land currently enjoys protected status and much of the rest remains untouched by development.

PARK	SIZE	FEATURES	PAGE
Peradayan Forest Reserve	10.7 sq km	Has a trail through the jungle to the summit of Bukit Patoi (310m)	p212
Ulu Temburong National Park	500 sq km	Untouched expanse of pristine forest accessible only by longboat; only a small area is open to the public	p212

Sarawak

National parks (www.sarawakforestry.com) cover 7% of Sarawak's territory. Many of them can be visited on a day trip from Kuching or Miri. Entry fees for foreigners, doubled in May 2012, are RM20 for adults, RM10 for people with disabilities and RM7 for children age six to 17; nature reserves cost about half that.

PARK	SIZE	FEATURES	PAGE
Bako National Park	27 sq km	Great place to spot wildlife, including proboscis monkeys; 17 trails lead through heath forest to coves and beaches	p142
Batang Ai National Park	240 sq km	Rainforest home for lots of wild orangutans; situated deep in Iban country; no facilities	p158
Gunung Gading National Park	41 sq km	Giant Rafflesia flowers and old-growth jungle	p155
Gunung Mulu National Park	529 sq km	Unesco World Heritage site with spectacular mountain treks, vast caves, millions of bats, clear rivers and great hiking	p180
Kubah National Park	22 sq km	Pristine rainforest, fine hiking trails and clear rivers you can swim in	p151
Kuching Wetlands National Park	66 sq km	Mangrove forest with proboscis monkeys, crocs and, offshore, Irrawaddy dolphins; no facilities	p148
Lambir Hills National Park	69 sq km	May have the greatest plant biodiversity on the planet	p173
Matang Wildlife Centre	1.8 sq km	Respected wildlife rehabilitation program for orangutans, sun bears and other rare mammals, reptiles and birds	p152
Niah National Park	32 sq km	The massive caves, once home to prehistoric humans, still shelter bats and swiftlets	p171
Pulong Tau National Park	598 sq km	Sarawak's newest park was gazetted in 2005 to preserve the rich jungle of the Kelabit Highlands	p192
Semenggoh Nature Reserve	6.8 sq km	One of the best places in the world to see semi-wild orangutans	p149
Similajau National Park	90 sq km	Coastal park with hiking trails, beaches, meandering rivers and beady-eyed estuarine crocodiles	p169
Talang-Satang National Park	19.4 sq km	Marine park that protects the waters off four islands used by sea turtles to lay their eggs	p157
Tanjung Datu National Park	13.8 sq km	Virgin rainforest, beautiful beaches, clear rivers and coral reefs at Sarawak's far western tip	p157

Kalimantan

Most of Borneo's untouched jungle is in Kalimantan but certain areas are designated as national parks.

PARK	SIZE	FEATURES	PAGE
Danau Sentarum National Park	1320 sq km	Seasonal wetland with many islands; offers intriguing villages and interesting boat journeys	p250
Kutai National Park	1980 sq km	Very little intact forest remains in this once-great park, considered almost a 'total loss' by environmentalists	p236
Tanjung Puting National Park	4150 sq km	One of the world's last great refuges of the orangutan	p251
Wehea Forest	380 sq km	Pristine rainforest, offering great hiking, managed using a community-based conservation model	p237

LOGGING

Despite the best efforts of local and international environmental groups, the governments that rule Borneo (except that of Brunei) tend to view rainforests as an impediment to progress or as political spoils, with a handful of well-connected people deriving profits from logging concessions granted without public oversight. The logging and oil-palm businesses generate millions of dollars for the local economy and provide jobs, but they have wreaked untold ecological damage. To learn more about the opposition perspective on Sarawak's environmental record, see www.stop-timber-corruption.org.

Deforestation

Borneo suffers from one of the highest rates of deforestation on earth. In the mid-1980s, about 75% of the island still had its original forest cover; by 2005, the figure was just 50%. Unless something is done, less than a third of the island will retain its forests by 2020. The WWF calculated that in 2005, Borneo was losing 2.5 hectares of rainforest per minute – that comes to 1.5 sq km every hour. The main markets for Bornean wood are China and Japan.

Only a tiny fraction of Borneo's land is protected by law, and even less is subject to laws that are systematically enforced. In recent years, government pronouncements in Sabah and Sarawak have been more attuned to international pressure, in part because there's not all that much rainforest left to log, but allegedly selective cutting is continuing in formerly pristine areas such as the Kelabit Highlands. Despite this, remote Dayak populations are still being displaced (see www.borneoproject.org). But the news is not all bad. Sabah has been taking some concrete steps to improve forest conservation: in 2012, for instance, the state upgraded the protection status of 700 sq km of forest near the Danum Valley.

In Kalimantan, which suffers from an almost complete lack of enforcement, illegal logging even extends into national park lands. Some ostensibly protected areas, such as Kutai National Park in East Kalimantan, have been devastated by a combination of logging and fires and are considered by scientists to be a 'total loss'. Malaysian Borneo is used as a sales conduit for illegal timber logged in Kalimantan.

Visit the website of GRID-Arendal (www.grida.no), which collaborates with the UN Environment Programme, and search for 'Borneo deforestation' to see maps tracing the disappearance of the island's forest cover from 1950 to the present and on to 2020.

Oil-Palm Plantations

Alongside logging, the greatest single threat to Borneo's biodiversity comes from the vast oil-palm plantations that are replacing tens of thousands of square kilometres of primary and secondary forest in Sabah, Sarawak and Kalimantan – with the encouragement of the governments of Malaysia and Indonesia, which together produce 85% of the world's palm oil.

Originally brought from Africa in 1848, oil palms produce more edible oil per hectare (about 5000kg, ie 6000L of crude oil) than any other crop, especially in Borneo's ideal growing conditions. The oil is extracted from the orange-coloured fruit, which grows in bunches just below the fronds. It is used primarily for cooking, although it can also be refined into biodiesel, an alternative to fossil fuels.

For all the benefits, there have been huge environmental consequences to the creation of vast plantations that have been replacing both previously logged forests and virgin jungle. In Kalimantan, the area given over to oil palms has increased by 300% since 2000, to 31,640 sq km (as of 2012); in Sabah, some 20% of the land – about 14,000 sq km – is now

Some species of tropical hardwood are so valuable that a single tree can be worth US$50,000. Such trees are sometimes selectively logged using heavy-duty helicopters.

carpeted with oil palms. To see what this means, just look out the window of any aeroplane flying over Malaysian Borneo or check out Google Earth.

Palm-oil plantations may appear green – after all, they are covered with living plants – but from an ecological point of view they are almost dead zones. Even forest land that has been clear-cut can recover much of its biodiversity if allowed to grow back as secondary forest, but palm-oil plantations convert land into a permanent monoculture (leases are usually for 99 years), reducing the number of plant species by 80% and resident mammal, reptile and bird species by 80% to 90%. Oil palms require large quantities of herbicides and pesticides that can seep into rivers, drainage may lower water tables and dry out nearby peat forests, and the plantations fragment or destroy the natural habitats that are especially important to large mammals.

The Palm Oil Action Group (www.palmoilaction.org.au) is an Australian pressure group raising awareness about palm oil and the need to use alternatives. Roundtable on Sustainable Palm Oil tries to look at the issue from all sides while seeking to develop and implement global standards. Proforest (www.proforest.net) has also been working with Wild Asia (www.wildasia.org) on the Stepwise Support Programme, designed to promote sustainability within the palm-oil industry.

Hydroelectric Dams

Hydroelectric dams are touted as sources of carbon-free energy, but these huge projects often have serious environmental impacts. In addition, indigenous people are often forcibly relocated to areas where they have a difficulty earning a living or maintaining their traditions. Such was the case with the controversial Bakun Dam (www.bakundam.com) in Sarawak.

In October 2010 the 207m high structure began flooding a reservoir that will eventually submerge an area of once-virgin rainforest about the size of Singapore (690 sq km). According to the Malaysian government, 'the second-highest concrete-faced rockfill dam in the world' will produce 2400MW of 'emission-free clean energy', giving a much needed boost to Sarawak's economy.

However, Malaysian and international watchdogs claim the whole project – including contracts to clear the site of biomass, which involves

Every year fires set to clear Indonesian forest land carpet much of Malaysia with haze. Air pollution often peaks in August and September and is worst in El Niño years.

PALM OIL: BIOFUELLING FOREST DESTRUCTION

Replacing fossil fuels with renewable biofuels made from palm oil sounds like a great way to reduce carbon emissions and thus mitigate global warming, but this simple formulation does not take into account the significant ecological damage done when rainforests are converted to oil-palm plantations.

For starters, creating a plantation means logging the plantation area, destroying plant and animal habitats and displacing indigenous people. Because young oil palms take five years to produce their first crop, timber sales subsidise the pre-production phase.

While palm oil is an extraordinarily versatile food product, it's remarkably lousy as a 'sustainable' fuel. Studies show that the conversion of forests to palm plantations releases far more carbon than all the biofuel they'll ever produce could possibly save. The equation is especially unbalanced when the plantation replaces a peat-swamp forest, which releases colossal quantities of greenhouse gases as it dries out; emissions are off the charts when burning is the final step in clearing branches and underbrush.

Plantation monoculture creates a 'green dead zone', robbing wildlife of native food sources, increasing conflicts between wildlife and humans – plantation owners often treat displaced orangutans as pests – and pushing indigenous shifting cultivators towards slash-and-burn agriculture in marginal habitats such as peat swamps.

HEART OF BORNEO

An initiative of the WWF (www.panda.org), Heart of Borneo has a hugely ambitious goal: to safeguard Borneo's biodiversity for future generations and to ensure indigenous peoples' cultural survival, by protecting 240,000 sq km of interconnected forest land in Sabah, Sarawak, Brunei and Kalimantan. That's almost a third of the island's land area.

Since Malaysia, Indonesia and Brunei signed the Heart of Borneo Declaration in 2007, well over 100 new species have been discovered in the area it covers, including a 57cm-long stick insect, the world's longest.

logging old-growth jungle – has been shot through with corrupt dealings designed to benefit the business associates of local politicians. Transparency International (www.transparency.cz/doc/ti_gcr_2005_1 .pdf) has declared the dam a 'monument of corruption.'

The power that the dam will produce exceeds the island's energy requirements; the original plan was to send 70% of the energy to Peninsular Malaysia along a 670km undersea cable. That part of the project has been shelved, however, leaving Sarawak with an over-capacity (when all turbines are operating, the dam will produce 2.5 times as many watts as Sarawak's current peak demand).

Despite this, a dozen more dams in highland Sarawak are in various stages of planning and execution, including the 944MW Murum Dam, located in a Penan area 60km upriver from Bakun.

Wildlife Trade

Although theoretically illegal, the hugely lucrative trade in wild animals continues. Baby orangutans are captured for sale as pets, sun bears are butchered so body parts such as gall bladders can be used in traditional Chinese medicine, and clouded leopards are killed for their teeth, bones and pelts.

A baby orangutan can be worth US$50,000 in Taiwan, Japan or the Middle East; poachers in Kalimantan, though, are usually paid just US$100, so the profits from smuggling can be enormous. For every baby orangutan taken into captivity, it's estimated that up to five orangutans are killed, including the baby's mother. Captive orangutans are cute until they're about five years old, at which point they stop being cuddly and start becoming dangerous – and are usually killed. The orangutans that live in rehabilitation centres, such as Sarawak's Matang Wildlife Centre, are among the few that manage to survive capture and captivity.

What You Can Do

Every time a traveller visits a nature site, hires a trekking guide, pays a boatman for transport to a remote longhouse, or provides custom for a local ecotourism initiative, they are casting a vote – by putting cash in local pockets – for the economic (as opposed to purely ecological) value of sustainability and habitat conservation.

Travellers might want to check out the website of Wild Asia (www.wild asia.org) to learn more about responsible tourism in the region. Wherever you go, tread lightly, buy locally, support responsible tourism and give respectful, constructive feedback to local operators.

To keep abreast of the campaign to save Borneo's jungles, visit the website of Mongabay (www.mongabay.com), which has worldwide news on rainforest conservation.

POLLUTION

Everything from mining chemicals to human waste pours into Kalimantan's rivers. In a single generation, the water at Samarinda has gone from drinkable to not bathe-able.

Wildlife

From breathtaking coral reefs to luxuriant rainforest, Borneo is one of the greatest showcases of life anywhere on the planet.

Borneo sits at the junction of Asian and Australian biomes, but its strongest affinity is with the Asian mainland because whenever an ice age causes sea levels to drop, Borneo hooks up with Peninsular Malaysia. This has happened on several occasions, once about 50 million years ago, and more recently during the ice ages that lasted from approximately 2.5 million years ago until 10,000 years ago. Such connections allowed a tremendous diversity of genetic material to migrate onto the island, turning it into a kind of steamy, tropical Noah's ark. When rising seas submerged the land bridges to the mainland, life on the island was left to evolve into fantastic new forms. The result is one of the world's great biodiversity hot spots. On average, scientists discover about three new species every month!

There are two superb WWF (www.panda.org) publications on Borneo's fauna and flora: *Borneo: Treasure Island at Risk* (2005) and *Borneo's Lost World: Newly Discovered Species on Borneo* (2005).

Animals

Borneo's 222 species of mammal – 44 of them endemic – include 13 primates and more than 100 kinds of rodents and bats. Snake species number 166, amphibians over 100.

If you head into the rainforest, bear in mind that most animals wisely keep their distance from humans and are thus nearly impossible to see. Even researchers with years of field experience have never seen especially shy creatures such as the Western tarsier or clouded leopard.

Orangutan

There's something entrancing about a 90kg animal whose physique, facial expressions and obvious intelligence are so eerily similar to our own.

Endemic to Borneo and Sumatra, the orangutan, or 'man of the forest' (in Bahasa, *orang* means 'person' and *hutan* means 'forest'), is Asia's only great ape. Even the most seasoned traveller will feel a rush of awe if they are lucky enough to cross paths with a wild orangutan swinging through the canopy.

About 40,000 orangutans live in Borneo, including 13,000 in Sabah, down from 60,000 just a decade ago. Some 78% live outside of protected parks and reserves – that is, in forests that could be logged or turned into oil-palm plantations at any time. Scientists estimate that before human encroachment, the world's orangutan population was roughly 100 times what it is today.

Ranging over large areas of rainforest in search of fruiting trees and insects (a fine source of protein), the orangutan has suffered greatly due to hunting and, especially, habitat loss from logging, oil-palm plantations and fire. Also contributing to their numerical decline is the fact that the interval between a female's pregnancies is usually about eight

'The orangutan's future is dependent on the forests. As more are cleared and converted to agricultural plantations orangutan populations will continue to decline.' Ashley Leiman, OBE, Director of Orangutan Foundation (UK)

RAFFLESIA: POWER FLOWER

One of the wonders of the botanical world, the Rafflesia flower is astonishing not only because of its world-record size – up to 1m in diameter – but also because of its extraordinary and mysterious lifestyle.

Rafflesias are parasites that lack roots, stems or leaves. In fact, they consist of just two parts: tiny filaments that burrow into the host vine – a member of the grape family called *Tetrastigma* – to extract nutrients, and the flower itself, which often erupts directly from the forest floor, bursting forth from a cabbage-sized bud that takes nine to 12 months to mature. Few buds survive that long as many are munched by small mammals, including civets and moon rats.

Scientists have yet to figure out the Rafflesia's sex life. The red flowers, whose five fleshy petals are covered with bumps and blotches, are either male or female – their reproductive organs are hidden under the spiky disk in the middle – but it's not clear how they manage to effect pollination given that two flowers rarely bloom anywhere near each other at the same time. The transfer of pollen is carried out by carrion flies, attracted by the flowers' revolting odour, which is said to resemble that of rotten meat. After the fruit ripens, about half a year after flowering, the seeds are distributed by small rodents such as tree shrews and squirrels, but precisely how the plants manage to attach themselves to their host vines, and why they grow only on *Tetrastigmas*, remains a mystery.

There are approximately 17 species of Rafflesia (estimates vary). Some are thought to be extinct and all – including the three species that live in Sarawak – are threatened to some degree, mainly by loss of habitat but also by bud poaching for medicinal use.

Featured over the years on Malaysian stamps and coins and ubiquitous on tourist brochures, the Rafflesia is named after Sir Stamford Raffles who, while heading an expedition to the Sumatran rainforest, 'discovered' the flower in 1818, the year before he founded Singapore.

The good news is that Borneo is one of the best places in the world to see Rafflesias. The bad news is that they bloom for just three to five days before turning into a ring of black slime. So it takes a fair bit of luck to see one. Rafflesias blossom pretty much all year round, but irregularly – for the low-down on when and where, ask at your guesthouse or hotel, or contact one of the following:

» In Sarawak, the park headquarters of Gunung Gading National Park (p155) or Kuching's National Park Booking Office (p139).

» In Sabah, Tambunan Rafflesia Reserve (p103). You can also look for signs around Poring Hot Springs.

years. The good news is that orangutans seem capable of adapting to new circumstances – in Sabah, for instance, some now live in commercial forest reserves.

Wild orangutans are now difficult to find except in places like Sabah's Danum Valley Conservation Area and Sarawak's Batang Ai region, but semi-wild animals can be seen at the Semenggoh Nature Reserve in Sarawak and the Sepilok Orang-Utan Rehabilitation Centre in Sabah.

The website of the Orangutan Conservancy (www.orangutan.com) is a good source of information about these great apes.

Proboscis Monkey

Borneo's most peculiar primate, named for the male's pendulous nose, lives mainly in coastal areas, including mangrove forests. It is strictly herbivorous, which is why both sexes need prodigious quantities of cellulose-digesting bacteria – stored in their distinctive pot bellies – to turn their food into useable energy.

Proboscis monkeys are relatively easy to spot as they perform incredible leaps from tree to tree, often at great heights, and then settle down to dine on choice young leaves, the males' noses flopping as they chew.

Proboscis monkeys can often be spotted in Sabah at the Labuk Bay Proboscis Monkey Sanctuary, and in Sarawak at Bako National Park and along the waterways of Kuching Wetlands National Park.

Gibbon

Swinging effortlessly from branch to branch, gibbons move with such speed and agility that it seems as if they are falling sideways. Unfortunately for primate lovers, gibbons are much easier to hear than see, so like most visitors you'll probably have to make do with scanning the canopy as their whooping songs echo through the rainforest. National parks with gibbon populations include Brunei's Ulu Temburong National Park.

Gibbons swing by their hands, a unique mode of travel called brachiation that isn't fail-safe; most gibbons have bone fractures from falling.

Elephant

Of the 2000 Borneo pygmy elephants (a subspecies of the Asian elephant) estimated to live in northeastern Borneo, the largest population is thought to roam the forests around Sungai Kinabatangan, where they've come into conflict with the owners of vast oil-palm plantations.

New genetic evidence puts to rest the theory that humans introduced the creatures to the island in the mid-1700s. It turns out they've been on the island for at least 18,000 years.

GIBBONS

Rhinoceros

Very little is known about the elusive and critically endangered Borneo rhinoceros, a subspecies of the Sumatran rhino. The world's smallest rhinoceros, its global population is estimated to be less than 50, all of them in Sabah.

A wild Borneo rhino was briefly caught on film, for the first time ever, by a camera trap in 2007 – the captivating clip can be found on YouTube. For more information, check out www.borneorhinoalliance.org.

Bearded Pig

Bearded pigs are encountered in nearly every type of forested area on the island. Following well-worn paths, these rotund animals, which can weigh up to 150kg, sometimes gather into large herds and migrate incredible distances in search of nuts and seeds. Although they are an extremely popular game animal (except, of course, among Muslims), they are one creature that hunters and predators truly fear. Except for the tame pigs who live in and around the headquarters of Bako National Park, be wary of these unpredictable animals and their sharp tusks – they are capable of goring a human in the flash of a whisker.

'We woke periodically throughout the night to peel off leeches. In the light of the head torch, the ground was a sea of leeches – black, slithering, standing up on one end to sniff the air and heading inexorably our way to feed.' Rich Mayfield, *Kinabalu Escape: The Soldiers' Story*

Mouse Deer

Few Bornean mammals are more surprising than the lesser mouse deer, the world's smallest hoofed animal, which is the size of a rabbit (it weighs just 2kg) but looks like a tiny deer. Males defend themselves and their mates using protruding canines instead of antlers. Skittish and generally nocturnal, they can sometimes be seen during the day by quiet hikers.

Leech

If you'd like to give something back to the rainforest ecosystem, the humble leech – slimy, squiggly and fond of taking up residence in very private places – can arrange an involuntary donation of blood (p22).

DIVERSITY

Birds

A fantastic assortment of birds belonging to at least 420 species, 37 of them endemic, fill the forests of Borneo with flashes of feather and ethereal calls.

The most famous of Borneo's birds are its eight species of hornbill, some of which have an oversized 'helmet' or 'horn' perched on their beak. The 105cm-long rhinoceros hornbill, with its orange-red horn and loud whooping calls, serves as Sarawak's state emblem. When the 125cm-long helmeted hornbill swoops across the sky, you might think you're seeing a pterodactyl. Revered and hunted by Borneo's indigenous peoples, hornbills are highly threatened by habitat loss.

In 2009 a new bird species, the spectacled flowerpecker, was discovered in Sabah's Danum Valley Conservation Area.

Websites with great photos that may be of interest to birdwatchers:
» www.borneobirdclub.blogspot.com
» www.borneobirdimages.com
» www.borneobirdfestival.com
» www.borneobirds.com

Borneo has about 15,000 species of flowering plant. All of North America – from the Panama Canal to the Arctic – only has about 20,000.

Plants

The stats on Borneo's flora are astonishing. The island has as many species of flowering plants as the entire continent of Africa, which is 40 times larger. In Lambir Hills National Park scientists found an astounding 1200 species of tree in a single 52-hectare research plot, and the island is home to more than 1000 species of fern. Of Borneo's 2000 species of orchid, over 1000 live on Mt Kinabalu.

Many of Borneo's plants struggle to survive in thin, nutrient-poor soils. Some trees hold themselves upright with wide, flaring buttresses that compensate for shallow root systems.

Strangler figs start life as tiny seeds that are defecated by birds in the rainforest canopy, where they sprout and then send spindly roots downward in search of the forest floor. Eventually, some figs grow large enough to embrace their host tree in a death grip. Once the host tree dies and rots away, the giant fig stands upright on a fantastic hollow latticework of its own interlaced air roots. Orangutans, wild pigs and birds are only some of the creatures that feed on the fruit of the strangler fig.

Survival Guide

Directory A–Z

Accommodation

Accommodation in Borneo runs the gamut from international-standard hotels to upland Dayak longhouses, which themselves range from mod-con central to wood-and-palm structures deep in the jungle. In smaller towns, on outlying islands and in the hinterlands, your options may be limited to very simple lodgings. Sabah and Sarawak have the best range of accommodation, particularly in the upper brackets, while Kalimantan has fewer top-end hotels and resorts. Brunei boasts one of the world's most opulent hotels but has limited budget options.

On the ceilings of some hotel rooms, arrows point towards Mecca so Muslim guests know which direction to face when praying.

International-Standard Hotels

» All of Borneo's major cities have hotels with the full range of mod cons and amenities, but standards vary, from topnotch in Kuching, Kota Kinabalu (KK), Bandar Seri Begawan (BSB) and Balikpapan to close-but-no-cigar in places like Miri and Sibu.

» All but a few top-end hotels are run by local companies rather than the worldwide chains, and many are oriented primarily towards domestic business travellers.

» Booking online is the way to go at most of these places, and you'll often find offers well below rack rates – in Malaysia, excellent rooms can be found for less than US$100 per night and sometimes much less, and in Kalimantan luxury comes even cheaper.

» In Malaysia and Brunei, most room rates include the 10% service charge. If you're unsure if a rate is all-inclusive, ask if the quote is 'plus-plus' – a 'yes' means the service charge and taxes have not been factored in.

Local Hotels

» The island's small hotels – in Malaysia often run by people of Chinese ancestry – have long been the mainstay of the domestic hospitality market. The more salubrious ones are a decent option for budget travellers (some that we don't mention double as brothels). Starting at about US$17 for a double room in Sarawak and Sabah, they're generally fairly spartan.

» Showers and toilets are usually en suite, but may be down the hall for cheaper rooms.

» Some places ask you to leave a deposit for the TV remote.

» Before you check in, make sure your room is properly ventilated (ideally with a window) and hasn't taken on a dank tropical fug.

Resorts

» Some places that style themselves as resorts have plenty of seaside (or jungle) activities and impeccable service, but others cater mainly for the domestic business-conference market.

» For a relaxing, resort-style holiday in Sabah, you can choose from several excellent seaside resorts in and near KK, or head to an offshore island such as Pulau Mantanani, Pulau Manukan, Pulau Tiga or Layang Layang, or the islands of the Semporna Archipelago.

» Sarawak's best-known resort area is the Santubong Peninsula but, to be frank, this isn't southern Thailand.

» Brunei will blow you away with the over-the-top Empire Hotel & Country Club, or you can relax at the jungle lodge in Ulu Temburong National Park.

BOOK YOUR STAY ONLINE

For more accommodation reviews by Lonely Planet authors, check out http://hotels.lonelyplanet.com. You'll find independent reviews, as well as recommendations on the best places to stay. Best of all, you can book online.

» Kalimantan has several seaside and island resorts, including places in Balikpapan and on Nabucco and Nunukan Islands in the Derawan Archipelago.

Guesthouses & Backpacker Accommodation

» Malaysian Borneo's main tourist cities offer laid-back accommodation designed for visitors on a budget. Ideal for meeting fellow travellers, these places generally offer a choice of dorm beds or small private rooms (usually with shared bathrooms), and also have a common area for lounging, an internet terminal or two, a basic kitchen and, if you're lucky, a washing machine and a rooftop garden for hanging out in the evening. Some rent bicycles and conduct tours of local sights; for many it's a point of pride to provide up-to-the-minute travel information (eg regarding transport).

» Dorm beds start at about US$5 per night, while private rooms are from US$17. If you want your own room, cheap hotels are often better value.

» Because many guesthouses (especially in Kuching) are in converted commercial buildings and old shophouses, not all rooms have windows. This might work with proper ventilation, but in some establishments the rooms are musty enough to choke a horse.

» Kalimantan does not yet have a hostel scene, so backpackers looking for cheap digs usually bed down in an inexpensive hotel or *losmen*.

Longhouses

Until the last decade or two, passers-by were always welcome to stay overnight at longhouses, the age-old dwellings of many (but not all) of the indigenous peoples of Borneo. But this is changing, especially in Malaysia. For details on Dayak culture and the etiquette of staying over, see p278.

ACCOMMODATION PRICE RANGES

The following price ranges refer to a double room with private bathroom, except in some budget places.

	SABAH & SARAWAK	BRUNEI	KALIMANTAN
$	less than RM100	less than B$60	less than 250,000Rp
$$	RM100–400	B$60–150	250,000–800,000Rp
$$$	more than RM400	more than B$150	more than 800,000Rp

Homestays

» Sabah and Kalimantan have plenty of welcoming homestays offering good value and a local vibe.

» Brunei's homestays tend to cater to tour groups and domestic tourists with their own cars.

» Sarawak's tourism authorities have been encouraging villagers to open homestays but haven't always quite nailed the right mix of training, infrastructure and quality control. Some of Sarawak's homestays are superb (eg in the Kelabit Highlands), while others are guest-ready only on paper, with rundown facilities, hosts who speak no English and nothing to do.

Camping

» In many national parks, camping is permitted only near park headquarters.

» If you pitch your tent in the vicinity of a longhouse, residents may get the impression you're spurning their hospitality. Some travellers pitch their tent on the longhouse's covered verandah.

» A two-season tent with mosquito netting is ideal, and a summer-weight sleeping bag or just a bag liner will usually suffice unless you intend to hike at altitude. Choose a site that won't be inundated if it rains.

Business Hours

» Opening hours for eateries vary widely. Many restaurants open from around 11.30am to 10pm or so. *Kopitiam* and *kedai kopi* (Borneo's ubiquitous coffee shops; ie no-frills restaurants) that cater to the breakfast crowd open very early – well before dawn – but may close in the mid-afternoon or even before lunch. Others (generally the newer ones) start service later in the morning and stay open until 9pm or 10pm.

» Bars usually open around dinner time and close at 2am.

» Bank hours are generally 10am to 3pm or 4pm on weekdays and 9.30am to 11.30am on Saturday.

» Shop hours are variable, although small shops are generally open Monday to Saturday from 9am to 6pm. Major department stores, shopping malls, Chinese emporiums and some large stores are open from around 10am until 9pm or 10pm seven days a week.

» Government offices are usually open Monday to Friday from 8am to 4.15pm, and on Saturday from 8am to 12.45pm. Most close for lunch from 12.45pm to 2pm; in Sarawak the Friday lunch break is from 12.15pm to 2.45pm to accommodate Muslim prayers at the mosque. In Brunei

PRACTICALITIES

» Malaysia, Indonesia and Brunei use the metric system.

» There are two English-language newspapers published in Borneo: the *Borneo Post* (www.theborneopost.com), the main English-language daily in Sabah and Sarawak, and the *New Sarawak Tribune* (http://tribune.my).

» Also available in Malaysian Borneo is the Kuala Lumpur–based *New Straits Times* (www.nst.com.my).

» In Brunei, the *Borneo Bulletin* (www.borneobulletin.com.bn) is filled with local and international news, none of it locally controversial. News stories refer to the sultan as 'the benevolent ruler' so no prizes for guessing that the paper steers clear of hard-hitting investigative reporting.

» Radio Televisyen Brunei (RTB) handles almost all domestic TV and radio broadcasts, including English news broadcasts on the Pilihan channel (95.9FM and 96.9FM).

» Top-end hotels usually have satellite-TV relays of CNN, BBC, Star and other English-language stations.

» Brunei's tough anti-smoking laws ban puffing not only inside shops and malls, but also in outdoor markets and around food stalls.

government offices are closed on Friday and Sunday.

» During Ramadan, business and office hours are often shortened and Muslim-owned restaurants may close during daylight hours. In Brunei, many offices end the day at 2pm from Monday to Thursday and at 11.30am on Friday and Saturday.

Children

» Malaysian Borneo and Brunei are great for family travel, especially if the kids like monkeys, flowers, bugs and vibrantly variegated temples, food and fauna. Babies will attract a lot of adoring attention.

» Destinations with facilities and activities for children include Kota Kinabalu (KK), Sandakan and Sepilok in Sabah; and Kuching, the Santubong Peninsula, Bako National Park, Semenggoh Nature Reserve and Gunung Mulu National Park in Sarawak.

» In Malaysia, children receive discounts for attractions and public transport. Chinese hotels are a good bargain as they charge by room rather than by number of people. However, cots are not widely available in cheaper accommodation. Some top-end places allow two children under 12 to stay with their parents at no extra charge.

» In Kalimantan, only Balikpapan has hotels that specially cater to children (eg by offering babysitting and activities).

» Baby food, formula and nappies (diapers) are widely available, but stock up on such items before heading to remote destinations or islands.

» Lonely Planet's *Travel with Children* is packed with useful information.

Customs Regulations

» Tourists to Malaysia and Indonesia can bring up to 1L of liquor and 200 cigarettes duty free. Signs at Malaysian airports inform visitors that items not allowed into the country include daggers, cloth decorated with verses from the Koran, piranha fish and anything made in Israel.

» Non-Muslim visitors to Brunei, provided they're 18 or older, are allowed to import 12 cans of beer and two bottles of wine or spirits for personal consumption. There is no longer an allowance for cigarettes, which are are taxed at a rate of B$5 per pack of 20 (B$0.25 each).

» For travellers coming from Malaysia, Singapore's duty-free liquor allowance is zero. Travellers to Singapore, whatever their port of embarkation, must declare all cigarettes they are carrying. Theoretically, failing to declare even one pack of smokes can incur a S$200 fine.

Electricity

The electricity supply is 220V AC, 50Hz. Sarawak and Sabah (Malaysia) and Brunei use UK-style plugs with three massive square pins. Kalimantan (Indonesia) uses European-style plugs with two round prongs.

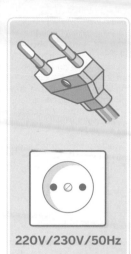

220V/230V/50Hz

24V/50Hz

Embassies & Consulates

Sabah

Australian Consulate (Map p42; ☑088-267151, in KL 03-2146 5555; www.malaysia .embassy.gov.au; Suite 10.1,

Level 10, Wisma Great Eastern, 65 Jln Gaya, Kota Kinabalu) Honorary consul; report emergencies to the High Commission in KL.

Indonesian Consulate Kota Kinabalu (Map p42; ☑088-218600; Lg Kemajuan, Kara-munsing; ⊙9am-5pm Mon-Fri); Tawau (off Map p98; ☑089-762069 084-772052; Jln Sinn Onn; ⊙9am-noon & 1-3pm)

UK Consulate (Map p42; ☑088-251775, 24hr in KL 03-2170 2200; www.ukinmalaysia. fco.gov.uk) Honorary consul; contact the High Commission in KL for emergency travel documents. Consul can visit UK citizens who are in hospital or prison.

Sarawak

Australian Consulate (☑082-313388, in KL 03-2146 5555; www.malaysia.embassy. gov.au; E39 Level 2, Taman Sri Sarawak Mall, Jln Tunku Abdul Rahman, Kuching) Honorary consul; report emergencies to the embassy in KL.

Indonesian Consulate (☑082-460734; www.kemlu.go .id; Jln Stutong, Kuching; ⊙visa applications 9am-noon Mon-Fri, visa collections 3-5pm Mon-Fri, closed Malaysian & Indonesian holidays) To get here from Saujana Bus Station (RM2), take City Public Link bus K8 (every 30 to 45 minutes) to Jln Song/Friendship Park or Sarawak Transport Compa-ny's buses 8G1, 8G2 or 8G3. A taxi from the centre costs RM2 one-way.

Brunei

All embassies and high com-missions are in Bandar Seri Begawan (BSB) or its sub-urbs unless otherwise noted.

Australian High Commis-sion (Map p200; ☑222 9435; www.bruneidarussalam.em-bassy.gov.au; 6th fl, Dar Takaful IBB Utama, Jln Pemancha)

Canadian High Commis-sion (Map p200; ☑222 0043; www.brunei.gc.ca; 5th fl, Jalan McArthur Bldg, 1 Jln McArthur)

Dutch Consulate (☑337 7285/2579; fax 337 4018; Brunei Shell Petroleum, Jln Utara, Panaga, Seria) Hon-orary consul.

French Embassy (Map p200; ☑222 0960; www .ambafrance-bn.org; Units 301-306, Kompleks Jalan Sultan, Jln Sultan)

German Embassy (Map p200; ☑222 5547; www.bandar-seri-begawan .diplo.de; 2nd fl, Unit 2.01, Block A, Yayasan Complex, Jln Pretty)

Indonesian Embassy (☑233 0180; http:// bandarseribegawan.kemlu.go .id; Lot 4498, Simpang 528, Jln Muara, Kampung Sungai Hanching)

Malaysian Embassy (☑238 1095-7; www.kln.gov .my/web/brn_begawan; No 61, Simpang 336, Jln Kebangsaan)

New Zealand Consulate (☑222 2422/5880; www.mfat .govt.nz; c/o Deloitte & Touche, 5th fl, Wisma Hajjah Fatimah, 22-23 Jln Sultan) Honorary consul.

Philippine Embassy (Map p200; ☑224 1465/6; www.philippine-embassybrunei .com; Simpang 336-17, Diplo-matic Enclave, Jln Kebangsaan)

Singaporean Embassy (☑226 2741; www.mfa.gov.sg/ brunei; No 8, Simpang 74, Jln Subok)

UK High Commission (Map p200; ☑222 2231/3121; www .ukinbrunei.fco.gov.uk/en; 2nd fl, Unit 2.01, Block D, Yayasan Complex, Jln Pretty)

US Embassy (☑238 4616; http://brunei .usembassy.gov; Simpang 336-52-16-9, Diplomatic Enclave, Jln Kebangsaan) About 5km northeast of downtown BSB.

Kalimantan

Malaysian Consulate (☑0561-736 061; www.kln.gov .my/web/idn_pontianak; Jln Perdana No 001, Pontianak)

EATING PRICE RANGES

The following price ranges are for the cheapest non-vegetarian main dish on the menu, plus a starter and a drink.

	SABAH & SARAWAK	BRUNEI	KALIMANTAN
$	less than RM10	less than B$6	less than 50,000Rp
$$	RM10–50	B$6–16	50,000–200,000Rp
$$$	more than RM50	more than B$16	more than 200,000Rp

Food

» A splendid array of delicious cuisines are cooked up by Borneo's many ethnic groups (see p281).

» During the month of Ramadan, Muslims are forbidden by Sharia law to eat or drink from dawn to sunset. But even in conservative Brunei, some restaurants continue to serve food to non-Muslims.

Gay & Lesbian Travellers

» Malaysia is by and large a socially conservative society and 'out' behaviour is looked upon disapprovingly; we strongly suggest discretion. According to the Australian government website www.smartraveller.gov.au, 'homosexual acts between males are illegal and penalties include corporal punishment and long prison sentences. Homosexual acts between women may be considered an "act of gross indecency with another" and penalties include imprisonment'.

» Brunei, a devoutly Muslim country, has an even sterner outlook. According to www.smartraveller.gov.au, 'consensual homosexual acts between adults (of either sex) are illegal and penalties include prison sentences'.

» Homosexuality is not illegal in Indonesia but Kalimantan is fairly conservative in these matters, so obviously 'out' behaviour is a very bad idea.

Insurance

» Do not travel without travel insurance. Before you buy a policy, check the fine print to see if it excludes 'risky' activities, such as scuba diving, mountain climbing or caving. If you'd like to do overnight trekking or visit remote areas, such as Sabah's Maliau Basin Conservation Area, make sure your plan covers emergency helicopter evacuation.

» Worldwide travel insurance is available at www.lonely planet.com/travel_services. You can buy, extend and claim online anytime – even if you're already on the road.

Internet Access

» Wi-fi is available at virtually all top-end hotels and backpackers guesthouses, at least in the lobby, though some fancy places have the cheek to charge outrageous sums to go online. These places almost always have one or more internet computers, for which there's often a nominal charge. Midrange places, including

Malaysia's Chinese hotels, are a mixed bag, though more and more offer wi-fi.

» Internet cafes (that double as video-game parlours) can still be found in cities and large towns, but they're becoming thin on the ground as smartphones proliferate. Access usually costs US$1 per hour or less.

» Western-style coffee shops and an increasing number of other eateries are wired for wi-fi.

» Areas without internet access include many of Borneo's offshore islands and huge swaths of the interior.

Legal Matters

» In Malaysia, certain drug crimes carry a 'mandatory death sentence', and when entering Brunei you'll see Singaporesque signs reading 'Warning: Death for drug traffickers under Brunei law'. Indonesia also has harsh penalties for the smuggling or possession of drugs.

» Gambling and possessing pornography are punishable by severe penalties.

» It is illegal to work without a proper working visa.

» The sale and public consumption of alcohol is forbidden in Brunei.

» Under Indonesian law, you must carry identification at all times.

Maps

Small-scale road maps of Borneo, some available online, are published by several companies:

World Express Mapping Sdn Bhd (www.wems.com.my) Based in Johor Bahru, Peninsular Malaysia. Publishes serviceable 1:900,000-scale maps of Sabah and Sarawak (sold in most bookshops in Malaysian Borneo) that include insets of major cities.

Periplus (www.periplus
.com) Publishes 1:1,000,000-
scale maps of Sabah and
Sarawak that include city
and town maps.

Globetrotter (www
.newhollandpublishers.com)
Has a 1:1,300,000-scale
map covering both Sabah
and Sarawak.

Nelles Verlag (www
.nelles-verlag.de) Based
in Munich. Produces a
1:500,000-scale map of
the entire island entitled
*Indonesia: Kalimantan,
East Malaysia & Brunei*.

Reise Know-How (www
.reise-know-how.de) Publishes
a 1:200,000-scale map of
the entire island (2011).

» Getting hold of accurate,
up-to-date topographical
maps of Borneo is nearly impossible. Malaysia still keeps
most hi-res maps classified,
partly as a holdover from the
Konfrontasi with Indonesia
(way back in the 1960s), and
partly to make it difficult for
indigenous groups to pursue
land claims against logging
companies. Brunei doesn't
officially release any of its
maps to non-Bruneians, and
accurate maps of Kaliman-
tan are simply impossible
to get.

» The most user-friendly
map of Brunei is the tourist
office's free *Official Map of
Brunei Darussalam*.

» **Google Earth** (www.google
.com/earth) is a very useful
resource, providing a fairly
clear overview of river and
road networks, particularly
along the northern coast. For
those planning a trek into the
sticks, it offers the best way
to check the extent of
remaining jungle cover.
Google Earth has especially
clear images of many of
urban areas. For Brunei, it's
easily the best supplement
to the maps in this book.

» The coverage of Borneo by
Google Maps (http://maps
.google.com) is spotty at best.

Money

Tipping is not practised
much in Borneo.

Sabah & Sarawak

» Malaysia's currency is
the ringgit (RM, for Ringgit
Malaysia, or MYR), which
is divided into 100 sen.
Banknote denominations are
RM1, RM5, RM10, RM50 and
RM100.

» The ringgit used to be
known as the Malaysian
dollar (M$) and Malaysians
sometimes still refer to a
ringgit as a *dolar*. To further
confuse things, in Bahasa
Malaysia, Singapore and
Brunei dollars are known as
ringgit.

» The amount of Malaysian
currency you are allowed
to bring into or take out of
the country is limited to
RM1000, a legacy of the 1997
Asian financial crisis. As a
result, outside of Malaysia
the exchange rates for ringgit
are often poor.

» ATMs are widely available
in cities, towns and big-city
airports but not in rural areas.
Some ATMs do not take international cards. Many banks
are able to do cash advances
at the counter.

» Credit cards can be used
at upscale hotels and restaurants, though some places
may only take cards with
embedded SIM chips, ruling
out lots of plastic issued in
North America.

» Banknotes in US, Australian and Singapore dollars
and pounds sterling are the
easiest to exchange. Moneychangers, some of which also
take other currencies, can
be found in cities and large
towns, and even smaller
towns often have a shop that
will change foreign currency.
Some banks aren't keen
on handling foreign cash,
and small-town branches
may not handle exchange
transactions at all.

Brunei

» The Brunei dollar (B$)
is available in denomina-
tions of B$1, B$5, B$10,
B$50, B$100, B$500 and
B$1000 and, believe it or
not, B$10,000. Thanks to the
1967 Currency Interchange-
ability Agreement between
Brunei and Singapore, the
two countries' dollars are
worth exactly the same and
can be used freely in both
countries. Singaporean
banknotes (with the possible
exception of S$2, which has
no Bruneian counterpart)
are universally accepted in
Brunei, and Brunei bank-
notes can be used almost
everywhere in Singapore.
To celebrate the pact's 40th
anniversary, a commemora-
tive B$20/S$20 note was
issued in 2007.

» For currency exchange,
moneychangers are gener-
ally a better bet than banks,
though some places in BSB
have a pretty hefty spread
between their buy and sell
rates.

» ATMs are widely available,
though not all take international credit/debit cards.

» Major credit cards are
widely accepted.

Kalimantan

» Indonesia's currency is the
rupiah (Rp). Banknotes come
in denominations of 1000Rp,
2000Rp, 5000Rp, 10,000Rp,
20,000Rp, 50,000Rp and
100,000Rp (sounds like a lot,
but it's worth just US$11).
Coins include 50Rp, 100Rp,
200Rp, 500Rp and 1000Rp;
newer ones are lightweight
aluminium, older ones are
either bronze-coloured or
bi-metal.

» ATMs can be found pretty
much everywhere this guide
goes except the Upper
Mahakam and the Derawan
Archipelago.

» All major cities have
exchange bureaux and/or
banks that handle foreign
currency.

» In general, credit cards are accepted at midrange and top-end hotels, as well as at the most fancy restaurants.

Public Holidays

The dates of Muslim, Buddhist and Hindu holidays, as well as some Christian festivals, follow lunar or lunisolar calendars and so vary relative to the Gregorian (Western) calendar. Muslim holidays fall 11 or 12 days earlier each year; their final dates are determined by the sighting of the moon and therefore may vary slightly relative to the dates below. The dates we give for some other religious holidays are also approximate. Many religious celebrations begin the night before the dates that appear in this section.

For details on public and religious holidays (as well as cultural events), see the events calendars posted by **Sabah Tourism** (www.sabah tourism.com), **Sarawak Ministry of Tourism** (www .mot.sarawak.gov.my) and **Brunei Tourism** (www.brunei tourism.travel)

Sabah & Sarawak

New Year's Day 1 January

Maulidur Rasul (Prophet's Birthday) 13 January 2014, 3 January 2015, 23 December 2016

Chinese New Year 31 January 2014, 19 February 2015, 8 February 2016

Federal Territory Day (Pulau Labuan) 1 February

Good Friday 29 March 2013, 18 April 2014, 3 April 2015

Labour Day 1 May

Wesak Day (Buddha's Birthday) 25 May 2013, 14 May 2014, 1 June 2015

Harvest Festival (Sabah) 30 & 31 May

Gawai Dayak (Sarawak) evening of 31 May to 2 June

Birthday of Yang di-Pertuan Agong First Saturday in June

Hari Raya Puasa (Eid al-Fitr) End of Ramadan; 8 August 2013, 28 July 2014, 17 July 2015

Independence Day 31 August

Sabah Head of State's Birthday (Sabah) First Saturday in October

Sarawak Head of State's Birthday (Sarawak) 8 September

Hari Raya Aidiladha (Eid al-Adha) 15 October 2013, 4 October 2014, 23 September 2015

Malaysia Day 23 October

Deepavali (not in Sarawak or Pulau Labuan) 3 November 2013, 23 October 2014, 11 November 2015

Awal Muharram (Muslim New Year) 4 November 2013, 25 October 2014, 14 October 2015

Christmas Day 25 December

Brunei

New Year's Day 1 January

Maulidur Rasul (Prophet's Birthday) 13 January 2014, 3 January 2015, 23 December 2015

Chinese New Year 31 January 2014, 19 February 2015, 8 February 2016

Brunei National Day 23 February

Royal Brunei Armed Forces Day 31 May

Gawai Dayak (Ibans only) Evening of 31 May to 2 June

Isra Mikraj (Prophet's Ascension) 6 June 2013, 27 May 2014, 16 May 2015

Sultan of Brunei's Birthday 15 July

First Day of Ramadan 9 July 2013, 28 June 2014, 18 June 2015

Nuzul Quraan (Koran Revelation Day) 26 July 2013, 14 July 2014, 4 July 2015

Hari Raya Aidil Fitri End of Ramadan; three-day holiday beginning 8 August 2013, 28 July 2014, 17 July 2015

Hari Raya Aidil Adha 15 October 2013, 4 October 2014, 23 September 2015

Islamic New Year 4 November 2013, 25 October 2014, 14 October 2015

Christmas Day 25 December

Kalimantan

Tahun Baru Masehi (New Year's Day) 1 January

Maulid Nabi Muhammed (Prophet's Birthday) 13 January 2014, 3 January 2015, 23 December 2015

Tahun Baru Imlek (Chinese New Year) 31 January 2014, 19 February 2015, 8 February 2016

Hari Raya Nyepi (Balinese Day of Silence) 12 March 2013, 31 March 2014, 21 March 2015

Wafat Yesus Kristus (Good Friday) 29 March 2013, 18 April 2014, 3 April 2015

Kenaikan Yesus Kristus (Ascension of Jesus Christ) 9 May 2013, 29 May 2014, 14 May 2015

Waisak (Buddha's Birthday) 25 May 2013, 14 May 2014, 1 June 2015

Isra' Mi'raj Nabi Muhammed (Prophet's Ascension) 6 June 2013, 27 May 2014, 16 May 2015

Idul Fitri End of Ramadan; 8 August 2013, 28 July 2014, 17 July 2015

Hari Proklamasi Kemerdekaan (Independence Day) 17 August

Idul Adha 15 October 2013, 4 October 2014, 23 September 2015

Tahun Baru Hijriyah (Islamic New Year) 4 November 2013, 25 October 2014, 14 October 2015

Hari Natal (Christmas Day) 25 December

Safe Travel

» The Australian government (www.smartraveller. gov.au) warns travellers of a 'high threat of kidnapping

GOVERNMENT TRAVEL ADVICE

The following government websites offer travel advisories and information on current hot spots:

» **Australian Department of Foreign Affairs** (www.smarttraveller.gov.au)

» **British Foreign Office** (www.fco.gov.uk)

» **Canadian Department of Foreign Affairs** (www.dfait-maeci.gc.ca)

» **US State Department** (www.travel.state.gov)

by terrorists and criminals' in 'the islands, dive sites and coastal areas of eastern Sabah', including Sipadan, Mataking and Pandanan. Concern about the area, ongoing as of 2012, dates from the abduction of 21 hostages from Sipadan by Philippines-based Abu Sayyaf terrorists in 2000.

» Borneo is generally very safe for travellers of both sexes, but in villages and logging camps things can get dodgy when alcohol enters the picture.

» Saltwater crocodiles are a very real danger in waterways, especially in muddy estuaries. Exercise caution when swimming in rivers, even far inland, and never swim near river mouths.

» In Kalimantan, transport standards on land and water and in the air are dodgy, roads and even bridges are frequently washed out, and some drivers are a menace to themselves and other road users.

» The Indonesian part of the island isn't anywhere near as dangerous as many Malaysians seem to think – violent crime is very rare – but keep your wits about you, especially in the cities.

Telephone

Cheap prepaid SIM cards make it easy and remarkably inexpensive to keep in touch, both with local contacts and family and friends around the world. If you bring your own gadget, make sure it can handle 900/1800MHz and is not locked. In Borneo, the cheapest Nokia mobile phones start at about US$40.

Sabah & Sarawak
PHONE CODES

» Malaysia's country code is 60. When calling Malaysia from overseas, dial the international access code followed by 60, then the area code or mobile-phone access code (minus the initial zero) and the local number (six to eight digits).

» Within Malaysia, the access code for making international calls is 00.

MOBILE PHONES

Sabah and Sarawak have three networks on which various companies buy air time: **Celcom** (www.celcom.com.my), **DiGi** (www.digi.com.my), and **Hotlink** (www.hotlink.com.my).

Celcom generally has the best coverage, making it possible to phone home from places like Bario (in the Kelabit Highlands) and the slopes of Mt Kinabalu.

A prepaid SIM card, available at shops and kiosks in all but the tiniest villages (as well as at Miri airport and on the Departure level of Kuching airport), costs just RM8.50, the equivalent of a minute or two of international roaming charges. It takes about 10 minutes to activate; you'll have to show your passport.

Recharge cardlets come in denominations ranging from RM5 to RM50. Calls cost just pennies per minute whether they're local or to landline phones around the world (calling mobile phones usually costs a bit more).

The best way to pay for 3G internet access, available mainly in the cities, is per day (Celcom charges RM5 for 500MB) or per week (RM18 for 1GB). Without a plan, you'll be charged a whopping RM10 per MB.

Brunei
PHONE CODES

» Brunei's country code is 673. There are no area codes.

» Within Brunei, the access code for making international calls is 00.

MOBILE PHONES

Bruneian prepaid SIM cards cost B$30 (including B$5 of credit) and must be registered within a week of activation (after that the number will be blocked). The cheapest and easiest way to buy one is to go to the office of **DST Communications** (www.dst-group.com) in central BSB; bring your passport.

Various shops also sell DST 'Easi' SIM cards but they often charge a premium and neglect to handle registration.

Local calls cost B$0.05 to B$0.30 a minute, depending on the time of day. For international calls, using the access code 095 ('IDD 095') is cheaper than 00; calls to Australia, the UK and the USA cost B$0.30 to B$0.50 a minute.

The sultanate's other mobile-phone service provider, **B-Mobile** (www.bmobile.com.bn) sells SIM-card starter packs for B$30.

If you have a Malaysian SIM card, it will not work in Brunei unless you pay astronomical roaming charges – or climb to the top of Ulu Temburong National Park's canopy walk for line-of-sight microwave reception.

Kalimantan

PHONE CODES

» Indonesia's country code is 62. When calling Indonesia from overseas, dial the international access code followed by 62, then the area code (minus the first zero) and local number.

» Within Indonesia, the access code for making international calls is 001.

MOBILE PHONES

Pulsa (www.pulsa-id.com) prepaid SIM cards can be bought in cities and towns for about 10,000Rp and need to be activated by the shop owner. **Telkomsel** (www.telkomsel.com) SIM cards are good for cheap overseas calls. Telcomsel is fine along the coast of East Kalimantan but in the interior **Indosat** (www.indosat.com) has better coverage.

Time

» Sabah, Sarawak and Brunei are all eight hours ahead of Greenwich Mean Time (GMT/UTC+8). They do not observe daylight-saving time.

» Kalimantan is divided into two time zones: Indonesian Western Standard Time (UTC+7), which is observed in West and Central Kalimantan, and Indonesian Central Standard Time (UTC+8), which is observed in East, North and South Kalimantan.

Toilets

» You'll find a lot of squat toilets in Borneo, particularly in public bathrooms.

» Western-style seated toilets are the norm in hotels and guesthouses. You may be expected to flush using water from a plastic bucket.

» Toilet paper is often unavailable in public toilets, including those with a fee, so keep a stash handy. In urban areas you can usually discard used toilet paper into the bowl without causing clogging, but if there is a wastepaper basket – as there often is in rural toilets – it's meant to be used.

Tourist Information

The best sources of information are often guesthouse owners, guides, tour agencies and, of course, fellow travellers.

Sabah & Sarawak

» The two state tourism authorities, the **Sabah Tourism Board** (www.sabahtourism.com) and **Sarawak Tourism Board** (www.sarawaktourism.com), have useful websites with details on festivals and events.

» Tourist information offices in larger cities generally have helpful staff and entire walls filled with up-to-date information.

» Sabah's national parks are run by **Sabah Parks** (www.sabahparks.org), which has an information office in KK.

» Sarawak's national parks are run by **Sarawak Forestry** (www.sarawakforestry.com), which has an especially informative website, publishes useful park brochures (RM1.50), and runs very helpful offices in Kuching and Miri. Staff even answer the phone! Accommodation at certain national parks can be booked at its offices, through its website or via http://ebooking.com.my.

Brunei

» **Brunei Tourism** (☎238-2822; www.tourismbrunei.com; Jln Menteri Besar, Ministry of Industry & Primary Resources) has a very useful – though not necessarily up-to-the-minute – website.

» KH Soon Resthouse in BSB can supply information on land transport to Miri (Sarawak) and Sabah.

Kalimantan

» Local tourist offices can be found in many of Kalimantan's bigger cities. They range from very helpful to well meaning but hopeless.

Travellers with Disabilities

» Borneo has a long way to go in this regard. Most buildings, tourist destinations and public transport in Borneo are not wheelchair accessible.

» Navigating Malaysian Borneo's city centres in a wheelchair can be tricky due to high kerbs and footpaths of varying heights.

» Most tour companies offering trips to the interior do not accommodate people with physical disabilities.

Visas

Make sure your passport is valid for at least six months beyond your date of entry and, if you'll be travelling overland through Brunei, that you have enough pages for lots of entry stamps (no fewer than 10 if you travel by road from Sabah to Sarawak).

Sabah & Sarawak

» Visas valid for three months are issued upon arrival to citizens of the US, Canada, Western Europe (except Greece, Monaco and Portugal, whose nationals get one month), Japan, South Korea and most Commonwealth countries.

» One-month visas are issued on arrival to citizens of Singapore, most countries in Latin America and most countries in the former Soviet Union.

» Israeli passport holders are issued Malaysian visas only in exceptional circumstances.

» For complete information on visa types, who needs them and how to get them, see the website of Malaysia's **Ministry of Foreign Affairs** (www.kln.gov.my) – next to

'Quick Info' (at the bottom of the page), click 'Visa Information', and then click 'Requirement for Foreigners'.

VISA EXTENSIONS

» Malaysian visas can be extended in the Sarawak towns of Kuching, Bintulu, Kapit, Lawas, Limbang, Miri and Sibu; and in the Sabah towns of KK, Keningau, Kudat, Lahad Datu, Sandakan, Semporna, Sipitang, Tawau and Tenom.

» In general, Malaysian visas can be extended for 60 days. Bring your departure ticket and be ready to explain why you would like to stay longer and where you'll be staying; a photo is not required. Approval is usually given same day.

» Extensions take effect on the day they're issued, so the best time to extend a visa is right before the old one expires. If your visa still has a month of validity left, that time will not be added to the period covered by the extension.

» Some travellers report they've been able to extend their Malaysian visas by going through Malaysian border control at the Brunei border and then, without officially entering Brunei, turning around and re-entering Malaysia. Others do visa runs by crossing from Sarawak into Indonesia at Tebedu–Entikong.

» Overstaying your visa by a few days is not usually a big deal, especially if you're a genuine tourist and have no prior offences. However, at the discretion of immigration officers, any violation of Malaysia's visa rules can result in your being turned over to the Immigration Department's enforcement section and, if you're in Sarawak, taken to Serian, 60km southeast of Kuching, for questioning. Bummer of a way to miss your flight.

SARAWAK & SABAH PASSPORT STAMPS

Under the terms of Sabah and Sarawak's entry into Malaysia, both states retain a certain degree of state-level control of their borders. Malaysian citizens from Peninsular Malaysia (West Malaysia) cannot work legally in Malaysian Borneo (East Malaysia) without special permits, and tourists travelling within Malaysia must go through passport control and have their passports stamped whenever they:

» Arrive in Sabah or Sarawak from Peninsular Malaysia or the federal district of Pulau Labuan

» Exit Sabah or Sarawak on their way to Peninsular Malaysia or Pulau Labuan

» Travel between Sabah and Sarawak

Note: When you enter Sabah or Sarawak from another part of Malaysia, your new visa stamp will be valid only for the remainder of the period left on your original Malaysian visa.

Brunei

» When it comes to getting into Brunei, Americans are luckiest (they receive a free 90-day visa on arrival) and Israelis the unluckiest (they aren't permitted to visit at all). Travellers from Western Europe, New Zealand, Singapore, Malaysia and a few other countries score 30 days at the border, while Canadians, Swiss and Japanese get 14 days.

» Australians don't need to apply for a visa in advance but do have to ante up B$5 (payable only in Brunei or Singapore dollars) for a three-day transit visa (you need to show a ticket out), B$20 for a single-entry visa valid for two weeks, or B$30 for a multiple-entry visa valid for a month (this is the one to get if you'll be going overland between Sarawak and Sabah).

» People of most other nationalities must obtain a visa (single/multiple entry B$20/30) in advance from a Brunei Darussalam diplomatic mission – unless, that is, they'll just be transiting through Brunei (defined as arriving from one country

and continuing on to a different country), in which case a 72-hour visa is available upon arrival.

» For more information, see the website of the **Immigration Department** (www.immigration.gov.bn/visiting.htm).

Kalimantan

» Tourists from 64 countries – including Australia, Canada, the EU, India, Japan, New Zealand, South Africa and the US – can receive a 30-day Indonesian visa on arrival (VOA) at three entry points to Kalimantan: the Tebedu–Entikong land crossing between Kuching (Sarawak) and Pontianak (West Kalimantan); Balikpapan (Sepinggan Airport); and Pontianak (Supadio Airport).

» The cost is US$25, payable in US dollars (at the Tebedu–Entikong crossing, at least, ringgit and rupiah may not be accepted). Once in the country, a VOA can be extended by another 30 days for US$25.

» If you arrive in Kalimantan – by land, sea or air – from outside Indonesia at any other entry point, or if

MALAYSIA'S STAR, STRIPES & CRESCENT

It's no coincidence that the Malaysian flag, based on a 1947 design, looks so much like its American counterpart. For a while after WWII, the US was very popular in Malaya, in part for having helped get rid of the Japanese, and the US flag was seen as an excellent way to represent a federal system of government.

The Malaysian flag has 14 horizontal red-and-white stripes (one more than the United States flag) representing the country's 13 states and either its federal government or, collectively, its three federal districts (the 14th stripe originally represented Singapore, which left the federation in 1965). In the upper left-hand corner is a field whose dark blue, taken from the Union Jack, was once seen as representing the Commonwealth but is now interpreted as signifying national unity. The crescent (representing Islam) and the 14-point star (representing the unity of the federation) are both yellow, the traditional royal colour.

your passport is not from one of the designated VOA countries, you must obtain a visa in advance. You might also want to apply for a visa ahead of time if you know you'll be staying in Kalimantan for longer than 30 days.

» In Sabah, Indonesia has consulates in KK and Tawau, and in Sarawak there's a consulate in Kuching. A 60-day visa costs RM170; bring a photo, your ticket out of Indonesia, and a credit card or cash to show that you've got funds. Visas are generally issued the same day.

» For a full list of the countries whose nationals score a VOA and details on the entry points at which they are issued, see www .embassyofindonesia.org /consular/voa.htm.

Volunteering

Pay-to-volunteer programs are available in Sabah at the Sepilok Orang-Utan Rehabilitation Centre (see www .travellersworldwide.com), and in Sarawak at the Matang Wildlife Centre (www. orangutanproject.com) and through Talang-Satang National Park's Sea Turtle Volunteer Programme (contact the National Park Booking Office in Kuching).

Women Travellers

» Borneo is a relatively easy and pleasant place for women travellers. Things are considerably more laid back and liberal in Borneo, including Kalimantan, than, say, in northeastern Peninsular Malaysia or Java. Brunei is more conservative than Sabah or Sarawak.

» Although local women (especially ethnic Chinese) wear shorts and tank tops in the cities, it's a good idea to dress fairly conservatively in Muslim areas and to cover up when visiting a mosque (robes and headscarves are sometimes provided).

» As with anywhere else, use common sense and caution. Do not get lulled into a false sense of security just because everyone seems so easygoing. Do not walk alone at night if possible and lock the door to your hotel room.

Transport

GETTING THERE & AWAY

Most travellers arrive in Borneo by air, most often from the gateway cities of Singapore, Kuala Lumpur (KL) and Jakarta. Kalimantan has ferry links to Java and Sulawesi, and there are also ferries between Sabah and the southern Philippines.

Many of the regional and low-fare airlines do not sell tickets through the major online fare aggregators.

Flights and tours can be booked online at www.lonely planet.com.

Air

Sabah

AirAsia (www.airasia.com) Kota Kinabalu (KK) to Peninsular Malaysia (KL, Johor Bahru and Penang), Singapore, Jakarta, Clark (Philippines), Taipei, Shenzhen and Hong Kong; Sandakan to KL; Tawau to KL; and Pulau Labuan to KL.

Malaysia Airlines (www .malaysiaairlines.com) KK to KL, Hong Kong, Tapei, Osaka and Perth.

Silk Air (www.silkair.com) KK to Singapore.

Tiger Airways (www.tiger airways.com) KK to Clark (Philippines).

Sarawak

AirAsia (www.airasia.com) Kuching to Singapore, KL, Johor Bahru and Penang; Miri to Singapore, KL and Johor Bahru; Sibu to KL and Johor Bahru; Bintulu to KL.

Malaysia Airlines (www .malaysiaairlines.com.my) Kuching to KL and Singapore.

Silk Air (www.silkair.com) Kuching to Singapore.

Tiger Airways (www.tiger airways.com) Kuching to Singapore.

Brunei

Royal Brunei Airlines (www.bruneiair.com) Bandar Seri Begawan (BSB) to London, Dubai, Hong Kong, Shanghai, Bangkok, Manila, Melbourne, Singapore, Surabaya, Jakarta and KL. Offers reasonably priced long-haul flights with a stopover in BSB. Flights are alcohol free.

AirAsia (www.airasia.com) BSB to KL.

Cebu Pacific Air (www. cebupacificair.com) BSB to Manila.

Malaysia Airlines (www .malaysiaairlines.com) BSB to KL.

Singapore Airlines (www .singaporeair.com) BSB to Singapore.

Kalimantan

Flying to and around Kalimantan is much safer than a few years ago.

AirAsia (www.airasia.com) Balikpapan to KL.

Batavia Air (www.batavia-air .com) Balikpapan to Jakarta, Surabaya, Jogjakarta and Manado; Banjarmasin to Jakarta and Surabaya; Berau to Surabaya; Pontianak to Jakarta, Jogjakarta, Batam (near Singapore) and Singapore.

Garuda (www.garuda -indonesia.com) Balikpapan to Jakarta, Surabaya, Jogjakarta and Makassar; Banjarmasin to Jakarta; Pontianak to Jakarta.

Kal Star (www.kalstaronline .com) Jakarta to various Kalimantan cities, plus intra-Kalimantan connections.

Lion Air (www2.lionair.co.id) Balikpapan to Jakarta, Surabaya, Jogjakarta and Makassar; Banjarmasin to Jakarta, Surabaya and Jogjakarta.

Silk Air (www.silkair.net) Balikpapan to Singapore.

Sriwijaya (www.sriwijayaair .co.id) Balikpapan to Jakarta, Surabaya, Jogjakarta and Makassar; Banjarmasin to Jakarta and Surabaya; Pontianak to Jakarta.

Sea

Sabah

Ferries link Sandakan with Zamboanga, on the Philippine island Mindanao, twice a week; see p77 for details.

Kalimantan

Ferries run by **Pelni** (www .pelni.co.id), **Dharma Lautan** (www.dluonline.co.id) and Prima Vista connect Balikpapan, Samarinda, Banjarmasin and Pontianak with

Java (Jakarta, Semarang and Surabaya) and Sulawesi (Makassar, Pare Pare and others).

GETTING AROUND

Air

Borneo is covered by a surprisingly extensive network of flights, and it's often remarkably cheap to hop around the island by air. Air travel is the only practical way to reach some destinations, such as Sarawak's Kelabit Highlands and Gunung Mulu National Park.

There's something incredibly exciting and romantic about buzzing over the jungle in a 19-seat DeHavilland Twin Otter turboprop – or bouncing around in a cloudburst, huge equatorial raindrops crashing furiously on the pilots' windshield, which passengers can see out of because the cockpit doesn't have a door.

Note: on some Twin Otter routes (eg up to Bario) there are strict limits on the weight of both carry-ons (5kg) and checked baggage (10kg). They even weigh the passengers!

In most cases, you can buy air tickets on relatively short notice, but for a few destinations, including Gunung Mulu National Park, Bario and Ba Kelalan (all in Sarawak), it's a good idea to book ahead, especially in July and August

and around holidays. Tickets for most flights can be purchased online.

Sabah & Sarawak

AirAsia (www.airasia.com) Kuching to Sibu, Bintulu, Miri and Kota Kinabalu (KK); KK to Tawau, Sandakan, Miri and Kuching.

Batavia Air (www.batavia-air .co.id) Kuching to Pontianak.

Malaysia Airlines (www .malaysiaairlines.com) Kuching to KK, Sibu and Bintulu; KK to Tawau, Labuan and Bintulu.

MASwings (www.maswings .com.my) Serves two dozen destinations in Sabah (including Sandakan, Lahad Datu and Tawau), Sarawak (including Lawas, Limbang, Bario, Miri, Gunung Mulu National Park, Bintulu and Sibu) and Brunei, plus handles Kuching to Pontianak. Has hubs in KK, Kuching and Miri. Member of Star Alliance. Allows liquids in carry-ons. ATRs and Twin Otters board from the tail so the most accessible seats are at the back of the plane.

Brunei

MASwings (www.maswings .com.my) Bandar Seri Begawan (BSB) to KK and Kuching.

Kalimantan

Kalimantan has a comprehensive network of air links.

Batavia Air (www.batavia-air .co.id) Balikpapan to Banjarmasin and Berau.

Kal-Star (www.kalstaronline .com) Has an extensive network of intra-Kalimantan flights.

Trigana Air (www.trigana-air .com) Intra-Borneo flights (eg to/from Berau and Pangkalan Bun).

Bicycle

Road and all-terrain cycling have recently taken off in the Kuching area, but it's unlikely that Borneo will become a popular bike-touring destination anytime soon. Few roads have shoulders/verges, many are in varying states of disrepair and heavy lorries often drive quite fast. There's also the climate – Borneo straddles the equator and the combination of heat, humidity, torrential rains and sun can be merciless. If you choose to ride, take extreme caution with traffic; drivers are not used to seeing bicycles and will give you precious little leeway. Remember to bring a helmet, a reflective vest, high-power lights and a wealth of inner tubes and spare parts.

Boat

Until the advent of aeroplanes and roads, boats were the only way to cover long distances in Borneo, both along the coast and in the interior. Rivers still play a major transport role, and in some trackless areas – such as Sarawak's Batang Rejang

---

CLIMATE CHANGE & TRAVEL

Every form of transport that relies on carbon-based fuel generates CO_2, the main cause of human-induced climate change. Modern travel is dependent on aeroplanes, which might use less fuel per kilometre per person than most cars but travel much greater distances. The altitude at which aircraft emit gases (including CO_2) and particles also contributes to their climate change impact. Many websites offer 'carbon calculators' that allow people to estimate the carbon emissions generated by their journey and, for those who wish to do so, to offset the impact of the greenhouse gases emitted with contributions to portfolios of climate-friendly initiatives throughout the world. Lonely Planet offsets the carbon footprint of all staff and author travel.

and much of Kalimantan – they're the only ride in town.

On wider rivers, 'flying coffins' – long, narrow express boats with about 60 seats – are the norm. Way upstream, the only craft that can make headway against the rapids and dodge submerged rocks are motorised wooden longboats, expertly manoeuvred by local boatmen and boatwomen.

Rates for water travel are often quite high, the crucial factor being the cost of petrol. Chartering a boat costs much more than taking a water taxi used by locals for commerce and commuting.

Sabah
Nature sites accessible by boat include Tunku Abdul Rahman National Park, the Semporna Archipelago and Pulau Tiga National Park.

In the west, sea ferries link Menumbok with Muara in Brunei; KK with Pulau Labuan; and Pulau Labuan with Muara. In Sabah's southeast corner, speedboats link Tawau with Tarakan and Nunukan in Kalimantan.

Sarawak
Sarawak's Batang Rejang is sometimes called the 'Amazon of Borneo' and a journey upriver is still very romantic, despite the lack of intact forest en route.

Along the coast, speedboats link Limbang with Pulau Labuan. In western Sarawak, motorboats are the only way to get to Bako, Tanjung Datu and Talang-Satang National Parks.

Brunei
Speedboats link BSB with Bangar (in Brunei's Temburong District), and car ferries leave from the Serasa Ferry Terminal in Muara, 25km northeast of BSB, to Pulau Labuan and the Sabah port of Menumbok. The only way to get to Ulu Temburong National Park is by longboat.

Kalimantan
At the time of research, the direct ferry from Tawau (Sabah) to Tarakan (North Kalimantan) wasn't operating, but there is a speedboat service from Tawau to Tarakan via Nunukan. A visa-on-arrival is available if you're entering Sabah but not if you're travelling in the other direction, into Kalimantan.

To get around Kalimantan, the only scheduled public boats are found on the Sungai Mahakam and sail as far as Long Bagun if the water is high enough, otherwise they stop at Tering. For other rivers, it's necessary to charter, or else wait for a local boat to fill up.

Bus, Van & Taxi
Malaysian Borneo's coastal cities are connected by a network of cheap and relatively comfortable buses.

Intercity buses generally depart from a long-distance bus terminal on the outskirts of town, linked to the city centre by bus and taxi. There's usually no need to purchase bus tickets in advance – just show up and shop around for the next departure (departure boards posted at bus-company counters make this easy). For many destinations, departures are most frequent in the mornings, but on some routes (eg Miri to Kuching) there are also afternoon and overnight buses.

Around most cities, including Kuching, short-haul bus services have been decimated by the proliferation of private cars and chaotic, privately operated minivans.

Sabah
An arc of excellent paved roads extends from KK southeast to Tawau, passing Mt Kinabalu, Sepilok, Sandakan, Lahad Datu and Semporna (gateway to Sipadan) along the way. Large buses ply this route on a daily basis, while even more frequent minivans and share taxis and jeeps connect both the main cities and secondary towns. Getting from KK to any towns north, all the way to Kudat, and southwest to the Brunei border, is easily done by share taxi or jeep. The same applies if travelling from Sandakan to any towns south to Tawau. Just keep in mind it's always hard to find any kind of public transport after 5pm.

The southern road that connects Tawau to Sapulot is not entirely paved yet, nor is it serviced by public transport, but you can arrange private transport down this way, and occasional (very occasional) minibuses ply the route. Getting to very remote villages by public transport is tougher – in these situations you need to hope share taxis and jeeps have enough passengers. These vehicles typically leave very early in the morning.

Sarawak
Frequent buses run by a clutch of companies ply the Pan Borneo Hwy from Kuching to Miri, stopping along the way in Sibu and Bintulu, near Niah National Park, and at Lambir Hills National Park. From Miri, several buses a day head via Brunei to Sabah

Long-haul buses link Sarawak's coastal cities, including Kuching, with Pontianak (West Kalimantan) via the Tebedu–Entikong border crossing.

Bus service from Kuching to destinations in Western Sarawak is very limited or non-existent, except to Lundu, Kubah National Park, Matang Wildlife Centre, Bako Bazaar (near Bako National Park) and Semenggoh Nature Reserve. For some destinations, the only transport options are hiring a car or taxi, or joining a tour group.

Border Crossings

Brunei

Only one company, known as Jesselton Express (for services heading from BSB towards KK) and PHLS (for services from BSB towards Miri), is allowed to pick up and drop off passengers inside the sultanate. Two buses a day run from BSB southwest to Miri (via Seria and Kuala Belait) and north-east to KK (via Limbang, Lawas and various destinations in Sabah).

Kalimantan

Buses and Kijang (4WD minivans that ply intercity routes) are a mixed affair, ranging from comfy to purgatorial. The same can also be said of Kalimantan's highways and minor roads, which vary from silk-smooth asphalt to muddy, potholed pumpkin soup during the wet season, when you may have to disembark and push. VIP-style buses with air-con operate between Balikpapan and Samarinda, and from Samarinda to Banjarmasin and Bontang. The rest of the country involves patchy roads, inhumanly quick drivers and, often, overcrowding on woefully smoky, dilapidated buses. Bring with you patience, an inflatable neck cushion, an iPod and anything else to ease the journey.

The only official land crossing between Kalimantan and Malaysian Borneo is at Tebedu–Entikong, in western Sarawak between Kuching and Pontianak. Long-haul buses link Pontianak with Kuching, the cities of Sarawak's central coast and Brunei.

Car & Motorcycle

Driving is on the left in all three countries that share Borneo. The (generally) nicely paved Pan Borneo Hwy runs all along Borneo's northern coast, from Sematan in Sarawak's far west via Brunei (and its many border crossings) to Tawau in the southeast corner of Sabah. Kalimantan's road network is limited, with lots of sections yet to be paved and frequent washouts and flash floods.

Road signage is often haphazard, with many junctions, including T-junctions, lacking any indication of where to go. Yogi Berra may have advised, 'when you get to a fork in the road, take it', but that's easier said than done.

Car Rental

Driving a rental car gives you maximum flexibility but can involve major hassles – in Borneo, these are likely to include poor or nonexistent road signage, a dearth of proper road maps, dilapidated vehicles, and small rental companies that may try to foist repair charges onto you. In Kalimantan you may have trouble asking for directions unless you speak Bahasa Indonesia. On the brighter side, in Malaysia petrol costs only about US$0.60 per litre (US$2.30 per US gallon).

Car-hire companies have desks in the arrivals halls of larger airports; in city centres, hotels and guesthouses can help find an agency. We've heard reports that small local companies sometimes try to rent out 10-year-old cars with bald tyres and leaky boots (trunks). Before you sign anything or hand over any cash, check over your vehicle very carefully (eg for seatbelts in back), especially if it's an older Malaysian-made model such as a tiny Perodua Kancil or Proton Wira.

In Sabah and Sarawak, prices for a very used 660cc Kancil start at an absolute minimum of RM90/500 per day/week at the cheapest outfits; a Perodua Viva or Proton Saga will cost a bit more. Renting a Hyundai Matrix through an international company such as **Hertz** (www.hertz.com) costs about double that, but your vehicle is likely to be newer, safer and better maintained.

As always, verify the insurance excess/deductible, whose default may be RM2000 or more; reducing this to RM500 can cost as little as RM15 a day.

In Brunei, prices start at about B$80 a day. In Kalimantan – where available – they start at about 1,500,000Rp per day.

With some Malaysian companies you can visit Brunei for no extra charge, while others charge a fee of RM50 or RM100. Renting a car in one city and returning it in another can be expensive – count on paying RM500 extra to pick up a vehicle in Miri and drop it off in Kuching. Some insurance plans are only valid in a limited geographical area.

A valid overseas licence is needed to rent a car. An International Driving Permit (a translation of your license and its provisions) is usually not required by local car-hire companies, but it's recommended that you bring one. Minimum age limits (generally 23, sometimes 21) often apply, and some companies won't rent to anyone over 60 or 65.

Taxi Hire

For travel to places within a 50km or 70km radius of where you're staying, hiring a taxi on a per-trip, half-day or per-day basis is often a good option, especially for three or four people. For day trips from public-transport-challenged Kuching, for instance, count on paying about RM250 for an eight-hour excursion. When you factor in fuel, this often works out only slightly more expensive than renting. Bonuses: you bear no liability in case the car is damaged, and you've got the driver to take care of navigation and mechanical problems – and to find places to eat.

In Kalimantan, the norm is to hire a Kijang (taxi), agreeing on remuneration for the driver in addition to paying for fuel.

Hitching

Hitching is never entirely safe anywhere in the world, but it's certainly possible to hitch in most parts of Borneo. It's usually relatively safe for male travellers, but we don't recommend it for female travellers. Some drivers will expect a small 'tip' or assistance with petrol costs for driving you. At the very least, if you stop for food, you should offer to pay for their meal.

Local Transport

Bicycle

Within cities, bicycles have become a rare sight as increased prosperity has brought the creature comforts of gas guzzling to Malaysia and Brunei. However, some guesthouses rent or lend bicycles to their guests. Out in the country, locals still use bicycles to get around small *kampung* (villages), and if you can get hold of a bicycle – rental options

are rare – this can be a very pleasant way to soak up the atmosphere.

Boat

Small motorboats and motorised longboats are often used for short trips across rivers and bays. Examples include traversing Kuching's Sungai Sarawak and transport from central BSB (Brunei) to the water village of Kampung Ayer.

Taxi

Taxis are common in Borneo's larger cities; meters, drivers who use them and fixed rates are less common, except in Kuching. Luckily, you'll find that most drivers in Borneo are quite honest. Just be sure to set the price before starting out and only pay upon arrival.

Tours

One way to get the most out of a national park visit, jungle trek or longhouse sojourn is to go with a guide who knows the territory (and, in the case of longhouses, the head-

man). Indeed, it's the only way to see some things – for instance, the summits of Gunung Mulu and Mt Kinabalu, the longhouses of Sarawak's Batang Ai region and the Kelabit Highlands, and Ulu Temburong National Park in Brunei.

Borneo has a wealth of excellent guides and tour agencies. Most guesthouses and hotels have relationships with at least one local tour operator, and some run their own in-house travel agencies. It's best to ask other travellers about their experiences with these before plunking down any money.

Train

Borneo's only railway line, run by the **Sabah State Railway** (www.sabah.gov.my/railway), runs two trains a day from Tanjung Aru, 4km southwest of central KK, south to Beaufort and Tenom, a distance of 134km. Inaugurated in 1896, this scenic line underwent a major renovation in 2011.

Health

Travellers tend to worry about contracting infectious diseases, but infections are not nearly as common in Borneo as you might think and rarely cause serious illness. Malaria does exist but is usually limited to isolated upland areas.

The following information should be used only as a general guide and should not replace the advice of a doctor trained in travel medicine.

Before You Go

If you take any regular medication, bring double your needs in case of loss or theft, and carry these supplies separately. You may be able to buy some medications over the counter in Borneo without a prescription, but it can be difficult to find some newer drugs, particularly the latest antidepressants, blood-pressure medications and contraceptive pills.

Insurance

Even if you're fit and healthy, don't travel without health insurance. Extra cover may be required for adventure activities, such as rock climbing, caving or scuba diving. If you're uninsured, emergency evacuation can be expensive; bills of over US$100,000 are not uncommon. Insurance is available online from www.lonelyplanet.com.

Vaccinations

Most vaccines don't produce immunity until at least two weeks after they're given, so visit a doctor four to eight weeks before departure. Ask for an International Certificate of Vaccination (known as the 'yellow booklet'), which will list all the vaccinations you've received.

Proof of vaccination against yellow fever will be required only if you have visited a country in the yellow-fever zone (parts of Africa and South America) within six days prior to entering Malaysia, Brunei or Indonesia. If you're coming from Africa or South America, check to see if you require proof of vaccination.

Medical Checklist

» Antibiotics – consider bringing if you're travelling well off the beaten track; see your doctor and carry the prescription with you

» Antifungal cream or powder – for fungal skin infections and thrush

» Antihistamine – for allergies such as hay fever; to ease the itch from insect bites or stings; and to prevent motion sickness

» Antiseptic (eg povidone-iodine or betadine) – for cuts and grazes

» Antispasmodic (eg Buscopan) – for stomach cramps

» Aspirin or paracetamol (acetaminophen in the USA) – for pain or fever

» Adhesive bandages and other wound dressings

» Calamine lotion, sting relief spray or aloe vera – to ease irritation from sunburn and insect bites or stings

RECOMMENDED VACCINATIONS

The World Health Organization recommends the following vaccinations for travellers to Borneo:
» Adult diphtheria and tetanus
» Hepatitis A
» Hepatitis B
» Measles, mumps and rubella
» Polio
» Typhoid
» Varicella

Recommended for longer term travellers (more than one month) or those at special risk:
» Japanese B Encephalitis
» Meningitis
» Rabies
» Tuberculosis

HEALTH ADVISORIES

Many government travel websites include health information:

» **Australia** (www.smartraveller.gov.au)
» **Canada** (www.travelhealth.gc.ca)
» **New Zealand** (www.safetravel.govt.nz)
» **United Kingdom** (www.dh.gov.uk)
» **United States** (www.cdc.gov/travel)

» Cold and flu tablets, throat lozenges, nasal decongestant
» Contraceptives
» DEET-based insect repellent
» Ibuprofen – or another anti-inflammatory
» Iodine tablets (unless you are pregnant or have a thyroid problem) – to purify water
» Loperamide or diphenoxylate – 'blockers' for diarrhoea
» Multivitamins – for long trips, when dietary vitamin intake may be inadequate
» Permethrin – to impregnate clothing and mosquito nets
» Prochlorperazine or metoclopramide – for nausea and vomiting
» Rehydration mixture – to prevent dehydration, which may occur, for example, during bouts of diarrhoea
» Scissors, tweezers and a thermometer (note that mercury thermometers are prohibited by airlines)
» Sterile kit – in case you need injections in a country with medical-hygiene problems; discuss with your doctor
» Sunscreen, lip balm and eye drops

Websites

There's a wealth of travel-health advice on the internet.
World Health Organization (www.who.int/ith) Publishes a superb book – *International Travel and Health* (downloadable) – and is the best source of information on disease distribution.
Centers for Disease Control & Prevention (USA) (www.cdc.gov) Excellent general information.

Further Reading

Lonely Planet's pocket-size *Asia & India: Healthy Travel* is packed with useful information, including pre-trip planning, emergency first aid, immunisation and disease information, and what to do if you get sick on the road. *Travel with Children* includes advice on travel health for young children.

Other references include the 5th (2012) edition of *Travellers' Health* by Dr Richard Dawood (Oxford University Press) and the 17th (2012) edition of *Travelling Well* by Dr Deborah Mills (available from www.travellingwell.com.au).

In Borneo

Availability & Cost of Health Care

There are good medical facilities – charging reasonable rates – in Borneo's larger cities. This is especially true in Sabah, Sarawak and Brunei, where even upland towns such as Bario and Belaga are now served by full-time doctors. As you head into the hinterlands, however, especially in Kalimantan, you'll find few if any medical facilities.

In Sabah, Sarawak and Brunei you will have no problem communicating with doctors in English, and almost all nurses know at least some English. Pharmacists also tend to speak reasonable English – this can be important, as many medications are marketed under a variety of names in different parts of the world.

Infectious Diseases

DENGUE FEVER

This mosquito-borne disease is present in Borneo. As there's no vaccine available, it can only be prevented by avoiding mosquito bites. The mosquito that carries dengue fever bites during both day and night, so use insect-avoidance measures at all times. Symptoms include high fever, severe headache and body ache. Some people develop a rash and experience diarrhoea. There's no specific treatment, just rest and paracetamol – don't take aspirin as it increases the likelihood of haemorrhaging. Some forms can be dangerous, so see a doctor to be diagnosed and monitored.

LEPTOSPIROSIS

Leptospirosis is a bacterial disease that's most commonly contracted after river rafting, canyoning or caving, sometimes as a result of contact with rat urine or faeces. Early symptoms are similar to the flu and include headache and fever. It can vary from a very mild to fatal disease. Diagnosis is through blood tests and it is easily treated with Doxycycline.

MALARIA

Malaria is not common but is present in Borneo, particularly in parts of Kalimantan. Brunei is malaria free; in Sabah and Sarawak, the disease is absent from coastal areas and only occasionally found in or around remote lumber camps. One reason for the relative rarity of malaria is the relatively low mosquito population in much of Borneo – thanks in part to the island's millions of cave-dwelling, insectivorous bats. Get up-to-date information on infected areas before your trip and as soon as you arrive in the country.

In areas with minimal to no risk of malaria, the potential side effects from antimalarial tablets may outweigh the risk of getting the disease. For some rural and upland areas, however, the risk of contracting the disease outweighs any tablet side effects. Remember that malaria can be fatal. Before you travel, seek medical advice on the right medication and dosage for you.

Malaria is caused by a parasite transmitted through the bite of an infected mosquito. The most important symptom is fever, but general symptoms such as headache, diarrhoea, cough or chills may also occur. Diagnosis can be made only by taking a blood sample.

Two strategies should be combined to prevent malaria: mosquito avoidance and antimalarial medications. Most people who catch malaria are taking inadequate or no medication. Travellers in malarial areas are advised to prevent mosquito bites by taking these steps:
» Use a DEET-containing insect repellent on exposed skin. Wash this off at night (if you're sleeping under a mosquito net treated with permethrin). Natural repellents such as citronella can be effective but must be applied more frequently than products containing DEET.
» Choose accommodation with screens and fans (if not air-con).
» Sleep under a permethrin-impregnated mosquito net.
» Wear long sleeves and trousers in light colours.
» Impregnate clothing with permethrin (in high-risk areas).
» Use mosquito coils.

RABIES
Rabies is present in Kalimantan but much less common in Sabah, Sarawak and Brunei. This fatal disease is spread by the bite or lick of an infected animal, most commonly a dog or monkey. Seek medical advice *immediately* after any animal bite.

Having pre-travel vaccination means the post-bite treatment is greatly simplified. If you are not pre-vaccinated, you will need to receive rabies immunoglobulin as soon as possible.

Environmental Hazards
DIVING
Divers and surfers should seek specialised advice before they travel, to ensure their medical kit contains treatment for coral cuts and tropical ear infections. Divers should ensure their insurance covers them for decompression illness – specialised dive insurance is available through **DAN Asia-Pacific** (Divers Alert Network; www.danasiapacific.org). Have a dive medical before you leave your home country.

HEAT
Borneo is hot and humid throughout the year. Most people take at least two weeks to adapt to the climate. Swelling of the feet and ankles is common, as are muscle cramps caused by excessive sweating. Prevent these by avoiding dehydration and too much activity in the heat. Take it easy when you first arrive. Don't eat salt tablets (they aggravate the gut), but drinking rehydration solution or eating salty food helps. Treat cramps by stopping activity, resting, rehydrating with double-strength rehydration solution and gently stretching.

Dehydration is the main contributor to heat exhaustion. Symptoms include feeling weak, headache, irritability, nausea or vomiting, sweaty skin, a fast, weak pulse and a slightly increased body temperature. Treatment involves getting the sufferer out of the heat and/or sun, fanning them and applying cool wet cloths to the skin, laying the victim flat with their legs raised and rehydrating with water containing a quarter of a teaspoon of salt per litre. Recovery is usually rapid, although it's common to feel weak for some days afterwards.

Heatstroke is a serious medical emergency. Symptoms come on suddenly and include weakness, nausea, a hot, dry body with a body temperature of over 41°C, dizziness, confusion, loss of coordination, fits, and eventual collapse and loss of consciousness. Seek medical help and commence cooling by getting the sufferer out of the heat, removing their clothes, fanning them and applying cool, wet cloths or ice to their body, especially to the groin and armpits.

Prickly heat is a common skin rash in the tropics, caused by sweat being trapped under the skin. The result is an itchy rash of tiny lumps. If you develop prickly heat, treat it by moving out of the heat and into an air-conditioned area for a few hours and by having cool showers. Creams and ointments clog the skin, so should be avoided. Locally bought prickly-heat powder can be helpful for relief.

INSECT BITES & STINGS
Ticks are contracted after walking in the bush and are commonly found behind the ears, on the belly and in armpits. If you have had a tick bite and experience symptoms such as a rash at the site of the bite or elsewhere, a fever or muscle aches, you should see a doctor.

Leeches are found in humid rainforest areas. They do not transmit any disease but their bites are often intensely itchy for weeks and can easily become infected. Apply iodine-based antiseptic to leech bites to help prevent infection. See p22 for more information.

Bee and wasp stings mainly cause problems for people who are allergic to them. Anyone with a serious bee or wasp allergy should carry an injection of adrenalin (eg an EpiPen) for emergency treatment. For others, pain is the main problem – apply ice to the sting and take painkillers.

Most jellyfish in Southeast Asian waters are not dangerous, just irritating. First aid for jellyfish stings involves pouring vinegar onto the affected area to neutralise the poison. Don't rub sand or water onto the stings. Take painkillers, and if you feel ill in any way after being stung seek medical advice. Take local advice if there are dangerous jellyfish around and keep out of the water.

SKIN PROBLEMS

Fungal rashes are common in humid climates. There are two common fungal rashes that affect travellers. The first occurs in moist areas that get less air, such as the groin, armpits and between the toes. It starts as a red patch that slowly spreads and is usually itchy. Treatment involves keeping the skin dry, avoiding chafing and using an antifungal cream such as Clotrimazole or Lamisil. Tinea versicolour is also common – this fungus causes small, light-coloured patches, most commonly on the back, chest and shoulders. Consult a doctor.

Cuts and scratches become easily infected in humid climates. Take meticulous care of wounds – immediately washing them in clean water and applying antiseptic – to prevent complications such as abscesses. If you develop signs of infection (increasing pain and redness), see a doctor. Divers and surfers should be particularly careful with coral cuts as they become easily infected.

TRAVELLER'S DIARRHOEA

Traveller's diarrhoea is by far the most common problem affecting travellers – between 30% to 50% of people will suffer from it within two weeks of starting their trip. In over 80% of cases, it's caused by a bacteria, and therefore responds promptly to treatment with antibiotics. Treatment will depend on your situation – how sick you are, how quickly you need to get better, where you are etc. Traveller's

TAP WATER

» Never drink tap water unless you've verified that it's safe (many parts of Sabah, Sarawak and Brunei have modern treatment plants).

» Bottled water is generally safe – check the seal is intact at purchase.

» Avoid ice in eateries that look dubious, especially in Kalimantan.

» Avoid fruit juices if they're not freshly squeezed or you suspect they have been watered down.

» Boiling water is the most efficient way to purify it.

» The best chemical purifier is iodine (not to be used if you are pregnant or have thyroid problems).

» Water filters should also filter out viruses. Ensure your filter has a chemical barrier such as iodine and a small pore size (ie less than 4 microns).

diarrhoea is defined as the passage of more than three watery bowel actions within 24 hours, plus at least one other symptom, such as fever, cramps, nausea, vomiting or feeling generally unwell. Treatment consists of staying well hydrated; rehydration solutions such as Gastrolyte are the best for this.

Always seek reliable medical care if you have blood in your diarrhoea.

Loperamide is just a 'stopper' and doesn't get to the cause of the problem (it can be helpful, for example, if you have to go on a long bus ride). Don't take it if you have a fever, or blood in your stools.

Ways to avoid traveller's diarrhoea include eating only freshly cooked food and avoiding shellfish and food that has been sitting around in buffets. Peel all fruit, cook vegetables, and soak salads in iodine water for at least 20 minutes. Eat in busy restaurants with a high turnover of customers.

Travelling with Children

Borneo is a great place to travel with children. However, there are specific health issues you need to consider.

All your children's routine vaccinations should be up

to date, as many of the common childhood diseases that have been eliminated in the West are still present in parts of Borneo. A travel-health clinic can advise you on specific vaccines, but think seriously about rabies vaccination if you're visiting rural areas or travelling for more than a month, as children are more vulnerable to severe animal bites.

Children are more prone to getting serious forms of mosquito-borne diseases such as malaria, Japanese B encephalitis and dengue fever. In particular, malaria is very serious in children and can rapidly lead to death – think seriously before taking your child into a malaria risk area. Permethrin-impregnated clothing is safe to use, and insect repellents should contain between 10% and 20% DEET.

Diarrhoea can cause rapid dehydration and you should pay particular attention to keeping your child well hydrated. The best antibiotic for children with diarrhoea is Azithromycin.

Women's Health

In urban areas, supplies of sanitary products are readily available. Birth-control options may be limited, so bring adequate supplies.

WANT MORE?

For in-depth language information and handy phrases, check out Lonely Planet's *Indonesian Phrasebook* and *Malay Phrasebook*. You'll find them at **shop.lonelyplanet.com**, or you can buy Lonely Planet's iPhone phrasebooks at the Apple App Store.

Language

Malay, or Bahasa Malaysia, is the official language of Malaysian Borneo (Sabah and Sarawak) and Brunei; it's the native language of people of Malay descent there. Indonesian, or Bahasa Indonesia, is the official language of Kalimantan and the mother tongue of most people of non-Chinese descent living there. The two languages are very similar, and if you can speak a little of either you'll be able to use it across the island. We've avoided duplication in this language guide by providing translations in both languages indicated by (I) and (M) – only where the differences are significant enough to cause confusion.

Each of Borneo's indigenous groups has its own language, but their members all speak Bahasa Malaysia or Bahasa Indonesia. Various dialects of Chinese are spoken by those of Chinese ancestry in Borneo, although Mandarin is fairly widely spoken and understood.

You'll find it easy to get by with only English in Borneo, particularly in Sabah, Sarawak and Brunei. English is the most common second language for Borneo's ethnic groups and is often used by people of different backgrounds, like ethnic Chinese and ethnic Malays, to communicate with one another.

In both Bahasa Malaysia and Bahasa Indonesia, most letters are pronounced more or less the same as their English counterparts, except for the letter *c* which is always pronounced as the 'ch' in 'chair'. Nearly all syllables carry equal emphasis, but a good approximation is to lightly stress the second-last syllable. The main exception to the rule is the unstressed *e* in words such as *besar* (big), which sounds like the 'a' in 'ago'.

Pronouns, particularly 'you', are rarely used in both Bahasa Malaysia and Bahasa Indonesia. *Anda* (in Indonesian) and *kamu* (in Malay) are the egalitarian forms designed to overcome the plethora of terms relating to a person's age and gender that are used for the second person.

BASICS

Hello.	*Salam./Helo.* (I/M)
Goodbye.	*Selamat tinggal/jalan.* (by person leaving/staying)
How are you?	*Apa kabar?*
I'm fine.	*Kabar baik.*
Excuse me.	*Maaf.*
Sorry.	*Maaf.*
Yes.	*Ya.*
No.	*Tidak.*
Please.	*Silakan.*
Thank you.	*Terima kasih.*
You're welcome.	*Kembali.* (I) *Sama-sama.* (M)

My name is ...
Nama saya ...

What's your name?
Siapa nama anda/kamu? (I/M)

Do you speak English?
Anda bisa Bahasa Inggris? (I)
Adakah anda berbahasa Inggeris? (M)

I (don't) understand.
Saya (tidak) mengerti. (I)
Saya (tidak) faham. (M)

ACCOMMODATION

Do you have any rooms available?
Ada kamar/bilik kosongkah? (I/M)

How much is it per day/person?
Berapa harga satu malam/orang?

Is breakfast included?
Makan pagi termasukkah?

campsite	*tempat kemah* (I)
	tempat perkhemahan (M)
guesthouse	*rumah yang disewakan* (I)
	rumah tetamu (M)
hotel	*hotel*
youth hostel	*losmen pemuda* (I)
	asrama belia (M)
single room	*kamar untuk seorang* (I)
	bilik untuk seorang (M)
room with a double bed	*tempat tidur besar satu kamar* (I)
	bilik untuk dua orang (M)
room with two beds	*kamar dengan dua tempat tidur* (I)
	bilik yang ada dua katil (M)
air-con	*AC* (pronounced 'a-se') (I)
	pendingin udara (M)
bathroom	*kamar mandi* (I)
	bilik air (M)
mosquito coil	*obat nyamuk*
window	*jendela/tingkap* (I/M)

DIRECTIONS

Where is ...?
Di mana ...?

What's the address?
Apa alamatnya?

Could you write it down, please?
Anda bisa tolong tuliskan? (I)
Tolong tuliskan alamat itu? (M)

Can you show me (on the map)?
Bisa tunjukkan kepada saya (di peta)? (I)
Tolong tunjukkan (di peta)? (M)

at the corner	*di sudut/simpang* (I/M)
at the traffic lights	*di lampu lalu-lintas* (I)
	di tempat lampu isyarat (M)
behind	*di belakang*
far (from)	*jauh (dari)*
in front of	*di depan*
near (to)	*dekat (dengan)*
opposite	*di seberang* (I)
	berhadapan dengan (M)

KEY PATTERNS

To get by in Indonesian and Malay, mix and match these simple patterns with words of your choice:

When's (the next bus)?
Jam berapa (bis yang berikutnya)?

Where's (the station)?
Di mana (stasiun)?

How much is it (per night)?
Berapa (satu malam)?

I'm looking for (a hotel).
Saya cari (hotel).

Do you have (a local map)?
Ada (peta daerah)?

Is there a (lift)?
Ada (lift)?

Can I (enter)?
Boleh saya (masuk)?

Do I need (a visa)?
Saya harus pakai (visa)?

I have (a reservation).
Saya (sudah punya booking).

I need (assistance).
Saya perlu (dibantu).

I'd like (the menu).
Saya minta (daftar makanan).

I'd like (to hire a car).
Saya mau (sewa mobil).

Could you (help me)?
Bisa Anda (bantu) saya?

Turn left/right.	*Belok kiri/kanan.*
Go straight ahead.	*Jalan terus.*

EATING & DRINKING

A table for (two), please.
Meja untuk (dua) orang.

What's in that dish?
Hidangan itu isinya apa? (I)
Ada apa dalam masakan itu? (M)

Bring the bill/check, please.
Tolong bawa kuitansi/bil. (I/M)

I don't eat ...	*Saya tidak mau makan ...* (I)
	Saya tak suka makan ... (M)
chicken	*ayam*
fish	*ikan*
(red) meat	*daging (merah)*
nuts	*biji-bijian/kacang* (I/M)

Signs

Buka	Open
Dilarang	Prohibited
Kamar Kecil (I)	Toilets
Keluar	Exit
Lelaki (M)	Men
Masuk	Entrance
Perempuan (M)	Women
Pria (I)	Men
Tandas (M)	Toilets
Tutup	Closed
Wanita (I)	Women

Key Words

bottle	*botol*
breakfast	*sarapan pagi*
cold	*dingin/sejuk* (I/M)
cup	*cangkir/cawan* (I/M)
dinner	*makan malam*
food	*makanan*
fork	*garpu/garfu* (I/M)
glass	*gelas*
hot	*panas*
knife	*pisau*
lunch	*makan siang/tengahari* (I/M)
market	*pasar*
menu	*daftar makanan* (I) *menu* (M)
plate	*piring/pinggan* (I/M)
restaurant	*restoran*
spicy	*pedas*
spoon	*sendok/sedu* (I/M)
vegetarian	*makanan tanpa daging* (I) *sayuran saja* (M)
with	*dengan*
without	*tanpa*

Meat & Fish

beef	*daging sapi/lembu* (I/M)
chicken	*ayam*
crab	*kepiting/ketam* (I/M)
fish	*ikan*
lamb	*daging anak domba* (I) *anak biri-biri* (M)
mussels	*remis/kepah* (I/M)
pork	*babi*
shrimp	*udang*

Fruit & Vegetables

apple	*apel/epal* (I/M)
banana	*pisang*
carrot	*wortel/lobak* (I/M)
cucumber	*ketimun/timun* (I/M)
jackfruit	*nangka*
mango	*mangga*
orange	*jeruk manis/oren* (I/M)
peanut	*kacang*
starfruit	*belimbing*
tomato	*tomat/tomato* (I/M)
watermelon	*semangka/tembikai* (I/M)

Other

bread	*roti*
cheese	*keju*
egg	*telur*
ice	*es/ais* (I/M)
rice	*nasi*
salt	*garam*
sugar	*gula*

Drinks

beer	*bir*
bottled water	*air botol*
citrus juice	*air jeruk/limau* (I/M)
coffee	*kopi*
milk	*susu*
tea	*teh*
water	*air*
wine	*anggur/wain* (I/M)

EMERGENCIES

Help!	*Tolong!*
Stop!	*Berhenti!*
I'm lost.	*Saya sesat.*
Go away!	*Pergi!*

There's been an accident.
Ada kecelakaan/kemalangan. (I/M)

Call the doctor/police!
Panggil doktor/polis!

I'm ill.
Saya sakit.

It hurts here.
Sakitnya di sini. (I)
Sini sakit. (M)

I'm allergic to (nuts).
Saya alergi terhadap (biji-bijian). (I)
Saya alergik kepada (kacang). (M)

SHOPPING & SERVICES

I'd like to buy ...
Saya mau/nak beli ... (I/M)

I'm just looking.
Saya lihat-lihat saja. (I)
Saya nak tengok saja. (M)

May I look at it?
Boleh saya lihat? (I)
Boleh saya tengok barang itu? (M)

How much is it?
Berapa harganya?

It's too expensive.
Itu terlalu mahal. (I)
Mahalnya. (M)

Can you lower the price?
Boleh kurang?

There's a mistake in the bill.
Ada kesalahan dalam kuitansi ini. (I)
Bil ini salah. (M)

ATM	*ATM* (pronounced 'a-te-em')
credit card	*kartu/kad kredit* (I/M)
internet cafe	*warnet* (I) *cyber cafe* (M)
post office	*kantor/pejabat pos* (I/M)
public phone	*telpon umum/awam* (I/M)
tourist office	*kantor pariwisata* (I) *pejabat pelancong* (M)

TIME & DATES

What time is it?
Jam berapa sekarang? (I)
Pukul berapa? (M)

It's (seven) o'clock.
Jam/Pukul (tujuh). (I/M)

It's half past (one).
Setengah (dua). (I)
  (lit: half two)
Pukul (satu) setengah. (M)

Question Words	
How?	*Bagaimana?*
What?	*Apa?*
When?	*Kapan?* (I) *Bila?* (M)
Where?	*Di mana?*
Who?	*Siapa?*
Why?	*Mengapa?*

in the morning	*pagi*
in the afternoon	*siang/tengahari* (I/M)
in the evening	*malam/petang* (I/M)
yesterday	*kemarin/semalam* (I/M)
today	*hari ini*
tomorrow	*besok/esok* (I/M)
Monday	*hari Senin/Isnin* (I/M)
Tuesday	*hari Selasa*
Wednesday	*hari Rabu*
Thursday	*hari Kamis*
Friday	*hari Jumat/Jumaat* (I/M)
Saturday	*hari Sabtu*
Sunday	*hari Minggu*
January	*Januari*
February	*Februari*
March	*Maret/Mac* (I/M)
April	*April*
May	*Mei*
June	*Juni/Jun* (I/M)
July	*Juli/Julai* (I/M)
August	*Agustus/Ogos* (I/M)
September	*September*
October	*Oktober*
November	*November*
December	*Desember*

TRANSPORT

Public Transport

What time does the ... leave?	*Jam/Pukul berapa ... berangkat?* (I/M)
boat	*kapal*
bus	*bis/bas* (I/M)
plane	*pesawat* (I) *kapal terbang* (M)
train	*kereta api*

I want to go to ...
Saya mau/nak ke ... (I/M)

Does it stop at ... ?
Berhenti di ...?

How long will it be delayed?
Berapa lama keterlambatannya? (I)
Berapa lambatnya? (M)

I'd like to get off at ...
Saya mau/nak turun di ... (I/M)

Numbers	
1	satu
2	dua
3	tiga
4	empat
5	lima
6	enam
7	tujuh
8	delapan (I)
	lapan (M)
9	sembilan
10	sepuluh
20	dua puluh
30	tiga puluh
40	empat puluh
50	lima puluh
60	enam puluh
70	tujuh puluh
80	delapan puluh (I)
	lapan puluh (M)
90	sembilan puluh
100	seratus
1000	seribu

Please put the meter on.
Tolong pakai argo/meter. (I/M)

Please stop here.
Tolong berhenti di sini.

I'd like a ... ticket.	*Saya mau/nak tiket ...* (I/M)
1st-class	*kelas satu* (I)
	kelas pertama (M)
2nd-class	*kelas dua* (I)
	kelas kedual (M)
one-way	*sekali jalan* (I)
	sehala (M)
return	*pulang pergi* (I)
	pergi balik (M)

the first	*pertama*
the last	*terakhir*
the next	*berikutnya*

bus station	*terminal bis* (I)
	stesen bas (M)
bus stop	*halte bis* (I)
	perhentian bas (M)
cancelled	*dibatalkan*
delayed	*terlambat/lambat* (I/M)
platform	*peron/landasan* (I/M)
ticket office	*loket/pejabat tiket* (I/M)
timetable	*jadwal/jadual waktu* (I/M)

Driving & Cycling

I'd like to hire a ...	*Saya mau sewa ...* (I)
	Saya nak menyewa ... (M)
bicycle	*sepeda/basikal* (I/M)
car	*mobil/kereta* (I/M)
jeep	*jip*
motorbike	*sepeda motor* (I)
	motosikal (M)

diesel	*solar/disel* (I/M)
helmet	*helem* (I)
	topi keledar (M)
petrol	*bensin/petrol* (I/M)
pump	*pompa/pam* (I/M)

Is this the road to ...?
Ini jalan ke ...?

Where's a service station?
Di mana pompa bensin? (I)
Stesen minyak di mana? (M)

(How long) Can I park here?
(Berapa lama) Saya boleh parkir di sini? (I)
(Beberapa lama) Boleh saya letak kereta di sini? (M)

I need a mechanic.
Saya perlu montir. (I)
Kami memerlukan mekanik. (M)

The car has broken down at ...
Mobil mogok di ... (I)
Kereta saya telah rosak di ... (M)

I have a flat tyre.
Ban saya kempes. (I)
Tayarnya kempis. (M)

I've run out of petrol/gas.
Saya kehabisan bensin. (I)
Minyak sudah habis. (M)

(m) indicates masculine gender, (f) feminine gender and (pl) plural

ai – small river

air – water

angkot – short for angkutan kota (city transport); small minibuses covering city routes in Kalimantan

Bahasa Indonesia – official language of Indonesia

Bahasa Malaysia – official language of Malaysia

bandar – seaport; town

bandung – floating general store (Kalimantan)

Barisan Nasional – National Front, commonly abbreviated as BN; Malaysia's federal ruling political force since independence

batang – stem; tree trunk; the main branch of a river

batik – technique of imprinting cloth with dye to produce multicoloured patterns

batu – stone; rock; milepost

becak – bicycle rickshaw (Kalimantan)

belian – ironwood

BSB – Bandar Seri Begawan; capital of Brunei

bukit – hill

bumiputra – literally, 'sons of the soil'; people considered indigenous under Malaysian law

ces – motorised canoe

Dayak – indigenous peoples of Borneo; term used mostly in Kalimantan and Sarawak

dipterocarp – family of commercially valuable rainforest trees

dusun – small town; orchard; fruit grove

gua – cave

gunung – mountain

ikat – fabric patterned by tie-dying the yarn before weaving

istana – palace

jalan – road (abbreviated as 'Jln' or 'Jl')

kampung – village; also spelt *kampong*

kapal biasa – river boats with second-storey accommodation (Kalimantan)

karst – characteristic scenery of a limestone region, including features such as underground streams and caverns

kedai kopi – eatery, often with several food stalls; literally, 'coffee shop' (Bahasa Malaysia)

kerangas – heath forest; in Iban, means 'land that cannot grow rice'

keraton – palace

Kijang – taxi (Kalimantan); Indonesian brand name of a Toyota minibus or pick-up

KK – Kota Kinabalu; capital of Sabah

klotok – houseboat (Kalimantan)

Konfrontasi – literally, 'confrontation'; catchphrase of the early 1960s when Soekarno embarked on a confrontational campaign against Western imperialism aimed at Malaysia

kopitiam – eatery, often with several food stalls; literally, 'coffee shop' (Chinese term)

kota – fort; city

kuala – river mouth; place where a tributary joins a larger river

langur – small, usually tree-dwelling monkey

laut – sea

lebuh – street

lorong – narrow street; alley (abbreviated 'Lg')

losmen – budget guesthouse

macaque – any of several small species of monkey

mandi – bathe; Southeast Asian wash basin

masjid – mosque

Melayu Islam Beraja – Malay Islamic Monarchy, known as MIB; Brunei's national ideology

merdeka – independence

muara – river mouth

muezzin – mosque official who calls the faithful to prayer

negara – country

negeri – state

ojek – motorcycle taxi (Kalimantan)

opelet – minibus (Kalimantan)

Orang Asli – literally, 'original people'; Malaysian aborigines

Orang Laut – literally, 'coastal people'

Orang Ulu – literally, 'upriver people'

padang – grassy area; field; also the city square

pantai – beach

parang – long jungle knife

pasar – market

pasar malam – night market

pegunungan – mountain (Kalimantan)

pelabuhan – port

pondok – hut or shelter

pulau – island

rajah – prince; ruler

ranee – princess or rajah's wife

rattan – stems from climbing palms used for wickerwork and canes

rimba – jungle

rumah – house

rumah batang – longhouse (Kalimantan)

rumah panjai – longhouse; also spelt rumah panjang

sarong – all-purpose cloth, often sewn into a tube, and worn by women, men and children; also spelt *sarung*

seberang – opposite side of road; far bank of a river

selat – strait

simpang – crossing; junction

songket – traditional Malay hand-woven fabric with gold threads

songkok – traditional Malay men's hat

sungai – river

tambang – river ferry; fare

tamu – market

tanjung – headland

teksi – taxi

teluk – bay; sometimes spelt *telok*

temenggong – Malay administrator

temuai – shallow-draft Iban longboat

transmigrasi – transmigration; Indonesian government policy to move people from densely populated islands such as Java, Bali and Madura to more remote areas, including Kalimantan

tuak – rice wine

tunku – prince

ulu – upriver

UMNO – United Malays National Organisation; Malaysia's largest political party

UNDP – United Nations Development Programme

warung – small eating stalls

White Rajahs – dynasty that founded and ruled the Kingdom of Sarawak from 1841 to 1946

wisma – office block or shopping centre

WWF – World Wide Fund for Nature

behind the scenes

SEND US YOUR FEEDBACK

We love to hear from travellers – your comments keep us on our toes and help make our books better. Our well-travelled team reads every word on what you loved or loathed about this book. Although we cannot reply individually to postal submissions, we always guarantee that your feedback goes straight to the appropriate authors, in time for the next edition. Each person who sends us information is thanked in the next edition – the most useful submissions are rewarded with a selection of digital PDF chapters.

Visit **lonelyplanet.com/contact** to submit your updates and suggestions or to ask for help. Our award-winning website also features inspirational travel stories, news and discussions.

Note: We may edit, reproduce and incorporate your comments in Lonely Planet products such as guidebooks, websites and digital products, so let us know if you don't want your comments reproduced or your name acknowledged. For a copy of our privacy policy visit lonelyplanet.com/privacy.

OUR READERS

Many thanks to the travellers who used the last edition and wrote to us with helpful hints, useful advice and interesting anecdotes:
Antonio Almeida, Alexandra Bardswell, Tamara Bedeaux, Neesha Copley, Augusto Garolla, Paul Gurn, Lloyd Jones, Laurel Kinrade, Cyril and Danielle Lousberg, Petra O'Neill, Bettina Ortmann, Christine Overvelde, Glenn Owens, Andrea Sanfilippo, Jeanie and Jim Schaden, Chronis Sofianidis, Fabian Spettel, Brian Strating, Eileen Synnott, Maurice van Dael, Johnno Van Havere, and Laszlo Wagner

AUTHOR THANKS

Daniel Robinson

Scores of people went out of their way to make this a better book, but I'm especially indebted to Amélie Blanc, Borbala Nyiri, Donald and Marina Tan, Eric and Annie Yap, Jacqueline Fong, Jo-Lynn Liao, Kelvin Egay, Polycarp, Mathew Ngau Jau, Philip Yong, Thomas Ulrich and Vernon Kedit (Kuching); Jessie, Noriza and Peter Tiong (Sibu); Paul Chuo, Sandra Kromdijk, Vincent Tiong and Wouter Mullink (Kapit); Camille de Kerchove, Captain David (Bennet), Elyn Chan and family, and Mrs Lee (Miri); Amy McGoldrick, Antonella Mori, Helen van Lindere, Jeremy Clark, Peter Hogge and my guides Bian Rumai, Esther Abu, Jeffry Simun, Susan Pulut and Syria Lejau (Gunung Mulu National Park); Apoi Ngimat, Jaman Riboh, Joanna Joy, Rebita Lupong, Rian John Pasan Lamulun, Stephen and Tine, and Stu Roach (Bario); Mr Lim (Chong Teah), Mr Chua (Eng Hin) and Ferdinand Gibson (Limbang); the dedicated staff of Sarawak's national parks; Glenn van Zutphen, Leonard Koh, Michelle Elias Solomon and Seng Beng Yeo and their families (Singapore); and, finally, my beloved wife Rachel Safman, our son Yair Lev and my mother-in-law Edie Safman (Los Angeles).

Adam Karlin

Terima kasih: Katie King, rockstar contact who redefines break dancing; the people who gave me insight, Charlie Ryan, Jessica Yew, Tom, Joel, Silas and Howard, I'm greatly privileged to have met you, and to have had the opportunity to explore your island with you; Angelica, the baddest ass bartender in Oakland, thanks for the laughs; Alex Zawadzki, Daniele Cohen, Serge, Johnny and the rest, your company was always hilarious; Mom and Dad, thanks for your constant support; and Rachel, for your love, and your voice every morning and evening when I'm away.

Paul Stiles

My thanks to the many people who guided me safely from one end of Kalimantan to the other, and back again: Lucas, Rahim, Ahmad Kaya and family, Alex, Erwin, Oaye, Aini, Shady. To my coauthors, for all their valuable advice and comments along the way. And to Ilaria, for making the Cross-Borneo Trek possible.

ACKNOWLEDGMENTS

Climate map data adapted from Peel MC, Finlayson BL & McMahon TA (2007) 'Updated World Map of the Köppen-Geiger Climate Classification', *Hydrology and Earth System Sciences*, 11, 163344.

Cover photograph: Danum Valley, Frans Lanting/National Geographic Stock

BEHIND THE SCENES

THIS BOOK

This 3rd edition of Lonely Planet's Borneo guidebook was researched and written by a stellar team of intrepid travel experts who have an unparalleled passion for adventure and the wilder parts of the world. LP veteran, passionate eco-traveller and Borneo-phile Daniel Robinson led the team. He researched Sarawak, and wrote the Plan, Understand and Survival Guide chapters. Paul Stiles survived his crazy research trip to Kalimantan, and the hilarious and charming Adam Karlin researched Sabah and wrote the Diving Pulau Sipadan chapter. Dr Trish Batchelor wrote the

Health chapter, which was then revised by Daniel Robinson. This guidebook was commissioned in Lonely Planet's Melbourne office, and produced by the following:

Commissioning Editors Suki Gear, Ilaria Walker

Coordinating Editors Catherine Naghten, Gabrielle Stefanos

Coordinating Cartographer James Leversha

Coordinating Layout Designer Clara Monitto

Managing Editors Sasha Baskett, Bruce Evans

Managing Cartographers Anita Bahn, Diana von Holdt

Managing Layout Designer Jane Hart

Cover Research Naomi Parker

Internal Image Research Aude Vauconsant

Language Content Branislava Vladisavljevic

Thanks to Elin Berglund, Jasna Bratic, Rebecca Chau, Lauren Egan, Ryan Evans, Larissa Frost, Chris Girdler, Bronwyn Hicks, Genesys India, Jouve India, Eva Murphy, Mardi O'Connor, Trent Paton, Kirsten Rawlings, Raphael Richards, Kate Sullivan, Gerard Walker

index

000 Map pages
000 Photo pages

how to use this book

These symbols will help you find the listings you want:

- ◉ Sights
- 🏄 Beaches
- 🏃 Activities
- 🚣 Courses

- 👆 Tours
- 🎊 Festivals & Events
- 🛏 Sleeping
- 🍴 Eating

- 🍷 Drinking
- ☆ Entertainment
- 🛍 Shopping
- ℹ Information/Transport

These symbols give you the vital information for each listing:

- ☎ Telephone Numbers
- ☉ Opening Hours
- P Parking
- ⊖ Nonsmoking
- ❄ Air-Conditioning
- @ Internet Access

- 🛜 Wi-Fi Access
- 🏊 Swimming Pool
- 🥗 Vegetarian Selection
- 📖 English-Language Menu
- 👪 Family-Friendly
- 🐾 Pet-Friendly

- 🚌 Bus
- ⛴ Ferry
- Ⓜ Metro
- Ⓢ Subway
- 🚊 Tram
- 🚉 Train

Reviews are organised by author preference.

Look out for these icons.

TOP CHOICE	Our author's recommendation
FREE	No payment required
🌿	A green or sustainable option

Our authors have nominated these places as demonstrating a strong commitment to sustainability – for example by supporting local communities and producers, operating in an environmentally friendly way, or supporting conservation projects.

Map Legend

Sights
- Beach
- Buddhist
- Castle
- Christian
- Hindu
- Islamic
- Jewish
- Monument
- Museum/Gallery
- Ruin
- Winery/Vineyard
- Zoo
- Other Sight

Activities, Courses & Tours
- Diving/Snorkelling
- Canoeing/Kayaking
- Skiing
- Surfing
- Swimming/Pool
- Walking
- Windsurfing
- Other Activity/Course/Tour

Sleeping
- Sleeping
- Camping

Eating
- Eating

Drinking
- Drinking
- Cafe

Entertainment
- Entertainment

Shopping
- Shopping

Information
- Bank
- Embassy/Consulate
- Hospital/Medical
- Internet
- Police
- Post Office
- Telephone
- Toilet
- Tourist Information
- Other Information

Transport
- Airport
- Border Crossing
- Bus
- Cable Car/Funicular
- Cycling
- Ferry
- Monorail
- Parking
- Petrol Station
- Taxi
- Train/Railway
- Tram
- Underground Train Station
- Other Transport

Routes
- Tollway
- Freeway
- Primary
- Secondary
- Tertiary
- Lane
- Unsealed Road
- Plaza/Mall
- Steps
- Tunnel
- Pedestrian Overpass
- Walking Tour
- Walking Tour Detour
- Path

Geographic
- Hut/Shelter
- Lighthouse
- Lookout
- Mountain/Volcano
- Oasis
- Park
- Pass
- Picnic Area
- Waterfall

Population
- Capital (National)
- Capital (State/Province)
- City/Large Town
- Town/Village

Boundaries
- International
- State/Province
- Disputed
- Regional/Suburb
- Marine Park
- Cliff
- Wall

Hydrography
- River, Creek
- Intermittent River
- Swamp/Mangrove
- Reef
- Canal
- Water
- Dry/Salt/Intermittent Lake
- Glacier

Areas
- Beach/Desert
- Cemetery (Christian)
- Cemetery (Other)
- Park/Forest
- Sportsground
- Sight (Building)
- Top Sight (Building)

OUR STORY

A beat-up old car, a few dollars in the pocket and a sense of adventure. In 1972 that's all Tony and Maureen Wheeler needed for the trip of a lifetime – across Europe and Asia overland to Australia. It took several months, and at the end – broke but inspired – they sat at their kitchen table writing and stapling together their first travel guide, *Across Asia on the Cheap*. Within a week they'd sold 1500 copies. Lonely Planet was born.

Today, Lonely Planet has offices in Melbourne, London, Oakland and Delhi, with more than 600 staff and writers. We share Tony's belief that 'a great guidebook should do three things: inform, educate and amuse'.

OUR WRITERS

Daniel Robinson

Coordinating Author, Plan Your Trip, Sarawak, Understand Borneo, Survival Guide Daniel has been covering Southeast Asia and its rainforests since 1989, when he researched Lonely Planet's first, award-winning guides to Vietnam and Cambodia. On his many visits to Sarawak, he has developed a fondness for travelling *ulu-ulu* (way upriver) by longboat, tramping through the jungle in search of gargantuan Rafflesia flowers, and slurping *Sarawak laksa*. Daniel, who holds a BA in Near Eastern Studies from Princeton University, writes on travel for a variety of magazines and newspapers, including the *New York Times*.

Read more about Daniel:
lonelyplanet.com/members/daniel_robinson

Adam Karlin

Diving Pulau Sipadan, Sabah, Brunei Adam thinks Borneo is like a savage garden, which may explain why he loves it truly, madly, deeply. On this trip, his second exploring Sabah (and third exploring Malaysia) for Lonely Planet, he glimpsed primates, hiked jungle mountains, held his own in expat drinking games and floated on his back down a river through virgin rainforest – a pretty good moment, that. He has written or contributed to some 30 titles for Lonely Planet.

Read more about Adam:
lonelyplanet.com/members/adamkarlin

Paul Stiles

Kalimantan Paul specialises in islands, ecotourism, and adventure travel for Lonely Planet, so Kalimantan was a natural fit. For this book he completed the entire Cross-Borneo Trek, crossing the Muller Range in five days. His only regret is that he did not have his camera when a rare clouded leopard swam right in front of his boat. Guide: 'I don't know, looks like a wild cat... Oh my god, *macan dahan!*'

Read more about Paul:
lonelyplanet.com/members/paulwstiles

Published by Lonely Planet Publications Pty Ltd
ABN 36 005 607 983
3rd edition – Jun 2013
ISBN 978 1 74220 296 9
© Lonely Planet 2013   Photographs © as indicated 2013
10 9 8 7 6 5 4 3 2 1
Printed in China